Chicago Sun Times "... a seductive volume for window shopping. ... Handsomely illustrated. ... Hotels that provide the atmosphere of a fine residence: beauty in design, color and furnishings, fresh flowers, luxurious toiletries and linens. Other considerations for select business and physical fitness facilities, excellence of cuisine and concierge services."

St. Louis Post-Dispatch "... these hotels lived up to the author's description. Fortunately the author covers a range of rates from affordable to expensive."

Cincinnati Enquirer "... unique places with exquisitely appointed rooms, interesting architecture, luxurious ambience and excellent food and service."

Dallas Morning News "The book may give in one volume readers everything they ever wanted to know."

Diversion "... well coded and full of practical information."

Los Angeles Times "... Definitive and worth the room in your reference library."

San Francisco Chronicle "A state-by-state and city-by-city guide researched listings ... an impressive number."

Elle "If elegant small hotel are your thing—and whose aren't they?—check out *Elegant Small Hotels*. Details 168 such establishments, complete with celeb comment on many of them."

USA Technical Information Center "... Lanier, as usual provides good value for the money."

Condo

VACATIONS

The Complete Guide™

Pamela Lanier

Lanier Publishing International, Ltd.

More Lanier Guides:
Golf Courses—The Complete Guide   from Lanier Publishing International, Ltd.
Golf Resorts—The Complete Guide
Golf Resorts International
Elegant Hotels of the Pacific Rim
Elegant Small Hotels
All Suite Hotel Guide
The Complete Guide to Bed & Breakfasts, Inns & Guesthouses in the United States and Canada
Cinnamon Mornings
Alaska in 22 Days

Copyright © 1997 Lanier Publishing International, Ltd.

1st Edition April 1989
2nd Edition April 1990
3rd Edition March 1991
4th Edition March 1992
5th Edition September 1993
6th Edition Spring 1997

Design & Production—J. C. Wright; Futura Graphics
Cover Design—Victor Ichioka
Published by Lanier Publishing International, Ltd.
    P.O. Drawer D
    Petaluma, CA 94953
Distributed by Ten Speed Press
    P.O. Box 7123
    Berkeley, CA 94707
Printed in the U.S.A. on recycled paper
Project Coordinator: J.C. Wright

American Hotel
& Motel Association
ALLIED MEMBER

Acknowledgements: I wish to acknowledge the following persons and organizations for their help in making this Guide a reality: Raymond C. Ellis, American Hotel Motel Association, Marianne Barth, Paul Gray, Carl Berry, all fifty state Departments of Tourism, Chambers of Commerce and Visitors Bureaus.

` **Library of Congress Cataloging-in-Publication Data**
Lanier, Pamela
Condo Vacations / Pamela Lanier
    p.   cm.
Includes index.
ISBN: 0-89815-888-5
    1. Resorts—United States—Directories.   2. Resorts—Directories.   3. Condominiums—United States—Directories.   4. Condominiums—Directories.   I. Title
TX907.2.L3598 1992
    647.9473—dc20   91-36569
                                                                                    CIP

Contents

VOTE

FOR YOUR CHOICE OF
CONDO OF THE YEAR

Did you find your stay at a Condominium listed in this Guide particularly enjoyable? Use the form in the back of the book or just drop us a note and we'll add your vote for the "Condo of the Year."

The winning entry will be featured in the next edition of **Condo Vacations—The Complete Guide.**™

Please base your decision on:
- Helpfulness of the Staff   • Quality of Service
- Cleanliness   • Amenities   • Decor   • Food

Look for the winning Condo in the new **Condo Vacations, The Complete Guide.**™

Introduction

You need a vacation. But where are you going to go? Why not take a condo vacation as an alternative to traditional hotels and motels? A new choice which offers greater flexibility at lower rates.

What Is A Vacation Condominium?

A vacation condominium is a lodging which features suites, rather than single rooms. Most condos have at least one separate bedroom. Others may have two or three. The vast majority of condos in this Guide have full kitchen facilities. Most of the conveniences of hotels, such as daily maid service are available, as well as individual air conditioning and heat control, and color, often cable, TV.

Who Stays In Vacation Condos?

The unique features of condos attract families, couples traveling together, business travelers who want a better working situation, and small business groups that are having meetings.

Why Stay In Vacation Condos?

Flexibility! And lower prices. Don't be crowded in a motel room where you can barely get by the TV to the bed. Condominiums, for a comparable price, offer a kitchen, bedroom, living room with a couch that opens up for extra sleeping space, and bathrooms with tubs—some even have jacuzzis in the master bath.

If you want to eat out, fine. There may be excellent restaurants in the area, but you can cut costs by eating in.

Staying at a condo can trim vacation expenses by up to fifty percent when compared with a stay in a similiarly located traditional hotel with all meals taken in a restaurant.

Family Fun!

Renting a condominium is like taking your home with you. The sheets are on the bed, the cable TV is ready, and the kitchen is waiting for you to prepare all the special treats your children love.

The staff at most condo resorts can recommend reliable babysitters, and offer daily maid service, giving everyone a break. Family reunions are also a natural for condominiums.

Business Meetings

Business groups benefit from the flexible accommodations and added privacy a condo affords, without the distracting hustle and bustle of a conventional resort hotel.

Group Vacations

For a few couples who want to get together for a vacation, why not rent a condominium? Condos are a great bargain for couples traveling together who can split the cost. Condo staffs are expert at arranging everything from ski lift tickets to equipment rental, which means less hassle and more fun for everyone!

Ski Vacations

Ski-area condominiums are especially appealing. Most ski condos offer a ski package which includes lift tickets, and many have ski schools and nurseries for children. Also, many condos are ski/in–ski/out so you can ski home whenever you want without the tedious job of piling your skis on the car and fighting the traffic home.

Beach Vacations

Rent a condominium on the beach and take the little ones to build sand castles while you relax and get a fantastic tan. Or maybe you're looking for a romantic hide-away for the two of you to celebrate a special occasion. Condos offer a couple the boon of extra space and privacy—something we can all appreciate!

We list additional condos at the back of this guide under "**More Condos.**" Please refer to the Table of Contents.

Whatever your vacation desire, a condominium vacation can fill it, and if you have specific ideas in mind, such as a spa where you can be pampered, special lessons from a golf or tennis pro, guided deep sea fishing, helicopter skiing or peace, quiet and seclusion—it's all there waiting for you.

Pamela Lanier
San Francisco
Spring 1997

Guide Notes

Prices

Our rate code reflects the most current information beginning with the least expensive condominiums off season. Generally, the rates are for the condo based on an average occupancy of up to 4 in a one-bedroom, or 6 in a two-bedroom. We give price codes as follows:

$	— to $50	Some places charge for extra
$$	— $51 to $100	persons in the room. Usually
$$$	— $101 to $150	nominal.
$$$$	— $151 to $399	
4$	— $400 to $499 5$ — $500 to $599, etc.	
10$	— anything over $1000	

These codes are designed to provide you with a *general* idea of the rates. Be sure to check for exact prices when you reserve.

Credit Cards And Checks

We make note of the credit cards which are accepted. Generally, personal checks are accepted with some restrictions. Be sure to inquire about this.

Reservations

The more popular condominiums fill up fast for peak season. Six months ahead is not too soon to reserve your place in the Hawaiian sun for Christmas; and Aspen area slopes are often booked by summer's end, so be sure to reserve early. However, last minute travelers are sometimes able to take advantage of last minute openings. When you make your reservation, be sure to confirm the availability of the amenities and services you require.

Pets, Smoking and Handicapped Access

We make note if you can bring your pet (it must be on a leash); however, some condominiums which allow pets limit the size, so if Bonzo is a Great Dane, be sure to check.

We make note where there are non-smoking rooms for the convenience of our readers who can't tolerate cigarette smoke.

We also make note of condominiums which have units accessible to the handicapped. Such rooms fill up early so be sure to reserve well in advance, and double check to make sure the facilities meet your requirements.

Maps

We include a map for each state to assist you in your planning. Also, at the back of the guide is a list of tourism offices. We recommend that you contact the tourist offices to get the general travel information before you go. It is a valuable free resource!

Deposit Policy

Generally, one or two nights' rate is required in advance, by check or credit card. Some condominiums have flat fees.

Cancellation Policy

Some places keep a percentage of the deposit, no matter when the cancellation is made. Deposits are usually refunded when cancellation is made by a specified time, anywhere from 72 hours to 2 months, depending on the resort's policy. Holiday seasons require a longer cancellation notice. Cancellation policies can be quite stringent, so be sure to check.

Check-in And Check-Out

The most popular check-out time tends to be noon, but can be as early as 10:00 a.m. Check-in times vary—2, 3 or 4 p.m. Please confirm check-in and check-out times when you make your reservations. If you have special time requirements, the condominium staff may be able to accommodate you.

Maid And Linen Service

Most condominiums have maid service; in some, included in the rate. For others it is an extra charge. Linens are generally provided as is kitchen equipment—often gourmet! It is important to check what service is provided when you book. Many beach properties request that you bring your own beach towels.

Hotel Amenities And Business Facilities

In our feature listing, we note which condominiums have full hotel services, i.e., front desk, message center, bell men, etc. Condominiums are increasingly popular for business meetings so we make note of conference facilities, conference room capacity and business services available which generally means on-site FAX, Xerox, message center, etc.

Recreational Facilities

We provide data on the gamut of recreational facilities available, from pool and sauna to nearby golf courses.

Room Amenities

Most condominiums these days feature over-size beds, king or queen. We make note of kitchen facilities, individual air conditioning and heating, TV, cable TV and VCR. Many condominiums have more facilities and amenities than we have space to note. We recommend that you narrow your choices to two or three condominiums and then write or call for their brochures and request information about your exact requirements.

Children

Most condominiums are very well prepared for family visits. Many make a special point of offering children's activities, such as play grounds, kiddie pool, movies, arts and crafts, ski nursery and other supervised activities.

Usually, the condominium staff can recommend a reliable baby sitter. Cribs and high chairs and extra cots are generally available at no extra charge. If you require children's equipment, be sure to reserve it in advance. In most condominium complexes there are plenty of families with kids, which means extra fun for everyone.

Location

In our feature listing, we note the distance to downtown, to airport, whether the property is beach front, and proximity to ski lifts.

Restaurant-Bar

We make note of the presence of on-site restaurants or bar when available.

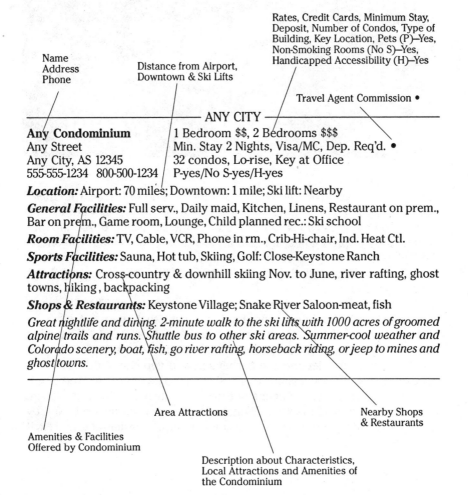

Rates, Credit Cards, Minimum Stay, Deposit, Number of Condos, Type of Building, Key Location, Pets (P)–Yes, Non-Smoking Rooms (No S)–Yes, Handicapped Accessibility (H)–Yes

Name
Address
Phone

Distance from Airport, Downtown & Ski Lifts

Travel Agent Commission •

—————————————— ANY CITY ——————————————

Any Condominium
Any Street
Any City, AS 12345
555-555-1234 800-500-1234

1 Bedroom $$, 2 Bedrooms $$$
Min. Stay 2 Nights, Visa/MC, Dep. Req'd. •
32 condos, Lo-rise, Key at Office
P-yes/No S-yes/H-yes

Location: Airport: 70 miles; Downtown: 1 mile; Ski lift: Nearby

General Facilities: Full serv., Daily maid, Kitchen, Linens, Restaurant on prem., Bar on prem., Game room, Lounge, Child planned rec.: Ski school

Room Facilities: TV, Cable, VCR, Phone in rm., Crib-Hi-chair, Ind. Heat Ctl.

Sports Facilities: Sauna, Hot tub, Skiing, Golf: Close-Keystone Ranch

Attractions: Cross-country & downhill skiing Nov. to June, river rafting, ghost towns, hiking, backpacking

Shops & Restaurants: Keystone Village; Snake River Saloon-meat, fish

Great nightlife and dining. 2-minute walk to the ski lifts with 1000 acres of groomed alpine trails and runs. Shuttle bus to other ski areas. Summer-cool weather and Colorado scenery, boat, fish, go river rafting, horseback riding, or jeep to mines and ghost towns.

Area Attractions

Nearby Shops
& Restaurants

Amenities & Facilities
Offered by Condominium

Description about Characteristics,
Local Attractions and Amenities of
the Condominium

1997
Condo of The Year

Our readers voted The Shores At Waikoloa "Condo of the Year for 1997."
Managed by Aston Hotels and Resorts, this AAA Three-Diamond resort is
located on the prestigious Kohala Coast of the Big Island of Hawaii. Surrounded by tropical landscaping and meandering fish ponds, The Shores
At Waikoloa offers spacious, luxurious accomodations with a full range of
vacation activities, including the Waikoloa Golf Club's championship Beach
and Kings' Courses.

Guests appreciate the comfort and convenience of The Shores At
Waikoloa's well-appointed condominiums, with their gourmet kitchens,
color TVs, washer/dryers, wet bars and private lanais. Add to this the luxury of daily maid service, along with such hotel amenities as a swimming
pool, tennis courts, jet spa and barbecues, and you can understand why
The Shores At Waikoloa is our readers' choice. The Shores At Waikoloa is
especially attentive to the needs of those traveling with children, offering
reasonable rates and an excellent atmosphere for the younger set. Nearby,
guests will find a variety of world-class shops, superb restaurants and exciting entertainment.

Alabama

Dadeville •

Gulf Shores

DADEVILLE

Still Waters
1000 Still Water Dr.
Dadeville, AL 36853
205-825-7021 800-633-4954

1 Bedroom $$, 2 Bedrooms $$$, Villas
Pool, Kitchen, Linens

Attractions: Montgomery attractions: Zoo, Planetarium, Fine Arts Museum, azalea trail, historic sights, Weight room, bicycles, Tennis, Golf

Individually appointed villas with lake or golf views, and decks with grills, in a resort that meets your every vacation requirement. Marina, lakeside beach, cabana and cafe. Active games and sports, theme parties, special social activities, boat rentals, stables.

GULF SHORES

Compass Point
1516 Sandpiper Lane
Gulf Shores, AL 36542
205-948-6411 800-344-8122

1 Bedroom $$, 2 Bedrooms $$, 3 Bedrooms $$
1 Bedrm/week $$$$, 2 Bed/week 4$,
3 Bed/week 5$
Min. Stay 2 Nights, Visa/MC, Dep. Req'd.
25 condos, Hi-rise, Key at Office

Location: Airport: 1 hour; Downtown: 1 mile; Need car

General Facilities: Conf. rm., Kitchen, Linens

Room Facilities: Pool, Putting green, Cable, Ind. AC Ctl., Ind. Heat Ctl.

Attractions: Charter boat rentals, 24 acre water park, sandy beaches, beach horseback riding

Shops & Restaurants: Tourist shops, Liz Claiborne-Ralph Lauren outlets; Nolans-variety

Surrounded by live oaks and oleanders, these units offer breathtaking views and master bedrooms with private bath and balcony. Heated swimming pool, fishing pier, boat ramp and putting green. History buffs will enjoy visiting Fort Morgan with its museum, gift shop and restaurant, or tour the historic districts of Mobile and Pensacola. The Lagoon has safe shallow waters for children and is perfect for water sports. Shopping, dining and nightlife are nearby, or take a stroll on the landscaped grounds.

Cabo Regis

--- GULF SHORES ---

Seabreeze Condominiums
West Beach Blvd., Rt. 1, Box 1994
Gulf Shores, AL 36542
205-948-6411 800-344-8122

2 Bedrooms $$
Min. Stay 2 Nights, Dep. Req'd.
Lo-rise, Key at Compass Pt. office

Location: Airport: 1 hour; Downtown: 1 mile; Need car
General Facilities: Daily maid, Kitchen, Linens
Room Facilities: Pool, Cable, Ind. AC Ctl., Ind. Heat Ctl.
Attractions: Naval Air Museum, Bellingrath Gardens, Fort Morgan, Mobile Bay Ferry, Country Club golfing
Shops & Restaurants: Rivera, Liz Claiborne, Ralph Lauren outlets; Fine seafood restaurants

Relax on the beautiful sandy beaches only steps away for a peaceful vacation, or for the more athletically inclined, try horseback riding on the beach or golf at the Country Club. Shopping, restaurants and many historical areas in Pensacola and Mobile, which also have greyhound racing. The Mobile Bay Ferry takes you to Fort Morgan, defended by David Farragut in the Battle of Mobile Bay.

Village By The Gulf
W. Beach Blvd., P.O. Box 2079
Gulf Shores, AL 36542
205-948-6832 205-948-6833

Arizona

Flagstaff

Lake Havasu
Pinetop
Carefree
Paradise Valley
Phoenix Scottsdale
Mesa

Tuscon

---------------------------- CAREFREE ----------------------------

Boulders Resort   120 condos
34631 N. Tom Darlington, Box 2090
Carefree, AZ 85377
602-488-9099 800-223-7636

Location: Downtown: nearby

General Facilities: Conf. rm. cap. 175, Kitchen, Restaurant on prem., Bar on prem., Lounge, Baby-sitter

Room Facilities: Pool, Tennis, Fitness Center, Golf: 3 courses

Attractions: Day trips and Grand Canyon flights, desert jeep tours, Taliesen West, ballooning, horses

Shops & Restaurants: Scottsdale shopping; Latilla Room, Palo Verde Room

120 Casitas blending in with the Sonoran desert north of Scottsdale. Contemporary in feeling, yet a place to unwind amid Indian handicrafts and regional art. Dining room menus feature innovative dishes and natural ingredients. You can be as active or as lazy as your spirit moves you.

---------------------------- FLAGSTAFF ----------------------------

Fairfield Flagstaff Comm. Club   1 Bedroom $$, 2 Bedrooms $$$, Hi-rise
1900 N. Country Club Dr., Box 1208   Pool, Kitchen, Linens
Flagstaff, AZ 86002
602-526-3232 800-526-1004

Attractions: Grand Canyon-80 miles, Sedona red rocks, Meteor Crater, Painted Desert-100 miles, Stables, mini golf, Tennis, Golf

Tastefully decorated units in the Arizona hill country. Sharpen your golf and tennis skills, swim in the pools or Lake Elaine, horseback ride through Coconino National Forest. 14 miles to Snowbowl winter skiing. Sunburst Lounge for late night dancing.

---------------------------- HOT SPRINGS ----------------------------

Willow Beach Lakefront Condos   1 Bedroom $$, Lo-rise
Route 3, Box 122   Pool, Kitchen, Linens, Phone in rm.
Hot Springs, AZ 71913
501-525-4398

Attractions: Lake, Oaklawn Race Track

9,000 acres of water sports on Lake Hamilton. Completely furnished lakefront view units with grill on balcony. Fishing docks, covered boat slips and a nearby marina.

—————————————— LAKE HAVASU CITY ——————————————

Nautical Inn Resort & Conf.   AmEx/Visa/MC •
Center   16 condos
1000 McCulloch Blvd.   No S-yes
Lake Havasu City, AZ 86403
602-855-2141 800-892-2141

Location: Airport: 4 minutes; Downtown: 4 min.; Beach front

General Facilities: Conf. rm. cap. 150, Kitchen, Restaurant on prem., Bar on prem.

Room Facilities: Pool, Sauna, Hot tub, Tennis, Golf: Nautical Inn course, TV, Phone in rm.

Attractions: London Bridge, complimentary round trips to Laughlin, Nevada, entertainment

Shops & Restaurants: London Bridge & K-Mart shopping centers, Bayless; Versaille/Fr., Capt's Table

Located on beautiful Lake Havasu and right across from the London Bridge. Captain's Table restaurant has a wide variety of cuisine and specializes in cakes and pies. Dance floor.

—————————————— LAKE HAVASU ——————————————

Inn at Tamarisk   Studio $$, 1 Bedroom $$, 2 Bedrooms $$
3101 London Bridge Road   1 Bedrm/week 9$, 2 Bed/week 10$
Lake Havasu, AZ 86403   Dep. Req'd.
602-764-3044   Lo-rise

General Facilities: Kitchen

Room Facilities: Pool, Tennis, Croquet, table tennis, TV

Attractions: World OutBoard Classic, Sailboat Regattas, Ski tournaments, International Jet Ski Race

Shops & Restaurants: English Village quaint shops under London Bridge; French, continental, American

Quiet desert oasis, a short walk to Lake Havasu beach. Comfortable condominiums, pool, barbecues and cabana area. Families also enjoy shuffleboard, horseshoes and the putting green. Scheduled free bus trips with fun packet to Laughlin, Nevada, casinos. English village along the water with unique shops beneath the London Bridge.

—————————————— MESA ——————————————

Arizona Golf Resort & Conf.   1 Bedroom $$, 2 Bedrooms $$$
Center   AmEx/Visa/MC, Dep. 1 Night
425 South Power Road   6 condos, Lo-rise
Mesa, AZ 85206   P-yes
602-832-3202 800-528-8282

Location: Airport: Phoenix 30 minutes; Downtown: 10 min.

General Facilities: Conf. rm. cap. 1000, Kitchen, Linens, Restaurant on prem., Bar on prem., Lounge

Room Facilities: Pool, Sauna, Hot tub, Tennis, Bikes, volleyball, Golf: Championship course, TV, Cable, Phone in rm., Ind.AC Ctl., Ind. Heat Ctl.

Attractions: Apache Trail & Tri Lakes Region, Champion Fighter Museum, Mormon Temple, Rockin R Ranch, entertainment

Shops & Restaurants: Fiesta Mall, VF Factory Outlet; Annabelle's/prime rib

One of Arizona's best golf resorts with a complete range of activities. Dance in the lounge after dinner at Anabelle's.

---------------------------- PARADISE VALLEY ----------------------------

Hermosa Inn Resort
5532 N. Palo Cristi Rd.
Paradise Valley, AZ 85253
602-955-8614

1 Bedroom $$$, Villas
Pool, Kitchen

Attractions: Putting green, Tennis, Golf

Comfortable seclusion and quiet elegance in Arizona's Valley of the Sun. Villas with mini-kitchens, private patios and Spanish-style beehive fireplaces. Peaceful relaxation by the pool. Play tennis, practice on the putting green, or play a full 18 holes of golf.

---------------------------- PHOENIX ----------------------------

The Wigwam
Litchfield Park
Phoenix, AZ 85340
602-935-3811

Dep. Req'd.
Lo-rise

Location: Airport: Sky Harbor; Downtown: 15 miles

General Facilities: Restaurant on prem., Bar on prem., Lounge

Room Facilities: Pool, Tennis, Trap skeet shooting, Ind. AC Ctl.

Attractions: Phoenix attractions, entertainment

Shops & Restaurants: Phoenix shops; Terrace Dining Room-on-site

Wigwam limousines meet you at the airport. Three championship golf courses, tennis courts, horseback riding, skeet shooting. Evening entertainment, dining under the stars. 60 acres of manicured lawns and flower gardens.

---------------------------- PINETOP ----------------------------

Roundhouse Resort
Buck Springs Rd., P.O. Box 1468
Pinetop, AZ 85935
602-369-4848

Studio $$, 1 Bedroom $$, 2 Bedrooms $$$$
AmEx/Visa/MC, Dep. 1 Night •
59 condos, Lo-rise, Key at Reserv. desk
H-yes

Location: Airport: Phoenix/Tucson 4 hrs; Downtown: 2 miles; Need car; Ski lift: 24 miles

General Facilities: Daily maid, Kitchen, Restaurant on prem., Bar on prem., Game room, Lounge, Baby-sitter

Room Facilities: Pool, Hot tub, Golf: ½ mile, TV, Cable, Phone in rm., Crib-Hi-chair, Ind. AC Ctl., Ind. Heat Ctl.

Attractions: Rodeos, parades, art shows, Petrified Forest Nat. Park, Painted Desert, Old West history, entertainment

Shops & Restaurants: Shops, boutiques and trading posts; Roundhouse-Southwest dining

Situated on the edge of the Sitgreaves National Forest in a natural setting. Outstanding athletic facilities and unlimited recreation and sightseeing. Barbecue and picnic area next door to the heated pool. Indoor handball and racquetball court, exercise room, basketball gymnasium and game room. On-site restaurant and various entertainment throughout the year. For stay-at-homes, the resort provides cards, board games and puzzles. 24 miles to skiing at Sunrise's 60 trails and 3 mountains.

Please mention *Condo Vacations the Complete Guide* when you reserve your condominium.

———————————— SCOTTSDALE ————————————

Scottsdale Camelback
Resort & Spa
6302 E. Camelback Rd.
Scottsdale, AZ 85251
602-947-3300

Studio $$, 2 Bedrooms $$, 3 Bedrooms $$$
2 Bedrooms/week 5$, 3 Bedrooms/week
6$
Min. Stay 2 Nights, Visa/MC
Dep. Required •
79 condos, Villas, Key at Front desk

Location: Airport: 8 miles; Downtown: 1 mile; Need car

General Facilities: Daily maid; Linens; Baby sitter; Crib-Hi-chair; Restaurant

Business Facilities: Conf. Room Cap. 80

Sports Facilities: Pool; Sauna; Hot tub; Tennis; Racketball, putting; 2 miles; Summer activities

Room Facilities: Kitchen; Cable; Phone; Ind.AC.Ctl; Ind.Heat Ctl.

Attractions: Sedma, Grand Canyon, Rawhide; Entertainment

Shops & Restaurants: Fashion Square, Old Town, Scottsdale, 5th Ave.; Avanti—Northern Italian

Luxurious, completely equipped villas nestled at the base of Camelback Mountain. Minutes from golf, fine dining and world famous Fifth Avenue shops. Complimentary tennis clinics Wednesday and Saturday. A vacation experience!

———————————————————————————————————————

Scottsdale Manor Suites
4807 N. Woodmere Fairway
Scottsdale, AZ 85251
602-994-5282 800-523-5282
FAX: 602-994-5625

2 Bedrooms $$$$, 3 Bedrooms $$$$
2 Bedrooms/week 10$
Min. Stay 3 nights, Dep. Required •
100 condos, Lo-rise, Key at Office or by
arrangement, P-No/H-Yes

Location: Airport: 20 minutes; Downtown: 5 minutes

General Facilities: Ltd. hotel service; Linens; Baby sitter; Crib-Hi-chair

Business Facilities: Bus. fac

Sports Facilities: Pool; Tennis; 120 Golf Courses nearby

Room Facilities: Kitchen; Cable; VCR; Ind.AC.Ctl; Ind.Heat Ctl.

Attractions: Old Town Scottsdale, Heard Museum, Sedona, Desert Bot. Garden, Cactus League, Grand Canyon

Shops & Restaurants: Fashion Square, Neiman Marcus, Scottsdale, Art Galleries; Lon's at Hermosa (Southwestern Cuisine)

Large 2- and 3-bedroom condo style suites (1150 to 1580 sq. ft.) in downtown Scottsdale. Secluded and quiet. 3 minutes from Fashion Square Mall and the arts and cultural district. 100+ golf courses, 200+ restaurants within an easy drive. Amenities include: pool, tennis, spas, golf center, concierge, weekly linen exchange and trolly service in season. Value accommodations; daily, weekly, and monthly rentals.

We want to hear from you—any comments regarding the condos or our publication may be noted on the form at the end of the book.

─────────────── TUCSON ───────────────

Villa Serenas
8111 E. Broadway
Tucson, AZ 85710
602-886-6761 800-345-3449

Studio $$, 1 Bedroom $$
AmEx/Visa/MC, Dep. Req'd. •
Hi-rise, Key at Leasing office
H-yes

Location: Airport: 12 miles; Downtown: 5 miles; Need car; Ski lift: Mt. Lemon

General Facilities: Conf. rm. cap. 50, Daily maid, Kitchen, Linens, Game room, Lounge

Room Facilities: Pool, Sauna, Hot tub, Tennis, Exercise, badminton, Golf: Putting greens, TV, Cable, Phone in rm., Crib-Hi-chair, Ind. AC Ctl., Ind. Heat Ctl.

Attractions: Old Tucson Amusement Park, Desert Museum, Colossal Cave, Saguaro Monument, Sabino Canyon, entertainment

Shops & Restaurants: Park Mall, Tucson Mall (all major dept. stores); The Tack Room/continental

Tucson's largest resort—award-winning landscaping, pools, fountains, spas, ponds and unmatched recreational facilities. Lounges, clubrooms, boat and trailer parking. Condominiums decorated in contemporary furnishings in soft desert colors. Everything under the sun for your vacation enjoyment.

Our listings—supplied by the managements—are as complete as possible. Many of the condos have more features than we list. Be sure to inquire when you book.

Arkansas

Lost Bridge Village, Garfield · Holiday Island · Siloam Springs · Cherokee Village · Fairfield Bay · Drasco · Higden, Greers Ferry · Arkadelphia · Hot Springs · Mount Ida

---

CHEROKEE VILLAGE

Los Indios
P.O. Box 840
Cherokee Village, AR 72714
501-257-2469

2 Bedrooms $$
Pool, Kitchen

Attractions: Pea Ridge Battlefield, ES&NA railroad, Passion Play, Beaver Lake, Arkansas football, Tennis

Two bedroom, two bath condomiums with fully equipped kitchens, microwave, laundry facilities and deck with barbecue. Master bath has jacuzzi.

DRASCO

Tyrolese Condominiums
P.O. Box 83
Drasco, AR 72530
501-362-3075

Lo-rise
Pool, Kitchen

Attractions: Boat ramp, horseshoes, Tennis

Tyrolese condominiums, Alpine Village in the Ozarks on Greers Ferry Lake. Lakeside decks, near pool, tennis courts and Cafe St. Clair. Badminton, shuffleboard, horseshoes, picnic area, boat ramp.

FAIRFIELD BAY

Fairfield Bay
P.O. Box 3008
Fairfield Bay, AR 72088
501-884-3333 800-643-9790

1 Bedroom $$, 2 Bedrooms $$, Villas
Kitchen, Linens

Attractions: Ozark Folk Center, Blanchard Springs Caverns, white river rafting, marina, bowling, Exercise complex, Tennis, Golf

Foothills of the Ozarks on Greers Ferry Lake, two championship golf courses, tennis, water sports paradise, Racquet Club memorable dining-dancing, skiing. Pre-1920 Ozark Folk Center and Blanchard Springs Caverns.

Shadow Mountain Resort

─────────── HIGDEN, GREERS FERRY ───────────

Devil's Fork Resort & Dock
Rt. 1, Box B
Higden, Greers Ferry, AR 72067
501-825-6240

2 Bedrooms $
2 Bedrms/week $$$$
Dep. Req'd.
Lo-rise, Key at Office

Location: Downtown: 35 miles; Need car

General Facilities: Kitchen, Linens, Child planned rec.: Playground

Room Facilities: TV, Cable, Crib-Hi-chair, Ind. AC Ctl.

Attractions: Sugar Loaf Mountain nature and hiking trails accessible only by water

Shops & Restaurants: Grocery, pharmacy, laundromat, hardware

A fisherman's paradise. Boat dock, ramp, boat slips, fishing supplies and free use of a fishing boat. Fish cleaning facilities and large freezers for storage. Water sport lovers will enjoy the pollution-free lake with its swimming area, ladder and float. Outdoor ball sports and indoor table games. Brick cottages have covered patios and fish cookers.

─────────── HOLIDAY ISLAND ───────────

Table Rock Landing On Holiday
1 Landing Dr.
Holiday Island, AR 72632
501-253-7561

1 Bedroom $$
Pool

Attractions: Recreation Center, Tennis, Golf

Comfortable, roomy, spaciously designed—two-story living room, mirrored whirlpool bath, grass-covered hillside leading to Table Rock Lake. Recreation Center, variety of activities, Eureka Springs sightseeing. Quiet, luxury living.

------------------- HOT SPRINGS -------------------

Belvedere Resort
317 Belvedere Drive
Hot Springs, AR 71901
501-624-4488

2 Bedrooms $$
Pool, Kitchen, Linens

Attractions: Pool table, exercise, Tennis, Golf

Escape from the pressures of everyday life to a special retreat in the Ouachita hills. Take lessons from the golf pro before trying the challenging course. Condos furnished with elegance and comfort in mind. Restaurant, lounge, art deco bar and antique pool table.

Buena Vista Resort
Route 3, Box 175
Hot Springs, AR 71913
501-525-1321 800-255-9030

Studio $, 1 Bedroom $, 2 Bedrooms $$,
    3 Bedrooms $$
Dep. Req'd.
Lo-rise

General Facilities: Kitchen, Game room, Child planned rec.: Fenced play-yard

Room Facilities: Pool, Tennis, Mini-golf, volleyball, TV, Phone in rm., Crib-Hi-chair, Ind. AC Ctl., Ind. Heat Ctl.

Attractions: Seasonal horse racing, bathhouses, Magic Springs, Mid-America Museum, observation tower

Shops & Restaurants: Mini store on grounds

Units on ten wooded acres on the shores of 22-mile Lake Hamilton. Your children can play in the fenced play-yard with slide and merry-go-round while you watch from the covered sitting dock, or help them feed the ducks and squirrels. Many recreational activities, including a summer game room with pool table, table tennis, video games, and pinball machines. Hot Springs is within a National Park and has many area attractions and lakes.

Emerald Isle Condominiums
7005 Central Ave.
Hot Springs, AR 71913
501-525-3696

2 Bedrooms $$$, Lo-rise
Pool

Attractions: Championship golf, Derby week, Hot Springs attractions, lakes, dinner/dance cruises, Spa, minature golf, tennis, golf

Just bring your suitcase and your food. Lakeside fun on the beach with floating platform, bank fishing, cookouts, boat docks, paddle boats. Bridges over the lake lead to the pool and gazebos with gas grills. Children enjoy the playground, splash pool and mini golf.

Los Lagos
P.O. Box 1600
Hot Springs, AR 71902
501-922-0200

2 Bedrooms $$
Pool, Kitchen

Attractions: Sailing, swimming, water sports, hiking, fishing, tennis, golf, Mini golf, shuffleboard

Pamper yourself in this year-round vacation resort. November to March temperatures are perfect for all sports and provide the best fishing. Natatorium and Fitness Center to keep you busy all day. Cortez Beach for swimming and picnics.

———————————— HOT SPRINGS ————————————

Sheraton Hot Springs Lakeshore   2 Bedrooms $$$, Hi-rise
3501 Albert Pike   Pool, Kitchen
Hot Springs, AR 71914
501-767-5511 800-426-3184

Attractions: Hot Springs Mountain Tower, Oaklawn, Mid-America Museum Complex, Exercise room, docks, Tennis

Views of Lake Hamilton and the Ouachita Mountains from almost anywhere on the property. Private sandy beach, atrium pool and jacuzzi, and boat dockage with water sports equipment rentals. Dine at Hanford's, dance at Champagne Alley, have a romantic evening by the Lake.

SunBay Resort & Condominiums   1 Bedroom $$, 2 Bedrooms $$$, Villas
6110 Central Avenue   Pool, Kitchen
Hot Springs, AR 71913
501-525-4691 800-847-0090

Attractions: Thoroughbred racing, Bathhouse Row, fishing, boating, water skiing, Athletic Club, Tennis

Exquisitely furnished condominiums on the shores of Lake Hamilton in the midst of carefully planned, colorful landscaping. Some units have jacuzzis, fireplaces, wet bars and private balconies. For a rigorous, fitness vacation, there's water sports, jogging and tennis.

The Wharf   2 Bedrooms $$$, Lo-rise
408 Long Island Drive   Pool, Kitchen, Linens
Hot Springs, AR 71913
501-525-4604

Attractions: Oaklawn Race Meet, Jan. 29 thru Apr. 23, Tennis

Wood and stone exteriors highlight these two-bedroom, two-bath condominiums with walkways down to the lake. Oversized whirlpool bath and glass-enclosed decks. Have fun fishing, skiing, boating or swimming in Lake Hamilton, surrounded by tall pines.

———————— LOST BRIDGE VILLAGE, GARFIELD ————————

Beaver Lake Lodge Resort
Route #1, 1653 Lodge Dr.
Lost Bridge Village, Garfield, AR 72732
501-359-3201

———————————— MOUNT IDA ————————————

Mountain Harbor Resort & Condo 2 Bedrooms $$, Lo-rise
P.O. Box 807   Pool, Daily maid, Kitchen, Linens
Mount Ida, AR 71957
501-867-2191

Attractions: Quachita Mountains, Hot Springs National Park quartz crystal dig, marina, playground, tennis

Individually decorated units nestled in a lush forest on the shores of Lake Ouachita. Coves for bass fishing, hiking trails, East Cove and Lodge Restaurants. Complete marina, breathtaking views, wildflowers, wildlife. Your needs carefully considered.

─────────── SILOAM SPRINGS ───────────

Smith's Landing Golf & Racquet   2 Bedrooms $
Siloam Springs, AR 72761   Pool, Kitchen

Attractions: Tennis, Golf

Townhouses with natural stone fireplaces, bedroom lofts and modern, complete kitchens. Golf, tennis and swimming in beautiful surroundings.

─────────── ARKADELPHIA ───────────

Iron Mountain Lodge & Marina   2 Bedrooms $$$, Lo-rise
25 IP Circle   Daily maid, Kitchen, Linens
Arkadelphia, AR 71923
501-246-4310

Attractions: De Gray Lake, Marina rentals

New log-style cottages among the oaks and hickories at the base of Iron Mountain. Boat storage, launching ramp, marina. Exceptional fishing and water sports.

Enter your favorite condo in our "Condo of the Year" contest (entry form is in the back of the book).

California

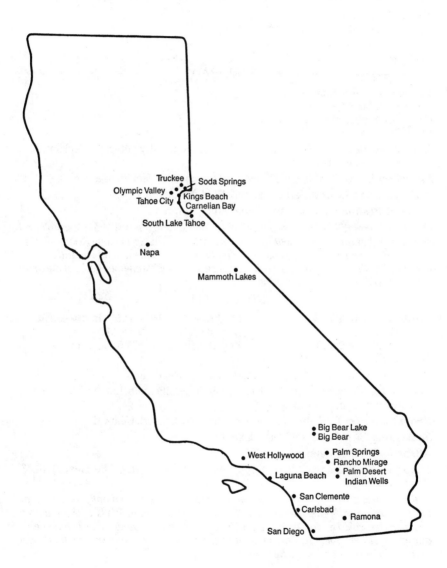

Truckee
Soda Springs
Olympic Valley
Tahoe City
Kings Beach
Carnelian Bay
South Lake Tahoe

Napa

Mammoth Lakes

Big Bear Lake
Big Bear

West Hollywood
Palm Springs
Rancho Mirage
Palm Desert
Laguna Beach
Indian Wells

San Clemente
Carlsbad
Ramona
San Diego

─────────────── BIG BEAR ───────────

North Shore Villas
39237 N. Shore Dr., Box 306
Big Bear, CA 92315
714-866-4948

─────────────── BIG BEAR LAKE ───────────────

Teola Pines Lodge
P.O. Box 1746, 547 Main St.
Big Bear Lake, CA 92315
714-866-2720

─────────────── CARLSBAD ───────────────

La Costa Hotel & Spa
Costa Del Mar Rd.
Carlsbad, CA 92009
619-438-9111 800-544-7483

General facilities: Conf. Rm. (cap. 1000), Kitchen, Baby sitter, Restaurant, Bar, Game room, Hot tub

Sports facilities: Pool, Tennis, 2 18-hole Golf courses, Health spa

Attractions: Sea World, San Diego Zoo, Wild Animal Park

Shops & Restaurants: Brasserie, Spa Dining Room

One of the world's leading resorts with extensive spa facilities. World-class golf and countless other amenities. Eight restaurants including the Spa Dining Room offering low-caloried meals. 23 tennis courts. Heated pools featuring a lovely aquatic center overlooking the golf course. Two highly-acclaimed eighteen-hole golf courses surrounded on three sides by towering hills.

─────────────── INDIAN WELLS ───────────────

Sands of Indian Wells   Studio $$, 1 Bedroom $$, 1 Bed/week 5$,
75-188 Hwy. 111   Min. stay 2 nights, Visa, MC
Indian Wells, CA 92210   Key at Front desk, 50 condos, H-yes •
619-346-8113

Location: Airport: 15 miles; Downtown: 2 miles; Need car

General facilities: Bus. fac., Conf. Rm. (cap. 10), Daily maid, Linens, Playground, Restaurant, Bar, Hot tub

Room facilities: TV, Cable, Phone, Crib, Ind. AC. Ctl, Ind. Heat Ctl.

Sports facilities: Pool, Golf very close by

Attractions: entertainment

Shops & Restaurants: Major Department stores nearby, The Nest/steak & seafood

Within a short drive to 30 championship golf courses and conveniently located near the Greater Palm Springs shops, The Sands Hotel of Indian Wells is the ultimate desert hideaway. By day enjoy tennis, golf, swimming, hiking or visit the scenic attractions. In the evening, fine dining and entertainment abound on-site at the nest or a few minutes away on restaurant row.

Please mention *Condo Vacations—the Complete Guide* when you reserve your condominium.

──────────────── INDIAN WELLS ────────────────

Indian Wells Racquet Club Resort   1 Bedroom $$$, 2 Bedrooms $$$, Lo-rise
46-765 Bay Club Drive   Pool, Kitchen
Indian Wells, CA 92210
619-345-2811

Attractions: Tennis, Golf

Nestled in a cove below the Santa Rosa mountains, your attractively styled townhouse has a private patio from which you can enjoy the desert flowers and sculptured landscape. Trained tennis instructors, golf across the street, and 8 private swimming pools.

──────────────── KINGS BEACH ────────────────

Brockway Springs Resort   1 Bedroom $$$, 2 Bedrooms $$$, 3 Bedrooms
P.O. Box 276 $$$
Kings Beach, CA 95719   1 Bedrm/week 8$, 2 Bed/week 10$,
916-546-4201   3 Bed/week 10$
                               Min. Stay 2 Nights, Visa/MC, Dep. Req'd.
                               Hi-rise, Lo-rise

Location: Need car; Beach front; Ski lift: 7 areas

General Facilities: Conf. rm. cap. 25, Kitchen, Linens, Child planned rec.: Wading pool

Room Facilities: Pool, Sauna, Tennis, Hot Springs, dock

Attractions: Truckee, Virginia City, casinos, seaplane rides, gliders, guided Forest Service outings

Shops & Restaurants: Truckee shops, Tahoe City shops

Lakefront units and crescent townhouse clusters on the lawn, on a wooded pine peninsula on the North Shore. Tahoe's only historic hot springs are here and they indirectly heat the pool. Wading pool, beach, tennis, fishing dock, shore boat and breakwater. Let the public shuttles take you to one of the 7 ski areas. Summer sports and sunbathing. Half mile to Stateline's casinos, dancing and entertainment.

Kings Wood   Lo-rise
P.O. Box 1919   Pool, Kitchen, Linens
Kings Beach, CA 95719
916-546-2501

Attractions: Volley, Badminton, Tennis

All season condominium living at Lake Tahoe. Two-to four-bedroom units with BBQ's, fireplaces, wood supplies, redwood paneling, beam ceilings and large decks. Pool, tennis, volleyball, horseshoes, badminton and foursquare hopscotch (in summer).

McKinney's Landing Townhouses   2 Bedrooms $$$, Lo-rise
P.O. Box 206   Daily maid, Kitchen
Kings Beach, CA 95719
916-546-4074

Attractions: 12 ski areas within easy driving distance, casinos, night spots, Boating

Individually decorated redwood townhouses set in pine and fir groves on the north shore of Lake Tahoe. Private 225-foot pier for boat docking and fishing and private beach swimming. Close to casinos, nightclubs and fine restaurants.

—————————————— LAGUNA BEACH ——————————————

Twin Palms
136 Cliff Drive
Laguna Beach, CA 92651
714-497-4773

1 Bedroom $$, 2 Bedrooms $$$
1 Bedrm/week 5$, 2 Bed/week 6$
Dep. Req'd.
Lo-rise

Location: Downtown: 5 min.

General Facilities: Kitchen, Linens

Room Facilities: TV

Attractions: Art festivals, Museum of Art, theatre, ballet, lawn bowling, parks, shuffleboard

Shops & Restaurants: Markets, village shops, art galleries, cafes

Located 1 block from beach, downtown Laguna, Art Festival. Easy gracious living close to beach, restaurants, shopping. Private balcony, barbecue. Attractively decorated, sheltered units.

—————————————— MAMMOTH LAKES ——————————————

1849 Condominiums
Box 835
Mammoth Lakes, CA 93546
619-934-7525 800-421-1849

Hi-rise
Pool, Kitchen

Attractions: Exercise equipment, Tennis

Luxury condominium units under the snow-capped Sierras. Summer serenity with cool mountain breezes. Pool, spas, tennis, exercise, endless activities. Friendly, courteous staff.

The Bridges
P.O. Box 1452
Mammoth Lakes, CA 93546
619-934-8919 800-654-1143

2 Bedrooms $$, Lo-rise
Kitchen, Linens

Private gated community with modern, beautifully furnished condominiums, half mile above Chairs 15 and 24. Ski home to a roaring fire, some TV watching, and retiring under designer sheets. Free local magazines, towel service to your door daily, and limo to airport.

Forest Creek Village
P.O. Box 7054
Mammoth Lakes, CA 93546
619-934-8372 800-325-8415

2 Bedrooms $$$, Lo-rise
Kitchen, Linens

Two master bedroom suites and three full baths. Kitchens with wet bars and trash compactors. After a day of skiing you'll be happy you have your own private spa under a greenhouse solarium.

Please mention *Condo Vacations the Complete Guide* when you reserve your condominium.

MAMMOTH LAKES

Mammoth Mountain Inn
P.O. Box 353
Mammoth Lakes, CA 93546
619-934-2581   800-228-4947

Lo-rise

Location: Ski lift: Nearby
General facilities: Conf. Rm., Kitchen, Summer/winter care, Restaurant, Bar, Game room, Lounge
Room facilities: TV, Phone
Attractions: Tennis, water skiing, golf, gondolas, sightseeing, horses, skiing, fishing, hiking
Shops & Restaurants: Gift shop and sports shop

Majestic mountains, beautiful forest, local flora, John Muir Wilderness area, winter skiing, special events, day care center, wine tasting room, shuttle service, indoor spas and game room. Be as active or as lazy as you want. Bed and breakfast getaway and complete day care facilities, winter or summer

---

Meadow Ridge
P.O. Box 8290
Mammoth Lakes, CA 93546
619-934-3808   800-468-5364

1 Bedroom $$$, 2 Bedrooms $$$
Lo-rise

General facilities: Kitchen, Linens
Room facilities: Phone
Sports facilities: Pool, Tennis

Located near Mammoth Mountain's chair 15 for easy access to downhill skiing. Complete comfort and relaxation with custom modern kitchens, fireplaces and stereos. For a special holiday.

Snowcreek Resort
P.O. Box 1647
Mammoth Lakes, CA 93546
619-934-3333   800-544-6007

1 Bedroom $$, 2 Bedrooms $$$,
3 Bedrooms $$$$
1 Bed/week 5$, 2 Bed/week 8$,
3 Bed/week 10$
Min. stay 2 nights, Visa, MC,
Dep. req'd
150 condos, Villas,
Key at Rental office
No S-yes

Location: Airport: 8 miles, Downtown: 2 miles, Need car, Ski lift: Mammoth
General facilities: Kitchen, Linens, Sauna, Hot Spa, Fax
Room facilities: TV, Cable, Phone, Ind.Heat Ctl.
Sports facilities: Golf, Tennis, Athletic Club
Attractions: Golf, tennis, Alpine and X-C skiing, hiking, fishing, horses, biking, sightseeing
Shops & Restaurants: Shopping malls and boutiques, Roget's/continental

Year-round resort living at its best. 1-4 bedroom luxury condominiums. Vast open spaces and majestic mountain views. Athletic Club with tennis, racquetball, swimming, aerobics, weights, gymnasium, golf course. Many special programs with golf included in rental package. On free shuttle route to ski area. The Golf Course and Athletic Club are all part of Snowcreek Resort.

──────────── NAPA ────────────

Silverado Country Club & Resort Lo-rise
1600 Atlas Peak Road
Napa, CA 94558
707-257-0200 800-532-0500

Location: Need car
General Facilities: Conf. rm. cap. 500, Kitchen, Restaurant on prem., Baby-sitter
Room Facilities: Pool, Jogging, Golf: 2 courses
Attractions: Winery tours, mud baths, Calistoga geyser, Napa Valley Wine Library, bicycle tours
Shops & Restaurants: Yountville shops; Vintner's Court, Royal Oak

All of Silverado centers around a historic mansion which was designed to incorporate adaptations of Italian and French architecture. Individual studios and suites are private, low-rise clusters around gardens and swimming pools. Twenty Plexipaved tennis courts, screened for privacy. An hour's jog takes you past as many as twenty wineries. Stop at a local market for picnic edibles; shop at Vintage 1870 Yountville; tour the area on a bicycle; go on a winery tour, or play the two 72-par golf courses.

──────────── OLYMPIC VALLEY ────────────

Squaw Valley Lodge
P.O. Box 2364
Olympic Valley, CA 95730
800-922-9970 800-992-9920

1 Bedroom $$$, Lo-rise
Pool, Daily maid, Kitchen, Linens

Attractions: Skiing, gambling casinos, nightlife, quaint Truckee, Exercise Room, Tennis

Wake up in your custom designed condominium under your goose down comforter to a continental breakfast. 84 steps from your front door is the Squaw Valley tram. Year-round paradise resort. 15 miles to casinos. Covered parking, daily maid.

Squaw Valley Townhouses
1604 Christy Hill Lane, Box 2008
Olympic Valley, CA 95730
916-583-3451

Studio $, 1 Bedroom $$, 2 Bedrooms $$$,
　3 Bedrooms $$$
Min. Stay 2 Nights, Dep. Req'd. •
40 condos, Lo-rise, Key at 1604 Christy Hill
H-yes

Location: Ski lift: Squaw
General Facilities: Conf. rm., Daily maid, Kitchen, Linens
Room Facilities: Tennis, Horseback riding, TV, Cable, Phone in rm., Ind. Heat Ctl.
Attractions: Squaw Valley skiing
Most units are two bedroom with ski area mountain views.

Subscribe to our newsletter *Mondo Condo* and hear about the latest special condo vacation values.

———————————— OLYMPIC VALLEY ————————————

Tavern Inn Condominiums   1 Bedroom $$$, 2 Bedrooms $$$$, 3 Bedrooms
P.O. Box 2741 $$$$
Olympic Valley, CA 95730   Lo-rise
916-583-1504

Location: Airport: Reno; Ski lift: Squaw
General Facilities: Kitchen
Room Facilities: Pool, Hot tub, Tennis, Activity area, TV, Cable, Phone in rm.
Attractions: Skiing, casinos, scenic drives and walks, golf, boating, fishing
Shops & Restaurants: Tahoe City, Truckee shops; River Ranch

European, Alpine architecture among the pines with scenic views of the Sierra Nevada mountains. Free shuttle to Squaw Valley skiing, minutes to 15 other ski areas. Be at Lake Tahoe's year-round playground in 10 minutes for boating, fishing, nightlife, casinos and sightseeing. Units have Jennair cooktop ranges, generous storage space, ceramic tile baths and fireplaces. Most units have skylights, wet bars and greenhouse bay windows.

———————————— PALM DESERT ————————————

Ironwood Country Club   1 Bedrm/week 8$, 2 Bed/week 10$,
49-200 Mariposa Drive   3 Bed/week 13$
Palm Desert, CA 92260   Min. Stay 7 Nights, Visa/MC, Dep. Req'd.
619-346-0551   200 condos, Lo-rise, Villas, Key at Office
                                     No S-yes

Location: Airport: 13 miles; Downtown: 2 miles; Need car
General Facilities: Full serv., Conf. rm. cap. 130, Daily maid, Kitchen, Linens, Restaurant on prem., Bar on prem., Lounge, Baby-sitter
Room Facilities: Pool, Hot tub, Tennis, Golf: 2 championship courses, TV, Cable, VCR, Phone in rm., Crib-Hi-chair, Ind.AC Ctl., Ind. Heat Ctl.
Attractions: Palm Springs Aerial Tramway, 100+ golf courses, entertainment
Shops & Restaurants: El Paseo Avenue, 2 shopping malls, Palm Springs; Clubhouse/elegant dining

Choose from four villa complexes with desert, mountain or garden views, all offering convenience and privacy. Golf and tennis privileges extended to guests. Swimming pools and whirlpools. Perfect relaxation spot, especially in the winter.

———————————————————————————————————————

The Lakes Country Club   1 Bedroom $$$, 2 Bedrooms $$$$
75-300 Country Club Drive   Kitchen, Linens, Phone in rm.
Palm Desert, CA 92260
619-345-5695

Attractions: Tennis, Golf

Condominiums with every modern convenience and luxury. 15 tennis courts, 8 lighted, surrounded by park-like grounds, and a clubhouse with pro shop and lounge overlooking the center court. 6,500-yard 18-hole golf course, two putting greens, chipping green.

—————————————— PALM DESERT ——————————————

Palm Desert Resort Country
Club
77-6222 Country Club Dr., Suite A
Palm Desert, CA 92211
619-360-6565 800-777-2615
FAX: 619-360-4238

1 Bedroom $$$, 2 Bedrooms $$$$
1 Bedroom/week 7$, 2 Bedrooms/week 9$
Min. Stay 2 Nights, Visa/MC •
200 condos, Villas, Key at Rental office,
P-No/No S-Yes/H-Yes

Location: Airport: Palm Springs, 20 min; Downtown: 10 minutes; Need car

General Facilities: Ltd. hotel service; Linens; Baby sitter; Lounge; Crib-Hi-chair; Restaurant on premises; Bar on premises

Business Facilities: Bus. fac.; Conf. Room Cap. 100+

Sports Facilities: Pool; Tennis; Biking, jogging; Palm Desert Resort CC

Room Facilities: Kitchen; Cable; VCR; Ind.AC.Ctl; Ind.Heat Ctl.

Attractions: Golf & tennis touranments, Aerial Tram, Living Desert Reserve, Bob Hope Cultural Center

Shops & Restaurants: El Paseo, Palm Desert Town Center; Morton's of Chicago, Gila Bar & Grill

Cove Condo Rentals prides itself in offering fully-equipped condos in attractive resort communities with the highest standards of cleanliness and service. Spacious patios offer dramatic views of lush fairways, emerald lakes and majestic mountain peaks. Warmth and beauty abound as you discover the desert lifestyle! Cove has been in business since 1981 and represents approximately 200 properties in all price ranges.

———————————————————————————————————————

PGA West
76-300 Country Club Dr.
Palm Desert, CA 92260
619-345-5695

1 Bedroom $$$, 2 Bedrooms $$$$
Lo-rise

General Facilities: Linens

Sports Facilities: Pool; Tennis; Golf

Room Facilities: Kitchen; Phone

20 miles southeast of Palm Springs, nestled against the Santa Rosa Mountains. Contemporary and Mediterranean condominiums with fairway or lakeside locations. Patio furniture and BBQ. Tennis pro shop, lounge and observation tower.

Please mention *Condo Vacations—the Complete Guide* when you reserve your condominium.

———————————————— PALM DESERT ————————————————

Palm Valley Country Club
76-200 Country Club Dr.
Palm Desert, CA 92260
619-345-7802

1 Bedroom $$$, 2 Bedrooms $$$$,
3 Bedrooms $$$$
Visa/MC, Dep. Required
95 condos, Lo-rise

Location: Airport: Palm Springs 20 min.; Downtown: 3 miles

General Facilities: Daily maid; Linens; Baby sitter; Lounge; Crib-Hi-chair; Restaurant; Bar

Business Facilities: Conf. Room Cap. 300

Sports Facilities: Pool; Sauna; Hot tub; Tennis; Racquetball Club; 36 holes

Room Facilities: Kitchen; Cable; Phone; Ind.AC.Ctl

Attractions: Annenberg Center for Health Sciences, balloon rides, horseback riding, theaters; Entertainment

Shops & Restaurants: Shops at Palm Desert Town Center; Seasonal dining room

Comfort, efficiency and beauty along lush fairways and crystal clear lakes. Walk to pools and spas. Weight room, exercise classes, cushioned jogging trail, beauty salon. Mediterranean-style condominiums on the golf course with front patios, gas barbeques and patio furniture. Some units have fireplaces and wet bars.

Shadow Mountain Golf & Tennis
45750 San Luis Rey
Palm Desert, CA 92260
619-346-6123 800-472-3713
FAX: 619-346-6518

Studio $$, 1 Bedroom $$$, 2 Bedrooms
$$$, 3 Bedrooms $$$
Min. Stay 1 Night, Visa/MC
Dep. Required •
125 condos, Lo-rise
Key at Lobby front desk, No S-Yes/H-Yes

Location: Airport: 13 miles; Downtown: 3 blocks

General Facilities: Full hotel service; Daily maid; Linens; Baby sitter; Lounge; Crib-Hi-chair; Restaurant on premises; Bar on premises

Business Facilities: Bus. fac.; Conf. Room Cap. 250

Sports Facilities: Pool; Sauna; Hot tub; Tennis; Paddle ten-volley; Tennis clinics

Room Facilities: Kitchen; Cable; Phone; Ind.AC.Ctl; Ind.Heat Ctl.

Attractions: Palm Springs Aerial Tram, Living Desert Wildlife Preserve, Joshua Tree National Park; Entertainment

Shops & Restaurants: Boutiques, specialty shops, Palm Springs, Fashion Mall; La Casuelas Nuevas (Mexican)

A relaxed condominium resort and racquet club on 21 beautifully landscaped acres. This is one of the top 50 tennis resorts in the U.S., offering extensive tennis clinics. Enjoy theme buffets and barbeques by the spectacular 165-ft. figure-eight swimming pool. Just steps away is the El Paseo shopping area and Bob Hope Cultural Center.

――――――――――――――― PALM SPRINGS ―――――――――――――――

Azure Sky Resort　　　　Studio $$, 1 Bedroom $$, 1 Bed/week 4$,
1661 Calle Palo Fierro　　Min. stay 2 nights, Visa, MC, Dep. 1 night,
Palm Springs, CA 92264　　Key at On-site office
619-325-9109　　　　　　　11 condos, Villas •

Location: Airport: 6 miles; Downtown: 2 miles

General facilities: Full serv., Daily maid, Kitchen, Linens, Lounge, Hot tub

Room facilities: TV, Cable, Phone, Crib-Hi-chair, Ind. AC. Ctl, Ind. Heat Ctl.

Sports facilities: Pool, Tennis

Attractions: Palm Springs Tramway, celebrity tour, golf courses, Indian Canyons, Sunshine

Shops & Restaurants: Palm Springs Fashion Plaza, Robbie Reeds/continental

―――――――――――――――――――――――――――――――――――――――

Casa Loma　　　　　　　Studio $, 1 Bedroom $, Dep. req'd,
275 Lugo Road, 225 Cahulla Rd.　　Key at Mt. View Inn
Palm Springs, CA 92262　　Lo-rise, P-yes
619-325-5281

Location: Airport: 10 min.; Downtown: 2 blocks

General facilities: Kitchen, Linens, Sauna

Room facilities: TV, Cable, Phone, Ind. AC. Ctl, Ind. Heat Ctl.

Sports facilities: Pool

Attractions: Celebrity tour, tram to mountaintop, Desert Museum

Shops & Restaurants: Bullocks, Saks, Gucci, I. Magnin, Le Vallarius/Fr.-Cedre
　Creek

―――――――――――――――――――――――――――――――――――――――

Doubletree Resort/Desert　　1 Bedroom $$$$, 2 Bedrooms $$$$,
Princess　　　　　　　　　3 Bedrooms $$$$, 1 Bed/week 10$,
P.O. Box 1644, Vista Chino　　2 Bed/week 10$, 3 Bed/week 10$, Min. stay
Palm Springs, CA 92263　　　　2 nights, Amex, Visa, MC, Dep. req'd
619-322-7000　800-637-0577　Key at Front desk, 85 condos, Lo-rise,
　　　　　　　　　　　　　　Villas, No S-yes, P-yes, H-yes •

Location: Airport: 5 miles; Downtown: 7 miles; Need car

General facilities: Full serv., Bus. fac., Daily maid, Kitchen, Linens, Baby sitter,
　Restaurant, Bar, Lounge, Sauna, Hot tub

Room facilities: TV, Cable, VCR, Phone, Crib, Ind. AC. Ctl, Ind. Heat Ctl.

Sports facilities: Pool, Tennis, Desert Princess on-site, Racquetball, Weights

Attractions: Aerial Tramway, Oasis Water Park, Cultural Center, Desert
　Museum, Living Desert Reserve, entertainment

Shops & Restaurants: El Paseo Drive, Towne Centre, Palm Springs, La Vallerius,
　Fr. Melvyn's, continental

*Year-round 345 acre resort with 289 room/suite hotel, 782 condo/executive homes,
Country Club with 27-hole championship golf course, fitness village with 10 tennis
courts, 2 racquetball courts, weight training and exercise room, full service spa with
saunas, whirlpool and massage. Golf/Tennis Pro shops offering great sports packages. Driving range and putting greens. Olympic-size pool, lap pools plus 35 other
pools and hydropathy pools. Restaurants, bars and room service available to all
rental guests.*

─────────────── PALM SPRINGS ───────────────

Palm Springs Marquis
150 South Indian Avenue
Palm Springs, CA 92262
619-322-2121

Location: Airport: Palm Springs 5 min.; Downtown: 2 blocks

General Facilities: Full serv., Kitchen, Restaurant on prem., Bar on prem.

Room Facilities: Pool, Tennis, Golf: 20 courses nearby

Attractions: Hot air ballooning, polo matches, championship golf, shopping

Shops & Restaurants: Saks, I. Magnin, Gucci

Elegantly contemporary villas with fireplaces and wet bars beneath the mountains in the desert. Spend your time being a sun worshiper by the pool. Play tennis on one of two championship courses, or have the hotel staff arrange your golf date and transportation to one of Palm Springs' many courses. A grand resort oasis in the wilderness.

───

Racquet Club of Palm Springs
2743 North Indian Ave.
Palm Springs, CA 92262
619-325-1281   800-367-0946

1 Bedroom $$$$, 2 Bedroom $$$$, Jr. $$$
1 Bedr m/week 9$, 2 Bedrm/week 10$
AmEx/MC/Visa/Other CC, Dep. 1 Night
130 condos, Lo-rise, Keys at Front office, P-yes, No S-yes, H-yes

Location: Airport: 7 miles; Downtown: nearby

General Facilities: Conf. rm. cap. 350, Full serv., Daily maid, Kitchen, Linens, Restaurant on prem., Bar on prem., Baby sitter, Lounge.

Room Facilities: Pool, Sauna, Hot Tub, Tennis, Gym., table tennis, Palm Springs C.C. adjacent, TV, Cable, Phone in rm., Ind. AC Ctl., Ind. Heat Ctl.

Attractions: Tram to Mt. San Jacinto, riding, water parks, home tours, Bob Hope Cultural Center, hiking, entertainment.

Shops & Restaurants: All major stores, boutiques, specialty shops; Bono's-Northern Italian

Located on 25 acres, amid palms, gardens and streams are 130 richly-appointed suites decorated in light desert colors with mountain, pool and garden views. Championship tennis courts, 4 olympic sized pools, complete spa, sauna and massage facilities, 4 jacuzzi's. Incomparable dining and personalized service. Villas and townhouses range from delightful single rooms to full suites with fireplaces, wet bars and full kitchens.

—————————————— SAN CLEMENTE ——————————————

Blarney Castle
509 Monterey Ln.
San Clemente, CA 92672
714-492-7576

2 Bedrooms $$$$, 2 Bedrm/week 5$, Min.
Stay: 3 Nights, Dep. Req'd, •
3 condos, Lo-rise, Key at Manager's
Apartment.

Location: Airport: 45 min. John Wayne; Downtown: 10 minutes, Need car.

Room Facilities: Kitchen, TV, Cable, Ind. Heat Ctl.

Attractions: 40 minutes-Disneyland, Knott's Berry Farm, baseball, football, Sea World, Zoo.

Shops & Restaurants: Local small shops, 15 miles to Mall, Delaney's/Charthouse/ Casa Mari.

Small, quiet, homelike atmosphere with only 4 units in the complex. Whitewalls, earthtone furnishings with views of the ocean. Close to every type of sport activity. A good place to come in winter to get away from the ice and snow and enjoy the San Clemente climate.

San Clemente Inn
2600 Ave. Del Presidente
San Clemente, CA 92672
714-492-6103

1 Bedroom $$, 2 Bedrooms $$$.
96 condos, Key at front desk.

Room Facilities: Kitchen.

Attractions: Beach, fishing, entertainment.

Shops & Restaurants: San Clemente shops, Swallows Cove on-site/gourmet.

Executive suites for 1 to four persons. The Inn borders the State Park and is only a three block walk to the beach, or use the pool on the property. Children's play area and weekly barbeques. Gourmet restaurant on-site.

—————————————— SANTA CRUZ ——————————————

Villa Vista
2-2800 East Cliff Dr.
Santa Cruz, CA 95062
408-866-2626 800-767-0322

3 Bedrooms $$$$, 3 Bedrm/week 10$, Min.
Stay: 2 Nights, •
2 condos, Lo-rise, Villas, H-yes, Key at
Lock box on-site.

Location: Airport: 45 minute; Downtown: 10 minutes, Need car.

General Facilities: Bus. fac., Conf. Rm. Cap.: 12, Lounge, Parasailing, surfing, Bar.

Room Facilities: Kitchen, TV, Cable, VCR, Phone, Ind. Heat Ctl.

Attractions: Championship golf courses in Monterey, U. C. Santa Cruz, wine tasting.

Shops & Restaurants: Carmel art galleries and upscale clothing shops, Verandah/continental.

Monterey Bay's finest view of sand, surf, sailboats, surfers, sunsets and city lights. 3 bedroom, 3 bath units with gourmet kitchens, Cuisinart, trash compactor, fireplace, CD and video players and board games. The deck/patio includes a BBQ, outside shower, patio chairs, umbrella and beach towels. Each unit sleeps six in twin beds, with down comforters. A quiet retreat ten minutes away from Santa Cruz, or 40 minutes away from Monterey and Carmel.

---------------------- SAN CLEMENTE ----------------------

Sea Horse Inn
602 Avenida Victoria
San Clemente, CA 92672
714-492-1720

1 Bedrm/week $$$$
AmEx/Visa/MC, Dep. Req'd.
P-yes

General Facilities: Daily maid, Kitchen, Linens
Room Facilities: TV
Attractions: Mexico, San Diego-1 hour, Disneyland-30 minutes, City park
Shops & Restaurants: Fisherman's Seafood

---------------------- SAN DIEGO ----------------------

Blue Sea Lodge
707 Pacific Beach Dr.
San Diego, CA 92109
619-483-4700 800-528-1234

Studio $$$, 1 Bedroom $$$$
AmEx/Visa/MC, Dep. 1 Night •
48 condos, Lo-rise, Key at Front desk
H-yes

Location: Airport: 7 miles; Downtown: 7 miles; Need car; Beach front
General Facilities: Daily maid, Kitchen, Linens, Baby-sitter
Room Facilities: Pool, Hot tub, TV, Cable, Phone in rm., Crib-Hi-chair, Ind. Heat Ctl.
Attractions: Sea World, San Diego Zoo, Cabrillo National Momument, Mission Bay Park
Shops & Restaurants: Promenade Center, boutiques and specialty shops; McCormick
    & Schmick-seafood

Contemporary beachfront condominiums decorated in peach and blue. Situated directly on the Pacific Ocean, across the street from Mission Bay Park with a full range of water sports. A fishing pier is a short walk away. Sea World, the San Diego Zoo and Cabrillo National Momument are all a short drive away.

Capri By The Sea
628 Missouri Street
San Diego, CA 92109
619-483-5011 800-542-2772

1 Bedroom $$$, 2 Bedroom $$$
1 Bedrm/week 5$, 2 Bedrm/week 7$
Min. Stay 3 Nights, MC/Visa, Dep. Req'd
50 condos, Hi-rise, Keys at Main office,
    N S-yes

Location: Airport: 10 minutes; Downtown: 10 minutes; Beach front
General Facilities: Daily maid, Kitchen, Linens, Baby sitter , Lounge.
Room Facilities: Pool, Sauna, Hot tub, TV, Cable, VCR, Phone in rm., Ind Heat Ctl.
Attractions: Sea World, Zoo, Old Town, beaches, La Jolla, Mission Bay, Wild Animal Park
Shops & Restaurants: All kinds of shopping nearby; Many fine restaurants.

Experience magnificent ocean views from spacious 1 or 2 bedroom condominiums. Also available for those special occasions are penthouse suites. Walk to many fine restaurants. Step out the front door onto the beachfront. B.B.Q. on the roof, sun-deck, and a relaxing spa. Special underground parking spaces. Stay any closer to the ocean and you'll get wet!

────────── SODA SPRINGS ──────────

Soda Springs Station
Old Highway 40
Soda Springs, CA 95728
916-622-3666

At the base of the Soda Springs Ski area offering wide-open skiing. Ski school and rental equipment available.

────────── SOUTH LAKE TAHOE ──────────

Bavarian Village Rentals
P.O. Box 709, 1140 Herbert
South Lake Tahoe, CA 96156
916-541-8191 800-822-6636
FAX: 916-544-3082

1 Bedrm $$, 2 Bedrms $$$, 3 Bedrms $$$
1 Bedrm/week 4$, 2 Bedrms/week 5$,
   3 Bedrms/week 5$
Min. Stay 2 Nights, 1 Night Dep. Req'd. •
72 condos, Lo-rise, Key at 1140B Herbert
Ave. H-Yes

Location: Airport: 5 miles; Downtown: 1 mile; Need car; Ski lift at Heavenly
General Facilities: Linens; Baby sitter; Crib-Hi-chair
Sports Facilities: Pool
Room Facilities: Kitchen; Cable; Phone; Ind.Heat Ctl.
Attractions: The Lake, boating, swimming, water skiing, skiing, casinos—Free casino shuttles
Shops & Restaurants: Crescent shopping, 1 mile, Safeway 5 blocks; Casinos-every cuisine

Clean, quiet, large condominiums. Centrally located to Lake Tahoe and casino areas. Fully equipped, fireplaces, BBQ area. Year-round recreation for the entire family. Save $$ at Lake Tahoe's Bavarian Village. Free Casino shuttles.

────────────────────────────

Lakeland Village Beach Resort
3535 Highway 50, P.O. Box 705002
South Lake Tahoe, CA 95705
916-541-7711 800-822-5969
FAX: 916-541-6278

Studio $$, 1 Bedroom $$$,
   2 Bedrooms $$$$, 3 Bedrooms $$$$
AmEx/Visa/MC, 1 Night Dep. Req'd. •
215 condos, Key at 24-hour front desk

Location: Airport: 7 miles; Downtown: 2 miles; Beachfront; Ski lift at Nearby
General Facilities: Full hotel service; Daily maid; Linens; Crib-Hi-chair
Business Facilities: Conf. Room Cap. 75
Sports Facilities: Game room; Pool; Sauna; Hot tub; Tennis; Watercraft rental
Room Facilities: Cable; Phone; Ind.Heat Ctl.
Attractions: Tahoe Queen paddlewheel boat 2 hour daily cruise. 2 miles to casinos.
Shops & Restaurants: Casual and fine restaurants

Ideallly located to experience all that Lake Tahoe offers. Heavenly Valley skiing 2 miles away. 19 secluded acres on 1,000 feet of private beach. Boat rental, parasailing, fishing, sailboards. Complimentary casino and ski shuttle. Within minutes are 24-hour casinos offering gaming, entertainment and fine restaurants. Truly a haven for those who want to escape anytime of the year.

──────────── SOUTH LAKE TAHOE ────────────

Lake Tahoe Accommodations   Studio $$, 1 Bedroom $$, 2 Bedrooms $$,
P.O. Box 7722, 2048 Dunlap Dr.   3 Bedrooms $$$, 1 Bed/week 5$, 2
South Lake Tahoe, CA 95731   Bed/week 7$, 3 Bed/week 10$, Min. stay 4
916-544-3234 800-544-3234   nights, Visa, MC, Key at Office, No S-yes •

Location: Need car; Beach front; Ski lift: Heavenly
General facilities: Kitchen, Linens
Room facilities: TV, Cable, Phone, Ind. AC. Ctl.
Sports facilities: Tennis, Sailing, some pools
Attractions: Skiing, casinos, water sports, hiking, horseback riding
Shops & Restaurants: Factory outlet stores—Mikasa-Gitano-Capezzio-Bass-
   Oneida, Los Tres Hombres/Mexican, Petrelio's/It.

Specializing in homes, condos and cabins in the South Lake Tahoe area, tastefully decorated and comfortably furnished with well equipped kitchens. Units are located in prime areas near the lake and beaches, close to ski areas, in quiet wooded seclusion,or near the nightlife of the Nevada casinos. Many of the accommodations allow use of pools, beaches, tennis courts and jacuzzis.

Tahoe Valley Motel and Condos   Studio $$, 1 Bedroom $$$, 2 Bedrooms
P.O. Box 7702, Hwy. 50 $$$, 3 Bedrooms $$$, 1 Bed/week 7$,
South Lake Tahoe, CA 95731   2 Bed/week 8$, 3 Bed/week 9$, Min. stay
916-541-0353 800-822-5922   2 nights, Dep. req'd, Key at Tahoe Valley
   Motel, 50 condos, Lo-rise

Location: Airport: 5 miles; Downtown: 7 miles; Need car; Beach front; Ski lift: 3
   nearby
General facilities: Daily maid, Kitchen, Linens, Baby sitter, Hot tub
Room facilities: TV, Cable, Phone, Crib-Hi-chair, Ind. AC. Ctl, Ind. Heat Ctl.
Sports facilities: Pool, Tennis, Putting green, Marina
Attractions: Casinos and show rooms, scenic & nature drives and walks, skiing,
   bicycles, horses
Shops & Restaurants: Local shops, Fresh Ketch-Tw.Panda-Sw.Chalet

Most condominiums are in the Tahoe Keys area with panoramic views of the Sierras and Lake Tahoe. Olympic size swimming pool, beaches, tennis courts, putting green and basketball court. Ski packages available. Cruise Lake Tahoe on the Tahoe Queen withbreakfast onboard, to Squaw Valley or Alpine Meadows, and have dinner on the return cruise with live music and dancing.

──────────── SQUAW VALLEY ────────────

Christy Hill Resort Rentals   Studio $, 1 Bedroom $$, 2 Bedrooms $$$,
1604 Christy Hill Ln.   3 Bedrooms $$$, Min. stay 2 nights
Squaw Valley, CA 95730   Dep. req'd
916-583-3451   32 condos, Lo-rise, H-yes •

Location: Airport: 45 min.; Downtown: 5 miles; Need car; Ski lift: Squaw
General facilities: Conf. Rm., Daily maid, Kitchen, Linens, Child planned rec.
Room facilities: TV, Cable, Phone, Ind. Heat Ctl.
Sports facilities: Tennis, Riding
Attractions: Lake Tahoe, Squaw Valley Mountain ski area, gaming casinos
Shops & Restaurants: Sportswear shops, art galleries, housewares, Le
   Petite/French

─────────────────────── TAHOE CITY ───────────────────────

O'Neal Associates, Inc.
P.O. Box 802
Tahoe City, CA 95730
916-583-7368 800-222-5758

1 Bedroom $$, 2 Bedrooms $$$,
3 Bedrooms $$$
1 Bedrm/week 4$, 2 Bedrms/week 5$,
3 Bedrms/week 6$
Min. Stay 2 Nights, Dep. Required •
100 condos, Lo-rise, Key at 1877 N. Lake
Blvd., P-yes/No S-yes/H-yes

Location: Airport: South Shore 30 miles; Downtown: ½ mile; Need car; Beach front; Ski lift at Nearby

General Facilities: Daily maid; Linens; Baby sitter; Crib-Hi-chair

Business Facilities: Conf. Room Cap. 30

Sports Facilities: Game room; Pool; Sauna; Hot tub; Tennis; Volleyball, skiing; Tahoe City

Room Facilities: Kitchen; Cable; VCR; Phone; Ind.Heat Ctl.

Attractions: Skiing, boating, horseback riding, sailing, swimming, casinos

Shops & Restaurants: Specialty shops; Le Petit Pier-French

Fully furnished condominium units on Tahoe's beautiful north shore. Units on the lake, or with lake or forest views, all with decks. Lake Tahoe is a winter wonderland, a summer paradise, and a relaxing place to spend a spring or fall vacation.

───

Prudential California Realty
3210 N. Lake Blvd., P.O. Box 5518
Tahoe City, CA 96145
916-583-7523 800-655-0608
FAX: 916-583-0407

Studio $$, 1 Bedroom $$, 2 Bedrooms $$,
3 Bedrooms $$$
1 Bedrm/week 6$, 2 Bedrms/week 7$,
3 Bedrms/week 9$
Min. Stay 2 Nights, Visa/MC, Key at Office,
P-No/No S-Yes/H-Yes

Location: Airport: Reno; 45 minutes; Downtown: 2-5 miles; Need car; Beachfront; Ski lift at Alpine, Squaw

General Facilities: Linens; Crib-Hi-chair

Sports Facilities: Pool; Sauna; Tennis; Waterski, Sled riding; Hiking, biking

Room Facilities: Kitchen; Cable; VCR; Ind.Heat Ctl.

Attractions: Lake Tahoe, Squaw Valley, Alpine Meadows, Casinos, Waterskiig

Shops & Restaurants: Cobblestone, The Boatworks; Sunnyside, Garwoods, Wolfdales, etc.

A wide assortment of rentals. From cabins and condos to spectacular lakefront estates. All located around the North Shore. Close to major ske areas. The North Shore of Lake Tahoe is a year-round family vacation area. Join us!

Be sure to call the condo to verify details and prices and to make your reservation.

Northstar-at-Tahoe

————————————————— TRUCKEE —————————————————

Donner Lake Village Resort
15695 Donner Pass Road, Box 11109
Truckee, CA 95737
916-587-6081

Studio $$, 1 Bedroom $$, 2 Bedrooms $$$
1 Bedrm/week 5$, 2 Bed/week 7$
AmEx/Visa/MC •
51 condos, Lo-rise, Key at Front desk, H-yes

Location: Airport: 5 miles; Downtown: 3 miles; Need car; Beach front; Ski lift: 6 areas

General Facilities: Bus. fac., Conf. rm. cap. 75, Daily maid, Kitchen, Linens, Bar on prem., Lounge, Baby-sitter

Room Facilities: Boating, fishing, Cable, Phone in rm., Crib-Hi-chair, Ind. Heat Ctl.

Attractions: Skiing, hiking, boating, museum, gambling, snowmobiling, biking, water-skiing

Shops & Restaurants: Historic downtown Truckee with specialty shops; The Left Bank/French

A great place for a Tahoe vacation. 51 units on Donner Lake for just relaxing or boating, fishing, swimming and hiking. For winter skiing drive to Boreal, Squaw Valley, Tahoe Donner, Northstar, Sugar Bowl, and Alpine, all within 15 minutes. Browse or shop in downtown Truckee, stop at the soda shop, have a gourmet dinner, or buy your own groceries and cook at home.

─────────────────── TRUCKEE ───────────────────

Northstar at Tahoe   Studio $$, 1 Bedroom $$, 2 Bedrooms $$,
P.O. Box 129   3 Bedrooms $$$
Truckee, CA 95734   225 condos, Lo-rise
916-562-1010 800-533-6787

Location: Airport: Truckee 3 miles; Downtown: 6 miles; Ski lift at Nearby

General Facilities: Lounge; Restaurant; Bar

Business Facilities: Conference Room

Sports Facilities: Pool; Sauna; Tennis; Bikes—horses—weights; Northstar at Tahoe

Attractions: Golf, tennis, horses, biking, swimming, skiing, weight room, Lake Tahoe activities; Entertainment

Shops & Restaurants: Outpost Store (video), gift shop, general store; Schaffer's Mill, Deli, Pizza

The 2,560 Northstar resort features golf, tennis, horseback riding, swimming, bike riding, volleyball and hayrides. Summer fun includes a jazz and brunch in the Village, art show, running race, food and wine festival and musical reviews. Minors' Camp is offered for children two through ten. A full-service alpine and cross-country ski resort with limited daily lift passes. Ski to the lifts from your condo or take the shuttle. All the attractions you need for your vacation.

─────────────── YOSEMITE NATIONAL PARK ───────────────

The Redwoods Guest Cottages   1 Bedroom $$, 2 Bedrooms $$$,
P.O. Box 2085 Wawona Station   3 Bedrooms $$$$
Yosemite National Park, CA 95389   Min. Stay 2 Nights, Visa/MC •
209-375-6666 FAX: 209-375-6400   123 condos, Homes, Key at Redwoods
                                   Office, P-No/No S-Yes/H-Yes

Location: Airport: Fresno, 1.5 hours; Downtown: Yosemite Valley; Need car; Riverfront; Ski lift at Badger 17 miles

General Facilities: Full hotel service; Daily maid; Linens; Parking service; Crib-Hi-Chair

Sports Facilities: Biking; Hiking, Ice skating; Wawona Golf cource; Junior Ranger Progrm

Room Facilities: Kitchen; TV; VCR; Ind.Heat Ctl.

Attractions: Only home rentals in Yosemite National Park w/ access to all activities available in Park

Shops & Restaurants: Wawona, Ahwahnee, Erna's Elderberry House

Visit Yosemite any season! Secluded in the Park is group of privately owned mountain homes, The Redwoods. Nestled among forest and mountain streams in community of Wawona. Many species of wildlife can be seen here at 4000 ft. elevation, where the air is clear and pure. Perfect place for family vacations, reunions, weddings, business retreats or that special getaway. Variety of homes from cozy 1-bedrooms to spacious 5-bedrooms, rustic to modern. Wide picture windows & spacious decks. Completely furnished.

Please mention *Condo Vacations—the Complete Guide* when you reserve your condominium.

Colorado

```
Steamboat Springs        Grand Lake
        •                      •              •
        Keystone • Winter Park     Beaver Creek
              •    Frisco   Lakewood  Silver Creek
        Mesa         Avon •• Vail  •
              •      Aspen • • Copper Mountain
        Snowmass Village •  • Dillon  Silverthorne
                              Breckenridge
        Crested Butte •


        Telluride •


                  • Durango      •
                            Pagosa Springs
```

———————————————— ASPEN ————————————————

Alpine Peaks
P.O. Box 3123
Aspen, CO 81612
303-925-7820
General Facilities: Daily maid; Linens
Sports Facilities: Pool; Tennis; Health Spa
Room Facilities: Kitchen
Attractions: Skiing, Health Spa with massages, steam, sauna, aqua exercise.

Spacious, individually owned apartments and personalized service. You don't have to be a skier to enjoy Aspen Alps. The desk will be happy to assist you with restaurant reservations, shopping, rental automobiles and ticket information.

Aspen Silverglo Condominiums   Studio $$$, 1 Bedroom $$$$,
940 Waters Ave.   2 Bedrooms $$$$, 3 Bedrooms $$$$
Aspen, CO 81611   Min. Stay 4 Nights, Dep. Required
970-925-8450 FAX: 970-920-3720   24 condos, Lo-rise
Location: Airport: Denver 4 hours; Downtown: 3 blocks; Ski lift at Aspen Mt.
General Facilities: Laundry
Sports Facilities: Game room; Pool; Sauna; Fireplace
Room Facilities: Kitchen; Phone
Attractions: Aspen Music Festival, Aspen Institute for Humanistic Studies, art
  galleries, 4 ski areas
Shops & Restaurants: Aspen shops; Restaurants-variety

Warm, intimate, with frontier congeniality. Beam ceilings, rock fireplaces, wood panelling. Convenient to ski areas. Summer wildflowers-hiking, fishing, golf, mountain climbing.

──────────────── ASPEN ────────────────

Aspen Ski Lodge   1 Bedroom $$, 2 Bedrooms $$$$, Lo-rise
101 W. Main St.   Pool, Kitchen
Aspen, CO 81611
800-356-6559

Small, intimate with a friendly staff. Continental breakfast, weekly champagne gathering, California wine tasting. An unforgettable holiday in a skier's paradise.

Durant Condominiums   1 Bedroom $$
718 South Galena Street   Pool, Daily maid, Kitchen
Aspen, CO 81611
303-925-7910 800-321-7025

Fireplaces and panoramic views, 1.5 blocks from Aspen Mountain Gondola and the center of town. Free shuttle bus to three other ski areas.

Fasching Haus   Studio $$, 1 Bedroom $$, 2 Bedrooms $$$,
747 Galena Street   3 Bedrooms $$$$
Aspen, CO 81611   AmEx, Dep. Req'd. •
303-925-5900 800-321-7025   30 condos, Lo-rise, Key at Front desk

Location: Airport: 5 miles; Downtown: 2 blocks; Ski lift: Aspen Mt.

General Facilities: Full serv., Conf. rm. cap. 30, Daily maid, Kitchen, Linens, Baby-sitter

Room Facilities: Pool, Sauna, Hot tub, TV, Cable, Phone in rm., Crib-Hi-chair, Ind. Heat Ctl.

Attractions: Music festival, Ballet Aspen, skiing, balloon rides, river rafting, horses, jeep tours, entertainment

Shops & Restaurants: Small boutiques, Esprit Store; Chart House/steak-seafood

Fully furnished, newly remodeled 1-3 bedroom condominiums and lodge rooms in Aspen's best location, 200 yards from the Aspen Mountain Gondola. Pool, jacuzzi, sauna and exercise room. Four mountains for beginners to experts to ski with groomed trails and Rocky Mountain powder. Discover "The Town" for apres-ski. Summer Aspen has music, ballet, art & film festivals, golf and tennis. Housemen on call. Lack of snow refund policy.

Fifth Avenue   1 Bedroom $$$, 2 Bedrooms $$
747 South Galena   Pool, Daily maid, Kitchen, Phone in rm.
Aspen, CO 81611
303-925-7397 800-321-7025

1.5 blocks from the gondola at Aspen mountain, one-to four-bedroom condominiums with fireplaces. Swimming, jacuzzi, sauna and guest laundry facilities.

Please mention *Condo Vacations the Complete Guide* when you reserve your condominium.

—————————————— ASPEN ——————————————

The Gant
610 West End St.
Aspen, CO 81612
970-925-5000 800-345-1471
FAX: 970-925-6891

1 Bedroom $$$$, 2 Bedrooms $$$$, 3
Bedrooms 4$
AmEx/Visa/MC, Dep. Required •
119 condos, Key at Gant office

Location: Airport: 2 miles; Downtown: 3 blocks; Ski lift at 2 blocks

General Facilities: Full hotel service; Daily maid; Linens; Baby sitter; Crib-Hi-chair

Business Facilities: Conf. Room Cap. 225

Sports Facilities: Pool; Sauna; Hot tub; Tennis; Ski, golf, horses, rafts

Room Facilities: Kitchen; Cable; Phone; Ind.Heat Ctl.

Attractions: Maroon Bells—wilderness, Gondola, Music festival, Ashcroft—old mining town

Shops & Restaurants: Ralph Lauren, Esprit, Benetton; French, Mexican, Chinese, Italian

The Gant is a self-contained retreat on five beautifully landscaped acres near the base of Aspen Mountain. Hiking trails lead from the forest and mountains in moments. Complimentary van service is available to shuttle guests on request. 5 tennis courts with a resident tennis pro, 2 pools, 3 jacuzzis, saunas, bicycles. Ski Aspen, raft the Colorado, attend the Aspen Music Festival-Ballet, and the Wheeler Opera House. The perfect blend of relaxation and stimulation.

The Gant

———————————————— AVON ————————————————

Beaver Creek West
P.O. Box 5290
Avon, CO 81620
303-949-4840 800-222-4840

1 Bedroom $$, 2 Bedrooms $$,
   3 Bedrooms $$$
Min. Stay 2 Nights, AmEx/Visa/MC,
   Dep. Required •
124 condos, Hi-rise, Lo-rise
Key at Front desk, H-yes

Location: Airport: Denver 100 miles; Downtown: 2 blocks; Ski lift at Vail

General Facilities: Daily maid; Linens; Baby sitter; Crib-Hi-chair

Sports Facilities: Pool; Sauna; Hot tub; Tennis; By public lake; 10 miles—4 courses; Vail Associates

Room Facilities: Kitchen; Phone; Ind.Heat Ctl.

Attractions: Snowmobiling, jeep tours, sleigh rides, concerts, weekend events, horses, fishing

Shops & Restaurants: Ralph Lauren, Gucci, Benetton, Golden Bear, Vail; Mirabelles French, Legends seafood

Comfortable, generously sized affordable lodging near Vail Mountain, home of the 1989 World Alpine Championships. Use the outdoor heated pool, sauna and hot tubs, or picnic on the public park and lake. All units have fireplaces and full baths for each bedroom. After a busy day try one of the many restaurants and clubs in Vail or Beaver Creek, or stay in your condo for a quiet family dinner and satellite TV watching.

———————————————————————————————————————

The Christie Lodge
0047 E. Beaver Creek Bl. Box 1196
Avon, CO 81620
303-949-7700 800-551-4326
FAX: 303-845-4535

1 Bedroom $$$, 3 Bedrooms $$$

General Facilities: Fireplaces; Linens

Sports Facilities: Pool; Hot tub; Fitness room

Room Facilities: Kitchen

Attractions: Skiing, cross country touring, golf, tennis, rafting, fishing

Ten minutes west of Vail, comfortable mini-kitchen condos with fireplace open onto a glass-domed atrium. On-site restaurants, sports shop, pools, hot tubs, exercise and conference rooms. Park in the underground garage and shuttle throughout the Vail valley.

———————————————— BEAVER CREEK ————————————————

Park Plaza Lodge
P.O. Box 36, 46 Avondale Lane
Beaver Creek, CO 81620
303-845-7700 800-525-2257

2 Bedrooms $$$, 3 Bedrooms $$$$
Min. Stay 7 Nights, AmEx/Visa/MC,
Dep. Req'd. •
36 condos, Hi-rise, Key at Front desk

Location: Airport: 2½ miles; Need car; Ski lift: Vail

General Facilities: Full serv., Conf. rm. cap. 500, Daily maid, Kitchen, Linens, Restaurant on prem., Bar on prem., Lounge, Baby-sitter, Child planned rec.: Nursery-Preschool

Room Facilities: Pool, Sauna, Hot tub, Tennis, Horses, rafting, fish, Golf: B.C. Golf Course-near, Cable, Phone in rm., Crib-Hi-chair, Ind. Heat Ctl.

Attractions: Skiing, rafting, hiking, golf, fishing, ballooning, Orvis Flyfishing School, entertainment

Shops & Restaurants: International selection of shops in Vail Village; Legends/seafood-LeRoy's/Amer.

Five-star condominiums just steps away from the ski slopes, adjacent to an 18-hole golf course. Indoor pool, jacuzzi, steam room, special programs for children and pop and classical concerts for adults. Units have mountain and valley views, and are furnished in blues and rusts with brass, crystal and wood appointments. Continental breakfasts, golf and tennis tournaments and bike races.

———————————————————————————————————

Poste Montane at Beaver Creek
76 Avon Dale Lane, Box 36
Beaver Creek, CO 81620
303-845-7500 800-525-2257

Studio $$, 1 Bedroom $$, 2 Bedrooms $$$
Min. Stay 7 Nights, AmEx/Visa/MC,
Dep. Req'd. •
24 condos, Hi-rise, Key at Front desk

Location: Airport: 2½ miles; Ski lift: Nearby

General Facilities: Full serv., Conf. rm. cap. 500, Daily maid, Kitchen, Linens, Restaurant on prem., Bar on prem., Lounge, Baby-sitter, Child planned rec.: Nursery, Kid's Spot

Room Facilities: Sauna, Hot tub, Tennis, Horses, Rafting, Golf: Beaver Creek Golf Course, Cable, VCR, Phone in rm., Crib-Hi-chair, Ind. Heat Ctl.

Attractions: Skiing, rafting, hiking, golf, fishing, ballooning, Orvis Flyfishing school, entertainment

Shops & Restaurants: International shops Vail Village, specialty shops; Legends/seafood-LeRoy's/Amer.

European mountain lodge, Laura Ashley wallpaper, rose and green color scheme. Children's ski school, theatre and petting zoo. Continental breakfast, steps from the ski lifts and adjacent to 18-hole championship golf course. Hot tub, sauna, bike racing and the 1989 host for the World Alpine Ski Championships.

We want to hear from you—any comments regarding the condos or our publication may be noted on the form at the end of the book.

--------------------------------- BEAVER CREEK ---------------------------------

The Charter at Beaver Creek   Studio $$, 1 Bedroom $$$, 2 Bedrooms $$$$,
120 Offerson Rd., P.O. Box 5310   3 Bedrooms $$$$
Beaver Creek, CO 81620   Min. Stay 2 Nights, AmEx/Visa/MC,
303-949-6660 800-824-3064   Dep. Req'd. •
                                          156 condos, Hi-rise, Key at Front desk

Location: Airport: Denver 110 miles; Ski lift: Beaver Cr

General Facilities: Full serv., Conf. rm., Daily maid, Kitchen, Linens, Restaurant on
prem., Bar on prem., Game room, Lounge, Baby-sitter

Room Facilities: Pool, Sauna, Hot tub, Tennis, Indoor lap pool, Golf: Beaver Creek PGA
Golf, TV, Cable, Phone in rm., Crib-Hi-chair, Ind. Heat Ctl.

Attractions: Golf, scenic chairlift rides, jeep tours, fishing, outdoor concerts, hiking, bik-
ing, entertainment

Shops & Restaurants: General store, sports shop, Beaver Creek Village; Terrace/
casual-First Season

*Quiet mountain retreat at the base of Beaver Creek Mountain. 200 feet to golf, walking dis-
tance to tennis and horseback riding. Surrounded by aspen and spruce-beautiful smog-
free air. Weight-aerobics room. Full breakfast included with winter rates. Piano player in
lounge.*

The Inn at Beaver Creek   Studio $$
P.O. Box 36, 10 Elk Track   Min. Stay 7 Nights, AmEx/Visa/MC,
Beaver Creek, CO 81620   Dep. Req'd. •
303-845-7800 800-525-7800   39 condos, Lo-rise, Key at Front desk
                                          H-yes

Location: Airport: 2½ miles; Need car; Ski lift: Beaver

General Facilities: Full serv., Conf. rm. cap. 500, Daily maid, Kitchen, Linens, Bar on
prem., Lounge, Baby-sitter, Child planned rec.: Preschool/Kid's Spot

Room Facilities: Pool, Hot tub, Tennis, horses, rafting, fish, Golf: B.C. Golf Course-near,
Cable, Phone in rm., Crib-Hi-chair, Ind. Heat Ctl.

Attractions: Orvis Flyfishing School, skiing, rafting, hiking, golf, ballooning, fishing,
entertainment

Shops & Restaurants: Vail Village international shops, specialty shops; Golden
Eagle/game-Mirabelles

*Quaint mountain lodge, 20 feet from chairlift, outdoor pool, hot tub, sauna, steam room,
lounge, underground parking. Pop and classical concerts, bike races, golf and tennis tournaments, 1989 World Alpine Ski Championships. For the children, nursery, preschool,
Small World, kid's spot, theatre and petting zoo. Units are furnished in blues and cranberry
and continental breakfast is offered.*

Subscribe to our newsletter *Mondo Condo* and hear about the latest
special condo vacation values.

--------------------------------- BRECKENRIDGE ---------------------------------

Beaver Run
P.O. Box 2115
Breckenridge, CO 80424
303-453-6000 800-525-2253

Studio $$, 1 Bedroom $$, 2 Bedrooms $$$,
3 Bedrooms $$$$
AmEx/Visa/MC, Dep. Required •
500 condos, Hi-rise
Key at Front desk, H-yes

Location: Airport: 81 miles; Downtown: ¼ mile; Need car; Ski lift at Nearby

General Facilities: Full serv.; Daily maid; Linens; Baby sitter; Lounge; Restaurant; Bar

Business Facilities: Conf. Room Cap. 800

Sports Facilities: Game room; Pool; Sauna; Hot tub; Tennis; Ski-in/ski-out

Room Facilities: Kitchen; Cable; Phone; Ind.Heat Ctl.

Attractions: Historic area, mines, museums, ski areas, lakes; entertainment

Shops & Restaurants: Resort town shopping; Over 120 in town

Modern, comfortable, contemporary suites in a fully self-contained resort. Ski to Breckenridge ski area or visit the historic town of Breckenridge. Live entertainment in the modern lounge. All summer outdoor activities.

Four Seasons Lodging, Inc.
P.O. Box 1356, 424 S. Ridge St.
Breckenridge, CO 80424
970-453-1403 800-848-3434
FAX: 970-453-7046

Studio $$$, 1 Bedroom $$$$,
2 Bedrooms $$$$, 3 Bedrooms $$$$
1 Bedrm/week 10$, 2 Bedrms/week 10$,
3 Bedrms/week 10$
Min. Stay Ask, Visa/MC, Dep. Required •
93 condos, Hi-rise, Lo-rise, Key at Approp.
office, P-No/No S-Yes

Location: Airport: 110 miles; Downtown: 1 block; Ski lift at 300 yards

General Facilities: Full hotel service; Linens; Baby sitter; Crib-Hi-chair

Sports Facilities: Pool; Sauna; Hot tub; Hiking, Riding; Golf, Fishing, Biking; Daycare & ski school

Room Facilities: Kitchen; Cable; VCR; Phone

Attractions: Historial tours thru Breckenridge. Summer music concerts at Breckenridge Riverwalk Center.

Shops & Restaurants: Many types specialty shops & factory outlet stores, 16 miles; Hearthstone Restaurant-American cuisine

We offer accommodations in the historic town of Breckenridge. Our properties are located at the south end of town close to the base of Peak 9. Either ski-in/ski-out, or take a short walk to lifts and downtown for restaurants, night clubs and shopping. Choose from the many activities offered in the area or relax in the tranquility of the mountains.

Enter your favorite condo in our "Condo of the Year" contest (entry form is in the back of the book).

———————————— BRECKENRIDGE ————————————

Gold Point Condominiums 1 Bedroom $$, 2 Bedrooms $$,
169 N. Fuller Placer Rd.-Box 568 3 Bedrooms $$, Min. stay 2 nights
Breckenridge, CO 80424 Amex, Visa, MC, Dep. req'd
303-453-1910 800-231-3780 Key at On site office, 36 condos
Lo-rise, H-yes •

Location: Airport: 80 miles; Downtown: 3 miles; Need car; Ski lift: Nearby

General facilities: Daily maid, Kitchen, Linens, Baby sitter, Hot tub

Room facilities: TV, Cable, Crib-Hi-chair, Ind. Heat Ctl.

Sports facilities: Breckenridge Golf Club, Athletic club

Attractions: Hiking, skiing, sailing, jeep rides, bike trails, gold mines

Shops & Restaurants: Breckenridge Victorian town, Vail, 60 restaurants in Breckenridge

For those who want the best, Gold Point offers quality accommodations with spacious townhouses and penthouses. Garages with automatic door openers, private balconies overlooking spectacular panoramic mountain views, and fully equipped kitchens. Hot tub,party room, Athletic Club with swimming, racquetball, nautilus, steam sauna, dining room and bar.

———————————————————————————————

Lake Cliffe 1 Bedroom $$, 2 Bedrooms $$$
160 East La Bonte
Breckenridge, CO 80424
303-468-2301

General facilities: Daily maid, Kitchen, Linens

Sports facilities: Pool

Attractions: National forest, golf, tennis, fishing, art shows, rodeos, craft fairs, film festivals

Views of Lake Dillon and the Ten Mile Range from these spacious lakefront units. Amenities include a clubhouse with pool, sauna and jacuzzi. Ski at five mountains, nearby golf, tennis, lake fishing, hiking, horseback riding and rafting for the rest of the year.

———————————————————————————————

Pine Ridge Condominiums 2 Bedrooms $$$$, 3 Bedrooms $$$$
P.O. Box 487
Breckenridge, CO 80424
303-453-6946 800-333-8833

Ski home at day's end to your individually decorated condominium, and relax in front of the fireplace while other skiers are still in the parking lot. Helpful, friendly staff to assist you all year long. Enjoy the hot tubs and pool. Short walk to Main Street or catch town trolley in front of the property.

Enter your favorite condo in our "Condo of the Year" contest (entry form is in the back of the book).

──────────────── BRECKENRIDGE ────────────────

Ski Hill Condominiums
250 Ski Hill Road
Breckenridge, CO 80424
303-453-2262 800-525-3882

Studio $$$, 1 Bedroom $$$, 2 Bedrooms $$$
AmEx/Visa/MC, Dep. Req'd. •
280 condos, Hi-rise, Key at 11072 N. Highway 9
No S-yes/H-yes

Location: Airport: 85 miles; Ski lift: Breckenridge

General Facilities: Kitchen, Linens, Baby-sitter, Child planned rec.: Ski lessons/day care

Room Facilities: Hot tub, Winter ski resort, Golf: Breckenridge—3 miles, Cable, VCR, Phone in rm., Ind. Heat Ctl.

Attractions: Skiing, snowmobile, sleigh ride, ice skating, horses, biking, fishing, boating

Shops & Restaurants: Over 300 shops, restaurants and bars

Deluxe one-and two-bedroom condominiums located in the heart of Breckenridge, one block to shops and restaurants and 2 blocks to the ski lifts and one block to free shuttle. Indoor hot tubs, central laundry facilities, covered parking and elevators. Spectacular alpine summers with sunny days and crisp nights, wildflowers, clear streams for fishing or just lazing in the sun until the cool of the evening.

The Gant

──────────────── BRECKENRIDGE ────────────────

Summit Ridge Lodgings
11072 US Hwy. 9
Breckenridge, CO 80424
303-453-2262 800-525-3882

Trails End Condominiums   1 Bedroom $$, 2 Bedrooms $$$
455 West Village Road   Pool, Daily maid, Kitchen, Phone in rm.
Breckenridge, CO 80424
303-968-2626 800-624-4242

Long a Breckenridge favorite, Trails End's tastefully appointed condominiums are within easy walking distance to Breckenridge's recreational facilities. Ski-in/ski-out, ski lockers, covered parking.

The Village At Breckenridge   1 Bedroom $$$, 2 Bedrooms $$$$
P.O. Box 8329   Pool, Daily maid, Kitchen, Phone in rm.
Breckenridge, CO 80424
303-453-2000 800-332-0424

Attractions: Health club, steam

You'll be treated with style and friendly service at this resort situated on the shore of historic Maggie Pond. Waterfront promenade and views of Colorado's great outdoors. The Village provides everything you need for a complete summer or winter vacation.

──────────────── COPPER MOUNTAIN ────────────────

Carbemate Property Management Studio $, 2 Bedrooms $$, 3 Bedrooms $$
Co.   AmEx/Visa/MC •
Box 3216   56 condos
Copper Mountain, CO 80443   H-yes
303-968-6854 800-526-7737

Location: Airport: Denver—15 miles; Downtown: 10 miles; Need car; Ski lift: Copper Mt.

General Facilities: Daily maid, Kitchen

Room Facilities: Sauna, Hot tub, Tennis, Hiking, fishing, spa, Golf: Nearby, TV, Phone in rm., Ind. Heat Ctl.

Attractions: Skiing, hiking, fishing

Shops & Restaurants: Frisco shops

Condominiums in a quiet, cool mountain setting. Southwestern motifs done in naturals with accents of mauve. Most units have mountain views and fireplaces. Free use of Athletic Club.

Subscribe to our newsletter *The Condo-Line* and hear about the latest special condo vacation values.

————————————— COPPER MOUNTAIN —————————————

Copper Mountain Inn
P.O. Box 3003
Copper Mountain, CO 80443
303-968-6477   800-525-3891

Studio $$, 1 Bedroom $$,
2 Bedrooms $$$, 3 Bedrooms $$$$
1 Bed/week 5$, 2 Bed/week 7$,
3 Bed/week 10$
Min. stay 3 nights, Amex, Visa, MC,
Dep. req'd Lo-rise No S-yes, H-yes •

Location: Airport: 2 hours, Downtown: 1 block, Ski lift: Copper. Mountain.
General facilities: Daily maid, Kitchen, Linens, Day care, Babysitter, Sauna
Room facilities: TV, Cable, Phone, Crib-Hi-chair, Ind.AC.Ctl, Ind.Heat Ctl.
Sports facilities: Pool, Tennis, Copper Creek Golf Club, Ice skating
Attractions: Summer and winter activities

Close to ski slopes, shops and restaurants. Fantastic scenery. All summer and winter sports for a great vacation any time.

Copper Mountain Resort
I-70 & US Hwy 91, Box 3001
Copper Mountain, CO 80443
303-968-2882   800-458-8386

Studio $$$, 1 Bedroom $$$,
2 Bedrooms $$$$, 3 Bedrooms $$$$
Amex, Visa, MC, Dep. req'd
650 condos, Hi-rise, Lo-rise,
Key at Mt. Plaza Guest Reg.
No S-yes, P-yes, H-yes •

Location: Airport: 75 miles, Downtown: 75 miles, Ski lift: Cpr. Mtn.
General facilities: Full serv., Bus. fac., Conf. Rm. (cap. 800), Daily maid, Kitchen, Linens, Child planned rec., Baby sitter, Restaurants, Bars, Game room, Lounges, Sauna, Hot tub, Concierge, Bell service
Room facilities: TV, Cable, Phone, Crib-Hi-chair, Ind.Heat Ctl., AAA 4-Diamond
Sports facilities: Pool, Tennis, Copper Creek Golf Club, Racquet and Athletic club
Attractions: Tennis/golf tournaments, International Festival, MM Murphey's WestFest, Nordic & Cross Country skiing
Shops & Restaurants: Village ski-golf shops, gifts, art and restaurants

This award winning resort treats you like royalty. All employees have completed training in guest services. After a day of skiing relax in the jacuzzi, work out in the Athletic Club, pamper yourself with a massage, or relax and enjoy the view of snow-covered mountains from your condo. A family resort with nursery and children's programs. Sleighrides through the woods, helicopter skiing, summer biking, golf, horseback riding, family picnics, fly fishing or shopping in the Village.

Foxpine Inn
P.O. Box 3296
Copper Mountain, CO 80443
303-968-2600   800-426-7400

1 Bedroom $$
2 Bedrooms $$
Hi-rise

General facilities: Daily maid, Kitchen, Linens
Sports facilities: Pool, Golf course
Attractions: Trail rides, tennis, hiking, biking, rafting, golf, skiing, Lake Dillon

30 paces to the ski lifts from your units, or drive to three other major ski areas. Ski home to your condominium and curl up in front of the warm fireplace. Summer brings lake boating, Colorado River rafting and hiking, biking or riding in beautiful mountain scenery.

─────────────── CRESTED BUTTE ───────────────

San Moritz Condominiums   1 Bedroom $, 2 Bedrooms $$, Lo-rise
P.O. Box 169   Kitchen, Linens, Phone in rm.
Crested Butte, CO 81224
303-349-5150

Attractions: Skiing, year-round vacation recreation

Ski-in, ski-out condominiums for an unforgettable winter vacation. Rock fireplaces and spectacular views. Hot tubs and saunas to ease stiff muscles unused to skiing. Friendly staff will be happy to arrange ski rentals, local transportation and grocery shopping.

The Columbine Condominiums   1 Bedroom $$, 2 Bedrooms $$, 3 Bedrooms $$
Drawer C, 51, Whetstone Road   AmEx/Visa/MC, Dep. 50% •
Crested Butte, CO 81225   30 condos, Lo-rise, Key at Three Seasons Condos
303-349-2448   800-821-3718

Location: Airport: 30 miles; Downtown: 3 miles; Ski lift: Nearby

General Facilities: Daily maid, Kitchen, Linens, Baby-sitter, Child planned rec.: Kids ski school

Room Facilities: Sauna, Hot tub, Golf: Skyland Resort-6 miles, TV, Cable, Phone in rm., Crib-Hi-chair, Ind. Heat Ctl.

Attractions: Skiing, ski-in, ski-out, Crested Butte National Historic District

Shops & Restaurants: Handmade items, souvenirs and pottery; Le Basquet-gourmet French

Casual, comfortable condominiums with magnificent mountain views from your balcony. Put your skis on and head for the chairlifts of Crested Butte. Three miles away is the National Historic District of Crested Butte where plenty of shopping and restaurants are available. For summer visitors, there's river rafting, jeeping, fishing, hiking, tennis, biking, kayaking and horseback riding.

─────────────── DILLON ───────────────

Buffalo Village   1 Bedroom $$, 2 Bedrooms $$
89400 Ryan Gulch Road   Pool
Dillon, CO 80435
303-468-6509

Attractions: Tennis

Nestled in the woods of Wildernest Mountain, 3 miles northwest of Dillon, in the heart of ski country. Rock fireplace, oak trim, large closets, tile baths. The best in Rocky Mountain living.

Chateau Claire Condos   1 Bedroom $$, 2 Bedrooms $$, Lo-rise
240 E. Labonte, Box 539
Dillon, CO 80435
303-468-2760   800-521-0531

Completely equipped condominiums in the Rockies. Great skiing, trout fishing, tennis, hiking, pool, hunting, golf, sailing on Lake Dillon. Close to shops, theatres, restaurants and parks.

────────────────── DILLON ──────────────────

Columbine Mgmt & Real Estate Co.
P.O. Box 2590, 348 Lake Dillon Dr
Dillon, CO 80435
970-468-9137 800-944-9601
FAX: 970-468-2556

Studio $$, 1 Bedroom $$$,
2 Bedrooms $$$$, 3 Bedrooms $$$$
1 Bedrm/week 6$, 2 Bedrms/week 8$,
3 Bedrms/week 10$
Min. Stay Ask, Visa/MC •
80 condos, Lo-rise, Villas, Key at Office or ski shop, P-No/No S-Yes/H-Ltd

Location: Airport: Denver, 80 miles; Downtown: Denver, 70 miles; Ski lift at 5-15 miles

General Facilities: Linens; Cribs

Sports Facilities: Game room; Pool; Sauna; Hot tub; Sailing, Biking; Cross-country skiing

Room Facilities: Kitchen; Cable; VCR; Phone; Ind.Heat Ctl.

Attractions: Skiing! Highest yacht club in the country, every outdoor activity imaginable.

Shops & Restaurants: 78 factory outlet stores 1 mile away, numerous boutiques; Ristorante al Lago-Northern Italian

Where else will you find 6,002 skiable acres with 1,454 of them snowmaking terrain? or 374 ski trails? With 59 lifts! Keystone, Arapaho Basin, Breckenridge & Copper Mountain within 12 miles. Vail, Beaver Creak, Loveland within 25 miles. Cross-country... Hand-picked finest condos, duplexes, private mountain homes to suit, and price ranges to fit any budget. Views! Views! Views! And summertime offers a plethora of fun-filled activities. Hike, climb, fish, sail, bike, roller blade, golf, raft, kayak, canoe.

───

Orofino
P.O. Box C
Dillon, CO 80435
303-468-5484 800-433-2815

2 Bedrooms $$
Lo-rise

Sports Facilities: Golf

Room Facilities: Kitchen; Phone

Attractions: Skiing, sailing, windsurfing, fishing, golf, horses, tennis, boating, white water rafting

Year-round sports and recreation in Summit County. Two story townhouses with washer/dryer and woodburning stove. Choose from four major ski areas. Minutes to shops, restaurants and nightlife. Three hot tubs open all year.

─────────────── DILLON ───────────────

Swan Mountain Resort
59 Soda Ridge Road, Box 95
Dillon, CO 80435
303-468-6595

1 Bedroom $$, 2 Bedrooms $$, Lo-rise
Pool, Kitchen, Linens

Attractions: Tennis, Golf

High in the Rockies, a four-season adventureland with exciting summer and winter sports. Pool, hot tub, barbecue, fireplace, microwave oven, balconies and patios.

─────────────────────────────────────

Yacht Club Condominiums, Inc.
410 Tenderfoot Box 397
Dillon, CO 80435
303-468-2703 800-999-2123

Studio $$, 1 Bedroom $$, 2 Bedrooms $$$,
  3 Bedrooms $$$
AmEx/Visa/MC, Dep. Req'd. •
40 condos, Lo-rise, Key at Office
H-yes

Location: Airport: 1½ hours Denver; Downtown: 3 miles; Need car; Ski lift: Keystone

General Facilities: Kitchen, Linens

Room Facilities: Sauna, Hot tub, Tennis, Sailing, boating, TV, Cable, Crib-Hi-chair, Ind. Heat Ctl.

Attractions: Summer: sailing, fishing, bicycle trails, hiking; Winter: 5 ski areas

Comfortable condominiums on the shore of Lake Dillon individually decorated with tasteful furnishings. Pick your season and enjoy the fabulous outdoor activities that surround you.

─────────────── DURANGO ───────────────

Cascade Village Resort
P.O. Box 2867, 50827 Hwy 550 N.
Durango, CO 81301
303-259-3500 800-525-0896

Studio $, 1 Bedroom $$, 2 Bedrooms $$,
  3 Bedrooms $$
1 Bedrm/week $$$$, 2 Bed/week 4$,
  3 Bed/week 5$
Min. Stay Ask, AmEx/Visa/MC, Dep. 1 Night •
125 condos, Lo-rise, Key at Benchmark Building

Location: Airport: 45 miles; Downtown: 30 miles; Need car; Ski lift: Nearby

General Facilities: Full serv., Conf. rm. cap. 100, Daily maid, Kitchen, Linens, Restaurant on prem., Bar on prem., Game room, Lounge, Baby-sitter

Room Facilities: Pool, Sauna, Hot tub, Tennis, Adjacent ski area, Golf: Durango-25 miles, TV, Cable, Phone in rm., Crib-Hi-chair, Ind. Heat Ctl.

Attractions: Durango/Silverton Narrow Gauge RR, Mesa Verde Nat. Park, Purgatory Theater, entertainment

Shops & Restaurants: Country store at Cascade, Historic Durango shops; Cafe Cascade-seafood, steaks

Luxury condominiums located in the two million acre San Juan National Forest adjacent to Purgatory ski area. Tennis lessons, horseback riding, river rafting, hiking, fishing, Alpine slide and trout pond. All this plus an indoor pool and jacuzzi make Cascade Village a wonderful summer or winter vacation spot.

———————————————— DURANGO ————————————————

Ferringway 1 Bedroom $$, 2 Bedrooms $$$
6 Ferringway Circle 1 Bed/week 4$, 2 Bed/week 5$
Durango, CO 81301 Amex, Visa, MC, Dep. 1 night
303-247-0441 800-624-9714 50 condos, Lo-rise, Key at Front desk
P-yes •

Location: Airport: 20 miles, Downtown: 0.5 mile, Need car, Ski lift: 26 miles

General facilities: Full serv., Conf. Rm. (cap. 50), Daily maid, Kitchen, Linens, Baby sitter, Game room, Lounge, Sauna, Hot tub

Room facilities: TV, Cable, Phone, Crib-Hi-chair, Ind.Heat Ctl.

Sports facilities: Pool, Hillcrest Golf Course, 2 ski lifts 15-26 miles

Attractions: Durango/Silverton Railroad, winter skiing, fall changing colors, lake fishing

Shops & Restaurants: Boutiques, shops up and down Main Avenue, Sweeny's Grubsteak duck and fish restaurant

Escape the summer heat in the cool air of the mountains. Ride the railroad or alpine slide. Clubhouse has pool, jacuzzi, dressing rooms, sauna and indoor entertaining facilities. Winter skiing at Purgatory for beginners, 2 half day free learn-to-ski lessons, to advanced. These are the only nightly condominiums in Durango, set on a mesa overlooking the city. Five models with well-appointed floorplans, fireplaces, lockable storage and assigned parking.

———

The Needles 2 Bedrooms $$
46850 Hwy 550 N., 10 Eolus Circle Lo-rise
Durango, CO 81301
303-259-5960

Location: Daily complementary shuttle service to and from ski slopes

General facilities: Kitchen, Linens, BB-Q, Hot tub

Room facilities: TV, Cable, Phone, Garages, Washer/Dryer, Ind. Heat Ctl

Sports facilities: Skiing, Seasonal hunting, Mountain lake fishing

Attractions: Durango & Silverton Narrow Gauge Railroad, downhill and cross country skiing at Purgatory, Animas river

Shops & Restaurants: Discount shopping at famous name brand outlet stores, Excellent eating establishments.

The Needles offers beautifully appointed 2- and 3-bedroom townhomes featuring vaulted ceilings, skylights, bay windows, ceiling fans, private balconies and whirl-pool tubs in the master bedroom/bath. Other amenities within each townhouse include modern and fully equipped kitchens with microwave and self-cleaning conventional ovens. Wall-to wall carpeting throughout, woodburning fireplaces, clean and comfortable electric baseboard heat and garages with automatic door openers.

Enter your favorite condo in our "Condo of the Year" contest (entry form is in the back of the book).

––––––––––––––––––––––––––– DURANGO –––––––––––––––––––––––––––

Purgatory-Village   Studio $$$, 1 Bedrm $$$$, 2 Bedrms $$$$,
175 Beatrice St., P.O. Box 666   3 Bedrooms $$$$, Min. stay 2 nights,
Durango, CO 81302   Amex, Visa, MC, Dep. req'd, Key at Village
303-247-9000 800-879-7879   Cntr desk, 178 condos, Hi-rise, No S-yes •

Location: Airport: 44 miles south; Downtown: 25 miles; Ski lift: Nearby

General facilities: Full serv., Bus. fac., Conf. Rm. (cap. 100), Kitchen, Skiing and day care, Baby sitter, Restaurant, Lounge, Sauna, Hot tub

Room facilities: TV, Cable, VCR, Phone, Crib-Hi-chair, Ind. Heat Ctl.

Sports facilities: Pool, Tennis, Tamarron Resort, Skiing

Attractions: Narrow gauge train, Mesa Verde Nat Park, Big Top Theatre, Alpine Slide, biking, skiing, entertainment

Shops & Restaurants: Village shops and Durango shops, Seafood and Mexican

Choose from units with heavy oak furniture, southwestern design or modern decor with deckside living or views of Needles Mountains. The best skiing in the West, 50 yards from base-area chairlifts with 630 acres of skiable terrain, plus cross-country trails. Beautiful summer surroundings for exploring the high country on foot or horseback, raft trips, Alpine Slide and nighttime entertainment at the Repertory Theatre or Big Top Tent.

––

The Ranch Townhomes   2 Bedrooms $$
33800 Highway 550
Durango, CO 81301
303-247-0762 800-525-0892

General facilities: Kitchen

Sports facilities: Tennis, Fishing, Golf, Chipping

Attractions: Bowling, golf, Mesa Verde National Park, fishing, skiing, narrow gauge train

Townhomes located on a 500 acre working ranch in the Animas Valley. Exceptionally large, beautifully planned units. Guests enjoy fishing and use of the wooded acres for hiking, picnics and wildlife observation. 15 miles to the north is Purgatory for winter skiing.

––

Tamarron   Studio $$, 1 Bedroom $$, 2 Bedrooms $$$,
P.O. Box 3131   3 Bedrooms $$$$, Amex, Visa, MC
Durango, CO 81302   Dep. req'd, Key at Registration desk,
303-259-2000 800-525-5420   Lo-rise, H-yes •

Location: Airport: 33 miles; Downtown: 17 miles; Ski lift: Purgatory

General facilities: Full serv., Conf. Rm. (cap. 500), Daily maid, Kitchen, Linens, Child planned rec., Baby sitter, Restaurant, Bar, Game room, Lounge, Sauna, Hot tub

Room facilities: TV, Cable, Phone, Crib-Hi-chair, Ind. AC. Ctl, Ind. Heat Ctl.

Sports facilities: Pool, Tennis, Health spa, Volleyball

Attractions: Mesa Verde National Park, Durango & Silverton narrow gauge train trip, sightseeing tours, Entertainment

Shops & Restaurants: Seven shops on property, art galleries, Palace-continental

Deluxe townhouses set amidst the spectacular San Juan Mountains. An award winning luxury retreat with restaurants, lounges, shopping arcade, health spa, fishing, riding, tours, sleigh rides, snowmobile and nightly live music in the bar.

—————————————— FRISCO ——————————————

Cedar Lodge
P.O. Box 2130
Frisco, CO 80443
303-668-0777 800-782-7699

1 Bedroom $$.
Golf, Kitchen.

Attractions: Skiing, rafting, fishing, hiking, sailing, golf, tennis, hunting, horses, sleigh rides.

European style condotel resembling a country inn. Free shuttle service to Breckenridge, Keystone and Copper Mountain. Shuttle to Vail, 25 miles away. Suites feature tile entries, oak doors and trim, kitchenettes, covered garage and ski storage.

————————————— ESTES PARK —————————————

Windcliff
P.O. Box 3990
Estes Park, CO 80517
305-586-4507 800-748-2181

2 Bedrooms $$$, 3 Bedrooms $$$$,
2 Bedrm/week 7$, 3 Bedrm/week 11$,
Min. Stay: 2 Nights, •
30 condos, Villas, NoS-yes, H-yes, Key at
guest office.

Location: Airport: 75 minutes; Downtown: 5 minutes, Need car.

General Facilities: Bus. fac., Conf. Rm. Cap.: 15, Pool, Sauna, Largest WMCA world, 15 minutes, Hikes, Golf nearby, X-country, downhill ski, Babysitter.

Room Facilities: Daily maid, Kitchen, TV, VCR, Phone, Crib-Hi-chair, Ind.Heat Ctl.

Attractions: Rocky Mountain National Park, gold mining towns, Skiing, Shopping, Stanley Hotel, Rafting., entertainment.

Shops & Restaurants: Quality boutiques, Indian art, one of a kind handcraft items, Fawn Brook Inn (Intercontinental).

All Windcliff condos are situated on the sunny Southwestern side of beautiful Rams Horn Mountain, each home captures the entire panorama of the majestic Rocky Mountains. Each unit is tastefully appointed; fireplaces, washer/dryer, fully equipped kitchens, TVs. Select units have water jet tubs, hot tubs, pool tables, saunas and VCRs. A great retreat for family reunions or memorable special occassions for couples. Great shopping in Estes Park.

Windcliff, Estes Park, CO

———————————— FRISCO ————————————

Tenmile Creek Condominiums
Resort
200 Granite St., P.O. Box 543
Frisco, CO 80443
303-668-3100

2 Bedrooms $$, 3 Bedrooms $$
Min. stay 3 nights, Amex, Visa, MC
Dep. req'd, Key at Office
60 condos, Lo-rise, No S-yes •

Location: Airport: 70 miles Denver; Downtown: 2 blocks; Ski lift: Nearby

General facilities: Conf. Rm. (cap. 50), Dishwasher, Kitchen, Linens, Fireplace,
Sauna, Hot tub

Room facilities: TV, Cable, Phone, Crib-Hi-chair, Ind. Heat Ctl.

Sports facilities: Indoor Pool, Free busses to skiing

Attractions: Downhill and x-country skiing, snowmobiling, sleigh rides, bikes,
boats, fish, windsurfing

Shops & Restaurants: 1 block to Village Center's restaurants/shops/equip.
rentals, Golden Annies/Mesquite-Mexican

*After a day of powder snow skiing, relax by the fireplace and watch TV or enjoy the
fine dining and nightlife of Frisco and Dillon. Pool, jacuzzi, sauna and party room.
Endless variety of summer and winter fun.*

———————————— GRAND LAKE ————————————

Soda Springs Ranch Resort
9921 U.S. Highway 34
Grand Lake, CO 80447
303-627-3486

1 Bedroom $$, 2 Bedrooms $$$

General facilities: Kitchen, Linens

Sports facilities: Tennis, Racquetball, Putt. green

*Newly built, completely furnished condominiums 5 miles south of Grand Lake.
Well-marked trails for every level of skier through meadows and pines. Athletic club,
racquetball court, weight room, restaurant. Summer-pool, fishing, jogging, horses.*

———————————— KEYSTONE ————————————

Hearthstone Mountain Homes
239099 U.S. Hwy. 6
Keystone, CO 80435
303-468-9291

———————————————— KEYSTONE ————————————————
Keystone Resort
Box 38
Keystone, CO 80435
303-534-7712 800-222-0188

AmEx/Visa/MC, Dep. Req'd.

Location: Airport: 68 miles Denver; Ski lift: Nearby

General Facilities: Bus. fac., Conf. rm. cap. 110, Daily maid, Kitchen, Linens, Restaurant on prem., Bar on prem., Lounge, Baby-sitter, Child planned rec.: Nursery-programs

Room Facilities: Pool, Sauna, Hot tub, Tennis, Fitness center, Golf: 18-hole course, TV, Cable, Phone in rm.

Attractions: Sailing, bicycling, hayride dinners, western melodrama, summer music festival, tours, entertainment

Shops & Restaurants: Pedestrian mall-gifts, clothing, arts and crafts; Garden Room/cont.-Bighorn Stk.

Condominiums have fireplaces with wood supply and television with HBO. Winter ski activities, and something for everyone in the summer. Tennis staff for instructions, golf course among pines, meadows and 9-acre lake. Golf clinics and Ranchhouse restaurant for lunch and dinner. Nursery for two months and up, picnics, crafts and pony rides for pre-schoolers and activity programs for older children. Hayrides to a cattle ranch for dinner. Guided tours to Old Keystone and Montezuma. Western melodrama.

Ski Run/Snowdance Manor
Keystone, CO 80435
303-468-9243

———————————————— LAKEWOOD ————————————————
Raintree Inn
3500 S. Wadsworth St.
Lakewood, CO 80235
800-824-3662

———————————————— MESA ————————————————
Goldenwoods Condominiums
Mesa, CO 81647
303-242-5637 800-876-9337

Studio $$$, 1 Bedroom $$$$, 2 Bedrooms $$$$
AmEx/Visa/MC, Dep. Req'd. •
78 condos, Lo-rise, Key at Powderhorn front dsk

Location: Airport: 40 miles; Downtown: 45 miles; Ski lift: Ski in

General Facilities: Full serv., Conf. rm., Daily maid, Kitchen, Linens, Restaurant on prem., Bar on prem., Game room, Lounge

Room Facilities: Sauna, Hot tub, TV, Cable, VCR, Phone in rm., Crib-Hi-chair

Attractions: Sleigh rides, torchlight parade, Colorado historian campfire, hiking, biking, entertainment

Shops & Restaurants: Resort convenience store, small town stores-6 mile; Fajita Willy's/Southwestern

Spectacular scenic playground for year-round activities. Breathtaking views of the valley, alpine and nordic skiing in the winter. Mountain bike touring in the summer. VIP service with a versatile arena for summer and winter activities.

—————————— MOUNT CRESTED BUTTE ——————————

Out Run Condominiums   3 Bedrooms $$
721 Gothic Road   3 Bedrms/week 5$
Mount Crested Butte, CO 81224   Min. Stay 3 Nights, AmEx/Visa/MC,
303-349-2800 800-821-7613   Dep. Req'd. •
                                    36 condos, Lo-rise, Key at Out Run, Birch Bldg.

Location: Airport: 30 miles; Downtown: 3 miles; Ski lift: Nearby

General Facilities: Conf. rm. cap. 30, Kitchen, Linens, Baby-sitter, Child planned rec.:
Nature walks, arts

Room Facilities: Sauna, Hot tub, Tennis, Golf: Golf—4 miles, TV, Cable, Phone in rm.,
Crib-Hi-chair, Ind. Heat Ctl.

Attractions: Snowmobile 8 miles to remote lodge for dinner, Black Canyon, Gunnison
boat tours

Shops & Restaurants: Small, locally owned shops; Soupcon-French/Penelope's

*Modern three-bedroom condominiums in the Rocky Mountains. Wonderful summer and
winter activities in a sparsely populated area that has the perfect blend of climate, scen-
ery and recreation. A variety of children's activities so that parents can have time to them-
selves. Ski in the winter, golf in the summer, or just read and enjoy the scenery.*

The Plaza at Woodcreek   2 Bedrooms $$
11 Snowmass Road, P.O. Box 5159
Mt. Crested Butte, CO 81224
303-349-6611 800-221-5228

Location: Ski lift: Crested B

General Facilities: Kitchen, Restaurant on prem., Game room

Room Facilities: Sauna, Hot tub, Tennis, TV, Cable, Phone in rm.

Attractions: Summer Shakespeare, wildflower festival, Crested Butte Victorian village

Shops & Restaurants: Crested Butte shops; The Black Bear

*A bottle of champagne in your unit is your arrival greeting at this picturesque mountain
resort offering endless year-round recreational opportunities. Continental breakfast served
daily during ski season. Spectacular scenery, pure air, majestic mountains.*

--------------------------- PAGOSA SPRINGS ---------------------------

Fairfield Pagosa
Hwy. 160, P.O. Box 4040
Pagosa Springs, CO 81157
303-731-4141 800-523-7704

Studio $$, 1 Bedroom $$, 2 Bedrooms $$,
3 Bedrooms $$
1 Bedrm/week 4$, 2 Bed/week 5$,
3 Bed/week 6$
AmEx/Visa/MC, Dep. 1 Night •
125 condos, Lo-rise, Key at Registr. desk
No S-yes/H-yes

Location: Airport: Pagosa Springs-2 Mi.; Downtown: 3 miles; Ski lift: Nearby

General Facilities: Full serv., Bus. fac., Conf. rm. cap. 350, Daily maid, Kitchen, Linens, Restaurant on prem., Bar on prem., Game room, Lounge, Baby-sitter, Child planned rec.: Sunburst program

Room Facilities: Pool, Sauna, Hot tub, Tennis, skiing, Golf: Fairfield Pagosa Pines, TV, Cable, VCR, Phone in rm., Crib-Hi-chair, Ind. AC Ctl., Ind. Heat Ctl.

Attractions: Indian Ruins, Durango-Silverton Train, entertainment

Shops & Restaurants: Small shops; South Face-Continental

Fairfield Paagosa is a four-season resort. A host of activities from ice fishing and cross-country skiing to trout fishing and mountain climbing. Located on 18,000 acres with seven lakes for canoeing and paddle-boating. Sunburst Kids program for children ages 4-12 offers adventures and crafts. Tennis and golf are also available. Escape to the Colorado wilderness, but have all the amenities of contemporary living.

--------------------------- SILVER CREEK ---------------------------

Mountainside at Silver Creek
P.O. Box 4104, 96 Mountainside Dr
Silver Creek, CO 80446
303-887-2571 800-223-7677

1 Bedroom $$, 2 Bedrooms $$
Min. Stay 2 Nights, AmEx/Visa/MC, Dep. 2
Nights •
90 condos, Lo-rise, Key at Front office

Location: Airport: 90 miles; Need car; Ski lift: Nearby

General Facilities: Full serv., Daily maid, Kitchen, Linens, Baby-sitter, Child planned rec.: Childrens Ski School

Room Facilities: Pool, Hot tub, Tennis, TV, Cable, Phone in rm., Crib-Hi-chair, Ind. Heat Ctl.

Attractions: Silver Creek & Winter Park Skiing, Rocky Mt. & Arapahoe Nat. Park areas

Shops & Restaurants: Gasthaus Eichler-German

The Mountainside at Silver Creek affords endless recreational opportunities or "doing nothing" in a picturesque Colorado setting. In the winter there is excellent skiing for beginners and intermediates at Silver Creek, or Winter Park for the advanced. Summertime brings tennis, golf, horseback riding, lake activities or river rafting. Al units have queen beds, rock fireplaces and in-room jacuzzis.

Please mention *Condo Vacations—The Complete Guide* when you reserve your condominium.

———————————————— SILVER CREEK ————————————————

Inn at Silver Creek
Box 4222
Silver Creek, CO 80446
303-887-2131 800-926-4386

Studio $, 1 Bedroom $$, 2 Bedrooms $$,
3 Bedrooms $$$
Amex, Visa, MC, Dep. req'd
342 condos, Lo-rise,
Key at Front desk
P-yes, H-yes •

Location: Airport: 90 miles Denver, Downtown: 85 miles, Need car, Ski lift:
Nearby

General facilities: Full serv., Conf. Rm. (cap. 600), Daily maid, Kitchen, Linens,
Deli, Game room, Lounge, Sauna, Hot tub

Room facilities: TV, Cable, Phone, Crib, Ind.Heat Ctl.

Sports facilities: Pool, Tennis, Near-Pole Creek/Grnd Lake, Racquetball, bikes

Attractions: Ski Winter Park and Silver Creek, gateway to Rocky Mtn. Nat. Park,
lakes, mountains, Entertainment

Shops & Restaurants: Grand Lake, Granby, Winter Park, Gausthouse Eichler/
German

*4 season resort and conference center located in the heart of the Colorado Rockies.
Moss rock fireplaces, baths with jacuzzi jets and steam closets. Gift shop, liquor store,
pantry, delicatessen and athletic club. Poolside lounging, summer and winter.*

———————————————— SILVERTHORNE ————————————————

Paradise Condominiums
221 Summit Blvd., Box 587
Silverthorne, CO 80498
303-468-5846 800-922-2590

1 Bedroom $, 2 Bedrooms $$,
3 Bedrooms $$
Min. stay 3 nights, Amex, Visa, MC,
Dep. 40%
30 condos, Lo-rise,
Key at Main office
No S-yes •

Location: Airport: 65 miles, Need car, Ski lift: Nearby

General facilities: Daily maid, Kitchen, Linens, Baby sitter, Game room, Sauna,
Hot tub

Room facilities: TV, Cable, Phone, Crib-Hi-chair, Ind.Heat Ctl.

Sports facilities: Pool, 3 miles, Skiing, golf

Attractions: Alpine/Nordic skiing, 4 golf courses, flyfishing, big game hunting,
sailing

Shops & Restaurants: Western and Indian art galleries, ski shops, Keystone
Ranch-Nouvelle/Amr.

*Contemporary mountain condominiums furnished in earthtones with interiors
detailed with fine woods, rock fireplaces and paintings. Four major ski areas, plus
miles of cross-country trails, ice skating and snowmobiling. Summer has tennis,
fishing, rafting, horseback riding and sailing on Lake Dillon. Music festivals, dining
and dancing, or just relax in the hot tub before the fireplace.*

Please mention *Condo Vacations—the Complete Guide* when you
reserve your condominium.

——————————— SNOWMASS VILLAGE ———————————

Chamonix at Woodrun
Box 6286
Snowmass Village, CO 81615
303-923-5543 800-635-7480

2 Bedrooms $$$, 3 Bedrooms $$$$
Min. Stay 1 Night, AmEx/Visa/MC
1 Night Dep. Req'd. •
27 condos, Hi-rise
Key at Front desk, H-yes

Location: Airport: 12 miles; Downtown: 1/4 mile; Ski lift at Snowmass

General Facilities: Full serv.; Daily maid; Linens; Baby sitter; Crib-Hi-chair

Business Facilities: Bus. fac.; Conf. Room Cap. 30

Sports Facilities: Pool; Hot tub; Slopeside access; Snowmass Club; Ski school/day care

Room Facilities: Kitchen; Cable; VCR; Phone; Ind.Heat Ctl.

Attractions: Skiing, sleighs, dog sleigh rides, ballooning, Aspen Music Festival, rafting, hiking

Shops & Restaurants: Ski/sport shops, designer shops in Aspen; Chez Crandmere/French

Located in the heart of the Elk Mountains of the Rockies with spectacular National Forest surroundings, having direct ski access in winter with complete staff to make a truly relaxed vacation. Lots of natural light, oak trim, high ceilings, individually designer-decorated with lots of southwest colors. Balconies with slope and valley view.

The Crestwood
P.O. Box 5460, 400 Wood Rd.
Snowmass Village, CO 81615
970-923-2450 800-356-5949
FAX: 970-923-5018

Studio $$, 1 Bedroom $$$,
2 Bedrooms $$$$, 3 Bedrooms $$$$
Min. Stay Ask, 1 Night Dep. Req'd., 141
condos, Hi-rise, Lo-rise, P-No

Location: Airport: Aspen; Ski lift at Ski-in/out

General Facilities: Full hotel service; Daily maid; Linens

Business Facilities: Bus. fac.; Conf. Room Cap. 175

Sports Facilities: Pool; Sauna; Golf Course

Room Facilities: Kitchen; Cable; VCR; Phone; Ind.Heat Ctl.

Attractions: Skiing, golf

The Crestwood offers condominium comfort on the slopes of Snowmass Village. Excellent ski-in/ski-out convenience, breathtaking scenery and unmatched hospitality. Deluxe condominiums featuring fully-equipped kitchens, fireplaces, balconies, BBQ grills and free laundry facilities. Heated outdoor pool, 2 therapy pools, a sauna and exercise room. At the Crestwood you will feel more than comfortable, you will feel right at home.

Be sure to call the condo to verify details and prices and to make your reservation.

---------------------------- SNOWMASS ----------------------------

Snowmass Lodging Company   Amex, Visa, MC
P.O. Box 6077   Key at Front desk
Snowmass, CO 81615   82 condos
303-923-3232 800-365-0410   Lo-rise, No S-yes, H-yes •

Location: Airport: 20 min.-Aspen; Downtown: 15 min.; Ski lift: Slopeside

General facilities: Full serv., Conf. Rm. (cap. 10), Daily maid, Kitchen, Linens, Child planned rec., Baby sitter, Sauna, Hot tub

Room facilities: TV, Cable, Phone, Crib-Hi-chair, Ind. Heat Ctl.

Sports facilities: Pool, Snowmass Club, Massage, small spa

Attractions: Skiing in Snowmass, Aspen,dog sledding, sleighrides, hot air balloon rides, Entertainment

Shops & Restaurants: Unique specialty gift stores, boutiques, ski shops, La Boheme/Fench Frabloonik/wild game

All three of these properties, Woodrun Place, The Enclave, and Chamonix, have superb slopeside locations. At either one you will enjoy luxury condominiums with all the conveniences of home. Ski at Snowmass Mountain, Aspen, Buttermilk, or Aspen Highlands—all on one ski ticket. Complimentary transportation between mountains. The most exciting ski vacation you have ever had.

---------------------------- SNOWMASS VILLAGE ----------------------------

Snowmass Club   1 Bedroom $$$, 2 Bedrooms $$$$,
P.O. Drawer G-2   3 Bedrooms 4$, Amex, Visa, MC
Snowmass Village, CO 81615   Dep. req'd, Key at Front desk
303-923-5600 800-525-6200   55 condos, Lo-rise, H-yes •

Location: Airport: 7 miles; Downtown: Aspen 15 min/11 mi; Need car; Ski lift: Snowmass

General facilities: Full serv., Conf. Rm. (cap. 200), Daily maid, Kitchen, Linens, Concierge, Restaurant, Bar, Bus Serv., Lounge, Sauna, Jacuzzi

Room facilities: TV, Cable, Phone, Newspaper, Deck, Ind. Heat Ctl.

Sports facilities: Pool, Tennis, 18-hole championship, Health Club, Squash/Racqt

Attractions: Aspen Music Festival, Repertory Theatre, Anderson Ranch Arts Center, dog sled rides, entertainment

Shops & Restaurants: Snowmass Village Mall, Aspen pedestrian mall, Four Corners on-site

Complimentary shuttle greets you at the Aspen/Snowmass Airport to take you to your condominium where you'll find a welcoming bottle of champagne. Read the morning newspaper before you start your skiing day. Afterwards, relax in front of the lobby's massive rock fireplace or cocktail lounge with its piano bar. When the snow melts, activities change to hiking, rafting, fishing, horseback riding, biking, hot air ballooning and gliding. Athletic Club has daily aerobics, massages, gym, pool and racquetball.

We want to hear from you—any comments regarding the condos or our publication may be noted on the form at the end of the book.

─────────────────── SNOWMASS VILLAGE ───────────────────

Timberline Condominiums
P.O. Box I-2, 0264 Snowmelt Rd.
Snowmass Village, CO 81615
303-923-4000 800-922-4001

Studio $$$, 1 Bedroom $$$, 2 Bedrooms
$$$$, 3 Bedrooms $$$$, Amex, Visa, MC,
Key at Front desk, 96 condos
Lo-rise •

Location: Airport: Aspen 20 minutes; Downtown: 5 minutes; Ski lift: Ski-in/out
General facilities: Full serv., Bus. fac., Conf. Rm. (cap. 50), Daily maid, Kitchen,
   Linens, Daily programs, Baby sitter, Restaurant, Bar, Lounge, Sauna, Hot tub
Room facilities: TV, Cable, VCR, Phone, Crib-Hi-chair, Ind. Heat Ctl.
Sports facilities: Pool, Biking, Rafting, Horses
Attractions: Aspen, Maroon Bells, Snowmass Wilderness, Theater, Music, Arts,
   Festival, receptions
Shops & Restaurants: Snowmass Village Mall, Aspen, Variety—from wild game
   to fine French cuisine

*Located in the heart of Snowmass' Upper Village. Home comforts and hotel service
in the heart of the Rockies. Whether summer or winter, you'll awaken each morning
with an endless variety of activities at your doorstep. Our staff will help you to
experience the Aspen Valley to its fullest. A comfortable resort atmosphere and
unmatched service make the Timberline a great get-away!*

Woodrun Place Condominiums
Box 6027, 0425 Wood Rd.
Snowmass Village, CO 81615
303-923-5392 800-635-7480

1 Bedroom $$$, 2 Bedrooms $$$,
3 Bedrooms $$$$, Min. stay 3 nights,
Amex, Visa, MC, Dep. req'd
Key at Front desk
54 condos, Lo-rise, Villas, H-yes •

Location: Airport: 12 miles; Downtown: 1/4 mile; Ski lift: Snowmass
General facilities: Full serv., Bus. fac., Conf. Rm. (cap. 120), Daily maid, Kitchen,
   Linens, Ski school/day care, Baby sitter, Sauna, Hot tub
Room facilities: TV, Cable, VCR, Phone, Crib-Hi-chair, Ind. Heat Ctl.
Sports facilities: Pool, Snowmass Club, Ski rent/tuning
Attractions: Wednesday night summer rodeos, horses, white water, Aspen
   Music Festival, sleigh rides.
Shops & Restaurants: Aspen designer shops and ski and sport shops, Krab-
   loonik/gourmet-game

*Each unit is designer decorated with a predominant southwest-French country flair
with lots of natural light and windows and pastel colors.*

─────────────────── STEAMBOAT SPRINGS ───────────────────

Bear Claw Condominiums
P.O. Box 774928
Steamboat Springs, CO 80477
303-879-6100

1 Bedroom $$$, 2 Bedrooms $$$

General facilities: Daily maid, Kitchen, Linens
Sports facilities: Pool
Attractions: Skiing, hike the Continental Divide, fishing

*Ski to the gondola from your condominium and ski back for a luncheon bowl of soup.
Overstuffed furniture and classic wood tables in units with private balconies and
fireplaces. Take time out to use the pool, sauna or jacuzzi. Serene summers ideal for
hiking.*

Ski Hill Condos

STEAMBOAT SPRINGS

Bronze Tree
1855 Ski Time Square Drive
Steamboat Springs, CO 80487
303-879-8811   800-228-2458

2 Bedrooms $$$, 3 Bedrooms $$$$
Min. stay ask, Visa, MC,
Dep. 2 nights
30 condos, Hi-rise,
Key at Torian Plum lobby •

Location: Airport: 8 miles, Downtown: 3 miles, Ski lift: Steamboat

General facilities: Full serv., Conf. Rm. (cap. 30), Daily maid, Kitchen, Linens, Ski free program, Concierge, Bell staff, Sauna, Hot tub

Room facilities: TV, Cable, Phone, Crib-Hi-chair, Ind.Heat Ctl.

Sports facilities: Pool, Free ski shuttle

Attractions: Ski-in and walk-out location adjacent to slopes

Shops & Restaurants: Unique gift shops and restaurants in the village below Bronze Tree and many others in downtown Steamboat.

Traditional, upholstered furniture, oak trim, tile and carpet throughout. Chairlift above, village below. Children 12 and under ski free when parents purchase a five-day ski ticket, one child per parent. Stone fireplaces are stocked with native pine. Individual ski lockers, covered parking and private balconies. Summer hikes among the wildflowers, fishing, whitewater rafting and ballooning.

Enter your favorite condo in our "Condo of the Year" contest (entry form is in the back of the book).

--------------------------------- STEAMBOAT SPRINGS ---------------------------------

Dulany Condominiums
P.O. Box 2995
Steamboat Springs, CO 80477
303-879-7900 800-525-5502

2 Bedrooms $$$, 3 Bedrooms $$$
2 Bedrms/week $$$$, 3 Bed/week $$$$
Min. Stay 7 Nights, AmEx/Visa/MC,
Dep. 1 Night •
20 condos, Hi-rise, Key at Front desk
H-yes

Location: Airport: Stolpt 7 miles; Downtown: 3 miles; Ski lift: Nearby

General Facilities: Full serv., Bus. fac., Conf. rm. cap. 75, Daily maid, Kitchen, Linens, Baby-sitter

Room Facilities: Hot tub, Golf: Sheraton Steamboat, TV, Cable, Phone in rm., Crib-Hi-chair, Ind. Heat Ctl.

Attractions: Ranching, hiking, hunting, skiing

Shops & Restaurants: Numerous retail stores-Old Town Steamboat; 50 restaurants-varied cuisine

Each of the Dulany condominiums has a personality & character distinctly its own. The wood and tile kitchens, private balconies, and fireplace areas open on a magical view of the mountains and forest trails. Dulany's condominiums nestle on the banks of Burgess Creek, a few easy glides from Mt. Werner's base gondola. You'll experience an exhilarating sense of Steamboat's special style of personal freedom at Dulany.

Four Seasons at Steamboat
2315 Apres Ski Way
Steamboat Springs, CO 80487
303-879-4445 800-492-8466

2 Bedrooms $$
Pool, Kitchen, Phone in rm.

Summer or winter, condominium vacationing at its best. After a day of skiing, take a romantic evening sleigh ride or a dip in the hot tub or pool. The rest of the year brings warm days, cool nights and clear skies for water sports, hiking, and wilderness backpacking.

Golden Triangle Condo Resort
P.O. Box 774847
Steamboat Springs, CO 80477
303-879-2931 800-822-7669

AmEx/Visa/MC, Dep. 1 Night •
24 condos, Lo-rise, Key at Front desk

Location: Airport: 5 miles; Downtown: 2 miles; Ski lift: Nearby

General Facilities: Full serv., Conf. rm. cap. 80, Daily maid, Kitchen, Linens, Lounge, Baby-sitter, Child planned rec.: Ski free program

Room Facilities: Pool, Sauna, Hot tub, Racquetball, steam room, Golf: Sheraton Golf—2 miles, TV, Cable, Phone in rm., Crib-Hi-chair, Ind. Heat Ctl.

Attractions: Winter-dinner steak sleigh rides, natural hot springs, powder, downhill & x-country skiing

Shops & Restaurants: Mattie Silks/French American

Condominiums are minutes away from the Steamboat ski area. The bus to town is one block from the property for dining, entertainment and shopping. Spa facilities, two jacuzzis, steam room sauna, indoor and outdoor pools.

────────────────── STEAMBOAT SPRINGS ──────────────────

Kutuk
P.O. Box 2995
Steamboat Springs, CO 80477
303-879-6605 800-525-5502

2 Bedrooms $$, 3 Bedrooms $$$
2 Bedrms/week $$$$, 3 Bed/week $$$$
Min. Stay 7 Nights, AmEx/Visa/MC,
Dep. 1 Night •
32 condos, Lo-rise, Key at Front desk

Location: Airport: Stolpt 7 miles; Downtown: 3 miles; Ski lift: Nearby

General Facilities: Full serv., Bus. fac., Daily maid, Kitchen, Linens, Baby-sitter

Room Facilities: Hot tub, Golf: Sheraton Steamboat, TV, Cable, Phone in rm., Crib-Hi-chair, Ind. Heat Ctl.

Attractions: Ranching, fishing, hiking, skiing

Shops & Restaurants: Numerous retail stores-Old Steamboat and ski area; 50 restaurants-varied cuisine

Situated at the base of Mount Werner, Kutuk Condominiums are adjacent to the Christie Lifts and the many specialty shops, restaurants and night spots of Ski Time Square. All units are uniquely decorated with magnificent views of Mount Werner. Bright, open, spacious, with large outdoor hot tubs and enormous sun deck. Complimentary bottle of wine on arrival.

──

La Casa at Steamboat
P.O. Box 2995
Steamboat Springs, CO 80477
303-879-6036 800-525-5502

2 Bedrooms $$$, 3 Bedrooms $$$
2 Bedrms/week $$$$, 3 Bed/week $$$$
Min. Stay 7 Nights, AmEx/Visa/MC,
Dep. 1 Night •
24 condos, Lo-rise, Key at Steamboat Lodge

Location: Airport: Stolpt 7 miles; Downtown: 3 miles; Ski lift: Nearby

General Facilities: Full serv., Bus. fac., Conf. rm. cap. 75, Daily maid, Kitchen, Linens, Baby-sitter

Room Facilities: Hot tub, Golf: Sheraton Steamboat, TV, Cable, Phone in rm., Crib-Hi-chair, Ind. Heat Ctl.

Attractions: Winter sports, fishing, hiking, hunting, golf.

Shops & Restaurants: Old Town Steamboat and ski area retail shops; 50+ restaurants

La Casa's striking sense of urban sophistication is at ease at the base of Steamboat's uncrowded ski runs. Two bubbling, soothing hot tubs, surrounded by pines and aspens, a secluded retreat from the neighboring gondolas, shops and nightlife of Ski Time Square. La Casa—for those who know that excellence is a matter of taste, not cost. A distinctly individual choice for your Steamboat vacation.

──

Meadows at Eagle-Ridge
Steamboat Springs, CO 80487
303-879-8811 800-228-2458

──

The Moraine at Steamboat
P.O. Box 771441
Steamboat Springs, CO 80488

2 Bedrooms $$$
Kitchen, Phone in rm.

Quietly elegant, meticulously appointed townhomes—private one-level spa/whirlpool hot tub, sauna, steam bath and dressing area. Mexican tile foyer, stereo intercom, heated garage, door opener. Idyllic spots for fishing, sailing, rafting. Wilderness.

─────────────────── STEAMBOAT SPRINGS ───────────────────

Pine Grove Village
P.O. Box 2995
Steamboat Springs, CO 80477
303-525-5502 800-332-5533

1 Bedroom $$, 2 Bedrooms $$
Min. Stay 7 Nights, AmEx/Visa/MC •
29 condos, Lo-rise, Key at Front desk
H-yes

Location: Airport: Stolpt 7 miles; Downtown: 3 miles; Ski lift: Steamboat

General Facilities: Daily maid, Kitchen, Linens, Baby-sitter

Room Facilities: Hot tub, Golf: Sheraton Steamboat-near, TV, Cable, Phone in rm., Crib-Hi-chair, Ind. Heat Ctl.

Attractions: Ranching, fishing, hunting town nestled to the world famous Steamboat ski area.

Shops & Restaurants: Retail stores in old town Steamboat and ski area; 50+ restaurants-varied cuisine

Friendly, neighborly mountain home with contemporary Western furnishings, clean-lined wood accented by earth and sky-tones. Pine Grove is midway between town and ski area with free city shuttle to ski area. Walk to neighboring stores and restaurants. Two new hot tubs and cozy club room.

───

Ptarmigan House Condominiums
P.O. Box 3626
Steamboat Springs, CO 80477
303-525-5502 800-332-5533

Studio $$, 1 Bedroom $$, 2 Bedrooms $$,
3 Bedrooms $$
1 Bedrm/week $$$$, 2 Bed/week $$$$,
3 Bed/week $$$$
Min. Stay 7 Nights, AmEx/Visa/MC,
Dep. 1 Night •
24 condos, Lo-rise, Key at Front desk, H-yes

Location: Airport: Stolpt 7 miles; Downtown: 3 miles; Ski lift: Nearby

General Facilities: Full serv., Bus. fac., Daily maid, Kitchen, Linens, Baby-sitter

Room Facilities: Pool, Hot tub, Golf: Sheraton Steamboat, TV, Cable, Phone in rm., Crib-Hi-chair, Ind. Heat Ctl.

Attractions: Ski-in, ski-out locations. A short stroll to village shops, & restaurants

Shops & Restaurants: Retail stores, Old Steamboat and at ski area; 50+ restaurant-varied cuisine

Ptarmigan House reflects the Old World heritage of Steamboat's first skiers. Built at Mt. Werner's base, it sits on one of the Mountain's finest ski-in/ski-out locations. The condominiums reflect a quiet grace and dignity with lustrous wood detailing welcoming warmth and windows and light fixtures sparkling in the fireplace light. A short stroll away are the ski village shops, clubs, restaurants and public transit to downtown Steamboat Springs.

───

The Rockies
P.O. Box 881120
Steamboat Springs, CO 88048
303-879-8300

1 Bedroom $, 2 Bedrooms $$, Lo-rise
Pool, Daily maid, Kitchen, Phone in rm.
Golf

The firewood is stacked and ready in your Rockies vacation home, 500 yards from the base of the mountain and the Ski Time Square shopping area with restaurants and bars. Go down to the hot tubs and heated year-round pool, or stay at home and watch HBO.

STEAMBOAT SPRINGS

Ski Trails Condominiums
P.O. Box 881120
Steamboat Springs, CO 88477
303-879-2135

1 Bedroom $, 2 Bedrooms $, Lo-rise
Daily maid, Kitchen

Warm, cozy, quiet condominiums, country wallpaper and plenty of wood for the brick fireplace. Located on Headall ski run, you have ski-in, ski-out convenience. Summer nature walks on Mt. Werner. Take the Silver Bullet Gondola to the top.

Snow Flower Condominiums
P.O. Box 4406
Steamboat Springs, CO 80477
303-879-5104   800-822-7669

AmEx/Visa/MC, Dep. 1 Night •
36 condos, Lo-rise, Key at Front desk
H-yes

Location: Airport: 5 miles; Downtown: 3 miles; Ski lift: Nearby

General Facilities: Full serv., Conf. rm. cap. 80, Daily maid, Kitchen, Linens, Lounge, Baby-sitter, Child planned rec.: Ski free program

Room Facilities: Pool, Hot tub, Tennis, Golf: 2 miles Sheraton Golf, TV, Cable, Phone in rm., Crib-Hi-chair, Ind. Heat Ctl.

Attractions: Winter-dinner steak sleigh rides, natural hot springs, powder cat, downhill, x-country ski

Shops & Restaurants: Mattie Silk's/French-American

Ski down and warm yourself in the fireside lobby accented with special country touches, and relax in all that Snow Country has to offer. Light and airy condominiums highlighted by one-of-a-kind country treasures and works of art, gas fireplaces and balcony views of the valley or ski area. Ski out to the "Silver Bullet," Steamboat's high speed passenger gondola and all the base area lifts. Just steps away you'll find dining, entertainment from western to jazz, and unique boutiques.

Storm Meadows Townhomes
2135 Burgess Creek Road
Steamboat Springs, CO 80487
800-332-5942   800-525-5921

Daily maid, Kitchen, Linens, Phone in rm.

Attractions: Athletic Club

Adjacent to the ski slopes of Mt. Werner, overlooking Yampa Valley. Completely furnished townhomes with mountain-lodge fireplaces and view balconies. Warm, friendly staff— laid-back Western hospitality.

SubAlpine
P.O. Box 881120
Steamboat Springs, CO 80488
800-654-7654   800-525-7654

2 Bedrooms $
Kitchen, Linens

Beautiful view of the Yampa Vallley highlight these quiet, affordable condominiums. Half mile from the base of Steamboat ski area with free shuttle to the slopes. Summer scenic walks and relaxing days after fishing, riding, or hot air ballooning.

———————————— STEAMBOAT SPRINGS ————————————

The Lodge At Steamboat
P.O. Box 2995
Steamboat Springs, CO 80477
303-525-5502   800-332-5533

1 Bedroom $$, 2 Bedrooms $$, 3 Bedrooms $$$
2 Bedrms/week $$$$
Min. Stay 7 Nights, AmEx/Visa/MC,
Dep. 1 Night •
120 condos, Lo-rise, Key at Front desk
H-yes

Location: Airport: Stolpt 7 miles; Downtown: 3 miles; Ski lift: Nearby

General Facilities: Full serv., Bus. fac., Conf. rm. cap. 75, Daily maid, Kitchen, Linens, Baby-sitter

Room Facilities: Pool, Sauna, Hot tub, Tennis, Skiing, Golf: Sheraton Steamboat, TV, Cable, Phone in rm., Crib-Hi-chair, Ind. Heat Ctl.

Attractions: Ranching, fishing, hiking, hunting, skiing, tennis, nightlife

Shops & Restaurants: Numerous retail stores-Old Steamboat and ski area; 50 restaurants-varied cuisine

Newly remodeled, private condominiums with floor to ceiling windows. Continuous daytime shuttle service to and from the Gondola. Hourly nighttime round-trip shuttle to shopping and entertainment. A full bathroom for every bedroom. Complimentary coffee and donuts in the Gathering Place. Large sauna, whirlpool and convenient changing rooms.

The Ranch at Steamboat
1 Ranch Road
Steamboat Springs, CO 80487
303-525-2002   800-237-2624

1 Bedroom $$, 2 Bedrooms $$, 3 Bedrooms $$$
Dep. Req'd.
Lo-rise, Key at Front desk

Location: Ski lift: Steamboat

General Facilities: Full serv., Bus. fac., Conf. rm. cap. 200, Daily maid, Kitchen, Linens, Bar on prem., Game room

Room Facilities: Pool, Sauna, Hot tub, Tennis, Nautilus-aerobic, Golf: Sheraton Steamboat, TV, Cable

Attractions: Natural hot mineral springs, rodeos, gondola rides, NASTAR ski racing, night ski, sleighs

Shops & Restaurants: Boutiques; Gourmet restaurants

Leave your car in the locked garage and let us chauffeur you through the complex or to the town of Steamboat Springs. Whether your dream is a winter ski vacation or a relaxing summer choosing your own activities, you'll enjoy the complimentary continental breakfast and daily Denver newspaper. Private balconies with electric barbecues and views of the Mt. Werner ski area.

Our goal is to provide as *complete* a listing of condo vacation properties as possible. If you know of a condo we don't list, please send us their name and address on the form at the back of this Guide.

──────── STEAMBOAT SPRINGS ────────

Timber Run
P.O. Box 2995
Steamboat Springs, CO 80477
303-879-7000 800-525-5502

1 Bedroom $$, 2 Bedrooms $$,
3 Bedrooms $$
2 Bedrms/week $$$$, 3 Bedrms/week $$$$
Min. Stay 7 Nights, AmEx/Visa/MC,
1 Night Dep. Req'd. •
80 condos, Lo-rise
Key at Front desk, H-yes

Location: Airport: Stolpt 7 miles; Downtown: 3 miles; Ski lift at Steamboat
General Facilities: Daily maid; Linens; Baby sitter; Crib-Hi-chair
Business Facilities: Bus. fac.; Conf. Room Cap. 75
Sports Facilities: Pool; Hot tub; Tennis; Skiing; Sheraton Steamboat-near
Room Facilities: Kitchen; Cable; Phone; Ind.Heat Ctl.
Attractions: Steamboat ski area with all winter sports. Summertime fishing,
hunting, and hiking.
Shops & Restaurants: Many retail stores in the ski area and Steamboat; Many
fine restaurants nearby

Three level timber-sided buildings in tawny wood tones and deep cushioned furniture under angled red roofs. Swimming pool, hot tubs and sauna to soothe your muscles, or take the shuttle to the base area, grocery store, gift shops and nightlife. If you prefer to just relax and stay at home, there is grocery delivery and complimentary coffee and donuts.

Torian Plum
1855 Ski Time Square Dr.
Steamboat Springs, CO 80487
970-879-8811 800-228-2458
FAX: 970-879-8485

1 Bedroom $$$$, 2 Bedrooms 5$,
3 Bedrooms 6$
Min. Stay Ask, Visa/MC,
2 Nights Dep. Req'd. •
45 condos, Hi-rise
Key at Torian Plum Lobby, No S-Yes

Location: Airport: 22 miles; Downtown: 3 miles; Ski lift at Free shuttle
General Facilities: Full hotel service; Daily maid; Linens; Baby sitter; Concierge;
Crib-Hi-chair; Restaurant on premises; Bar on premises
Sports Facilities: Pool; Sauna; Hot tub; Tennis; Athletic Club; Ski area nursery
Room Facilities: Kitchen; Cable; VCR; Phone; Stereo/CD; Ind.Heat Ctl.
Attractions: Ski-in and ski-out location at the base of Mt. Werner
Shops & Restaurants: Several shops and restaurants are located in Torian
Plum and; other are located in downtown Steamboat.

Traditional furnishings in pastel colors, oak trim, brass accessories, all with balconies overlooking the ski area. Ski lockers next to each condominium and underground parking. In summer, white water rafting, horseback riding, steak-fry, hayrides, rodeo, or leave it all behind in the basket of a hot air balloon, mountain biking on Mt. Werner.

Tamarron

———————————————— STEAMBOAT SPRINGS ————————————————

Trappeurs Crossing
1855 Ski Time Square Drive
Steamboat Springs, CO 80487
303-879-8811   800-228-2458

2 Bedrooms $$, 3 Bedrooms $$$
Min. stay ask, Visa, MC,
Dep. 2 nights
34 condos, Lo-rise,
Key at Torian Plum Lobby •

Location: Airport: 9 miles, Downtown: 4 miles, Ski lift: Nearby

General facilities: Full serv., Conf. Rm. (cap. 150), Daily maid, Kitchen, Linens, Kids ski free, Concierge, Sauna, Hot tub

Room facilities: TV, Cable, Phone, Crib-Hi-chair, Ind.Heat Ctl.

Sports facilities: Pool, Tennis, Free ski shuttle, Golf, horses, rafting

Attractions: Just 2 blocks from the gondola/Steamboat ski area; One of the area's finest Amenity Center

Shops & Restaurants: Many retail stores, Over 70 fine restaurants in Steamboat

Special touches at Trappeur's Crossing include gourmet kitchen and wet bar, private balconies, gas-log fireplaces, heated parking and an emphasis on rich oak trim, brass and soft colors. Carve up Steamboat's powdery slopes on over 90 different runs for all levels of skiing. Or discover the pleasures of the warm months in the Rocky Mountains with sparkling summer days, just right for hikes among the wildflowers and other outdoor activities.

Please mention *Condo Vacations—the Complete Guide* when you reserve your condominium.

─────────────────── STEAMBOAT SPRINGS ───────────────────

Waterford Townhomes   3 Bedrooms $$$
P.O. Box 2995   3 Bedrms/week 4$
Steamboat Springs, CO 80477   Min. Stay 7 Nights, AmEx/Visa/MC,
303-879-7000 800-525-5502   Dep. 1 Night •
28 condos, Lo-rise, Key at Front desk
H-yes

Location: Airport: Stolpt 7 miles; Downtown: 3 miles; Ski lift: Nearby

General Facilities: Full serv., Bus. fac., Conf. rm. cap. 75, Daily maid, Kitchen, Linens, Baby-sitter

Room Facilities: Pool, Hot tub, Golf: Sheraton Steamboat, TV, Cable, Phone in rm., Crib-Hi-chair, Ind. Heat Ctl.

Attractions: Winter sports, fishing, hiking, hunting, sightseeing.

Shops & Restaurants: Old Town Steamboat and ski area retail stores; 50+ restaurants-varied cuisine

The Waterford's timber-beamed ceilings, massive stone fireplaces, enclosed by wood-paneled walls are reminiscent of a secluded mountain lodge. Tradition blends harmoniously with contemporary convenience. The townhomes overlook the ski village and the Yampa Valley. Complimentary bottle of wine, private outdoor swimming pool in summer, guest bus service and grocery delivery on request.

West Condominiums
Steamboat Springs, CO 88477

Whistler Village on the Creek
Steamboat Springs, CO 88477

Winterwood Townhomes   2 Bedrooms $$
P.O. Box 2995   2 Bedrms/week $$$$
Steamboat Springs, CO 80477   Min. Stay 7 Nights, AmEx/Visa/MC,
303-879-6605 800-525-5502   Dep. 1 Night •
16 condos, Lo-rise, Key at Res. Mgrs. Condo
H-yes

Location: Airport: Stolpt 7 miles; Downtown: 3 miles; Ski lift: Nearby

General Facilities: Daily maid, Kitchen, Linens, Baby-sitter

Room Facilities: Hot tub, Golf: Sheraton Steamboat-near, TV, Cable, Phone in rm., Crib-Hi-chair, Ind. Heat Ctl.

Attractions: Winter sports, fishing, hiking and hunting

Shops & Restaurants: Old Town Steamboat and ski area—retail shops; 50+ restaurants-varied cuisine

Private, multi-level townhomes sheltered from the outside world by towering stands of spruce and pine. An intimate mountain hideaway, tucked away in a secluded forest glen by a crystal stream. The master bedroom suite features window seats, large, multi-drawered polished wood furnishings, queen-size bed and glass-enclosed private spa. A very personal, elegant greenhouse retreat to enjoy with your complimentary bottle of wine.

─────────── TELLURIDE ───────────

Riverside of Telluride
Box 276
Telluride, CO 81435
303-728-4311 800-852-0015

1 Bedroom $$, 2 Bedrooms $$,
3 Bedrooms $$
1 Bedrm/week 4$, 2 Bedrms/week 5$,
3 Bedrms/week 6$
AmEx/Visa/MC, Dep. Required •
20 condos, Lo-rise, Key at 250 South Fir
H-yes

Location: Airport: 5 miles; Downtown: 3 blocks; Ski lift at Telluride

General Facilities: Full serv.; Daily maid; Linens; Hi-chair

Sports Facilities: Hot tub; Learn to ski

Room Facilities: Kitchen; Cable; Phone; Ind.Heat Ctl.

Attractions: Telluride Ski area, historic town of Telluride, mountain scenery

Shops & Restaurants: Resort town gift shops and art galleries; La Marmotle-French

One-level or townhouse with oak trim and oak dining furniture decorated in muted colors. On the San Miguel River, 2½ blocks from the ski lift and the heart of historic Telluride. All the creature comforts in these spacious units. Year-round activities and summer music festivals.

The Peaks at Telluride Condos
Box 2702, 136 Atop Country Club
Telluride, CO 81435
970-728-6800 800-789-2220
FAX: 970-728-6567

Studio $$$$, 1 Bedroom 8$,
2 Bedrooms 10$
AmEx/Visa/MC •
7 condos, Hi-rise, Key at Front desk,
P-Yes/No S-Yes/H-Yes

Location: Airport: 7 miles, 15 minutes; Downtown: 7 miles, 15 minute; Ski lift at Ski-in/out

General Facilities: Concierge; Daily maid; Linens; Baby sitter; Lounge; Crib-Hi-Chair; Restaurant on premises; Bar on premises

Sports Facilities: Game room; Pool; Tennis; Full health spa; Telluride Golf Course; Kidspa 8:30–6 daily

Room Facilities: Kitchen; Cable; VCR; Phone; Ind.Heat Ctl.

Attractions: Mesa Verde National Park, ski-in/ski-out, golf-in/golf-out; Entertainment

Shops & Restaurants: La Marmotte-French cuisine

Surrounded by the San Juan Mountains, The Peaks at Telluride offers ideal ski-in/ski-out and golf-in/golf-out convenience. The Spa at the Peaks is rated one of the largest in North America; 42,000 sq.ft. spread over 4 levels, 44 treatment rooms, cardiovascular desk, lap pool, indoor/outdoor pool, jacuzzis, steam rooms, sauna, squash and racquetball courts, climbing wall and kidspa. The Peaks is only 10 minutes from the historic town of Telluride with scheduled, complimentary shuttle service.

Enter your favorite condo in our "Condo of the Year" contest (entry form is in the back of the book).

─────────────────── VAIL ───────────────────

Apollo Park Lodge
P.O. Box 2157
Vail, CO 81658
303-476-5881 800-872-8281

1 Bedroom $$, 2 Bedrooms $$$
AmEx/Visa/MC, Dep. Req'd.
Lo-rise, Key at Front desk

Location: Airport: Avon-winter pickup; Downtown: 3 blocks; Ski lift: Vail
General Facilities: Full serv., Daily maid, Kitchen, Linens
Room Facilities: Pool, Golf: 18-hole championship near, TV, Crib-Hi-chair
Attractions: Vail Mountain, Apres-ski, hiking, gondola rides, fishing, horses, concerts
Shops & Restaurants: 100-plus Vail Village shops and boutiques; 85 restaurants

Delightful, tastefully furnished units in the heart of Vail Village with balcony views of the mountain and Gore Creek. 19 lifts for all levels of skiing ability with minimum waits. Ski school class lessons to improve your skills. Day and night ice skating, winter or summer. Lift tickets can be ordered 3 weeks prior to your arrival. Outstanding summer activities, cultural events and concerts.

Bighorn Condominium
P.O. Box 400
Vail, CO 81658
303-476-5532

1 Bedroom $$
Min. Stay 4 Nights, AmEx/Visa/MC,
   Dep. Req'd. •
60 condos, Key at 4327 Steamside, H-yes

Location: Airport: 2 hours; Ski lift: Vail
General Facilities: Daily maid, Kitchen, Linens, Baby-sitter
Room Facilities: Pool, Sauna, Hot tub, Golf: Vail Golf Course near, TV, Cable, Phone in rm., Ind. Heat Ctl.
Attractions: Cross-country skiing, snowmobiling, ice skating, hiking, biking, rafting
Shops & Restaurants: Cartier, Polo, Benetton; Left Bank/French

Privately owned clean and comfortable condominiums with views of the woods and open fields. The shuttle takes you to the village or ski area in just 15 minutes. Winter ice skating. Summer hiking, biking, rafting and swimming.

Coldstream Condominiums
1476 Westhaven Drive
Vail, CO 81657
303-476-6106

1 Bedroom $$$, 2 Bedrooms $$$$, 3 Bedrooms
   $$$$
1 Bedrm/week 5$, 3 Bed/week 8$
Min. Stay 2 Nights, AmEx/Visa/MC,
   Dep. Req'd. •
35 condos, Lo-rise, Key at Office

Location: Airport: 2 hours Denver; Downtown: 1 mile; Ski lift: Nearby
General Facilities: Daily maid, Kitchen, Linens, Baby-sitter
Room Facilities: Pool, Sauna, Hot tub, Tennis, Racquetball, TV, Cable, VCR, Phone in rm., Crib-Hi-chair, Ind. Heat Ctl.
Attractions: Colorado Mountain College, Cascade Club, Cascade Village, movies
Shops & Restaurants: Vail is known internationally for its shopping and food

Creekside setting offers guests a special kind of solitude and privacy. Custom designed accommodations are appealingly furnished, fireplaces, electric kitchens, covered parking, private balconies and patios with view of the Rockies and within walking distance of a host of summer and winter activities, in the heart of Cascade Village.

—————————————————— VAIL ——————————————————

Fallridge at Vail
1650 E. Vail Valley Dr.
Vail, CO 81657
303-476-1163 800-742-8245

1 Bedroom $$, 2 Bedrooms $$$, 3 Bedrooms
$$$$
Min. Stay 4 Nights, Dep. 1 Night •
50 condos, Hi-rise, Key at Front desk, H-yes

Location: Airport: Avon 9 miles; Downtown: 2 miles; Ski lift: Nearby

General Facilities: Conf. rm. cap. 60, Daily maid, Kitchen, Linens, Baby-sitter

Room Facilities: Pool, Sauna, Hot tub, Cross country skiing, Golf: Vail Golf Course, TV, Cable, Phone in rm., Crib-Hi-chair, Ind. Heat Ctl.

Attractions: Winter sports-hiking-biking-ballooning-gondola rides-rafting-photography

Shops & Restaurants: European import shops, upscale American shops, ski; Tyrolean Inn-Continental

Fallridge has been planned for relaxation and privacy. It has beautiful, unobstructed views of Vail Valley from private sun decks. Fallridge is located on the first tee of Vail's 18-hole PGA championship golf course to challenge golfers from mid-May through October, and providing an ideal touring area for cross-country skiers in winter. At day's end, gaze at the setting sun or the splendor of the alpenglow on the Gore Range.

———

Holiday Inn At Vail/Holiday House
13 Vail Road
Vail, CO 81657
303-476-5631 800-872-7221

1 Bedroom $$, 2 Bedrooms $$$, 3 Bedrooms
$$$
Dep. Req'd.
21 condos, Hi-rise, Key at Front desk

Location: Airport: Avon 10 miles; Downtown: 2 min.; Ski lift: Vail

General Facilities: Full serv., Daily maid, Kitchen, Linens, Restaurant on prem., Bar on prem., Lounge

Room Facilities: Pool, Sauna, Hot tub, Golf: Vail 18-hole courses, TV

Attractions: Colorado Ski Museum/Ski Hall of Fame, craft fairs, bicycle race, pro-circuit tennis, fish, entertainment

Shops & Restaurants: Vail Village shops; Gold Rush Restaurant-at Inn

Condominiums ranging in size from one to five bedrooms set in a charming European-style village. All units have fireplaces, balconies, jacuzzis, underground, heated parking and laundry facilities. Skiing and winter play in the fresh, cold air, endless summer fun. Gold Rush Restaurant, Fondue Stube, Fireside Bar. Free shuttle buses throughout Vail Village.

———

Homestake Condominiums
1081 Vail View Drive
Vail, CO 81657
303-476-3950

1 Bedroom $, 2 Bedrooms $$, Lo-rise
Kitchen, Phone in rm.

Attractions: Skiing, Ski Museum

Condominiums in the Sandstone Lionsridge area of Vail. Studios and one bedrooms with lofts to sleep two. Underground parking, kitchenettes, superb mountain views and fireplaces with wood provided. Sandstone Shuttle to Village and ski mountain.

--- VAIL ---

Lion Square Lodge
660 W. Lion Head Place
Vail, CO 81657
303-476-2281 800-525-5788

Studio $$, 1 Bedroom $$$, 2 Bedrooms $$$$, 3
 Bedrooms $$$$
AmEx/Visa/MC, Dep. Req'd.
90 condos, Hi-rise, Key at Front desk
H-yes

Location: Downtown: 1 block; Ski lift: Vail

General Facilities: Full serv., Conf. rm. cap. 400, Daily maid, Kitchen, Linens, Restaurant on prem., Lounge

Room Facilities: Pool, Sauna, Hot tub, Tennis, Golf: Vail Golf Course, TV, Cable, Crib-Hi-chair

Attractions: Jerry Ford Invitational Golf Tournament, World Forum, music and theatrical performances

Shops & Restaurants: Vail shopping; KB Ranch Company/steak, seafood

An Alpine village 100 miles west of Denver offering an endless variety of year-round activity. Luxurious accommodations enhancing your memorable vacation in Vail's international atmosphere.

Lodge at Vail/Towers
174 E. Bore Creek Dr.
Vail, CO 81659
800-231-0136

Manor Vail Lodge
595 East Vail Valley Drive
Vail, CO 81657
303-476-5651 800-525-9165

Studio $, 1 Bedroom $$$, 2 Bedrooms $$$$
Min. Stay 7 Nights, AmEx/Visa/MC,
Dep. Req'd. •
170 condos, Lo-rise, Key at Front desk
No S-yes/H-yes

Location: Airport: 100 miles; Downtown: 1 block; Ski lift: Vail

General Facilities: Full serv., Bus. fac., Conf. rm. cap. 600, Daily maid, Kitchen, Linens, Restaurant on prem., Bar on prem., Lounge, Baby-sitter, Child planned rec.: Day care, ski school

Room Facilities: Pool, Sauna, Hot tub, Tennis, Skiing, Golf: Vail Golf Club, TV, Cable, Phone in rm., Crib-Hi-chair, Ind. Heat Ctl.

Attractions: Gerald Ford Amphitheater, ski, Vail Village, winter/summer mountain activities

Shops & Restaurants: Vail Village-European style pedestrian village; Lord Gore Terrace

Unique personalized units with moss rock fireplaces, ideally located to enjoy the entire Vail resort, walk to ski lifts, amphitheatre, tennis, fish Gore Creek for trout, rent a bicycle, or take a gondola ride to the top of the mountain. In summer, attend art festivals, music concerts, ballet and community theater. Discos, bars, rock and roll, and quiet lounges. Ski accessories and equipment rental are available.

——————————————— VAIL ———————————————

Montaneros Condominiums in Vail
641 W. Lionshead Circle
Vail, CO 81657
303-476-2491 800-523-6327

1 Bedroom $$, 2 Bedrooms $$$, 3 Bedrooms $$$$
Min. Stay 2 Nights, AmEx/Visa/MC,
Dep. 3 Nights •
42 condos, Hi-rise, Key at Front desk

Location: Airport: Avon 10 miles; Downtown: 1 block; Ski lift: Vail

General Facilities: Full serv., Bus. fac., Conf. rm. cap. 100, Daily maid, Kitchen, Linens

Room Facilities: Pool, Sauna, Hot tub, Golf: Vail Golf course 3 miles, TV, Cable, Phone in rm., Crib-Hi-chair, Ind. Heat Ctl.

Attractions: Glenwood Hot Springs, Aspen, Leadville, Estes Park, Breckenridge-all within 2 hours

Shops & Restaurants: Ski shops, Ralph Lauren, Cartier, Gucci, novelty; Chanticler/con.-Tyrolean/Aus.

Located on the Lionshead Mall, Montaneros is close to Vail's boutiques and restaurants, yet steps away from the gondola and chairlift. You'll enjoy the heated outdoor pool, whirlpool, sauna and hot tub. Picnics after golf, tennis, hiking or riding. All condominiums are privately owned and decorated differently in colonial, southwestern and contemporary.

——————————————————————————————————————

Mountain Haus at Vail
P.O. Box 1748
Vail, CO 81658
303-476-2434 800-237-0922

Studio $$$$, 1 Bedroom $$$$, 2 Bedrooms $$$$, 3 Bedrooms $$$$
Dep. Req'd.
Hi-rise, Key at Front desk

Location: Airport: Avon 10 miles; Downtown: 1 block; Ski lift: Vail

General Facilities: Full serv., Conf. rm. cap. 100, Daily maid, Kitchen, Linens, Restaurant on prem., Bar on prem., Game room

Room Facilities: Pool, Sauna, Hot tub, Golf: PGA courses near, TV

Attractions: Hiking, gondola rides, stream and lake fishing, horseback riding, river rafting

Shops & Restaurants: Vail elegant shops; Alain's/French country-on-site

Next to the covered bridge, these condominiums are all casually decorated by individual owners. Fireplace, balcony, color TV and all the services found in the best hotels. Superior service in a prime location. Winter enchantment of powder snow and ice skating at the Olympic Ice arena. Summer golf, tennis, fishing, hiking, horseback riding, river rafting, dining at one of Vail's patio restaurants, and shopping.

Please mention *Condo Vacations the Complete Guide* when you reserve your condominium.

—————————————— VAIL/LAKEWOOD ——————————————

Raintree Inn
3500 S. Wadsworth St.
Lakewood, CO 80235
303-476-3890
800-543-2814

1 Bedroom $$, 2 Bedrooms $$$,
3 Bedrooms $$$
Min. Stay 2 Nights, AmEx/Visa/MC,
Deposit Req'd. •
Key at Front Desk, 19 condos, Hi-rise,
S-Yes/H-Yes

Location: Airport: Denver-100 miles; Downtown: 2 miles; Ski lift at Vail

General Facilities: Daily maid; Linens; Baby sitter; Crib-Hi-Chair; Restaurant;
Bar

Business Facilities: Business facilities, Conf. Rm. Cap: 120.

Sports Facilities: Game room; Pool, Sauna; Hot tub; Horseshoes; Volleyball;
Golf; Child planned recreation—ski area.

Room Facilities: Kitchen; Cable TV; Phone in room; Ind. Heat Ctl.

Attractions: Skiing, hiking, rafting, shopping, biking, tours, sleigh rides, nightlife,
golf.

Shops & Restaurants: Vail Village, Lionshead; Shopping center next door;
Pepi's European-German

*100 miles west of Denver within 10 minutes of Vail and Beaver Creek ski areas. Cozy,
southwestern decor with fireplaces, decks and lofted bedrooms. Live guitar on
weekends. Full shuttle service to enjoy the variety of winter and summer activities.
Complimentary continental breakfast. Cozy lobby with fireplace. Football-game
parties in the lounge on Sundays.*
——————————————— VAIL ———————————————

Simba Resort
1100 N. Frontage Rd.
Vail, CO 81657
970-476-0344 800-746-2278
FAX: 970-476-0888

1 Bedroom $$$, 2 Bedrooms $$$
Min. Stay Ask, AmEx/Visa/MC,
25% Dep. Req'd. •
70 condos, Hi-rise, Key at Front desk
No S-Yes

Location: Airport: Denver-120 miles; Downtown: 2 miles; Ski lift at Nearby

General Facilities: Full hotel service; Daily maid; Linens; Lounge

Sports Facilities: Game room; Pool; Sauna; Hot tub; Tennis; Racquetball, exer-
cise; Vail golf course-3 miles

Room Facilities: Kitchen; Cable; HBO; Phone

Attractions: Skiing, snowmobile, rafting, horseback riding, fishing, hiking,
mountain bike, jeep tours.; Entertainment

*Sunny one and two bedroom condominiums cheerfully decorated in earth tones.
Located just one and a half miles from the Village of Vail and the ski slopes. Ride our
courtesy shuttle to and from the slopes. Simba offers year-round beauty, diversified
recreational activities, hospitality and charm. The resort atmosphere and privacy are
quietly apart from the activity of the village.*

─────────────── VAIL ───────────────

Sonnenalp Hotel
20 Vail Road
Vail, CO 81657
303-476-5656 800-654-8312

1 Bedroom $$$$, 2 Bedrooms 4$
Pool, Kitchen

Attractions: Guided bicycle rides, hiking, jeep trip to Colorado ghost town, white-water rafting, Cosmetique Spa, Tennis, Golf

Lobby with hand-crafted woodwork and Bavarian decor. Suites are furnished in an Alpine motif with down comforters and plush terry robes for your nightly comfort. Plenty of sunshine, clear, warm air and dry temperatures. Year-round sports activities and cultural events.

Streamside at Vail
2264 S. Frontage Rd.
Vail, CO 81657
303-476-6000 800-223-8245

Studio $, 1 Bedroom $, 2 Bedrooms $$,
    3 Bedrooms $$$
Min. Stay 2 Nights, AmEx/Visa/MC,
    Dep. 20% •
109 condos, Lo-rise, Key at Front desk
No S-yes/H-yes

Location: Airport: Avon-5 miles; Downtown: 3 miles; Ski lift: Nearby

General Facilities: Full serv., Bus. fac., Conf. rm. cap. 45, Daily maid, Kitchen, Babysitter, Child planned rec.: Nightly movies

Room Facilities: Pool, Sauna, Hot tub, Racquetball, handball, TV, Cable, Phone in rm., Crib-Hi-chair, Ind. Heat Ctl.

Attractions: Winter sports-Narrow Gauge RR-whitewater rafting-hot springs-backpacking, entertainment

Shops & Restaurants: Polo Ralph Lauren-Esprit-Bogner-Cartier-Crabtree; Left Bank-Fr. Ore House-stks

Tastefully appointed southwestern condominiums in earth tone colors on an open, wooded hillside. Streamside offers guests the quieter side of the mountains, the relaxing beauty of a serene wooded setting, the sounds of Gore Creek, and vistas of distant forests and snowy peaks. Nightly wine and cheese parties and movies. Shuttle service, indoor/outdoor pool, racquet-handball courts and exercise equipment.

The Lodge At Lionshead
P.O. Drawer 1868 380 E. Lionshead
Vail, CO 81658
303-476-2700

Studio $$, 1 Bedroom $$, 2 Bedrooms $$, 3
    Bedrooms $$$$
Min. Stay 2 Nights, AmEx/Visa/MC,
    Dep. 3 Nights •
54 condos, Lo-rise, Key at Mgt. Office

Location: Airport: Denver 100 miles; Ski lift: Vail

General Facilities: Daily maid, Kitchen, Linens, Baby-sitter

Room Facilities: Pool, Sauna, Golf: Vail Golf Club nearby, TV, Cable, Phone in rm., Crib-Hi-chair, Ind. Heat Ctl.

Attractions: Skiing, golf, tennis

Shops & Restaurants: Vail Village & Lionshead, shops, boutiques; Tea Room, Vail Valley dining

Situated along scenic Gore Creek, amid aspen and pines, providing a unique combination of seclusion and convenience. Family-oriented for summer and winter vacation experiences. Ski-in/ski-out. Shuttle to golf, tennis, hiking and bike trails.

──────────────── VAIL ────────────────

The Lodge at Vail
174 East Gore Creek Drive
Vail, CO 81657
303-476-5011 800-223-6800

1 Bedroom $$$$, 2 Bedrooms 5$, 3 Bedrooms
7$
Dep. Req'd.
Lo-rise, Key at Lobby

Location: Airport: 100 miles; Downtown: 1 block; Ski lift: Vail

General Facilities: Full serv., Kitchen, Linens, Restaurant on prem., Bar on prem., Baby-sitter

Room Facilities: Pool, Sauna, Hot tub

Attractions: Golf, tennis, horseback riding, hiking, fishing white water, vintage car races, ballooning

Shops & Restaurants: Vail shops, Lodge—15 shops; Wildflower Inn

European in commitment to service and elegance, attendant to take your skis before you check your dinner reservations or use the jacuzzi or pool. Swiss chalet style condos. Summer celebrity tournaments, vintage car races, hot air ballooning.

The Wren Condominiums
500 South Frontage Road, #116
Vail, CO 81657
303-476-0052 800-345-5415

Studio $$, 1 Bedroom $$$, 2 Bedrooms $$$$
Min. Stay 3 Nights, AmEx/Visa/MC,
Dep. 3 Nights
Hi-rise, Key at Front desk

Location: Airport: Stapleton; Downtown: 2 blocks; Ski lift: Vail

General Facilities: Kitchen

Room Facilities: Pool, TV, Cable, Phone in rm., Crib-Hi-chair

Attractions: 2 ski mountains, 4 18-hole golf courses, 60 tennis courts, ice skating, horses

Shops & Restaurants: Vail shops; Vail Village restaurants

All units designed for maximum privacy and unobstructed mountain views. Vail Valley winter and summer sports. Nature trails next door to your condominium. Friendly staff makes you feel at home.

Vail Hotel and Athletic Club
352 East Meadow Drive
Vail, CO 81657
303-476-0700 800-822-4754

Studio $$$$, 2 Bedrooms $$$$
AmEx/Visa/MC, Dep. Req'd. •
38 condos, Lo-rise, Key at Front desk

Location: Airport: 10 miles; Downtown: 50 yds.; Ski lift: Nearby

General Facilities: Full serv., Conf. rm. cap. 55, Daily maid, Kitchen, Linens, Restaurant on prem., Bar on prem., Lounge, Baby-sitter, Child planned rec.: Nursery

Room Facilities: Pool, Sauna, Hot tub, Athletic club, Golf: Vail Golf Club, TV, Cable, Phone in rm., Crib-Hi-chair, Ind. Heat Ctl.

Attractions: World-famous ski resort. Four 18-hole golf courses, tennis, shopping, dining, entertainment

Shops & Restaurants: Large amount of shops within walking distance; 352 East/Nouvelle American

Small, distinctive, elegant with full service spa and athletic club on the premises. Most rooms face the mountain. Complete amenity package in room, robes, newspapers. Band entertainment in the bar and restaurant. Golf and tennis nearby, and excellent skiing.

———————————— VAIL ————————————

Vail International
300 E. Lionshead Circle, Box 877
Vail, CO 81658
303-476-5200

1 Bedroom $$, 2 Bedrooms $$, 3 Bedrooms $$$
Min. Stay 2 Nights, Visa/MC, Dep. Req'd. •
56 condos, Hi-rise, Key at Front desk
H-yes

Location: Airport: 7 miles; Downtown: 10 min.; Ski lift: 400 yds

General Facilities: Daily maid, Kitchen, Linens, Baby-sitter

Room Facilities: Pool, Sauna, Hot tub, Ski Vail, Golf: Vail Golf Course, TV, Cable, Phone in rm., Crib-Hi-chair, Ind. Heat Ctl.

Attractions: Vail Mountain, ice skating, cross-country skiing, snowmobiling

Shops & Restaurants: Vail's famous shops; Left Bank/French

For the family planning a ski vacation. 400 yards to "Born Free" express and gondola. Walk to Vail for shops, restaurants and nightlife. Contemporary furnishings in fully equipped condominiums with fireplaces and mountain views.

Copper Mountain Resort

―――――――――――――――――― VAIL ――――――――――――――――――

Vail Racquet Club
4690 Vail Racquet Dr., Box 1437
Vail, CO 81657
303-476-4840

1 Bedroom $$, 2 Bedrooms $$, 3 Bedrooms $$$
Min. Stay 1 Night, AmEx/Visa/MC,
Dep. 1 Night •
Key at R. Club sales office
H-yes

Location: Airport: Avon 20 miles; Downtown: 4 miles; Ski lift: Vail

General Facilities: Conf. rm. cap. 110, Daily maid, Kitchen, Linens, Restaurant on prem., Bar on prem., Game room, Lounge, Baby-sitter, Child planned rec.: Swimming, hiking

Room Facilities: Pool, Sauna, Tennis, Ski Vail, Golf: Vail golf course-1 mile, TV, Cable, Phone in rm., Crib-Hi-chair, Ind. Heat Ctl.

Attractions: World-class ski area, golfing, tennis

Shops & Restaurants: Clothing, sportswear; Vail Racquet Club-French-Amr.

Fully equipped condominiums and townhouses with fireplaces and kitchens. Full health facility with indoor/outdoor jacuzzis, 25 meter lap pool, Olympic outdoor pool, Kaiser and Nautilus equipment, and 18 tennis courts, three of them indoors. All of this in beautiful Gore Range, 4 miles from Vail Village on free bus route.

―――

Vail Run Resort
1000 Lions Ridge Loop
Vail, CO 81657
303-476-1500

Studio $$, 1 Bedroom $$, 2 Bedrooms $$$,
3 Bedrooms $$$$
Min. Stay 2 Nights, AmEx/Visa/MC,
Dep. 1 Night •
54 condos, Hi-rise, Key at Registr. desk

Location: Airport: 10 miles; Downtown: 1 mile; Ski lift: Vail

General Facilities: Full serv., Daily maid, Kitchen, Linens, Restaurant on prem., Game room, Baby-sitter

Room Facilities: Pool, Sauna, Hot tub, Tennis, Nautilus, TV, Cable, Phone in rm., Crib-Hi-chair, Ind. Heat Ctl.

Attractions: Rafting, horseback riding, jeep tours, fishing, hiking, tennis, golf, entertainment

Shops & Restaurants: Boutique shops throughout the village; Mataam Fez-Moroccan

Be in the middle of what's happening throughout the valley. Summer activities during cool, sunny days. World class skiing in winter. Vail's Alpine Village for shopping and dining. Free shuttle bus. Furnishings are contemporary in this complete resort with nautilus, tanning bed, indoor tennis, pool and 3 restaurants. In-room movies. Sunday keg parties.

Enter your favorite condo in our "Condo of the Year" contest (entry form is in the back of the book).

————————————————— VAIL —————————————————

Vail Spa
710 West Lionshead Circle
Vail, CO 81657
303-476-0882

2 Bedrooms $$$$, 3 Bedrooms $$$$
Dep. Req'd.
Hi-rise

Location: Airport: Avon; Downtown: 2 blocks; Ski lift: Vail
General Facilities: Daily maid, Kitchen, Linens, Restaurant on prem.
Room Facilities: Pool, Sauna, Hot tub, Exercise, weight room, TV, Crib-Hi-chair
Attractions: Sleigh rides, snowshoe treks, snowmobiling, ice skating
Shops & Restaurants: Vail specialty shops, stores, services; On-site restaurant

Ski Vail and Beaver Creek on a single lift ticket by taking the shuttle bus service. The Spa offers a courtesy van to and from Avon Airport, and one to Safeway twice daily. Condominiums with washer/dryer, fireplaces and a Briggs Spa whirlpool bathtub. If you're not too tired after skiing, use the outdoor pool, indoor lap pool, heated whirlpool, or steam and dry heat saunas. For non-skiers who want to stay in shape there is an exercise and weight room. Go out to dinner at the Spa or Vail restaurants.

Village Inn Plaza Condominiums
100 East Meadow Drive
Vail, CO 81657
303-476-5622 800-445-4014

Studio $$$$, 1 Bedroom $$$$, 2 Bedrooms
$$$$, 3 Bedrooms 5$
Min. Stay 7 Nights, AmEx/Visa/MC,
Dep. 2 Nights •
45 condos, Hi-rise, Key at Front desk at Inn

Location: Airport: Avon-20 miles; Downtown: 1 block; Ski lift: Vail
General Facilities: Full serv., Bus. fac., Conf. rm. cap. 50, Daily maid, Kitchen, Linens, Restaurant on prem., Bar on prem., Lounge, Baby-sitter, Child planned rec.: Ski classes
Room Facilities: Pool, Sauna, Hot tub, Golf: Vail golf course-2 miles, TV, Phone in rm., Ind. Heat Ctl.
Attractions: Snowmobiling, day/night sleigh rides with lunch or dinner, nature walks
Shops & Restaurants: All types of shops in the on-site Plaza; Ambrosia-cont/ Alpenpose-Ger.

In the center of Vail Village, a block and a half from the Vista-Bon high speed quad chair, charming Alpine style condominiums with all the creature comforts. Non-skiers enjoy ice skating, snowmobiling, sleigh rides, shopping, dining, museums and art galleries throughout the village. Summer outdoor sports including gondola rides and western cookouts. Year-round heated pool and sun deck. Winter movies for the children. Continental breakfast.

─────────────── VAIL ───────────────

The Willows Condominiums   Studio $$, 1 Bedroom $$, 2 Bedrooms $$$
74 Willow Road   Lo-rise
Vail, CO 81657
970-476-2233 800-826-1274
FAX: 970-476-5714

General Facilities: Full hotel service; Daily maid; Linens

Sports Facilities: Tennis; Ski; Golf Course

Room Facilities: Kitchen

In the heart of Vail Village, at the base of Vail Mountain, privately owned condominiums with all the comforts, convenience, service and amenities desired. Close to shopping, dining and entertainment. Jacuzzi, steam room, complimentary parking. Winter rates include complimentary continental breakfast. Select The Willows for home comforts with hotel services.

─────────────── WINTER PARK ───────────────

Beaver Village Condominiums   1 Bedroom $$, 2 Bedrooms $$$,
50 Village Drive, P.O. Box 349   3 Bedrooms $$$
Winter Park, CO 80482   1 Night Dep. Req'd. •
970-726-8813 800-824-8438   115 condos, Lo-rise
FAX: 970-726-5313   Key at Clubhouse front desk

Location: Airport: Denver, 85 miles; Downtown: 4 blocks; Ski lift at 2 miles

General Facilities: Full hotel service; Linens

Business Facilities: Bus. fac.; Conf. Room Cap. 110

Sports Facilities: Pool; Sauna; Hot tub

Room Facilities: Kitchen; Cable; VCR; Phone; Ind.Heat Ctl.

Attractions: Major ski area, sleigh rides, tubing, snowmobiling, horses, fishing, mountain biking, golf

Shops & Restaurants: Small mountain retail shops, Safeway-3 miles; 25 different restaurants

Enter your Beaver Village condominium and notice the bag of potpourri on your vanity. Firewood is right outside your door. Nearby is the Amenity Center where you can take a soothing hot tub or play a game of backgammon. Get updates on current ski conditions and take complimentary transportation from your doorstep to the slopes. Go home with memories of fantastic skiing, crackling fires, wonderful dining and sincere personal attention.

———————————————————— VAIL ————————————————————

Hi Country Haus Resort   1 Bedroom $$, Lo-rise
P.O. Box 3095   Pool, Kitchen, Phone in rm.
Winter Park, CO 80482
303-726-9421 800-228-1025

Attractions: Tennis, swimming, hiking, rodeos, Alpine Slide, golf

Just a short 15 minute walk to downtown Winter Park's shops, restaurants and nightlife. Secluded condominiums adjacent to all activities. All the comforts of home, plus swimming pool, hot tub and sauna.

Iron Horse Resort Retreat Studio $$, 1 Bedroom $$$, 2 Bedrooms $$$$
P.O. Box 1286, 257 Winter Park Dr. Min. Stay 2 Nights, AmEx/Visa/MC,
Winter Park, CO 80482   Dep. 2 Nights •
303-726-8851 800-621-8190 126 condos, Hi-rise, Key at Lobby check-in desk
            H-yes

Location: Airport: 67 miles Denver; Ski lift: Winter Pk

General Facilities: Full serv., Conf. rm. cap. 120, Daily maid, Kitchen, Linens, Restaurant on prem., Bar on prem., Lounge, Baby-sitter, Child planned rec.: 5 & under ski free

Room Facilities: Pool, Sauna, Hot tub, Golf: Pole Creek-drive, TV, Cable, VCR, Phone in rm., Crib-Hi-chair, Ind. Heat Ctl.

Attractions: Jeep tours, Winter Park

Shops & Restaurants: Cooper Creek Square, Safeway Shopping Mall

Set in the rugged beauty of the Colorado Rockies, this unique vacation resort offers a perfect setting for a romantic retreat or family vacation. Magical moments in every season. Ski-in/ski-out to two mountains. Picnic at Alpine Meadows among the wildflowers or changing fall colors. Trout streams, lakes, trails for walking or riding. Friendly staff and luxury vacation homes with all the amenities.

Lookout Village Condominiums 1 Bedroom $$, 2 Bedrooms $$
P.O. Box 3157   1 Bedrm/week $$$$, 2 Bed/week $$$$
Winter Park, CO 80482   Dep. Req'd.
303-726-8821 800-443-2781 13 condos, Villas, Key at The Summit #10

Location: Airport: 67 miles; Downtown: 3 miles; Ski lift: Winter Pk

General Facilities: Daily maid, Kitchen, Linens

Room Facilities: Sauna, Hot tub, Tennis, Exercise equipment, Golf: Pole Creek 7 miles, TV, Cable, Phone in rm., Crib-Hi-chair, Ind. Heat Ctl.

Attractions: Snow tubing, alpine slide, rafting, bike trails, sleigh rides, horses, hiking, Nat. Park

Shops & Restaurants: Yellow Front, Ben Franklin, Safeway, ski, gifts; Lani's Place/ Mex-Gasthaus/Ger.

Vaulted ceilings, oak cabinetry and woodwork, upholstered furniture custom decorated in earthtones and oak on landscaped grounds with views of pines, aspens and mountain peaks. Five minute walk to Ridge Club for tennis, swimming, racquetball, game room, restaurant and lounge.

---------------------------- WINTER PARK ----------------------------

Silverado II Resort 1 Bedroom $$, 2 Bedrooms $$$$
380 Alpine Vista Lane, POB 3368 Lo-rise
Winter Park, CO 80482
303-726-5753 800-654-7157
Sports Facilities: Pool
Room Facilities: Kitchen

No matter what the season, this is the place for fun. Learn to ski, or improve your techinque. For warmer weather, raft the Colorado, backpack, hike or ride. Outdoor pool, sauna, jacuzzi, recreation room, ski shop, restaurant and bar.

The Summit At Winter Park Studio $$, 1 Bedroom $$, 2 Bedrooms $$$,
P.O. Box 3157 3 Bedrooms $$$
Winter Park, CO 80482 Dep. Required, 10 condos, Lo-rise,
515-292-9546 800-443-2781 Key at Office Summit #10, No S-yes
FAX: 515-292-3670

Location: Airport: 67 miles; Downtown: 3 miles; Ski lift at Winter Park

General Facilities: Daily maid; Linens; Crib-Hi-chair

Sports Facilities: Videos; Pool; Basketball; Hot tub; Ski shop; Horseshoes, racquetball; Pole Creek Golf 7 miles

Room Facilities: Kitchen; Cable; VCP; Phone; Ind.Heat Ctl.

Attractions: Grand Lake/Lake Granby recreational area, Rocky Mt. National Park, summer festivals, bikes; nightclubs

Shops & Restaurants: Safeway, 7-11, video, ski, gift shops, drug store; Lani's Place Mexican, Gasthaus Eichler

The Summit offers a variety of condos located in several smaller condominium communities nestled in the woods on a mountain highland overlooking the Winter Park/Fraser Valley. We specialize in high quality condominiums with complete furnishings. A free shuttle transports you to skiing, shopping and other activities. For a ski trip or a summer vacation, it's your home away from home.

Winter Park 1 Bedroom $$
P.O. Box 36
Winter Park, CO 80482
303-726-5587 800-453-2525

Never a dull moment in the friendliest valley in the Rockies. Children's center with specially trained instructors during ski season. Wildflowers cover the landscape in summer, with fishing, rodeo, rafting, golf and hiking. Unpretentious hospitality.

Delaware

South Bethany
Beach

─────────── SOUTH BETHANY BEACH ───────────

King's Grant
Route 1
South Bethany Beach, DE
301-524-1200 800-437-7600

Lo-rise
Pool, Kitchen

Oceanfront and bayfront condominiums with European-styled gourmet kitchens, lofts, garden baths and fireplaces, one and a half miles between Bethany Beach, Delaware and Ocean City, Maryland. Three and four bedroom units with sun decks and jacuzzis.

We want to hear from you—any comments regarding the condos or our publication may be noted on the form at the end of the book.

Florida

Pensacola Niceville
Panama City Beach
Destin
Fort Walton
Beach   Santa Rosa
Navarre Beach Beach Seagrove
Perdido Key   Beach   Winter Garden
Redington   Tarpon Springs
Beach   Crystal Beach
Indian Rocks St. Petersburg Beach
Beach   Longboat Key
         Captiva Island
Englewood Sanibel Island
Cape Haze Fort Myers Beach
Bonita Springs   Marco Island

Amelia Island
Middleburg
St. Augustine
Ormond Beach
Daytona Beach
New Smyrna Beach
Orlando   Cocoa Beach
Lake Buena Vista
Kissimmee   Satellite Beach
Tampa   Vero Beach Grenelefe
Indian Shores   Hutchinson Island
Sarasota   Jensen Beach   Indian Harbour
Punta Gorda   Jupiter   Beach
         Sebring Delray Beach Stuart
Naples   Fort   Boca Raton   Howey-In-The- Hills
         Lauderdale Deerfield Beach Pompano Beach
West Palm   Miami Beach   Sunny Isles   Hillsboro
Beach   Gulfstream   Treasure Island Beach
         Key Largo
Duck Key   Islamorada
Key West
         Marathon

-------------------- AMELIA ISLAND --------------------

Amelia Island Plantation
Box 758, Highway A1A South
Amelia Island, FL 32034
904-261-6161 800-874-6878

1 Bedroom $$$$, 2 Bedrooms $$$$, 3 Bedrooms $$$$
AmEx/Visa/MC, Dep. 1 Night •
549 condos, Villas
H-yes

Location: Airport: Jacksonville-35 min.; Downtown: 4 miles; Beach front

General Facilities: Conf. rm., Daily maid, Kitchen, Linens, Restaurant on prem., Bar on prem., Game room, Lounge, Baby-sitter, Child planned rec.: Seasonal 3-12 years

Room Facilities: Pool, Sauna, Tennis, Golf: Amelia Links & Long Point, TV, Cable, Phone in rm., Crib-Hi-chair, Ind. AC Ctl., Ind. Heat Ctl.

Attractions: Fernandina Beach, local historic shrimping village, Disney World, St. Augustine, entertainment

Shops & Restaurants: Jacksonville shopping malls; Dune Side Club, Verandah

Villa complexes with your choice of views. Boardwalk to the beach from oceanfront villas. Honeymoon villas with private indoor pools. Wake up to the morning sounds of Amelia, have breakfast and grab your golf clubs, tennis racquet, fishing gear or bathing suit to start your day. Children love the playground, kiddie pool, their own fishing pond and the Coop's fast food. 5 restaurants, ranging from romantic to casual, the Beach Club, dancing, Admiral's Lounge, music, cocktails. Too much to do to list.

──────────────── AMELIA ISLAND ────────────────

Amelia Island Lodging Systems Studio $$, 1 Bedroom $$, 2 Bedrooms $$$,
584 S. Fletcher Ave. 3 Bedrooms $$$, 1 Bed/week 5$, 2
Amelia Island, FL 32034 Bed/week 7$, 3 Bed/week 8$, Amex, Visa,
904-261-4148 800-872-8531 MC, Dep. req'd, Key at Office #1735
115 condos, Hi-rise, Lo-rise, Villas, No
S-yes, H-yes

Location: Airport: 3 miles; Downtown: 3 miles; Beach front

General facilities: Full serv., Conf. Rm. (cap. 10), Kitchen, Linens, Child planned
rec., Baby sitter

Room facilities: TV, Cable, Phone, Ind. AC. Ctl., Ind. Heat Ctl.

Sports facilities: Pool, Tennis, Boating, Fishing

Attractions: Fort Clinch, 13 mile beach, Victorian village and shrimp fleet,
antiques, State Park

Shops & Restaurants: Antique shops, restored Victorian City of Fernandina
Beach, Brett's Waterway Cafe

*Choice of 115 completely equipped oceanfront condos, villas and townhouses with
modern Florida decor, nestled on Barrier Island. Unspoiled solitude, beauty and
nature on Amelia Island, a pre-Civil War fort. Shopping and fine seafood restaurants
at the restored shrimping village of Fernandina. Play golf, tennis, horseback ride
along the beach; go sailing, surfing or charter a boat for deep-sea fishing. Special
off-season rates.*

──────────────── BOCA RATON ────────────────

La Boca Casa by the Ocean 1 Bed/week $$, Min. stay 7 nights, Amex,
365 North Ocean Blvd. Visa, MC, Dep. req'd
Boca Raton, FL 33432 Key at Office by the pool
407-392-0885 19 condos, Lo-rise •

Location: Airport: 20 miles; Downtown: 1 mile; Need car

General facilities: Kitchen, Linens, Hot tub

Room facilities: TV, Cable, Phone, Crib-Hi-chair, Ind. AC. Ctl, Ind. Heat Ctl.

Sports facilities: Pool, Executive Golf/4 blocks

Attractions: Superior restaurants, shopping, jai alai, polo, racing, golf, cruises,
snorkeling

Shops & Restaurants: Saks, Lord & Taylor, Bloomingdales, Burdine's, La Vielle
Maison-5-star

*Earth tones, wicker and plants decorate these 1 bedroom condos. Prestigious Boca
Raton offers polo matches, five-star dining and exceptional shopping. Just steps away
from a quiet beach, surrounded by bicycling and jogging paths, or use the heated
swimming pool and jacuzzi. Nearby are tropical parks and reefs for snorkeling.
Thoroughbred and harness racing, or one day cruises to the Bahamas.*

Be sure to call the condo the verify details and prices and to make
your reservation.

Bronze Tree

BONITA SPRINGS

Bonita Beach Resort
26395 Hickory Boulevard
Bonita Springs, FL 33923
813-992-2137

Studio $, 1 Bedroom $
1 Bedrm/week $$$$
Lo-rise

Location: Airport: Southwest Florida
General Facilities: Kitchen, Linens
Room Facilities: Fishing
Attractions: Beaches, dog track, golf course, Thomas Edison Lab., Shell Factory, Everglades Gardens
Shops & Restaurants: Fort Myers and Naples shopping

An original Florida fishing camp, now a comfortable resort. Tropical plants and palm trees shade the children's play area and picnic tables. Boat ramp and docks behind the apartments, lighted for night fishing. Beach with a 5 mile unbroken shoreline for swimming and boating, or look for some of the 300 varieties of shells found on the beach and sand bars.

———————————————— CAPE HAZE ————————————————

Palm Island Resort
7092 Placida Rd.
Cape Haze, FL 33946
813-697-4800 800-824-5412
FAX: 941-697-0696

1 Bedroom $$$, 2 Bedrooms $$$$,
3 Bedrooms $$$$
1 Bedrm/week 5$, 2 Bedrms/week 7$,
3 Bedrms/week 9$
Min. Stay 2 Nights, AmEx/Visa/MC
Dep. Required •
160 condos, Lo-rise
Key at Reception-Mainland

Location: Airport: Sarasota-45 miles; Downtown: 6 miles; Need car; Beachfront

General Facilities: Full hotel service; Linens; Baby sitter; Store; Restaurant on premises; Bar on premises

Business Facilities: Bus. fac.; Conf. Room Cap. 100

Sports Facilities: Pool; Hot tub; 11 tennis courts with pro; 3 Golf courses-10 miles; Fishing poles, bikes

Room Facilities: Kitchen; Cable; Phone; Ind.AC.Ctl; Ind.Heat Ctl.

Attractions: Sarasota-1 hour, John Ringling, Jungle Gardens, St. Armands Circle, Mote Marine Laboratory; Entertainment

Shops & Restaurants: Boca Grande Boutiques, Venice: Avenue of Boutiques; Garfields, The Pink Elephant

Deluxe accommodations located on an island with no bridges or causeways from the mainland, no cars and no crowds, quiet and unspoiled surroundings, all Gulf-front views with 3 miles of shell-laden beach. Private launch between island and mainland for guests only, open air tram continually circles resort. Great place for couples/honeymooners, families and small groups. Florida's only true out-island resort. Golf carts, tandem bikes and canoes available for rent.

———————————————— CLEARWATER ————————————————

Executive/Clearwater House
P.O. Box 7642
Clearwater, FL 33518
813-797-1140

1 Bedroom $, 2 Bedrooms $$, 3 Bedrooms
$$, 1 Bedrm/week $$$$, 2 Bedrm/week
4$, 3 Bedrm/week 5$
Min. Stay 7 Nights; Deposit Required
Key in Lock Box; 4 condos; Hi-Rise

Location: Airport: 25 min.; Downtown: 1 mile.

General Facilities: Daily maid; Linens

Sports Facilities: Pool, Hot Tub, Chi Chi Rodriguez Club

Room Facilities: Kitchen; VCP; Phones; Ind. Heat Ctl.; Ind. AC Ctl.

Attractions: Busch Gardens, Sea World, Walt Disney World, beaches, swimming, water sports

Shops & Restaurants: Countryside Mall, Sears, Maas Bros, K-Mart; Jesses' Landing–Seafood

Large, luxurious 2,650 sq.ft., two-bath home located on 1/3 acre lot overlooking pool and golf course. Custom designed kitchen, family room with stone fireplace, 4 dining areas, lanai, solarium, 6-jet whirlpool bath. Bedrooms are located in separate wings. May be rented as a 1-, 2-, or 3-bedroom home. Housekeeping service available. For the executive business person: Fax, computer, paging and answering equipment on-site.

──────── COCOA BEACH ────────

Ocean Landings Resort
900 North Atlantic Ave.
Cocoa Beach, FL 32931
407-783-9430
FAX: 407-783-1339

1 Bedroom $$$, 2 Bedroom $$$$, Jr. $$
1 Bedrm/week 6$, 2 Bedrm/week 9$
AmEx/MC/Visa/Other CC, Dep. 1 Night
228 condos, Hi-rise, Lo-rise, Keys at
Front lobby, H-yes

Location: Airport: 50 miles-Orlando; Downtown: 1 mile, Beach front

General Facilities: Full serv., Bus. fac., Daily maid, Kitchen, Linens, Restaurant on prem., Bar on prem., Baby sitter, Gameroom, Lounge.

Room Facilities: Pool, Sauna, Hot Tub, Tennis, Racquetball/nautilus, TV, Cable, Phone in rm., Ind. AC Ctl., Ind. Heat Ctl.

Attractions: EPCOT, Kennedy Space Center, Port Canaveral cruises, deep sea fishing, equipment rentals, entertainment.

Shops & Restaurants: Ron Jon's Surf Shop, Malls; Cocoa Cabana/continental.

95 oceanfront units in contemporary, casual style. A complete resort with tennis, racquetball, 2 pools, heated spa, sauna, exercise equipment, barbeques, aerobics classes and get-together breakfasts. The closest beach to Disney World and a perfect alternative to the crowded Orlando scene.

──────── CRYSTAL BEACH ────────

Sutherland Crossing
962 Seaview Circle, P.O. Box 883
Crystal Beach, FL 34681
813-786-2287

3 Bedrooms $$
3 Bedrms/week 6$
Min. Stay 2 Nights, Visa/MC, Dep. 25% •
Villas, Key at Clubhouse

Location: Airport: 35 minutes; Downtown: 10 min.; Need car

General Facilities: Daily maid, Kitchen, Linens, Restaurant on prem., Game room, Lounge, Baby-sitter

Room Facilities: Pool, Hot tub, Tennis, Mini golf, TV, Cable, Phone in rm., Crib-Hi-chair, Ind. AC Ctl., Ind. Heat Ctl.

Attractions: Busch Gardens, EPCOT Center, entertainment

Shops & Restaurants: Countryside and Clearwater Malls, Burdines, Sears; Jesse's Dockside-seafood

Single-family, "tree house style" villas in a natural, quiet setting, beautifully furnished in blues, mauve and green. Heated pool, jacuzzi, mini-golf, tennis, basketball and trips to "Honeymoon Island" via the Sutherland Express pontoon boat.

Subscribe to our newsletter *Mondo Condo* and hear about the latest special condo vacation values.

─────────────── DAYTONA BEACH SHORES ───────────────

Dolphin Beach Club
3355 South Atlantic Avenue
Daytona Beach Shores, FL 32018
904-761-8130

Pool, Kitchen, Phone in rm.

Attractions: Daytona International Speedway, Shuffleboard

Water activities during the sunny days, glorious sunsets and the many activities of Daytona Beach. Efficiency and 1 bedroom units with complete kitchens.

Fantasy Island Resort II
3175 S. Atlantic Ave.
Daytona Beach Shores, FL 32018
904-756-9446

Pool, Kitchen, Phone in rm.

Attractions: Daytona International Speedway

Beautiful weather and many water activities make this a favorite family resort. Barbecue grills and picnic areas for casual meals. Daytona Beach nightlife.

Seven Seas Resort Condo
2433 S. Atlantic Ave.
Daytona Beach Shores, FL 32018
904-257-1180

Sunglow
3647 S. Atlantic Avenue
Daytona Beach Shores, FL 32019
904-756-4005 800-225-3396

1 Bedroom $$, 2 Bedrooms $$$, Hi-rise
Pool, Kitchen

Attractions: Jai alai, greyhound racing, ten golf courses, Daytona Speedway

A luxury condominium for the price of a hotel room on Florida's picturesque coastline. Professionally decorated with all the comforts of home and close to Florida's major attractions. Game room, pool, jacuzzi, sauna. Oceanfront.

─────────────── DEERFIELD BEACH ───────────────

Avalon
735 South A1A
Deerfield Beach, FL 33441
305-427-6611 800-424-1943

Lo-rise
Pool, Kitchen

Attractions: Golf, tennis, fishing, boating, surfing, shuffleboard, put. green

A place to relax, soak up the sun and change to a leisurely life-style. Many area activities, a few miles to Boca Raton and Fort Lauderdale.

Emerald Seas
660 N. Ocean Blvd.
Deerfield Beach, FL 33441
305-427-1300

1 Bedroom $$, 2 Bedrooms $$$, Lo-rise
Pool, Daily maid, Kitchen
Shuffleboard

On Florida's Gold Coast, large beach, almond/blue designer kitchens, restful furnishing accentuating the colors of the outdoors. Two pools, unsurpassed fishing, charter boats, spectator sports, nightlife. A pleasurable experience in a tranquil setting.

————————————————— DEERFIELD BEACH —————————————————

Inn At Deer Creek Racquet Club
9 Deer Creek Road, A105
Deerfield Beach, FL 33442
305-421-7800 800-327-1699

1 Bedroom $$, Jr. $, 1 Bedrm/week 4$,
AmEx/Visa/MC, Dep. Req'd, •
25 condos, Villas, H-yes, Key at front desk.

Location: Airport: Ft. Lauderdale; Downtown: 3 miles, Need car.

General Facilities: Bus. fac., Conf. Rm. Cap.: 160, Lounge, Pool, Child planned rec., Tennis, Deer Creek Country Club, Restaurant.

Room Facilities: Daily maid, Kitchen, TV, Cable, Phone, Crib, Ind. AC. Ctl, Ind. Heat Ctl.

Attractions: Nearby golf, beaches, water ski, Everglades, airboats, Ocean World, cruises.

Shops & Restaurants: Bloomingdales, Lord & Taylor, Boca Town Center, Sea Watch/seafood/continental.

Villas with lofts, private jacuzzis, and balconies set among palms, lakes, fountains and tropical landscaping. Play an early morning set of tennis, round of golf, or dip in the pool, then lunch at the Matchpoint Lounge or have a poolside snack. Atlantic Ocean beaches are minutes away. 15 minutes to entertainment, parks, shopping, sports and restaurants. Golf Club dining room offers gourmet meals.

———————————————— DELRAY BEACH ————————————————

Spanish River Resort Beach Club
1111 E. Atlantic Ave.
Delray Beach, FL 33483
407-243-7946 800-543-7946
FAX: 407-276-9634

Studio $$, 1 Bedroom $$$,
2 Bedrooms $$$$
1 Bedrm/week $$$$, 2 Bedrms/week 6$
Disc/Visa/MC, Dep. Required •
72 condos, Hi-rise, Key at Desk in Lobby
H-Yes

Location: Airport: W. Palm Beach 15 mi.; Downtown: 3 blocks

General Facilities: Full hotel service; Daily maid; Linens; Baby sitter; Lounge; Crib-Hi-chair; Restaurant on premises; Bar on premises

Business Facilities: Bus. fac.; Conf. Room Cap. 50

Sports Facilities: Game room; Pool; Sauna; Tennis; Volleyball

Room Facilities: Kitchen; Cable; VCR; Phone; Ind.AC.Ctl.; Ind.Heat Ctl.

Attractions: Sightseeing cruises, Fishing, Horse/Dog Races, Horses, Jai Alai, Spg. Training, Everglades

Shops & Restaurants: Worth Ave., Lord & Taylor, Bloomingdales, Saks; 6 restaurants within 2 blocks

Affordable, luxurious 11-story hi-rise with balconies and breathtaking views overlooking public beach and intercoastal waterway. Nestled in quaint shopping district midway between Palm Beach and Boca Raton. Traditionally furnished with the most modern kitchen conveniences for stay-at-home dinners. Call ahead for limo pickup from the airport.

Spanish River Resort Beach Club

――――――――――――――――― DESTIN ―――――――――――――――――

Beach House Condominiums　　1 Bedroom $$
4800 Highway 98 East　　　　　　　Min. Stay 3 Nights, Visa/MC, Dep. Req'd. •
Destin, FL 32541　　　　　　　　　106 condos, Hi-rise, Key at Beach House
904-837-6131 800-874-8914

Location: Airport: Elgin 25 miles; Downtown: 7 miles; Need car; Beach front

General Facilities: Full serv., Kitchen, Linens, Game room, Child planned rec.: Easter
  to Labor Day

Room Facilities: Pool, Tennis, Shuffleboard, volleyball, Golf: 6 miles two courses, TV,
  Cable, VCR, Phone in rm., Crib-Hi-chair, Ind. AC Ctl., Ind. Heat Ctl.

Attractions: Sailing, fishing, diving, scuba, swimming, golf, tennis, water skiing.

Shops & Restaurants: Shoreline Village Mall, Downtown Destin, Shores; Marina Cafe-
  Flamingo Cafe

*Gulf-front condominiums on the quiet side of Destin, away from the crowds, yet close to
vacation pleasures. Swimming pool, gazebo, kiddie pool, teen room, tennis, organized
summer recreation. Something for the whole family.*

Breakers East
1010 Highway 98 East
Destin, FL 32541
800-338-4418

*Summer or winter, a great vacation. Shopping, golf, fishing, dining within a two-mile
radius. Improve your tan by the Gulfside pool or on the sand dune beach. New con-
dominiums with two lighted tennis courts.*

Cabana Club　　　　　　　　　1 Bedroom $$
Hwy. 98 East
Destin, FL 32541
904-837-4853 800-874-8914

*Overlooking the sparkling blue-green waters of the Gulf of Mexico. Perfect vacation retreat
for beach lovers. Relax in your private jacuzzi, enjoy a cool drink on your balcony while
watching the sunset, spend a day on the uncrowded beach.*

Coral Reef Club　　　　　　　　1 Bedroom $$
Hwy 98 East
Destin, FL 32541
904-837-4853 800-874-8914

*East of Henderson Beach State Park, two miles from Destin, new condominiums close to
golf and fishing. Enjoy beach activities or sunbathe by the covered, heated pool.*

Crystal Villas　　　　　　　　1 Bedroom $$
2850 Hwy. 98 East
Destin, FL 32541
904-837-4853 800-874-8914

*Watch your children build sandcastles or swim in the shallows and tidal pools of this quiet
beach. Shopping, fishing, golf, restaurants are all close. Enclosed heated pool and beach
service.*

──────────────── DESTIN ────────────────

Destin Beach Club
1150 Hwy. 98 East
Destin, FL 32541
904-837-3985

1 Bedrm/week $$$$
Min. Stay 3 Nights, AmEx/Visa/MC, Dep.
Req'd.
47 condos, Lo-rise

Location: Airport: Destin Airport; Downtown: 5 min.; Beach front
General Facilities: Kitchen
Room Facilities: Pool, Hot tub, TV
Attractions: Destin Racquet Club, Bayou Golf Course, fishing charters
Shops & Restaurants: Shores Shopping Center; Seafood

Enjoy Florida's romantic sunsets in this beachfront getaway paradise. Contemporary designed units set in a fishing village atmosphere. 10:00 p.m. to 10:00 a.m. quiet time.

Destin Towers Condominiums
1008 Highway 98 East
Destin, FL 32541
904-837-7002 800-338-4418

2 Bedrms/week $6
Min. Stay 7 Nights, Dep. Req'd.
Hi-rise

Location: Airport: Destin Airport; Beach front
General Facilities: Kitchen, Linens
Room Facilities: Pool, Tennis, Golf: Indian Bayou Golf 1 mile
Attractions: Indian Bayou Golf and Country Club, fishing, sailing, surfing

Take one of two elevators to your condominium in the 16-story Destin Towers. Full balcony overlooking the pool, clubhouse and gulf. Beach service rental of Hobie Cats, cabanas, chairs and umbrellas. Protected walkway from covered parking to the Towers. Family oriented, convenient to Destin activities and entertainment.

Destin Yacht Club
320 Hwy 98 East
Destin, FL 32541
904-837-4853 800-874-8914

Panoramic views of Destin Harbor and the Gulf, boat docks, large balconies. Master bath jacuzzi, second bath sauna. Pool, restaurant and bar. 5 minute drive to beach.

East Pass Towers
100 Gulfshore Drive
Destin, FL 32541
904-837-4191 800-541-4191

Studio $$, 2 Bedrooms $$, 3 Bedrooms $$$
Min. Stay 3 Nights, Visa/MC, Dep. Req'd. •
55 condos, Hi-rise, Key at Office

Location: Airport: 2.5-3 miles; Downtown: 2.5 mile; Beach front
General Facilities: Bus. fac., Daily maid, Kitchen, Linens
Room Facilities: Pool, Hot tub, Marine facility, TV, Cable, VCR, Phone in rm., Crib-Hi-chair, Ind. AC Ctl., Ind. Heat Ctl.
Attractions: Sport fishing, snorkeling, diving trips, golf courses
Shops & Restaurants: Shores Shopping Center, Shoreline Mall; Marina Cafe

On the tip of Holiday Isle, breathtaking views from large balconies, miles of fine sugar-white beaches to enjoy and explore. Pool, jacuzzi, exercise room, marina, beach service, security. Minutes from downtown. Diving and fishing trips. Boat slip available with power, phone, TV cable. Large boats welcome.

———————————— DESTIN ————————————

Edgewater Beach Condominium 1 Bedroom $$, 2 Bedrooms $$, 3 Bedrooms $$$
5000 Highway 98 East   1 Bedrm/week 4$, 2 Bed/week $5,
Destin, FL 32541   3 Bed/week 6$
904-837-5800 800-322-7263   Min. Stay 3 Nights, Visa/MC, Dep. Req'd.
                                  Hi-rise, Key at Office

Location: Downtown: 5 min.; Beach front

General Facilities: Kitchen, Linens, Restaurant on prem.

Room Facilities: Pool, Tennis, TV, Cable, Phone in rm.

Shops & Restaurants: Edgewater shopping

The French Riviera in Florida. Unique condominiums with cultured marble baths, mirrored closets, hanging gardens on your private balcony. Lush landscaping with three pools fed by a waterfall, illuminated at night. Private beach in a natural paradise.

Emerald Towers   2 Bedrooms $$
1044 Highway 98 East   Min. Stay 3 Nights, Visa/MC, Dep. Req'd.
Destin, FL 32541   82 condos, Hi-rise, Key at Office
904-837-6575 800-874-8914

Location: Airport: 20 miles; Downtown: 1 mile; Beach front

General Facilities: Full serv., Daily maid, Kitchen, Linens, Child planned rec.: Mem. Day-Labor Day

Room Facilities: Pool, Sauna, Tennis, TV, Cable, VCR, Phone in rm., Crib-Hi-chair, Ind. AC Ctl., Ind. Heat Ctl.

Attractions: Fishing charters, sailing, waterpark, golf, beach service, skiing, tennis, entertainment

Shops & Restaurants: Gayfers, McRae's, Penney, Sears, Shoreline Mall; Marina Cafe/Capt. Dave's/Pier98

Two and three bedroom units with private steam, sauna and whirlpool. Pool, tennis, beach service, exercise rooms. Walk to shopping, restaurants. Luxury and quality for your season in the sun.

Gulf Terrace Condominiums
Hwy. 98 East
Destin, FL 32541
904-837-4720 800-992-4720

Holiday Beach Resort—Destin 1 Bedroom $, 2 Bedrooms $$, Lo-rise
U.S. 98 East, P.O. Box 125   Pool, Kitchen, Linens
Destin, FL 32541
904-932-4298 800-874-0402

Attractions: Spa, Tennis

Emerald gulf waters and white sugar sand beach to get rid of your everyday cares. Boardwalks, pool, spa, tennis.

Trappeur's Crossing

—————————————— DESTIN ——————————————

Holiday Surf & Racquet Club Hi-rise
510 Gulf Shore Drive Pool, Kitchen
Destin, FL 32541
904-837-6108 800-833-6108

Attractions: Shuffleboard, Volleyball, Tennis

Your family will love the summer here, while spring and fall are ideal times for adults. Pool, tennis, health clubs, shuffleboard, volleyball, barbecues, swing sets and miles of beautiful, white beach.

———————————————————————————————————

Huntington by the Sea 1 Bedroom $$
Hwy. 98 East Min. Stay 3 Nights, Visa/MC, Dep. Req'd.
Destin, FL 32541 21 condos, Hi-rise, Key at Office
904-837-7811 800-874-8914

Location: Airport: 20 miles; Downtown: 6 miles; Need car; Beach front

General Facilities: Full serv., Kitchen, Linens

Room Facilities: Pool, TV, Cable, VCR, Phone in rm., Ind. AC Ctl., Ind. Heat Ctl.

Attractions: Deep-sea fishing, charters for sailing, golf, tennis, swimming

Shops & Restaurants: Shoreline Village Mall, The Market, downtn Destin; Marina Cafe-Flamingo-Scampi's

If you want privacy and seclusion, this is for you. Like being on a tropical island. Swim in the gulf or pool, or take a quiet walk. Barbecues, gazebo, private view balconies. All units individually furnished with modern decor.

────────────────── DESTIN ──────────────────

Inlet Reef Club
506 Gulf Shore Drive
Destin, FL 32541
904-837-6100

2 Bedrooms $$, Hi-rise
Pool, Kitchen

Attractions: Sport fishing, Exercise room, Tennis, Golf

Large apartments with Gulf view private terraces on architecturally designed property. Separate utility rooms, wet bar and pass-through, covered parking. Beach, tennis, pool, sauna and exercise room.

The Islander Condominium
502 Gulf Shore Drive
Destin, FL 32541
904-837-1000

2 Bedrooms $$, Hi-rise
Pool, Kitchen, Linens, Phone in rm.

Attractions: Tennis

On Holiday Isle, a short drive to 5 golf courses and the deep-sea fishing fleet. Beachside cabanas with barbecue, picnic tables, palm trees. Carefree vacation living.

Jetty East Condominium Assoc.
500 Gulf Shore Dr.
Destin, FL 32541
904-837-2141 800-368-0222

Hi-rise
Pool, Kitchen, Linens, Phone in rm.

Attractions: October festivals, sailing, fishing, windsurfing, scuba, snorkeling, tennis, golf

Water sports for everyone and the world's luckiest fishing fleet. Personally decorated completely furnished units. Pool, tennis, 900 feet of beach.

Mainsail
5100 Hwy 98 East
Destin, FL 32541
904-837-7711 800-874-8914

Studio $$, 2 Bedrooms $$, 3 Bedrooms $$$
Min. Stay 3 Nights, Visa/MC, Dep. Req'd. •
189 condos, Hi-rise

Location: Airport: 25 miles; Downtown: 5 miles; Need car; Beach front

General Facilities: Full serv., Daily maid, Kitchen, Linens, Game room, Child planned rec.: Mem.Day-Labor Day

Room Facilities: Pool, Sauna, Hot tub, Tennis, Shuffleboard, TV, Cable, Phone in rm., Crib-Hi-chair, Ind. AC Ctl., Ind. Heat Ctl.

Attractions: Charter fishing, sailing, water sports, tennis, water skiing, windsurfing

Shops & Restaurants: Destin, Shoreline Village Mall, The Market; Marina Cafe-Pier 98-Scampi's

Eight miles east of Destin's Main Street on a 15-acre tract on the Gulf. 4 tennis courts, 2 pools, 2 kiddie pools, walk to 3 shopping centers. Unforgettable combination of sand, sun and surf. Units with wet bars, jacuzzis and ceiling fans.

Sailfish Yacht Club
504 Hwy. 98 East
Destin, FL 32541
904-837-6027

DESTIN

Sandestin Beach Resort
Emerald Coast Parkway
Destin, FL 32541
904-267-8000 800-874-3950

1 Bedroom $$$, 2 Bedrooms $$$, 3 Bedrooms
$$$
1 Bedrm/week 5$, 2 Bed/week 6$,
3 Bed/week 7$
175 condos, Hi-rise

Location: Airport: Pensacola; Beach front

General Facilities: Bus. fac., Conf. rm. cap. 600, Kitchen, Restaurant on prem., Bar on prem., Game room, Lounge, Child planned rec.: Organized day camps

Room Facilities: Pool, Sauna, Tennis, Health facilities, Golf: 2 18-hole courses

Attractions: Golf, tennis, fishing, marina, October Destin Fishing Rodeo and Seafood Festival, entertainment

Shops & Restaurants: Complete array of clothing and specialty shops; Elephant Walk, Babe's Seafood

Choose from villas or tower units in this award-winning 2800-acre resort with 7.5 miles of waterfront. Golf and tennis packages, lessons and pro shops. Fishing charters, freshwater fishing in stocked lakes, marina for your boat. Water sport rentals available on the beach for Hobie catamarans, sailboards, Aqua Trikes or lie in the sun and get a golden tan. Four restaurants, on-site shopping. Honeymoon package with champagne, decorative glasses, fruit basket, dinner for two and half-day bicycle rental.

Sandestin High Rise
Highway 98 E
Destin, FL 32541
904-267-8000 800-874-3900

Sandpiper Cove Resort
Hwy. 98 Box 158
Destin, FL 32541
904-837-9121 800-874-0448

1 Bedroom $$, 2 Bedrooms $$, Villas
Pool, Kitchen

Elegant condominium living on 43 acres—tennis, 9-hole golf, 4 pools, boat ramp, waterfront restaurant and lounge, beachside pavilion with refreshment center.

Sealoft
3460 Hwy. 98 East
Destin, FL 32541
904-837-4853 800-874-8914

2 Bedrooms $$

Adjacent to State Wayside Park overlooking the Gulf of Mexico. Fireplace, jacuzzi, washer/dryers. For the vacationer who wants a relaxing beach vacation.

Seascape
100 Seascape Drive
Destin, FL 32541
904-837-9181 800-874-9106

1 Bedroom $$, 2 Bedrooms $$$, Lo-rise, Villas
Pool, Kitchen

Attractions: Gulfarium Zoo, Roller Skating, Indian Museum, Biking, hiking, Tennis

Located on Florida's Emerald Coast, 18-hole golf course, 8 tennis courts, both with pro shops, lessons, clinics and tournaments, 5 pools, 1500 feet of unspoiled beach with unmatched solitude and beach club. Freshwater lakes, subtropical vegetation.

———————————— DESTIN ————————————

Shoreline Towers & Townhomes   2 Bedrooms $$, Hi-rise
P.O. Box 1006   Pool, Kitchen
Destin, FL 32541
904-837-9163 800-874-0162

Attractions: Golf, sailing, tennis, scuba, charter fishing, Racquetball

Towers have large two and three bedroom condos on the Gulf of Mexico with Clubhouse, tennis, racquetball and pool. Townhomes with parquet floors, carpeting, cathedral ceilings, marble fireplaces and private access to the beach.

Summer Breeze   1 Bedroom $$
Hwy. 98 East
Destin, FL 32541
904-837-4853 800-874-8914

Affordable vacation in a low-density project away from traffic noise. Close to shopping, restaurants and entertainment. Pool, jacuzzi and barbecue.

SunDestin   1 Bedroom $$
1040 Hwy. 98 East   AmEx/Visa/MC, Dep. Req'd. •
Destin, FL 32541   280 condos, Hi-rise, Key at Front desk
904-837-7093 800-874-8914 H-yes

Location: Airport: Destin 2 miles; Downtown: 1 mile; Beach front

General Facilities: Daily maid, Kitchen, Linens, Restaurant on prem., Game room, Lounge, Baby-sitter, Child planned rec.: May thru Labor Day

Room Facilities: Pool, Sauna, Hot tub, Shuffeboard, TV, Cable, Phone in rm., Crib-Hichair, Ind. AC Ctl., Ind. Heat Ctl.

Attractions: Sailing, fishing, swimming

Shops & Restaurants: Marina Cafe, Flamingo Cafe

Less than 5 minutes from shopping, golf and Destin airport. Room service, restaurant and lounge. Organized activities and babysitting for children. Outdoor and indoor pool, fitness center, shuffleboard, 24-hour front desk.

Sunchase Townhouses   1 Bedroom $$
Hwy. 98 East
Destin, FL 32541
904-837-4853 800-874-8914

Intimate townhouse complex with spectacular view and beach at your back door. Away from the crowds, yet convenient to shopping, restaurants and deep-sea fishing.

Our listings—supplied by the managements—are as complete as possible. Many of the condos have more features than we list. Be sure to inquire when you book.

———————————————— DESTIN ————————————————

Surfside Resort
4701 Highway 98 East
Destin, FL 32541
904-837-4700 800-432-7882

Studio $$, 1 Bedroom $$, 2 Bedrooms $$$,
  3 Bedrooms $$$
1 Bedrm/week 5$, 2 Bedrms/week 6$,
  3 Bedrms/week 8$
AmEx/Visa/MC, 1 Night Dep. Req'd. •
117 condos, Hi-rise, Key at Front desk

Location: Airport: Ft. Walton 30 miles; Beach front

General Facilities: Full serv.; Daily maid; Linens; Baby sitter; Lounge; Crib-Hi-chair; Restaurant; Bar

Business Facilities: Bus. fac.; Conf. Room Cap. 100

Sports Facilities: Game room; Pool; Sauna; Tennis; Exercise room, picnic; Seascape; Rainy day program

Room Facilities: Kitchen; Cable; Phone; Ind.AC.Ctl; Ind.Heat Ctl.

Attractions: All water sports, fishing, access to 4 championship golf courses; Entertainment

Shops & Restaurants: Sandestin Village; Flamingo Cafe, L. Laniappe

Angular rooms with high ceilings and contemporary pastel furnishings. Pool, wading pool, whirlpool, saunas, tennis and skywalk to the beach. Balconies with safety glass railings to block the winds. Casual living at its best. Hotel Services plans volleyball and beach activities. Children's rainy day activity program.

———————————————— DUCK KEY ————————————————

Hawk's Cay Resort And Marina
Mile Marker 61
Duck Key, FL 33050
305-743-7000 800-432-2242
FAX: 305-743-5215

2 Bedrooms $$$$
2 Bedrms/week 10$
Min. Stay 4 Nights, Lo-rise, Villas

Location: Airport: Marathon, 8 miles; Beachfront

General Facilities: Daily maid; Linens; Restaurant on premises

Sports Facilities: Pool; Hot tub; Childrens programs

Room Facilities: Kitchen; Cable

Shops & Restaurants: Palm Terrace, Porto Cayo, Cantina.

Private Island Resort in the heart of the Florida Keys. 60-acre private island, fishing, tennis, sandy beach lagoon, heated swimming pool, childrens programs, diving and snorkeling, conference facilities, 60-slip full-service marina, gift shop, game room, boat tours, water sports. Rooms feature 2 full baths, walk-in closets, separate bath area with vanity, private large screened wrap-around verandas.

────────────────── ENGLEWOOD ──────────────────

The Castaways Condominiums Lo-rise
2240 N. Beach Road Pool, Kitchen
Englewood, FL 33533
813-474-4078

On beautiful Manasota Key, these condominiums are on 300 feet of private beach for shelling, boating, swimming or fishing. Unusual architecture in these modern, round units.

El Galeon Condominium Resort Lo-rise
1770 Gulf Boulevard Pool, Kitchen
Englewood, FL 33533 Golf
813-474-2709

New villas on the lower west coast of Florida fronting the Gulf of Mexico and Lemon Bay, which has private fishing and boat dock. A great beach for shelling and superior fishing.

Englewood Beach & Yatch Club Pool, Kitchen
1815 Gulf Boulevard
Englewood, FL 34223
813-474-7761

Attractions: Deepwater marina, sailing, windsurfing, fishing, boat docks, fishing

Condominiums on a private Gulf of Mexico beach, fully furnished down to books and games. Lounge by the pool and watch the sailboats. Dock your boat and be ready for early morning fishing and afternoon water sports.

Fantasy Island Condominiums 2 Bedrooms $$
2765 N. Beach Road 2 Bedrms/week 5$
Englewood, FL 34223 Dep. Req'd.
813-475-2108 20 condos, Lo-rise, Key at Office

Location: Airport: 40 minutes; Downtown: 1 mile; Need car
General Facilities: Kitchen, Linens
Room Facilities: Pool, Golf: 3 mile radius, TV, Phone in rm., Ind. AC Ctl., Ind. Heat Ctl.
Attractions: Island outings, home of Edison, Busch Gardens, Ringling Museum
Shops & Restaurants: 3 shopping centers for daily needs, Mall; Greek/Italian/fish

28 large, 2-bedroom, 2-bath units, enclosed 2-car garages, two balconies, private entranceway and lots of storage space. Screened balconies overlook Lemon Bay, and across the street is access to the Gulf of Mexico. A peaceful, relaxing atmosphere.

LaCoquina Beach Condominium Lo-rise
2800 North Beach Road Pool, Kitchen, Linens
Englewood, FL 33533
813-474-0846

Attractions: Fishing, boat-docks

Condominiums available for weekly rentals in April, Easter, Thanksgiving and Christmas only. 2 story condominiums on the Gulf of Mexico with screened lanais.

──────────── ENGLEWOOD ────────────

Sandpiper Key Condominium Assoc.
1601 Beach Road
Englewood, FL 34223
813-475-3108

2 Bedrms/week $$$$, 3 Bed/week 4$
Dep. Req'd.
215 condos, Hi-rise, Key at Rental office
No S-yes

Location: Airport: Sarasota 1 hour; Need car

General Facilities: Kitchen, Linens

Room Facilities: Pool, Golf and tennis nearby, TV, Cable, Phone in rm., Ind. AC Ctl., Ind. Heat Ctl.

Attractions: Englewood is located on the Gulf of Mexico. Ringling Museum, Jungle Gardens, Edison Home, entertainment

Shops & Restaurants: Quaint boutiques, art galleries, St. Armands Circle; Barnacle Bill's-seafood

Waterfront condominiums within walking distance to Gulf beaches. A mangrove-fringed tropical paradise surrounded by tranquil emerald waters, so bring your own boat since boat docks are available. Indulge yourself in this elegant resort. Swim, fish, shell or just relax listening to the chirping of crickets, splashing of fish or the gentle rolling of the waters.

Torian Plum

─────────────── ENGLEWOOD ───────────────

SunBurst Condominiums   1 Bedroom $, 2 Bedrooms $$
2450 N. Beach Road   1 Bedrm/week $$$$, 2 Bed/week 4$
Englewood, FL 34223   Min. Stay 2 Nights, Dep. Req'd.
813-474-0096   30 condos, Lo-rise, Key at Office

Location: Airport: 45 miles; Downtown: 1 mile; Need car; Beach front
General Facilities: Kitchen, Linens
Room Facilities: Pool, TV, Cable, Crib-Hi-chair, Ind. AC Ctl., Ind. Heat Ctl.
Attractions: Charter boats
Shops & Restaurants: Small area shops; Seafood and Italian

This is a small complex located on the Bay and Gulf. Each unit is individually furnished and decorated. Heated swimming pool, boat and fishing dock. Conveniently located to attractions on Florida's West Coast.

Tamarind Gulf & Bay Condominium Hi-rise
Manasota Key   Pool, Kitchen
Englewood, FL 34223
813-475-2275

Attractions: Golf, swimming, boating, water skiing, sailing, fishing, boat ramp, dockage

Units have roof deck, patios or screened lanai and sheltered parking spaces. Bayfront living with easy access to all water activities, dining, golfing and shopping. Tropically landscaped. Boat ramp and docking facilities on Lemon Bay.

─────────────── FORT LAUDERDALE ───────────────

Bahia Cabana Beach Resort   1 Bedroom $$, 2 Bedrooms $$
3001 Harbor Drive   AmEx/Visa/MC, Dep. 1 Night
Fort Lauderdale, FL 33316
305-524-1555 800-BEACHES

Location: Airport: Ft. Lauderdale 5 mi.
General Facilities: Daily maid, Kitchen, Linens, Restaurant on prem., Bar on prem.
Room Facilities: Pool, Hot tub, Marina, TV, Ind. AC Ctl., Ind. Heat Ctl.
Attractions: Cruise ships, 3½ hrs. Disney World, Swimming Hall of Fame, Ocean World
Shops & Restaurants: Dockside Bar/dining room

Owner-operated resort almost entirely surrounded by water. One and two bedroom apartments with private terraces, tropical grounds, sheltered sun decks and unmatched views. Marina with yacht dockage, miles of beach and picnic area. Food served dockside at the Patio Bar from 11:30 a.m.

Banyan Marina   1 Bedroom $$, 2 Bedrooms $$$, Lo-rise
111 Isle of Venice   Pool, Daily maid, Kitchen, Linens
Fort Lauderdale, FL 33301
305-524-4430

Modern, nicely furnished units on an island, just a few blocks to the beach. Tropical landscaping by the pool and sun deck, large outdoor barbecue. Sit under the shade of the banyan tree. Dockage for 8 yachts.

---------------------- FORT LAUDERDALE ----------------------

Coconut Bay Resort Hotel Studio $$, 1 Bedroom $$, 2 Bedrooms $$$
919 N. Birch Rd.   1 Bedrm/week 4$, 2 Bed/week 6$
Fort Lauderdale, FL 33304   Lo-rise, Key at Front desk
305-563-4229

General Facilities: Full serv., Daily maid, Kitchen, Linens
Room Facilities: Pool, Hot tub
Attractions: Jai alai, Indian reservations, Planetarium, zoo, Sea & Disney World
Shops & Restaurants: Galleria Plaza, Saks, Neiman Marcus

Unpack your suitcase and start to relax and enjoy this waterfront paradise. Walk to most daytime activities. Designer decorated condominiums, kitchens with microwaves. Well-kept recreation areas and tropical gardens.

Inverrary House   1 Bedrm/week $$$$, 2 Bed/week 4$,
3363 Spanish Moss Terrace   3 Bed/week 5$
Fort Lauderdale, FL 33319   Min. Stay 7 Nights, Dep. Req'd. •
305-731-9278   6 condos, Lo-rise, Key at At building

Room Facilities: Pool, Sauna, Tennis, Golf: Inverrary C.C. 3 courses, TV, Crib-Hi-chair, Ind. AC Ctl., Ind. Heat Ctl.
Attractions: Ocean World, jai alai, Horse racing, Everglades, Coral reefs, diving, fishing, cruises
Shops & Restaurants: Galeria Mall/Coral Square Mall/department stores; By Word of Mouth/gourmet

Six spacious luxury apartments on a private lake in the heart of Inverrary, steps to pool-fine dining and theaters nearby. 24-hour security gate for privacy in a tropical setting. Tropical print sofas, rattan, glass tables and screened patios with lounge furniture. There are 30 tennis courts, 8 lighted, 3 challenging golf courses, pool and restaurant.

Radisson Ocean Resort   1 Bedroom $$$, 2 Bedroom $$$$, Jr. $$
4040 Galt Ocean Drive   AmEx/MC/Visa/Other CC, Dep. 1 Night
Fort Lauderdale, FL 33308   145 condos, Hi-rise, Keys at Front desk,
305-566-7500 800-333-3333   C-yes, No S-yes, H-yes
FAX: 305-564-3075

Location: Airport: 8 miles 20 minutes; Downtown: 6 miles, Beach front
General Facilities: Conf. rm. cap. 225, Full serv., Bus. fac., Daily maid, Kitchen, Linens, Restaurant on prem., Bar on prem., Baby sitter, Gameroom, Lounge.
Room Facilities: Pool, Rental catamaran, American Golf Course, Child planned rec., TV, Cable, Ind. AC Ctl., Ind. Heat Ctl.
Attractions: Deep sea fishing and diving arrangements, beach, tennis, golf, entertainment.
Shops & Restaurants: Galleria & Coral Ridge Malls, Shoppes on the Galt; Yesterday's—continental, American.

Most suites have a predominant pink and burgundy color scheme, individually decorated, with ocean facing balconies that can be enclosed during stormy weather. Directly on the beach. Weekend barbeques, lounge entertainment and weekend brunches. Rent a catamaran or windsurfer while the children are enjoying volleyball, games in the pool. Pay TV.

──────────── FORT LAUDERDALE ────────────

Silver Seas
101 N. Atlantic Blvd.
Fort Lauderdale, FL 33304
305-522-8723

Amex, Visa, MC,
Key at Front desk,
27 condos, H-yes •

Location: Airport: 12 miles; Downtown: 15 miles; Need car; Beach front

General facilities: Daily maid, Kitchen, Linens

Room facilities: TV, Cable, Phone, Crib-Hi-chair, Ind. AC. Ctl, Ind. Heat Ctl.

Sports facilities: Pool

Shops & Restaurants: Galleria Malls, French, Italian, Continental

Ocean beach, sailing, boating, snorkeling, diving and parasailing.

**The Breakers of Fort
Lauderdale**
909 Breakers Ave.
Fort Lauderdale, FL 33304
305-566-8800 800-776-8770

Studio $$, 1 Bedroom $$$, 2 Bedrooms
$$$$, 1 Bed/week 10$, Min. stay 3 nights,
Amex, Visa, MC, Dep. 1 night,
Key at Front desk,
210 condos, Hi-rise, H-yes •

Location: Airport: 15 minutes; Downtown: 1 block; Beach front

General facilities: Full serv., Bus. fac., Daily maid, Kitchen, Linens, Games by
  social dir., Baby sitter, Restaurant, Bar, Lounge, Sauna, Hot tub

Room facilities: TV, Phone, Crib-Hi-chair, Ind. AC. Ctl, Ind. Heat Ctl.

Sports facilities: Pool, Tennis, Fishing, Boats, Swiming

Attractions: Public tours at Bonnett Estate, State Park at Northside, one block
  to beach, watersports, entertainment

Shops & Restaurants: Nieman Marcus, Lord & Taylor, Jordan Marsh, Mall, La
  Ferme-French, seafood, Italian

*Pastel colors of these suites tantalize your senses and prepare you for a relaxed
vacation. Dining and dancing go hand in hand, as the Brass Monkey Lounge features
piano bar entertainment and late night jazz. Motto: hospitality. Goal: satisfied guests.*

The Boardwalk Caper
1301 San Carlos Blvd.
Fort Myers Beach, FL 33931
813-466-3500

General facilities: Kitchen

Room facilities: Phone

Sports facilities: Pool, Tennis

*Townhouses located on a deep 200' wide waterway 5 minutes to the Gulf of Mexico
and a 3 minute drive to Estero Island's beach. "Vacation equipped" units with choice
of water, pool or garden views. 4 swimming pools, 2 tennis courts and spa.*

Be sure to call the condo the verify details and prices and to
make your reservation.

———————————— FORT MYERS BEACH ————————————

Caribbean Beach Club   Lo-rise
7600 Estero Blvd.   Pool, Kitchen
Fort Myers Beach, FL 33931
813-463-6111

Located on the Gulf side of Estero Island, overlooking a lagoon, just off the beach. One bedroom apartments viewing the Gulf or tropical courtyard and pool area.

Estero Island Beach Club   Lo-rise
1840 Estero Boulevard   Pool, Kitchen
Fort Myers Beach, FL 33931
813-463-6116

This complex offers two styles of one bedroom apartments. Within walking distance to all beach activities.

Island Towers   Hi-rise
4900 Estero Blvd.   Pool, Kitchen
Fort Myers Beach, FL 33931   Shuffleboard
813-463-5795

One bedroom units for one to five persons with king-size bed, queen sofa-sleeper and twin bed lounge chair. On property laundry facilities, grills and bicycles.

Kahlua Beach Club   Hi-rise
4950 Estero Boulevard   Pool, Kitchen
Fort Myers Beach, FL 33931
813-463-5751

One bedroom apartments facing the Gulf of Mexico with beach view balconies.

Lahaina Inn Resort   Lo-rise
5580 Estero Blvd.   Pool, Kitchen, Phone in rm.
Fort Myers Beach, FL 33931
813-463-4414

Attractions: Thomas Edison's winter home and laboratory, Jungle Larry's African Safari Park, Golf

A bit of old Hawaii in Florida. Laze in the sun and soak up Lahaina Inn's Southern hospitality or pursue the endless recreational possibilities. On-site swimming, fishing, volleyball, shelling on the island's seven miles of beach.

Marina Village at Snug Harbor   2 Bedrooms $$$, Hi-rise
645 San Carlos   Pool, Kitchen
Fort Myers Beach, FL 33931
813-463-3949

Attractions: Nautilus gym

Attractively decorated 2 bedroom, 2 bath units, washer/dryers, microwaves and waterfront balconies amid garden boardwalks, tropical gardens and palms. Work out at the Nautilus gym, sunbathe on the rooftop with dining gazebos and Jacuzzi, or boating.

—————————————— FORT MYERS BEACH ——————————————

Mariner's Boathouse Beach
Resort
7630 Estero Blvd.
Fort Myers Beach, FL 33931
813-463-8787 800-237-8906

1 Bedroom $$
1 Bedrm/week 4$
Min. Stay 2 Nights, AmEx/Visa/MC
1 Night Dep. Req'd. •
22 condos, Lo-rise
Key at Office on property

Location: Airport: 20 miles; Downtown: 30 min.; Need car; Beach front
General Facilities: Daily maid; Linens; Baby sitter; Crib-Hi-chair
Sports Facilities: Game room; Pool; Hot tub; across street
Room Facilities: Kitchen; Cable; Phone; Ind.AC.Ctl; Ind.Heat Ctl.
Attractions: Edison winter home & laboratory, Everglades National Park, wild-life refuges
Shops & Restaurants: Boutiques, Edison Mall, Maison Blanche, Sears; Mucky Duck/seafood

Nautically themed resort, with brass and teak fittings for sun-seekers who want the pleasures of a cruise without leaving land. Units resemble a luxury yacht with screened terrace overlooking the pool, spa and private beach. Boat launching ramps, fishing and deep sea charters, tennis and golf across the street. A short drive to shopping, restaurants and attractions. Perfect for families with small children.

———

Pointe Estero Resort
6640 Estero Blvd.
Fort Myers Beach, FL 33931
813-765-1155 800-237-5141
FAX: 813-765-0657

1 Bedroom Suite, 2 Bedrooms Suite
Min. Stay Ask, Visa/MC,
2 Nights Dep. Req'd. •
60 condos, Hi-rise

Location: Airport: 20 miles; Downtown: 25 miles; Need car; Beachfront
General Facilities: Daily maid; Linens; Baby sitter; Crib-Hi-chair
Business Facilities: Conf. Room Cap. 30
Sports Facilities: Pool; Hot tub; Tennis; Volleyball; Family rec. programs
Room Facilities: Kitchen; Cable; VCR; Phone; Ind.AC.Ctl.; Ind.Heat Ctl.
Attractions: Thomas Edison Winter Home, Naples-Ft. Myers dog track, Shell Factory, cruises, theatre
Shops & Restaurants: Villa Santini Plaza, Edison Mall, Bell Tower

Luxury and quality with oversized marble jacuzzi tubs in every master suite and screened balconies overlooking the Gulf of Mexico. Tiki Hut, eating areas, foot-bridges and a romantic gazebo overlooking a lush, tropical pond. Short distance from grocery stores, shopping, boat rentals, fishing charters, a golf course and several excellent restaurants. Barbecue grills. Penthouses available.

We want to hear from you—any comments regarding the con-dos or our publication may be noted on the form at the end of the book.

FORT MYERS BEACH

Royal Beach Club
800 Estero Blvd.
Fort Myers Beach, FL 33931
813-463-9494

1 Bedrm/week $$$$, 2 Bed/week $$$$,
3 Bed/week 4$
Min. Stay 3 Nights, Dep. Req'd.
27 condos, Lo-rise, Key at 800 Estero Blvd.

Location: Airport: 13 Miles; Downtown: 16 miles; Beach front

General Facilities: Kitchen, Linens, Lounge, Baby-sitter

Room Facilities: Pool, Hot tub, TV, Cable, Phone in rm., Crib-Hi-chair, Ind. AC Ctl., Ind. Heat Ctl.

Attractions: Edison House, Shell Factory, Everglades, Deep-sea fishing

Shops & Restaurants: Edison Mall, Metro Mall; Pelican, Mucky Duck, C. Browns

Charming townhouse unit decorated in earth tones and wicker surround the courtyard with its heated pool, and hot tub, shuffleboard and picnic area. All units fully equipped. Tan on the beach right out front.

Tropical Sands Resort
7785 Estero Blvd.
Fort Myers Beach, FL 33931
813-463-1133

2 Bedrooms $$, Lo-rise
Pool, Kitchen

Attractions: Exercise, video room

Nautically decorated condominiums to accommodate six adults with wet bar, ceiling fans and two color T.V.'s with Atari computer. Tropically landscaped grounds surround the pool area, chickee huts and gas grills. Adjacent health spa and recreation complex and beach access.

Windward Passage Resort
418 Estero Boulevard
Fort Myers Beach, FL 33931
813-463-1194

1 Bedroom $$, 2 Bedrooms $$, Hi-rise
Pool, Kitchen, Phone in rm.

Attractions: Volleyball, Shuffleboard, Tennis, Golf

For those who love the beach and all it has to offer. . .calm, warm water and white sand beach. These fine accommodations also have a pool, spa and tennis court and are close to shops, restaurants, charter fishing and golf.

FORT MYERS

Bahama Beach Club
5370 Estero Blvd.
Fort Myers, FL 33931
813-463-3148

1 Bedroom $$, Lo-rise
Pool

Affordable, spacious condominiums on the Gulf of Mexico. One bedroom units have gulf front screened porches; two bedrooms have poolside front and back porches. Park your car in the covered parking area, put on your suit and enjoy the seawalled private beach.

──────────────── FORT MYERS BEACH ────────────────

Cane Palm Beach Club   Hi-rise
600 Estero Blvd.   Pool, Kitchen, Linens
Fort Myers, FL 33931
813-463-3222

Attractions: Dog racing, baseball spring training, fishing, championship golf, shuffleboard

If you're a sun worshiper, this is the place to stay. Private white sand beach guarded by palms, heated freshwater pool, outdoor barbecues and screened patios. Nearby activities for young and old, or relax and enjoy your leisure time.

Gulfview Manor Club   Hi-rise
6530 Estero Blvd.   Pool, Kitchen
Fort Myers, FL 33931
813-463-4446

Attractions: Charter fishing, golf, tennis, dog racing, Sanibel & Captive Islands, Everglades trips, shuffleboard

Watch the sunset over the Gulf of Mexico from your private, screened balcony. Swim on the "front door" sands of Ft. Myers beach, collect shells, or sunbathe in the warm sun. Heated pool in a tropical setting. Take a romantic walk along the water's edge of Ft. Myers.

Seawatch On The Beach   1 Bedroom $$, 2 Bedrooms $$$, Hi-rise
6550 Estero Blvd.   Pool, Kitchen
Fort Myers, FL 33931
813-463-4469

You know you are in Florida when you enter the modern building and see the tropical atrium. Open kitchens, screened terraces, washer/dryers and microwaves. Wide beach, pool, spa and tennis court.

Smugglers Cove Condominiums Hi-rise
5100 Estero Blvd.   Pool, Kitchen, Linens
Fort Myers, FL 33931
813-463-4128

Attractions: Shuffleboard

Headquarters for your tropical vacation on the Gulf of Mexico. Freshwater pool and outdoor barbecues on the premises. Island sailing, fishing, water-jet skiing, para-sailing, tennis and golf are all available on the Island.

Sonesta Sanibel Harbor Resort Pool, Kitchen
15610 McGregor Blvd.
Fort Myers, FL 33908
813-466-4000 800-343-7170

Attractions: Spa & Fitness Center, Tennis, Golf

Relax by the pool or beach, pamper yourself with health and beauty treatments, work out in the weight room, improve your tennis, then unwind at Jimmy's restaurant for drinks, dinner and live entertainment, and retire to your condo and view San Carlos Bay.

———————————————— FORT WALTON BEACH ————————————————

Breakers   1 Bedroom $
381 Santa Rosa Blvd.   2 Bedrooms $$
Fort Walton Beach, FL 32548   3 Bedrooms $$$
904-244-9127 800-395-4853
General facilities: Kitchen
Room facilities: Phone
Sports facilities: Pool, Tennis, Golf, Exercise facilities
Attractions: Destin fishing fleet, water sports, golf

Suites with balconies, cable T.V.s with HBO and washer/dryers. Four passenger elevators, plus two elevators for beach, pool and service. Market Deli on the premises and also a video store.

El Matador Condominiums   2 Bedrooms $$
909 Santa Rosa Blvd.   Hi-rise
Fort Walton Beach, FL 32548
904-244-3299
General facilities: Kitchen, Linens
Room facilities: Phone
Sports facilities: Pool, Tennis

Very large condominium complex with well-designed, individually decorated one and two bedroom units. Serene beachfront living above the sand dunes. Two pools, two tennis courts, gameroom and private white sand beach. 24-hour security. Rentals limited to families only.

Island Echoes Condominiums   1 Bedroom $$
676 Nautilus Ct.
Fort Walton Beach, FL 32548
904-837-4853 800-874-8914

On the sugar white beaches of Okaloosa Island, this popular vacation getaway features pool, tennis, shuffleboard, beach service and is close to family entertainment attractions, shopping, golf and restaurants.

Pirates Bay Condominium   Studio $, 1 Bedroom $$
214 Miracle Strip Pkwy.   1 Bed/week $$$$
Fort Walton Beach, FL 32548   Amex, Visa, MC, Dep. 1 night
904-243-3154 800-356-1861   120 condos, Hi-rise,
                                      Key at Front desk
                                      H-yes •
Location: Airport: 12 miles, Downtown: 1 mile
General facilities: Full serv., Bus. fac., Daily maid, Kitchen, Linens
Room facilities: TV, Cable, Phone, Crib-Hi-chair, Ind.AC.Ctl, Ind.Heat Ctl.
Sports facilities: Pool, Boating
Attractions: Gulf intercoastal waterway, marina facility, water slide for children
Shops & Restaurants: Santa Rosa Mall, souvenir shops, department stores, The
  Sound-seafood/steaks

———————————————— FORT WALTON BEACH ————————————————

Sandcastle
461 Abalone Ct.
Fort Walton Beach, FL 32548
904-837-4853 800-874-8914

Secluded beach-front vacationing for the sun-loving, beach-loving family. Fully furnished three bedroom duplexes convenient to downtown Fort Walton Beach.

Sea Oats Resort Condominium   2 Bedrooms $$, Hi-rise
1114 Santa Rosa Blvd.   Pool, Kitchen, Linens, Phone in rm.
Fort Walton Beach, FL 32548
904-244-5200 800-451-2343

Attractions: Okaloosa Island fishing pier, Gulfarium, picnic parks, amusement parks, golf, Shuffleboard, Tennis, Golf

Security entrance to Sea Oats ideal location on the Gulf beach. Each unit has energy efficient windows, tile baths and oversized view balconies. A short walk or bike ride to the amusement parks, picnic parks, fishing piers and golf courses on "The Playground."

Seaspray Condominium   1 Bedroom $$, 2 Bedroom $$$, 3
1530 U.S. Highway 98 E.   Bedroom $$$
Fort Walton Beach, FL 90424 1 Bedrm/week 5$, 2 Bedrm/week 7$, 3
904-244-1108 800-428-2726   Bedrm/week 8$
                             Min. Stay 2 Nights, MC/Visa, Dep. Req'd
                             Lo-rise, Keys at At front office, P-yes,
                             C-yes

Location: Airport: 5 miles; Downtown: 1 mile, Beach front

General Facilities:, Kitchen, Linens

Room Facilities: Pool, Sauna, Athletic Club, TV, Cable, Phone in rm., Ind. AC Ctl., Ind. Heat Ctl.

Attractions: 9-hole nearby golf course, fishing, Gulfarium, water slide, beach

Shops & Restaurants: Unlimited shopping malls; Seafood and steak house.

Townhousse condominium units commmplete with color cable 32 channel and movie channel TV. These two story units offer a grass courtyard, uncrowded beach, parking at each unit, and no elevators. Stroll the beach, picnic in the park, exercise in the fully equipped athletic club, relax in the sauna, or take a cool dip in the pool. Seaspray is just a short walk to Okaloosa Island Fishing Pier or four miles from Destin, "The World's Luckiest Fishing Village."

———————————————— FORT WALTON BEACH ————————————————

Steamboat Landing
161 S.E. Brooks Street
Fort Walton Beach, FL 32548
904-244-1391

1 Bedroom $$
1 Bedrm/week 5$
Visa/MC,Dep. Req'd.
18 condos, Lo-rise, Key at Office

Location: Airport: 12 miles; Downtown: 1 block

General Facilities: Kitchen, Linens, Game room

Room Facilities: Pool, TV, Cable, Phone in rm., Ind. AC Ctl., Ind. Heat Ctl.

Attractions: Sport fishing, charter parties, surf-casting, amusements centers, zoo, museum

Shops & Restaurants: Unlimited shopping malls, souvenir shops; The Seagull-seafood

Completely furnished condominiums on the Intercoastal Waterway with living room and bedroom color T.V. Recreational activities include an Amenity Building, pool table, indoor heated pool, ping pong, large screen T.V./VCR, jacuzzi, basketball, horseshoes, badminton and outdoor pool. Gas grills are available for your favorite barbecued feast.

———————————————— FORT WALTON ————————————————

Sea Oats
1114 Santa Rosa Boulevard
Fort Walton, FL 32548
904-244-5200 800-451-2343

———————————————— GRENELEFE ————————————————

Grenelefe Resort
3200 State Road 546
Grenelefe, FL 33884
813-422-7511 800-237-9549
FAX: 813-421-1694

1 Bedroom $$, 2 Bedroom $$$$, Jr. $$
1 Bedrm/week 5$, 2 Bedrm/week 9$

Location: Airport: 45 minutes; Downtown: nearby

General Facilities: Conf. rm. cap. 2000, Kitchen, Restaurant on prem., Bar on prem., Baby sitter, Gameroom.

Sports Facilities: Pool, Tennis, Sailing, 54 holes of golf

Attractions: Disney World/EPCOT Center, MGM Studios, Sea World, Cypress Gardens, Boardwalk, baseball, entertainment.

Shops & Restaurants: Convenience store, 3 pro-shops, gift shop; Camelot-Grene, Heron-Forest

Located 45 minutes south of the Orlando International Airport and just minutes from the Central Florida attractions. The resort embraces 1,000 lush, wooded acres along the shores of Lake Marion. 20 court tennis complex, 5 swimming pools, full-service marina with excellent bass fishing and 54 holes of championship golf.

The Summit

GULFSTREAM

Gulfstream Manor
3901 N. Ocean Blvd. (A-1-A)
Gulfstream, FL 33444
305-272-6300

1 Bedroom $$, Lo-rise
Pool, Kitchen, Linens, Phone in rm.

Attractions: Shuffleboard, BBQ, Golf

Located directly on the ocean, one bedroom units accommodate 4 people. 2 televisions, microwave and washer/dryer. Close to tennis, golf, shopping and restaurants.

HILLSBORO BEACH

The Barefoot Mailman Resort
1061 Hillsboro Mile
Hillsboro Beach, FL 33062
305-941-0100 800-327-1584

Lo-rise
Pool, Kitchen

Clean air, low pollen count, private beach, manicured lawns, palm trees and large pool make for a most relaxing vacation in sunny Hillsboro Beach.

HOLLYWOOD

Enchanted Isle Resort
1601 S. Surf Rd.
Hollywood, FL 33019
305-922-1508

1 Bedroom $$, 2 Bedrooms $$, Lo-rise
Pool, Kitchen, Phone in rm.

Attractions: Shuffleboard

Four condominium buildings surrounding a pool and courtyard. Oceanfront lawn terrace and private beach. Plan to relax in the quiet atmosphere.

—————————————— HOLLYWOOD ——————————————

Hollywood Beach Resort
101 N. Ocean Dr.
Hollywood, FL 33019
305-921-0990 800-331-6103

Studio $$, 1 Bedroom $$$
AmEx/Visa/MC •
360 condos, Hi-rise, Key at Front desk,
P-yes/H-yes

Location: Airport: 11.2 miles; Downtown: 1 mile; Beach front

General Facilities: Full serv.; Daily maid; Linens; Baby sitter; Lounge; Crib-Hi-chair; Restaurant; Bar

Business Facilities: Bus. fac.; Conf. Room Cap. 50

Sports Facilities: Game room; Pool; Hot tub; Spa

Room Facilities: Kitchen; Cable; Phone; Ind.AC.Ctl; Ind.Heat Ctl.

Shops & Restaurants: Oceanwalk Grill continental

Completely refurbished historical, art deco building, suites done in pastel colors. Relax in your private suite, shop the exciting mall, enjoy the beach. Fun for families or great for romance. Pick your own atmosphere for the best of all worlds.

———

Hollywood Sands Resort
2404 N. Surf Rd.
Hollywood, FL 33019
305-925-2285 800-269-6192
FAX: 305-927-0665

Studio $$, 1 Bedroom $$$,
  2 Bedrooms $$$$
1 Bedrm/week 8$, 2 Bedrms/week 10$
Min. Stay 3 Days, AmEx/Visa/MC
2 Day Dep. Req'd., 25 condos, Lo-rise
Key at Front desk, P-No/H-Yes

Location: Airport: 6 miles; Downtown: 7 miles; Boardwalk

General Facilities: Linens; Crib-Hi-Chair

Sports Facilities: Pool; Nearby; All water sports,; Golf Course nearby

Room Facilities: Kitchen; Cable; VCR; Phone; Ind.AC Ctl.; Ind.Heat Ctl.

Attractions: Sightseeing tours, day and evening boat trips, some with gambling. 30 minutes from Miami.

Shops & Restaurants: World's largest discount mall—Sawgrass Mills. Beachfront; Billy's Crab House—seafood

Location of Hollywood Sands put you right on the famous Boardwalk in the heart of Hollywood Beach with all its colorful shops and restaurants. Situated midway between Ft. Lauderdale and Miami. Fully equipped apartments with all the comforts of home. Heated pool, hot tub, sundecks, barbecue grills, bicycles for family fun. All water sports, golf and tennis nearby. Relax on the beach, pool or hot tub. Ride bikes on the Boardwalk.

─────────────── HOWEY-IN-THE-HILLS ───────────────

Mission Inn Golf & Tennis Resort   Location: Airport: Orlando
Box 441
Howey-In-The-Hills, FL 32737
904-324-2101 800-874-9053

General Facilities: Conf. rm. cap. 350, Kitchen, Restaurant on prem., Bar on prem.,
Game room, Baby-sitter, Child planned rec.: Children's program

Room Facilities: Pool, Tennis, Sailing, fishing, Golf: 18-hole golf course

Attractions: Disney World/EPCOT, Sea World, Cypress Gardens, cocktail cruises, Lake
Harris

Shops & Restaurants: Orlando; El Conquistador/continental

*A country-inn hideaway, 45 minutes from Walt Disney World in the foothills of Orlando.
Spanish in style reminiscent of Florida's early days with fountains, gardens, birds and
waterfalls lining the covered walkways. Work out in the spa, fish, sail, and speedboat on
Lake Harris, play tennis and swim. Hilly 18-hole golf course with varied landscaping.*

─────────────── HUTCHINSON ISLAND, STUART ───────────────

Plantation Beach Club   1 Bedroom $$$, 2 Bedrooms $$$, Hi-rise
329 N.E. Tradewind Lane   Pool, Kitchen
Hutchinson Island, Stuart, FK 34996
813-481-3636 800-237-8096

Attractions: Golf, tennis, water sports

*A resort within a resort away from the city, yet only a short distance to Palm Beach activi-
ties. Oceanfront suites have screened porches, bathtubs with whirlpools and home entertainment centers. Gas grill and picnic area for outdoor cooking, pool, hot tub and sauna.*

─────────────── HUTCHINSON ISLAND ───────────────

Indian River Plantation Resort   1 Bedroom $$$, 2 Bedrooms $$$$
555 N.E. Ocean Blvd.   AmEx/Visa/MC, Dep. 1 Night •
Hutchinson Island, FL 34996   56 condos, Lo-rise, Key at Registr. desk
407-225-3700 800-327-4873   H-yes

Location: Airport: 45 minutes; Downtown: 3 miles; Beach front

General Facilities: Full serv., Conf. rm. cap. 525, Daily maid, Kitchen, Linens, Restau-
rant on prem., Bar on prem., Lounge, Baby-sitter, Child planned rec.: Daily activities

Room Facilities: Pool, Hot tub, Tennis, Golf, boating, TV, Cable, Phone in rm., Crib-Hi-
chair, Ind. AC Ctl., Ind. Heat Ctl.

Attractions: Elliott Museum, House of Refuge, sailfish capital of the world, enter-
tainment

Shops & Restaurants: Treasure Coast Mall-Jordan Marsh, Lord & Taylor; Benihana
of Tokyo/Japanese

*56 oceanfront suites on this 200-acre resort, with golf, lighted tennis court and a marina
with 77 slips for boats with maximum 6-foot draft MLT, water and electrical hook-ups, on-
board yacht telephone service and cable TV. Entertainment and dancing at one of the three
lounges. Ideal year-round weather. Golf and tennis pros for clinics, lessons or tournaments.
Outdoor spa and cabana bar.*

––––––––––––––––––– INDIAN HARBOUR BEACH –––––––––––––––––––

Oceanique   2 Bedrooms $$$, Lo-rise
2105 Highway A1A   Pool, Kitchen
Indian Harbour Beach, FL 32937
305-777-6512

Attractions: Disney World, Spaceport U.S.A., tennis, golf, sailing, fishing

Midway between Jacksonville and Miami, in a quiet residential community, yet close to Florida's major tourist attractions. Private beach club and pool.

––––––––––––––––––––– INDIAN ROCKS BEACH –––––––––––––––––––––

Bay Shores Yacht & Tennis Club   1 Bedroom $$, 2 Bedrooms $$, Lo-rise
19451 Gulf Blvd.   Pool, Kitchen, Linens
Indian Rocks Beach, FL 34635
813-595-9313

Attractions: Disney World, Busch Gardens, Tiki Gardens, deep-sea fishing, jai alai, Sunken Gardens, Putting green, Shuffleboard, Tennis, Golf

Hi-rise condominiums with view balconies for your complete Florida vacation. Boat docks, fishing and barbecue grills.

––––––––––––––––––––––––– INDIAN SHORES –––––––––––––––––––––––––

Holiday Villas II   1 Bedroom $$, 2 Bedrooms $$, Lo-rise
P.O. Box 738, 19610 Gulf Blvd.   Pool, Kitchen, Linens
Indian Shores, FL 33535
813-595-7392

Attractions: Disney World, Busch Gardens, Sea World, Cypress Gardens, Circus World, Golf

Luxury apartments with terraces. Swim, fish, look for shells or run barefoot through the white sands. Many local amenities including tennis, golf, restaurants and after-hour entertainment. Small, well-trained, non-shedding dogs permitted in some units.

Holiday Villas III   1 Bedroom $$, 2 Bedrooms $$, Hi-rise
18610 Gulf Blvd.   Pool, Kitchen, Linens
Indian Shores, FL 34635
813-595-2335

Attractions: Disney World, EPCOT Center, tennis, golf, Dock, fishing pier

Great family vacation living on one of Florida's major boating areas. Play volleyball on the beach, have an evening cookout or daytime picnic at the barbecue area, or relax with a game of pool. All ages like to play the video machines. Free green fees.

118 Florida

Sand Dollar Resort
18500 Gulf Blvd.
Indian Shores, FL 34635
813-595-8109

1 Bedroom $$, 2 Bedrooms $$, 3 Bedrooms $$
1 Bedrm/week 5$, 2 Bed/week 6$,
3 Bed/week 6$
Min. Stay 3 Nights, AmEx/Visa/MC,
Dep. Req'd. •
50 condos, Lo-rise, Key at Front desk
No S-yes/H-yes

Location: Airport: 30 miles; Downtown: 10 min.; Beach front

General Facilities: Full serv., Daily maid, Kitchen, Linens, Baby-sitter

Room Facilities: Pool, Hot tub, Sailing, windsurfing, Golf: Nearby, TV, Cable, Phone in rm., Crib-Hi-chair, Ind. AC Ctl., Ind. Heat Ctl.

Attractions: Busch Gardens, Dali Museum, Wagon Wheel Flea Market, charter boats, Walt Disney World

Shops & Restaurants: Maas Brothers, Burdines, boutiques, shopping plaza; Wine Cellar/variety

Gulf-front condominiums with private balconies. Beautiful sunsets and a white sandy beach for bathing and long moonlit walks. Swimming pool, jacuzzi and surfside cabanas. A few minutes to discos, clubs, shopping and restaurants. If you like to gamble, there is parimutuel betting: greyhounds, horses and jai alai not far away.

Caloosa Cove Resort
Mile Mrk 73.8-73801 OversHwy. US#1
Islamorada, FL 33036
305-664-8811

1 Bedroom $$$, Lo-rise
Pool, Kitchen, Linens

Attractions: Sports, Back Country Fishing, scuba diving, snorkeling, reefs, Shuffleboard, marina, tennis

Thoughtfully furnished units with personalized custom details. Full service marina with dockage for boating and fishing pleasure. Beach for barbecueing and relaxing, solar heated pool. Cocktails at the Safari Lounge with authentic African artifacts.

Morada Wells Resort & Club
M.M. 80½, P.O. Box 1361
Islamorada, FL 33036
305-664-8849

Villas
Pool, Kitchen, Linens

Attractions: Therapy spa, racquetball

Hidden behind tropical trees in natural woodlands are these fully furnished villas and townhouses. Walk along the boardwalk and nature trail, swim, fish, dock your boat for water sports.

─────────────────── ISLAMORADA ───────────────────

Ocean 80 Resort
U.S. 1, Mile Marker 80, Box 949
Islamorada, FL 33036
305-664-4411

1 Bedroom $$, 2 Bedrooms $$$
Pool, Daily maid, Kitchen

Attractions: Handball, badminton, Tennis

Choice of studio, one or two bedroom units with bar unit, entertainment center and ceiling fans. Adult recreational center with two jumbo TV screens, children's pool and playground. Boat dockage and launching facilities, sailboats, jet skis and bicycles.

─────────────────── JENSEN BEACH ───────────────────

Turtle Reef II
10740 So. Ocean Drive A1A
Jensen Beach, FL 34957
305-229-9200

2 Bedrooms $$, Hi-rise
Pool, Kitchen, Linens

Attractions: Disney World, Cape Canaveral, Tennis, Golf

Fully furnished units with split floor plans. Large balconies, dining rooms adjoining breakfast bar and master bath oversized Roman tub. The beach, pool and tennis are just outside your door. Deep sea and surf fishing in the carefree atmosphere of Hutchinson Island.

─────────────────── JUPITER ───────────────────

Jupiter Bay Resort & Tennis Club
350 S. US Highway 1
Jupiter, FL 33477
407-744-0210 800-228-5152

1 Bedroom $$$, 2 Bedrooms $$$$
1 Bedrm/week 6$, 2 Bed/week 8$
AmEx/Visa/MC, Dep. Req'd. •
224 condos, Lo-rise, Key at Front desk

Location: Airport: 25 Minutes; Downtown: 2 Miles; Need car; Beach front

General Facilities: Full serv., Conf. rm. cap. 125, Daily maid, Kitchen, Linens, Restaurant on prem., Bar on prem., Baby-sitter

Room Facilities: Pool, Hot tub, Tennis, TV, Cable, Phone in rm., Crib-Hi-chair, Ind. AC Ctl., Ind. Heat Ctl.

Attractions: Cruises to Bahamas, Deep-sea fishing, Burt Reynolds Theater, Boating

Shops & Restaurants: Worth Avenue and six large malls

Park-like environment, one block walk to the beach. Jogging heart trail with scenic views of lake and waterfalls.

Jupiter Reef Club
1600 S. Ocean Dr.
Jupiter, FL 33477
407-747-7788

1 Bedroom $$$, 2 Bedrooms $$$
Pool, Daily maid, Kitchen, Linens

Attractions: Burt Reynolds Dinner Theater, water sports

Units decorated by Roland Lee and the firm of Childs Dreyfus with at least one view deck. Jupiter Reef Club has private beach access, oceanside pool and spa. Patio area with gazebo and deck chairs graced by tropical greenery.

─────────────── KEY LARGO ───────────────

Marina Del Mar
P.O. Box 1050
Key Largo, FL 33037
305-451-4107 800-451-3483

1 Bedroom $$$, 2 Bedrooms $$$$, Hi-rise
Pool, Kitchen

Attractions: John Pennekamp Coral Reef State Park, Key Largo Marine Sanctuary, Everglades, Fitness, dive center, Tennis

Located on a deep water marina, complete lodging, entertainment and water sports base. Ocean Divers dive center and full service marina make this an ideal spot for fishing, scuba and snorkeling enthusiasts. Pool, sun deck, tennis and fitness center.

Anchorage Resort & Yacht Club
107500 Overseas Highway
Key Largo, FL 33037
305-451-0500

1 Bedroom $$
1 Bedrm/week 6$
AmEx/Visa/MC, Dep. Req'd. •
28 condos, Hi-rise, Key at Front desk

Location: Airport: Miami 55 miles; Need car; Beach front

General Facilities: Bus. fac., Daily maid, Kitchen, Linens, Game room, Baby-sitter

Room Facilities: Pool, Hot tub, Tennis, Shuffleboard, boats, TV, Phone in rm., Crib-Hi-chair, Ind. AC Ctl., Ind. Heat Ctl.

Attractions: Bayside water shuttle, John Pennekamp Coral Reef State Park, Everglades, entertainment

Shops & Restaurants: Coral Gables, Bayside, 1 hr. Key West, 2 hours; Quay Rest-Fisherman-Sundowners

Balmy year-round weather, tropical sunsets, casual dress. Tropically decorated one bedroom units. Fine restaurants, glassbottom boat tours of John Pennekamp Coral Reef Park, as well as scuba and snorkeling excursions. All water sports. Furnished in bright, airy Florida rattan. Relaxed island ambience, yet 1 hour from Miami's culture and nightlife.

Moon Bay Condominium
4700 Overseas Highway
Key Largo, FL 33130
305-451-4161

2 Bedrooms $$
2 Bedrms/week 6$
Dep. Req'd.
Lo-rise

Location: Airport: Miami 55 miles; Downtown: 60 miles; Need car

General Facilities: Daily maid, Kitchen, Linens, Game room, Lounge

Room Facilities: Pool, Sauna, Tennis, TV, Phone in rm., Crib-Hi-chair, Ind. AC Ctl., Ind. Heat Ctl.

Attractions: Scuba diving, snorkeling, windsurfing, deep-sea fishing, jet, water skiing, Coral Reef

Shops & Restaurants: Cutler Ridge Mall, Lord & Taylor, Burdines; Quay/gourmet seafood

Beautiful waterfront resort with magnificent seascapes and spectacular sunsets. Completely equipped for pleasure and comfort. Clubhouse, marina and private boat slip. Tropical island landscaping with stunning views from nearly every room.

Lookout Village

KEY WEST

1800 Atlantic   Pool, Kitchen
1800 Atlantic Blvd.
Key West, FL 33040
305-294-0878

Attractions: Hemingway's house, Conch Train, theaters, sailing, windsurfing, parasailing, Recreation center, Golf

1657-square-foot condominiums with oversized sunken tub, mirrored dressing area, oversized closets, kitchen pantry and breakfast area. Pool and spa set in a tropical garden. Fitness, exercise room and sauna in the recreation center with its party kitchen.

Bay Villas
32 Hilton Haven Road
Key West, FL 33040

Galleon Marina & Beach Resort   1 Bedroom $$$$
617 Front St., P.O. Box 409   Kitchen
Key West, FL 33040
800-544-1010 800-544-3030

Tropical furnishings in seaside colors furnished with everything you need. Pool, private beach, exercise club, water sports. Key West offers exotic gardens, wild orchids, night spots, international cuisine, museums, art galleries, plays and musicals.

──────────── KEY WEST ────────────

The Galleon
617 Front St.
Key West, FL 33040
305-296-7711 800-544-3030

1 Bedroom $$$$, 2 Bedrooms $$$$, Hi-rise
Pool, Kitchen

Attractions: Exercise club

Airy rooms with tropical furnishings in seaside pastel colors. Relax in your private jacuzzi or with your complete entertainment system, VCR, tape deck, stereo and cable TV. Even games are provided. Explore Key West's Victorian homes, museums, and art galleries.

La Brisa Condominium
1901 S. Roosevelt Blvd.
Key West, FL 33040
305-294-4770

1 Bedroom $$, 2 Bedrooms $$$, Hi-rise
Pool, Kitchen, Linens, Phone in rm.

Attractions: Recreation Center, Tennis

Just west of the airport on the ocean, opulent master suites, contemporary kitchens, panoramic views. Complete recreational complex. Overlooking protected nature preserve for native wildfowl. Traditional setting.

Pelican Landing
915 Eisenhower Drive
Key West, FL 33040
305-296-7583 800-527-8108

AmEx/Visa/MC •
16 condos, Hi-rise, Key at Office on premises

Location: Airport: 1½ miles; Downtown: 1 mile
General Facilities: Full serv., Daily maid, Kitchen, Linens, Baby-sitter
Room Facilities: Pool, TV, Cable, Phone in rm., Crib, Ind. AC Ctl., Ind. Heat Ctl.
Attractions: Tour train of city, many historical sites
Shops & Restaurants: Souvenir shops, clothing shops; Numerous and varied

Luxury condominiums at affordable prices, balconies with harbor views, catering primarily to boating, fishing, diving, and water sports. Dockage available. Convenient location on the outskirts of Old Town. Tennis, golf, water sports, and shopping all close by.

Reflections On Key West
0 Duval St.
Key West, FL 33040
305-296-7701

Enter your favorite condo in our "Condo of the Year" contest (entry form is in the back of the book).

——————————— KEY WEST ———————————

The Banyan Resort
323 White Head Street
Key West, FL 33040
305-294-9573 800-225-0639

Studio $$, 1 Bedroom $$$, 2 Bedrooms $$$
AmEx/Visa/MC, Dep. 1 Night •
38 condos, Key at Front desk

Location: Airport: 1½ miles; Downtown: 1 block

General Facilities: Conf. rm. cap. 30, Daily maid, Kitchen, Linens, Bar on prem.

Room Facilities: Pool, Hot tub, TV, VCR, Phone in rm., Ind. AC Ctl., Ind. Heat Ctl.

Attractions: Diving, fishing, swimming, boating, charters, museums, art galleries, theaters, biking, entertainment

Shops & Restaurants: Fast Buck Freddies, J. Byrons, food stores; The Battery

A compound of eight restored Victorian houses with all modern interiors surrounded by lush tropical gardens. Decorated in tropical wicker with ceiling fans and french doors. 2 pools, 2 jacuzzis, conveniently located in old town for walking to shopping, restaurants, nightlife and museums. Brunches, aerobics and a Tiki bar by the pool, serving sandwiches, beer and wine.

——————————— KISSIMMEE ———————————

Club Sevilla
4646 W. Irlo Bronson Memorial Hwy
Kissimmee, FL 32741
305-396-1800

1 Bedroom $$, 2 Bedrooms $$
1 Bedrm/week 5$, 2 Bed/week 5$
Dep. Req'd.
Lo-rise

General Facilities: Kitchen, Linens, Bar on prem., Lounge, Child planned rec.: Playground

Room Facilities: Pool, Tennis, TV, Cable

Attractions: Disney World, Sea World, Wet 'N Wild, Spaceport U.S.A., Circus World, Busch Gardens

Shops & Restaurants: Kissimmee-St. Cloud shopping

Club Sevilla is located in the middle of the Kissimmee-St. Cloud resort area. Accommodations with a Spanish feeling and designer decor. Pool, and children's playground.

Fortune Place Resort
1475 Astro Lake Dr.
Kissimmee, FL 32743
407-348-0330 800-624-7496

1 Bedroom $$, 2 Bedrooms $$$, 3 Bedrooms $$$$
1 Bedrm/week $$, 2 Bed/week $$$,
3 Bed/week $$$$
AmEx/Visa/MC, Dep. 1 Night •
46 condos, Villas, Key at desk, P-yes/H-yes

Location: Airport: 14 miles; Downtown: 20 miles; Need car

General Facilities: Full serv., Daily maid, Kitchen, Linens, Baby-sitter

Room Facilities: Pool, Tennis, Pad-Rac-VB-Shuffleboard, Golf: Buena Ventura Lakes, TV, Cable, VCR, Phone in rm., Crib-Hi-chair, Ind. AC Ctl., Ind. Heat Ctl.

Attractions: Disney World, EPCOT, Sea World, Gatorland, baseball, entertainment

Shops & Restaurants: Florida Mall-largest mall in Florida; Murphy's Lobster House

The luxury and privacy of a modern villa close to Disney World, EPCOT, Sea World and other area attractions, but removed from traffic congestion and noise. A large fenced playground, gas grills and picnic tables. Complimentary breakfast, Saturday evening barbecue and free daily newspaper. Vacationing families with children are especially welcome.

--- KISSIMMEE ---

High Point World Resort
2951 High Point Blvd.
Kissimmee, FL 32741
407-396-9600 800-637-8893

2 Bedrooms $$$
Min. Stay 2 Nights, AmEx/Visa/MC,
Dep. 1 Night •
108 condos, Key at Front desk

Location: Airport: 30-40 minutes; Downtown: 15 miles; Need car

General Facilities: Daily maid, Kitchen, Linens, Baby-sitter

Room Facilities: Pool, Hot tub, Tennis, TV, VCR, Phone in rm., Crib-Hi-chair, Ind. AC Ctl., Ind. Heat Ctl.

Attractions: Disney World/EPCOT, Sea World, Cypress Gardens, Busch Gardens, Space Cntr.

Shops & Restaurants: Florida & Oscgola Malls, Belz Factory Outlet; Townsend Plantation/Olive Grdn

Luxury townhomes and villas exquisitely furnished in navy and earth tones. Guest services committed to maximum hospitality; just one mile from Disney World entrance in the heart of vacationland.

Lago Vista Vacation Resort
180 Royal Palm Drive
Kissimmee, FL 32743
305-348-5246

2 Bedrooms $$, Lo-rise
Pool, Kitchen

Attractions: Disney World, Wet 'N Wild, Sea World, Houston Astros Training Camp, EPCOT, Golf

Complete condominiums away from traffic noise and congestion. Pool and lakefront beach for bass and bream fishing, just outside your apartment. The Country Club with golf, tennis and dining is down the street. Ocean beaches can be reached in an hour's drive.

Lifetime of Vacations Resort
7770 W. Irlo Bronson Memorial Hwy
Kissimmee, FL 32741
407-396-3000 800-527-9132

1 Bedroom $$, 2 Bedrooms $$, 3 Bedrooms $$$
Visa/MC
100 condos

Location: Airport: Orlando 30 minutes; Downtown: 25 min.; Need car

General Facilities: Kitchen, Child planned rec.: Playground

Room Facilities: Pool, Boat dock, horseshoes, Golf: Lake Buena Vista nearby, TV

Attractions: Disney World, EPCOT, Sea World, Cypress Gardens, Boardwalk and Baseball

Shops & Restaurants: Florida Mall, Altamonte Mall

Each unit overlooks Lake Wilson with its white sand beach, picnic, barbecue area and children's playground. Moor your boat at the boat dock to be ready for bass fishing and boating. Comfortably furnished units even have a table for cards and games. Bedroom with jacuzzi and steam/sauna shower. Housekeeping available.

─────────────── KISSIMMEE ───────────────

Magic Tree Resort   Pool, Kitchen, Linens
2795 State Road 545 S.
Kissimmee, FL 32741
305-396-2300

Attractions: Walt Disney World, Circus World, Sea World, rapids at River Country, Sea World, Shuffleboard, bikes, Tennis

Visit Walt Disney World and then come back to the relaxation of Magic Tree for a swim or to unwind in the whirlpool spa. Kiddie pool, playground, game room, bicycling, shuffleboard and Tiki Gazebos. Have a drink at the Patio Bar and cook dinner on the gas barbecue grills.

Orange Lake Country Club   2 Bedrooms $$
8505 W. Space Coast Pkwy., Rt 192W   Dep. 1 Night
Kissimmee, FL 32741   Villas, Key at Front desk
305-239-0000 800-327-4444

General Facilities: Kitchen, Restaurant on prem., Bar on prem., Game room, Lounge, Baby-sitter, Child planned rec.: Pool/playground/bike
Room Facilities: Pool, Sauna, Tennis, Racquetball, Golf: 27-hole course, Crib-Hi-chair
Attractions: 4½ miles west of The Magic Kingdom Entrance, Orange Lake
Shops & Restaurants: General store; Citrus Room, Coffee Shop

Luxury accommodations on 400 acres. Championship golf and golf school, tennis courts, sauna, jacuzzis, pools, racquetball, basketball. 80-acre Orange Lake for water sports and fishing. Children are special here, kiddie pool, playground, bicycling, miniature golf, shuffleboard, video game room and a movie theatre. On-site restaurant and coffee shop, exercise room, and even a beauty shop.

Orbit One Vacation Villas   Villas
2950 Entry Point Blvd.   Pool, Kitchen
Kissimmee, FL 32741
407-396-1300

Attractions: Horseshoes, Tennis

Enjoy fresh orange juice from fruit picked outside your condominium. White architecture among palm trees, flower-lined pathways, sculptured ponds with a wooden bridge and waterfalls. Ceramic tile entryways, wicker and rattan furniture, stereo units, and 5 by 7 tub.

Polynesian Isles Resort   1 Bedroom $$, 2 Bedrooms $$$, Lo-rise
3045 Polynesian Isles Blvd.   Pool, Kitchen
Kissimmee, FL 32741
305-396-1622

Attractions: EPCOT, Sea World, Wet 'n Wild, Space Center, Busch Gardens, Cypress Gardens, Shuffleboard, Tennis

Located in the heart of Central Florida among palms, tropical gardens, lagoons, waterfalls and orange trees. Native wood and coral rock exteriors. Suites with designer furnishings, full dining rooms, tinted windows and covered balconies.

KISSIMMEE

Resort World of Orlando
2794 N. Poinciana Blvd.
Kissimmee, FL 34746
305-396-8300 FAX: 407-396-6403

1 Bedroom $$$, 2 Bedrooms $$$,
  3 Bedrooms $$$$
AmEx/Visa/MC, 1 Night Dep. Req'd. •
300 condos, Lo-rise, Key at Front desk,
  24 hours

Location: Airport: 18 miles; Downtown: 1 block; Need car

General Facilities: Full hotel service; Daily maid; Linens; Baby sitter; Lounge; Crib-Hi-chair; Restaurant on premises; Bar on premises

Sports Facilities: Pool; Sauna; Hot tub; Tennis; Racquetball, bicycles

Room Facilities: Kitchen; Cable; VCR; Phone; Ind.AC.Ctl.; Ind.Heat Ctl.

Attractions: Disney World, EPCOT, Sea World, Wet N Wild, Kennedy Space Ctr., Cypress Gardens, Universal

Shops & Restaurants: Disney Village, Florida Mall; Olive Garden/Italian-TGI Fridays/America

Award winning decorated villas, most with jacuzzi baths. 4 miles from Disney World. You'll enjoy 4 pools, hot tubs, saunas, 4 tennis courts, 4 racquetball courts and video games in the gameroom. A restaurant/lounge with terraces on site. Free bicycles available and periodic cookouts.

Westgate Vacation Villas   Villas
2770 Old Lake Wilson Rd.
Kissimmee, FL 32741
407-351-3351 800-992-2990

General Facilities: Linens

Sports Facilities: Pool; Tennis

Room Facilities: Kitchen

Attractions: Walt Disney, Sea World, EPCOT Center

Villas on a lake amidst 170 acres of orange groves. Living room with 27" TV and mirrored wet bar, master bedroom with king-size bed, 19" TV and mirrored closets, double jacuzzi and separate shower, extra bedroom with 19" TV and double-access bathroom.

——————————————— LAKE BUENA VISTA ———————————————

Vistana Resort
8800 Vistana Centre Dr, Box
22051
Lake Buena Vista, FL 32830
407-239-3100 800-327-9152
FAX: 407-239-3131

Studio $$, 1 Bedroom $$$,
2 Bedrooms $$$$
AmEx/Visa/MC, 1 Night Dep. Req'd. •
976 condos, Lo-rise, Villas, Key at
Registration desk H-Yes

Location: Airport: 15 miles; Downtown: 17 miles

General Facilities: Full hotel service; Daily maid; Linens; Baby sitter; Crib-Hi-chair; Restauranton premises; Bar on premises

Sports Facilities: Game room; Pool; Sauna; Hot tub; Tennis; Basketball, Shuffle-board; Walt Disney Golf Course; Full-time activities

Room Facilities: Kitchen; TV; VHS; Phone; Ind.AC.Ctl; Ind.Heat Ctl.

Attractions: 1 mile from Disney World Complex, Sea World, Wet & Wild, Kennedy Space Ctr., Universal; Entertainment

Shops & Restaurants: Disney World Shopping, Church St. Exchange; Several on premises and in area

Spacious, deluxe, designer furnished, contemporary villas. Vistana Resort places its guests in a hub of limitless vacation opportunities. There are two types of accommodations-villas and townhomes. The townhomes offer a two-story living room with floor-to-ceiling windows. Villas have two color TVs, video players and oversized whirlpool tub. Be as active as you like, or just sit back and "reenergize." 11 tennis courts and 6 swimming pool.

——————————————— LAUDERDALE-BY-THE-SEA ———————————————

Driftwood Beach Club
4417 El Mar Drive
Lauderdale-By-The-Sea, FL 33308
305-776-4441

Studio $, 1 Bedroom $$, 2 Bedrooms $$$
Dep. Required, 40 condos, Lo-rise

Location: Beach front

General Facilities: Daily maid; Linens; Baby sitter

Sports Facilities: Pool; Shuffleboard, horseshoes

Room Facilities: Kitchen

Attractions: Fishing pier, marina, tennis courts, Water Kingdoms, Bahama Islands, Everglades, golf; Entertainment

Shops & Restaurants: Lauderdale gift shops, take-out, service stores

Monday morning orange juice wake-ups with coffee and donuts, Wednesday night chicken and ribs barbeques and manager's informal talk about the area are some of the weekly happenings here. Use the private beach with its shuffleboard courts and horseshoe pits or walk two blocks to fishing pier and marina. Pool, grills and large patio—close to tennis and playground.

Be sure to call the condo to verify details and prices and to make your reservation.

------------------------------ LAUDERDALE-BY-THE-SEA ------------------------------

Howard Johnson Resort and Villas
4660 N. Ocean Drive
Lauderdale-By-The-Sea, FL 33308
305-776-5660 800-327-5919

Studio $$, 1 Bedroom $$, 2 Bedrooms $$$
Dep. 1 Night
Villas, Key at Front desk
No S-yes/H-yes

Location: Airport: Ft. Lauderdale; Beach front

General Facilities: Full serv., Conf. rm., Kitchen, Linens, Restaurant on prem., Bar on prem., Lounge, Child planned rec.: Activities Director

Room Facilities: Pool, Health Club, TV, Cable, VCR, Phone in rm., Ind. AC Ctl., Ind. Heat Ctl.

Attractions: Jai alai, horse/dog racing, Ocean World, Cruise Harbor, State parks, night-club circuit

Shops & Restaurants: Sea Ranch Shopping Village, On-site gift shop; Howard Johnson restaurant

Check into your Villa and sip the complimentary Perrier. Complimentary coffee and newspaper to start your day before you head for the beach, pools or exercise and steam rooms. Children have their own pool as well as craft classes and supervised activities. Movies and entertainment in the lobby lounge, Oceanfront Patio Bar with BBQ, and family-priced Howard Johnson's restaurant. 5 minute walk to the ocean pier. The staff will be happy to arrange your visit to area attractions.

Morningstar Condominium
223 Marine Court
Lauderdale-By-The-Sea, FL 33308
305-771-5924

1 Bedroom $$, 2 Bedrooms $$
Min. Stay 7 Nights, Dep. Req'd.
11 condos, Lo-rise, Villas, Key at Apt. 206
H-yes

Location: Airport: 7 miles; Need car

General Facilities: Kitchen, Linens

Room Facilities: Pool, Tennis, TV, Cable, Crib-Hi-chair, Ind. AC Ctl., Ind. Heat Ctl.

Attractions: Paddlewheel Queen, Jungle Queen, sightseeing, Ft. Lauderdale

Shops & Restaurants: Shopping malls; Raindancer Wharf, Benihana

Completely furnished apartments in modern decor. The beach is just around the corner. Tropical patio, small pool, shuffleboard, laundry facilities and free parking. 10 minute walk to stores, restaurants, post office and nightlife.

Villas By The Sea
4500 Ocean Drive
Lauderdale-By-The-Sea, FL 33308
305-722-3550 800-247-8963

1 Bedroom $$, Villas
Pool, Daily maid, Kitchen, Linens, Phone in rm.

Attractions: Fitness room, Tennis

Six adjoining properties, four of which are on the beach. All but one property have their own pools. Free weekly continental breakfast. Monthly calendar of events with various activities, games and parties. Weekly bingo and monthly barbecue.

─────────────────── LEHIGH ───────────────────

Lehigh Resort Club
225 East Joel Blvd.
Lehigh, FL 33936
813-369-2121 800-843-0971

Studio $$, 1 Bedroom $$, 2 Bedrooms $$$
1 Bedrm/week 5$, 2 Bed/week 6$
AmEx/Visa/MC, Dep. 1 Night •
140 condos, Lo-rise, Key at Front desk
H-yes

Location: Airport: 20 miles; Downtown: 20 miles; Need car

General Facilities: Full serv., Conf. rm. cap. 200, Kitchen, Linens, Restaurant on prem., Bar on prem., Game room, Lounge, Baby-sitter, Child planned rec.: Recreation director

Room Facilities: Pool, Hot tub, Tennis, Shuffleboard, Basketball, Golf: 36-holes on property, TV, Cable, Phone in rm., Crib-Hi-chair, Ind. AC Ctl., Ind. Heat Ctl.

Attractions: Thomas Edison winter home, golf, tennis, entertainment

Shops & Restaurants: Burdines, Robinsons, Mass Brothers, Jacobsons

Complete golf and tennis resort, bordering two 18-hole championship golf courses. Four lighted tennis courts and a recreational director with planned activities for all ages. Nightly entertainment in the lounge.

─────────────── LIDO BEACH, SARASOTA ───────────────

Sarasota Sands
2150 Benjamin Franklin Dr.
Lido Beach, Sarasota, FL 34236
813-388-2138

1 Bedroom $$, 2 Bedrooms $$, Hi-rise
Pool, Kitchen, Linens, Phone in rm.

Attractions: Ringling Museum, Jungle Gardens, Lionel Train and Seashell Museum, V. Wezel Performing Arts, Basketball, racquetball, Tennis

Relaxed, casual, informal atmosphere. Professionally furnished gulf-front condominiums on Lido Beach. Recreation facilities include tennis, racquetball, basketball, shuffleboard, pool, sauna and hot tub.

─────────────── LONGBOAT KEY, SARASOTA ───────────────

Veranda Beach Club
2509 Gulf Of Mexico Drive
Longboat Key, Sarasota, FL 34228
813-383-5511

2 Bedrm/week 8$
Min. Stay 7 Nights
Hi-rise

Location: Downtown: minutes away; Beach front

General Facilities: Kitchen, Linens

Room Facilities: Pool, Sauna, Hot tub, Tennis, Health-exercise center, Area golf courses.

Attractions: Deep sea fishing, golf, tennis, White Sox spring training, Disney World, Busch Gardens

Shops & Restaurants: Longboat and Sarasota shops

Spacious 38 foot covered porches with Gulf and Bay views span each unit. Each unit is built around a central landscaped courtyard with wrought-iron and a bubbling fountain. Your complete vacation home has a private, furnished, ceramic floored terrace, designer fabric furnishings and whirlpool tub. Handball, racquetball, squash and tennis courts, indoor/outdoor pools. Bicycles to explore the island, surf sailboats, fishing equipment and cabanas are provided.

—————————————————— LONGBOAT KEY ——————————————————

Colony Beach & Tennis Resort 1 Bedroom $$$$, 2 Bedrooms $$$$, Amex,
1620 Gulf of Mexico Dr. Visa, MC, Key at Front desk/Lobby
Longboat Key, FL 34228 235 condos, Villas, H-yes

Location: Airport: 11 miles; Downtown: Sarasota: 5 miles; Beach front

General facilities: Full serv., Conf. Rm. (cap. 250), Daily maid, Kitchen, Linens,
Child planned rec., Baby sitter, Restaurant, Bar

Room facilities: TV, Cable, Phone, Cribs $15, Ind. AC Ctl., Ind. Heat Ctl.

Sports facilities: Pool, Tennis, Golf nearby, Health Spa

Attractions: Ringling Estate, Mote Marine Laboratory, Selby Gardens, Asolo
Theatre, Sarasota Opera, entertainment

Shops & Restaurants: St. Armands Circle, Michael's On East/Continental cuisine

*235 luxurious one- and two-bedroom villas, complimentary tennis (21 courts, 10
soft), health spas, fitness center and supervised children's programs along with the
award winning Colony Restaurant create casual island luxury in a private club
atmosphere on lush, tropical Longboat key located 15 minutes from Sarasota/Bradenton Airport. Tampa International Airport—1 hour.*

The Resort at Longboat Key Club

———————————————— LONGBOAT KEY ————————————————

The Resort at Longboat Key Club
301 Gulf of Mexico Dr.
Longboat Key, FL 34228
941-383-8821 800-237-8821
FAX: 941-383-0359

Studio $$, 1 Bedroom $$$$,
  2 Bedrooms $$$$
AmEx/Visa/MC, 1 Night Dep. Req'd. •
232 condos, Hi-rise
Key at Reception Center, H-Yes

Location: Airport: 15 minutes; Downtown: 10 minutes; Need car; Beachfront

General Facilities: Full hotel service; Daily maid; Linens; Baby sitter; Lounge; Crib-Hi-chair; Restaurant on premises; Bar on premises

Business Facilities: Bus. fac.; Conf. Room Cap. 150

Sports Facilities: Pool; Sauna; Hot tub; Tennis; Sail, Fish, Bike, Beaches; 45-holes Golf on-site; Kids Klub—seasonal

Room Facilities: Kitchen; Cable; Phone; Ind.AC.Ctl; Ind.Heat Ctl.

Attractions: John Ringling Home, Asolo Theatre, Performing Arts Hall, Marie Selby Botanical Gardens

Shops & Restaurants: St. Armands Circle shops, Avenue of the Flowers; Plaza on Longboat Key

Elegant vacation suites, light tropical colors, contemporary styling, balconies with views of the Gulf, lagoons or golf course. A family resort with games, nature walks, tours and movies for the children, four restaurants on the property, and entertainment by a harpist in the Orchid Room. Also nearby Sarasota Ballet, Opera.

─────────────── LONGBOAT KEY ───────────────

White Sands of Longboat   Lo-rise, Villas
5114 Gulf of Mexico Drive
Longboat Key, FL 34228
813-383-2428
General facilities: Kitchen, Linens
Sports facilities: Pool, Tennis, Putting green

Bermuda-style villa, or gracious townhouse overlooking gardens, the Gulf or Bay. Professionally designed interiors with whirlpool tubs, screened and open porches, even board games. Bay-front fishing and boat dock for your complimentary dory.

─────────────── MARATHON ───────────────

Buccaneer Resort Hotel   2 Bedrooms $$$$
2600 Overseas Highway   Villas
Marathon, FL 33050
305-743-9071 800-237-3329
General facilities: Daily maid, Kitchen, Linens
Attractions: Charter boats, jet skis, sailing, reef trips, rental boats, tennis, pool

Villas with jacuzzis, two T.V.'s and fully equipped kitchens on a tropically landscaped 10 acre resort on the Gulf. Private beach and dock with full service dive shop. Exotic drinks at the Sunset Café and nightly specials in the dining room.

───

Casa Cayo Condominiums   Hi-rise
12690 Overseas Highway
Marathon, FL 33050
305-743-7562
General facilities: Kitchen
Sports facilities: Pool, Golf, Dockage
Attractions: Gulf of Mexico, golf, tennis, fishing, boating, diving

16-unit condominium on a private peninsula with 270 degree views. Security gates at entrance and free dockage. Access to Gulf and Atlantic waters.

───

Cocoplum Beach & Tennis Club   2 Bedrooms $$
109 Cocoplum Dr.   2 Bed/week 6$
Marathon, FL 33050   Min. stay 2 nights, Dep. req'd
305-743-0240 800-228-1587   20 condos, Villas, Key at Main office •
Location: Airport: 2 miles, Downtown: 6 miles, Need car, Beach front
General facilities: Kitchen, Linens, Hot tub
Room facilities: TV, Cable, Crib-Hi-chair, Ind.AC.Ctl., Ind.Heat Ctl.
Sports facilities: Pool, Tennis, Volleyball, boats, beach
Attractions: Old town Key West, scuba, snorkeling, state parks
Shops & Restaurants: Unique shopping in the 125 mile chain of islands; The
   Quay-French

Two bedroom, two bath villas in the fabulous Florida Keys. Stuffed furniture in muted mauves, pinks and beiges, glass top dining table, large screened porch. Take an excursion boat or a drive to Key West, or just relax and enjoy the pool or beach.

MARATHON

Gulfpointe I
12690 Overseas Hwy.
Marathon, FL 33050
305-743-75622
FAX: 305-743-6918

2 Bedroom $$$$, Jr. $$
2 Bedrm/week 9$
Min. Stay 3 Nights, Dep. Req'd
30 condos, Lo-rise, Keys at 12690
Overseas Highway.

Location: Airport: Marathon 2 miles; Downtown: nearby

General Facilities: Daily maid, Kitchen, Linens, Baby sitter

Room Facilities: Pool, Tennis, Boat dockage, Sombrero C. Club near, Child planned rec., TV, Cable, Phone in rm., Ind. AC Ctl., Ind Heat Ctl.

Attractions: Beautiful seaside community with fishing, diving, snorkeling, sightseeing

Shops & Restaurants: Marathon shopping centers; Seafood, steaks, tiki bar.

Island lifestyle and tropical climate for a relaxed vacation. Two bedroom, two level condominiums have 1400 square feet of living space and wrap-around six foot wide terraces off the living room and master bedroom providing panoramic and sunset views. Ceramic tile living areas with carpeted bedrooms, bahama fans and fully equipped kitchens. Enjoy a day of fishing, snorkeling and diving, dock your boat at the pier, play tennis or relax by the pool.

The Hawks Nest
One Kyle Way South
Marathon, FL 33050
305-743-6711

1 Bedroom $$, 2 Bedrooms $$, Hi-rise
Pool, Daily maid, Kitchen, Linens

Attractions: Bay and deep-sea fishing, snorkeling, diving, water skiing, Boat docking, Tennis

Functional spacious units with golf or ocean views from the terrace. Bring your boat or rent a canoe or power boat. Snorkel, swim and dive and explore the reef. Catch your dinner in the Keys water and barbecue it for dinner at the picnic facility.

Marathon Key Beach Club
4590 Overseas Highway
Marathon, FL 33050
305-743-6522

Lo-rise
Pool, Daily maid

Attractions: Hemingway haven, treasure reefs, historic homes, theater, golf, helicopter rides, Boat ramp, bicycles, Tennis

Leave your business suit at home for this casual resort. No telephones to disturb you, just many water sports, tennis and the largest pool in the Keys. Tropical grounds have barbecue pit and picnic area. Screened patios, laundries, carport and three dining areas.

The Reef at Marathon
6800 Overseas Highway
Marathon, FL 33050
305-743-7900 800-327-4836

1 Bedroom $$$, 2 Bedrooms $$$, Lo-rise, Villas
Pool, Kitchen

Attractions: Boat slip, ramp, tennis

Villas on 6 acres of Florida Bay. Small private boat marina with ramp, small, pebble beach and slip included with villa. Complimentary canoes, paddle boats, sailboats and windsurfers. Tennis, pool and grills.

─────────────────── MARATHON ───────────────────

Sombrero Resort & Lighthouse   1 Bedroom $$$
19 Sombrero Blvd.   1 Bedrm/week 7$
Marathon, FL 33050   AmEx/Visa/MC, Dep. 1 Night •
305-743-2250 800-433-8660   105 condos, Lo-rise, Key at Front desk
H-yes

Location: Airport: 2 Miles; Downtown: 1 mile; Beach front

General Facilities: Full serv., Conf. rm. cap. 100, Daily maid, Kitchen, Linens, Restaurant on prem., Bar on prem., Lounge

Room Facilities: Pool, Sauna, Tennis, Golf: Sombrero Country Club, TV, Cable, VCR, Phone in rm., Crib, Ind. AC Ctl., Ind. Heat Ctl.

Attractions: Bahia Honda State Park, Sombrero Beach, 7-Mile Bridge, Dolphin Research Ctr, entertainment

Shops & Restaurants: K-Mart, Grocery store, Eckerd Drugs; Kelseys-Gourmet

Lounging at pool, fishing, dining. Lovely one-bedroom suites, live entertainment, lush tropical grounds; family oriented; deep water protected marina; tennis pro shop.

─────────────────── MARCO ISLAND ───────────────────

Beach Club Of Marco   1 Bedroom $$, 2 Bedrooms $$
901 S. Collier Blvd.   1 Bedrm/week 4$, 2 Bed/week 5$
Marco Island, FL 33937   AmEx/Visa/MC, Dep. 1 Night •
813-394-8860 800-323-8860   52 condos, Hi-rise, Key at Registr. desk

Location: Airport: Naples 20 miles; Downtown: 3 miles; Need car

General Facilities: Daily maid, Kitchen, Linens, Restaurant on prem., Bar on prem., Lounge, Baby-sitter

Room Facilities: Pool, Racquetball, TV, Cable, Phone in rm., Crib-Hi-chair, Ind. AC Ctl., Ind. Heat Ctl.

Attractions: Everglades boat tours, seashelling trips, paddle boat tours, charter boat fishing trips, entertainment

Shops & Restaurants: Sears, Maison Blanche, grocery, boutiques, K-Mart; French/Italian/German/Mexican

Gracious, Florida-style furnishings with private balconies. Spend a calm, leisurely vacation or take advantage of the abundant sporting life. Margo II trolley takes you on an island historical tour and to island shops. 3.5 miles to the beach. Heated pool, shuffleboard, racquetball, gazebos with barbecue. Ensign's Quarters Restaurant and nightly entertainment in the Upper Deck Lounge.

Charter Club of Marco Beach   Hi-rise
700 S. Collier Blvd.   Pool, Kitchen, Linens
Marco Island, FL 33937
813-394-4192 800-237-4411

Attractions: Putting green, fitness center, Tennis

On Marco Island, a bridge away from the mainland, condominiums overlooking the Gulf of Mexico. Enter the round-robin tennis tournaments held twice weekly. Fitness room instructors, sailing lessons, social building, pools and barbecue pavilion.

──────────────── MARCO ISLAND ────────────────

Marco House
Shadowridge Court
Marco Island, FL
813-797-1140

1 Bedroom $$, 2 Bedroom $$$, 3
Bedroom $$$
2 Bedrm/week 6$, 3 Bedrm/week 8$
Min. Stay 7 Nights, Dep. Req'd
3 condos, Villas, Keys at Lock box

Location: Airport: 50 miles; Downtown: 1 mile
General Facilities:, Kitchen, Linens
Room Facilities: Pool, Tennis, Island Country Club, TV, Cable, Phone in rm., Ind. AC Ctl., Ind. Heat Ctl.
Attractions: Airboat rides through the Everglades, Marco Island Trolley, shelling, Corkscrew sanctuary
Shops & Restaurants: Many fine shops, grocery stores; O'Sheas-seafood
Private, spacious 2800 sq. ft. home, overlooking spectacular view of golf course and ten acre lake. Custom decorated, marble fireplace, 3 dining areas, covered lanai, and large pool. Ideal for couples sharing a vacation. Minutes from the Gulf, private beach pass, boating, tennis, golf, nightlife. Contact Profinmar Home Rentals, P.O. Box 7642, Clearwater, Florida 34618 to rent this property.

───

Marco Bay Resort
1001 N. Barfield Dr.
Marco Island, FL 33937
813-394-8881 800-228-0661

1 Bedroom $$, 2 Bedrooms $$
1 Bedrm/week $$$$, 2 Bed/week 4$
AmEx/Visa/MC, Dep. 1 Night •
200 condos, Hi-rise, Key at Front desk
H-yes

Location: Airport: Ft. Meyers-55 min.; Downtown: 1 mile; Need car
General Facilities: Full serv., Bus. fac., Conf. rm. cap. 250, Daily maid, Kitchen, Linens, Restaurant on prem., Bar on prem., Baby-sitter, Child planned rec.: Activities director
Room Facilities: Pool, Hot tub, Tennis, Golf: Nearby, TV, Cable, Phone in rm., Crib-Hichair, Ind. AC Ctl., Ind. Heat Ctl.
Attractions: Shelling, Sunset cruises, paddlewheeler, Island trolley and Everglades tours
Shops & Restaurants: Port of Marco shopping village; Old Marco Inn-European
Light, airy suites with ample dockage for your boat. Explore the many secluded islands nearby, or charter a fully equipped boat with a licensed captain for serious fishing. The Chickee Bar is at water's edge, and the Hawk's Nest cafe is at poolside. Relax by the pool or take provided transportation to Tigertail Beach. Planned recreational activities for children, plus a video arcade. Marco Bay Resort is a "suite treat."

───

Sea Winds Beach Resort
890 S. Collier Blvd.
Marco Island, FL 33937
813-642-6262 800-237-4155

Hi-rise
Pool, Kitchen

Attractions: Exercise room, Tennis
Magnificently furnished 2 bedroom condominiums on 3.5 miles of crescent beach. Amenities include pool, whirlpool, tennis, sauna, exercise room, poolside bar and barbecue.

─────────────── MARCO ISLAND ───────────────

Sunrise Bay Resort & Club   1 Bedroom $$
10 Tampa Place   1 Bedrm/week 5$
Marco Island, FL 33937   Visa/MC,Dep. Req'd. •
813-394-5280   20 condos, Hi-rise, Key at Front desk

Location: Airport: Ft. Myers 40 miles; Downtown: 1 mile; Need car; Beach front

General Facilities: Kitchen, Linens

Room Facilities: Pool, Hot tub, Bikes, boat rentals, TV, Cable, Phone in rm., Crib, Ind. AC Ctl., Ind. Heat Ctl.

Attractions: Rosie O'Shea Paddlewheel, Island trolley tours, charter fishing, entertainment

Shops & Restaurants: Island boutiques, Naples 15 miles, 3rd St. South; O'Shea's/seafood, variety

Peaceful, tropical area in historic Marco. Units are partially encircled in walls of mirrors and windows including screened balconies with table and chairs. Shades of blue, brown, wood grains, brass and tweed enhance the nautical theme of this boating and fishing resort. Largest privately owned fishing pier on the Island, with slip space, Seminole-built "chickee hut," pool, spa, bikes, and grills in picnic area. Just a few minutes to sports, dining, shopping and entertainment. Sunday aft. dock parties.

The Surf Club of Marco   2 Bedrooms $$$, Hi-rise
540 S. Collier Blvd.   Pool, Kitchen, Linens
Marco Island, FL 33937
813-642-5800

Attractions: Charter fishing, shelling, bike rentals, parasailing, water skiing, sailing, Tennis, Golf

Located on Marco Island's crescent beach, two-bedroom, two-bath suites with everything you need for your vacation. Tennis, pool with patio and deck, spa.

─────────────── MIAMI BEACH ───────────────

Golden Strand Ocean Resort   Studio $$, 1 Bedroom $$, 2 Bedrooms $$$
17901 Collins Avenue   Villas
Miami Beach, FL 33160
305-931-7000 800-327-4008

Location: Beach front

General Facilities: Kitchen, Restaurant on prem., Bar on prem., Lounge

Room Facilities: Pool, Hot tub, Spa, gym, putt green

Attractions: Deep-sea fishing, sailing, surfing, golf, jai alai, horse/dog racing

Shops & Restaurants: Aventura Mall, Bal Harbour-Saks, Gucci's, Neiman M; Ocean View, Terrace Cafe

Unusual attention to service, private and exclusive. Villas decorated with meticulous attention to detail. Tile floors, skylights, wet bars. Full service spa, evaluation, exercise program and diet planned especially for you. Yoga, aerobics, weight-training instructors. Pool and putting green for those who prefer a less strenuous vacation.

──────────────── MIAMI BEACH ────────────────

Roney Plaza   1 Bedroom $$, 2 Bedrooms $$$, Hi-rise
2301 Collins Ave.   Pool, Kitchen, Linens
Miami Beach, FL 33139
305-531-8811 800-432-4317

Attractions: Art Deco district, theatre, museums, galleries

Ideally located in fabulous Miami Beach with its many attractions and activities. Olympic-sized pool, restaurant, lounge. Do it all, or do nothing.

──

Seacoast Towers Apartment Hotel 1 Bedroom $$, 2 Bedrooms $$$, Hi-rise
5151 Collins Avenue   Pool, Daily maid, Kitchen, Linens
Miami Beach, FL 33140
305-865-5152 800-523-3671

Attractions: Marina, Tennis, Golf

Commitment to excellence in the designer decorated suites, equipped with video players, mini-bars and walk-in closets. 600-foot stretch of beach and private marina. Courteous, hospitable staff provides maid service and valet parking.

Marco Bay Resort

———————————— MIDDLEBURG ————————————

The Inn at Ravines
2932 Ravines Road
Middleburg, FL 32068
904-282-2843

1 Bedroom $$, 2 Bedrooms $$, 3 Bedrooms $$
Visa/MC •
50 condos

Location: Airport: 50 miles; Downtown: 45 miles

General Facilities: Conf. rm. cap. 75, Kitchen, Restaurant on prem., Bar on prem.

Room Facilities: Pool, Tennis, Putting course, Golf: Ravines, TV, Cable, Ind.AC Ctl., Ind. Heat Ctl.

Attractions: St. Augustine, Jacksonville Landing

Shops & Restaurants: Orange Park Mall (15 miles) 120 stores; Hilltop/continental, Ravines'

Warm, comfortable condominiums on 450 acres of planned beauty. The natural terrain of the area has steep hills that rise some 90 feet above sea level with drastic drops of more than 60 feet to the ravine bottom. There are many species of wildlife and more than 50 varieties of trees. All the diversions you could ask for with the ambience of a country inn.

———————————— N. REDINGTON BEACH ————————————

Emerald Isle
17334 Gulf Blvd.
N. Redington Beach, FL 33708
813-397-0441

2 Bedrooms $$, 3 Bedrooms $$$
2 Bedrms/week 6$, 3 Bed/week 6$
Min. Stay 7 Nights, AmEx/Visa/MC,
Dep. Req'd.
Hi-rise, Key at Office, No S-yes/H-yes

Location: Airport: 30 miles; Downtown: 10 min.; Beach front

General Facilities: Daily maid, Kitchen, Linens, Baby-sitter

Room Facilities: Pool, Sailing, windsurfing, TV, Cable, Phone in rm., Crib-Hi-chair, Ind. AC Ctl., Ind. Heat Ctl.

Attractions: Busch Gardens, Dali Museum, charter boats, Disney World, St. Petersburg pier, Flea market

Shops & Restaurants: Small shopping plaza, Maas Brothers, Burdines; Wine Cellar/wide variety

Located directly on the Gulf of Mexico between St. Petersburg and Clearwater. Private terraces overlooking the beach, large closets and fully equipped kitchens.

———————————————————————————————

Redington Ambassdor
16900 Gulf Blvd.
N. Redington Beach, FL 33708
813-391-9646

2 Bedrooms $$, Hi-rise
Pool, Kitchen

Built directly on the Gulf of Mexico, within walking distance to shops, stores, restaurants and Redington fishing pier. Two-bedroom, two-bath units with ceiling fans and abundant storage. Recreational deck area, pool, jacuzzi and inside atrium with walk.

———————————— NAPLES ————————————

Beachcomber Club
290 Fifth Avenue South
Naples, FL 33940
813-262-8112

1 Bedroom $$, 2 Bedrooms $$, Lo-rise
Pool, Kitchen

Mostly efficiencies and one bedroom units with screened porches, cable color TV, telephones, heated pools, landscaped patios.

─────────────────── NAPLES ───────────────────

Charter Club of Naples Bay 2 Bedrooms $$
1000 10th Ave. S 2 Bedrms/week 6$
Naples, FL 33940 Min. Stay 3 Nights, Dep. Req'd.
813-261-5559 800-445-3623 Lo-rise

General Facilities: Kitchen, Bar on prem., Child planned rec.: Kiddie pool

Room Facilities: Pool, Badminton, Horseshoes, TV

Polynesian motif exteriors and light rattan interiors for casual, comfortable vacation living. King-size bed and color TV in the master bedroom. 30 ft. screened lanai covers the master bedroom and living room for Naples Bay views. Rolling terrain with tropical landscaping, winding paths and shade trees. Bicycles, fishing poles, badminton, horseshoes, pool and kiddie pool. Boat rental at the Marina, or slip for boats up to 18 feet. 8 blocks to the beach.

Edgewater Beach Hotel 1 Bedroom $$
1901 Golfshore Blvd. N. AmEx/MC/Visa/Other CC
Naples, FL 33940 115 condos, Hi-rise, Villas
813-262-6511 800-821-0196
FAX: 813-262-1243

Location: Airport: Naples-10 miles; Downtown: 5 miles, Beach front

General Facilities: Conf. rm. cap. 100, Kitchen, Restaurant on prem., Bar on prem., Lounge.

Attractions: Tennis, golf, sailing, boating, sightseeing, fishing, shelling excursions

Shops & Restaurants: Olde Naples shops; Crystal Parrot on-site

Concerned professionals greet you as you enter the imported Italian marble lobby. When you are settled, walk to the beach or swim in the heated pool with its gulf side bar. Nearby golf and tennis, trolley outside the lobby for trips to Olde Naples for browsing and shopping. Two lounges, gift shop and view dining in the Crystal Parrot. 5:00 p.m. Happy Hour with hors d'oeuvres. Microwave ovens for fast dining "at home."

Golden Isle Apartments 1 Bedroom $$, 2 Bedrooms $$
430 Fourth Ave. S. 1 Bedrm/week 4$, 2 Bed/week 5$
Naples, FL 33940 MC,Dep. 25%
813-261-8104 18 condos, Hi-rise, Key at Office

Room Facilities: TV, Cable, Ind. AC Ctl., Ind. Heat Ctl.

Attractions: Naples beach, fishing, charter boats, Jungle Larry's, Everglades

Shops & Restaurants: Grocery, drug and specialty stores; Kelly's, Red Lobster, Chinese

Golden Isle is a small place appealing to couples and families who appreciate a quiet environment among congenial neighbors. Free use of bicycles and 16' Sunfish sailboat. 3 blocks to Naples beach and fishing pier. Public tennis and golf courses are nearby. The simple design of the furnishings create a relaxed atmosphere for vacation enjoyment.

─────────────── NAPLES ───────────────

Naples Bath & Tennis 1 Bedroom $$, 2 Bedrooms $$$, 3 Bedrooms
4995 Airport Rd. N. $$$
Naples, FL 33942   1 Bedrm/week 6$, 2 Bed/week 7$,
813-261-5777 800-225-9692   3 Bed/week 9$
                         AmEx/Visa/MC, Dep. Req'd. •
                         80 condos, Lo-rise, Key at Resort office, No S-yes

Location: Downtown: 4 miles; Need car

General Facilities: Full serv., Bus. fac., Conf. rm. cap. 450, Daily maid, Kitchen, Linens, Restaurant on prem., Bar on prem., Lounge, Baby-sitter

Room Facilities: Pool, Sauna, Hot tub, Tennis, Health Club, Golf: Naples Beach & Vineyards, TV, Cable, Phone in rm., Crib-Hi-chair, Ind. AC Ctl., Ind. Heat Ctl.

Attractions: Everglades cruise, deep-sea fishing, dinner cruise, African Safari, Edison Home, entertainment

Shops & Restaurants: Burdines, Maas Bros. Third Street boutiques; Villa Pescatore/George & Dragon

Premier tennis resort community, official home of the 1987-88 Tennis Grand Masters. The place to go if you really care about improving your tennis. 160 acres of tropical paradise. Lakes, pools, jacuzzi, health clubs, planned barbecues, dances, tennis tournaments, aerobics, bridge, recreational activities, shopping, sports, and a nearby beach—all for a complete family vacation.

Park Shore Resort   1 Bedroom $$, 2 Bedrooms $$, Lo-rise
4535 Tamiami Trail North   Pool, Kitchen
Naples, FL 33940
813-481-3636 800-237-8096

Attractions: Golf, fishing, water sports, beach, Racquetball, Tennis

13 acres of lush, tropical landscaping. Lake with an island in the center housing a pool with sparkling waterfall and the Island Club lounge and restaurant. Suites with private patios and sleeper sofas in the living area.

Sandrift Club Condominium   Lo-rise
613 E. Lake Dr.   Pool, Kitchen, Phone in rm.
Naples, FL 33940
813-261-2380

Attractions: Cambier Park, Candy Cane Park, Naples Recreation Center

Heated pool with deck area and self-service poolside bar, jacuzzi, and gas grills surrounded by lawns, tropical flowers and carpeted walkways. Color-coordinated mahogany, period furniture, large-screen color television, and private patio or balcony.

White Sands Resort Club   1 Bedroom $, 2 Bedrooms $$, Lo-rise
260 Third St. So.   Pool, Kitchen, Linens, Phone in rm.
Naples, FL 33940
813-261-4144

Attractions: Water sports, deep-sea fishing, scuba diving, golf, tennis, Shuffleboard

2.5 blocks from the Gulf of Mexico. Units overlook green courtyard with palm trees and umbrella covered tables by the heated pool and spa. Chickee bar, shuffleboard court, and grills. Ride one of the free bicycles to the beach. Quiet, private atmosphere.

─────────────────────── NAPLES ───────────────────────

World Tennis Center
4800 Airport Road
Naples, FL 33942
813-263-1900 800-292-6663

2 Bedrooms $$
2 Bedrms/week 4$
Min. Stay 2 Nights, Visa/MC, Dep. Req'd. •
160 condos, Lo-rise, Villas, Key at Rental office
P-yes

Location: Airport: Naples-3 miles; Downtown: 5 miles; Need car

General Facilities: Bus. fac., Daily maid, Kitchen, Linens, Restaurant on prem., Bar on prem.

Room Facilities: Pool, Sauna, Hot tub, Tennis, TV, Cable, Phone in rm., Crib, Ind. AC Ctl., Ind. Heat Ctl.

Attractions: Dog racing, hot air balloon festival, African Safari park, airboat rides, Indian villages, entertainment

Shops & Restaurants: Fifth Avenue South and 3rd Street, Olde Naples; Chef's Garden-continental

1100-square-foot condominiums, white stucco exteriors and Mediterranean-style architecture with rattan furnishings. 11 clay, 5 hard tennis courts, 10 of them lighted. Poolside cafe/bar, Pro Shop, beach three miles away. A family resort for tennis and non-tennis players alike.

─────────────────────── NAVARRE BEACH ───────────────────────

Beach Resort
8459 Gulf Blvd.
Navarre Beach, FL 32561
904-939-2324 800-344-7368

1 Bedroom $$
1 Bedrm/week 5$
Min. Stay 3 Nights, Dep. Req'd.
30 condos, Hi-rise, Key at Realty office onsite
H-yes

Location: Airport: 30 miles; Downtown: 15 miles; Need car; Beach front

General Facilities: Daily maid, Kitchen, Linens, Restaurant on prem., Bar on prem.

Room Facilities: Pool, Hot tub, Tennis, TV, Cable, Phone in rm., Ind. AC Ctl., Ind. Heat Ctl.

Attractions: Zoo, Pensacola historical district, Fort Pickens, Air Force/Navy & Indian museums

Shops & Restaurants: Shopping Malls, McRae's, Gayfers, Parisian; Navarre Orleans, Destinees

Secluded family oriented island living. Bedroom has two queen-size beds, living room with sofa sleeper, balcony and private Gulf beach. Barbecue grills, party room and excellent seafood restaurant on property; Pensacola's historic district and deep-sea fishing just 30 minutes away.

Beachview
8425 Gulf Blvd.
Navarre Beach, FL 32561

──────────── NAVARRE BEACH ────────────

Emerald Surf 2 Bedrooms $$, 2 Bedrms/week 5$
8245 Gulf Blvd. Min. Stay 2 Nights, Visa/MC
Navarre Beach, FL 32561 Dep. Required, 33 condos, Hi-rise
904-939-3450 800-331-0540 Key at In office

Location: Airport: 35 miles; Downtown: 25 miles; Need car

General Facilities: Linens

Business Facilities: Conference room

Sports Facilities: Pool; Activities room

Room Facilities: Kitchen; Cable; Ind.AC.Ctl; Ind.Heat Ctl.

Attractions: Charter boats for rent in Pensacola or Fort Walton, water activities; Entertainment

Shops & Restaurants: Gift shops; Pensacola/Fort Walton

Enjoy the sun, sea and rolling dunes on this tranquil barrier island to the Gulf Islands National Seashore. Gulf front suites with whirlpool tubs and private balconies in an unsurpassed water sports playground. Covered shuffle-board court, VCR and tape rental, beach service for chairs, umbrellas, and sailboats available. Activity room for your pleasure. Minutes away from historic Pensacola and fun-loving Ft. Walton. Area tennis courts and golf, plus our magnificent sunsets.

──────────── NEW SMYRNA BEACH ────────────

Islander Beach Resort Studio $$, 1 Bedroom $$, 2 Bedrooms $$
1601 S. Atlantic Ave. 1 Bedrm/week 5$, 2 Bedrms/week 6$
New Smyrna Beach, FL 32169 Min. Stay 3 Nights, AmEx/Visa/MC
904-427-3452 FAX: 904-426-5606 114 condos, Hi-rise
  Key at Front desk, H-Yes

Location: Airport: 20 miles; Downtown: 2 miles; Need car; Beachfront

General Facilities: Linens; Lounge; Crib-Hi-chair; Restauranton premises

Sports Facilities: Pool; Hot tub; Nautilus room, Volleyball; Child planned recreation

Room Facilities: Kitchen; Cable; VCR; Phone; Ind.AC.Ctl.; Ind.Heat Ctl.

Attractions: Disney World, Sea World, Kennedy Space Center, Blue Springs State Park, Universal Studios; Entertainment

Shops & Restaurants: Specialty boutiques abound, grocery store, pharmacy; Fine local seafood restaurants

Far from the crowds, but an hour's drive to most Florida attractions. Tastefully furnished condominium apartments. Lounge with entertainment, bingo, covered dish dinner. Nautilus, game and activity rooms. Most rooms have private balconies. Free HBO plus on-site movie rentals. Arcade daily activities. All units are suites with full kitchen.

We want to hear from you—any comments regarding the condos or our publication may be noted on the form at the end of the book.

NORTH REDINGTON BEACH

Ram Sea I and Ram Sea II
17200 Gulf Blvd.
North Redington Beach, FL 33708
813-397-0441

1 Bedroom $$, 2 Bedrooms $$$, 3 Bedrooms $$$
1 Bedrm/week 5$, 2 Bed/week 6$,
   3 Bed/week 6$
Min. Stay 3 Nights, AmEx/Visa/MC,
   Dep. Req'd.
60 condos, Hi-rise, Key at Front desk
No S-yes/H-yes

Location: Airport: 30 miles; Downtown: 10 min.

General Facilities: Full serv., Daily maid, Kitchen, Linens, Baby-sitter

Room Facilities: Pool, Hot tub, Windsurfing, sailing, Golf: Nearby, TV, Cable, Phone in rm., Crib-Hi-chair, Ind. AC Ctl., Ind. Heat Ctl.

Attractions: Busch Gardens, Dali Museum, Disney World, Sunken Gardens, Flea market, pier

Shops & Restaurants: Beach boutiques, small shopping plaza, Burdines; Wine Cellar/variety

Uniquely furnished units overlooking the Gulf. Bathe in the pool, jacuzzi or Gulf, or relax in a surfside cabana. Tour Disney World or go deep-sea fishing, windsurfing or sailing. Shops and restaurants within minutes.

Redington Ambassador Resort
16900 Gulf Blvd.
North Redington Beach, FL 33708
813-391-9646

2 Bedrooms $$
2 Bedrms/week 5$
Min. Stay 5 Nights, Visa/MC, Dep. Req'd. •
20 condos, Hi-rise, Key at At resort
H-yes

Location: Beach front

General Facilities: Kitchen, Linens, Baby-sitter

Room Facilities: Pool, Hot tub, TV, Cable, Phone in rm., Crib-Hi-chair, Ind. AC Ctl., Ind. Heat Ctl.

Attractions: Redington fishing pier

Shops & Restaurants: Redington Beach shops

Spacious, modern units carefully planned and decorated. Swimming pool with recreational deck area, jacuzzi and inside atrium with walks and landscaping. Built directly on the beach for those who want to splash in the surf. Walk to shops, restaurants and Redington Fishing Pier. Come to the Ambassador and enjoy the "suite life."

Please mention *Condo Vacations the Complete Guide* when you reserve your condominium.

——————————————————— ORLANDO ———————————————————

Club Orlando
5305 San Antonio St.
Orlando, FL 32809
407-351-3351 407-352-2237

1 Bedroom $$, 1 Bed/week 4$
Min. stay 2 nights, Amex, Visa, MC
Key at Front desk
60 condos, Lo-rise, H-yes •

Location: Airport: 15 miles; Downtown: 8 miles; Need car
General facilities: Full serv., Kitchen, Linens
Room facilities: TV, Cable, Crib-Hi-chair, Ind. AC. Ctl., Ind. Heat Ctl.
Sports facilities: Pool, Tennis, .5 miles to The Greens
Attractions: Universal Studios, Wet-n-Wild Sea World, Mystery Fun House
Shops & Restaurants: Florida Mall, Maison Blanche, Burdines, Belzmalls (discount), Full range of restaurants available

One bedroom, 2 bath condos centrally located to downtown entertainment, shopping, Tupperware Convention Center, Disney, Seaworld, Universal Studios, and all major attractions.

———

Orlando International Resort
5353 Del Verde Way
Orlando, FL 32819
407-351-2641 800-222-6472

2 Bedrooms $$$, 2 Bed/week 8$
Amex, Visa, MC, Dep. req'd
Key at Management office
63 condos, Lo-rise, H-yes •

Location: Airport: 9 miles; Downtown: 6 miles; Need car
General facilities: Kitchen, Linens
Room facilities: TV, VCR, Phone, Crib-Hi-chair, Ind. AC. Ctl, Ind. Heat Ctl.
Sports facilities: Pool, Tennis
Attractions: Disney World, EPCOT, Wet'N Wild, Sea World, Universal Studios
Shops & Restaurants: Beltz factory outlet, Townsend's/Florida seafood

Two bedroom luxury units with balconies and washer/dryer on Orlando's popular International Drive. Heated pool, lighted tennis courts and gas barbecue grills. Minutes away from Disney World, Wet and Wild, Universal Studios.

———

Sonesta Village Hotel
10000 Turkey Lake Rd.
Orlando, FL 32819
305-352-8051

Villas

General facilities: Kitchen
Sports facilities: Pool, Tennis
Attractions: Disney World

Villas on Sand Lake featuring lakefront beach, pool, water sports, tennis and play area for children. Just 10 minutes from Walt Disney World.

Please mention *Condo Vacations—the Complete Guide* when you reserve your condominium.

———————————— ORLANDO ————————————

The Seasons
5736 Texas Ave.
Orlando, FL 32809
407-351-3351 800-768-2341

Min. stay 2 nights, Amex, Visa, MC
Key at Front desk
48 condos, Lo-rise, H-yes •

Location: Airport: 15 miles; Downtown: 8 miles; Need car

General facilities: Full serv., Conf.fac, Kitchen, Linens, Playgound/kiddiepool, Sauna, Spa

Room facilities: TV, Cable, Phone, Crib-Hi-chair, Ind. AC. Ctl., Ind. Heat Ctl.

Sports facilities: Pool, Tennis, .5 miles to The Greens

Attractions: Universal Studios, Wet 'N Wild Sea World, Disney World, Mystery Fun House

Shops & Restaurants: Florida Mall, Maison Blanche, Burdines & Belz Malls-discount, Full range of dining available

Luxuriously decorated 2 bedroom, 2 bath villas, each with a private balcony or patio. Elegant surroundings with a casual atmosphere, convenient to all of Orlando's attractions.

The Villas of Grand Cypress   Villas
One North Jacaranda
Orlando, FL 32819
407-239-4700 800-835-7377

Location: Airport: Orlando-18 miles

General facilities: Full serv., Bus. fac., Conf. Rm. (cap. 200), Daily maid, Kitchen, Linens, Restaurant, Bar, Lounge

Room facilities: TV

Sports facilities: Tennis, 45-hole Golf course, Lake, Equestrian Center

Attractions: Walt Disney's EPCOT, Sea World, Entertainment

Shops & Restaurants: Black Swan, Ballybunion

Get on the turn-of-the century Belgian trolley for a scenic 7 mile drive throughout the resort while you decide which activities you prefer-45 hole Nicklaus designed golf course and Academy of Golf with special programs, tennis, racquetball, volleyball,water sports on Lake Windsong, 45-acre nature area for jogging/biking, or the Equestrian Center. Mediterranean Villas, sunlit interiors, vaulted ceilings, morning newspapers, evening turn-down service and twice daily housekeeping-a truly luxurious resort

---------------------------- ORLANDO ----------------------------

Ventura
3100 Raper Dairy Road
Orlando, FL 32822
407-273-8770 800-247-8417

1 Bedrm/week $$$$, 2 Bed/week 4$,
3 Bed/week 5$
Min. Stay 7 Nights, Visa/MC, Dep. Req'd.
350 condos, Lo-rise, Villas, Key at 3100 Raper Dairy Rd.
H-yes

Location: Airport: 6 miles-Orlando; Downtown: 5 miles; Need car

General Facilities: Kitchen, Linens

Room Facilities: Pool, Hot tub, Tennis, Golf: Ventura, TV, Cable, Phone in rm., Ind. AC Ctl., Ind. Heat Ctl.

Attractions: Disneyland, Sea World, Boardwalk, Baseball, Space Center, Rosie O'Grady, entertainment

Shops & Restaurants: Florida, Fashion, Altamonte & Beltz Outlet Malls; Barneys-Steak/South Seas

Live like a Floridian in garden condominiums, modern, furnished in rattan. Unwind with golf or tennis, or jog, bike or stroll down walks alive with oleanders and tropical foliage. Sunbathe on a tropical beach, splash in the Clubhouse pool, or spend the day on the shores of Lake Ventura. Symphony, ballet, opera and first-run New York shows are at Bob Carr Auditorium. Most vacation attractions are within an hour's drive. Your passport to fun and sun.

------------------------- ORMOND BEACH -------------------------

Aquarius Ocean Front Condominiums
1575 Ocean Shore Boulevard
Ormond Beach, FL 32074
904-441-2050

Ocean East Resort Club
867 S. Atlantic Ave
Ormond Beach, FL 32176
904-677-8111

1 Bedroom $$, 2 Bedroom $$, Jr. $$
1 Bedrm/week 7$, 2 Bedrm/week 8$
Min. Stay 3 Nights, AmEx/MC/Visa, Dep. 1 Night
114 condos, Hi-rise, Keys at Front desk, C-yes

Location: Airport: 15 miles; Downtown: 6 miles, Beach front

General Facilities: Full serv., Daily maid, Kitchen, Linens, Restaurant on prem., Baby sitter, Gameroom.

Room Facilities: Pool, Sauna, Hot Tub, Exercise rooms, Child planned rec., TV, Cable, Phone in rm., Ind. AC Ctl., Ind. Heat Ctl.

Attractions: Disney World, Sea World, Kennedy Space Center, Daytona Speedway, St. Augustine, entertainment.

Shops & Restaurants: Volusia Mall, Daytona Mall, Bellaire Plaza.

A complete family vacation resort that even supplies family games in your suite. Cook in your condo or dine at one of the restauranats on the property. Splash in the Atlantic, or spend your time enjoying walks on the beach, dips in the pool and all the planned recreational activities presented by the Recreation Director. Units with fully equipped kitchens, decorated in pleasant Florida style, some with direct ocean front views. Most Florida attractions are close enough for a day trip.

Indian River Plantation Resort

——————————— ORMOND BEACH ———————————

Seascape & Sunrise
Condominiums
2290 Ocean Shore Boulevard
Ormond Beach, FL 32074
904-441-1058

2 Bedrms/week 4$
Min. Stay 7 Nights, Dep. Req'd. •
39 condos, Hi-rise, Key at Office

Location: Airport: 5 miles; Downtown: 2 miles; Need car; Beach front
General Facilities: Kitchen, Linens, Game room
Room Facilities: Pool, Sauna, TV, Cable, VCR, Phone in rm., Crib, Ind. AC Ctl., Ind. Heat
Ctl.
Attractions: 1½ hours to Disney, 1 hr. St. Augustine, 1 hr. to Cape Canaveral
Shops & Restaurants: Mall with grocery, drug, clothing—2 miles; Captain Coty's

*Large vistas of glass enhance the panoramic view of the Atlantic Ocean from the living
room and master bedroom. Units are complemented by lush tropical landscaping. Walk
to the beach, swim in the pool, relax in the sauna. Minutes to places of interest.*

Traders Inn Beach Club
1355 Ocean Shore Boulevard
Ormond Beach, FL 32074
904-441-1111

1 Bedroom $
Pool, Kitchen

*A neighboring community of Daytona Beach, convenient to area attractions, malls,
restaurants and speedway. Units are oceanfront and sleep 4.*

———————————————— ORMOND-BY-THE SEA ————————————————

Ocean Beach Condominiums
2220 Ocean Shore Boulevard #106
Ormond-By-The Sea, FL 32074

———————————————— PALM BEACH GARDENS ————————————————

PGA National Club Cottages   Villas
300 Avenue Of The Champions   Pool, Kitchen, Linens
Palm Beach Gardens, FL 33418
305-627-3000 800-325-3535

Attractions: Palm Beach, jai alai, polo, horse and greyhound racing, deep-sea fishing, sailing, Health & Racquet Club, Tennis, Golf

Single-level, two and three bedroom villas with Mediterranean architecture. Vaulted ceilings, master suites with marble baths and oversized sliding glass doors opening onto screened view patios. European flavor landscaping with tiered fountains.

———————————————— PALM BEACH SHORES ————————————————

Ocean Club of Palm Beach   1 Bedroom $$, Lo-rise
155 Ocean Ave.   Linens, Phone in rm.
Palm Beach Shores, FL 33404
407-842-9966

Attractions: Golf, tennis, swimming

Sand Dunes Shores   1 Bedroom $$, 2 Bedrooms $$, Lo-rise
165 Ocean Ave.   Pool, Kitchen
Palm Beach Shores, FL 33404
407-848-2581

Attractions: Amusement Center, scuba, snorkeling, fishing, charters, jai alai, Lion Country Safari, Bicycles

Oceanfront condominiums on Singer Island, which has some of the widest beaches in the State. Pool, spa, grills and bicycles. Amusements, sports, shopping, dining and entertainment within half mile.

———————————————— PALM BEACH ————————————————

Palm Beach Resort-Beach Club   Lo-rise
3031 South Ocean Blvd.   Pool, Kitchen
Palm Beach, FL 33480
800-826-1943 800-424-1943

Attractions: Fishing, golf, tennis, polo, private boat dock

Fully equipped units between the Intracoastal Waterway and the Atlantic Ocean on Lake Worth. One block from the beach, private boat dock. The place for a leisurely vacation on the lake.

———————————————— PANAMA CITY BEACH ————————————————

Casa Blanca Resort   Pool, Kitchen, Phone in rm.
11115 U.S. Hwy 98 W   Exercise room
Panama City Beach, FL 32407
904-234-5245

The beach is right outside the door of these one bedroom units. Pool, sauna, spa, hot tubs, games and party rooms on the property.

―――――――――――――――――― PANAMA CITY BEACH ――――――――――――――――――

Colonial Shores Condominiums   Lo-rise
8512 Surf Dr.   Pool, Daily maid, Kitchen
Panama City Beach, FL 32407
904-234-6054

Turn-of-the-century charm in quiet neighborhood, steps away from the beach and an easy drive to restaurants, State park, fishing fleet and golf.

Continental Condominiums   Studio $$, 1 Bedroom $$, 2 Bedrooms $$$
15413 W. Hwy. 98   1 Bedrm/week 5$, 2 Bed/week 6$
Panama City Beach, FL 32407   Min. Stay 2 Nights, AmEx/Visa/MC,
904-234-3720 800-222-2728   Dep. Req'd.
    111 condos, Hi-rise, Key at Main complex office
    No S-yes/H-yes

Location: Airport: 20 miles; Downtown: 16 miles; Need car; Beach front

General Facilities: Daily maid, Kitchen, Linens, Baby-sitter

Room Facilities: Pool, Fishing, sailboats, Golf: 2 miles, TV, Cable, Phone in rm., Crib, Ind. AC Ctl., Ind. Heat Ctl.

Attractions: Amusement Park with Shipwreck Island, water slides, go-cart track, Sportspark, Gulf World

Shops & Restaurants: Food World, Winn-Dixie, fast foods, 6-movie theater; Capt. Anderson's, Boar's Head

Classically appointed vacation residences in the center of the "World's Most Beautiful Beaches." Dolphin & Sea Life shows, amusement-shopping centers, Sports park and famous restaurants, fishing pier, all a short walk away. Family condos, individually owned and decorated.

Dunes of Panama   1 Bedroom $$, 2 Bedrooms $$, Hi-rise
Bldg. C, 7205 Thomas Dr.   Pool, Kitchen
Panama City Beach, FL 32407
800-874-0751 800-874-2412

Attractions: Picnic pavilion, Tennis

How about a night swim cooled by the Gulf evening breezes or some night tennis? Graciously furnished with Gulf views near golf, shopping and amusements. 3 pools, sauna, jacuzzi, clubhouse and picnic pavilion on this lavish resort.

Edgewater Beach Resort   1 Bedroom $$, 2 Bedrooms $$
11212 W. Hwy. 98A
Panama City Beach, FL 32407
800-874-8686 800-327-8686

Choice of Towers, Gulf Front or Golf Villa condominiums in this tropical seaside resort in this self-contained environment secured by gatehouses. Pedestrian overpass to golf, tennis, shuffleboard, lagoon pool and beach. Shopping village adjacent.

──────────────── PANAMA CITY BEACH ────────────────

Endless Summer Condominiums   1 Bedroom $
Front Beach Rd. Hwy 98-Shalimar St   Pool, Kitchen, Phone in rm.
Panama City Beach, FL 32407
904-234-9205

Quality constructed units with unrestricted Gulf access. Clubhouse, swimming pool, shuffleboard. Professionally landscaped.

Gulf Highlands Beach Resort   2 Bedrooms $$, Lo-rise
10997 W. Alt. 98   Pool, Kitchen
Panama City Beach, FL 32407
904-235-1591 800-826-1442

Townhomes finished in stucco with weathered grey accents, 2 bedrooms, 1.5 baths, ceiling fans, private parking. Private beach, large sunning decks, pools surrounded by green lawns, tennis, shuffleboard, putting greens, volleyball. Children welcomed.

Gulfgate Condominiums   1 Bedroom $$, 2 Bedrooms $$, Hi-rise
8200 Surf Dr.   Pool, Kitchen
Panama City Beach, FL 32407
904-234-3623

Open your wall of glass and step onto your private patio to view the ocean and beach activities. Swimming and wading pools, saunas and dressing rooms. Everything for the recreational minded family can be found at Panama City Beach.

Horizon South I Condominiums   1 Bedroom $, 2 Bedrooms $, Lo-rise
17462 West Highway 98   Pool, Kitchen
Panama City Beach, FL 32407
904-234-6633

Bright, attractively furnished residences overlooking an uncluttered white sand beach. Recreation area has 2 swimming pools, sauna, billiards, table tennis, shuffleboard. Two lighted tennis courts, minature golf, video game room.

Horizon South II Condominiums   1 Bedroom $, 2 Bedrooms $$, 3 Bedrooms $$
17462 W. Hwy. 98   1 Bedrm/week $$$$, 2 Bed/week 4$,
Panama City Beach, FL 32407   3 Bed/week 5$
904-234-8329 800-334-4010   Min. Stay 3 Nights, AmEx/Visa/MC,
Dep. Req'd.
152 condos, Villas, Key at office, No S-yes/H-yes

Location: Airport: 12 miles; Need car
General Facilities: Conf. rm. cap. 80, Kitchen, Linens, Game room, Baby-sitter
Room Facilities: Pool, Sauna, Tennis, Shufflebrd, Mini-golf, TV, Cable, Ind. AC Ctl., Ind. Heat Ctl.
Shops & Restaurants: Boars Head-seafood

A family oriented resort community in a friendly, relaxed atmosphere of fun and entertainment. Palm trees and shrubbery lead your way to the beach across the road and the pool and club facilities in the middle of the property. Putt-putt, tennis court, baby pool, shuffleboard, pool tables, table tennis and exercise room. Large clubhouse with kitchen, television room and activity room.

———————————— PANAMA CITY BEACH ————————————

Landmark Holiday Beach Resort   1 Bedroom $, 2 Bedrooms $$, 3 Bedrooms $$
17501 U.S. Highway 98 W.   1 Bedrm/week $$$$, 2 Bed/week 4$,
Panama City Beach, FL 32407   3 Bed/week 4$
904-235-3100 800-433-7059   Min. Stay 2 Nights, AmEx/Visa/MC,
Dep. Req'd. •
95 condos, Hi-rise, Key at At the resort

Location: Airport: 15 miles; Downtown: 5 miles; Beach front

General Facilities: Full serv., Kitchen, Game room, Lounge, Baby-sitter, Child planned rec.: Ice cream social

Room Facilities: Pool, Sauna, Hot tub, Golf: Nearby, TV, Cable, Phone in rm., Crib-Hi-chair, Ind. AC Ctl., Ind. Heat Ctl.

Attractions: Amusement Park, miniature golf, water slides, cruise ships with dining/dancing, state park, entertainment

Shops & Restaurants: Promenade Mall, Panama City Mall; The Lighthouse/seafood

Warm, inviting white sand beaches; unsurpassed boating and fishing; manicured golf courses; tennis and water sports. Condominiums overlook the Gulf of Mexico and white sands beach, and are designer decorated with tropical touches. Wine and cheese parties, bingo, continental breakfast, and children's ice cream social.

The Landmark Holiday Beach Resort
17501 US Highway 98
Panama City Beach, FL 32407
904-235-1118

Quality accommodations created for your vacation fun. Hi-rise condominium with gulf front view from private balconies. Spa, sauna, indoor pool and tennis.

Largo Mar   1 Bedroom $$, 2 Bedrooms $$$, 3 Bedrooms
5715 Thomas Drive $$$$
Panama City Beach, FL 32407   1 Bedrm/week 5$, 2 Bed/week 6$,
904-234-5750 800-645-2746   3 Bed/week 10$
Min. Stay 3 Nights, Visa/MC, Dep. Req'd. •
72 condos, Lo-rise, Key at Office-from security

Location: Airport: 8 miles; Downtown: 15 miles; Need car; Beach front

General Facilities: Kitchen, Linens, Game room

Room Facilities: Pool, Sauna, Hot tub, TV, Cable, Phone in rm., Ind. AC Ctl., Ind. Heat Ctl.

Attractions: Fishing, pleasure cruises, dining, dancing, gambling, Shipwreck Island

Shops & Restaurants: Alvins Island & Panama City Malls, gift shops; Capt. Anderson's, Hamilton's

A family place located on the Gulf of Mexico. Golfing, swimming, sailing, boating, sunning-it's all here. Full-time security and the greatest sunsets on the world's most beautiful beaches.

——————————— PANAMA CITY BEACH ———————————

Latitude 29
21703 W. Hwy. 98
Panama City Beach, FL 32407
904-234-5583

1 Bedroom $$, Lo-rise, Villas
Pool, Kitchen

Versatile one-bedroom units become two by using the living room as a bedroom at night. Architecturally attractive condominiums with large pool and private beach. Minutes drive to golf, tennis, fishing, restaurants and amusements.

Mariner East & West Condominiums
6211-6213 Thomas Drive
Panama City Beach, FL 32407
904-234-9468

1 Bedroom $$, Hi-rise
Pool, Daily maid, Kitchen, Linens

Convenience and comfort in a fine resort. Swim or sunbathe by the pool, collect shells along the beach, play tennis or shuffleboard. Game room with pool table, video games and ping pong. Lounge area, exercise room, saunas.

Moondrifter
8815 Thomas Drive
Panama City Beach, FL 32407
904-234-5564 800-232-6636

1 Bedroom $$, 2 Bedrooms $$
1 Bedrm/week $$$$, 2 Bed/week 4$
Min. Stay 2 Nights, AmEx/Visa/MC,
Dep. Req'd., Hi-rise, No S-yes/H-yes

Location: Airport: 15 miles; Downtown: 7 miles; Need car; Beach front

General Facilities: Full serv., Bus. fac., Kitchen, Linens, Game room, Lounge, Baby-sitter

Room Facilities: Pool, Sauna, Hot tub, Tennis, Shuffleboard, Golf: Near Signal Hill, TV, Cable, VCR, Phone in rm., Crib-Hi-chair, Ind.AC Ctl., Ind. Heat Ctl.

Attractions: Gulf World, glass bottom boats, deep-sea fishing, snorkeling

Shops & Restaurants: Shopping center, food, gifts; Capt. Anderson/seafood

View the crystal clear waters of the Gulf of Mexico from your private balcony. Swim in the pool or beach, sail, fish, play tennis or shuffleboard.

Moonspinner Condominiums
4425 Thomas Dr.
Panama City Beach, FL 32407
904-234-8900 800-223-3947

2 Bedrooms $$$, 3 Bedrooms $$$
2 Bedrms/week 6$, 3 Bed/week 9$
Min. Stay 3 Nights, AmEx/Visa/MC,
Dep. Req'd.
162 condos, Hi-rise, Key at Reserv. office

Location: Airport: 5 miles; Downtown: 12 miles; Beach front

General Facilities: Conf. rm. cap. 100, Daily maid, Kitchen, Linens, Game room, Baby-sitter

Room Facilities: Pool, Sauna, Hot tub, Tennis, TV, Cable, Phone in rm., Crib-Hi-chair, Ind. AC Ctl., Ind. Heat Ctl.

Attractions: Beach resort activities, dog track, cruises, fishing

Shops & Restaurants: Gayfers, Sears, Penney; Capt. Andersons, Boars Head

Complex with full-time security staff and friendly personnel to serve you. Oceanfront pool, rental sailboats, beach service which even provides tanning lotion. Shuffleboard, day and night tennis. Adjacent to St. Andrew State Park and minutes to Panama City Beach.

PANAMA CITY BEACH

Nautical Watch Condominiums
6205 Thomas Dr.
Panama City Beach, FL 32407
904-234-6876 800-621-2462

1 Bedroom $, 2 Bedrooms $$, 3 Bedrooms $$
1 Bedrm/week $$$$, 2 Bed/week $$$$,
  3 Bed/week $$$$
Min. Stay 3 Nights, Visa/MC, Dep. Req'd.
81 condos, Lo-rise, Key at Nautical Watch

Location: Airport: 5 miles; Downtown: 1.5 mi.; Need car; Beach front

General Facilities: Kitchen, Linens

Room Facilities: Pool, TV, Cable, Ind. AC Ctl., Ind. Heat Ctl.

Attractions: Trips to Shell Island, dinner cruises from Capt. Anderson's, summer-the Miracle Strip

Shops & Restaurants: Promenade Mall, Panama City Mall, St. Thomas square; Captain Anderson's/seafood

Beautifully furnished condominiums with beach or pool views. Close to fine restaurants and entertainment. Take a trip to Shell Island or enjoy a dinner cruise.

Ocean Terrace Condominiums
8618 Surf Dr.
Panama City Beach, FL 32407
904-234-5631

1 Bedroom $, 2 Bedrooms $$, Lo-rise
Pool, Daily maid, Kitchen

Attractions: Kiddie pool

A small complex catering to family groups. Sun deck with gazebo and kiddie pool, large pool overlooking the gulf, barbecues, cable and HBO. The ideal place for a quiet, peaceful vacation.

Ocean Towers Beach Club
11211 West Highway 98
Panama City Beach, FL 32407
904-235-4050

Hi-rise
Pool, Kitchen, Phone in rm.

Attractions: Exercise room, Golf

Twin towers of this complex border on the clubhouse with enjoyment for the whole family. Free golf and tennis nearby, bicycles, barbecue and heated pool.

Oceanna Condominiums
8000 Surf Dr.
Panama City Beach, FL 32407
904-234-9384

1 Bedroom $$, Lo-rise
Pool, Daily maid, Kitchen, Linens

Attractions: Amusement Parks, deep sea fishing, golf, Shuffleboard

Fully furnished units on the beach away from congestion. Courtyard with gazebo overlooking the pool with picnic tables and barbecue grills.

The Beach Club

——————————— PANAMA CITY BEACH ———————————

Panama City Resort & Club   Studio $, 1 Bedroom $$$$
16709 W. Hwy 98   1 Bedrm/week $$
Panama City Beach, FL 32407   Min. Stay 2 Nights, Visa/MC, Dep. Req'd. •
904-235-2002   40 condos, Hi-rise, Key at At resort

Location: Airport: 17 miles; Downtown: 20 miles; Need car; Beach front

General Facilities: Full serv., Kitchen, Linens, Game room, Baby-sitter

Room Facilities: Pool, Hot tub, Tennis, Free golf, Golf: 3 miles east, TV, Cable, Phone in rm., Crib-Hi-chair, Ind. AC Ctl., Ind. Heat Ctl.

Attractions: Gulf World Dolphin Show, Casino & Dolphin cruises, two amusement parks, entertainment

Shops & Restaurants: Shops at Edgewater, Magic Mountain; Capt.Andersons-seafood

Friendly, informal atmosphere in this family resort located on the beach. Play golf, tennis, fish, swim, sail, horse races and jai alai. Welcome breakfast on Saturday, potluck lunch, bingo, scavenger hunt and crazy hat contest. Varied pleasures in this year-round playground-relaxed or active, exotic or romantic, peaceful or lively, or a combination of all these.

──────────────── PANAMA CITY BEACH ────────────────

Pelican Walk
6905 Thomas Drive
Panama City Beach, FL 32407
904-234-9255

1 Bedroom $$, 2 Bedrooms $$, 3 Bedrooms $$$
1 Bedrm/week 4$, 2 Bed/week 6$,
3 Bed/week 7$
Min. Stay 2 Nights, AmEx/Visa/MC,
Dep. Req'd. •
Hi-rise
No S-yes/P-yes/H-yes

Location: Airport: 15 miles; Downtown: 7 miles; Need car; Beach front

General Facilities: Full serv., Bus. fac., Kitchen, Linens, Game room, Lounge

Room Facilities: Pool, Sauna, Hot tub, Tennis, Racquetball, Shuffleboard, Golf: Near Signal Hill, TV, Cable, VCR, Phone in rm., Crib-Hi-chair, Ind.AC Ctl., Ind. Heat Ctl.

Attractions: Gulf World, amusement parks, glass bottom boat, deep sea fishing, windsurfing

Shops & Restaurants: Shopping center, food, gifts; Capt. Anderson/seafood

Four spacious floor plans with contemporary furnishings, ideally located. Two level clubhouse, social lounge, racquetball, saunas, glass enclosed whirlpool solarium, tennis and 2 beachside pools.

Pinnacle Port Condominiums
23223 W. Hwy. 98
Panama City Beach, FL 32407
904-234-8813 800-874-8823

1 Bedroom $$, 2 Bedrooms $$, Hi-rise
Pool, Kitchen, Phone in rm.

Attractions: Golf, amusement attractions, shopping, Shuffleboard, Tennis

Jutting out into the blue-green waters of the Gulf of Mexico and surrounded by natural landscaping, Pinnacle Port has half mile of secluded beach. Leave your boat at the dock so you're ready for water-skiing, sailing or fishing. Use the beach, two pools.

Portside Resort
17620 West Alt. Hwy. 98
Panama City Beach, FL 32407
904-235-0244 800-443-2737

2 Bedrooms $$
Pool, Kitchen, Linens

Attractions: Shuffleboard, Tennis

Palms, evergreens and flowering plants surround the tennis courts, clubhouse, shuffleboard and pools. The main pool features a Polynesian thatched palapa surrounded by two freeform pools and a cascading waterfall. Decorator furnished two-story townhomes.

Subscribe to our newsletter *The Condo-Line* and hear about the latest special condo vacation values.

———————————— PANAMA CITY BEACH ————————————

Ramsgate Harbour
23011 W. Hwy.
Panama City Beach, FL 32407
904-235-2667 800-423-1889

2 Bedrooms $$$
2 Bedrms/week 6$
Min. Stay 3 Nights, Visa/MC, Dep.
Required •
66 condos, Lo-rise, Key at On-site office
No S-yes

Location: Airport: 30 minutes; Downtown: 30 min; Beach front
General Facilities: Daily maid; Linens
Sports Facilities: Game room; Pool; Shuffleboard; Bay Point Lagoon 20 min.
Room Facilities: Kitchen; Cable; Phone; Ind.AC.Ctl; Ind.Heat Ctl.
Attractions: Miracle Strip Amusement Park-Shipwreck Island Water Park-Shell
Island-Casino cruise ship
Shops & Restaurants: Panama City Mall, Promenade Mall, outdoor market;
Captain Anderson's/seafood

*Stucco and weathered grey cedar, enclosed stairwells and covered balconies with
Gulf views set among lighted tropical landscaping. Private beach, sun deck, pool and
clubhouse with refrigerator, sink and restrooms. Carpeted condominiums with
quarry tile in kitchen, baths and foyer. Washer and dryer, ceiling fans.*

———————————————————————————————————————

Seachase Condominiums
17351 Front Beach Rd.
Panama City Beach, FL 32407
904-235-1300 800-457-2051
FAX: 904-235-4854

2 Bedrooms $$$
Min. Stay 2 Nights, Disc/Visa/MC,
Dep. Required •
64 condos, Hi-rise
Key at Office on property, H-Yes

Location: Airport: 15 miles; Downtown: 15 miles; Beachfront
General Facilities: Linens; Crib-Hi-chair
Sports Facilities: Pool; Volleyball, wave runners; Golf Course nearby
Room Facilities: Kitchen; Cable; Phone; Ind.AC.Ctl; Ind.Heat Ctl.
Attractions: Amusement & water parks, Putt-Putt golf, Gulf World "The world's
most beautiful beaches"; Entertainment
Shops & Restaurants: Individual shops, grocery, gifts, pharmacy, liquor; Boars
Head—Prime Rib/Seafood

*Luxurious condos, directly on the beach with view from ceiling to floor of the world's
most beautiful beaches. Excellent seafood restaurants and beach shopping within
walking distance. A family-oriented condominium. Colors vary from peach and
seafoam green to misty mauve and blues. Airy modern wicker furniture. Facilities
include washer/dryer, dishwasher, microwave and trash compactor. Units are available for rent or sale.*

──────────────── PANAMA CITY BEACH ────────────────

St. Andrew Bay Resort Mgmt. Inc.
726 Thomas Drive
Panama City Beach, FL 32408
904-235-4075 800-621-2462
FAX: 904-769-3939

Min. Stay: 3 Nights, Visa/MC, •
400 condos, Hi-rise, Lo-rise, Villas, H-yes,
Key at check-in offices.

Location: Airport: 15-20 minutes; Downtown: 20 minutes, Beach front.

General Facilities: Lounge, Pool, Hot tub, Tennis, Golf nearby, Bar.

Room Facilities: Daily maid, Kitchen, TV, Cable, VCR, Phone, Ind. AC. Ctl., Ind. Heat Ctl.

Attractions: Day trips: Florida Caverns, Falling Waters, Wakulla Springs, Shell Island, Eden Mansion.

Shops & Restaurants: Panama City Mall offers Gayers, J. C. Penney, specialty shops, Capt. Anderson's.

We've got the sand . . . we've got the sun . . . we've got the water and all that goes with it to make Panama City Beach one of the favorite vacation spots in Florida. Townhouses and condominiums on the Gulf or across the street priced to fit all budgets. Lie back and relax on the beautiful beaches, or use your vacation time for fishing, diving, golf, tennis and boating.

───

Summer House
6505 Thomas Dr.
Panama City Beach, FL 32407
904-234-1112 800-354-1112

1 Bedroom $$, 2 Bedrooms $$.
Hi-rise condos.
Pool, Shuffleboard, Racquetball.
Kitchen.

Continuously upgraded units, clean and well-kept on a pearly white beach. Beautifully landscaped grounds, friendly personnel and security guards to ensure your privacy. Lounge by one of the pools near the gazebo, play tennis or games in the lobby gameroom.

───

Sunbird
8850 S. Thomas Drive
Panama City Beach, FL 32407
904-235-4300 800-433-8240

1 Bedroom $$.
Hi-rise condos.
Pool, Tennis, Shuffleboard.
Kitchen, Phone.

Contemporary style furnishings in gulf front condominiums. Five different one bedroom floor plans. Three pools, large deck, clubhouse and game room.

───

The Summit
8743 Thomas Dr.
Panama City Beach, FL 32407
904-234-7890 800-824-5048

1 Bedroom $$, 2 Bedrooms.
Hi-rise condos
Pool, Tennis, Weight rooms.
Kitchen, Phone.

Gulfside highrise condominiums with 24 hour security. Tennis, pools, weight rooms, whirlpools, hot tubs and snack bar.

─────────────────── PANAMA CITY BEACH ───────────────────

Tropical Breeze
1701 W. Hwy. 98
Panama City Beach, FL 32407
904-234-2228

─────────────────── PANAMA CITY ───────────────────

Bay Point Yacht and Country Club   1 Bedrm/week $$$$, 2 Bed/week $$$$,
100 Delwood Beach Rd., Box 314   3 Bed/week 4$
Panama City, FL 32407   Min. Stay 7 Nights, AmEx/Visa/MC,
904-234-1618 800-543-3307   Dep. Req'd.
                                        557 condos, Lo-rise, Key at Bay Pt. office

General Facilities: Conf. rm. cap. 44, Daily maid, Kitchen, Linens, Restaurant on
prem., Bar on prem., Lounge, Baby-sitter

Room Facilities: Pool, Sauna, Tennis, Health club, bikes, Golf: 2 18-hole courses, TV,
Cable, Phone in rm.

Attractions: Shell Island, Gulf of Mexico fishing, marina, deep sea/sailing charters,
entertainment

Shops & Restaurants: The Terrace Court/nouvelle

Privately owned villas meeting the high decor and equipment standards of the Club. 5 minute drive to public beaches, or launch to undeveloped, isolated beaches. Marina with 154 slips, children's play area, driving range, tennis, golf and health club. There is always music someplace at the Club, fashion shows and theme parties. Proper golf or tennis attire must be worn on the course and courts. An outstanding resort combining casual luxury with southern charm and service by an experienced staff.

─────────────────── PENSACOLA BEACH ───────────────────

Holiday Beach Resort   2 Bedrooms $$, Lo-rise
19 Via Deluna   Pool, Kitchen, Linens
Pensacola Beach, FL 32561
904-436-4500

Attractions: Spa, Tennis

On the quiet side of Pensacola Beach for a beach vacation and sightseeing in historic Pensacola. Fishing pier, pool, beach, spa, tennis and whirlpool tubs.

Palm Beach Club Condominiums
1390 Fort Pickens Rd.
Pensacola Beach, FL 32561
904-932-1399 800-932-6667

Sabine Yacht & Racquet Club   1 Bedroom $$, 2 Bedrooms $$
330 Fort Pickens Rd.   Pool, Kitchen, Phone in rm.
Pensacola Beach, FL 32561
904-932-7290 800-343-0344

Attractions: Exercise room, Tennis

1, 2, and 3 bedrooms units on the azure waters of Sabine Bay. Pool, exercise room, boat dock, tennis, large balconies.

─────────────────── PENSACOLA BEACH ───────────────────

Tristan Towers
1200 Fort Pickens Rd.
Pensacola Beach, FL 32561
904-932-9341 800-826-0614

2 Bedrooms $$, 3 Bedrooms $$
2 Bedrms/week 4$, 3 Bed/week 5$
Min. Stay 3 Nights, Visa/MC, Dep. Req'd.
90 condos, Hi-rise, Key at Office

Location: Airport: 10 miles; Downtown: 5 miles

General Facilities: Kitchen, Linens

Room Facilities: Pool, Tennis, Putting green, TV, Cable, Phone in rm., Crib-Hi-chair, Ind. AC Ctl., Ind. Heat Ctl.

New beautiful 15-story white building with blue trim on the beach. Tennis, Olympic-size pool, Clubhouse with fireplace, lighted tennis courts, putting green. Residences have washer/dryers and large closets. Boardwalk to beach gazebo, picnic tables and barbecues on a grassy area by the private beach.

─────────────────── PENSACOLA ───────────────────

Perdido Towers
16785 Perdido Key Dr.
Pensacola, FL 32507
904-492-2809 800-492-2809

2 Bedroom $$$$, 3 Bedroom $$$$
2 Bedrm/week 7$, 3 Bedrm/week 8$
Min. Stay 3 Nights, MC/Visa, Dep. Req'd
66 condos, Hi-rise, Keys at Office, No S-yes, H-yes

Location: Airport: 22 miles; Downtown: 22 miles, Beach front

General Facilities:, Daily maid, Kitchen, Linens, Baby sitter

Room Facilities: Pool, Tennis, Racquetball, TV, Cable, VCR, Phone in rm., Ind. AC Ctl., Ind. Heat Ctl.

Attractions: Beach, boat-fishing, golf, zoo's, Gulfarium, Pensacola, Naval museum.

Shops & Restaurants: Malls, factory outlet shopping center in Foley, The Oyster Bar/seafood

All the comforts of home with resort amenities. All apartments on Gulfside, fully equipped, spacious and most are professionally decorated. Tropical beach decor, sleeper sofas, washers and dryers. 28-slip boat dock and launching ramp on Old River. Pool, raised sundeck, tennis, racquetball, views. Quiet complex, excellent security.

─────────────────── PERDIDO KEY, PENSACOLA ───────────────────

Vista Del Mar Condominiums
13-333 Johnson Beach Road
Perdido Key, Pensacola, FL 32507
904-492-0211

1 Bedrm/week $$$$, 2 Bed/week $$$$, 3 Bed/week 4$
Min. Stay 4 Nights, Dep. Req'd.
64 condos, Hi-rise, Key at Office on property

Location: Airport: 40 Minutes; Downtown: 9 miles; Need car; Beach front

General Facilities: Kitchen, Linens

Room Facilities: Pool, Tennis, Cable, Phone in rm., Crib-Hi-chair, Ind. AC Ctl., Ind. Heat Ctl.

Attractions: Gulf Islands Nat. Seashore, jet ski, sailing, boating, para-sailing, fish.

Adjacent to the Gulf Islands National Seashore with 20 miles of rolling dunes. Excellent surf fishing, plus sailing, jet skiing, wind surfing, speed boating and para-sailing. Several championship golf courses are nearby. Historic Pensacola is just 15 minutes away with many museums and gourmet dining.

———————————————— PERDIDO KEY ————————————————

Sandy Key Condominiums   2 Bedrooms $$
13575 Perdido Key Dr.   Hi-rise
Perdido Key, FL 32507
904-492-3084 800-351-8266
Sports Facilities: Pool; Tennis; Exercise facility; Golf
Room Facilities: Kitchen

Casually furnished, sliding glass doors to oversize balcony with its tables and chairs for dining or relaxing, whirlpool tub in master bath. Adjacent to Gulf Islands National Seashore. On-site tennis, spa, health facililty, volleyball, basketball, steam room, and pool.

Sea Spray Luxury   2 Bedrooms $$
Condominiums   Hi-rise
16287 Perdido Key Dr.
Perdido Key, FL 32507
904-492-2200 800-824-2231
General Facilities: Linens
Sports Facilities: Pool; Tennis; Exercise room
Room Facilities: Kitchen

Get ready for beach fun or launch your boat at the marina. Three buildings with 2 and 3 bedroom units. Complete use of all amenities inclluding pools, spa, tennis, exercise and rec room.

Shipwatch Condominium   Hi-rise
16787 Perdido Key Dr.
Perdido Key, FL 32507
904-492-0111 800-228-3732
General Facilities: Linens
Sports Facilities: Pool; Tennis; Health club
Room Facilities: Kitchen; Cable; Phone

Make the Gulf your personal playground, or try Old River for water-skiing and fishing. High ceilings, marble vanities, recessed lighting. Pool, health club, spa, sauna, 3 lighted tennis courts. Choose between 2-bedroom/2-bath and 3-bedroom/2-bath individually decorated units. Kitchens are fully equipped.

Sundown Condominium
16470 Perdido Key Dr.
Perdido Key, FL 32507
904-492-1816
General Facilities: Linens
Sports Facilities: Pool; Tennis; Golf
Room Facilities: Kitchen; Phone

Exceptionally spacious units half way between Gulf Shores and Pensacola. Close to the Gulf and Perdido Bay for sailing, fishing and shrimping. Pool and tennis. Minutes to golf.

──────────── POMPANO BEACH ────────────

Canada House Beach Club
1704 North Ocean Boulevard
Pompano Beach, FL 33062
305-942-8200

Studio $, 1 Bedroom $$
Min. Stay 2 Nights, AmEx/Visa/MC,
   Dep. Req'd. •
88 condos, Hi-rise, Key at Front desk
H-yes

Location: Airport: 12 miles; Need car; Beach front

General Facilities: Full serv., Daily maid, Kitchen, Linens, Restaurant on prem., Baby-sitter

Room Facilities: Pool, Hot tub, Minature golf, TV, Cable, Phone in rm., Crib-Hi-chair, Ind. AC Ctl., Ind. Heat Ctl.

Attractions: Cruises from local port (Everglades), fishing, golf, tennis facilities available nearby, entertainment

Shops & Restaurants: Pompano Fashion Square, Burdines, Penny; Sea Watch-Harris-Chinese

Uncluttered, homelike atmosphere with modern style rattan furnishings. Two swimming pools, shuffleboard, putting green, barbecue facilities, bicycles, paddle boats, and Wednesday night cook-outs. Full-time activities director on staff. Game fishing in the Gulf Stream or Bahamas, horse racing, nightlife, or just bask in the sun and enjoy a memorable Florida vacation.

La Costa Beach Club Resort
1504 N. Ocean Blvd.
Pompano Beach, FL 33062
305-942-4900

1 Bedroom $$, 2 Bedrooms $$
Pool, Kitchen, Phone in rm.

Attractions: Ex. room, shuffleboard

All new furnishings in these individually owned condominiums. If the weather should turn cold, use the indoor pool and jacuzzi. Beach and outdoor pool for the usual sunny days.

Ocean Ranch and Villas
1110 South Ocean Boulevard
Pompano Beach, FL 33062
305-941-7100

1 Bedroom $, Lo-rise
Pool, Daily maid, Kitchen, Linens, Phone in rm.

Attractions: Putting green

You'll have access to 250 feet of private beach when you stay at Ocean Ranch with its pool, whirlpool, rental cabanas, exercise room and putting greens. Dining room, piano lounge and glass-enclosed patio bar for relaxation after a day at the beach. Nightclub tours.

Palm Ocean Villas
1430 South Ocean Boulevard
Pompano Beach, FL 33062
305-941-7330

1 Bedroom $$, Lo-rise
Pool, Kitchen

Attractions: Tennis

Let the staff make all arrangements for the many sports and entertainment facilities, or stay at your Villa and do nothing except swim in the ocean or pool. If you bring your boat, there is free boat dockage.

─────────────── POMPANO BEACH ───────────────

Sea Garden
615 N. Ocean Blvd.
Pompano Beach, FL 33062
305-943-6200 800-327-8920

Studio $$, 1 Bedroom $$, 2 Bedrooms $$
1 Bedrm/week 4$, 2 Bed/week 5$
AmEx/Visa/MC, Dep. 1 Night •
40 condos, Lo-rise, Key at Front desk
H-yes

Location: Airport: 10 miles; Downtown: 4 miles; Need car; Beach front

General Facilities: Full serv., Bus. fac., Conf. rm. cap. 300, Daily maid, Kitchen, Linens, Restaurant on prem., Bar on prem., Lounge, Baby-sitter

Room Facilities: Pool, Hot tub, Tennis, Volleyball, Golf: Pompano Municipal close, TV, Cable, Phone in rm., Crib-Hi-chair, Ind. AC Ctl., Ind. Heat Ctl.

Attractions: One day Bahama cruises, Everglades, Jungle Queen & Paddlewheel Queen tours, jai alai, entertainment

Shops & Restaurants: Pompano Fashion Square, Galleria & Town Cntr. Malls; Rinaldo's/It-Le Vieulle Maison

Tropical settinng and lush gardens set on 7.5 acres with 300 feet of beachfront. Restaurant and lounge, two bars with piano entertainment, two pools and fourteen tennis courts.

───────────────────────────────────

Sea Side Beach Club
501 Briny Ave.
Pompano Beach, FL 33062
305-941-7650

1 Bedroom $$, 2 Bedrooms $$
Pool, Kitchen

Attractions: Jai alai, dog races, golf, tennis, concerts, discos

Designer coordinated suites for contemporary living. Lay on the beach or by the pool for complete relaxation, or be active and participate in area sports. 5 minute walk to fishing pier, and a short drive to Fort Lauderdale nightlife.

───────────────────────────────────

Surf Rider Resort Condominium
1441 S. Ocean Blvd. (AIA)
Pompano Beach, FL 33062
305-785-8991

1 Bedroom $$, 2 Bedrooms $$
Pool, Kitchen, Phone in rm.

Attractions: 200-foot dock, Tennis

Intimate villa hideaways with designer furnishings. Private beach, olympic pool, tennis, docking facilities. Gold Coast restaurants, nightlife and boutiques.

─────────────── PUNTA GORDA ───────────────

Burnt Store Marina Resort
3150 Matecumbe Key Road
Punta Gorda, FL 33955
813-481-3636 800-237-8906

1 Bedroom $$, 2 Bedrooms $$$, Lo-rise
Pool, Kitchen

Attractions: Sailing, boating, fishing, tennis, golf, Marina

Complete resort with 400 wet slip marina and fuel dock. Emphasis on marine recreation, but there is also golf, tennis and a heated pool. Condominiums and lanais overlooking the marina, golf course or pool. Live entertainment in the lounge and property restaurant.

─────────────── PUNTA GORDO ───────────────

Fishermen's Village Resort Club   1 Bedroom $$, Lo-rise
1200 W. Retta Esplande   Pool, Kitchen
Punta Gorda, FL 33950
813-639-8721

Attractions: Tennis

Apartments with king-size bed in master bedroom, den sleeper sofa and loft area with two twin beds. Above 30 fashion, gift, and specialty shops and 8 restaurants. Balconies over-look the harbor with its 98-slip yacht basin. Pool and tennis.

─────────────── REDINGTON BEACH ───────────────

Suncoast Resort Rentals
16401 Gulf Blvd.
Redington Beach, FL 33708
800-237-6586

Dune House Condominiums

—————————————— REDINGTON SHORES ——————————————

San Remo
18320 Gulf Blvd.
Redington Shores, FL 33708
813-398-5591

2 Bedrms/week 5$, 3 Bed/week 6$
Min. Stay 7 Nights, AmEx/Visa/MC,
Dep. Req'd. •
87 condos, Hi-rise, Key at On-site office
P-yes/H-yes

Location: Airport: Tampa 30 minutes; Beach front

General Facilities: Daily maid, Kitchen, Linens

Room Facilities: Pool, Hot tub, Tennis, Volleyball, Golf: Nearby, TV, Cable, Phone in rm., Crib-Hi-chair, Ind. AC Ctl., Ind. Heat Ctl.

Attractions: Disney World, Sea World, Sunken Gardens, Busch Gardens, Wax Museum, Tiki Gardens

Shops & Restaurants: Tyrone shopping mall, Seminole Mall, other shops; Wine Cellar/Ger.-Amer.-French

Very large units that look like houses, high ceilings, lots of windows and large porches. Tennis across the street, storage for bikes, skateboards, surf and sailboards. Laundry rooms in units. Walk to shops, parks, fishing and restaurants.

—————————————— SANIBEL ISLAND ——————————————

Caribe Beach Resort
2669 W. Gulf Dr., P.O. Box 158
Sanibel Island, FL 33957
813-472-1166

Studio $, 1 Bedroom $
1 Bedrm/week $$$$
Visa/MC, Dep. 1 Night
27 condos, Lo-rise, Key at Office
H-yes

Location: Airport: 25 miles; Downtown: 1 mile; Need car; Beach front

General Facilities: Daily maid, Kitchen, Linens

Room Facilities: Pool, Hot tub, Horseshoes, volleyball, TV, Cable, Phone in rm., Crib-Hi-chair, Ind. AC Ctl., Ind. Heat Ctl.

Attractions: Wildlife refuge, underdeveloped surroundings for shelling and boating

Shops & Restaurants: Unique shops all over the Island; Casual seafood restaurants

When you want to get away from it all. Relax on the beach in the Florida sunshine and work on your tan. Collect shells, go biking, or explore the wildlife refuge. When you're ready to eat retire to the lovely groove area with picnic tables and charcoal grills for easy barbecueing right on the edge of the beach. Pool, spa, horseshoes, shuffleboard and volleyball, if you must exercise.

———————————————————————————————————————

Casa Ybel Resort
2255 W. Gulf Dr., P.O. Box 167
Sanibel Island, FL 33957
813-481-3636 800-282-8906

1 Bedroom $$, 2 Bedrooms $$$, Villas
Pool, Daily maid, Kitchen, Linens

Attractions: Shuffleboard, volleyball, Tennis, Golf

Condominiums surround the award-winning Thistle Lodge restaurant recreating the home that the first Sanibel settler built for his daughter as a wedding gift. Suites overlook the Gulf of Mexico. In the center of the resort are the pool with waterslides.

SANIBEL ISLAND

Hurricane House
2939 W. Gulf Drive
Sanibel Island, FL 33957
813-481-3636 800-237-8906

2 Bedrooms $$$, Villas
Pool, Kitchen, Linens

Attractions: Tennis, golf, swimming

Opened in 1987, townhouses with modern kitchens, screened terraces and washer/dryers. Pool, tennis court, and beach for sunning and beachcombing.

Sanibel Cottages
2341 W. Gulf Drive
Sanibel Island, FL 33597
813-481-3636 800-237-8906

2 Bedrooms $$$, Villas
Pool, Kitchen

Attractions: Tennis

Victorian elegance and "Old Florida" style architecture and decor in these two bedroom vacation retreats. Bay windows, window seats and huge tubs with whirlpool jets in the master bath. Green lawn with footbridge and gazebo. Golf, water sports, and dining are nearby.

Sanibel Siesta Condominiums
1246 Fulger Street
Sanibel Island, FL 33957
813-472-4117 800-548-2743
FAX: 800-472-6826

2 Bedroom $$$
2 Bedrm/week 8$
Min. Stay 4 Nights, Dep. Req'd
62 condos, Hi-rise, Lo-rise, Keys at
Complex office, P-yes, C-yes, H-yes

Location: Airport: 27 miles; Downtown: 20 minutes, Beach front

General Facilities:, Kitchen, Linens

Room Facilities: Pool, Tennis, Shuffleboard, Beachview public course, TV, Cable, VCR, Phone in rm., Ind. AC Ctl., Ind. Heat Ctl.

Attractions: Deep sea & bay fishing, bay shelling, trolley tour of Sanibel/ Capitva Isles.

Shops & Restaurants: 30 boutiques and gift shops; 50+ restaurants

Sanibel Siesta is an island paradise in the shimmering Gulf of Mexico, enjoying a tropical climate, clothed with lush tropical vegetation, and an abundance of shells, birds and other wildlife. A beachfront condomminium with shuffleboard, heated pool and wheelchair ramp to the beach. Tennis courts are available and golf course is a block away. For those who seek the carefree life in surroundings of unparalleled natural beauty and privacy.

Song of the Sea
863 E. Gulf Drive
Sanibel Island, FL 33957
813-472-2220 800-237-8906

1 Bedroom $$, Lo-rise
Pool, Kitchen

Attractions: Tennis, golf, shelling, boating, fishing, bird watching

Efficiency units with kitchenettes and terraces, casually decorated one bedroom apartments overlooking the Gulf of Mexico, all in an Old World Inn with whitewashed walls and red tile roofs. Palm trees and shrubbery surround the walkways and parking.

―――――――――――――――――― SANIBEL ISLAND ――――――――――――――――――

Sundial Beach & Tennis Resort
1451 Middle Gulf Dr.
Sanibel Island, FL 33957
813-472-4151 800-237-4184
FAX: 813-472-0554

1 Bedroom $$$, 2 Bedrooms $$$,
AmEx/Visa/MC, Dep. 1 Night, •
230 condos, Lo-rise, NoS-yes, H-yes, Key
at front desk.

Location: Airport: 21 miles, Need car, Beach front.

General Facilities: Conf. Rm. Cap: 250, Lounge, Game room, Pool, Recreation Dept., Tennis, Dunes—2 miles, Bike and boat, Baby sitter, Restaurant, Bar.

Room Facilities: Daily maid, Kitchen, TV, Cable, Phone, Crib-Hi-chair, Ind. AC. Ctl., Ind. Heat Ctl.

Attractions: Ding Darling Wildlife Refuge, Shelling beaches, windsurfing, bikes, entertainment.

Shops & Restaurants: Unique specialty shops and boutiques, Windows, Noopies/ Japanese, The Shoppe.

Sundial Beach Resort is located on Sanibel Island, just off the southwest coast of Florida. Sundial is the only full service resort and conference facility on Sanibel. Walk in cool tropical breezes stirring the native palms and gentle waves lapping the beaches. Stroll barefoot on the shell-strewn beach under the morning sun, or witness the brilliant sunset and gaze at the blanket of stars above the tranquil surf.

―――

Tortuga Beach Club
959 E. Gulf Dr.
Sanibel Island, FL 33957
813-481-3636 800-237-8906

2 Bedrooms $$$.
Lo-rise condos.
Pool, Golf. Kitchen.

54 lavish townhouse suites in a Caribbean style island resort. Three-story cluster buildings for those who need privacy. Or socializing at the gameroom/clubhouse, pool or beach for the gregarious.

―――――――――――――――――― SANTA ROSA BEACH ――――――――――――――――――

One Seagrove Place
Route 2, Box 650
Santa Rosa Beach, FL 32459
904-231-5032 800-368-9100

2 Bedrooms $$.
Hi-rise condos.
Pool, Tennis, Golf. Kitchen.

You'll feel you're on a secluded island at this family resort with its white sand beach, pool and tennis court, yet you're close to golf, dining, shopping and recreation. Complete electric kitchens with breakfast bar pass-thrus, wide balconies, washers & ceiling fans.

―――――――――――――――――――――――― SARASOTA ――――――――――――――――――――――――

Calini Beach Club
1030 Seaside Dr.
Sarasota, FL 34242
813-349-2500

2 Bedrooms $$.
Hi-rise condos.
Pool. Kitchen.

Two bedroom, two bath condominiums with luxurious modern furnishings, marble baths, Italian ceramic floor tile, decorator linens, ceiling fans, mirrored walls and private veranda with gulf or garden views.

——————————— SARASOTA ———————————

Limetree Beach Resort
1050 Ben Franklin Dr.
Sarasota, FL 34236
813-388-2111
FAX: 813-388-1408

1 Bedrm/week 5$, 2 Bedrm/week 7$, Min.
Stay: 3 Nights, Visa/MC, Dep. Req'd.
67 condos, Lo-rise, H-yes, Key at office.

Location: Airport: 7 miles; Downtown: 5 miles, Need car; Beach front.

General Facilities: Game room, Pool, Hot tub, Tennis, Exercise room.

Room Facilities: Kitchen, TV, Cable, Phone, Crib-Hi-chair, Ind. AC. Ctl., Ind. Heat Ctl.

Attractions: Sarasota Jungle Gardens, Ringling Museum, deep sea fishing, Disney World, Busch Gardens.

Shops & Restaurants: St. Armand's Circle, Charley's Crab.

Warm weather, beautiful pool and right on Lido Beach, Limetree Beach Resort is within walking distance to St. Armands Circle, one of Florida's finest shopping and dining areas. Visit the Jungle Gardens or Ringling Museum, or take an hour's drive to Busch Gardens, or just lie around the pool.

Sea Club V
6744 Sara Sea Circle
Sarasota, FL 34242
813-349-1176

1 Bedrm/week 7$, 2 Bedrm/week 8$,
3 Bedrm/week, Min. Stay: 7 Nights,
AmEx/Visa/MC, Dep. Req'd, •
41 condos, Lo-rise, H-yes, Key at front office.

Location: Airport: 15 miles; Downtown: 10 miles, Need car; Beach front.

General Facilities: Pool, Hot tub.

Room Facilities: Kitchen, TV, Cable, Phone, Crib-Hi-chair, Ind. AC. Ctl, Ind. Heat Ctl.

Attractions: Ringling Estate and Museum, Bellm's Cars & Music of Yesterday, Sarasota Jungle Gardens, entertainment.

Shops & Restaurants: St. Armand's Circle, Maas Brothers, Burdines, Miguel's, French, Sugar & Spice/Amish.

Sea Club V gives you a private, white sand beach which slopes to the Gulf of Mexico. You can wander out hundreds of feet in these clear waters. Hobie cats, sunfish, wind surfers, sun canoes, snorkeling gear, rafts and beach cabanas are at your doorstep. Nearby is Sarasota with sports from baseball to dog racing, plus many cultural attractions and fine restaurants and shopping.

Suntide Island Beach Club
850 Ben Franklin Dr.
Sarasota, FL 34236
813-388-2151

1 Bedroom $$, 2 Bedrooms $$.
Lo-rise condos.
Pool, Kitchen.

Attractions: Jungle Gardens, Botanical Gardens, Busch Gardens, Van Wezel Theatre, Cypress Gardens.

All the comforts of home in your tropically furnished condominium surrounded by palms. Pool, jacuzzi and beach. Monday night barbeque with live entertainment.

─────────────────────── SARASOTA ───────────────────────

The Meadows Golf & Tennis   Studio $$
Resort   AmEx/Visa/MC, Dep. 1 Night •
3101 Longmeadow   12 condos, Villas, Key at Resort check-in
Sarasota, FL 34235   H-yes
813-378-6660 800-428-0808

Location: Airport: 5 miles; Downtown: 6 miles; Need car

General Facilities: Daily maid, Kitchen, Linens, Restaurant on prem., Bar on prem., Lounge, Baby-sitter

Room Facilities: Pool, Sauna, Tennis, 3 golf courses, Golf: Meadows, Highlands, Grove, TV, Cable, Phone in rm., Crib-Hi-chair, Ind. AC Ctl., Ind. Heat Ctl.

Attractions: White beaches, theatre and art, Ringling Museum, entertainment

Shops & Restaurants: St. Armand's Circle; Cafe L'Europe/continental

Located minutes from the cultural delights of Sarasota and the white sands of the Gulf Beaches, The Meadows offers world class golf, a professional tennis centre, swimming pools and an abundance of lakes. Three restaurants and four bars on the property. Various planned social events for your entertainment.

───

Tivoli By The Sea   2 Bedrooms 4$, Hi-rise
625 Beach Road, Siesta Key   Pool, Daily maid, Kitchen, Linens, Phone in rm.
Sarasota, FL 34242
813-349-5544

Attractions: Florida Symphony, Ringling Museum of Art, Jungle Gardens, greyhound racing, Ca'd 'Zan, Putting green, Tennis, Golf

Situated on semi-tropical Siesta Key and linked by two bridges to Sarasota for shopping, entertainment and sightseeing. Dramatically styled two bedroom split-plan apartments with 26-foot balconies and washer/dryers, facing the powdery sands of Siesta Beach and the Gulf.

─────────────────────── SATELLITE BEACH ───────────────────────

Las Olas Beach Club   2 Bedrooms $$$
1215-25 Highway A1A   2 Bedrms/week 6$
Satellite Beach, FL 32937   Min. Stay 3 Nights, Visa/MC, Dep. Req'd. •
407-777-3224   40 condos, Hi-rise, Key at Reception desk
                                      H-yes

Location: Airport: Melborne-20 minutes; Downtown: 1 hour; Need car; Beach front

General Facilities: Kitchen, Linens, Baby-sitter

Room Facilities: Pool, Hot tub, TV, Cable, Phone in rm., Crib-Hi-chair, Ind. AC Ctl., Ind. Heat Ctl.

Attractions: Kennedy Space Center and easy access to all Orlando attractions, entertainment

Shops & Restaurants: Large indoor mall as well as shopping villages; Italian, French, Seafood

Come to lovely Las Olas and enjoy Central Florida beaches. All units afford gorgeous oceanfront views from private balconies. Welcome continental breakfast, wine & cheese parties and weekly potluck cook-out. Very family oriented, weekly get-togethers and activities organized by the staff, such as volleyball and sand castle building.

————————————— SEAGROVE BEACH ——————————————

Beachside Condominiums   1 Bedroom $$
Highway 365   1 Bedrm/week 4$
Seagrove Beach, FL 32459   Dep. Req'd.
904-231-4205 800-443-3146   3 condos

Location: Airport: 25 miles; Downtown: 10 miles; Need car

General Facilities: Kitchen, Linens

Room Facilities: Pool, Cable, Ind. AC Ctl., Ind. Heat Ctl.

Attractions: Beach activities

Shops & Restaurants: Destin, Panama City

This is the place to get away from it all and forget your cares by relaxing at the beach or sunbathing by the pool.

Beachwood Villas
Route 2, Box 640
Seagrove Beach, FL 32459
904-231-4031 800-537-5387

All units face the two kidney shaped pools set among attractive, spacious, landscaped common areas. 2 tennis courts, clubhouse, direct beach access. On-site office.

Cassine Gardens   2 Bedrooms $$
Route 2, Box 658, Highway 30-A   2 Bedrms/week 4$
Seagrove Beach, FL 32459   Min. Stay 3 Nights, Dep. Req'd. •
904-231-4851 800-346-0128   72 condos, Lo-rise, Key at On site office
                                     No S-yes

Location: Airport: 40 miles; Downtown: 30 miles; Need car

General Facilities: Kitchen, Linens

Room Facilities: Pool, Tennis, Nature/fitness trail, TV, Cable, Phone in rm., Crib-Hi-chair, Ind. AC Ctl., Ind. Heat Ctl.

Attractions: Gulf of Mexico-Emerald Green Waters, world's whitest beaches

Shops & Restaurants: Santa Rosa/Panama City Mall, Village at Sandestin; Capt.' Andersons/Daves/Bayou Bill

Cassine Gardens is 1 mile east of Seagrove Beach on a 25-acre site. Walk miles crunching in the beach sand looking for shells, or picnic on your private dune. Bicycle down the scenic coastal highway, or jog through two miles of nature trails among cyress groves and estuaries. Take a short walk to White Sand Gulf Beach, or play tennis or volleyball, or sun and swim at the pool.

SEBRING

Ridge Resort at Sun 'n Lake
4101 Sun 'n Lake Blvd.
Sebring, FL 33872
813-385-2561 800-237-2165
FAX: 813-385-2563

1 Bedrm/week $$$$, 2 Bedrm/week 5$,
Min. Stay: 7 Nights, AmEx/Visa/MC.
85 condos, Lo-rise, Villas, H-yes.

Location: Airport: 86 miles-Orlando; Downtown: 7 miles

General Facilities: Conf. Rm Cap.: 250, Pool, Tennis, Bikes, Horseshoes, Restaurant, Bar.

Room Facilities: TV, Cable, Phone, Ind. AC. Ctl., Ind. Heat Ctl.

Attractions: Highlands Hammock State Park, Cypress Swamp, wildlife, guided tours & museum, entertainment.

Shops & Restaurants: Penney, Byrons, Beall's, Zayre's, Wal-Mart & K-Mart, Pierre's/ French, Candlelight/Amr.

This small condominium resort is nestled within a residential community in the "unspoiled" heart of Florida, offering the comforts of home with fully-furnished, totally equipped one and two bedroom villas and townhouses, all with semi-private pool. Experience complete comfort, sincere hospitality and friendly service. Great for a secluded "get-away."

Sun 'n Lake Estates
4101 Sun 'n Lake Blvd.
Sebring, FL 33872
813-385-2561 800-237-2165

1 Bedroom $, 2 Bedrooms $$,
1 Bedrm/week $$$$, 2 Bedrm/week 4$,
Min. Stay: 2 Nights, AmEx/Visa/MC,
Dep. Req'd, •
115 condos, Lo-rise, Villas, Key at
registration desk.

Location: Airport: Orlando 86 miles; Downtown: 7 miles, Need car.

General Facilities: Conf. Rm Cap.: 250, Lounge, Pool, Tennis, Sun 'n Lake of Sebring, Shuffleboard, Horseshoes, Baby sitter, Restaurant, Bar.

Room Facilities: Kitchen, TV, Cable, Phone, Crib-Hi-chair, Ind. AC. Ctl, Ind. Heat Ctl.

Attractions: Highlands Hammock State Park, Cypress Swamp, guided tours, entertainment.

Shops & Restaurants: Penney, Byrons, Beall's, Zayre's, Wal-Mart, K-Mart, Candlelight-Amr./Pierre's-Fr. .

Tastefully decorated villas and townhouses nestled within a residential community in "unspoiled" south central Florida. Family recreation and relaxation for get-togethers or secluded get-aways. Complete comfort, hospitality and friendly service.

——————————————— SIESTA KEY, SARASOTA ———————————————

House of the Sun
6518 Midnight Pass Rd.
Siesta Key, Sarasota, FL 34242
813-349-4141 800-618-6948
FAX: 813-346-0749

2 Bedrms/week 6$
Min. Stay 7 Nights, Dep. Required
58 condos, Hi-rise, Key at Office

Location: Airport: 10 miles; Downtown: 5 miles; Need car; Beachfront

General Facilities: Linens; Crib-Hi-chair

Sports Facilities: Pool; Tennis

Room Facilities: Kitchen; Cable; Phone; Ind.AC.Ctl.; Ind.Heat Ctl.

Attractions: Mote Marine-Longboat Key, Jungle Gardens, Myakka State Park, Public golf courses

Shops & Restaurants: Publics grocery, Gulf Gate Mall, Sarasota Square; Italian, French, seafood

Sliding glass doors in the living/dining area lead to your private terrace for partying as you watch the sunset over the Gulf. Frost-free refrigerator freezer with ice maker, kitchen pass-thru snack bar, separate beverage bar in dining area. Underground parking, two elevators. Tennis on the beach with heated swimming pool and game-room directly on the water. Walking distance to points of interest, shopping and dining.

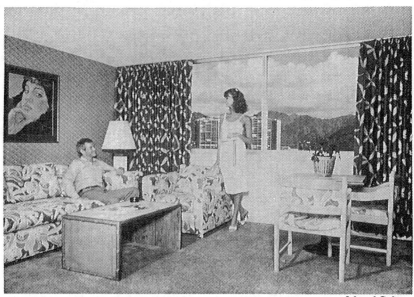

Island Colony

―――――――――――――――――――――― ST. AUGUSTINE ――――――――――――――――――――――

Anastasia Condominiums
Two Dondanville Road
St. Augustine, FL 32084
904-471-2800 800-458-7345

2 Bed/week $$$$
3 Bed/week 4$
Hi-rise

Location: Need car, Ocean front, 5 miles to historic area. 40 miles to Daytona, 50 miles to Jacksonville, easy access from I-95, US 1

General facilities: 7 floors of fully furnished & equipped spacious 2 & 3 bedroom apartments, 2 full baths, private oceanview terrace.

Room facilities: TV, Cable, Phone, Linens, total electrical kitchens including ice makers, microwave, washer/dryer, small appliances, kitchen equipment. Everything except disposables, groceries and you.

Sports facilities: Pool, Tennis, 3 elevators

Attractions: NATIONS OLDEST CITY with many tours, shops, dozens of good restaurants, carriage rides, river cruises, deep sea fishing. 20 minutes to Marineland, golf courses, 2 hours to Orlando, Cape Kennedy.

Oversized rooms on a choice location overlooking St. Augustine Beach. Total-electric kitchens even have trash compactors. Lounge by the pool and patio area or enjoy the miles of sandy beach.

Beach Club At St. Augustine Beach
A1A at 2 Ocean Trace Rd.
St. Augustine, FL 32084
904-471-2626

1 Bedroom $$
2 Bedrooms $$
Hi-rise

General facilities: Kitchen, Linens

Room facilities: Phone

Sports facilities: Pool, Tennis, Exercise room, bikes

Attractions: Walt Disney EPCOT, Sea & Circus Worlds, Kennedy Space Center, Daytona Speedway, Dog Track

Appealing, comfortable, designer selected furnishings in one and two bedroom units with shower massages, hair dryers and family games. A planned environment along the beach for fun and leisure. Pro shop, clubhouse, and snack bar.

Beachers Lodge
6970 A1A South
St. Augustine, FL 32084
904-471-8849 527-8849

Studio $$, 1 Bedroom $$
  2 Bed/week 4$
Visa, MC, Dep. 1 night
142 condos, Hi-rise, Key at Front desk
No S-yes, H-yes

Location: Airport: 50 miles, Downtown: 10 miles, Beach front

General facilities: Daily maid, Kitchen, Linens, Baby sitter

Room facilities: TV, Cable, Phone, Ind.AC.Ctl, Ind.Heat Ctl.

Sports facilities: Pool

Attractions: Historically restored area of St. Augustine, the nation's oldest city.

Shops & Restaurants: Several malls; Salt Water Cowboys seafood restaurant.

Newly refurbished ocean front condominium hotel with kitchenettes, king or queen beds, sofa opening to sleep two. Mauve, sea green and blue color schemes. 10 miles south of historical St. Augustine and only 8 miles north of fabulous Marineland Boardwalk to one of the most beautiful wide beaches in the south. Pool on property. Easy acces from Interstate 95, US1 and A1A. Families welcome, and 10% discount on AARP and AAA.

────────────────────── ST. AUGUSTINE ──────────────────────

Colony Reef Club
4670 A1A South
St. Augustine, FL 32084
904-471-2233 800-624-5965
FAX: 904-471-6429

2 Bedrms/week 4$, 3 Bedrms/week 5$
Min. Stay 2 Nights, AmEx/Visa/MC
132 condos, Lo-rise, Villas

Location: Airport: Daytona, 1 hour; Beachfront

Sports Facilities: Pool; Tennis; Racquetball

Room Facilities: Kitchen; HBO

Attractions: Historic downtown St. Augustine, Marineland, Alligator Farm, Lighthouse Museum

Shops & Restaurants: Shopping centers nearby.; Nearby

All family members will find something to do at this complete oceanfront resort. Sauna, jacuzzi, kiddie pool, jungle gym, exercise room. 120 oceanview units offer 1200 sq.ft. of luxury with sleeping accommodations for 8 people. Watch the sun rise from your private balcony. 12 Tennis villas. One hour to Jacksonville or Daytona Airports. Gas grills and washer/dryers. Private boardwalk over dunes to 24 miles of white sandy beach.

───

Four Winds Condominiums
8130 A1A South
St. Augustine, FL 32086
904-471-0683

Lo-rise

General Facilities: Linens

Sports Facilities: Pool

Room Facilities: Kitchen

Attractions: Marineland, Ocala National Forest, Disney World, Kennedy Space Center

Ideally located apartments on a crescent shaped beach. Heated pool for non-beach lovers. Swimming, sunbathing, beachcombing and salt water fishing in a tranquil setting for full Florida vacation enjoyment.

───

Ocean Village Management
3689 Hwy A1A South
St. Augustine, FL 32084
904-471-9329 800-447-0004

1 Bedroom $$, 2 Bedrooms $$
1 Bedrm/week $$$$, 2 Bedrms/week $$$$
Min. Stay 2 Nights, Visa/MC
Dep. Required •
348 condos, Lo-rise
Key at Rental office/site, No S-yes/H-yes

Location: Airport: 45 minutes; Downtown: 10 Min; Need car

General Facilities: Linens; Crib-Hi-chair

Sports Facilities: Pool; Hot tub; Tennis

Room Facilities: Kitchen; Cable; Phone; Ind.AC.Ctl; Ind.Heat Ctl.

Attractions: Many guided tours, horse and carriage rides, Marineland-15 min.

Shops & Restaurants: Cobblestone streets closed to traffic-many shops; Salt Water Cowboys/seafood

Oceanfront properties with washers and dryers and small kitchen appliances in each unit. 10 minutes from the historic downtown area of St. Augustine with its many fine retaurants. Swimming pool and hot tub, with North Florida's finest beaches at your door.

─────────────── ST. AUGUSTINE ───────────────

Ponce de Leon Resort & Conf. Ctr.   AmEx/Visa/MC
4000 US 1 North   30 condos, Villas, Key at Hotel lobby
St. Augustine, FL 32085
904-824-2821 800-824-2821

Location: Airport: Jacksonville 50 mi.; Downtown: 2 miles; Need car

General Facilities: Conf. rm. cap. 480, Kitchen, Restaurant on prem., Bar on prem.

Room Facilities: Pool, Tennis, Fishing, sailing, Golf: Ponce de Leon course, TV, Cable, Phone in rm., Ind.AC Ctl., Ind. Heat Ctl.

Attractions: St. Augustine, Marineland, greyhound racing, sailing, deep-sea fishing, entertainment

Shops & Restaurants: Historic district shops, sundries shop; Michaels/seafood and steaks

Resort on 350 landscaped acres, adjacent to the inland waterway. Villas are traditionally furnished in pastel colors. Some have whirlpools and sleeping lofts. Six Deco Turf II tennis courts, huge pool and 18-hole putting course with hazards disguised as fountains. Area tours, deep-sea fishing, sailing and water skiing are easily scheduled through the resort.

───

Sand Dollar Condominiums   3 Bedrms/week 5$
8050 South AIA Street   Min. Stay 7 Nights, Dep. Req'd.
St. Augustine, FL 32086   166 condos, Hi-rise
904-471-1733   No S-yes/H-yes

Location: Airport: 1½ hour; Downtown: 11 miles; Need car; Beach front

General Facilities: Kitchen, Linens

Room Facilities: Pool, Tennis, TV, Cable, Phone in rm., Crib-Hi-chair, Ind. AC Ctl., Ind. Heat Ctl.

Attractions: St. Augustine—the nation's oldest city, sightseeing of historical areas, Marineland, tours, entertainment

Shops & Restaurants: Fiddlers Green/seafood

These large, 1700-square-foot units overlook the Atlantic Ocean and Intercoastal Waterway. Miles of white beach, pools and tennis on beautiful spacious grounds. Winter entertainment includes coffee hour, bridge and social events. Eleven miles to St. Augustine.

───

Sea Place Condominiums   2 Bedrooms $$, 3 Bedrooms $$$
4400 A1A South   2 Bedrms/week $$$, 3 Bed/week 6$
St. Augustine, FL 32084   Min. Stay 2 Nights, AmEx/Visa/MC, Dep. Req'd. •
904-471-3881 800-242-7999   42 condos, Lo-rise, Key at Rental office
                             No S-yes/H-yes

Location: Airport: Jacksonville; Downtown: 10 miles; Need car; Beach front

General Facilities: Kitchen, Linens, Baby-sitter

Room Facilities: Pool, Hot tub, Tennis, Racquetball, TV, Cable, Phone in rm., Crib-Hi-chair, Ind. AC Ctl., Ind. Heat Ctl.

Attractions: Historical St. Augustine, Marineland, Alligator Farm

Shops & Restaurants: Ponce de Leon Mall, St. Augustine shops & boutiques; Salt Water Cowboy's/seafood

Centrally located villas with private patios. Step outside your door on paths set in a manicured lawn and swim, surf, sun and sail. Pool, tennis, racquetball and jacuzzi.

——————————— ST. AUGUSTINE ———————————

Spanish Trace   Lo-rise
1 Ocean Trace Rd.
St. Augustine, FL 32084
904-471-2535
General facilities: Kitchen, Linens
Sports facilities: Pool, Tennis, Shuffleboard
Attractions: Disney World, Sea World, Circus World, Kennedy Space Center,
   Marineland
South of St. Augustine, right on the ocean with view of the landscaped courtyard, ocean and dunes. Individually furnished units. Safe ocean swimming, pool, tennis and shuffleboard.

St. Aug. Beach and Tennis Club   2 Bed/week $$$$, 3 Bed/week $$$$
4 Ocean Trace Rd.   Min. stay 7 nights, Dep. req'd
St. Augustine, FL 32084   Key at Office
904-471-2880   96 condos, Hi-rise, No S-yes, H-yes
Location: Airport: 50 miles; Downtown: 5 miles; Need car; Beach front
General facilities: Kitchen, Linens, Baby sitter, Bar, Sauna
Room facilities: TV, Cable, Phone, Crib-Hi-chair, Ind. AC. Ctl, Ind. Heat Ctl.
Sports facilities: Pool, Tennis
Attractions: Scenic carriage rides, boat excursion, historical sights, Marineland,
   Disney World
Shops & Restaurants: Fiddlers Green/seafood
Modern, comfortable, homelike units furnished to the owners' preference. Walk on the beach, keep fit at the health and fitness center, or relax in the jacuzzi after your tennis game.

Summerhouse   2 Bedrooms $$$, 3 Bedrooms $$$,
8550 A1A South-Anastasia Island   2 Bed/week 4$, 3 Bed/week 5$, Min. stay
St. Augustine, FL 32086   2 nights, Visa, MC, Dep. req'd, Key at Site
904-471-1503 800-334-2160   rental office, 256 condos, Lo-rise, H-yes •
Location: Airport: 45 minutes; Downtown: 15 min.; Need car; Beach front
General facilities: Conf. Rm. (cap. 200), Daily maid, Kitchen, Linens
Room facilities: TV, Cable, Phone, Crib-Hi-chair, Ind. AC. Ctl, Ind. Heat Ctl.
Sports facilities: Pool, Tennis, Racquetball
Attractions: River cruises, horse carriage tours, Marineland sea shows, oldest
   USA city
Shops & Restaurants: Anastasia shopping mall, tourist shops, Conch House-
   seafood, steaks
Tropical rattan in summer colors make for a truly relaxed vacation in these two and three bedroom condominiums. 4 swimming pools, 6 tennis courts and 6 racquetball courts with courtyard or ocean views from the balconies. 2 miles from Marineland, less than two hours to Disney World.

Be sure to call the condo the verify details and prices and to make
your reservation.

---------------------------- ST. AUGUSTINE ----------------------------

The Coquina
7900 A1A South
St. Augustine, FL 32086
904-471-0055

2 Bedrms/week 4$
Dep. Req'd.
42 condos, Lo-rise

Location: Downtown: 10 miles; Beach front

General Facilities: Kitchen, Linens, Child planned rec.: Wading pool

Room Facilities: Pool, Tennis, Golf: Nearby, TV, Cable, Ind. AC Ctl., Ind. Heat Ctl.

Attractions: Disney World, Marineland, Daytona Beach, Old Fort, Alligator Farm

Shops & Restaurants: Historical Restoration Area shops, St. Augustine

Well-decorated units in V-shaped construction. Pool and wading pool on the oceanfront by the sea wall with steps leading to the wide, hard sand, unspoiled beach. Friendly, quiet, refined atmosphere.

Tradewinds Condominiums
7750 South A1A
St. Augustine, FL 32084
904-471-0113

1 Bedroom $, 2 Bedrooms $$, Hi-rise
Pool, Kitchen, Linens

Attractions: Disney World, Jacksonville, Daytona Beach, Tennis

Family-oriented condominiums with private pier and secured boat storage, on fourteen miles of unbroken white sand beach. Tennis, pool and clubhouse.

---------------------------- ST. PETERSBURG BEACH ----------------------------

Breckenridge Resort Beach Club
5700 Gulf Blvd.
St. Petersburg Beach, FL 33706
813-828-3371   800-237-3371

Studio $$, 1 Bedroom $$$
AmEx/Visa/MC, Dep. 1 Night •
200 condos, Hi-rise, Key at Front desk
No S-yes/H-yes

Location: Airport: 35 minutes; Downtown: 15 min.; Beach front

General Facilities: Full serv., Bus. fac., Conf. rm. cap. 250, Daily maid, Kitchen, Linens, Restaurant on prem., Bar on prem., Game room, Lounge, Baby-sitter

Room Facilities: Pool, Tennis, Golf: Pasadena Country C. 5 min, TV, Cable, Phone in rm., Crib-Hi-chair, Ind. AC Ctl., Ind. Heat Ctl.

Attractions: Busch Gardens Theme Park and Zoo, SeaEscape 1 day cruise/casino, museums, entertainment

Shops & Restaurants: Boutiques, resort wear, outlet mall; Wine Cellar/European

Gulf-front studios in mauve color scheme, dinette area, mirrored closet doors, built-in cabinetry. A guitarist to entertain you during the day, and evening comedian/pianist in the lounge. Have fun on the beach or join in the many water sports available on the premises. Two tennis courts, game room and pool.

———————————— ST. PETERSBURGH BEACH ————————————

Camelot
1801 Gulf Way, Pass-A-Grille Bch
St. Petersburg Beach, FL 33706
813-360-6988

1 Bedrm/week $$$$, 2 Bed/week 4$
Dep. Req'd.
Lo-rise

Location: Downtown: 5 minute

General Facilities: Kitchen

Room Facilities: Pool, Sauna, Hot tub, Bikes, Shuffleboard, Golf: Nearby, TV, Phone in rm., Ind. AC Ctl.

Attractions: Tennis, golf, water activities

Shops & Restaurants: Convenience market—5 minutes

Two-story resort condominium with friendly, southern style atmosphere. Fully carpeted with designer coordinated furnishings overlooking the beach. Lounge around the pool, tan on the sun deck or picnic on the beach.

Coral Reef Beach Resort
5800 Gulf Blvd.
St. Petersburg Beach, FL 33706
813-360-0821 800-553-6599

1 Bedroom $$, 2 Bedrooms $$$, Hi-rise
Pool, Kitchen

Look out at night at the beautiful, lighted, unusually shaped pool under walkways and surrounded by umbrella covered tables. This five acre resort has a private beach and its own restaurant and deluxe one and two bedroom units.

Hideaway Sands Resort
3804 Gulf Blvd.
St. Petersburg Beach, FL 33706
813-367-2781

1 Bedroom $$, 2 Bedrooms $$, Hi-rise
Pool, Kitchen, Phone in rm.

Attractions: Disney World, Busch Gaardens, dog/horse racing, NASL soccer, jai alai, Exercise room, Golf

Located directly on the beach and convenient to shopping and dining, these units have washer/dryers, microwaves and private balconies. Pool, jacuzzi, billiards and exercise room, BBQ grills, covered pavilion on beach side and complimentary membership to the golf club.

Mariner Beach Club
4220 Gulf Blvd.
St. Petersburg Beach, FL 33706
813-367-3721

1 Bedroom $$, 2 Bedrooms $$$, Lo-rise
Pool

Overlooking the Gulf of Mexico, one and two bedroom condominiums with special touches such as track lighting, ceiling fans, games, books and a daily newspaper. Swimming pool, two jacuzzis and barbecue.

———————————————— STUART ————————————————

Indian River Plantation
Resort
555 N.E. Ocean Blvd.
Stuart, FL 34996
407-225-3700 800-444-3389

1 Bedroom $$$$, 2 Bedroom $$$$
AmEx/MC/Visa, Dep. 1 Night
54 condos, Hi-rise, Keys at Hotel front
desk, C-yes

Location: Airport: 45 minutes; Downtown: 10 minutes, Beach front

General Facilities: Conf. rm. cap. 525, Full serv., Bus. fac., Daily maid, Kitchen, Linens, Restaurant on prem., Bar on prem., Baby sitter, Gameroom, Lounge.

Room Facilities: Pool, Hot Tub, Tennis, Boating, 18-hole, 61 par, Child planned rec., TV, Cable, Phone in rm., Ind. AC Ctl., Ind. Heat Ctl.

Attractions: Elliott Museum, House of Refuge, Oceanographic Society, Jai Alai, Historic homes tour, entertainment.

Shops & Restaurants: Treasure Coast Mall-Jordan Marsh, Lord & Taylor; Benihana/Jap. Helga's/gourmet.

Luxury, oceanfront one and two bedroom condos with private balconies, located on 200-acre, self-contained, ocean-to-river resort on uncrowded Hutchinson Island; reminiscent of "old Florida" with golf, lighted tennis court and a 77-slip marina, water and electrical hook-ups, yacht telephone service and cable TV. Luxury excursion boat, 5 restaurants and 3 lounges with variety of atmospheres, entertainment and dancing. Golf and tennis pros for clinics, lessons. Outdoor spa, cabana bar and gourmet grocery.

———————————————— TARPON SPRINGS ————————————————

Innisbrook
P.O. Drawer 1088
Tarpon Springs, FL 34688
813-942-2000 800-237-0157

1 Bedroom $$, 2 Bedrooms $$$
Dep. Req'd.
Key at Reception Center
H-yes

Location: Airport: Tampa--25 minutes

General Facilities: Kitchen, Linens, Restaurant on prem., Bar on prem., Child planned rec.: Zoo Crew ages 4-12

Room Facilities: Pool, Sauna, Tennis, Health club, bikes, Golf: 3 on-site courses

Attractions: Disney World, Sea World, Kennedy Space Center, Busch Gardens, Circus World, Weeki Wachee, entertainment

Shops & Restaurants: Le Market Place on-site, gifts, sundries, liquors; 6 restaurants, 2 snack bars

World class golf with 35 clinics and summer junior program. Terry Addison's Australian Tennis Institute with 2 clinic programs and summer junior program. Rich flowering wooded acres with gleaming lakes, citrus groves, pine trees and a wildlife preserve. Zoo Crew activities program for 4-to 12-year-olds. 6 pools, lake or sport fishing, beach shuttle service, bicycle or jog. Day trips arranged to attractions. Dress for dining at the Island Clubhouse and Copperhead nightclub, or relax with room service.

———————————————— TREASURE ISLAND ————————————————

Jamaican On The Gulf
11660 Gulf Blvd.
Treasure Island, FL 33706
813-360-6981

1 Bedroom $$, 2 Bedrooms $$$, Hi-rise
Kitchen

Contemporary resort with one and two bedroom suites directly on the Gulf of Mexico. Beach level sun deck and rooftop patio for sunbathing.

──────────────── TREASURE ISLAND ────────────────

Land's End Resort
7500 Bayshore Drive
Treasure Island, FL 33706
813-367-7859 800-382-8883

Lo-rise
Pool, Kitchen

Attractions: Tennis

A beachfront hideaway for a leisurely, relaxing vacation. On a peninsula surrounded by tranquil, blue water. Pool, tennis, gazebos. Be pampered at this romantic, Mediterranean style resort. Close to shopping, restaurants and nightlife.

Nordvind
12700 Gulf Blvd.
Treasure Island, FL 33706
813-360-7037 800-237-5897

1 Bedroom $$, 2 Bedrooms $$, Hi-rise
Kitchen, Linens

Quality, craftsmanship and Scandinavian detail with ceramic tile and oak cabinetry. Lawn and beach views from every suite.

Sand Pebble Resort
12300 Gulf Blvd.
Treasure Island, FL 33706
813-360-1845

Studio $, 1 Bedroom $$, 2 Bedrooms $$,
  3 Bedrooms $$$
1 Bedrm/week 5$, 2 Bed/week 5$,
  3 Bed/week 7$
Min. Stay 2 Nights, AmEx/Visa/MC,
  Dep. Req'd. •
45 condos, Lo-rise, Key at Front desk, H-yes

Location: Airport: 40 minutes; Downtown: 15 min.; Need car; Beach front

General Facilities: Daily maid, Kitchen, Linens, Baby-sitter, Child planned rec.: Activity Director

Room Facilities: Pool, Hot tub, Tennis, Golf: 1 mile, TV, Cable, Phone in rm., Crib-Hichair, Ind. AC Ctl., Ind. Heat Ctl.

Attractions: John's Pass Fishing Village, Busch Gardens, Adventure Island, sailing, deep-sea fishing, entertainment

Shops & Restaurants: John's Pass Village, Tyrone Square Mall; Wine Cellar/Lobster Pot/Pompano

Sand Pebble was designed with families in mind and is situated on the Gulf of Mexico on the white sand beach of Treasure Island. Full activity schedule for all ages, swimming pool, in-ground spa and barbecue. Fine shops, restaurants, sailing fishing and spring training baseball camps are all close.

Treasure Island Beach Club
11750 Gulf Blvd.
Treasure Island, FL 33706
813-360-7096

1 Bedroom $$, 2 Bedrooms $$
Pool, Kitchen, Linens, Phone in rm.

Attractions: Disney World, EPCOT, Busch Gardens, major league teams spring training

Units with ultra-modern kitchens, tile baths and convenience appliances. Most have balconies. Beach, pool and in-ground spa for passive fun. Game room with pool table and video games. Dinner cruises and fishing charters available.

———————————— TREASURE ISLAND ————————————

Treasure Shores   1 Bedroom $$, Lo-rise
10360 Gulf Blvd.   Pool, Kitchen
Treasure Island, FL 33706
813-367-5989

Decorator accessories in these units with video disc players and on-site laundry facilities. If you tire of the beach, try the pool and jacuzzi. Barbecue area. Tennis and golf nearby.

Voyager Beach Club   1 Bedroom $$, 2 Bedrooms $$
11860 Gulf Blvd.   Pool, Kitchen, Linens, Phone in rm.
Treasure Island, FL 33706   Putting green, Tennis
813-360-5529

Enjoy the sunsets over the Gulf of Mexico from your private balcony. All your favorite water sports, heated pool, jacuzzi and rooftop sun deck with shuffleboard. Jog on the beach, and then retire to your condominium for a relaxing jacuzzi.

———————————— VANDERBILT BEACH, NAPLES ————————————

Vanderbilt Beach & Harbour Club Pool, Kitchen, Linens
9301 Gulfshore Drive
Vanderbilt Beach, Naples, FL 33940
813-597-5098 800-331-4941

Attractions: Jungle Larry's, sailing, golf, tennis, theatres, Ritz-Carlton, Greyhound racing, Exercise room, bikes

Spacious, airy units furnished with everything you need for your vacation. Eating table in kitchen, screened in, furnished balcony, dining table, washer/dryers. All of this plus lush landscaping, pools, jacuzzis, sauna, exercise room, and bicycles.

Waikiki Beach Tower

---------------------- VENICE/SARASOTA CITY ----------------------

Plantation Golf & Country Club   Min. stay 7 nights, Visa, MC
800 Rockley Blvd.   150 condos, Lo-rise
Venice   Key at Plantation Rental Office
Sarasota City, FL 34293   No S-yes •
813-493-2146   800-826-4060

Location: Airport: 45 minutes, Downtown Sarasota: 7 miles, Need car

General facilities: Kitchen, Linens, Restaurant, Bar, Lounge, Jacuzzi

Room facilities: Cable, Phone, Crib-Hi-chair, Ind.AC.Ctl., Ind.Heat Ctl.

Sports facilities: Junior Olympic-Size Pool, 13 Har-Tru Tennis Courts, 2 18-hole Golf courses, Fitness trail, bike, fishing.

Attractions: Ringling Museums, Chicago White Sox, Texas Rangers, Barnum/Bailey Circus winter homes, entertainment

Shops & Restaurants: Shops of Venice, St. Armand's Circle, Sarasota Square Mall, Manor/continental on premises

Winter, spring, summer, fall, we have it all. No matter when you stay with us, you'll find great hospitality, 36 holes of golf, tennis, restaurant and Gulf beaches nearby. Rent private golf course homes or condominiums by the week, month, or year. This all-season resort is spread over 1300 acres of Florida's beautiful west coast.

---------------------- VERO BEACH ----------------------

Sea Oaks   1 Bed/week 4$, 2 Bed/week 6$
8850 North AIA   Min. stay 7 nights, Dep. req'd
Vero Beach, FL 32963   47 condos, Lo-rise,
407-231-5656   800-231-6227   Key at Office/guard house
                                 No S-yes, H-yes

Location: Airport: 45 min., Downtown: 10 min., Need car, Beach front

General facilities: Daily maid, Kitchen, Linens, Tennis clinics, Baby sitter, Restaurant, Bar, Sauna, Hot tub

Room facilities: TV, Cable, Phone, Crib-Hi-chair, Ind.AC.Ctl, Ind.Heat Ctl.

Sports facilities: Pool, Tennis, Marina

Attractions: Vero Beach attractions, L.A. Dodgers sprg. training, museums, libraries, Riverside Theater, Entertainment

Shops & Restaurants: Boutiques, Worth Avenue in Palm Beach, Ocean Grill/seafood-cont.

Five-star tennis and beach resort community bordering the Atlantic Ocean on the east and Indian River on the west. Elegant, old-Florida style architecture on a secluded beach. Gourmet dining in the Oak Room, piano bar, and casual dining in the Beach Club Lounge. Water sports in the Gulf Stream and fishing in the Indian River. Protected, wooded trails along the river's edge for strolling, biking, jogging or bird watching.

Be sure to call the condo to verify details and prices and to make your reservation.

--------------------- WESLEY CHAPEL ---------------------

Saddlebrook Golf & Tennis Resort
100 Saddlebrook Way
Wesley Chapel, FL 33543
813-973-1111 800-729-8383
FAX: 813-973-4504

1 Bedroom $$, 2 Bedrooms $$,
3 Bedrooms $$$, 1 Bedrm/week 4$,
2 Bedrm/week 5$, 3 Bedrm/week 8$,
AmEx/Visa/MC, •
700 condos, Lo-rise, H-yes, Key at front desk.

Location: Airport: 30 minutes—Tampa; Downtown: 15 miles.

General Facilities: Bus. fac., Conf. Rm Cap.: 10, Lounge, Pool, Child planned rec., Tennis, Golf on premises, Fishing, Bicycling, Baby sitter, Restaurant, Bar.

Room Facilities: Daily maid, Kitchen, TV, Cable, Phone, Crib-Hi-chair, Ind. AC. Ctl., Ind. Heat Ctl.

Attractions: Busch Gardens, Cypress Gardens, Orlando attractions, Gulf of Mexico beaches, entertainment.

Shops & Restaurants: University Square Mall, J. C. Penney, Sears, Maas Brothers, 4 on-site restaurants.

Saddlebrook, at 480 acre award-winning golf and tennis resort is located just 15 miles north of Tampa. Features include two 18-hole championship golf courses, 37 tennis courts, half-million gallon superpool and complete fitness center. One and two bedroom units feature fully equipped kitchens with serving bar. Four restaurants ranging from outdoor casual to elegant and two lounges offering dancing and entertainment nightly.

--------------------- WEST PALM BEACH ---------------------

Palm Beach Polo & Country Club
13198 Forest Hill Blvd.
West Palm Beach, FL 33414
407-798-7000 800-327-4202
FAX: 407-798-7052

1 Bedroom $$$$, 2 Bedrooms 4$, Jr. $$$$,
3 Bedrooms 4$
120 condos, Lo-rise, Villas.

Location: Airport: 12 miles; Downtown Palm Beach: 15 miles, Need car.

General Facilities: Conf. Rm Cap.: 60, Pool, Spa, Sauna, Child planned rec., Tennis, 45-holes, Riding, Squash, Baby sitter, Restaurant, Bar.

Room Facilities: Daily maid, Kitchen, TV, Cable.

Attractions: Polo equestrian events, museums, Jai Alai, deep sea fishing, horse racing, rowing clinics.

Shops & Restaurants: Neighborhood shops, 9 plex theater, Three dining rooms on-site.

Guests stay in contemporary Florida-style condominiums with fairway or lake views, and have use of a tennis center with 24 courts featuring all three surfaces and a full health spa. 3 clubhouses scattered about the grounds house 3 dining rooms. The ocean is half hour away, full-service concierge will be happy to arrange a deep-sea fishing excursion. Croquet lawns, numerous swimming pools, rowing clinics, 3 golf courses designed by Dye, Garl/Pate and Fazio.

———————————————— WINTER GARDEN ————————————————

Windtree Villas
12 Windtree Ln.
Winter Garden, FL 32787
407-656-1577 800-423-7498

2 Bedrooms $$
2 Bedrms/week 5$
Min. Stay 4 Nights, AmEx/Visa/MC,
   Dep. Req'd. •
186 condos, Lo-rise, Villas, Key at Office
No S-yes/P-yes/H-yes

Location: Airport: 24 miles; Downtown: 2 miles; Need car

General Facilities: Full serv., Conf. rm. cap. 150, Kitchen, Linens, Restaurant on prem.,
Baby-sitter

Room Facilities: Pool, Tennis, TV, Phone in rm., Crib-Hi-chair, Ind. AC Ctl., Ind. Heat
Ctl.

Attractions: Disney World, EPCOT, Wet 'N Wild, Sea World, Orlando

Shops & Restaurants: Reginal Mall, Zayres, small shops, EPCOT shops; Christini's-
Lake Buena Vista

*Wintree Villas are all two-bedroom, two-bathroom condos, furnished with custom-made
furniture in an art deco feeling in shades of mauve, black and peach. Windtree Villas are
just 20 minutes from Disney World and 15 minutes from Sea World. Private patios or ter-
races to enjoy the beautiful Florida sunsets. Pool and tennis are also included on this
16-acre resort.*

Georgia

Dillard
Ellijay • • Helen
• Pine Mountain
• Tybee Island
St. Simons Island • • Sea Island

DILLARD

Sky Valley Resort
Dillard
Dillard, GA 30537
404-746-5301

2 Bedrooms $$, 3 Bedrooms $$$
Lo-rise, Key at Front desk

Location: Airport: Atlanta; Need car; Ski lift: Nearby

General Facilities: Kitchen, Restaurant on prem., Lounge, Child planned rec.: Playground-day camp

Room Facilities: Pool, Tennis, Fishing, hiking, Golf: 18-hole course

Attractions: Tallulah Gorge, Rabun Bald, Black Rock Mountain State Park, river rafting, hiking

Shops & Restaurants: Full-service grocery store, antiques and crafts; The Chateau at SV/nouvelle

Located in the foothills of the Blue Ridge Mountains, fully equipped chalets and condominiums with fireplaces, two to four bedrooms. Wilderness trails for hiking and horseback riding, clean, public beaches for water lovers, mountain streams for fishing. A variety of things to do for the active sportsperson; pool swimming and communing with nature for the less ambitious. Winter skiing. Summer day camp and teen center. Friendly, homespun atmosphere with real Southern hospitality.

ELLIJAY

Blue Ridge Mountain Marina Resort
100 Beaver Lake Dr., Carters Lake
Ellijay, GA 30540
404-276-4891

1 Bedroom $$, Lo-rise
Kitchen

Attractions: Smoky Mountains, Carters Lake, Marina, boat rentals

Cabins on Carters Lake's sixty-two miles of shoreline. The only commercial facility on the Lake. Marina and convenience store with everything for the boater and fishing equipment rental.

---------------------------- HELEN ----------------------------

Loreley
1 Bruckenstrasse, P.O. Box 116
Helen, GA 30545
404-878-2236 800-631-6291

1 Bedroom $$, 2 Bedrooms $$
1 Bedrm/week 4$, 2 Bed/week 4$
Min. Stay 2 Nights, AmEx/Visa/MC,
Dep. Req'd.
93 condos, Lo-rise, Key at Manager's office
H-yes

Location: Airport: 95 miles Atlanta; Downtown: 2 miles; Need car; Ski lift: Sky Vly.

General Facilities: Kitchen, Linens, Game room, Lounge

Room Facilities: Pool, Sauna, Hot tub, Tennis, Indoor pool, Golf: Innsbruck Golf, TV, Cable, VCR, Crib-Hi-chair, Ind. AC Ctl., Ind. Heat Ctl.

Attractions: The beauty and serenity of Georgia mountains, cascading waterfalls, lakes, rivers & parks, entertainment

Shops & Restaurants: Outlet Mall, recreated Bavarian Village; Chef Hans/German & American

Southern hospitality mixed with Alpine charm, set along the Chattahoochee River. Activities Director plans trips, bingo, dancing, rafting, horseback riding, cook-outs, panning for gold and games for children. Helen's year-round festivities include Octoberfest, Fasching Carnival, Mayfest, hot air balloon race, and canoe and kayak sprints. Tennis, golf, badminton, volleyball, horseshoes, plus safety, security and a good time for family fun.

-------------------------- PINE MOUNTAIN --------------------------

Calloway Gardens
US Highway 27
Pine Mountain, GA 31822
404-663-2281 800-282-8181

Studio $$$, 1 Bedroom $$$$, 2 Bedrooms $$$$,
    3 Bedrooms $$$$
Dep. 1 Night •
200 condos, Villas, Key at Front desk

Location: Airport: Atlanta 1 hour; Downtown: 2 miles; Need car

General Facilities: Full serv., Conf. rm. cap. 1000, Daily maid, Kitchen, Linens, Restaurant on prem., Bar on prem., Baby-sitter, Child planned rec.: Summer day camp

Room Facilities: Pool, Sauna, Hot tub, Tennis, Trap & skeet range, Golf: Calloway Garden 4 courses, TV, Phone in rm., Crib-Hi-chair, Ind. AC Ctl., Ind. Heat Ctl.

Attractions: Calloway Gardens, Warm Springs, FDR Little White House, entertainment

Shops & Restaurants: Tennis, golf shops, country store on property; Hamilton House/continental

Award-winning resort with lakes, scenic trails, rare azaleas, and wildlife woodlands. John A. Sibley Horticultural Center and Cecil B. Day Butterfly Center. Elegantly furnished villas with stone fireplaces and private patios. A wealth of recreational opportunities and five restaurants to choose from. Evening live entertainment, music and dancing. Fishing and sailing on Mountain Creek Lake, 4 golf courses, 17 tennis courts and 3 pools.

─────────────────── SEA ISLAND ───────────────────

The Cloister
Sea Island, GA 31561
912-638-3611 800-732-4752

Location: Beach front

General Facilities: Conf. rm. cap. 450, Kitchen, Restaurant on prem., Bar on prem., Game room, Lounge, Baby-sitter

Room Facilities: Pool, Tennis, Croquet, trap-skeet, Golf: 54-holes

Attractions: Historic retreat plantation, artists' colony, horseback riding, boating

Shops & Restaurants: Area shops; Restaurants on property

A massive fireplace and grand piano set in a romantic Spanish-style lounge with chandeliered high ceiling and stained glass windows greets your arrival at this island resort. Azaleas, a quaint covered bridge and lagoons guard the fairways of The Cloister's 54 holes of legendary golf. Listen to the Sea Island singers Friday at plantation supper.

─────────────────── ST. SIMONS ISLAND ───────────────────

River Watch Inn
1 Marina Drive
St. Simons Island, GA 31522
912-638-4092

Studio $$, 1 Bedroom $$$, 2 Bedrooms $$$$
AmEx/Visa/MC
33 condos, Lo-rise, Key at Froont office
H-yes

Location: Airport: 15-20 minutes; Downtown: 2 miles; Need car

General Facilities: Kitchen, Linens, Restaurant on prem., Bar on prem.

Room Facilities: Pool, Marina, Golf: Close by, TV, Cable, Phone in rm., Crib-Hi-chair, Ind. AC Ctl., Ind. Heat Ctl.

Attractions: Fort Frederica, Christ Church, Lighthouse, Okefenokee Swamp, Sapelo Island tours, entertainment

Shops & Restaurants: 25 gift and specialty shops, Marina Village; Emmeline & Hessie/seafood-steaks

View St. Simons Sound, the Marshes of Glynn, and inland waterways from the rooftop swimming pool. 25 gift and specialty shops and 3 great restaurants. Full service marina-charter fishing, sailing cruises and lessons, tour boats. Sandy beach, horses, biking.

Sea Palm Resort Golf Club
5445 Frederica Rd.
St. Simons Island, GA 31522
912-638-3351 800-841-6268

1 Bedroom $$$, 2 Bedrooms $$$$, Villas
Pool, Kitchen

Attractions: Pier, lighthouse, Museum of Coastal History, Bloody Marsh, Christ Church, tours, Health Club, jogging, Tennis, Golf

Choose a golf course villa set among the oaks or condominium with marsh view, both elegantly decorated. Located in the center of St. Simons Island with its many specialty shops and fine restaurants. 27 holes of chammpionship golf, 12 tennis courts, 2 pools.

─────────────────── TYBEE ISLAND ───────────────────

Trbrisa Beach Resort
1 15th St., P.O. Box 26
Tybee Island, GA 31328
912-786-4080

Villas
Pool, Kitchen, Linens
Sun, sailing, fishing, beach, tennis

Relax in the master suite jacuzzi, have a romantic dinner on your balcony, enjoy the holiday pleasures of the beach or pool. Two-bedroom, two-bath fully equipped villas, with bicycles on the property for touring Tybee Island.

Hawaii

--------- HANA, MAUI ---------

Hana Kai Maui Resort (on Hana Bay)
P.O. Box 38
Hana, Maui, HI 96713
808-248-8426 800-346-2772

Studio $$$, 1 Bedroom $$
Amex, Visa, MC, Dep. 50%
12 condos, Lo-rise, Key at Office •
Fax: 808-248-7482

Location: International Airport: 2 hours 30 minutes, Municipal Airport: 3.5 miles, Need car, Beach front

General facilities: Daily maid, service, Linens, Oceanside Luau, BB-Q, Refrigerator, Parking

Room facilities: Fully equipped kitchens, private oceanview lanais

Attractions: Whale watching, hiking, fishing, swimming, snorkeling, horseback, Seven Pools, Hana Ranch, Botanical Gardens, Piilanihale Heiau, Waianapanapa State Park

Shops & Restaurants: Hasegawa General Store, grocery store, Restaurants, Tutu's carryout

Tucked away in a sheltered cove amidst lush foliage on the blue Pacific. Spend lazy days at the beach or explore spectacular waterfalls, lava tubes caverns, unspoiled picnic areas, cliff enclosed beaches, or swim in the hidden pools, once bathing spots of kings and queens. A unique, lovely and very special part of the Islands.

--------- HANALEI, KAUAI ---------

Albert Road House
P.O. Box 1109
Hanalei, Kauai, HI 96714
808-826-9833

Alii Kai I
P.O. Box 1109
Hanalei, Kauai, HI 96714
808-826-9833 800-367-8047

———————————————— HANALEI, KAUAI ————————————————

Cliffs
P.O. Box 1005
Hanalei, Kauai, HI 96714
808-826-6219 800-367-6046

1 Bedroom $$, 2 Bedrooms $$$
AmEx/Visa/MC, 1 Night Dep. Req'd. •
100 condos, Lo-rise
Key at Registration lobby, H-yes

Location: Airport: 30 miles; Downtown: 30 miles; Need car; Beach front

General Facilities: Full serv.; Daily maid; Linens; Baby sitter; Crib-Hi-chair

Sports Facilities: Pool; Sauna; Hot tub; Tennis; Putting green; Princeville Makai Golf

Room Facilities: Kitchen; Cable; VCR; Phone

Attractions: Zodiac coast rides, whale watching, windsurfing, horseback & helicopter rides, hiking; entertainment

Shops & Restaurants: Princeville & Kukui Shopping Cntrs, Coconut Mall; Nobles-Mirage-Princeville

There is a unique tranquility in these spacious villas with luscious surroundings. Ten minute drive to the beach, four tennis courts, barbeque facilities, putting green and Friday night cocktail party. Private recreation pavilion, pool and jacuzzis. All units furnished in rattan with tropical printed fabrics, with lanai furniture for four.

Hale Moi Resort
P.O. Box 1185
Hanalei, Kauai, HI 96714
808-826-9602 800-367-7042

Studio $$, 1 Bedroom $$
1 Bedrm/week 5$
Min. Stay 2 Nights, AmEx/Visa/MC,
    1 Night Dep. Req'd. •
40 condos, Lo-rise, Key at Front office

Location: Airport: Princeville-3 miles; Downtown: 30 min.; Need car

General Facilities: Linens; Baby sitter; Crib-Hi-chair

Sports Facilities: Princeville's Oceans

Room Facilities: Kitchen; Phone

Attractions: Hanalei Town, water sports, Princeville Racquet and Health Club

Shops & Restaurants: Princeville Center; Beamreach-casual fine dining

Tropical, Hawaiian, modern furnishings with natural tones and mountain and water-fall views, and an abundance of outdoor activities.

Hanalei Bay Resort
P.O. Box 220
Hanalei, Kauai, HI 96714
808-826-6522 800-367-5004
FAX: 808-596-0158

Studio $$$, 1 Bedroom $$$$, 2 Bedrooms
$$$$, 3 Bedrooms 6$
Min. Stay 2 Nights, AmEx/Visa/MC,
    1 Night Dep. Req'd. •
200 condos, Key at Front desk

Location: Airport: 32 miles; Downtown: 1 mile; Need car

General Facilities: Full serv.; Baby sitter; Lounge; Crib-Hi-chair; Restaurant; Bar

Sports Facilities: Pool; Sauna; Hot tub; Tennis; Princeville

Room Facilities: Cable

Attractions: Hanalei Bay, Kaulaulau Valley

Shops & Restaurants: Princeville shopping center; Nobel's

Tropical furnishings in these 1, 2 and 3 bedroom units. Babysitting, ice machines, safety deposit boxes, wake-up calls, tennis pro shop, recreation room, bar on property, and nearby shopping center, bank and restaurants.

---------------------- HANALEI, KAUAI ----------------------

Hanalei Colony Resort
P.O. Box 206
Hanalei, Kauai, HI 96714
808-826-6235 800-367-8047

2 Bedrooms $$
2 Bedrms/week 5$
Min. Stay 3 Nights, AmEx/Visa/MC,
Dep. Req'd. •
49 condos, Lo-rise, Key at At office

Location: Airport: 6 mi. Princeville; Need car; Beach front

General Facilities: Daily maid, Kitchen, Linens, Restaurant on prem., Bar on prem., Baby-sitter

Room Facilities: Pool, Hot tub, Golf: Golf 6 mi. S. Princeville; Crib-Hi-chair

Attractions: Napali Coast, boat & helicopter rides, whale watching, snorkling, Tropical Gardens, surf

Shops & Restaurants: Mall 35 miles, small unique shops from Haena south; Dolphin, Lanai, Shell, Tahiti

Secluded two-bedroom condos on beachfront property, located two miles from the beautiful Napali coastline. Swimming, snorkeling, fishing and hiking. Golf is 6 miles away. Fine restaurants and shops. For honeymooners and families.

Pali Ke Kua at Princeville
P.O. Box 899
Hanalei, Kauai, HI 96714
808-826-9066 800-367-7042

1 Bedroom $$, 2 Bedrooms $$
1 Bedrm/week 4$, 2 Bed/week 6$
Min. Stay 2 Nights, AmEx/Visa/MC,
Dep. 1 Night •
98 condos, Lo-rise, Key at Central office

Location: Airport: Princeville-3 miles; Downtown: 30 min.; Need car

General Facilities: Kitchen, Linens, Restaurant on prem., Baby-sitter

Room Facilities: Pool, Hot tub, Putting green, Golf: Princeville's Oceans; TV, Phone in rm., Crib-Hi-chair

Attractions: Hanalei Town, water sports, Princeville Racquet Club and Health Club

Shops & Restaurants: Princeville Center; Beamreach-casual fine dining

For the best golf in Hawaii, come to Pali Ke Kua with its tropical Hawaiian furnishings. Seaside picnic pavilion and private beach cove with breathtaking views.

Paliuli Cottages
P.O. Box 351
Hanalei, Kauai, HI 96714
808-826-6264

Lo-rise
Pool

Attractions: Golf

Unusual cottages on a knoll adjacent to Princeville's golf course and surrounded by mountain and ocean scenery. Split-level two-bedroom, two-bath units with a foyer looking over a bannister into the beamed-ceiling sunken living room.

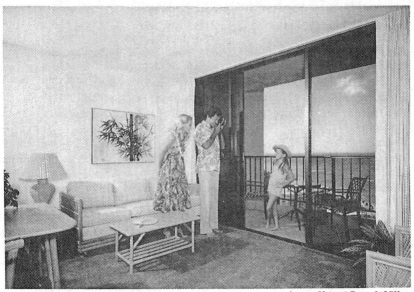

Aston Kauai Beach Villas

Pu'U Po'A
P. O. Box 1185, Ka Haku Road
Hanalei, Kauai, HI 96714
808-826-9602   800-367-7042

2 Bedrooms $$$
2 Bed/week 6$
Min. stay 2 nights, Amex, Visa, MC,
Dep. 1 night
56 condos, Hi-rise,
Key at Central office •

Location: Airport: Princeville-3 miles, Downtown: 30 min., Need car
General facilities: Kitchen, Linens, Baby sitter, Hot tub
Room facilities: TV, Phone, Crib-Hi-chair
Sports facilities: Pool, Tennis, Princeville's Oceans, Putting green
Attractions: Hanalei Town, golf, tennis, water sports, Princeville Racquet and
   Health Club
Shops & Restaurants: Princeville Center, Beamreach-casual fine dining

*Two bedroom condominiums, tropically furnished, set high on the cliffs of Princeville.
Secluded, white sand beach, spectacular sunsets, next to world famous Princeville's
Oceans Golf Course.*

Puamana
P.O. Box 1109
Hanalei, Kauai, HI 96714
808-826-9833   800-367-8047

--------------------------------- HAUULA, OAHU ---------------------------------

Pat's at Punaluu Condo
53-567 Kamehameha Highway
Hauula, Oahu, HI 96717
808-293-8111

Studio $, 1 Bedroom $$, 3 Bedrooms $$
Visa, MC, Dep. 1 night
40 condos, Hi-rise, Key at Front desk
H-yes

Location: Airport: 45 min., Downtown: 32 miles, Need car, Beach front
General facilities: Bus. fac., Conf. Rm. (cap. 20), Kitchen, Linens, Restaurant, Bar, Lounge, Sauna
Room facilities: TV, Crib-Hi-chair
Sports facilities: Pool
Attractions: Polynesian Cultural Center, Pipe Line surfing area
Shops & Restaurants: 2 small shopping centers, IGA, Pay-N-Save, Turtle Bay Hilton continental cuisine

On the windward north shore side of Oahu-beautiful beach with tropical country living. Nearby golf, tennis, Waikiki nightlife, Diamond Head, Punalulu Beach. Complimentary happy hour hors d'oeuvres, restaurant, convenience store, clothing and gift shops. All units are self-contained with ocean view and sandy beach frontage with sheltered reef.

--------------------------------- HILO, HAWAII ---------------------------------

Waiakea Villas
400 Hualani St.
Hilo, Hawaii, HI 96720
808-961-2841   800-367-7042

1 Bedroom $,   1 Bed/week $$$$
Amex, Visa, MC, Dep. 1 night
155 condos, Lo-rise,
Key at Front desk; H-yes •

Location: Airport: Hilo-1 mile, Downtown: 5 min., Need car
General facilities: Full serv., Daily maid, Kitchen, Linens, Restaurant, Bar
Room facilities: TV, Crib-Hi-chair, Ind.AC.Ctl, Ind.Heat Ctl.
Sports facilities: Pool, Tennis
Attractions: Volcano National Park, Wailoa State Park, Liliuokalani Gardens & Rainbow, Akaka Falls, Entertainment
Shops & Restaurants: Prince Kuhio Plaza, Harrington's-seafood

Amidst 14 acres of exotic plants, trees, flowers, rolling lawns and beautiful waterways. Borders Wailoa pond fresh water reserve, black sand beaches, and snow-capped mountains. Tropical, wicker and rattan furnishings in earth tones. Live entertainment in the lounge.

--------------------------------- HONOLULU ---------------------------------

Aston at the Waikiki Banyan
201 Ohua Ave.
Honolulu, Oahu, HI 96815
808-922-0555 800-922-7866

1 Bedroom $$$
Amex, Visa, MC, Dep. 1 night
328 condos, Hi-rise, Key at Front desk

General facilities: Full serv., Conf. Rm. (cap. 50), Daily maid, Kitchen, Linens, Childrens playground, Minimart, BBQ, Snack bar, Sauna
Room facilities: TV, Lanai, In-room safe, Ind.AC Ctl.
Sports facilities: Pool, Tennis, Activities desk
Attractions: Honolulu Zoo, Kapiolani Park, Aquarium, shopping, Bishop Museum

Each one bedroom suite is beautifully furnished. Spacious recreation deck with pool, tennis court, barbecue, children's play area, sauna, snack bar and minimart. Hotel services, laundry. Ideally located one block from Waikiki Beach on a quiet street. Diamond Head views.

--------------------------- HONOLULU, OAHU ---------------------------

Aston At The Waikiki Shores   Studio $$$$, 1 Bedroom $$$$, 2 Bedrooms
2161 Kalia Rd. $$$$
Honolulu, HI 96815   AmEx/Visa/MC, 1 night Dep. Req'd.
808-926-4733 800-922-7866   96 condos, Hi-rise, Key at Front desk

Location: Airport: Honolulu Intl. 10 mi; Beachfront
General Facilities: Parking; Daily maid; Linens; Dry cleaning
Room Facilities: Kitchen; Cable TV; Phone; Ind.AC.Ctl.; Washer/dryer
Attractions: Honolulu Zoo, Waikiki Aquarium, Kapiolani Park, Punchbowl
Shops & Restaurants: Ala Moana Center, International Marketplace

The only condominium resort located directly on Waikiki Beach. Each unit has a private lanai and panoramic ocean and mountain views.

Aston Pacific Monarch   Studio $$$, 1 Bedroom $$$$
142 Uluniu Avenue   AmEx/Visa/MC, 1 Night Dep. Req'd. •
Honolulu, Oahu, HI 96815   147 condos, Hi-rise, Key at Front desk
808-923-9805 800-922-7866
FAX: 808-924-3220

Location: Airport: Honolulu, 10 miles; Downtown: 5 miles
General Facilities: Laundry service; Daily maid; Linens; Travel desk; Lanai; Crib
Sports Facilities: Pool; Sauna; Jet spa
Room Facilities: Kitchen; Cable; Phone; Ind.AC Ctl.
Attractions: Bishop Museum, Honolulu Zoo, Aquarium, Kapiolani Park, Diamond Head
Shops & Restaurants: Ala Moana Center, International Market Place

Ideally located in the heart of Waikiki, just a block and a half to famous Waikiki Beach, surrounded by shopping and restaurants and just steps away from International Marketplace.

Aston Waikiki Beach Tower   1 Bedroom $$$$, 2 Bedrooms 4$
2470 Kalakaua Ave.   AmEx/Visa/MC, 1 Night Dep. Req'd. •
Honolulu, Oahu, HI 96815   94 condos, Hi-rise, Key at Front desk
808-926-6400 800-922-7866
FAX: 808-926-7380

Location: Airport: 10 miles; Downtown: 5 miles; Beachfront
General Facilities: Valet parking; Daily maid; Linens; Concierge
Business Facilities: Conf. Room Cap. 10
Sports Facilities: Pool; Sauna; Jet Spa; Shuffleboard
Room Facilities: Kitchen; Cable TV; Phone; Ind.AC.Ctl.; Washer/dryer
Attractions: Bishop Museum, International Marketplace, Diamond Head, Polynesian Cultural Cntr.
Shops & Restaurants: Ala Moana Center, International Marketplace

An excellent choice for discerning guests. Richly furnished 1- and 2-bedroom condominiums with unsurpassed views and private lanais overlooking Waikiki Beach. Only four suites per floor. A four-diamond award recipient. Gracious, personalized service. AAA 4-diamond award.

---------------------- HONOLULU, OAHU ----------------------

Aston Waikiki Sunset
229 Paoakalani Ave.
Honolulu, Oahu, HI 96815
808-922-0511 800-922-7866
FAX: 808-923-8580

Studio $$$, 1 Bedroom $$$$,
2 Bedrooms $$$$
AmEx/Visa/MC, 1 Night Dep. Req'd. •
355 condos, Hi-rise, Key at Front desk

Location: Airport: 10 miles; Downtown: 5 miles

General Facilities: Travel desk; Daily maid; Linens; Baby sitter; Restaurant on premises; BBQ

Business Facilities: Conf. Room Cap. 50

Sports Facilities: Game room; Pool; Sauna; Tennis; Shuffleboard

Room Facilities: Kitchen; Cable TV; Phone; Ind.AC.Ctl.

Attractions: Bishop Museum, Honolulu Zoo, Aquarium, Kapiolani Park, Diamond Head

Shops & Restaurants: Ala Moana Center, International Marketplace

On the picturesque Diamond Head side of Waikiki, 2 blocks from Kapiolani Park and the Honolulu Zoo. Spacious 1- and 2-bedroom suites with private lanais and charming poolside cafe. Unlimited free tennis, shuffleboard, swimming pool, sauna, barbeque grills. A great view—a great location!

Aston at the Waikiki Banyan
201 Ohua Ave.
Honolulu, Oahu, HI 96815
808-922-0555 800-922-7866
FAX: 808-922-0906

1 Bedroom $$$
AmEx/Visa/MC, 1 Night Dep. Req'd., 294 condos, Hi-rise, Key at Front desk

General Facilities: Parking; Daily maid; Linens

Business Facilities: Conf. Room Cap. 10

Sports Facilities: Game room; Activity desk; Sauna; Jet spa; Children's playground; Ala Wai Golf Course; Childrens playground

Room Facilities: Kitchen; Cable TV; Phone; Ind.AC Ctl.

Attractions: Honolulu Zoo, Kapiolani Park, Aquarium, shopping, Bishop Museum

Each one-bedroom suite is beautifully furnished with accommodations for four. Spacious recreation deck with pool, tennis court, barbeque, children's play area, sauna, locker room, game room, snack bar and minimart. Full hotel services, laundry. One Block from Waikiki Beach on a quiet street. Diamond Head/ocean views.

Please mention *Condo Vacations—the Complete Guide* when you reserve your condominium.

─────────────── HONLULU ───────────────

Royal Kuhio
2240 Kuhio Ave.
Honolulu, Oahu, HI 96815
808-923-2502 800-367-5205

1 Bedroom $$
Dep. 3 nights
Key at Front office
389 condos, Hi-rise, H-yes •

Location: Airport: 10 miles; Downtown: 1 block

General facilities: Kitchen, Linens, Child planned rec., Game room, Sauna

Room facilities: TV, Cable, Crib-Hi-chair, Ind. AC. Ctl

Sports facilities: Pool, Shuffleboard, Put. green

Attractions: Waikiki, Paradise Park, Sea Life Park, Polynesian Cultural Center, beaches

Shops & Restaurants: Ala Moana Shopping Center, Waikiki shopping, Matteo's-Italian

Completely furnished one-bedroom apartments with twin beds and queen pullout sleeper sofa in the living room. Large swimming pool, paddle tennis, basketball court, putting green, sauna, shuffleboard, and Waikiki beach two blocks away.

───

Waikiki Lanais
2452 Tusitala St.
Honolulu, Oahu, HI 96815
808-923-0994 800-367-7042

1 Bedroom $$, 2 Bedrooms $$,
1 Bed/week 4$, 2 Bed/week 5$, Amex,
Visa, MC, Dep. 1 night
Key at Front desk
160 condos, Hi-rise, H-yes •

Location: Airport: 12 miles; Downtown: 5 miles; Need car

General facilities: Kitchen, Linens, Baby sitter, Sauna, Hot tub

Room facilities: TV, Phone, Crib-Hi-chair, Ind. AC. Ctl, Ind. Heat Ctl.

Sports facilities: Pool, Exercise room

Attractions: Zoo, Aquarium, Kapiolani Park, beach

Shops & Restaurants: Royal Hawaiian Shopping Plaza, Ala Moana Center, Hy's Steakhouse

In the heart of Waikiki, tucked away in a garden setting, not far off the beaten track, are the Waikiki Lanais with views of the mountains and ocean. There is a rooftop recreation area, swimming pool, mini-gym and Waikiki Beach, Diamond Head, and the Honolulu Zoo are right outside your door. Units feature tropical, Hawaiian decor so you know you are really in Hawaii.

———————— KAANAPALI, LAHAINA, MAUI ————————

International Colony Club 1 Bedroom $$, 2 Bedrooms $$,
2750 Kalapu Drive 3 Bedrooms $$$
Kaanapali, HI 96761 Min. Stay 4 Nights, Dep. Required •
808-661-4070 800-367-8047 45 condos, Lo-rise
Key at Manager's office, H-yes

Location: Airport: 30 miles; Downtown: 3 miles; Need car
General Facilities: Linens
Sports Facilities: Pool; Shuffleboard; Royal Kaanapali
Room Facilities: Kitchen; Cable; Phone
Attractions: All ocean activities, thrill craft, fishing, snorkeling, tours, luaus, tropical gardens
Shops & Restaurants: Whaler's Village, hotel shops; Bay Club/Bar & Grill/Veranda.

Hawaiian decor with use of rattan and wicker furniture in a private area, with fruit trees and beautiful landscaping. Each cottage is unique. Relaxed carefree living by the pools, but close to beaches, water sports, shops and dining.

Maui Eldorado Resort Studio $$$, 1 Bedroom $$$$,
2661 Kekaa Dr. 2 Bedrooms $$$$
Kaanapali, Lahaina, Maui, HI AmEx/Visa/MC, 1 night Dep. Req'd. •
96761 102 condos, Lo-rise, Key at Front desk
808-661-0021 800-367-5004
FAX: 808-667-7039

Location: Airport: Kapalua West, 5 min.; Beach front
General Facilities: Full serv.; Daily maid; Linens; Baby sitter
Sports Facilities: Pool; Lawn Bowl, shuffleboard; Golf
Room Facilities: Kitchen; Cable; Phone
Attractions: Golf, tennis, beach recreation, shuttle to beach club
Shops & Restaurants: Whaler's Village an other resorts within walking distance

The Maui Eldorado is conveniently located in the center of the Kaanapali resort area. This 1st class condominium is located 5 minutes from Kapalua West Maui Airport and 45 minutes from Kahului Airport. Guests can enjoy the property's 3 swimming pools and Maui's only private beach club on Kaanapali Beach. Maui Eldorado's Beach Club is on one of Hawaii's most beautiful white sand swimming beaches and offers guests a weekly complimentary cocktail reception, beach equipment and full kitchen facilities.

---------------------------- KAANAPALI, MAUI ----------------------------

Kaanapali Alii
50 Nohea Kai Dr.
Kaanapali, Maui, HI 96761
808-667-1400 800-642-6284

1 Bedroom $$$$, 2 Bedrooms $$$$
Min. Stay 3 Nights, AmEx/Visa/MC,
Dep. 3 Nights •
264 condos, Hi-rise, Key at Front desk
H-yes

Location: Airport: West Maui—15 min.; Downtown: 3 miles; Beach front

General Facilities: Full serv., Conf. rm. cap. 14, Daily maid, Kitchen, Linens, Baby-sitter, Child planned rec.: Hawaiian handicrafts

Room Facilities: Pool, Sauna, Hot tub, Tennis, Beach activities, Golf: Royal Kaanapali; TV, Phone in rm., Crib-Hi-chair, Ind. AC Ctl., Ind. Heat Ctl.

Attractions: Swimming, snorkeling, golfing, scuba diving, catamaran cruises, helicopter rides, horses

Shops & Restaurants: Whaler's Village, Old Lahaina Town, hotels; La Bretagne-French

Comfortable elegance reflecting the spirit of Hawaiian hospitality. Beachfront on Kaanapali Beach for swimming in the warm Pacific, freshwater pools, jacuzzi, saunas, and exercise room. Watch the whales spout or take a ride on the Sugar Cane Train. Fine restaurants and shopping within walking distance, full hotel services including Concierge and beach activities.

---------------------------- KAHUKU ----------------------------

Kuilima Estates
P.O. Box 899
Kahuku, HI 96731
808-293-2494 800-367-7040

Studio $, 1 Bedroom $$, 2 Bedrooms $$$
Min. Stay 2 Nights, AmEx/Visa/MC,
Dep. 1 Night •
80 condos, Lo-rise, Key at Kahuku Sugar Mill

Location: Airport: 1½ hours; Downtown: 1 hour; Need car

General Facilities: Kitchen, Linens, Baby-sitter

Room Facilities: Sauna, Tennis, Golf: Kuilima at Turtle Bay; TV, Cable, Phone in rm., Crib-Hi-chair

Attractions: Polynesian Cultural Center, Kahuku Sugar Mill, surfing, water sports, polo, horses

Shops & Restaurants: Haleiwa Town; The Mill

A wind-surfing paradise near famous beaches, just an hour away from Waikiki. Situated on an 18-hole championship golf course with pools and tennis courts, these tropically furnished units are within walking and driving distance to shopping and dining. The perfect Hawaiian vacation on the "other side."

Our listings—supplied by the managements—are as complete as possible. Many of the condos have more features than we list. Be sure to inquire when you book.

----------------------- KAILUA, KONA -----------------------

Keauhou Resort Condominiums	1 Bedroom $, 2 Bedrooms $$
78-7039 Kamehameha III Rd.	1 Bedrm/week $$$$, 2 Bed/week 5$
Kailua, Kona, HI 96740	Min. Stay 5 Nights, Dep. Req'd. •
808-322-9122 800-367-5286	48 condos, Lo-rise, Key at Front office
	H-yes

Location: Airport: 12 miles; Downtown: 6 miles; Need car

General Facilities: Kitchen, Linens

Room Facilities: Pool, Golf: Kona Country Club; TV, Cable, VCR, Phone in rm., Crib-Hi-chair

Attractions: Golf, island tours, charter fishing, snorkeling, diving, swimming

Shops & Restaurants: Keauhou shopping village

A cluster of one-and two-level townhouses, nestled in a 5-acre tropical garden. Most units have ocean views with one or two lanais flowering with bougainvillea. Drowse and laze by the pool, or delight in the brilliant treasure trove of marine life in the underwater world of the sparkling waters of the Kona Coast. Glass-bottom viewing boats, charter fishing and dinner sails. Golf at your doorstep.

Kona Alii	1 Bedroom $$
75-5782 Kuakini Highway	1 Bedrm/week $$$$
Kailua, Kona, HI 96740	Min. Stay 3 Nights, Dep. Req'd. •
808-329-2000 800-553-5035	70 condos, Hi-rise, Key at Office on site
	H-yes

Location: Airport: 7 miles; Downtown: 1 block; Beach front

General Facilities: Kitchen, Linens

Room Facilities: Pool, Golf: Kona Golf Course—close; TV, Cable

Attractions: Snorkeling, swimming, sightseeing, volcano, fishing, parasailing

Shops & Restaurants: Tourist shops; Various cuisines

Kona Alii overlooks the Kona coast and is located on Kailua Bay's rugged lava rim. Each one bedroom suite has two baths and sleeps up to six. Large pool and barbecues on the grounds, and tennis courts next door. Walk to Kailua Village with its many fine shops and restaurants. Kona, the largest and youngest island, is famous for black sand beaches, rain forests, volcanoes, and a year-round temperature of 72.

Kona Bali Kai	155 condos
76-6246 Alii Dr.	
Kailua, Kona, HI 96740	
800-272-3282 800-243-2992	

An intimate resort situated between quaint Kailua-Kona and the Keauhou resort area. Oceanfront suites with sweeping views of Kona Coast on meticulously landscaped grounds surrounding a freshwater swimming pool, jet spa, and sandy sunning area. Kailua-Kona is the capital of deep-sea fishing and the site of the Ironman Triathlon. Arrangements can be made for daily excursions to all the historical sites of the Big Island, or just lie back and relax at Kona by the Sea.

———————————— KAILUA-KONA, HAWAII ————————————

Kona Reef
75-5888 Alii Dr.
Kailua, Kona, Hawaii, HI 96740
808-329-2959 800-367-5004
FAX: 808-329-2762

1 Bedroom $$$, 2 Bedrooms $$$$
Min. Stay 2 Nights, AmEx/Visa/MC,
1 Night Dep. Req'd. •
56 condos, Lo-rise, Key at Front desk

Location: Airport: 10 miles; Downtown: 1 mile; Need car; Beach front

General Facilities: Full serv.; Daily maid; Linens; Baby sitter; Lounge; Crib-Hi-chair

Sports Facilities: Pool; Sauna; Spa; Nearby; Nearby

Room Facilities: Kitchen; Cable; Phone; Ind.AC.Ctl

Attractions: Volcano, Parker Ranch, Fishing. Historic Kailua-Kona.

Shops & Restaurants: Kailua Village and shopping arcade within walking distance.; Restaurants featuring fish nearby

Built in 1980. The Kona Reef is conveniently located oceanfront on the sunny Kona Coast of the Big Island. Enjoy a great vacation in the comfort and privacy of your own 1- or 2-bedroom condominium suite. All suites have a full kitchen equipped with refrigerator, oven/stove and dishwasher. Swimming pool, sundeck and barbecue area is available for all guests.

———————————————————————————————

Aston Royal Sea Cliff Resort
75-6040 Alii Dr.
Kailua-Kona, Hawaii, HI 96740
808-329-8021 800-922-7866
FAX: 808-326-1887

Studio $$$, 1 Bedrm $$$$, 2 Bedrms $$$$
AmEx/Visa/MC, 1 Night Dep. Req'd. •
148 condos, Lo-rise, Key at Front desk

Location: Airport: 10 miles; Downtown: 1 mile; Need car; Oceanfront

General Facilities: Daily maid; Linens; Inroom safe; Washer/Dryer; BBQ

Sports Facilities: Pool; Sauna; Jet Spa; Tennis; Activities desk

Room Facilities: Kitchen; Cable; VCR; Phone; Ind.AC.Ctl.

Attractions: Trips around the Island and to the volcano.

Handsome units furnished in comtemporary style. Lovely grounds with fresh and salt water pools. Lanais with ocean view or garden views. Convenience store for sundries. A spectacular oceanfront resort on the Kona Coast.

———————————————————————————————

Kona By The Sea
75-6106 Alii Dr.
Kailua-Kona, Hawaii, HI 96740
808-327-2300 800-922-7866

Studio $$$$, 1 Bedrm $$$$, 2 Bedrms $$$$
AmEx/Visa/MC, 1 Night Dep. Req'd. •
75 condos, Lo-rise, Key at Front desk

Location: Airport: 10 miles; Downtown: 2 miles; Need car; Oceanfront

General Facilities: Daily maid; Linens; Lanai; Washer/Dryer; BBQ

Sports Facilities: Pool; Jet spa; Activities Desk

Room Facilities: Kitchen; Cable; Phone; Ind.AC.Ctl.

Attractions: Hawaii Volcanoes National Park, Parker Ranch, historical attractions

Shops & Restaurants: Kailua-Kona town, 2 miles

Just south of historic Kailua-Kona town, many suites offer sweeping views of the fabulous Kona Coast. Spacious privacy in 1 bedroom and 2 bedroom/2 bath suites with designer furnishings. Lush tropical landscaping. Five minutes away from tennis and the championship Keauhou Golf Course. An optimum value. AAA 3-Diamond Award.

Royal Sea Cliff

———————————— KAILUA, KONA ————————————

Kona White Sands
Box 594
Kailua, Kona, HI 96745
808-329-9393 800-553-5035

Studio $, 1 Bedroom $
1 Bedrm/week $$$$
Min. Stay 3 Nights, Dep. Req'd. •
10 condos, Lo-rise, Key at on-site office
H-yes

Location: Airport: 9 miles; Downtown: 5 miles; Need car; Beach front
General Facilities: Kitchen, Linens
Room Facilities: TV, Cable
Attractions: Boat and fishing trips, volcano sightseeing, many nearby golf courses
Shops & Restaurants: Tourist shops

Located four miles from Kailua Village, twelve miles from Kona Airport, the ten fully equipped kitchenette suites in a two-story building have private lanais overlooking white sands beach. Golf, tennis, swimming, body-surfing, snorkeling, scuba-diving and fishing are close by. Relax while viewing palms, surf, sparkling blue seas and memorable sunsets.

──────────────── KAILUA, KONA ────────────────

Sea Village
75-6002 Alii Dr.
Kailua, Kona, HI 96740
808-329-1000 800-367-5205

1 Bedroom $, 2 Bedrooms $$, Min. stay
3 nights, Amex, Visa, MC, Dep. 3 nights
Key at Front desk
131 condos, Lo-rise, H-yes •

Location: Airport: 10 miles; Downtown: 1 mile; Need car; Beach front

General facilities: Kitchen, Linens, Hot tub

Room facilities: TV, Crib-Hi-chair

Sports facilities: Pool, Tennis

Attractions: Historic Mokuaikauna Church, Hulihee Palace, Captain Cook Monument, Painted Church

Shops & Restaurants: Kona Coast and Lanihau Shopping Center, Uncle Billy's/steak-seafood

One and two bedroom units with completely furnished kitchens with washer and dryer. Spacious paatio area, view lanais, ocean-side pool, therapeutic jacuzzi, picnic area with barbeques, tennis courts and all water sports. Hawaii's special place in the sun.

White Sands Village
74-6469 Alii Dr.
Kailua, Kona, HI 96740
808-329-6402 800-345-2823

2 Bedrooms $$, 2 Bed/week 5$, Min. stay
3 nights, Amex, Visa, MC, Dep. req'd
Key at Office on grounds
108 condos, Lo-rise, H-yes

Location: Airport: 20 miles; Downtown: 4 miles; Need car

General facilities: Daily maid, Kitchen, Linens, Baby sitter, Bar, Game room, Lounge, Sauna

Room facilities: TV, Cable, Crib-Hi-chair, Ind. AC. Ctl

Sports facilities: Tennis, 3 miles to Golf course

Attractions: Volcanoes National Park, para-sailing, snorkeling, big-game fishing

Shops & Restaurants: Keauhou Shopping Village, grocery, retail outlets, Dorian's By the Sea/steak-sea

Charm and friendliness away from big cities, sun-filled days, freedom from wind. Take the elevator down to the tennis courts and pool area. Game room with pool table and barbeque. Crescent, white sand beach. Comfortable, roomy family condominiums with air conditioning, modern decor and lanais open to garden or pool. Beach is directly across the street.

———————————— KAILUA-KONA ————————————

Hale Kona Kai   1 Bedroom $$, Min. Stay: 3 Nights, Dep.
75-5870 Kahakai Rd.   Req'd.
Kailua-Kona, Hawaii, HI 96740   39 condos, Lo-rise, NoS-yes, Key at
800-421-3696   condominium office.

Location: Airport: 7 miles; Downtown: 1 mile, Need car; Ocean front.

General Facilities: Pool.

Room Facilities: Elevator, Kitchen, TV, Cable, Ind. AC. Ctl.

Attractions: Whale watching, coast cruises, charter fishing boats, diving, snorkeling Hulihee Palace.

Shops & Restaurants: 2 village shopping complexes, gift and small shops, Galley/fish, Huggo's/fish.

A rare find at ocean's edge, each unit has a private lanai overlooking the sparkling poolside terrace and the gentle waves of Kailua Bay. Casual dress appropriate; mid-70's year-round temperatures. The beach is only 10 minutes away from your home by the sea.

Kanaloa at Kona   1 Bedroom $$.
78-261 Manukai St.
Kailua, Kona, Hawaii, HI 96740
808-322-2272 800-367-6046

Charming Hawaiian village architecture in these low-rise condominiums. Large lanais with wet bars and jacuzzis in oceanfront suites. 3 pools, 1 adults only, 2 tennis courts, recreation center, adjacent 18 hole golf. Abundant palm trees above the calm Pacific.

Kona Bay Hotel, Uncle Billy's
75-5739 Alii Dr.
Kailua, Kona, Hawaii, HI 96740
808-329-1393 800-367-5102

Kona Islander Inn
P.O. Box 1239
Kailua, Kona, Hawaii, HI 96740
808-329-3181 800-367-5124

Kona Magic Sands   Lo-rise condos.
77-6452 Alii Dr.
Kailua, Kona, Hawaii, HI 96740
808-329-9177

All units are ocean front studios with full kitchens. Informal and relaxed vacationing, sunning by the pool while watching the playful dolphins. White sand beach next door.

———————————————— KAMUELA ————————————————

Aston The Shores at Waikoloa
69-1035 Keana Place
Kamuela, HI 96743
808-885-5001 800-922-7866
FAX: 808-885-8414

1 Bedroom $$$$, 2 Bedrooms $$$$
AmEx/Visa/MC, 1 Night Dep. Req'd.,
64 condos, Lo-rise
Key at Front desk

Location: Airport: 18 miles Keahole; Downtown: 25 mi, Kailua-Kona; Need car

General Facilities: Laundry facility; Daily maid; Linens; Lanai; Crib; Activities Desk; BBQ

Sports Facilities: Pool; Jet Spa; Tennis; Waikoloa Resort Course; In-room safe

Room Facilities: Kitchen; Cable; Phone; Ind.AC.Ctl.

Attractions: Hawaii Volcanos National Park, Parker Ranch, historical attractions

Shops & Restaurants: Nearby shops; Nearby restaurants

Luxury resort along the prestigious Kohala Coast, amidst lush tropical gardens, fronting the fairways of Waikoloa's Beach Course. AAA 3-diamond award.

——

Elima Lani At Waikoloa Village
68-3883 Lua Kula St., #1704
Kamuela, HI 96743
808-883-8288 800-367-5004
FAX: 808-883-8170

Studio $$, 1 Bedroom $$, 2 Bedrooms $$$
AmEx/Visa/MC ●
216 condos, Lo-rise
Key at Front desk

Location: Airport: Keahole-Kona, 30 min; Downtown: Waikoloa Village

General Facilities: Full serv.; Daily maid; Linens

Sports Facilities: Pool; Spas; Waikoloa Village G.C.

Room Facilities: Kitchen; Cable; VCR; Phone

Shops & Restaurants: Waikoloa Shopping Village

Elima Lani presents a lifestyle which few condominiums can match. Its name, which translates to "Heavenly Five," reflects the beautiful view of the 5 surrounding mountains—Haleakala, Kohala, Hualalai, Mauna Kea and Mauna Loa. Elmina Lani's locale on the Kohala Coast is ideal. A short 30-minute drive from the Keahole-Kona Airport, our all-suite resort is situated in Wailoloa Village and is conveniently located for exploring the exciting Big Island of Hawaii.

———————————————— KAMUELA ————————————————

Villas & Fairway Homes, Mauna Kea
62-100 Mauna Kea Beach Dr.
Kamuela, HI 96743
808-880-3491 800-880-6060
FAX: 808-880-3489

1 Bedroom 6$, 2 Bedrooms 8$, 3 Bedrooms 9$
Min. Stay Ask, AmEx/Visa/MC, Villas

Location: Beachfront
General Facilities: Linen
Sports Facilities: Pool; Jacuzzi; Golf Course nearby
Room Facilities: Kitchen

Villas are 2,700 sq.ft. air conditioned living areas with 2 master bedrooms, two and a half baths, dining room, sunken living room with bar and very spacious kitchen with all amenities. Laundry with washer and dryer. 1,200 sq.ft. lanai with pool or jacuzzi. Full carging privileges throughout the Mauna Kea Resort at hotel guest rates, including Mauna Kea Beach Hotel, Hapuna Beach Prince Hotel and both golf courses.

———————————————————————————————————————

Waikoloa Villas
Box 3066
Kamuela, HI 96743
808-883-9588 800-367-7042

1 Bedroom $$, 2 Bedrooms $$, 3 Bedrooms $$$
1 Bedrm/week 4$, 2 Bedrms/week 5$, 3 Bedrms/week 6$
Min. Stay 2 Nights, AmEx/Visa/MC, 2 Nights Dep. Req'd. •
40 condos, Lo-rise
Key at Administration,. No S-yes/H-yes

Location: Airport: 30 miles; Downtown: 20 miles; Need car
General Facilities: Linens; Crib-Hi-chair
Business Facilities: Conf. Room Cap. 30
Sports Facilities: Pool; Hot tub; Waikoloa Golf Course
Room Facilities: Kitchen; Cable
Attractions: Home of Parker Ranch, Volcano National Park, Snow on Mauna Kea often, two beaches—15 min.
Shops & Restaurants: Waimea-20 miles-nontourist shops, supermarket; Edelweiss-German

These condominiums are on 7 luxuriously landscaped acres fronting the Waikoloa Golf Course. Fully equipped units for all meals or just snacks; lanais feature wet bars and ocean or garden views. Outside are two pools, whirlpools, cabanas and gazebo area. Golf, riding stables and two beaches are nearby, while tennis is just across the street.

Enter your favorite condo in our "Condo of the Year" contest (entry form is in the back of the book).

--------- KAPAA, KAUAI ---------

Kapaa Sands
P.O. Box 3292
Kapaa, Kauai, HI 96746
808-822-4901 800-222-4901

Studio $$, 2 Bedrooms $$
Min. Stay 3 Nights, Dep. Required •
24 condos, Lo-rise
Key at Dining room table

Location: Airport: 7 miles; Downtown: 5 miles; Beach front

General Facilities: Daily maid; Linens; Baby sitter

Sports Facilities: Pool

Room Facilities: Kitchen; Cable

Attractions: Opaeka's Falls, hike up the Sleeping Giant, ski on the Wailua River

Shops & Restaurants: Plantation Marketplace includes shops/restaurants

A secluded private paradise tucked away on the famed Coconut Coast. Walk to the sea from your ocean front unit. A low-key vacation hideaway within walking distance to shopping and restaurants. Centrally located between road ends of the island's only highway-70 miles along the coast, ending at the rugged Na Pali mountain range.

Lanikai
390 Papaloa Road
Kapaa, Kauai, HI 96746
808-822-7456 800-367-5004
FAX: 808-822-9293

1 Bedroom $$$$, 2 Bedrooms $$$$
AmEx/Visa/MC •
18 condos, Lo-rise, Villa
Key at Front desk

Location: Need car; Beach front

General Facilities: Full serv.; Daily maid; Linens

Sports Facilities: Pool

Room Facilities: Kitchen; Cable; VCR; Phone

Shops & Restaurants: Coconut Plantation Marketplace within walking distance

Renovated in 1993. Experience the ultimate in beach front luxury. A few exceptionally large apartments set in lush gardens leading to a sandy beach on Wailua Bay in Kauai's most convenient yet absolutely private location. Spacious 1- and 2-bedroom condominium suites with full kitchens and balconies overlooking the water but within walking distance of restaurants and shops.

─────────────── KIHEI, MAUI ───────────────

Aston Maui Hill
2881 S. Kihei Rd.
Kihei, Maui, HI 96753
808-879-6321 800-922-7866
FAX: 808-879-8945

1 Bedroom $$$$, 2 Bedrooms $$$$,
3 Bedrooms $$$$
AmEx/Visa/MC, 1 Night Dep. Req'd. •
42 condos, Lo-rise, Key at Front desk

Location: Airport: 16 miles Kahului; Downtown: 15 min. Kahului; Need car
General Facilities: Daily maid; Linens; Baby sitter; Washer/Dryer; BBQ
Sports Facilities: Pool; Jet Spa; Tennis; Shuffleboard; Putting green; Activities Desk
Room Facilities: Kitchen; Cable; Phone; Ind.AC.Ctl.
Attractions: Haleakala Crater, whale watching cruises
Shops & Restaurants: Azeka and Wailea Shopping Centers, supermarkets

A quiet, exclusive hideaway just minutes from Wailea. Fully furnished 1-, 2- and 3-bedroom suites with air conditioning BBQ, cable TV and pool. Enjoy the sunsets from your private lanai.

Aston Maui Vista
2191 Kihei Rd.
Kihei, Maui, HI 96753
808-879-7966 800-922-7866
FAX: 808-874-5612

1 Bedroom $$, 2 Bedrooms $$
AmEx/Visa/MC, 1 Night Dep. Req'd. •
90 condos, Hi-rise, Key at Front desk

Location: Airport: 15 miles Kahului
General Facilities: Full serv.; Daily maid; Linens; Laundry; BBQ
Sports Facilities: Pool; Activity Desk
Room Facilities: Kitchen; Cable; Phone; Ind.AC.Ctl.; Washer/dryer
Attractions: Haleakala Crater, Kamaole Beach Park
Shops & Restaurants: 3 shopping centers within 2 miles, boutiques

Ten acres of tropical retreat across from sandy Kamaole Beach near Wailea. Spacious 1 and 2 bedroom suites with private lanais and fully furnished kitchens. 3 pools, 6 championship tennis courts, spacious grounds and outdoor BBQ. Championship golf, shopping and restaurants nearby.

Kamaole Sands
2695 S. Kihei Road
Kihei, Maui, HI 96742
808-874-8700 800-367-5004
FAX: 808-879-3273

Studio $$, 1 Bedroom $$$,
2 Bedrooms $$$$, 3 Bedrooms $$$$
AmEx/Visa/MC •
268 condos, Hi-rise, Key at Front desk

General Facilities: Full serv.; Daily maid; Linens; Restaurant
Sports Facilities: Pool; Spas; Tennis; Volleyball, bike, snorkel; Golf
Room Facilities: Kitchen; Cable; Phone
Attractions: Water sports, health club

Renovated in 1991, one of the most popular condominium resorts in Maui. Accommodations are spacious and comfortable, offering all the conveniences for a fun filled vacation experience. All studios and suites have fully equipped kitchen and private lanai. Guests can enjoy complimentary tennis, swimming pool and sundeck, 2 jet spas, 8 BBQ areas and free parking. Just across from the beach, the Kamaole Sands offers its guests 15 acres of tropical gardens, complete with fish ponds and spectacular waterfalls.

——————————————— KIHEI, MAUI ———————————————

Aston At The Maui Banyan
2575 South Kihei Rd.
Kihei, Maui, HI 96853
808-875-0004 800-922-7866
FAX: 808-874-4035

Studio $$$, 1 Bedrm $$$, 2 Bedrms $$$$
AmEx/Visa/MC, 1 Night Dep. Req'd.
113 condos, Hi-rise, Key at Front desk

Location: Airport: Kahului, 10 miles; Downtown: Kahului, 15 min.; Need car; Beachfront

General Facilities: Parking; Daily maid; Linens; Drycleaning; Lanai; BBQ facilities

Sports Facilities: Pool; Jet spa; Tennis; 4 golf courses nearby; Activities Desk

Room Facilities: Kitchen; Cable; Phone; Ind.AC.Ctl.

Attractions: Haleakala Crater, whale watching cruises

Shops & Restaurants: Azeka & Wailea Shopping Centers

Overlooking the sunny shores of Kamaole Beach Park, every suite has a private lanai. Four championship golf courses minutes away.

——

Haleakala Shores
Condominiums
2619 S. Kihei Rd.
Kihei, Maui, HI 96753
808-879-1218 800-869-1097
FAX: 808-879-2219

2 Bedrooms $$
2 Bedrms/week 5$
Min. Stay 5 Nights, 76 condos, Lo-rise
Key at Haleakala Shores, H-Yes

Location: Airport: 20 minutes; Downtown: 20 minutes; Need car

General Facilities: Linens; Baby sitter; Crib-Hi-chair

Sports Facilities: Pool; Tennis; Snorkeling, fishing; Near Wailea Golf Courses

Room Facilities: Kitchen; Cable; Phone; Ind.AC.Ctl.

Attractions: Haleakala Volcano, Maalaea Harbor, Women's Kemper Open at Wailea Blue Golf Course

Shops & Restaurants: Azeka's Place, Kukui Mall, specialty shops; Kihei Prime Rib, Fairway Restaurant

Hawaiian-style buildings with elevators in a Polynesian garden setting. Spacious 2-bedroom, 2-bath residences with private lanais, dressing areas and generous closets. Barbeques, leisure areas and pool in a lush garden setting. Across the street from the beautiful beach of Kamaole Park Three. Fine dining, exceptional golf and tennis facilities are only minutes away.

Kona By The Sea

——————————————— KIHEI, MAUI ———————————————

Kihei Alii Kai
2387 S. Kihei Rd., P.O.Box 985
Kihei, Maui, HI 96753
808-879-6770 800-888-6284
FAX: 808-874-0844

1 Bedroom $$, 2 Bedroom $$, 3
  Bedroom $$
1 Bedrm/week 4$, 2 Bedrm/week 5$, 3
  Bedrm/week 6$
Min. Stay 3 Nights, AmEx/MC/Visa/
  Other CC, Dep. Req'd
127 condos, Hi-rise, Keys at Front office

Location: Airport: 20 minutes; Downtown:

General Facilities: Kitchen, Linens

Room Facilities: Pool, Sauna, Hot tub, Tennis, Silver Sword 1½ mile, TV,
  Cable, Phone in rm.

Attractions: Ocean activities, luaus, tours of island.

Shops & Restaurants: Foodland, ABC store, Kihei town center; Kihei prime
  rib & seafood.

*300 feet to one of the largest beaches on Maui. Spacious units with ocean and
mountain views from the balconies. Pool and jacuzzi surrounded by a flower-
covered fence. Two tennis courts when you feel the need for more strenuous
activity. Fine restaurants within walking distance, or barbeque your dinner at
"home."*

──────── KIHEI, MAUI ────────

Kihei Beach Resort
36 S. Kihei Rd.
Kihei, Maui, HI 96753
808-879-2744 800-367-6034

1 Bedroom $$, 2 Bedrooms $$$
Min. Stay 3 Nights, 3 Nights Dep. Req'd. ●
53 condos, Hi-rise, Key at Office in lobby

Location: Airport: Kahului-15 minutes; Downtown: 2 miles; Need car; Beach front

General Facilities: Daily maid; Linens; Baby sitter; Crib-Hi-chair

Sports Facilities: Pool

Room Facilities: Kitchen; Cable; Phone; Ind.AC.Ctl

Attractions: Haleakala Crater, IAO Needle, Hana, Lahaina

Shops & Restaurants: Lahaina, Kahului, Sears, Liberty House; Wailea Steak House/fish-steak

Accommodations with all the essentials, including maid service to get you away from home housekeeping. Daily coffee in the lobby. Family oriented resort with an excellent climate, fine swimming beach for walking, shelling and snorkeling. Settle down on your lanai overlooking the pool and ocean with a good book. Area restaurants, 15 minutes to the Kahului airport, Maui's major seaport and a great place for shopping.

──────────────────────────────

Kihei Sands
115 North Kihei Road
Kihei, Maui, HI 96753
808-879-2624 800-882-6284
FAX: 808-875-1928

1 Bedroom $$, 2 Bedrooms $$
Min. Stay 4 Nights, Dep. Required ●
30 condos, Lo-rise, Key with Manager

Location: Airport: 20 minutes; Downtown: 3 miles; Need car; Beachfront

General Facilities: Linens

Sports Facilities: Pool

Room Facilities: Kitchen; Cable; Phone; Ind.AC.Ctl

Attractions: Snorkeling, boogie boards, windsurfing, swimming, sightseeing and golf.

Shops & Restaurants: Costco, Liberty House, Longs; Margaritas, Waterfront

Stay at Kihei Sands on the tranquil and beautiful island of Maui. Freshwater pool in a tropical Polynesian setting overlooks the beach and offshore islands of Kahoolawe and Molokini. Centrally located for sightseeing to Lahaina, Hana, Iao Valley, Haleakala, and The Seven Sacred Pools. Ten miles of golden sand beaches are a step away.

Enter your favorite condo in our "Condo of the Year" contest (entry form is in the back of the book).

―――――――――――― KIHEI, MAUI ――――――――――――

Kihei Surfside Resort
2936 South Kihei Rd.
Kihei, Maui, HI 96753
808-879-1488 800-367-5240

1 Bedroom $$, 2 Bedrooms $$$
Min. Stay 3 Nights, AmEx/Visa/MC, 3
Nights Dep. Req'd. •
83 condos, Hi-rise
Key at Office-Unit 105, H-yes

Location: Airport: 16 miles; Downtown: 1 mile; Need car; Beach front

General Facilities: Daily maid; Linens; Baby sitter; Crib-Hi-chair

Sports Facilities: Pool; Shuffleboard; Wailea

Room Facilities: Kitchen; Cable; Phone

Attractions: Ocean excursions, tours to Molokai, luaus, pineapple plantation tours, Haliakala, fishing

Shops & Restaurants: Wailea tourist shopping, Kihei shopping centers; Continental-Oriental-Hawaiian

Delightful accommodations with rattan furnishings, adjacent to an uncrowded swimming beach, for swimming, skin diving or beach-bumming. Explore the green grottoes and coral caves ... delight in the tropical blossoms, volcanic mountains and waterfalls. Charter boats are available for blue marlin fishing, or cast from the shore. A great place for a family vacation.

Leinaala Condominiums
998 S. Kihei Rd.
Kihei, Maui, HI 96753
808-879-2235 800-334-3305
FAX: 808-879-8366

Studio $$, 1 Bedroom $$, 2 Bedrooms $$$
Min. Stay 5 Nights, Dep. Required •
25 condos, Hi-rise, H-Yes

Location: Beachfront

General Facilities: Linens

Sports Facilities: Pool; Tennis

Room Facilities: Kitchen; Cable; Phone; Ind.AC.Ctl

Off the beaten path, but only a 20 minute drive from Kahului Airport and a half mile from shopping. Palm trees and green lawns lead to the beach for ocean sports. Frequent barbeques and pupu parties. Views of West Maui mountains and Haleakala from the beach front in Kihei.

──────────── KIHEI, MAUI ────────────

Luana Kai
940 S. Kihei Rd.
Kihei, Maui, HI 96753
808-879-1268 800-367-7042

1 Bedroom $$, 2 Bedrooms $$,
3 Bedrooms $$$
1 Bedrm/week 4$, 2 Bedrms/week 5$
AmEx/Visa/MC, 1 Night Dep. Req'd. •
114 condos, Lo-rise, Key at Front desk
H-yes

Location: Airport: 15 Min-Kahalui; Downtown: ½ mile; Need car; Beach front

General Facilities: Linens; Baby sitter; Crib-Hi-chair

Sports Facilities: Pool; Sauna; Hot tub; Putting green

Room Facilities: Kitchen; Phone

Attractions: Water sports, IAO Valley; Entertainment

Shops & Restaurants: Kihei town, Azekas Place, Dolphin Center; Stouffer's Raffles

Vacationer's paradise with tropical style furnishings amidst warm and friendly people. Barbeque area for cook-outs, morning coffee, orientation, aerobic classes, snorkeling lessons, hula lessons and a dive clinic. Garden and ocean views from your balconies.

──────────────────────────

Maalaea Surf Resort
12 South Kihei Rd.
Kihei, Maui, HI 96753
808-879-1267 800-423-7953

1 Bedroom $$$, 2 Bedrooms $$$$
Min. Stay 3 Nights, Dep. Required •
59 condos, Lo-rise, Key at Office, H-yes

Location: Airport: 8 miles; Downtown: 2½ miles; Need car

General Facilities: Daily maid; Linens; Baby sitter

Sports Facilities: Pool; Tennis

Room Facilities: Kitchen; Cable; Phone; Ind.AC.Ctl

Attractions: Snorkel and dinner cruises, luaus, windsurfing, golf within 2½ miles

Shops & Restaurants: Azeka shopping center, Kahului shopping centers; Azeka's Ribs-Pancake House

Truly luxurious accommodations in one or two-story townhouses amid tall palms. South Seas furnishings. Two swimming pools, two tennis courts, and several shuffleboards. Golden sand beach and gorgeous sunsets. A very private resort on peaceful Maui.

----------------------------------- KIHEI, MAUI -----------------------------------

Nani Kai Hale
73 North Kihei Road
Kihei, Maui, HI 96753
808-879-9120 800-367-6032

Studio $, 1 Bedroom $$,
2 Bedrooms $$$
Min. stay 3 nights, Dep. required
46 condos, Hi-rise,
Key at Office or Apt. 409
H-yes •

Location: Airport: 9 miles, Downtown: 2 miles, Need car, Beach front, Ski lift: and Ocean View

General facilities: Kitchen, Linens, Baby sitter, Microwave, BBQ, Parking, Pool

Room facilities: TV, Cable, Phone, Crib-Hi-chair, Ceiling Fans, Washer/Dryer, some A/C

Attractions: 5 miles of walking and swimming beach, whale watching, snorkeling, windsurfing, Haleakala Crater, professional golf and tennis.

Shops & Restaurants: Kihei—2.5 miles, Kahului—7 miles, many restaurants in the Kihei area

Delightful condominiums with ratan furnishings located on an excellent five mile walking, uncrowded, swimming beach. Nani Kai Hale (Beautiful Sea House) is centrally located to any activity that you might do. Professional golf, tennis, also shopping, hiking, water sports are located within ten miles. Excellent view of Haleakala and West Maui Mountains. A great place to bring your family for vacation.

Royal Mauian
2430 South Kihei Rd.
Kihei, Maui, HI 96753
808-879-1263 800-367-8009

1 Bedroom $$, 2 Bedrooms $$,
3 Bedrooms $$$
Min. stay 5 nights, Dep. req'd
107 condos, Hi-rise,
Key at Front desk •

Location: Airport: 12 miles, Downtown: 2 miles, Need car, Beach front

General facilities: Kitchen, Linens, Baby sitter

Room facilities: TV, Cable, Phone, Crib-Hi-chair

Sports facilities: Pool, Silver Sword-3 miles

Attractions: Sun, beach, golf, tennis, Haleakala Crater, winter whale watching

Shops & Restaurants: Lahaina shops, Steak-seafood in Lahaina

Tastefully furnished units for island living. Large pool where complimentary coffee and tea are served each morning. Carpeted Roof Garden with refrigerated bar, and gas grills for daytime sunning or evening cocktails. Snorkel to lava reefs to watch exotic fish, swim, tan or stroll on the beach.

──────── KIHEI, MAUI ────────

Shores of Maui　　　　　　　1 Bedroom $$, 2 Bedrooms $$
2075 S. Kihei Rd.　　　　　　　1 Bedrm/week $$$$, 2 Bedrms/week 6$
Kihei, Maui, HI 96753　　　　　Min. Stay 3 Nights, Visa/MC •
808-879-9140　800-367-8002　50 condos, Lo-rise, Key at Front desk
FAX: 808-879-6221

Location: Airport: 20 minutes; Downtown: 1 block; Beachfront

General Facilities: Linens

Sports Facilities: Pool; Hot tub; Tennis

Room Facilities: Kitchen; Cable; Phone

Attractions: Ocean activities, Haleakala Volcano; Entertainment

Shops & Restaurants: Star, Foodland, ABC, Dolphin Center, Rainbow Mall; Kihei
　　PrimeRib-Stoffer Hotel

Clean, comfortable, brightly decorated condominiums across the street from snorkeling. Pool, hot tub, tennis, winter whale watching. Brightly decorated condominiums with Hawaiian style furniture, kitchen microwaves and washer/dryers.

───────────────────────────────

Sugar Beach Resort　　　　1 Bedroom $$, 2 Bedrooms $$$
145 N. Kihei Rd.　　　　　　　1 Bedrm/week 4$, 2 Bedrms/week 8$
Kihei, Maui, HI 96753　　　　　Min. Stay 4 Nights, Dep. Required •
808-879-2778　800-367-5242　240 condos, Hi-rise, Key at Front office

Location: Airport: 8 miles; Downtown: 2 miles; Need car; Beach front

General Facilities: Linens; Baby sitter; Crib-Hi-chair; Restaurant; Bar

Sports Facilities: Pool; Sauna; Hot tub; Tennis; Silver Sword—2 miles

Room Facilities: Kitchen; Cable; Phone; Ind.Heat Ctl.

Attractions: Scuba, snorkeling, fishing, surfing, windsurfing, luaus, jet ski,
　　parasailing; Entertainment

Shops & Restaurants: Tourist shops; Chinese

Ocean-front one and two bedroom units located on a five mile stretch of white sandy beach in north Kihei. Fully furnished with color cable TV, central air conditioning and full kitchens. Polynesian dancing once a month in the winter.

───────────────────────────────

Hale Kamaole Condominiums　　　1 Bedroom $$, 2 Bedrooms $$
2737 South Kihei Rd.
Kihei, Maui, HI 96753
808-879-2698　800-367-2970

One-bedroom and split-level two-bedroom/two-bath units across from beach park. Telephone, ceiling fans, TVs, two pools, tennis court on landscaped grounds.

————————————————— KIHEI —————————————————

Kauhale Makai
938 S. Kihei Road
Kihei, HI 96753
808-879-8888 800-367-2954

1 Bedroom $$, 2 Bedrooms $$, Hi-rise
Pool, Phone in rm.

Attractions: Snorkeling, windsurfing, beachcombing, Shuffleboard, volleyball, tennis, golf

300 feet of grass in front of the pool and jacuzzi leads to the sandy beach. Units with kitchenettes, color TV's and balconies. Outdoor barbecues, shuffleboard, volleyball and mini-golf.

Kihei Kai Nani
2495 South Kihei Road
Kihei, HI 96753
808-879-9088 800-367-8047

1 Bedroom $$
Min. Stay 7 Nights, Dep. Req'd. •
185 condos, Lo-rise, Key at Main office

Location: Airport: 11 miles; Downtown: 3 miles; Need car

General Facilities: Kitchen, Linens

Room Facilities: Pool, Shuffleboard, Golf: Nearby; TV, Cable, Phone in rm., Crib-Hi-chair

Attractions: All water sports, golf, tennis, beach

Shops & Restaurants: Kai Nani Village convenience market, shops; Prime Rib House

Across the road from Kamaole Beach II, low-rise condominiums in a Polynesian garden environment with palms and pulmeria. Owner-furnished units have lanais with varying views and comfortably accommodate four persons. Spend the sunny days at the beach, swimming, snorkeling, windsurfing, sailing, fishing or sunbathing. Outdoor barbecues and a garden pavilion for private meetings and entertainment.

————————————————— KOHALA —————————————————

Mauna Lani Point
HCR 2, Box 4600, Kohala Coast
Kohala, HI 96743
808-885-5022 800-642-6284

1 Bedroom $$$, 2 Bedrooms $$$$, 3 Bedrooms
$$$$
Min. Stay 3 Nights, AmEx/Visa/MC,
Dep. 3 Nights •
116 condos, Lo-rise, Key at Front office

Location: Airport: 20 miles; Downtown: 30 miles; Need car

General Facilities: Full serv., Bus. fac., Conf. rm. cap. 60, Daily maid, Kitchen, Linens, Baby-sitter, Child planned rec.: Summer day camp

Room Facilities: Pool, Sauna, Hot tub, Tennis, Recreation area, Golf: Francis H. I'i Brown; TV, Cable, Phone in rm., Crib-Hi-chair, Ind. AC Ctl.

Attractions: Deep-sea marlin fishing, scuba diving, historic royal fishponds, jogging

Shops & Restaurants: Mauna Lani Bay Hotel shops, art galleries; Gallery Restaurant/nouvelle

Spacious, sophisticated rattan furnished units with postcard views of the golf course and ocean. The pool has its own waterfall surrounded by spectacular exotic flowers, as well as a jacuzzi and sauna. Recreation area pavilion has barbecue and cooking facilities. Go to the Racquet Club for tennis, steam room and exercise work-out and stay for lunch or dinner. The Mauna Lani Beach Club lets you laze on the white sand cove in quiet, beautiful surroundings.

────────────────── KOLOA ──────────────────

Embassy Vacation Resort
Poipu Pt.
1613 Pe'e Road
Koloa, HI 96756
808-742-1888 800-922-7866
FAX: 808-742-1924

1 Bedroom $$$$, 2 Bedrooms $$$$,
3 Bedrooms 10$
AmEx/Visa/MC, 1 Night Dep. Req'd., 200
condos, Lo-rise, Key at Front Desk

General Facilities: Concierge; Daily maid; Linens; Drycleaning; Lanai; BBQ facilities; Laundry service

Sports Facilities: Pool; Spa; Fitness center; Activities Desk

Room Facilities: Kitchen; Cable; Phone; Ind.AC.Ctl.

Luxury oceanfront resort amidst 22 acres of lush tropical gardens. Relax in the luxury of your spacious suite with gourmet kitchen, oversize master bath and private lanai.

──

Makahuena Resort at Poipu
1661 Pe'e Road
Koloa, Kauai, HI 96756
808-742-7555 800-367-5004

1 Bedroom $$$, 2 Bedrooms $$$
Visa/MC, 1 Night Dep. Req'd. •
75 condos, Lo-rise, Key at Front desk

Location: Airport: 30 minutes; Downtown: 30 minutes; Need car; Ocean front

General Facilities: Full serv.; Daily maid; Linens; Crib-Hi-chair

Sports Facilities: Pool; Jacuzzi; Tennis; Snorkeling; Kiahuna Golf Course-near

Room Facilities: Kitchen; Cable; Phone

Attractions: Near Poipu Beach and historic Koloa town, a distance from Waimea Canyon and Wailua Falls

Shops & Restaurants: Poipu Shopping Village a short drive away; Dozens of restaurants nearby

On the southernmost point of the island of Kauai. Offers the rare opportunity for viewing both sunrise and sunset from its oceanfront location. This all-suite condominiumn consists of beautifully furnished 1- and 2-bedroom units with swimming pool, sundeck, hydro-spa, tennis court and barbecue area. With Keoniloa Bay and Shipwreck Beach to the east and Brennecke's and Poipu Beach to the west, Makahuena is within walking distance to some of the most beautiful beaches on the island.

---------- KOLOA, KAUAI ----------

Kiahuna Plantation
2253 Poipu Rd.
Koloa, Kauai, HI 96756
808-742-6411 800-367-7052
FAX: 808-742-7233

1 Bedroom $$$$, 2 Bedrooms $$$$, Min.
Stay: 2 Nights, AmEx/Visa/MC, Dep.
Req'd, •
333 condos, Lo-rise, H-yes, Key at front
desk.

Location: Airport: 14 miles; Downtown: 1 mile, Need car; Beach front.

General Facilities: Lagoon fishing, Tennis, Kiahuna, Horses, surfing, Baby sitter, Restaurant, Bar.

Room Facilities: Daily maid, Kitchen, TV, Phone, Crib-Hi-chair.

Attractions: Scenic attractions-Waimea Canyon (hiking), Spouting Horn, Fern Grotto, Kokee State Park, entertainment.

Shops & Restaurants: Liberty House, Sears, Plantation Gardens/seafood.

Condominiums on sunny south shore of Kauai with garden or ocean views. Kiahuna Shopping Village is across the street, and Old Koloa Town, a showpiece of Kauai's plantation past is two miles away. Rent boogie boards, snorkeling gear or surf boards. White sand beach. Pool at tennis complex. Surfing, tennis and scuba lessons available. Golf and honeymoon packages.

Lawai Beach Resort
5017 Lawai Rd.
Koloa, Kauai, HI 96756
808-742-9581 800-367-6046

On Kauai's sunny south shore facing a world-famous surfing beach. Two pools, two tennis courts, minutes to Kiahuna Golf Village.

Makahuena at Poipu
1661 Pe'e Road
Koloa, Kauai, HI 96756
808-742-7474 800-367-5124

2 Bedrooms $$$, 2 Bedrm/week 8$, Min.
Stay: 4 Nights, Dep. Req'd.
78 condos, Lo-rise, H-yes.

Location: Airport: 20 miles, Need car; Beach front.

General Facilities: Pool, Hot tub, Tennis, Kiahuna, Baby sitter.

Room Facilities: Kitchen, TV, Cable, Crib-Hi-chair.

Attractions: Snorkeling, scuba diving, helicopter rides, deep sea fishing, boat tours, beaches.

Built on cliff side with dramatic ocean views to the east and south. Two bedroom units with swimming pool, jacuzzi, barbeque area and two tennis courts.

———————————— KOLOA, KAUI ————————————

Manualoha at Poipu Kai
RR 1
Koloa, Kauai, HI 96756
808-742-7555 800-367-8022

1 Bedroom $$
1 Bedrm/week 5$
Lo-rise
H-yes

Location: Airport: 20 miles; Need car

General Facilities: Kitchen, Linens, Restaurant on prem., Bar on prem., Baby-sitter

Room Facilities: Pool, Hot tub, Tennis, Golf: ½ mile Kiahuna; TV, Cable, Phone in rm., Crib-Hi-chair

Attractions: Helicopter rides, tours of Waimea Canyon, boat tours, deep-sea fishing

Shops & Restaurants: Three separate shopping villages; Keoki's/seafood-continental

Tropically furnished, beautifully appointed units built along the Greenbelt of Poipu Kai Resort leading to the Maunaloha pool and on to Brennecke's Beach for body surfing.

Sea Village

────────────── KOLOA, KAUAI ──────────────

Nihi Kai Villas
1870 Hoone Rd.
Koloa, Kauai, HI 96756
808-742-1412 800-325-5701
FAX: 808-742-9001

1 Bedroom $$$, 2 Bedrooms $$$,
3 Bedrooms $$$$, Min. Stay: 3 Nights,
AmEx/Visa/MC, Dep. 2 Nights, •
70 condos, Lo-rise, Key at office.

Location: Airport: 15 miles; Downtown: 15 miles, Need car; Beach front.

General Facilities: Pool, Tennis, Kiahuna, Baby sitter, BBQ.

Room Facilities: Kitchen, TV, Cable.

Attractions: Waimea Canyon, beaches, snorkeling, scuba diving, helicopter rides, boat tours, fishing.

Shops & Restaurants: Three separate shopping villages, Keoki's/seafood-continental.

This complete resort complex is located 20 yards from Brennecke Beach, famous for body surfing. One block further is Poipu Beach Park with safe swimming for everyone. These condominiums are furnished with complete kitchens, washer/dryer, lanais, televisions and telephones. Balconies with garden or ocean views. Two tennis courts, paddle tennis and pool.

───

Poipu Crater Resort
RR 1, Box 101
Koloa, Kauai, HI 96756
808-742-7400 800-367-8020
FAX: 808-742-9121

2 Bedrooms $$, 2 Bedrm/week 6$.
30 condos, Lo-rise, H-yes.

Location: Airport: 20 miles, Need car.

General Facilities: Game room, Pool, Hot tub, Sauna, Tennis, Kiahuna, Baby sitter.

Room Facilities: Kitchen, TV, Cable, Phone, Crib-Hi-chair.

Attractions: Waimea Canyon, deep sea fishing, boat tours, snorkeling, helicopter rides, scuba diving.

*Shops & Restaurants:*Three separate shopping villages, Keoki's/seafood-continental.

These two-story, townhouse style units are built entirely in the caldera of an extinct volcanic crater. Swimming beaches are 600 yards away. The resort is 100 yards inland. Tropically furnished with lanais.

———————————— KOLOA, KAUAI ————————————

Poipu Kapili
2221 Kapili Rd.
Koloa, Kauai, HI 96756
808-742-6449

1 Bedroom $$$$, 2 Bedrooms $$$$,
Min. stay 3 nights, Visa, MC, Dep. 2 nights
Key at Front office
60 condos, Lo-rise, H-yes •

Location: Airport: 25 minutes; Need car; Ocean front

General facilities: Kitchen, Linens

Room facilities: TV, Cable, Phone, Ocean views

Sports facilities: Pool, Tennis, Golf course near

Attractions: Waimea Canyon, Napali Coast, mountains, valleys, gardens, beaches and views all around

Shops & Restaurants: Old Koloa Town, Kiahuna Village, Kukui Grove Cntr., Plantation Gardens/seafood

A classic, architecturally designed oceanside condominium resort. Louvered wood sliding doors, high ceilings, tropical fans and private lanais. Pool, tennis and 1 mile from golf. Morning rainbows and golden sunsets. 3 minute walk to Poipu Beach and fine restaurants. A good base for sightseeing the island's many attractions.

Poipu Kapili

We want to hear from you—any comments regarding the condos or our publication may be noted on the form at the end of the book.

—————————————— KOLOA, KAUAI ——————————————

Prince Kuhio Resort
P.O. Box 1060, 5160 Lauai Road
Koloa, Kauai, HI 96756
808-742-1409 800-722-1409

Studio $, 1 Bedroom $$
Min. Stay 5 Nights, Dep. Req'd. •
69 condos, Lo-rise, Key at Office on premises

Location: Airport: 14 miles; Need car

General Facilities: Kitchen, Linens

Room Facilities: Pool, Golf: 2 blocks; TV, Cable, Crib-Hi-chair, Ind. AC Ctl.

Attractions: Tours to any place on the island. Horseback, sailing, helicopter, kayaking, scuba

Shops & Restaurants: Liberty House, Andrade's, Koloa Town shops; Beach House-Koala Broiler

Three-story garden resort overlooking Prince Kuhio Park and the ocean. Three lovely beaches within 1.5 miles, plus a little lagoon a block away for sunning and swimming. The pool is surrounded by tropical plants and there is also a barbecue area. Golf, tennis, shopping, dining and dancing are not far away. Centrally located for sightseeing, 44 miles to the end of the road each way.

Sunset Kahili Condo Apt.
R.R. 1, Box 96, 1763 Pe'e Road
Koloa, Kauai, HI 96756
808-742-1691 800-367-8047

1 Bedroom $$, 2 Bedrooms $$$
1 Bedrm/week 5$
Min. Stay 3 Nights, Visa/MC, Dep. 3 Nights •
36 condos, Hi-rise, Key at Office
H-yes

Location: Airport: 13 miles; Downtown: 3 miles; Need car; Beach front

General Facilities: Daily maid, Kitchen, Linens, Lounge, Baby-sitter

Room Facilities: Pool, Golf: ¼ mile Kiahuna; TV, Cable, Phone in rm., Crib-Hi-chair

Attractions: Beaches and water sports on sunny Poipu

Shops & Restaurants: Kiahuna, Koloa Town stores; Beach House-Keoki's-Plantation

Lower floor views of ocean, plumeria, pool; upper floor ocean and Poipu Beach. Join the surfers, sunbathers, fishermen and swimmers, or be a spectator watching the porpoise, turtles and whales. Located midway between Waimea Canyon and the Na Pali Cliffs, Sunset Kahili is a 25-minute drive amidst rural sugar cane plantation from Lihue Airport. Walk to Brennecke body surfing beach and Poipu State Park.

Wailkomo Stream Villas
Poipu Road
Koloa, Kauai, HI 96756
808-742-7220 800-325-5701

1 Bedroom $$

Extensive greenery, tropical flowers, large lanais, ceiling fans. Walk to beach. Tennis court and pool. Adjacent to golf.

---------------------------------- KOLOA ----------------------------------

Kahala at Poipu Kai
2827 Poipu Road
Koloa, HI 96756
808-742-7555 800-367-8022

1 Bedroom $$
1 Bedrm/week 5$
Min. Stay 4 Nights, Visa/MC, Dep. Req'd. •
82 condos, Lo-rise
H-yes

Location: Airport: 20 miles; Need car; Beach front

General Facilities: Kitchen, Linens, Restaurant on prem., Bar on prem., Baby-sitter

Room Facilities: Pool, Hot tub, Tennis, Golf: Kiahuna— ½ mile; TV, Cable, VCR, Phone in rm., Crib-Hi-chair

Attractions: Tours of Waimea Canyon, beaches, snorkeling, scuba diving, helicopter rides, fishing

Shops & Restaurants: Three separate shopping villages; Keoki's, House of Seafood

Tropically furnished one bedroom condominiums directly adjacent to the 8 court Racquet Club. Garden and ocean views, and an easy walk to Poipu Beach Park.

Kuhio Shores Condominiums
Lawai Road
Koloa, HI 96756
808-742-6120 800-367-8022

1 Bedroom $$, 2 Bedrooms $$$
1 Bedrm/week 5$, 2 Bed/week 7$
Min. Stay 4 Nights, Dep. Req'd.
76 condos, Lo-rise
H-yes

Location: Airport: 20 miles; Need car; Beach front

General Facilities: Kitchen, Linens, Restaurant on prem., Bar on prem., Baby-sitter

Room Facilities: TV, Cable, Phone in rm., Crib-Hi-chair

Attractions: Helicopter sightseeing, fishing, boating, beach activities, Spouting Horn

Shops & Restaurants: Kiahuna, Old Koloa Town shops; Beachhouse Restaurant

Each unit in this four-story condominium has beautiful ocean views. Located on the rocky shoreline, just 15 feet from the Pacific Ocean. Relax, read, sunbathe and enjoy the playful waves of the crescent beaches.

Makanui at Poipu Kai
Koloa, HI 96756

1 Bedroom $$, 2 Bedrooms $$$
1 Bedrm/week 5$, 2 Bed/week 8$
Min. Stay 4 Nights, Dep. Req'd.
22 condos, Lo-rise
H-yes

Location: Airport: 20 miles; Need car

General Facilities: Kitchen, Linens, Restaurant on prem., Bar on prem., Baby-sitter

Room Facilities: Pool, Hot tub, Tennis, Golf: Kiahuna ½ mile; TV, Phone in rm., Crib-Hi-chair

Attractions: Many beautiful beaches, snorkeling, scuba diving, deep-sea fishing, boat tours

Shops & Restaurants: Local shops; Restaurant on premises

These large, beautifully appointed units have access to all the amenities of Poipu Kai. Fantastic panoramic mountain and ocean views, and, of course, easy walking distance to two sandy beaches. On-site pool and hot tub.

—————————————— KOLOA, KAUAI ——————————————

Poipu Sands at Poipu Kai
Poipu Rd.
Koloa, Kauai, HI 96756

1 Bedroom $$$, 2 Bed/week 12$, Min. stay
4 nights, Dep. req'd, 72 condos, Lo-rise,
H-yes

Location: Airport: 20 miles; Need car; Beach front

General facilities: Kitchen, Linens, Baby sitter, Restaurant, Bar, Lounge, Hot tub

Room facilities: TV, Cable, Phone, Crib-Hi-chair

Sports facilities: Pool, Tennis, Near Kiahuna Golf course

Attractions: Beach activities, deep sea fishing, scuba diving, snorkeling

Shops & Restaurants: Local shops, House of Seafood

Sandy Shipwreck Beach is immediately adjacent to the Poipu Sands Condominiums. Tropically furnished with private lanais. These luxury units have microwaves and ceiling fans. Large swimming pool and nearby barbecue area. Brennecke's body surfing beach for the more adventurous is close, as is Poipu Beach Park with safe sandy swimming for everyone.

Poipu Kai
R.R. 1 Box 173
Koloa, Kauai, HI 96756
808-742-6464 800-367-6046

1 Bedroom $$$, 2 Bedrooms $$$$, 3
Bedrooms $$$$, Amex, Visa, MC, Dep. 1
night, Key at Administration, 240 condos,
Lo-rise, H-yes

Location: Airport: 17 miles; Downtown: 2 miles; Need car; Beach front

General facilities: Full serv., Conf. Rm. (cap. 150), Daily maid, Kitchen, Linens,
Baby sitter, Restaurant, Bar, Lounge, Hot tub

Room facilities: TV, Cable, Phone, Crib-Hi-chair

Sports facilities: Pool, Tennis, Kiahuna Golf course

Attractions: Spouting horn, Waimea Canyon, Poipu Beach Park, boat excursions
from Kukuiula Harbor, Entertainment

Shops & Restaurants: Kiahuna shopping village, Old Koloa Town Center, House
of Seafood

Luxuriously appointed vacation suites covering over 100 acres, anchored at one end by Brennecke Beach and the other end by Keoniloa Bay. Nine tennis courts with daily tennis activities. Five swimming pools and 1/2 mile from Kiahuna Golf Village.

We want to hear from you—any comments regarding the condos or
our publication may be noted on the form at the end of the book.

─────────────── KOLOA, KAUAI ───────────────

Whalers Cove
2640 Puuholo Rd.
Koloa, Kauai, HI 96756
808-742-7272 800-367-7040

2 Bedrooms $$$$
Min. Stay 2 Nights, AmEx/Visa/MC,
1 Night Dep. Req'd. •
34 condos, Lo-rise, Key at Front desk

Location: Airport: 12 miles; Downtown: 1 mile; Need car

General Facilities: Full serv.; Daily maid; Linens; Baby sitter; Lounge; Crib-Hi-chair

Sports Facilities: Pool; Sauna; Kiahuna

Room Facilities: Kitchen; Cable; Phone; Ind.AC.Ctl

Attractions: Koloa Town, Waimea Canyon, Kilohana

Shops & Restaurants: Kiahuna shopping center; Keoki's

Oceanfront extra spacious units, master bedroom features jacuzzi tub, deluxe furniture, and ocean views in a private location.

─────────────── LAHAINA, MAUI ───────────────

Aston Kaanapali Shores
3445 Honoapiilani Highway
Lahaina, Maui, HI 96761
808-667-2211 800-922-7866
FAX: 808-661-5474

1 Bedroom $$$, 2 Bedrooms $$$$
AmEx/Visa/MC, 1 Night Dep. Req'd. •
426 condos, Hi-rise, Key at Front desk

Location: Airport: 2 miles Kapalua; Downtown: 10 min. Lahaina; Need car; Beachfront

General Facilities: Full hotel service; Daily maid; Linens; Safe box; Travel desk; Lounge; Restaurant on premises

Business Facilities: Conf. Room Cap. 10

Sports Facilities: Pool; Sauna; Jet Spa; Tennis

Room Facilities: Kitchen; Cable; Phone; Ind.AC Ctl.

Attractions: Kaanapali beach, historic Lahaina, whale watching cruises (Dec.-April), Haleakala Crater.

Shops & Restaurants: Lahaina shops; Aston Beach Club restaurant

Located on Kaanapali Beach, spacious studio, one- and two-bedroom units featuring luxury baths, family sized lanais and gourmet kitchens. Four championship golf courses nearby. Guest activities desk, and summer children's activities program including nature walks, arts, crafts, hula lessons, lei-tying classes, treasure hunts, trips and kite flying.

─────────────── LAHAINA, MAUI ───────────────

Hale Mahina Beach Resort
3875 L. Honoapiilani Rd.
Lahaina, Maui, HI 96761
808-669-8441   800-367-8047

1 Bedroom $$$, 2 Bedroom $$$
1 Bedrm/week 6$, 2 Bedrm/week 9$
52 condos

At the "House of the Pale Moon" relax at the beach front pool, jacuzzi or beach. Barbeque your dinner, walk on the beach, then let the sound of the surf lull you to sleep.

Hale Ono Loa
3823 Lower Honoapiilani Rd.
Lahaina, Maui, HI 96761
808-669-6362   800-367-2927

All of these cool, airy, spacious apartments are oriented to the trade winds. Lanais, pool. Shop Whaler's Village, golf at Kapalua or Kaanapali. Carefree living.

Hololani Resort Condo
4401 Honoapiilani Rd.
Lahaina, Maui, HI 96761
808-669-8021   800-367-5021

1 Bedroom $$, 2 Bedrooms $$$
Min. Stay Ask, Dep. Req'd. •
62 condos, Hi-rise, Key at Office
H-yes

Location: Airport: Maui/Kapalua 5 min.; Downtown: 6 miles; Need car; Beach front

Room Facilities: Pool, Golf: Kapalu-Kaanapali near; TV, Cable, Phone in rm., Crib-Hi-chair

Attractions: Many aquatic attractions. Historic area. Humpback whales play close to shore in winter, entertainment

Shops & Restaurants: Neighborhood grocery store, Whalers Village shops; Erik's/seafood-Grill & Bar

Fully equipped two-bedroom, two-bath units with color TV and double lanai for winter whale watching. A mile of swimming beach, pool, not far from tennis and golf. A short drive brings you to Lahaina for shopping, dining or harbor activities.

Hono Koa Resort
3801 Lower Honoapiilani Rd.
Lahaina, Maui, HI 96761
808-669-0979   800-367-7042

2 Bedrooms $$
2 Bedrms/week 5$
AmEx/Visa/MC, Dep. 1 Night •
28 condos, Hi-rise, Key at Front desk, H-yes

Location: Airport: Kapalua—4 miles; Downtown: 10 min.; Need car

General Facilities: Daily maid, Kitchen, Linens, Baby-sitter

Room Facilities: Pool, Hot tub, Golf: Royal Kaanapali 4 miles; TV, Phone in rm., Crib-Hi-chair

Attractions: Fishing, sailing, scuba diving, parasailing, beaches, golf, tennis, entertainment

Shops & Restaurants: Lahaina shops, supermarket nearby, Kapalua; Leilani's/fine dining

Recently completed resort condominiums with lanai ocean or garden views. Swimming pool with entertainment and barbecue areas in the center of tropical trees and plants. A short walk to two beaches, large park for picnics and supermarket. All two-bedroom, two-bath units have oak and tile kitchens and tropical furnishings.

Kappa Sands

LAHAINA, MAUI

Honokeana Cove
5255 Lower Honoapiilani Road
Lahaina, Maui, HI 96761
808-669-6441 800-237-4948

1 Bedroom $$, 2 Bedrooms $$$, 3 Bedrooms $$$
1 Bedrm/week 5$, 2 Bed/week 7$, 3 Bed/week 9$
Min. Stay 5 Nights, Dep. 5 Nights •
38 condos, Lo-rise, Key at Office

Location: Airport: 5 minutes; Downtown: 7 miles; Need car; Beach front
General Facilities: Kitchen, Linens, Baby-sitter
Room Facilities: Pool, Golf: Kapalua near; TV, Cable, Phone in rm., Crib-Hi-chair
Attractions: Parasailing, golf, tennis, cruises, sunset sails, surfing, snorkeling, entertainment
Shops & Restaurants: Kapalua shops; Kapalua Grill & Bar/fish-steak

In the Napili section of West Maui, on a private, picturesque cove offering some of the best snorkeling on Maui. Napili Bay's crescent beach is reached in a 5 minute walk along a shoreline path. Lanais, ocean views, barbecues, and some with VCR's and radios. When you tire of the pool and beach, Lahaina is within easy reach. Weekly mai-tai or pu-pu parties at this romantic hideaway.

———————————— LAHAINA, MAUI ————————————

Hoyochi Nikko
3901 Lower Honoapiilani Rd.
Lahaina, Maui, HI 96761
808-669-8343

1 Bedroom $$
Min. Stay 5 Nights, Dep. Req'd. •
18 condos, Lo-rise, Key from manager
H-yes

Location: Airport: 2 miles; Downtown: 10 miles; Need car; Beach front
General Facilities: Daily maid, Kitchen, Linens, Baby-sitter
Room Facilities: Pool, Tennis, Surfing, snorkeling, Golf: Kapalu-Kaanapali near; TV, Cable, Phone in rm., Crib-Hi-chair
Attractions: Lahaina Town, Haleakala, Hana beaches, entertainment
Shops & Restaurants: Lahaina shops; Kapalua Grill & Bar

A small, friendly spot with a great view, oriental in design. Low density units face the ocean with the pool surrounded by a large lawn and attractive tropical garden. Bay protected barrier reef makes for safe ocean swimming and snorkeling. Golf, tennis, shopping and restaurants within a few miles. Soak up the sun and scenery and view the incredible sunsets.

Hyatt Regency Maui
200 Kohea Kai Drive
Lahaina, Maui, HI 96761
808-667-7474

Kaanapali Plantation
150 Puukolii Rd.
Lahaina, Maui, HI 96761
808-661-4446

Kaanapali Royal
2560 Kekaa Drive
Lahaina, Maui, HI 96761
808-667-7200 800-367-7040

1 Bedroom $$$, 2 Bedrooms $$$
AmEx/Visa/MC, Dep. 1 Night •
36 condos, Villas, Key at Front desk

Location: Airport: 45 minutes; Downtown: 2 miles; Need car
General Facilities: Full serv., Daily maid, Kitchen, Linens, Baby-sitter
Room Facilities: Pool, Sauna, Hot tub, Tennis, Golf: Royal Kaanapali; TV, Cable, Phone in rm., Crib-Hi-chair, Ind. AC Ctl.
Attractions: Lahaina, whaling port, Kaanapali Resort, beaches
Shops & Restaurants: Kaanapali; Kimos

Kaanapali Royal condominiums are nearly twice the size of many typical units. Sunken living rooms and spacious master bedroom suites with tropical furniture. Seven acres of lush tropical landscape adjacent to Kaanapali North Golf Course. Pool, spa, sauna, tennis on the water's edge.

Kaanapali Shores Resort
100 Kaanapali Shores Place
Lahaina, Maui, HI 96761
714-497-4253 800-854-8843

──────────────── LAHAINA, MAUI ────────────────

Kahana Sunset　　　　　　　　1 Bedroom $$$
P.O. Box 10219
Lahaina, Maui, HI 96761
808-669-8011　800-367-8011

One bedroom apartments, two bedroom townhouses with trellised lanais upstairs and down set among exotic plants, flowers and shrubs. Reef protected beach safe for children, windsurfing, pool, patios, barbecues. Grocery stores and restaurants.

Kahana Village　　　　　　　2 Bedrooms $$$$, 3 Bedrooms $$$$
4531 Honoapiilani Rd.　　　　　Min. Stay 5 Nights, Dep. Required ●
Lahaina, Maui, HI 96761　　　　42 condos, Lo-rise, Key at Office on site
808-669-5111　800-824-3065
FAX: 808-669-0974

Location: Airport: West Maui, 1 mile; Downtown: 6 miles; Need car; Beachfront
General Facilities: Washer/Dryer; Linens; Baby sitter; Crib-Hi-chair
Sports Facilities: Pool; Snorkeling
Room Facilities: Kitchen; Cable; VCR; Phone; Microwave
Attractions: Close to four of the best snorkeling beaches on Maui, golf and tennis; Entertainment
Shops & Restaurants: Hotel area shopping, Safeway, The Cannery; Eric's Seafood-China Boat-Grotto

You know you're in Hawaii when you stay at Kahana Village situated at the foot of pineapple and sugar cane fields. The white sand beach is set in a picturesque reef protected cove. The open air beachhouses in early missionary style architecture have large lanais with island views. Vaulted ceilings and skylights in 2nd story units, sunken tubs and wet bars in ground level units. Heated pool.

Kahana Villas　　　　　　　Hi-rise
4242 Lower Honoapiilani Rd.
Lahaina, Maui, HI 96761
808-669-5613　800-367-6046

General Facilities: Daily maid
Sports Facilities: Pool; Tennis
Room Facilities: Kitchen

Two story, two bedroom villas for your home away from home. Complimentary play at the tennis court. Pool, jacuzzi and 2 saunas. On-site convenience store and restaurant. 10 minutes to Old Lahina. Across from Kahana Beach.

Please mention *Condo Vacations—the Complete Guide* when you reserve your condominium.

———————————————— LAHAINA, MAUI ————————————————

Kaleialoha Resort Condominium Studio $$, 1 Bedroom $$
3785 Lower Honoapiilani Rd.   1 Bedrm/week 4$
Lahaina, Maui, HI 96761   Min. Stay 3 Nights, Visa/MC, Dep. 3 Nights •
808-669-8197 800-222-8688   35 condos, Hi-rise, Key at Office on property
                                 H-yes

Location: Airport: 5 Min.; Downtown: 5 miles; Need car; Beach front

General Facilities: Kitchen, Linens, Baby-sitter

Room Facilities: Pool, TV, Cable, Phone in rm., Crib-Hi-chair

Attractions: Kaanapali Resort area, Old Lahaina Town

Shops & Restaurants: Kaanapali-Liberty House and specialty shops; Grill & Bar-casual dining

Hawaiian style living by the ocean. The beach is inside a protected outer reef. An interior courtyard shelters the pool. Five minutes from this peace and quiet is Kaanapali Resort area which features great entertainment, restaurants, shopping and golf course. "Old Lahaina Town" is ten minutes away. Bus service available.

Kapalua Villas   1 Bedroom $$$$, 2 Bedrooms $$$$
One Bay Drive   AmEx/Visa/MC, Dep. 1 Night •
Lahaina, Maui, HI 96761   180 condos, Villas, Key at Kapalua Bay Hotel
808-669-0244 800-367-8000   H-yes

Location: Airport: 4 miles; Downtown: 11 miles; Beach front

General Facilities: Full serv., Conf. rm. cap. 200, Daily maid, Kitchen, Linens, Restaurant on prem., Bar on prem., Lounge, Baby-sitter, Child planned rec.: Children's programs

Room Facilities: Pool, Tennis, Water sports, Golf: Bay Course-Village Course; TV, Cable, Phone in rm., Crib-Hi-chair, Ind. Heat Ctl.

Attractions: Historic whaling town of Lahaina, museums, galleries, Haleakala downhill bike ride, entertainment

Shops & Restaurants: Kapalua shops, jewelry, art, clothing, Market Cafe; The Bay Club/seafood-continent

Contemporary styling in soft colors to complement the harmonious, lush tropical landscaping. Artfully tucked into its surroundings, this resort offers the ultimate in privacy, luxury and tranquility. A children's program is offered in summer, and at Christmas and Easter. Live dinner music in the restaurants.

Konokeana Cove
5255 Lower Honoapiilani Rd.
Lahaina, Maui, HI 96761
808-669-6441

---------------------------- LAHAINA, MAUI ----------------------------

Kulakane
3741 L. Honoapiilani Rd.
Lahaina, Maui, HI 96761
808-669-6119 800-367-6088

1 Bedroom $$, 2 Bedrooms $$$, 1
Bed/week 5$, 2 Bed/week 8$, Min. stay
3 nights, Visa, MC, Dep. req'd, Key at
Rental office, 42 condos, Lo-rise •

Location: Airport: Kapalua-1 mile; Downtown: 7 miles; Need car; Beach front
General facilities: Kitchen, Linens, Hula lessons
Room facilities: TV, Cable, Phone, Crib-Hi-chair
Sports facilities: Pool, Near Kiahuna Golf course
Shops & Restaurants: Whaler's Village, Lahaina Cannery shopping center, Kapalua Bay Club, Seahouse

Six miles from the old Whaling port of Lahaina, ten minutes to championship golf courses. Townhouse units with private lanais and ocean views. Surf, snorkel, swim and sunbathe.

Kuleana Maui
3959 L. Honoapiilani Rd.
Lahaina, Maui, HI 96761
808-669-8080 800-367-5633

1 Bedroom $$, 2 Bedrooms $$$,
1 Bed/week 4$, 2 Bed/week 6$, Min. stay
3 nights, Visa, MC, Dep. 3 nights
Key at Manager's office
40 condos, Lo-rise, H-yes •

Location: Airport: West Maui-5 Min.; Downtown: 10 min.; Need car; Beach front
General facilities: Kitchen, Linens, Baby sitter, Game room, Lounge
Room facilities: TV, Cable, Phone, Crib-Hi-chair
Sports facilities: Pool, Tennis, Shuffleboard, Snorkel
Attractions: Valleys and mountains of Maui, Haleakala Crater, Falls/pool at Hana, Lahaina whaling port
Shops & Restaurants: Whaler's Village, Liberty House, Kimo's/cont-Longhi's/ Italian

Colorful tropical color scheme and furnishings in these condominiums, all with ocean view from private lanais. The grounds are filled with lush tropical foliage and you can walk along the lighted pathway at night. A private snorkeling area lets you view colorful tropical fish.

Lahaina Roads
1403 Front Street
Lahaina, Maui, HI 96761
808-661-3166 800-624-8203

1 Bedroom $$, 2 Bedrooms $$$, Min. stay
3 nights, Dep. req'd
Key at Office on property
42 condos, Hi-rise, Lo-rise •

Location: Airport: 45 minutes; Downtown: 1 mile; Need car; Beach front
General facilities: Kitchen, Linens
Room facilities: TV, Cable, Phone, Crib-Hi-chair
Sports facilities: Pool
Attractions: Scuba, snorkeling, surfing, trip to Hana, Haleakala Crater, glass bottom boat, luaus, entertainment
Shops & Restaurants: Safeway, Longs Drug, shopping mall with boutiques, Seafood-Steak-French/5 star

Comfortable, well equipped condos with ocean front views from private lanais. Reef protected beach for water sports, and park and swimming beach minutes away. 5 minute walk to shopping, golf and tennis. Pool overlooks beach and the islands of Lanai and Molokai.

---------------------------- LAHAINA, MAUI ----------------------------

Lahaina Shores Beach Resort Studio $$, 1 Bedroom $$$
475 Front St. 1 Bedrm/week 6$
Lahaina, Maui, HI 96761 AmEx/Visa/MC, 1 Night Dep. Req'd. •
808-661-4835 800-367-2972 199 condos, Hi-rise, Key at Front desk
H-yes

Location: Airport: Kapalua 4 miles; Downtown: 2 blocks; Need car; Beach front
General Facilities: Full serv.; Daily maid; Linens; Baby sitter; Crib-Hi-chair
Sports Facilities: Pool; Hot tub; Nearby
Room Facilities: Kitchen; Cable; Phone; Ind.AC Ctl.; Ind.Heat Ctl.
Attractions: Water sports, tennis, historic Lahaina Town, whale watching, Iao Needle Park
Shops & Restaurants: Lahaina Town shops; Swan Court/Longhi's/La Bretone

The only beachfront hotel in historic Lahaina Town. Newly renovated with tropical furnishings in pastel colors. Spacious lanais with incredible views of the ocean and mountains. Two blocks from the center of town. Water sports and activities at the harbor. Tennis across the street, luau feast next door. Take time out to watch the special sunset before you begin your evening.

Lokelani 1 Bedroom $$, 2 Bedrooms $$$
3833 Lower Honoapiilani Rd. Lo-rise
Lahaina, Maui, HI 96761
808-669-8110 800-367-2976
General Facilities: Linens
Sports Facilities: Pool
Room Facilities: Kitchen; Phone
Attractions: Whale watching, swimming, golf, tennis, scuba diving, snorkeling

No schedules to keep here. Be as active or inactive as you like. Spend your day at the beach or sunbathing by the pool. Enjoy your fresh Hawaiian pineapple on the lanai overlooking the islands of Molokai and Lani. Listen to the surf and feel the cooling winds at night.

Aston Mahana At Kaanapali Studio $$$, 1 Bedroom $$$$,
110 Kaanapali Shores Pl. 2 Bedrooms $$$$
Lahaina, Maui, HI 96761 Min. Stay 3 Nights, AmEx/Visa/MC
808-661-8751 800-922-7866 1 Night Dep. Req'd. •
FAX: 808-661-5510 140 condos, Hi-rise, Key at Front desk

Location: Airport: 2 miles Kapalua; Downtown: Lahaina 10 min.; Need car; Beachfront
General Facilities: Washer/Dryer; Daily maid; Linens; Laundry; BBQ
Sports Facilities: Pool; Tennis; Shuffleboard
Room Facilities: Kitchen; Cable; Phone; Ind.AC Ctl.
Attractions: Kaanapali beach, Lahaina Town, whale watching cruises (Dec. to April), Haleakala Crater
Shops & Restaurants: Lahaina Town, Whaler's Village

A secluded resort on Kaanapali Beach where every guest has a beachfront condominium suite. Tastefully appointed units. Beachfront pool, complete gourmet kitchens. 3-night minimum stay. 3-diamond AAA award.

———————————— LAHAINA, MAUI ————————————

Makani Sands 1 Bedroom $$, 2 Bedrooms $$$
3765 Honoapiilani Rd. Lo-rise
Lahaina, Maui, HI 96761
808-669-8223 800-227-8223
Sports Facilities: Pool
Room Facilities: Kitchen; Phone
Attractions: Scuba, snorkeling, surfing

A wide range of individully furnished accommodations with private lanais. 2 miles to the Tennis Ranch and 5 miles to golf. Colorful tropical landscaping, sparkling pool, and golden beach make this a real Hawaiian retreat.

Maui Kai Studio $$, 1 Bedroom $$$,
106 Kaanapali Shores Pl. 2 Bedrooms $$$$
Lahaina, Maui, HI 96761 Min. Stay 2 Nights, Visa/MC,
808-667-3500 800-367-5635 2 Nights Dep. Req'd. •
FAX: 808-667-3660 60 condos
Location: Airport: West Maui 5 miles; Downtown: Lahaina 5 miles
General Facilities: BBQ
Sports Facilities: Pool; Hot tub; Ping pong, snorkeling; On premises
Room Facilities: Kitchen; Phone; Ind.AC.Ctl.
Attractions: Royal Kaanapali Golf Course, horseback riding, tours to Hana/Haleakala Crater-condo pickup
Shops & Restaurants: Within walking distance

Oceanfront property located on Kaanapali beach offering reasonable rates and all the comforts of home. Unobstructed ocean view from each unit complete with spectacular sunsets and whale watching in season. After savoring the many ocean activities, relax in the jacuzzi, cook dinner by the pool, and share the unique Maui Kai Aloha. Guest activity desk to book all island tours.

Aston Maui Kaanapali Villas Studio $$$$, 1 Bedroom $$$$
45 Kai Ala Dr. Min. Stay 1 Night, AmEx/Visa/MC
Lahaina, Maui, HI 96761 1 Night Dep. Req'd. •
808-667-7791 800-922-7866 161 condos, Lo-rise, Key at Front desk
FAX: 808-667-0366
Location: Airport: 23 miles Kahului; Downtown: Lahaina 10 minutes; Need car; Beachfront
General Facilities: Laundry; Daily maid; Linens; Dryclean; Restaurant on premises
Sports Facilities: Pool; Shuffleboard; Activities desk
Room Facilities: Kitchen; Cable; Phone; Ind.AC.Ctl.
Attractions: Kaanapali Beach, Lahaina, Haleakala Crater, whale watching cruises, chartered sails
Shops & Restaurants: Historic Lahaina Town, on-site sundry store; 3 restaurants next door

An 11-acre garden estate fronting Kaanapali Beach. Spacious studio or 1-bedroom suites with full kitchens. Easy access to nearby Kaanapali Resort, Tennis Ranch and golf. Ideal location, excellent weather, near harbor for sport fishing, scuba or snorkel dives. 3-diamond AAA award.

———————————————— LAHAINA, MAUI ————————————————

Maui Park　　　　　　　　　Studio $$, 1 Bedroom $$$,
3626 Lower Honoapiilani　　　2 Bedrooms $$$
Highway　　　　　　　　　　Amex, Visa, MC, Dep. 1 night
Lahaina, Maui, HI 96761　　　205 condos, Lo-rise,
808-669-6622　800-922-7866　Key at Front desk •

Location: Airport: 1 mile Kapalua

General facilities: Daily maid, Laundry facilities, Linens, Activities desk, Dry cleaning, BBQ, Safe Box

Room facilities: TV, Cable, Phone, Lanai, Ind.AC Ctl., Kitchen

Sports facilities: Pool, Jet Spa

Attractions: Kaanapali Beach, Lahaina Town, Haleakala Crater, whale watching cruises, chartered sails

Shops & Restaurants: Lahaina Village, Whaler's Village

Maui Park is the perfect place for those who seek comfort and value. Across from Honokowai Beach Park midway between Kapalua and Kaanapali.

Napili Point　　　　　　　1 Bedroom $$$, 2 Bedrooms $$$$
5295 L. Honoapiilani Rd.　　　Amex, Visa, MC, Dep. 1 night
Lahaina, Maui, HI 96761　　　103 condos, Lo-rise,
808-669-9222　800-367-5124　Key at Front desk •

Location: Airport: 15 min., Downtown: 15 min., Need car

General facilities: Full serv., Daily maid, Kitchen, Linens

Room facilities: TV, Cable, Phone, Crib-Hi-chair

Sports facilities: Pool, Snorkeling

Attractions: Whale watching cruises, visits to Lahaina and Haleakala Crater

Shops & Restaurants: Lahaina

Beautifully decorated and conveniently furnished condominiums with breathtaking views of Lanai and Molokai from your private lanai. Two bedroom suites are split level. Complimentary manager's get-acquainted party. Experience all the comforts and space of a condominium with all the services and amenities of a fine resort.

Napili Shores Resort　　　Studio $$, 1 Bedroom $$$
5315 L. Honoapiilani Rd.　　　Amex, Visa, MC, Dep. 1 night
Lahaina, Maui, HI 96761　　　152 condos, Lo-rise,
808-669-8061　800-367-6046　Key at Front desk •

Location: Airport: 3 miles-Kapalua, Downtown: 9 miles, Need car, Beach front

General facilities: Full serv., Daily maid, Kitchen, Linens, Baby sitter, Restaurant, Bar, Hot tub

Room facilities: TV, Cable, Phone, Crib-Hi-chair

Sports facilities: Pool, Shuffleboard

Attractions: Haleakala National Park, snorkeling, diving, Entertainment

Shops & Restaurants: Orient Express/Thai-Chinese

Secluded hideaway on the leeward side of West Maui with enchanting garden estate landscaping. Two freshwater pools, one with jacuzzi, shuffleboard, croquet and nearby golf. Friday night mai-tai parties, gazebo on the pool terrace and an excellent restaurant overlooking the gardens. Free scuba lessons, snorkeling or just soak up the sun.

———————————— LAHAINA, MAUI ————————————

Napili Village Hotel
5425 Honoapiilani Hwy.
Lahaina, Maui, HI 96761
808-669-6228 800-336-2185

Studio $$, 1 Bedroom $$
1 Bedrm/week 4$
Min. Stay 3 Nights, Visa/MC,
3 Nights Dep. Req'd. •
30 condos, Lo-rise, Key at Office ,H-yes

Location: Airport: 2 miles; Downtown: 8 miles; Need car
General Facilities: Daily maid; Linens; Crib-Hi-chair
Sports Facilities: Pool; Kapalua - ½ mile
Room Facilities: Kitchen; Cable
Attractions: Luaus, dinner cruises, fishing charters, surfing, tours; Entertainment
Shops & Restaurants: Whalers Village, Lahaina Village; American

Napili Village Hotel consists of a few low-rise buildings in Polynesian style clusters with wall-to-wall carpeting and tropical furnishings. Private lanais, pool, barbeque, village store and beauty shop. Set on an uncrowded beach for full family fun. Pool party once a week with live entertainment.

———————————————————————————————

Nohonani
3723 Lower Honoapiilani Road
Lahaina, Maui, HI 96761
808-669-8208 800-822-7368
FAX: 808-669-2388

1 Bedroom $$, 2 Bedrooms $$$
Min. Stay 4 Nights, •
25 condos, Lo-rise, Key at Office

Location: Airport: Maui Kapalua-1 mile; Need car; Beachfront
General Facilities: Linens; Baby sitter; Crib-Hi-chair
Sports Facilities: Pool; Kapalua/Kaanapali-closeby
Room Facilities: Kitchen; Phone
Attractions: Haleakala, IAO Valley, Seven Sacred Pools, cocktail cruises, sailing, windsurfing
Shops & Restaurants: Lahaina Village; 50 fine restaurants

A small condominium complex, with spacious lanais, ocean front living room and bedroom. Golden sand beaches, sparkling surf, plumeria and ginger on nicely landscaped grounds which include picnic tables, large pool and barbeques. A grocery store and post office are located one block away, as well as a public park and playground. Enjoy the fiery sunsets and star-studded nights from the comfort of your lanai.

Be sure to call the condo to verify details and prices and to make your reservation.

Aston at the Waikiki Shore

———————————— LAHAINA, MAUI ————————————

Paki Maui Resort
3615 Lower Honoapiilani Hwy.
Lahaina, Maui, HI 96761
808-669-8235 800-922-7866

Studio $$, 1 Bedroom $$,
2 Bedrooms $$$
Amex, Visa, MC, Dep. 2 nights
80 condos, Hi-rise, Key at Front desk
H-yes •

Location: Airport: 10 minutes, Downtown: 10 min., Need car, Beach front
General facilities: Full serv., Daily maid, Kitchen, Linens, Baby sitter, Hot tub
Room facilities: TV, Cable, Phone
Sports facilities: Pool, Tennis, Nearby, Snorkeling
Attractions: Lahaina, Haleakala Crater, whale watching cruises, chartered sails, helicopter sightseeing
Shops & Restaurants: Lahaina Village

Oceanfront between Kaanapali and Kapalua. Tastefully appointed units with easy access to local recreation and restaurants. Pack a picnic and leave early to watch the spectacular sunrise at Haleakala Crater, or toast a Maui sunset from the lanai of your own private suite. Superb accommodations, gracious service, and good value for your vacation dollar.

Please mention *Condo Vacations—the Complete Guide* when you reserve your condominium.

─────────────── LAHAINA, MAUI ───────────────

Papakea Beach Resort RPI's Rental
3543 L. Honoapiilani Rd.
Lahaina, Maui, HI 96761
808-669-4848 800-367-5637

Studio $$$, 1 Bedroom $$$, 2 Bedrooms $$$$, Amex, Visa, MC, Dep. 1 night
Key at Front desk
120 condos
Lo-rise, H-yes •

Location: Airport: West Maui-10 min.; Downtown: 10 min.; Need car; Beach front
General facilities: Full serv., Daily maid, Kitchen, Baby sitter, Sauna, Hot tub
Room facilities: TV, Cable, Phone, Crib-Hi-chair
Sports facilities: Pool, Tennis
Attractions: Lahaina Town, Kaanapali and Kapalua golf courses, Entertainment
Shops & Restaurants: Sundry and grocery stores adjacent to property, Beach
    Club/continental
Your island home framed by coconut palms with all the conveniences of home. Three lighted tennis courts, 2 18-hole putting greens, two pools, saunas. Lahaina is just down the road when you tire of beach sun and fun. Some units have VCR's. Tennis clinics, round robins and swimmercize classes.

Polynesian Shores
3975 Honoapiilani Rd.
Lahaina, Maui, HI 96761
808-669-6065 800-433-6284

1 Bedroom $$, 2 Bedrooms $$$, 3 Bedrooms $$$$, Min. stay 3 nights, Visa, MC, Dep. req'd, Key at Office on property, 52 condos, Lo-rise, H-yes •

Location: Airport: 45 minutes; Downtown: 6 miles; Need car; Ocean front
General facilities: Kitchen, Linens, Baby sitter
Room facilities: TV, Cable, Phone, Crib-Hi-chair
Sports facilities: Pool
Attractions: Snorkel, sail, luaus, Haleakala Crater, dinner and island cruises,
    Hana Waterfall, entertainment
Shops & Restaurants: Kapalua & Kaanapali shopping, Lahaina Village, Eric's
    Seafood Grotto
Airy, polynesian style condominiums stressing rattan, glass and pastels on two tropical oceanfront acres. Pupu party on ocean deck, pool and barbeques. Relaxed, carefree atmosphere for your vacation, but only minutes away from Lahaina, Kaanapali and Kapalua resort areas with golf, tennis, sailing, sport fishing, shopping, restaurants and nightlife.

Puamana
P.O. Box 515
Lahaina, Maui, HI 96761
808-667-2551 800-367-5630

1 Bedroom $$$, 2 Bedrooms $$$, 3 Bedrooms $$$$, Min. stay 3 nights, Visa, MC, Dep. 3 nights, Key at Pumana Clubhouse, 230 condos, Lo-rise, No S-yes •

Location: Airport: 25 miles; Downtown: 1 mile; Beach front
General facilities: Daily maid, Kitchen, Linens, Lounge, Sauna
Room facilities: TV, Cable, Phone, Crib-Hi-chair
Sports facilities: Pool, Tennis
Attractions: Haleakala Crater, Iao Valley,Hana, beaches, fishing, authentic luaus
Shops & Restaurants: Cannery Mall, fine shops, local shops, Gerards/European

---------------------- LAHAINA, MAUI ----------------------

Royal Kahana Resort
4365 Honoapiilani Highway
Lahaina, Maui, HI 96761
808-669-5911 800-535-0085
FAX: 808-669-5950

Studio $$$, 1 Bedroom $$$$,
  2 Bedrooms $$$$
AmEx/Visa/MC, 2 Nights Dep. Req'd. •
205 condos, Hi-rise, Key at Front desk

Location: Airport: Kapalua, W. Maui; Downtown: 5 miles; Need car; Beachfront
General Facilities: Full hotel service; Daily maid; Linens; Baby sitter
Business Facilities: Bus. fac.; Conf. Room Cap. 50
Sports Facilities: Pool; Sauna; Tennis; Shuffleboard; Kapalua Golf Course
Room Facilities: Kitchen; Cable; Phone; Ind.AC.Ctl.
Attractions: Windsurfing, golf, tennis, Sugar cane train, Hana
Shops & Restaurants: Variety & convenience store, market, sundries; Eric's
  Seafood Grotto, Roy's Kahana

*Enter the inviting Hawaiian style lobby and ride one of the three high-speed elevators
to your comdominiums with sweeping views of the ocean. Beach, pool, his and her
saunas, tennis, putting green and volleyball courts. Meet new friends by the pool, or
reserve the poolside cabana for a private party.*

Sands of Kahana
4299 Honoapiilani Rd.
Lahaina, Maui, HI 96761
808-669-0400 800-922-7866

1 Bedroom $$$, 2 Bedrooms $$$$,
  3 Bedrooms $$$$
AmEx/Visa/MC, 1 Night Dep. Req'd. •
182 condos, Hi-rise, Key at Front desk

Location: Airport: l0 minutes; Downtown: 10 minutes; Need car; Beach front
General Facilities: Full serv.; Daily maid; Linens; Lounge; Crib-Hi-chair; Restaurant; Bar
Sports Facilities: Pool; Hot tub; Tennis; Putting green; Nearby; Child planned
  rec.
Room Facilities: Kitchen; Cable; Phone
Attractions: Haleakala Crater and whale watching tours from Mid-December to
  late April; Entertainment
Shops & Restaurants: Lahaina Village; Aston Beach Club

*Uncommon in their sumptuous luxury, these condominiums are exquisitely deco-
rated. Private lanais overlooking a magnificent ocean channel and the islands of
Lanai and Molokai in the distance. Camp Kahana for the children offering arts, crafts,
hula, tennis, pool, nature activities and Hawaiiana classes. With space, comfort and
luxury, Sands of Kahana has to be experienced to be believed.*

LIHUE, KAUAI

Aston Kauai Beach Villas
4330 Kauai Beach Dr.
Lihue, Kauai, HI 96766
808-245-7711 800-922-7866

1 Bedroom $$$$, 2 Bedrooms $$$$
AmEx/Visa/MC, 1 night Dep. Req'd.
114 condos, Lo-rise
Key at Front desk

Location: Airport: Lihue, 2 miles; Downtown: 2 miles; Need car; Beachfront
General Facilities: Laundry facilities; Daily maid; Linens; Drycleaning; Washer/Dryer; BBQ
Sports Facilities: Pool; Jet spa; Tennis; Volleyball; Adj. Wailua Golf Course
Room Facilities: Kitchen; Cable; Phone; Ind.AC.Ctl.
Attractions: Fern Grotto, Wailua River, Waimea Canyon
Shops & Restaurants: Coconut Plantation Marketplace

The AAA 3-Diamond Aston Kauai Beach Villas is a beachfront condominium resort situated on 13 acres of landscaped gardens. The resort is adjacent to Wailua Golf Course.

Banyan Harbor
3411 Wilcox Rd.
Lihue, Kauai, HI 96766
808-245-7333 800-422-6926

2 Bedrooms $$
Visa/MC, 1 Night Dep. Req'd. •
148 condos, Lo-rise, Key at Front desk

Location: Airport: Lihue 2 Miles; Downtown: 2 miles; Need car
General Facilities: Linens; Crib-Hi-chair
Sports Facilities: Pool; Tennis; Shuffleboard; Kauai Hotel–Kauai Lagoons
Room Facilities: Kitchen; Cable; Phone
Attractions: Boat tours, circle island plane/helicopter rides, luaus, scuba & snorkel tours, fishing; Entertainment
Shops & Restaurants: Kukui Grove Center; Tempura Garden–Prince Bill's

Your home away from home, with rich decor and distinctive furnishings. Free scuba/snorkel lessons, cabana/BBQ, and adjacent to the Westin Kauai Hotel with 30 shops, 8 restaurants, carriage rides and nightlife. Cruise the Wailua River to the fern grotto, visit Waimea Canyon—the Grand Canyon of the Pacific, drive to Hanalei where "South Pacific" was filmed, or just stay by the pool, surrounded by tropical foliage.

Kaha Lani
4460 Nehe Rd.
Lihue, Kauai, HI 96766
808-822-9331 800-922-7866

1 Bedrm $$$, 2 Bedrms $$$$,
3 Bedrms $$$$
AmEx/Visa/MC, 1 Night Dep. Req'd. •
65 condos, Lo-rise, Key at Front desk
H-yes

Location: Airport: Lihue 5 miles; Need car; Beachfront
General Facilities: Laundry facilities; Daily maid; Linens; Drycleaning; Iron/board; BBQ
Sports Facilities: Pool; Tennis; Snorkeling, Volleyball; Adj. Wailua Golf Course
Room Facilities: Kitchen; Cable; Phone
Attractions: Waimea Canyon, Wailua River, Fern Grotto
Shops & Restaurants: Coconut Plantation Marketplace

A tranquil, secluded setting on one of Kauai's loveliest beaches. Beautiful 1, 2 and 3-bedroom suites. Hawaiian for Heavenly Place, Kaha Lani lives up to its name, providing a truly relaxing vacation.

Kauai Aston Beach Villas, Lihue, Kauai, HI

———————————— MAALAEA VILLAGE, MAUI ————————————

Kanai A Nalu　　　　　　　　1 Bedroom $$, 2 Bedrooms $$
R.R. 1, Box 389
Maalaea Village, Maui, HI 96793
808-244-5627　800-367-6084
General facilities: Kitchen, Linens
Sports facilities: Pool

All units face the ocean in these specially designed condominiums. Lounge on the lawn under palms. Inner courtyard featuring waterfall, barbecue, swimming pool.

We want to hear from you—any comments regarding the condos or our publication may be noted on the form at the end of the book.

——————————— MAALAEA VILLAGE, MAUI ———————————

Maalaea Banyans   1 Bedroom $$, 2 Bedrooms $$
Hauoli St.   Lo-rise
Maalaea Village, HI 96793
808-242-5668 800-367-5234

General facilities: Kitchen, Linens
Sports facilities: Pool
Attractions: Swimming, snorkeling, scuba diving

Step outside your door to the pool surrounded by a wide green lawn, tropical plants, jacuzzi and barbeque. Below is the blue Pacific and nearby golden sand beach. Two bedroom units have beamed ceilings and lofts. Sliding glass doors lead to your spacious lanai.

——————————— MAALAEA, MAUI ———————————

Maalaea Bay Rentals   1 Bedroom $$, 2 Bedrooms $$
RR 1, Box 389   Min. stay 5 nights
Maalaea, Maui, HI 96793   Key at Hono Kai office
808-244-7012 800-367-6084   140 condos, Hi-rise •

Location: Airport: 20 minutes; Downtown: 20 minutes; Need car; Beach front
General facilities: Kitchen, Linens
Room facilities: TV, Cable, Phone, Microwave, Ceiling fans
Attractions: Golf, ocean activities from nearby harbor, restaurants, fresh fish, deli
Shops & Restaurants: Nearby towns have all types of shops, Waterfront-fresh fish, steak

Oceanfront community offers a variety of properties with a variety of rates. Host of ocean activities offered from nearby harbor. Amenities include furnished units, pools, beach access, laundry facilities and much more. Restaurants, deli within walking distance. Shopping, golf, tennis and other activities close by. Maalaea is Maui's best kept secret. Discover why.

——————————— MAKENA, MAUI ———————————

Polo Beach Club   2 Bedrooms $$$$
20 Makena Rd.   Hi-rise
Makena, Maui, HI 96753
808-879-8847 800-367-6046

General facilities: Daily maid, Kitchen, Linens
Sports facilities: Pool, Golf course
Attractions: Surfing, scuba diving, port of Lahaina, Hana's Seven Sacred Pools, sightseeing

A private resort with deluxe condominiums matching the outdoors with the indoors. Marble floored entrances and koa wood accents. 180-degree views from balconies with rattan chairs and table shaded by palms. Large free form pool and spa. Two minutes to Wailea.

We want to hear from you—any comments regarding the condos or our publication may be noted on the form at the end of the book.

———————————————— MAUI ————————————————

Puene Towers Condominium
1063 East Main
Maui, HI 96753
808-244-0564

Deluxe units with marble floored entrances, accented by rich koa wood. Secluded Pacific white sand beach. Free form pool, spa, sundeck overlooking the beach. Tennis, golf, shops and restaurants in Wailea.

———————————— MAUNALOA, MOLOKAI ————————————

Ke Nani Kai
P. O. Box 126
Maunaloa, Molokai, HI 96770
808-552-2761 800-922-7866

1 Bedroom $$$, 2 Bedrooms $$$$
Amex, Visa, MC, Dep. 50%
Key at Front desk
45 condos, Lo-rise •

Location: Need car
General facilities: Full serv., Daily maid, Kitchen, Linens, Hot tub
Room facilities: TV, Cable, Phone
Sports facilities: Pool, Tennis, Golf-Kaluakoi
Attractions: Pleasant hiking trails and a donkey ride to Father Damien's Leper Colony, Walk to beach

On the sunny west shore, surrounded by the championship Kaluakoi Golf Course, spacious, richly furnished units in Polynesian decor have fully equipped kitchens. Private lanais overlook 15 manicured acres and the unspoiled Molokai scenery. Sun on Hawaii's longest white sand beach or take to the pleasant hiking trails.

Paniolo Hale
P.O. Box 146
Maunaloa, Molokai, HI 96770
808-552-2731 800-367-2984

Studio $$, 1 Bedroom $$, 2 Bedrooms $$$,
Min. stay 3 nights, Amex, Visa, MC
Dep. 2 nights, Key at Office
77 condos, Lo-rise, H-yes •

Location: Airport: 12 Miles; Downtown: 22 miles; Need car
General facilities: Kitchen, Linens, Baby sitter
Room facilities: Phone, Crib-Hi-chair, Color TV
Sports facilities: Pool, Tennis, Golf-Kaluakoi, Water sports
Attractions: Snorkeling, Safari tour, Father Damien's Leper Colony-Halawa Valley & Falls, Next to golf.
Shops & Restaurants: 22 miles to variety of stores, 7 miles to grocery, Restaurant next door.

Far from the hustle and bustle, undiscovered, unspoiled, the last of the Hawaiian Islands to be developed. Paniolo Hale, built in the true Hawaiian tradition, screened lanais, open beam ceilings, hardwood floors and ceiling fans. Molokai offers the serene tranquility of bygone years-the "do nothing island." Wild turkeys roam the golf course, deer take an evening stroll, and a wildlife safari is nearby. Pool, sandy beaches, picnic tables and barbeques. Molokai-The Friendly Island.

We want to hear from you—any comments regarding the condos or our publication may be noted on the form at the end of the book.

─────────────── NAPILI BAY, LAHAINA, MAUI ───────────────

Napili Kai Beach Club
5900 Honoapiilani Road
Napili Bay, Lahaina, Maui, HI
96761
808-669-6271 800-367-5030
FAX: 808-669-5740

Studio $$$, 1 Bedroom $$$$
2 Bedrooms 4$
2 Nights Dep. Req'd.
162 condos, Lo-rise, Key at Lobby

Location: Airport: Kahului Airport; Downtown: 9 miles; Need car; Beachfront

General Facilities: Full hotel service; Daily maid; Lounge; Restaurant on premises

Business Facilities: Conf. Room Cap. 80

Sports Facilities: Pool; Hot tub; 18-hole putting green; Kapalua Golf Course

Room Facilities: Kitchen; Phone

Attractions: Lahaina Town, golf, water sports, West Maui Mountains; Entertainment

Shops & Restaurants: Breezeway gift shop, Lahaina shops; Sea House, Whale Watcher's Bar

Charming Polynesian condominiums scattered over 10 acres of private refuge. Private view lanais. Stroll or lounge on the beach after your complimentary coffee in the cabana. Swim in one of the 4 pools, use the large jacuzzi or recreation facilities with equipment supplied. Daily cabana coffee and tea party, weekly Mai Tai party and putting party, nightly entertainment and dancing at the Sea House. Warm and friendly staff makes you feel at home. Tennis and golf at Kapalua across the road.

───

Napili Surf Beach Resort
50 Napili Pt.
Napili Bay, Maui, HI 96761
808-669-8002

Studio $$, 1 Bedroom $$$
Min. Stay 5 Nights, Dep. Required •
54 condos, Lo-rise, Key at Front desk

Location: Airport: Kapalua-3 miles; Downtown: 10 miles; Need car; Beach front

General Facilities: Full serv.; Daily maid; Linens; Baby sitter; Crib-Hi-chair

Sports Facilities: Shuffleboard; Kapalua-2 courses

Room Facilities: Kitchen

Attractions: Haleakala Crater, Hana; Entertainment

Shops & Restaurants: Kapalua shops, Kaanapali shops; Kapalua Hotel, The Bay Club

Modern decor in ocean or garden view units, off the highway at the end of a tree-lined country road. Two pools, three shuffleboards, two barbeques and outdoor lanais. The beach is on a secluded crescent bay. One mile to golf and tennis, close to Lahaina for fishing, boating, shopping. To insure a truly relaxed, quiet vacation, there are no telephones in the rooms.

We want to hear from you—any comments regarding the condos or our publication may be noted on the form at the end of the book.

Poipu

———————————— NAPILI, MAUI ————————————

Coconut Inn
P.O. Box 10517, 181 Hui Road "F"
Napili, Maui, HI 96761
808-669-5712 800-367-8006

Studio $$, 1 Bedroom $$
Dep. 2 Nights •
40 condos, Lo-rise, Key at Front desk
H-yes

Location: Airport: Kapalua-25 miles; Downtown: 9 miles; Need car

General Facilities: Full serv., Daily maid, Kitchen, Linens, Game room, Baby-sitter

Room Facilities: Pool, Hot tub, Golf: Kapalua adjacent; TV, Cable, Phone in rm., Crib-Hi-chair

Attractions: Horseback riding, snorkeling, scuba diving, helicopter tours, entertainment

Shops & Restaurants: Lahaina Town—9 miles; Grill & Bar, fresh seafood

A lush tropical retreat tucked in the pineapple covered hills of West Maui. Early Hawaiian architecture, tropical cane and floral print furnishings in a cozy, homey atmosphere. Start your morning with a complimentary continental breakfast in the poolside breakfast room. After a day of swimming and sightseeing, enjoy the evening Mai Tai party. Snorkel classes available.

———————————————— LIHUE, KAUAI ————————————————

Alii Kai II Hanalei
P.O. Box 3292
Lihue, Kauai, HI 96766
808-826-9988

———————————————— PAHALA, HAWAII ————————————————

Colony One at SeaMountain   Studio $$, 1 Bedroom $$$, 2 Bedrooms $$$
P.O. Box 70   Min. Stay 2 nights, Visa/MC, Dep.
Pahala, Hawaii, HI 96777   Required, 30 condos, Lo-rise
808-928-8301 800-488-8301   Key at At office on site, H-Yes
FAX: 808-928-8008

Location: Airport: Hilo 56 mi, Kona 65; Downtown: Village 7 miles; Need car;
   Beachfront

General Facilities: Daily maid; Linens; Baby sitter; Crib; Restaurant on prem-
   ises; Bar on premises

Sports Facilities: Pool; Hot tub; Tennis; Golf–SeaMountain

Room Facilities: Kitchen; TV; Phone

Attractions: 26 miles to Volcano National Park, 24 miles to southernmost point
   in the United States

Shops & Restaurants: Basics only at village stores, restaurant 10 minutes away;
   Limited menu at Seamountain

*Secluded, elegant condominiums, neutral walls, rattan, harmonious furnishings. On
the coast 30 minutes south of Volcano Park. Unhurried play on splendid 18-hole golf
course. Black sand beach, tennis, clubhouse, pool and jacuzzi.*

———————————————— POIPU, KAUAI ————————————————

Poipu Shores   1 Bedroom $$$$, 2 Bedrooms $$$$,
1775 Pe'e Road   3 Bedrooms $$$$
Poipu, Kauai, HI 96756   Min. Stay 3 Nights, AmEx/Visa/MC,
808-742-7700 800-367-5004   3 Nights Dep. Req'd. •
FAX: 808-742-9720   39 condos, Lo-rise, Key at Front desk

Location: Airport: 15 miles; Need car

General Facilities: Full serv.; Daily maid; Linens; Crib-Hi-chair

Sports Facilities: Pool; Tennis; Bikes, ride, water sports; Kiahuna-1 mile

Room Facilities: Kitchen; Cable; Phone

Attractions: Free tennis at Waiohai Tennis Club, golf at Robert Trent Jones
   course

Shops & Restaurants: Poipu Shopping Village & Historic Koloa Town nearby;
   Beach House-Keoki's-P. Gardens

*Renovated in 1994, the Poipu Shores is conveniently located oceanfront on Kauai's
sunny south shore and is situated within the world famous Poipu Resort destination.
Guests can choose from 1-, 2- or 3-bedroom condominium suites. All suites are
spacious with beautiful ocean views and feature fully-equipped kitchen, beautiful
island-style furniture, color TV, washer/dryer, and private lanai. Enjoy a memorable
vacation in one of Kauai's most popular condominium resorts.*

─────────────── PRINCEVILLE, KAUAI ───────────────

Mauna Kai
Country Club Drive, P.O. Box 3006
Princeville, Kauai, HI 96722
808-826-6855

2 Bedrooms $$, 3 Bedrooms $$
2 Bedrms/week 4$, 3 Bed/week 4$
Min. Stay 3 Nights, Dep. Req'd.
46 condos, Villas, Key at Manager's office

Location: Airport: 30 miles; Downtown: 30 miles; Need car
General Facilities: Kitchen, Linens
Room Facilities: Pool, Golf: Makai at Princeville; TV, Cable, Phone in rm., Crib-Hi-chair
Attractions: Boat cruises, helicopter sightseeing, fishing, snorkeling, beaches, golf, tennis
Shops & Restaurants: Princeville Center-grocery-gifts-post office-bank; Steak-Chinese-Mexican-Italian

Two-and three-bedroom condominiums with Hawaiian style furnishings, large open beams and cedar walls. Beautiful grounds highlighted by a large swimming pool. Property sits along the famous Princeville Makai Golf Course and there are 6 tennis courts a half mile away at the Princeville clubhouse. Shopping, restaurants and beaches are only a one minute drive away.

Pahio
P.O. Box 3099
Princeville, Kauai, HI 96722
808-826-6549

2 Bedrooms $$$$, Lo-rise
Pool, Kitchen

2300-square-foot, 2-bedroom vacation suites with fireplace, wet bar, spa and entertainment center complete with 67" TV, radio and cassette deck. Rattan furniture, ceiling fans, large lanais with deck furniture. Shopping, dining, golf at Princeville. Secluded beaches.

Sandpiper Village
P.O. Box 460, 4770 Pepelani Loop
Princeville, Kauai, HI 96722
808-826-1176 800-367-7040

2 Bedrooms $$, 3 Bedrooms $$
Min. Stay 2 Nights, AmEx/Visa/MC,
Dep. 1 Night •
30 condos, Lo-rise, Key at Front desk

Location: Airport: 33 miles; Downtown: 1 mile; Need car
General Facilities: Full serv., Daily maid, Lounge, Baby-sitter
Room Facilities: Pool, Sauna, Golf: Princeville; Cable, Crib-Hi-chair
Attractions: Golf, Hanalei Bay, Kalaulau Valley
Shops & Restaurants: Princeville shops; Nobel's

In the heart of master planned Princeville, commanding a scenic view of mountains and the ocean, Sandpiper Village's suites have all the necessities for easy living. Swimming pool, spa, sauna, golf and tennis, or drive to Hanalei for uncrowded beaches. After a day of rafting, snorkeling or surfing, relax in front of your TV or drive to Princeville for dinner, entertainment and shopping.

─────────────── WAIANAE ───────────────

Maili Cove
87-561 Farrington Hwy, Room 110
Waianae, HI 96792
808-696-4447

Pool, Daily maid, Kitchen, Linens, Phone in rm.

Exclusive year-round hideaway on Oahu's dry and sunny west coast. Peace and quiet with nothing to do but swim and lie in the sun. Access to golf, restaurants, shopping, horseback riding, deep-sea fishing.

---------------------------------- WAIKOLOA ----------------------------------

The Shores at Waikoloa
5460 Beach Club Drive
Waikoloa, HI 96743
808-885-5001 800-922-7866

1 Bedroom $$$$, 2 Bedrooms $$$$
Amex, Visa, MC, Dep. 1 night
72 condos, Lo-rise, Key at Front desk •

Location: Airport: 17 miles Keahole, Downtown: 24 mi. Kailua-Kona, Need car

General facilities: Full serv., Daily maid, Linens, Activities desk, Laundry fac,
BBQ

Room facilities: TV, Cable, Phone, Lanai, Wetbar, Ind.AC.Ctl., Washer/dryer,
Kitchen

Sports facilities: Pool, Tennis, Jet spa

Attractions: The varied terrain on the Big Island lends to lots of sightseeing.

Shops & Restaurants: Nearby restaurants and shops

*World class luxury and style on the prestigious Kohala Coast. Nearby beach for water
activities, or take a trip around the Island. AAA 3-Diamond award. **Voted Condo of
The Year by our readers for 1992!***

------------------------- WAILEA, KIHEI, MAUI -------------------------

Wailea Ekahi
3300 Wailea Alanui Dr.
Wailea, Kihei, Maui, HI 96753

1 Bedroom $$, 2 Bedrooms $$$
1 Bed/week 6$, 2 Bed/week 8$
Dep. req'd
Lo-rise
H-yes

Location: Airport: 14 Miles, Downtown: 5 miles, Need car

General facilities: Kitchen, Linens

Room facilities: TV, Cable, Phone, Crib-Hi-chair

Sports facilities: Pool, Tennis, Golf course nearby, Ocean activities

Attractions: Glass bottom boats, dinner cruises, snorkeling, biking, tennis, golf,
lauas

Shops & Restaurants: Kaahumanu Shopping Center, resort shops at hotels,
Stouffers "Raffles"—Continental cuisine.

*Luxury condominium homes offering pools, beaches, snorkeling, ocean activities,
luaus. Tennis and golf discounts. Near restaurants, hotels and shopping. Tropical
garden setting-pool, kiddie pool, jacuzzi, putting green.*

------------------------------ WAILEA, MAUI ------------------------------

Destination Resorts Hawaii
Condos
3750 Wailea Alanui Dr.
Wailea, Maui, HI 96753
808-879-1595 800-367-5246
FAX: 808-874-3554

Studio $$$, 1 Bedroom $$$, 2 Bedrooms
$$$$, 3 Bedrooms $$$$
Min. Stay 3 Nights, AmEx/Visa/MC,
3 Nights Dep. Req'd. •
300 condos, Villas, Key at Rental office,
P-No/No S-Yes/H-No

Location: Airport: 20 miles; Downtown: In Wailea Resort; Need car

General Facilities: Concierge; Daily maid; Linens; Baby sitter

Sports Facilities: Pool; Tennis; Watersports, shuffleboard; Wailea & Makena Golf; Childrens programs

Room Facilities: Kitchen; Cable; Phone; Ind.AC.Ctl

Attractions: All water sports, helicopter rides, horseback riding, tennis, 5 championship golf courses

Shops & Restaurants: Wailea shopping village, Kihei town, Wailea area; Seawatch Restaurant—seafood, Pacific

Six distinctive condominium properties are set amid tropical gardens and secluded beaches. Swimming pools, putting green, jacuzzi, paddle tennis court, barbeque grills are available. Tennis and golf packages are available. Polo Beach Club and Makena Surf are oceanfront properties in Makena. Elua and Ekahi are beachside in Wailea. Grand Champions and Ekolu are on the fairway of the Wailea Blue Golf Course.

Wailea Elua Village '
3600 Wailea Alanui Dr.
Wailea, Maui, HI 96753
808-878-4726 800-231-0611

1 Bedroom $$$, 2 Bedrooms $$$,
3 Bedrooms $$$$
Min. Stay 5 Nights, 3 Nights Dep. Req'd. •
152 condos, Lo-rise, Key at Rental office
H-yes

Location: Airport: 30 minutes; Need car; Beach front

General Facilities: Daily maid; Linens; Baby sitter; Lounge; Crib-Hi-chair

Business Facilities: Bus. fac.

Sports Facilities: Pool; Hot tub; Paddle ball; Put. green; Wailea Blue & Orange

Room Facilities: Kitchen; Cable; Phone

Attractions: Swimming, golf, beach, snorkeling

Shops & Restaurants: Grocery, complete shopping areas; Raffles-Stouffer-Wailea Hotel

Casually elegant, completely furnished beachside condominiums with private lanais for an ocean view. Ceiling fans keep you cool when you come in from the beach or pool. Play paddleball or practice on the putting green.

Be sure to call the condo to verify details and prices and to make your reservation.

Idaho

Sun Valley
Ketchum

--------------- KETCHUM ---------------

Stone Hill Condominiums
Valleywood Drive
Ketchum, ID 83340
208-726-5149

2 Bedrooms $$$
Min. Stay 4 Nights, 1 Night Dep. Req'd. •
9 condos, Lo-rise, Key on arrival

Location: Airport: 12 miles; Downtown: 1 mile; Need car
General Facilities: Linens; Crib-Hi-chair
Sports Facilities: Sauna; Hot tub
Room Facilities: Kitchen; Cable; Phone; Ind.Heat Ctl.
Attractions: Skiing, rafting, hiking, fishing, golfing, biking, winter and summer ice skating
Shops & Restaurants: Small, unique specialty shops; French-Austrian-Continental

Professionally decorated townhouses overlooking the slopes of Baldy and the rugged Sawtooth Range. Wet rooms for skis and boots and whirlpool tub in each unit. Minutes from a winter and summer sports playground. Trout fishing, hiking, golfing and tennis. Shopping, restaurants and exciting night life, or bask in the sun on wide decks.

Christophe Condo-Hotel
351 2nd Ave. S.
Ketchum, ID 83340
208-726-5601 800-521-2515
FAX: 208-726-5617

1 Bedroom $$$$, 2 Bedrooms $$$$
AmEx/Visa/MC •
30 condos, Lo-rise
Key at Office on site, P-No

Location: ; Downtown: 5 blocks
General Facilities: Full serv.; Daily maid; Linens; Baby sitter; Crib-Hi-chair
Business Facilities: Conf. Room Cap. 150
Sports Facilities: Pool; Whirlpool; Hiking, bikes, fishing; Golf
Room Facilities: Kitchen; Cable; VCR; Ind.Heat Ctl.
Attractions: National Recreation Area, Craters of the Moon Natl. Monument, bike path, Big Wood River.
Shops & Restaurants: Many kinds of shops; Vegetarian, Thai

Sun Valley's only condominium hotel, located within walking distance to Bold Mountain ski lifts and central Ketchum. Spacious, contemporary non-smoking 1- or 2-bedroom flats. Each bedroom has its own entrance, phone line, full bath and TV. Condos have full kitchens, sofa sleepers, gas fireplaces. We have Ketchum's only 4 season outdoor pool. Underground parking, 2 outdoor hot tubs and elevators.

--- SUN VALLEY ---

Bluff Condominium
P.O. Box 186
Sun Valley, ID 83353
208-726-0110

2 Bedrooms $$, 2 Bedrm/week 7$, Min.
Stay: 7 Nights, Visa/MC, Dep. Req'd, •
90 condos, Lo-rise.

Location: Airport: 12 miles; Downtown: 1 mile.

General Facilities: Pool, Hot tub, Sauna, Child planned rec., Tennis, Elkhorn at Sun Valley, Skiing, Baby sitter.

Room Facilities: Daily maid, Kitchen, TV, Cable, Phone, Crib-Hi-chair, Ind. Heat Ctl.

Attractions: Downhill and cross-country skiing, golf, tennis, river rafting, entertainment.

Shops & Restaurants: Many types of shops, Evergreen.

2 bedroom condominiums in Sun Valley with wonderful views. Summer and winter activities for children. Great skiing at Sun Valley Resort.

Dollar Meadows
Sun Valley Co
Sun Valley, ID 83353
800-635-8261

1 Bedroom $$$.

Elkhorn Resort
Box 6009
Sun Valley, ID 83354
208-622-4511 800-635-9356
FAX: 208-622-9705

1 Bedroom $$$, 2 Bedrooms $$$$, Jr. $$$,
3 Bedrooms $$$$, Dep. Req'd.
300 condos, Hi-rise, Key at Lobby.

Location: Airport: Horizon Airlines.

General Facilities: Conf. Rm. Cap.: 400, Lounge, Pool, Recreation Center, Sun Valley, Tennis, 18-hole, Health club, Restaurant, Bar.

Room Facilities: Kitchen, TV, Ind. Heat Ctl.

Attractions: Hemingway haunts, Ketchum Ore Wagon Museum, ice skating, white water float trips, horses, entertainment.

Shops & Restaurants: Elkhorn's shopping plaza, Tequila Joe's, Dino's Bistro.

Year-round award winning resort. 66 world class ski runs nearby. Return to a welcome fire and kitchen fully stocked according to your pre-arrival instructions. Jesses Clubhouse in the summer, 5 swimming pools, 7 spas. A premier vacation resort, year-round, for the whole family, with day care, happy hour, live entertainment, trout streams, biking trails and visits to the haunts of Hemingway.

Copper Mountain Resort

─────────────── SUN VALLEY ───────────────

Knob Hill Ridge
Sun Valley, ID 83353
208-726-4340 800-251-3037

2 Bedrooms $$$$, 3 Bedrooms $$$$
Min. Stay 2 Nights, AmEx/Visa/MC, Dep.
Req'd. •
200 condos, Lo-rise, Key at 380 Washington-#101
No S-yes/H-yes

Location: Airport: 15 miles; Downtown: 1 block; Ski lift: Nearby

General Facilities: Bus. fac., Conf. rm., Daily maid, Kitchen, Linens, Game room, Lounge, Baby-sitter, Child planned rec.: Local day care

Room Facilities: Pool, Sauna, Hot tub, Tennis, Ice skating, fly fishing, TV, Cable, VCR, Phone in rm., Crib-Hi-chair, Ind. Heat Ctl.

Attractions: Fly fishing guides, glider rides, helicopter skiing

Shops & Restaurants: Everything from grocery to sheepskin coats; International cuisine

Lovely surroundings amidst spectacular mountain views. Many activities, skiing, golf, tennis, shopping, dining and entertainment. Sun Valley for great skiing or summer adventures.

Mountain Resorts
Box 1710
Sun Valley, ID 83353
208-622-4511 800-635-4444

———————————— KETCHUM ————————————

Warm Springs Resort at Sun Valley
P.O. Box 10009
Ketchum, ID 83340
208-726-8274 800-635-4404

Studio $$, 1 Bedroom $$,
2 Bedrooms $$$, 3 Bedrooms $$$
1 Bed/week $$$$, 2 Bed/week 5$,
3 Bed/week 7$
Min. stay 2 nights, Amex, Visa, MC,
Dep. req'd
130 condos, Lo-rise,
Key at Front desk •

Location: Airport: 12 miles, Downtown: 2 miles, Ski lift: Mt. Baldy

General facilities: Full serv., Bus. fac., Conf. Rm. (cap. 25), Daily maid, Kitchen, Linens, Baby sitter, Sauna, Hot tub

Room facilities: TV, Cable, Crib-Hi-chair, Ind.Heat Ctl.

Sports facilities: Pool, Tennis, TV, Golf, Cable, Phone in rm.

Attractions: Skiing on Mt. Baldy, water sports nearby, fishing, mountain biking

Shops & Restaurants: Hamburgers and pizza to Continental cuisine, Various small village shops.

Warm Springs Resort at Sun Valley manages 130 completely equipped condominium packages with sizes ranging from convenient, economical studios to deluxe, spacious four bedroom units. All properties are located within easy walking distance of the Warm Spring lift. Unlimited winter activities, and diverse summertime activities, such as steelhead fishing, golf, horseback riding, windsurfing and white water rafting. Rodeo, arts and crafts festivals and Wagon Days celebration.

———————————— SUN VALLEY ————————————

River Run Lodge
P.O. Box 1298
Sun Valley, ID 83353
208-726-9086

1 Bedroom $$$, 2 Bedrooms $$
Lo-rise

Sun Valley Resort
Sun Valley, ID 83353
208-622-4111 800-SUN-VALY

Location: Airport: 12 miles

General facilities: Kitchen, Restaurant, Bar

Sports facilities: Pool, Tennis, 18-hole course, Bikes, ice skating

Attractions: Sun Valley wine auction, Ketchum rodeo, Wagon Days, skiing, bikes, ice skating

Shops & Restaurants: Ketchum galleries, shops, mall adjoining lodge, Lodge dining room

Stay in the condominiums of this family resort with top-notch facilities. Imposing Lodge conveying an air of genteel luxury and understated elegance. Several bars around the premises and wood paneled Lodge dining room. A Bavarian-looking mall adjoins the Lodge, offering irresistible shops and eateries. Hike in the Sawtooths. This is without a doubt, America's premier four season resort featuring world class recreation, accommodations, shopping and dining all nestled into a quaint mountain village.

─────────── SUN VALLEY ───────────

Wildflower
Sun Valley Co
Sun Valley, ID 83353
800-635-8261

─────────── SUN VALLEY (KETCHUM) ───────────

Spa Suite Hotel & Condominiums 1 Bedroom $$
P.O. Box 2771, 351 Second Ave
Sun Valley (Ketchum), ID 83353
208-726-0999 800-321-6447

Make these condominiums your Sun Valley vacation headquarters. Located at the base of Mt. Baldy, suites have ultra-modern kitchens, woodburning fireplaces and large spa master bath in deluxe suites. 4 season activities, such as ice skating, fishing, golf, and tennis.

We want to hear from you—any comments regarding the condos or our publication may be noted on the form at the end of the book.

Illinois

Galena

GALENA

Eagle Ridge Inn & Resort
Box 777, US Route 20
Galena, IL 61036
815-777-2444   800-892-2269

1 Bedroom $$$, 2 Bedrooms $$$$,
3 Bedrooms $$$$
Amex, Visa, MC, DS, CB, DC
Dep. req'd
H-yes ●

Location: Airport: Dubuque - 20 miles, Downtown: 6 miles, Ski lift: nearby

General facilities: Full serv., Bus. fac., Conf. Rm. (cap. 1000), Daily maid, Kitchen, Linens, Recreation programs, Restaurant, Bar, Game room, Lounge, Sauna, Jacuzzi

Room facilities: TV, A/C, VCR, Fireplace, Washer/dryer, Room service

Sports facilities: Pool, Tennis, Golf courses— 45 holes, Lake Galena

Attractions: Historic Galena, Home of U.S. Grant,

Mississippi river-boat cruises, Galena Wine Cellars, entertainment

Shops & Restaurants: Antique shops, Galena shops, Authentic Nineteenth Century downtown, Inn's restaurant/continental & American

Located amidst rolling hills, surrounded by 6,800 acres of woods, grassy meadows and native prairie. Choose from golf course condominiums, townhouses overlooking the lake, or homes tucked deep in the woods, all luxuriously furnished and equipped with every convenience. 3 championship golf courses, 3 full-service pro shops, golf school, practice fairway. Indoor/outdoor pools, water sports on 220-acre fully stocked lake. Hay rides, horseback riding/lessons, fitness and hiking trails. In winter, X-C skiing, sledding, skating, horse-drawn sleigh rides.

Indiana

French Lick

─────────────── FRENCH LICK ───────────────

French Lick Spring Villas Pool
127 South Maple Street
French Lick, IN 47432
812-935-9381 800-457-4042
Attractions: Exercise room, golf

French Lick Springs Golf & Tennis Villas
French Lick, IN 47432 P-yes
812-936-9981 800-457-4042

General Facilities: Conf. rm., Kitchen, Restaurant on prem., Bar on prem., Game room, Baby-sitter

Room Facilities: Pool, Hot tub, Tennis, Croquet, skeet-trap, Golf: Two 18-hole courses

Attractions: Kimball Piano Factory tour, House of Clock Museum, steam train rides, West Baden tours, entertainment

Shops & Restaurants: Le Bistro, Mr. G's Pizzeria

Lobby with mosaic floor, seating areas overlooking the veranda and marble columns recalling an era of graciousness and quiet charm where high tea is served on Friday and Saturday afternoons. Five full service dining rooms. European mineral spa featuring complete beauty and health regimens. Game room with video games, pool tables, big screen TV. Top name entertainment. Variety of interesting packages. Two exciting golf courses.

Kentucky

Gilbertsville
Cadiz

──────────────── CADIZ ────────────────

Vacation Club International   1 Bedroom $, 2 Bedrooms $$, Lo-rise
Route 2   Pool, Kitchen, Linens
Cadiz, KY 42211
502-924-5814

Attractions: Lake Barkley State Resort Park, golf, beaches, boating, horses, trapshooting, exercise room, tennis

One-and two-bedroom villas with screened porches, wall-to-wall carpeting and paddle fans. Comfortably appointed with all household accessories. Rent a boat for fishing or skiing on Lake Barkely. Play tennis, pool, shuffleboard and video games.

──────────────── GILBERTSVILLE ────────────────

Ken-Bar Inn Resort and Club   1 Bedroom $$
Highway 641, P.O. Box 66   Lo-rise
Gilbertsville, KY 42044
502-362-8652

General Facilities: Conf. rm. cap. 500, Kitchen, Restaurant on prem., Game room, Child planned rec.: Playgrd.-pool-pond

Room Facilities: Pool, Sauna, Hot tub, Volley, basketball

Attractions: Empire Farms, Homeplace-1850, Environmental Education Center, hiking, jeep touring, fishin, entertainment

Shops & Restaurants: Harbor House/on-site

Set in the lakes region of southwestern Kentucky, known for its two parallel lakes, forming the world's largest man-made body of water. Half mile to the beach, but you may be too busy with the resort activities, such as indoor/outdoor pools, exercise room, hot tub, saunas, game room, volleyball, shuffleboard, horseshoes, basketball, aerobics, nature trail, picnic area and tennis. Younger guests enjoy their own pool, fishing pond and playground. Square or ballroom dancing, country entertainment often.

Louisiana

New Orleans

─────────────── NEW ORLEANS ───────────────

The Quarter House   1 Bedroom $$$, 2 Bedrooms $$$$
129 Chartres St.
New Orleans, LA 70130
504-523-5906

General Facilities: Daily maid
Sports Facilities: Pool
Room Facilities: Kitchen; Phone
Attractions: French Quarter, Basin Street

One- and two-bedroom suites have whirlpool baths, color television and smoke detectors. Swimming pool, jacuzzi and tropical courtyard. Restaurant and tour reservation service. Accommodations noted for privacy, yet the location is excellent for sightseeing.

Avenue Plaza/Eurovita Spa
2111 St. Charles Ave.
New Orleans, LA 70130
504-566-1212

Windsor Court Hotel
300 Gravier St.
New Orleans, LA 70140
504-523-6000

Maine

Carrabasset Valley

Bethel

Rockport

Kennebunkport
Ogunquit

─────────────────── BETHEL ───────────────────

Sunday River Ski Resort
P.O. Box 450
Bethel, ME 04217
200-824-2187 800-543-2754
FAX: 207-824-2111

1 Bedroom $$$$, 2 Bedrooms $$$$, Jr. $$$,
3 Bedrooms $$$$, 1 Bedrm/week 10$,
2 Bedrm/week 10$, 3 Bedrm/week 10$,
Min. Stay: 2 Nights on Wkends.,
AmEx/Visa/MC/Disc., Dep. Req'd, •
680 condos, Hi-rise, Lo-rise, H-yes, Key at
Welcome center.

Location: Airport: 1.5 hrs from Portland; Downtown: 5 miles; Ski lift: on mountain.

General Facilities: Conf. Rm. Cap.: 500, Lounge, Pool, Hot tub, Sauna, Day care/
nursery, Slopeside, Tennis, 5 miles-Bethel Inn CClub, Mountain bike park,
Baby sitter, Restaurant, Bar.

Room Facilities: Daily maid, Kitchen, TV, Cable, Phone, Cribs, Ind. Heat Ctl.

Attractions: Skiing, sleigh rides, White Mountains, Sunday River Fall Festival,
Mardi Gras, Mt. bikes, entertainment.

Shops & Restaurants: Outlet shopping, antiques, on-mountain ski shop, Ros-
setto's, Fall Line/Amr, Bumps/Pubfood.

*Fully equipped condos right on the mountain with free shuttle to all 3 base lodges and
condos. Sunday River has 89% snowmaking coverage from top to bottom! Modern full
kitchens, ski storage in most units, some fireplaces, and heated pools. Dine in our
fine restaurants followed by a fun evening of live entertainment and dancing.
Summer activities include a Mountain Bike Park, tennis, swimming and nearby golf.*

─────────────────── CARRABASSETT VALLEY ───────────────────

Sugarloaf Mountain Resort
Carrabassett Valley
Carrabassett Valley, ME 04947
207-237-2000 800-457-0002

Game room, Pool, Hot tub, Tennis, Health
spa, Baby sitter, Kitchen.

Attractions: Hartford Ballet Residency, nature walks, Seasons' Restaurant.

─────────────────── KENNEBUNKPORT ───────────────────

Nonantum Resort
P.O. Box 2626, Ocean Ave.
Kennebunkport, ME 04046
207-967-4050

—————————————— OGUNQUIT ——————————————

Hillcrest Inn Resort
Shore Rd., P.O. Box 2000
Ogunquit, ME 03907
207-646-7776

Studio $$, 1 Bedroom $$$, 2 Bedrooms
$$$, 1 Bed/week 6$, 2 Bed/week 8$
Min. stay 3 nights, Visa, MC
Key at Front office

Location: Airport: 45 miles; Downtown: 2 miles; Need car; Ski lift: ¼ mi. X-C

General facilities: Kitchen, Linens

Room facilities: TV, Cable, Phone, Crib-Hi-chair, Ind. AC Ctl., Ind. Heat Ctl.

Sports facilities: 3/4 mi. Cape Neddick CC, Indoor pool, Sailing

Attractions: Summer playhouse, Galleries, Fishing, Boating, Swimming, coffee hours

Shops & Restaurants: 20 minutes to outlet shopping, Many excellent restaurants

The Hillcrest Condominiums offers a relaxing vacation in a charming Maine town complete with fine sandy beaches, rugged rocky coast, excellent dining, renowned summer theater, unique shops and galleries galore—all within walking distance from your spacious apartment or compact studio fully equipped to meet your vacation needs. Open year round.

Be sure to call the condo the verify details and prices and to make your reservation.

Maryland

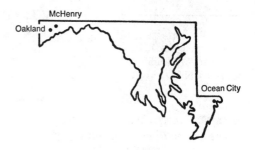

McHenry
Oakland
Ocean City

──────────────── MCHENRY ────────────────

Sunplace   2 Bedrooms 4$
P.O. Box 215
McHenry, MD 21541
301-387-7866 800-544-7754

Deep Creek Lake for summer fun, mountains for winter skiing. Cedar exteriors, master bath jacuzzi, garden tub, fireplace. Pool, community building, golf.

───

Villages of Wisp
P.O. Box 390
McHenry, MD 21541
301-387-4966

Colonial style modern townhouses on Deep Creek Lake along the slopes of Wisp Ski Resort. Serene retreat in beautiful West Maryland.

OAKLAND

Will O' Wisp
Star Route 1, Box 124
Oakland, MD 21550
301-387-5503

1 Bedroom $$, 2 Bedrooms $$$, 3 Bedrooms $$$$
1 Bedrm/week 5$, 2 Bed/week 8$, 3 Bed/week 10$
AmEx/Visa/MC, Dep. Req'd.
Hi-rise

Location: Beach front; Ski lift: Wisp Ski

General Facilities: Conf. rm. cap. 150, Kitchen, Linens, Restaurant on prem., Bar on prem., Game room, Lounge

Room Facilities: Pool, Sauna, Racquet, exercise, Golf: Wisp; TV, Cable, Phone in rm., Ind. AC Ctl., Ind. Heat Ctl.

Attractions: Wisp ski area, Deep Creek Lake

Shops & Restaurants: Four Seasons/continental

Just bring your food, clothes and beach towels. Individually decorated units with sliding glass doors and windows overlooking the lake, patios or balconies for lounging. Elevators, 4th floor washers and dryers. Allegheny mountain skiing. Torchlight ski parade at end of Winterfest weekend. Boat docks, lake cruises, protected swimming area, boat rentals. Indoor pool, full gym, game room, golf and gourmet restaurant. Special vacation plans available.

OCEAN CITY

Boardwalk One
First St. & Boardwalk, Box 762
Ocean City, MD 21842
301-289-3161

Pool, Kitchen

Attractions: Amusements, arcades, shops, ocean

Oceanfront efficencies with private balconies. Choice location on the Boardwalk for area amusements. Atlantic Ocean at your front door. Limited membership to Ocean City Health and Racquetball Club for weight room, aerobic dancing and indoor-heated pool.

The Quay
107th Street & Coastal Highway
Ocean City, MD 21842
800-437-7600

Hi-rise
Pool, Kitchen

Attractions: Miniature golf, tennis

Spacious two-and three-bedroom condominiums with panoramic views of both ocean and bay. 24-hour security, outdoor and indoor pools, nautical recreation area with billiards room.

Sea Watch
115th Street & Coastal Highway
Ocean City, MD 21842
800-437-7600

Hi-rise
Pool, Kitchen

Attractions: Basketball court, tennis

Everything you need within walking distance of these individually decorated apartments. Enjoy sunny days on the white sand beach. Take advantage of the lighted tennis courts, pool, game room, adult billiard room and the relaxing atmosphere of the green atrium.

Massachusetts

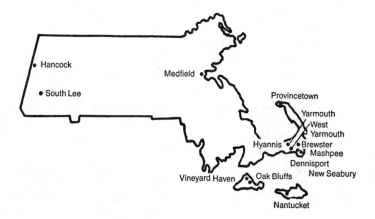

Hancock

Medfield

South Lee

Provincetown

Yarmouth
West
Yarmouth

Hyannis • Brewster
Mashpee
Dennisport

Vineyard Haven Oak Bluffs New Seabury

Nantucket

BREWSTER

Brewster Green
South Pond Rd.
Brewster, MA 02631
617-896-5772

Ocean Edge Resort   1 Bedroom $$, 2 Bedrooms $$, Lo-rise
1 Village Dr., Route 6A   Pool, Kitchen, Linens
Brewster, MA 02631
508-896-2781 800-221-1837

Attractions: Melody Tent, Cape Cod Playhouse, Whale Watches, golf, tennis, Basketball, Drive range, tennis, golf

Private designer-decorated villas and townhouses with views of ponds, woods or golf course. Playground and structured activities for children. Golf, tennis lessons and tournaments. Play at the beach or pools, bicycle on the Cape Cod trail. Sunday evening cocktail.

DENNISPORT

Delray Beach Club   1 Bedroom $, 2 Bedrooms $$
188 Captain Chase Rd, Box 1247   Pool, Kitchen, Linens
Dennisport, MA 02639
508-398-3441

Attractions: One block to beach

Efficiency and one bedroom units one block from the beach. Heated outdoor pool, June to September. Outdoor gas grills.

———————————————— DENNISPORT ————————————————

Oceanside Resort   Lo-rise
Condominiums
154 Old Wharf Rd. at Glendon Rd.
Dennisport, MA 02639
617-394-5359

General facilities: Kitchen

Sports facilities: Pool, Golf course, Fishing

Attractions: Nantucket Island, Martha's Vineyard, deep sea fishing, National Seashore hiking

Modern condominiums on a gentle rise, steps away from Nantucket Sound beach fun. Oceanfront views and some private porches. In the center of Cape Cod's vacation wonderland.

———————————————— HANCOCK ————————————————

Country Village At Jiminy Peak 1 Bedroom $$$, 2 Bedrooms $$$$,
Corey Rd.   3 Bedrooms $$$$, 1 Bed/week 7$, 2
Hancock, MA 01237   Bed/week 10$, 3 Bed/week 10$, Min. stay 2
413-738-5500   nights, Amex, Visa, MC, Dep. 1 night, Key
          at Front desk, 20 condos, Lo-rise, H-yes

Location: Airport: 45 min.; Downtown: 20 min.; Need car; Ski lift: Jiminy

General facilities: Full serv., Conf. Rm. (cap. 200), Daily maid, Kitchen, Linens, Ski Wee, Patriot Pk., Baby sitter, Restaurant, Bar, Game room, Lounge, Sauna, Hot tub

Room facilities: TV, Cable, Phone, Crib-Hi-chair, Ind. AC. Ctl, Ind. Heat Ctl.

Sports facilities: Pool, Tennis, Waubeeka Golf course, Alpine Slide

Attractions: Williamstown Theatre Festival, Tanglewood, Jacob's Pillow, Entertainment

Shops & Restaurants: Jardin/French

Nestled in the scenic Jericho Valley, these units are furnished in old New England style with neutral color schemes. Ski Wee and patriots program for the children, and planned winter activities, plus bingo. Larger units have lofts, fireplaces and decks.

The Shores

———————————————— HYANNIS ————————————————

Hyannis Harborview Resort   1 Bedroom $$
213 Ocean Street
Hyannis, MA 02601
617-775-4420

Location: Downtown: 5 min.
General Facilities: Conf. rm. cap. 150, Restaurant on prem., Bar on prem., Lounge
Room Facilities: Pool, Sauna, Hot tub, Health spa, Ind. AC Ctl., Ind. Heat Ctl.
Attractions: Nantucket and Martha's Vineyard
Shops & Restaurants: Hyannis shops; Neptune Room

Courtesy van picks you up at the airport or bus terminal and brings you to this complete year-round resort. Spacious two-level units with everything you need for your vacation. Sun on the beach, lunch by the pool, watch the fishing boats and sailing ships. In winter walk through the hallways to the indoor pool oasis. Fine dining spots and Crow's Nest Lounge on the premises. 5 minutes to downtown Hyannis shops and attractions. Step out of the courtyard for a day trip to Martha's Vineyard or Nantucket.

Subscribe to our newsletter *Mondo Condo* and hear about the latest special condo vacation values.

─────────────── HYANNIS ───────────────

The Breakwaters
Box 118, 432 Sea Street
Hyannis, MA 02601
617-775-6831

1 Bedroom $$, 2 Bedrooms $$, 3 Bedrooms $$
1 Bedrm/week $$$$, 2 Bed/week 4$, 3 Bed/
week 5$
Min. Stay 3 Nights, Dep. Req'd.
18 condos, Lo-rise, Key at Office

Location: Airport: 2 miles; Downtown: 1 mile; Beach front

General Facilities: Daily maid, Kitchen, Linens, Baby-sitter

Room Facilities: Pool, Golf: 2 miles; TV, Cable, Crib-Hi-chair, Ind. Heat Ctl.

Attractions: Whale watching, fishing, excursions to Nantucket and Martha's Vineyard

Shops & Restaurants: Hyannis Center Shops; Marie Jeans-Up The Creek/fish

The Breakwater is on the beach of Nantucket Sound in a residential area one mile from town and docks. Charming, weathered, gray cottages, blue rugs, white wallpapers with country house furnishings in the Laura Ashley fashion. Swimming pool and decks with harbor views. Three diamond award rating from the American Automobile Association.

**The Yachtsman
Condominiums**
P.O. Box 939, 500 Ocean St.
Hyannis, MA 02601
508-771-5454
FAX: 508-775-1695

1 Bedrm/week, 2 Bedrm/week 9$,
3 Bedrm/week 10$
Min. Stay 7 Nights, AmEx/MC/Visa, Dep.
Req'd
125 condos, Villas, Keys at Rental
office, C-yes

Location: Airport: 2 miles; Downtown: 1 mile, Beach front

General Facilities:, Kitchen, Baby sitter

Room Facilities: Pool, TV, Cable, Phone in rm., Ind. Heat Ctl.

Attractions: Whale watching, Nantucket and Martha's Vineyard, Plymouth Rock, Provincetown, seashore

Shops & Restaurants: Cape Cod Mall, Filenes, Jordans; Chillingsworth/ French

Multi-level townhouses, full kitchens with dishwashers, washers and dryers and decks. Views of Nantucket Sound. Private beach and heated pool, just minutes away from shopping, dining and sport activities. A convenient, elegant retreat.

─────────────── MASHPEE ───────────────

Southcape Resort & Club
Route 28, RFD 1
Mashpee, MA 02649
617-477-3990

2 Bedrooms $$, Lo-rise
Pool, Kitchen, Linens

Attractions: Golf, fishing, Martha's Vineyard, Nantucket, Steam rooms, tennis

Pine scented land with country roads for jogging and quaint villages. Two-bedroom condominiums have entertainment areas with hi-fi, fireplaces or jacuzzis and living room big-screen color televisions. Seashore and park are five minutes away.

─────────────── MEDFIELD ───────────────

Ocean Watch
14 The Paddock Lane
Medfield, MA 02052
617-956-7640

——————————————— Nantucket ———————————————

Monomoy Village
8 Federal Street
Nantucket, MA 02554
617-228-4449

1 Bedrm/week 8$, 2 Bed/week 9$
Min. Stay 7 Nights, Dep. Req'd.
8 condos, Villas

Location: Airport: 1 mile; Downtown: 1 mile; Need car

General Facilities: Kitchen, Linens

Room Facilities: ¼ mile to beach, TV, Cable, Phone in rm., Ind. Heat Ctl.

Attractions: The unique island of Nantucket, preserved as it was in the 19th century.

Shops & Restaurants: 21 Federal/The Boarding House

Newly renovated cottages with pine floors, Shaker furnishings and color coordinated fabrics. Fully equipped kitchens, fireplace, washer/dryer, cable TV, deck or courtyard with furniture and barbecue, all set in a landscaped private compound. Beach sports, art galleries, museums and historic sites.

Tristram's Landing
Madaket
Nantucket, MA 02554
508-228-0359

Min. Stay 3 Nights, Visa/MC, Dep. Req'd.
Lo-rise, Villas, Key at Main office

Location: Airport: 5 miles; Downtown: 5 miles; Need car; Beach front

General Facilities: Daily maid, Kitchen, Linens, Game room, Baby-sitter, Child planned rec.: Play area

Room Facilities: Tennis, Sailing, Canoeing, Phone in rm., Crib-Hi-chair, Ind. Heat Ctl.

Attractions: Fabulous beaches, super ocean activities, sailing, swimming, Great Point excursions

Shops & Restaurants: Nantucket restaurants

Multi-level townhouses with sleeping quarters well separated from living areas. Almost snow-free winters, delightful, warm spring and fall days. Beach, swimming hole, tennis, recreation hall and outdoor play area. Fishing, nature trails, Nantucket Town.

——————————————— NEW SEABURY ———————————————

New Seabury Cape Cod
P.O. Box B
New Seabury, MA 02649
617-477-9111   800-222-2044

Villas

Location: Airport: Boston—1½ hours; Beach front

General Facilities: Conf. rm. cap. 125, Daily maid, Kitchen, Linens, Restaurant on prem., Bar on prem., Game room, Baby-sitter

Room Facilities: Pool, Tennis, Health spa, jogging, Golf: 2 championship courses

Attractions: Sandwich Glass Museum, Heritage Plantation, fishing excursions, jogging and bike trails

Shops & Restaurants: Boutiques, Popponesset Market Place; New Seabury Restaurant

Seaside villas with full housekeeping services on Cape Cod's southern tip. Decor ranges from 19th century Nantucket style with antiques, wide plank floors and French doors, to cool California contemporary. Something for every age, starting with three miles of sandy white beach. Numerous children's activities—movies, waterbug slalom race, beach blanket bingo. Tennis instruction and health spa with Nautilus equipment. Two championship golf courses.

──────────────── OAK BLUFFS ────────────────

Island Country Club Inn   Studio $$, 1 Bedroom $$, 2 Bedrooms $$
P.O. Box 1585   1 Bedrm/week 4$, 2 Bed/week 5$
Oak Bluffs, MA 02557   AmEx/Visa/MC, Dep. Req'd. •
617-693-2002   51 condos, Lo-rise, Key at Registr. office
                                     H-yes

Location: Airport: 10 miles; Downtown: 1 mile; Need car

General Facilities: Conf. rm. cap. 200, Daily maid, Kitchen, Linens, Restaurant on prem., Bar on prem., Lounge, Baby-sitter

Room Facilities: Pool, Tennis, Golf: Farm Neck Golf adjacent; TV, Cable, Phone in rm., Crib

Attractions: Bus tours, fishing, charters, sailing

Shops & Restaurants: Anthony's

Informal resort-like property on Martha's Vineyard. Patios and decks with views of Nantucket Sound and Sengekontacket Pond. 24 post and beam suites with fireplaces. Beachcomb, swim, bicycle on scenic paths, fish, windsurf. Three Har-Tru tennis courts, pro shop, tennis pro, lessons. Relax in leisure in this island resort for all seasons.

──────────────── PROVINCETOWN ────────────────

Eastwood At Provincetown   Kitchen, Linens
324 Bradford St.
Provincetown, MA 02657
508-487-0760 800-462-1126

Attractions: First landing place of Pilgrims, playhouse, Boston ferry boat, Provincetown Heritage Museu, putting green, shuffleboard, tennis

Bright, airy, professionally decorated condominiums with coordinated carpeting, ceramic tiled kitchen and bathroom floors and custom designed draperies. Clubhouse with fireplace, wet bar, food preparation unit. Picnic tables, gazebo, lawns, shrubs and shade trees.

Fishermans Cove Condominiums
145 Commercial Street
Provincetown, MA 02657
516-487-1397

Sandcastle Condominiums   1 Bedroom $$
Route 6A, P.O. Box 576
Provincetown, MA 02657
617-487-9300

Kitchens, phones, TV's and balconies overlooking Cape Cod Bay. Beach, indoor and outdoor pools and tennis. Hike among the dunes or browse the shops and art galleries of quaint, historic Provincetown.

SOUTH LEE

Oak 'n Spruce Resort
P.O. Box 237, Meadow Street
South Lee, MA 01260
413-243-3500 800-341-5700

1 Bedroom $$$$, 2 Bedrooms $$$$
1 Bedrm/week 8$, 2 Bed/week 10$
Dep. Req'd.
Lo-rise

Location: Ski lift: x-country

General Facilities: Kitchen, Linens, Restaurant on prem., Bar on prem., Game room, Lounge, Child planned rec.: Supervised activity

Room Facilities: Pool, Sauna, Hot tub, Tennis, Health Club, Golf: 3 par 9-hole course

Attractions: Tanglewood, Norman Rockwell Museum, Jacob's Pillow Dance Festival, Beartown State Forest, entertainment

Shops & Restaurants: On-site restaurant/continental

Year-round resort in the Berkshires. Informal atmosphere with recreation department offering planned activities for children and adults. Have a snack in front of the game room fireplace, fish for trout in the nearby stream, participate in aerobics and water aerobics. Golf, tennis and x-c ski trails. Restaurant features special events, buffets and cookouts.

VINEYARD HAVEN

Causeway Harborview
Skiff Avenue, Box 450
Vineyard Haven, MA 02568
508-693-1606

Studio $$, 1 Bedroom $$, 2 Bedrooms $$,
3 Bedrooms $$
1 Bedrm/week $$$$, 2 Bed/week $$$$,
3 Bed/week $$$$
Dep. Req'd., 24 condos, Lo-rise, Key at Office

Location: Airport: 15 minutes; Downtown: 10 min.

General Facilities: Daily maid, Kitchen, Linens

Room Facilities: Pool, Water sports, harbor, TV, Crib-Hi-chair, Ind. Heat Ctl.

Attractions: Martha's Vineyard-beautiful scenery, beaches, boating

Shops & Restaurants: Small stores; Black Dog Tavern/New England

Comfortable, homey apartments and cottages in a hillside setting overlooking the beautiful harbor. Minutes walk to town and waterfront activities. The spacious, well-landscaped property has a large pool and picnic sites with barbecues.

WEST YARMOUTH, CAPE COD

The Englewood Townhouses
60 Broadway
West Yarmouth, Cape Cod, MA 02673
617-775-3900

Two-story townhouses, second-story balconies, first-floor patios. 100 yards to beach, outdoor and indoor pools, tennis, shuffleboard, barbecue area. Weekly rentals.

YARMOUTH

The Cove at Yarmouth
P.O. Box 1000, Route 28
Yarmouth, MA 02673
617-771-3666

1 Bedroom $$
Pool, Kitchen

Attractions: Hyannis Harbour tours, Kennedy Compound, Martha's Vineyard, Nantucket Island, health spa, racquetball, tennis

Townhouses in the heart of Cape Cod with stereo systems and whirlpool baths. Total recreation environment, area beaches, picnic and barbecue areas. Try windsurfing or deep-sea fishing, ride on the Cape Cod & Hyannis Railroad.

Michigan

Wakefield

Boyne Falls
Bellaire
Traverse City Acme
Thompsonville

--- ACME ---

Grand Traverse Resort Village
6300 North US-31
Acme, MI 49610
616-938-2100 800-678-1308

Studio $$, 1 Bedroom $$$, 2 Bedrooms $$$, 3 Bedrooms $$$$
AmEx/Visa/MC, Dep. 1 Night •
293 condos, Hi-rise, Lo-rise, Key at Lobby area
No S-yes/H-yes

Location: Airport: Traverse 5 miles; Downtown: 6 miles; Beach front; Ski lift: 6 areas

General Facilities: Full serv., Bus. fac., Conf. rm. cap. 1750, Daily maid, Kitchen, Linens, Restaurant on prem., Bar on prem., Game room, Lounge, Baby-sitter, Child planned rec.: Crafts, recreation

Room Facilities: Pool, Sauna, Hot tub, Tennis, Health-Racquet Club, Golf: Nicklaus designed "Bear"; TV, Cable, Phone in rm., Crib-Hi-chair, Ind. AC Ctl., Ind. Heat Ctl.

Attractions: Cherry orchard tours, skiing, Winery tours, Sleeping Bear Dunes, Interlochen Music Camp, entertainment

Shops & Restaurants: Tower Gallery of shops, art, wines, clothes; Trillium, Hannah Lay Gourmet

For a carefree getaway, romantic escape or fun-filled family vacation, stay in these golf or lakefront condominiums. Cherry blossoms in the spring and golden leaves in the autumn surround the renowned golf course. Winter skiing, complete Nordic ski center. Charter fishing boats, private game reserve. Complete resort activities including children's programs, video games and pinball. Outdoor cooking facilities at the Beach Club. Casual to elegant dining and nightly entertainment, deli, homemade pizza.

———————————————— BELLAIRE ————————————————

Shanty Creek-Schuss Mtn.
Resort
Bellaire, MI 49615
Location: Beach front; Ski lift at Nearby
General Facilities: Restaurant
Business Facilities: Conference Room
Sports Facilities: Pool; Tennis; Health Club, fishing; "Legend" and Schuss Mt.; Activity programs
Room Facilities: Kitchen
Attractions: Canoes, paddleboats, skeet shooting, orchard tours, hayrides, fishing, Lake Bellaire
Shops & Restaurants: Ivanhof

These two resorts recently merged to form this complex on northern Michigan's Gold Coast. Rolling wooded country dotted with natural lakes and streams. Wide variety of activities for children, winter skiing, summer fishing, hiking and watersports. Private beach club on the lake. Arnold Palmer- and Billy Diddel-designed golf courses.

———————————————— THOMPSONVILLE ————————————————

Crystal Mountain Resort   Studio $$, 1 Bedroom $$$,
12500 Crystal Mountain Dr.   2 Bedrooms $$$$, 3 Bedrooms $$$$
Thompsonville, MI 49683   Visa/MC, Dep. Required
616-378-2911 800-968-7686   141 condos, Lo-rise
FAX: 616-378-2998   Key at Front Desk, No S-Yes

Location: Airport: 40 minutes; Downtown: 40 minutes; Ski lift at On-site
General Facilities: Daily maid; Linens; Baby sitter; Lounge; Restaurant on premises; Bar on premises
Business Facilities: Bus. fac.; Conf. Room Cap. 300
Sports Facilities: Game room; Pool; Tennis; Canoeing, fishing; Crystal Mountain Resort; Children's programs
Room Facilities: Kitchen; Cable; Phone; Ind.AC Ctl.; Ind.Heat Ctl.
Attractions: Sleeping Bear Dunes National Lakeshore, Center for the Arts-Interlochen, Lake Michigan; Entertainment
Shops & Restaurants: Traverse City, local gift shops, small town shops; Wildflower Dining Room-American

This year-round resort and conference center offers fine dining, downhill & cross country skiing, golf and tennis. Sightseeing and water sports abound with Lake Michigan and numerous inland lakes just minutes away. A family resort with nightly activities for guests. Crystal's scenic rural location and recreational amenities make it a popular vacation destination.

─────────────── TRAVERSE CITY ───────────────

The Beach Condominiums
1995 U. S. 31 North
Traverse City, MI 49648
616-938-2238
FAX: 616-938-9774

1 Bedroom $$$$, 2 Bedrooms,
AmEx/Visa/MC, •
30 condos, Lo-rise, NoS-yes, H-yes, Key at
front desk.

Location: Airport: 1 mile; Downtown: 2 miles, Need car; Beach front.

General Facilities: Bus. fac., Lounge, Pool, Hot tub, Miniature golf, Grand Traverse Resort, Sailing, water skiing, Baby sitter, Restaurant, Bar.

Room Facilities: Daily maid, Kitchen, TV, Cable, Phone, Crib-Hi-chair, Ind. AC. Ctl., Ind. Heat Ctl.

Attractions: Sleeping Bear Dunes, Machinac Island, Leland, North Port, Petoskey, Night club.

Shops & Restaurants: Traverse City, Harbor Springs, Leland, Chalevoix, Bowers Harbour Inn/gourmet.

The finest accommodations on Grand Traverse Bay in Northern Michigan. Resort oriented condominiums in decorator colors and large private decks with bay views. 300 feet of gorgeous sugar sand beach is raked daily. Heated pool and spa. Close to golf, downhill and cross-country skiing and shopping. Adjacent boat launch.

Our goal is to provide as *complete* a listing of condo vacation properties as possible. If you know of a condo we don't list, please send us their name and address on the form at the back of this Guide.

Minnesota

Park Rapids • • Hill City   Lutsen
Grand Rapids
Detroit Lakes • • • Breezy Point
Nisswa Brainerd • • Deerwood
• Alexandria

Minnetonka •

───────────── ALEXANDRIA ─────────────

Lake Carlos Villas   1 Bedroom $
R.R. #5, South Lake Carlos
Alexandria, MN 56308
612-846-1784

Sunshine or snow, an outstanding family fun region. Fireplaces with wood, TV, radio, decks with grill and furniture. Smowmobile and x-country ski trails. Clubhouse, indoor and outdoor pools, hot tub and sauna. In summer each unit is furnished a boat.

───────────── BRAINERD ─────────────

Causeway On Gull   2 Bedrooms $$$
Route 6, Box 116
Brainerd, MN 56401
218-963-3510 800-247-1216

Room Facilities: Pool, Tennis, Lake, Golf: Gull Lake golf course

Attractions: Sailing, water skiing, fishing, windsurfing, speedboats, snowmobiles, x-country skiing

Rich in architectural design surrounded by more than an acre of wooded land, wooded nature trail outside your door. Tennis courts with ball machine, golf practice facility, 18-foot speedboat. Pool surrounded by plush gardens, stone waterfall and towering pines. Yamaha snowmobiles available for winter use. Four passenger golf cart for riding around.

─────────────── BRAINERD ───────────────

Cragun's Pine Beach Lodge
2001 Pine Beach Road
Brainerd, MN 56401
218-829-3591 800-272-4867

Alpine designed cottages and townhouses with fireplaces, in-house audio-visual equipment, smoke alarms and color TV. Sandy beaches, marina, indoor pool, fishing, hunting, tennis, golf, volleyball. Winter x-country skiing, dog and sleigh rides, and skating.

─────────────── BREEZY POINT ───────────────

Breezy Point International
HCR2, Box 70
Breezy Point, MN 56472
218-562-7811 800-328-2284

Studio $$, 1 Bedroom $$, 2 Bedrooms $$$$
AmEx/Visa/MC, Dep. Req'd. •
Lo-rise, Key at Front desk
H-yes

Location: Airport: Brainerd 20 miles; Downtown: 20 miles; Need car; Beach front; Ski lift: Ski Bull

General Facilities: Bus. fac., Conf. rm. cap. 750, Daily maid, Kitchen, Linens, Restaurant on prem., Bar on prem., Game room, Lounge, Baby-sitter, Child planned rec.: Full program

Room Facilities: Pool, Sauna, Hot tub, Tennis, Boating, bikes, hike, Golf: Breezy Point 36 holes; TV, Cable, Phone in rm., Crib-Hi-chair, Ind. AC Ctl., Ind. Heat Ctl.

Attractions: Lake, fishing, hiking, golf, skiing, tennis, boating, entertainment

Shops & Restaurants: Antiques and local boutiques, Nisswa Mall; Marina Dining Room/American

Deluxe resort set on the shores of Big Pelican Lake. Rustic elegance, blue, moss green and rust color schemes, fireplaces, jacuzzis and some VCRs. Top 40 band, easy listening music, adult and children recreation programs. Excellent food and entertainment. State-of-the-art convention and meeting facilities. An upbeat fun resort with something for everyone.

─────────────── DEERWOOD ───────────────

Ruttgers Bay Lodge & Conf. Center
Box 400
Deerwood, MN 56444
218-678-2885 800-328-0312

1 Bedroom $$, 2 Bedrooms $$$$
Dep. 1 Night
Key at Front desk

Location: Beach front; Ski lift: x-country

General Facilities: Bus. fac., Conf. rm., Daily maid, Kitchen, Linens, Restaurant on prem., Child planned rec.: Summer activities

Room Facilities: Pool, Sauna, Hot tub, Tennis, Volleyball, marina, Golf: Bay Lodge-two 9-hole; TV, Phone in rm., Ind. AC Ctl.

Attractions: Brainerd Lakes Area, summer theatre, historical museums, antique shows, regional festivals, entertainment

Shops & Restaurants: The Country Store, Pro Shop, Corner Sportswear; Colonial Room, on-site

Golf Course condominiums with walkouts overlooking the golf course, and villas adjoining the indoor pool. Modified American Plan packages with special activities available year-round. Marina has boat rentals, tackle and bait. Full range of dining from elegant to casual. Pine-scented forest, daily activity programs and summer Kid's Kamp. X-country ski trail and sleigh rides for winter vacationers. Townhomes, 1 mile from the Lodge, with dockage, launching, tennis court, pool, whirlpool and sauna.

---------------------------- DETROIT LAKES ----------------------------

Breezy Shores Resort   2 Bedrooms $$, Lo-rise
1275 West Lake Drive   Pool, Kitchen, Linens
Detroit Lakes, MN 56501
218-847-2695 800-346-4978

Attractions: Boating, golf, tennis, fishing, ice fishing, snowmobiling, skiing, ice skating, Activity Center, golf

Two-story townhouses with fireplaces-wood supplied-decks and balconies on 800 feet of private beach. Activity center has indoor pool, sauna, whirlpool, game room and social area. Summer boating and water sports, plus nearby golf and tennis.

Edgewater Beach Club   2 Bedrooms $$, Lo-rise
321 Park Boulevard   Pool, Kitchen, Phone in rm.
Detroit Lakes, MN 56501
218-847-1351

Attractions: Detroit Mt. skiing, Tamarac Wildlife Refuge, Soo-Pass "Dude Ranch," Itasca State Park, Marina, golf

Country life with the convenience of town living. Area ski slopes-6 tows. Indoor and outdoor pools and sauna. Lake sports. Beach, marina, tennis, minature golf, park and playground adjacent. Tamarac Wildlife Refuge. Restaurants and entertainment nearby.

---------------------------- GRAND RAPIDS ----------------------------

Sugar Hills Resort   1 Bedroom $, 2 Bedrooms $$, Lo-rise
P.O. Box 369   Pool, Kitchen
Grand Rapids, MN 55744
218-326-9461 800-752-5263

Attractions: Golf, tennis, boating, skiing, fishing, windsurfing, paddleboats, sailing, Volleyball, hiking

Western ski style condominiums at the base of the hills near the indoor pool, or townhouses surrounded by trees on the golf course near beach, tennis courts and indoor pool. Supervised programs for 4 years and older. Clubhouse dining and cocktails.

---------------------------- HILL CITY ----------------------------

Quadna Mountain Vacation Club   1 Bedroom $$
100 Quadna Rd.
Hill City, MN 55748
218-697-8133 800-422-6649

Villas and townhouses for modern living in a rustic setting. Winter skiing, fall colors and superb hunting, spring and summer fishing and water sports. Indoor/outdoor pools-tennis, horseshoes, badminton, croquet, bocce, shuffleboard, dining, bar and entertainment.

Kana Lani

LUTSEN

The Village Inn and Resort
P.O. Box 26
Lutsen, MN 55612
218-663-7241 800-642-6036

1 Bedroom $$, 2 Bedrooms $$$, Lo-rise
Pool, Kitchen

Attractions: Boundary Waters Canoe Area, alpine slide, hiking, fishing, music festivals, art fairs, volleyball, lawn games, tennis, golf

Condominiums and townhouses on Lake Superior's North Shore and the Sawtooth Mountain Range. Breakfast rides, overnights and hay rides. Indoor pool, jacuzzi, tennis, volleyball, lawn games, Alpine Slide. Recreation programs for children and naturalist programs.

MINNETONKA

Breezy Point Resort
10560 Wayzata Boulevard
Minnetonka, MN 55343
218-562-7811 800-328-2284

Lo-rise
Kitchen

Attractions: Skiing, snowmobiling, fishing, boating, ice fishing, ice skating, Dockside-entertainment, Trapshooting, volleyball, tennis, golf

———————————————— NISSOVA ————————————————

Grand View Lodge
134 Nokomis
Nissova, MN 56468
218-963-2234 800-432-3788

AmEx/Visa/MC •
16 condos
No S-yes/H-yes

Location: Airport: 17 miles—Brainerd; Downtown: 17 miles

General Facilities: Bus. fac., Conf. rm. cap. 350, Kitchen, Restaurant on prem., Bar on prem., Child planned rec.: Activities program

Room Facilities: Pool, Sauna, Hot tub, Tennis, Sailing, riding, TV, Cable, Phone in rm., Ind. AC Ctl., Ind. Heat Ctl.

Attractions: Grand View Gardens, entertainment

Shops & Restaurants: Sundries, gift shop; Kavanaughs/French

Located in northern Minnesota lake country, Grand View Lodge sits among tall pines, sandy beaches and deep blue waters. Exceptional dining, friendly service and a vacation with activities for the entire family. You'll especially enjoy the resort's famous flower gardens.

———————————————— PARK RAPIDS ————————————————

North Beach Vacation Club
Niawa Star Route
Park Rapids, MN 56470
218-732-9708 800-362-3145

Townhouses with views of the lake. Winter skiing, summer sailing, canoeing, swimming. Jog or bike on scenic trails in the crystal clear air. Shipwreck Supper Club for dining and entertainment. Playground for the children.

Our listings—supplied by the managements—are as complete as possible. Many of the condos have more features than we list. Be sure to inquire when you book.

Mississippi

Gulfport

GULFPORT

Shoreline Oaks
30 East Beach Blvd, P.O. Box 6823
Gulfport, MS 39501
601-868-1916

1 Bedroom $$, 2 Bedrooms $$
1 Bedrm/week $$$$, 2 Bed/week 4$
Min. Stay 2 Nights, Visa/MC, Dep. Req'd.
10 condos, Lo-rise, Key will be arranged
H-yes

Location: Airport: 5 minutes; Downtown: 5 min.; Need car; Beach front

General Facilities: Kitchen, Linens

Room Facilities: Pool, Hot tub, TV, Cable, Ind. AC Ctl., Ind. Heat Ctl.

Attractions: Excursions to the islands, Marine life, water activities, Casino cruise ships, historical

Shops & Restaurants: Edgewater Mall and individual specialty stores; Cajun, Mexican, Italian

A five minute drive from the airport and you're in your Shoreline Oaks condominium. The beach is across the street, and should you tire of the water activities, take an island excursion, visit the many historical attractions, or board a casino cruise ship. Shaded grounds for a family picnic or barbecue, private patio or deck and even an ice bucket and corkscrew for the wine!

Missouri

Osage Beach
Lake Ozark

Joplin Galena
Lakeview Branson
Kimberling City   Reeds Spring

─────────── BRANSON ───────────

Alpine Lodge
S.R. 1, Box 795 Indian Point
Branson, MO 65616
417-338-2514

1 Bedroom $, 2 Bedrooms $

Less than 1 mile from Silver Dollar City in Shepherd of the Hills country, individual Alpine lodges and two-bedroom A-Frame cottages overlooking Table Rock Lake and the Ozark hills. Each unit has picnic tables and grills. Spend the day at the pool with a slide.

Bentree Lodge
Indian Point Road, Box 967
Branson, MO 65616
417-338-2218 800-272-6766

1 Bedroom $$
AmEx/Visa/MC, Dep. 1 Night •
20 condos, Lo-rise, Key at Front desk

Location: Airport: 45 miles; Need car

General Facilities: Conf. rm. cap. 200, Daily maid, Kitchen, Linens, Restaurant on prem., Bar on prem., Game room, Lounge, Baby-sitter

Room Facilities: Pool, Sauna, Hot tub, Tennis, Fitness center, TV, Phone in rm., Crib-Hi-chair, Ind. AC Ctl., Ind. Heat Ctl.

Attractions: Boating, skiing, fishing, Silver Dollar City, music shows

Shops & Restaurants: Bentree Restaurant/continental

Set on 15 acres, 1.5 miles south of Silver Dollar City on Indian Point Road, overlooking beautiful Table Rock Lake. Two pools, jacuzzi, sauna, tennis courts, game room, restaurant and lounge. Elegantly furnished suites with color TV, queen-sized beds and direct dial phones.

—————————————————— BRANSON ——————————————————

Del Mar Resort on Lake   1 Bedroom $, 2 Bedrooms $
Taneyco   Lo-rise
Lakeshore Dr. S.R. 4, Box 2193
Branson, MO 65616
417-334-6241

General facilities: Kitchen, Linens

Sports facilities: Pool, Horseshoes, Badminton

Attractions: Silver Dollar City, White Water, Shepherd of the Hills Farm, Country Music shows

On the shores of Lake Tanneycomo in the Ozark Mountains. Open acreage with trees, playground with horseshoes, tetherball, volleyball, badminton and plenty of room for softball and soccer. Fishing dock where boats, licenses, bait, tackle, gas and oil are available.

Happy Valley Lodge   1 Bedroom $, 2 Bedrooms $
S.R. 1, Box 849   Lo-rise
Branson, MO 65616
417-338-2342

General facilities: Kitchen, Linens

Sports facilities: Pool, Horseshoes

Attractions: Car museum, trout hatchery, School of the Ozarks Museum, Sammy Lane Pirate cruise, crafts

When you want to get away from city living into the serenity of the mountains. Pool with water slide, playground with swings and slide, games, ski and pontoon boat rentals. All fishing needs available for bass fishing in the clean, unpolluted lake.

Pointe Royale Village   1 Bedroom $$, 2 Bedrooms $$$,
4CV Pointe Royale Dr.   3 Bedrooms $$$$, 1 Bed/week 4$,
Branson, MO 65616   2 Bed/week 8$, 3 Bed/week 10$
417-334-5614 800-962-4710   Min. stay 2 nights, Amex, Visa, MC
                                     Key at Front desk
                                     120 condos, Lo-rise, No S-yes, H-yes •

Location: Airport: 45 miles; Need car

General facilities: Full serv., Conf. Rm. (cap. 120), Kitchen, Linens, Baby sitter, Restaurant, Bar, Lounge, Sauna

Room facilities: TV, Cable, Phone, Crib, A/C, heat, Washer/dryer

Sports facilities: Pool, Tennis, Golf-Pointe Royale, Fishing, boating

Attractions: Silver Dollar City, 20 Country Music Shows, Whitewater Park, Shepherd of the Hills Farm

Shops & Restaurants: Antique shops, Factory Merchants Outlet Mall

Vacation condominiums along a scenic 18 hole golf course, swimming pool and tennis courts. Just 3 miles to music shows and attractions, 9 miles to Silver Dollar City. Situated on Lake Tanycomo (trout fishing) and 4 miles from Table Rock Lake (bass fishing and water sports). Restaurant, lounge and meeting facilities for groups of 120 people. AAA three diamond rating.

-------------------------------- BRANSON --------------------------------

Riverpoint Estates Luxury Condos   2 Bedrooms $$
Box 966   Pool, Kitchen
Branson, MO 65616
417-334-6721

Attractions: Silver Dollar City, country music shows, fish hatchery, pirate cruise, white water, playground, tennis

Two-and three-bedroom condominiums with fireplaces, caarpeted living rooms, 7-foot beds, pool and lake views. Club House lounge with wet bar and refrigerator-freezer. Excellent trout fishing, launching ramp, and private dock slips steps away from your front door.

-------------------------------- GALENA --------------------------------

Lake Country Resort & Golf Club   1 Bedroom $$, 2 Bedrooms $$, 3 Bedrooms $$
Hwy. Y-18, Route 3, Box 91   1 Bedrm/week $$$$, 2 Bed/week $$$$, 3 Bed/
Galena, MO 65656   week $$$$
417-538-2291   Min. Stay 2 Nights, AmEx/Visa/MC, Dep. 2
                                         Nights
                                       16 condos, Lo-rise, Villas, Key at Infor. center
                                       H-yes

Location: Airport: 1 hour; Downtown: 30 min.; Need car

General Facilities: Full serv., Bus. fac., Conf. rm. cap. 50, Daily maid, Kitchen, Linens, Restaurant on prem.

Room Facilities: Pool, Hot tub, Tennis, Hike, Bike, Water, Golf: On site; TV, Crib-Hi-chair, Ind. AC Ctl., Ind. Heat Ctl.

Attractions: Silver Dollar City, Shepherd of the Hills, music shows

Shops & Restaurants: Battlefield & Lakeview shopping, antiques & crafts; Wooden Nickel/steaks-ribs-fish

Super comfortable condominiums with views of the lake, golf course, or bluffs. There are numerous recreational and entertainment facilities within a short drive. Many guests prefer to stay at the Village condominiums with its wood and homey earth tones, electric fireplaces and cathedral ceilings, and just enjoy the quiet and privacy of the pool or 9-hole golf course.

-------------------------------- JOPLIN --------------------------------

**Loma Linda Estates & Country
Club**
Route 5, P.O. Box 1000
Joplin, MO 64801
417-781-2620

─────────────── KIMBERLING CITY ───────────────

Idyllwilde Reosrt 1 Bedroom $, 2 Bedrooms $$
Route 3, Box 674 Dep. 2 Nights •
Kimberling City, MO 65686 13 condos, Lo-rise, Key at Office
417-739-4951

Location: Airport: 45 minutes; Downtown: 5 miles; Need car; Beach front

General Facilities: Kitchen, Linens, Game room, Baby-sitter

Room Facilities: Pool, Putting green, Golf: 4 miles; TV, Crib-Hi-chair, Ind. AC Ctl., Ind. Heat Ctl.

Attractions: Shepherd of the Hills, golf, Talking Rocks Caverns, Lost Silver Mine Play

Shops & Restaurants: Shopping centers, antiques, crafts, pottery, gifts; All types

Nicely furnished apartments among oak and hickory trees on Table Rock Lake for active vactioners. Little ones will love fenced-in playground especially for them. Also a playground with climbing ropes and tree house. Covered boat dock with electrical hook-up, boat rentals, pool, shuffleboard, horseshoes, and miniature putting green. Game room, picnic area, grills.

Kimberling Inn Resort & Vacation Studio $, 1 Bedroom $$, 2 Bedrooms $$$
P.O. Box 159, Highway 13 Dep. 1 Night •
Kimberling City, MO 65686 100 condos, Lo-rise, Key at Lobby
417-739-4311 800-833-5551 P-yes/H-yes

Location: Airport: 45 miles; Need car

General Facilities: Bus. fac., Conf. rm. cap. 200, Daily maid, Kitchen, Linens, Restaurant on prem., Bar on prem., Game room, Lounge, Baby-sitter, Child planned rec.: Games, golf

Room Facilities: Pool, Sauna, Hot tub, Tennis, Boat docks, Golf: Kimberling Hills CC near; TV, Cable, Phone in rm., Crib-Hi-chair, Ind. AC Ctl., Ind. Heat Ctl.

Attractions: Silver Dollar City, 1880's Theme Park, country music shows, Shepherd of the Hills

Shops & Restaurants: Pier Supper Club/steaks-fish

Lakefront condominiums adjacent to Kimberly Inn Resort, with full use of all resort amenities. Exclusive and private family vacation atmosphere, but within walking distance to Kimberling City for shopping, browsing and dining. Full fun opportunities on Table Rock Lake. Easy drive to area attractions.

─────────────── LAKE OZARK ───────────────

Holiday Shores Pool, Kitchen
Hwy. 54, P.O. Box 812
Lake Ozark, MO 65049
314-348-3438

Attractions: Ha Ha Tonka Castle & Park, Bagnell Dam, Bridal Cave, Grand Glaize Bridge, Ozarks Watershow, Lake, fishing, golf

Two-bedroom loft units for six with large balconies. Some units have whirlpool tubs and lake views. Set on a wooded hillside above the Lake of the Ozarks with local marinas to provide your boating and fishing needs. Lake of the Ozarks Park is nearby.

--------------------------- LAKE OZARK ---------------------------

Southwood Shores Condo Rentals
790 Highway HH
Lake Ozark, MO 65049
314-365-4644 800-331-0965

Studio $$, 1 Bedroom $$, 2 Bedrooms $$$, 3 Bedrooms $$$, 1 Bed/week 5$, 2 Bed/week 6$, 3 Bed/week 9$, Min. stay 2 nights, Amex, Visa, MC, Key at Front desk, 80 condos, Hi-rise, No S-yes, H-yes

Location: Downtown: 10 miles; Need car; Lake front

General facilities: Conf. Rm. (cap. 100), Kitchen, Linens, Jacuzzi

Room facilities: TV, Cable, Crib, Ind. AC. Ctl., Ind. Heat Ctl

Sports facilities: Pool, Tennis, 3 mi. to Seasons Ridge

Attractions: Boat excursions on lake, Bagnell Dam, Miniature Golf, Shopping, Golf, Water Park, Fishing

Shops & Restaurants: Osage Village Factory Outlet Mall, Wal-mart, Gift shops, Blue Heron/steak & lobster

Located on beautiful Horseshoe Bend at Lake of the Ozarks. Situated on 21 acres with 2200 feet of shoreline. Indoor and outdoor pools, tennis courts. Easy access, open year round. Just three miles from a public golf course. Fully furnished condos with fully equipped kitchens available for nightly or weekly rentals.

--------------------------- LAKEVIEW ---------------------------

Notch Estates Condominiums
P.O. Box 2097
Lakeview, MO 65737
417-338-2941

1 Bedroom $$, 2 Bedrooms $$, Min. stay 2 nights, Amex, Visa, MC, Dep. 1 night Key at Registration Lobby 36 condos, Lo-rise

Location: Airport: 45 miles; Downtown: 6 miles; Need car

General facilities: Daily maid, Kitchen, Linens

Room facilities: TV, Ind. AC. Ctl, Ind. Heat Ctl.

Sports facilities: Pool, Hiking trail

Attractions: Silver Dollar City, Shepherd of the Hills play, Music shows

Shops & Restaurants: Two miles to small shopping area, Wooden Nickel/steaks-seafood

All new units with walk out decks overlooking scenic countryside located in the heart of the Ozark Mountains, just one mile west of Silver Dollar City, yet away from the congested traffic.

--------------------------- OSAGE BEACH ---------------------------

Lake Chalet Resort
Route 2, Box 3986
Osage Beach, MO 65065
314-348-4718

Amex, Visa, MC, Dep. req'd
Key at Best Western Inn
7 condos
Lo-rise, H-yes

Location: Airport: 55 miles; Need car

General facilities: Full serv., Kitchen, Linens, Play area, Baby sitter, Restaurant, Bar, Game room, Lounge

Room facilities: TV, Cable, VCR, Phone, Crib-Hi-chair, Ind. AC. Ctl, Ind. Heat Ctl.

Sports facilities: Pool, Shuffleboard

Attractions: Water Theme Park, caves, Ha-Ha Tonka State Park, fish, boating, music shows, Bagnell Dam

Shops & Restaurants: Osage Village Factory, Merchant Mall, Oneida store, Blue Heron/intercontinental

─────────────── OSAGE BEACH ───────────────

Lakewood Condominiums
RR #2, Box 59-401
Osage Beach, MO 65065
314-348-1721

Marriott's Tan-Tar-A Resort   Villas
State Road K.K.
Osage Beach, MO 65065
314-348-3131 800-392-5304

Location: Airport: St. Louis—30 min.

General Facilities: Kitchen, Restaurant on prem., Bar on prem., Game room, Lounge, Child planned rec.: Planned activities

Room Facilities: Pool, Hot tub, Tennis, Aerobics, bowling, Golf: One 9-hole, one 18-hole

Attractions: Bridal Cave and Ha Ha Tonka State Park, excursion boat rides, Stephens College Theatre

Shops & Restaurants: Outlet mall, antique shops; Wildrose on the Water

Water sports and golf are given top priority here. Lakefront villas with incredible views peek out of trees. Organized recreational programs for children 5 years and older, and special teen programs. Nightly, live entertainment and wide screen T.V. Full health spa, indoor and outdoor tennis, jogging trails, fishing, horseback riding and choice of two golf courses.

─────────────── REEDS SPRING ───────────────

Bar M Ranch   1 Bedroom $, 2 Bedrooms $, Lo-rise
HCR 4, Box 2990
Reeds Spring, MO 65737
417-338-2593

Off the beaten track, on a private road, spacious property with a Western atmosphere. Quiet walks, pool sunbathing, hot and cold whirlpool spas. Steel dock opening on a wide waterway for fishing, water skiing, swimming. Boat rentals. Woods for walking.

Please mention *Condo Vacations the Complete Guide* when you reserve your condominium.

Montana

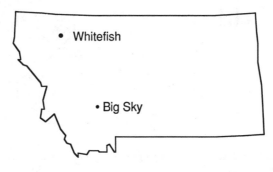

Whitefish

Big Sky

────────────────── BIG SKY ──────────────────

Silverbow
P.O. Box 8
Big Sky, MT 59716
406-995-4800 800-548-4488
FAX: 406-995-2447

1 Bedroom $$, 2 Bedrooms $$$,
3 Bedrooms $$$, 1 Bedrm/week 5$,
2 Bedrm/week 6$, 3 Bedrm/week
8$, Min. Stay: 2 Nights,
AmEx/Visa/MC, •
70 condos, Lo-rise, NoS-yes, H-yes,
Key at Golden Eagle office.

Location: Airport: 1 hour, Need car.

General Facilities: Bus. fac., Conf. Rm. Cap.: 100, Pool, Hot tub, Sauna, Tennis, Big Sky course, Riding, Baby sitter.

Room Facilities: Daily maid, Kitchen, TV, Cable, VCR, Phone, Crib-Hi-chair, Ind. Heat Ctl.

Attractions: Yellowstone, rodeos, summer theater, ghost towns, museums, classical music festival, fair.

Shops & Restaurants: Country store, gift shops, bakery, Edelweiss/Austrian-German-American.

Nestled in a meadow among the grand mountains of Montana, these units are individually decorated and have views of the mountains from their decks. Walk to the outdoor pool, jacuzzi, shops and restaurants. Play a round of golf, go trout fishing, or take a drive down the Gallatin Canyon on your way to Yellowstone National Park. Summer or winter, this is a vacation place to be.

────────────────── WHITEFISH ──────────────────

Bay Point Estates
300 Bay Point Dr.
Whitefish, MT 59937
406-862-2331

1 Bedroom $, Visa/MC, •
50 condos.

Location: Airport: Glacier-9 miles; Downtown: 1 mile.

General Facilities: Conf. Rm. Cap.: 50, Pool, Hot tub, Sauna, Child planned rec., Big Mtn., Whitefish Lake, Hiking, fishing.

Room Facilities: Kitchen, TV, Cable, Phone, Ind. Heat Ctl.

Attractions: 25 miles to Glacier National Park, Big Mountain Ski Resort, Whitefish Lake, Flathead Lake.

Shops & Restaurants: Art galleries, clothing, sporting goods, Whitefish Lake Restaurant.

Nevada

Incline Village
Lake Tahoe
Zephyr Cove
Stateline

Las Vegas

—————————— INCLINE VILLAGE ——————————

All Seasons Resorts
P.O. Box 4268, 807 Alder Avenue
Incline Village, NV 89450
702-831-2311 800-322-4331

1 Bedroom $$, 2 Bedrooms $$
Pool, Daily maid, Kitchen, Linens

Attractions: Lake Tahoe, Diamond Peak ski area, casinos, golf, tennis, Weight Center

Condominiums with fireplaces, wood not provided, at Incline Village, a planned recreational community. On-site clubhouse with pool, spa-whirlpool, weight center and sun deck. Passes for Incline's private beaches are available at the front desk.

Club Tahoe
914 Northwood Boulevard, Box 4650
Incline Village, NV 89450
702-831-5750 800-527-5154

2 Bedrooms $$$, Lo-rise
Pool, Kitchen, Linens, Phone in rm.

Attractions: Reno, Tahoe and Carson City casinos, boating, swimming, fishing, hiking, skiing, gym, racquetball, tennis, golf

10,000-square-foot facility houses these two-bedroom condominiums with sleeping loft. Two TVs, multiplex stereo, washer/dryer, and fireplace. Workout in the universal gym and racquetball courts, lighted tennis courts, horseshoe pits and swimming pool.

Coeur du Lac Condominiums
Lakeshore Blvd. & Juanita
Incline Village, NV 89450
702-831-3318

1 Bedroom $$, 2 Bedrooms $$, Lo-rise
Pool, Kitchen, Linens

Attractions: Skiing, golf, water ski, fish, casinos, Recreation Center

Secluded condominiums 1 block from a private beach. Rustic, roomy interiors with beamed ceilings, redwood paneled walls and wood burning fireplaces. Recreation center with pool, jacuzzi and saunas. Ski a different area every day.

Popu Kapili

———————————— INCLINE VILLAGE ————————————

Forest Pines Condos
P.O. Box 4057
Incline Village, NV 89450
702-831-1307 800-458-2463

1 Bedroom $$, 2 Bedrooms $$, Lo-rise
Pool, Kitchen, Linens

Attractions: Lake Tahoe, casinos, skiing, tennis, golf, swimming, fishing, boating

Condominiums in a pine tree studded landscape with uncluttered views. Central parking and minimum interior roadways for less automobile noise. Recreation building with outdoor pool, indoor jacuzzi, sauna and game room. Close to Lake Tahoe beaches and winter skiing.

L'Ermitage
Southwood Blvd.
Incline Village, NV 89450
702-813-3318

Lo-rise
Kitchen

Attractions: Skiing, golf, boating, water sports, sailing, water skiing, jet skiing

Park-like setting with pines. Architecturally designed, decorator condominiums with wood burning fireplaces, fully equipped wet bar, master bedroom walk-in closet, trash compactor and barbecue on dining room deck. Walk to beaches, boat launch, pool and tennis.

—————————————— INCLINE VILLAGE ——————————————

Lakeside Tennis & Ski Resort
P.O. Box 5576
Incline Village, NV 89450
702-831-5258 800-222-2612

Studio $$, 1 Bedroom $$, 2 Bedrooms $$$,
3 Bedrooms $$$$
1 Bedrm/week 5$, 2 Bedrms/week 6$,
3 Bedrms/week 9$
Min. Stay 2 Nights, AmEx/Visa/MC,
1 Night Dep. Req'd. •
36 condos, Lo-rise, Key at Front desk
H-yes

Location: Airport: 45 minutes; Downtown: 3 min.; Need car; Ski lift at Incline
General Facilities: Full serv.; Daily maid; Linens; Baby sitter; Crib-Hi-chair; Restaurant; Bar
Business Facilities: Bus. fac.; Conf. Room Cap. 20
Sports Facilities: Pool; Hot tub; Tennis; Incline Golf Course
Room Facilities: Kitchen; Cable; Phone; Ind.Heat Ctl.
Attractions: M.S. Dixie dinner/dance on the lake, Ponderosa Ranch, Truckee raft rides, water skiing
Shops & Restaurants: Le Petite Pier/French

Contemporary furnishings to rustic and modern with varying color schemes. A five minute walk to the beach or drive to Ski Incline. Tennis packages and clinics are available. Water sports in the summer or winter skiing in this beautiful Tahoe setting.

————————————— INCLINE VILLAGE/LAKE TAHOE —————————————

Vacation Station/Mccloud Condos
P.O. Box 7180
Incline Village/Lake Tahoe, NV 89452
702-831-3664 800-841-7443
FAX: 702-832-4844

1 Bedroom $$$, 2 Bedrooms $$$$,
3 Bedrooms $$$$
Min. Stay 2 Nights, Disc/Visa/MC •
30 condos, Key at Office, No S-Yes/H-Yes

Location: Airport: Reno, 45 minutes; Downtown: Reno, 45 minutes; Need car; Ski lift at 3 miles
General Facilities: Linens; Baby sitter
Sports Facilities: Sauna; Jacuzzi; Tennis; Hiking, Sailing, Riding; Incline Championship Golf
Room Facilities: Kitchen; Cable; Phone; Ind.Heat Ctl.
Attractions: Lake Tahoe-Emerald Bay, lake cruises, Ponderosa-Home of Bonanza, Hyatt Regency Casino
Shops & Restaurants: Raleys; La Bistro-French, Austins-American

All units (1-, 2- and 3-bedroom) are fully equipped, all you need to bring is your toothbrush. McCloud Condominium Project is centrally located in Incline and is within walking distance to the beach and tennis complexes. A short drive will take you to the golf course and ski hill. A modern complex nestled in the trees, beautifully landscaped, each section has its own jacuzzi-style tub and sauna. Fireplaces.

───────────────── LAS VEGAS ─────────────────

The Carriage House
105 East Harmon Ave.
Las Vegas, NV 89109
702-798-1020 800-777-1700
FAX: 702-798-1020

1 Bedroom $$, 2 Bedrooms $$$, Jr. $$,
AmEx/Visa/MC, •
143 condos, Hi-rise, Key at front desk.

Location: Airport: 3 miles; Downtown: 6 miles.

General Facilities: Lounge, Pool, Hot tub, Complimentary airport shuttle, Tennis, Tropicana Golf Course, Baby sitter, Restaurant, Bar.

Room Facilities: Daily maid, Kitchen, TV, Cable, Phone, Cribs, Ind. AC. Ctl., Ind. Heat Ctl.

Attractions: Las Vegas Strip, Wet N Wild, Lake Mead, Guiness World Records, Hoover Dam, Red Rock tours.

Shops & Restaurants: Fashion Show Mall, Lord & Taylor, Saks Fifth Avenue, Kiefer's/American cuisine.

A charming 143 room condominium suite hotel located 1 block from the famous Las Vegas Strip, 3 miles from the airport and 1 mile from the Las Vegas Convention Center. Each suite offers color cable TV, in-room movies, complimentary first morning coffee and fully equipped kitchens. Pool, whirlpool, tennis court, courtesy transportation and a weekly wine and cheese party. VCR rentals available.

───────────────── STATELINE ─────────────────

Ridge Tahoe
P.O. Box 5790
Stateline, NV 89449
702-588-3553 800-648-3341

2 Bedrooms $$$, Min. Stay: 2 Nights, Dep.
Req'd
Key at front desk.

Location: Airport: Reno International; Downtown: 6 miles, Need car.

General Facilities: Conf. Room, Lounge, Game room, Pool, Hot tub, Tennis, Weight room, racquetball, Restaurant, Bar.

Room Facilities: Daily maid, Kitchen, TV, Cable, VCR.

Attractions: Stateline Casinos, skiing, lake cruises, horseback riding, fishing, yachting, entertainment.

Shops & Restaurants: Ridge Club 5-star dining room.

Elegant, casual rustic interiors in these suites perched on a mountain peak, minutes from Heavenly Valley, casinos and Tahoe's beaches. Enjoy the soothing rooftop spa beneath the stars, overlooking the mountains and valley. Spend the evening dining and dancing at the Ridge Club, after skiing or tennis. Summer lake activities, miles of trails to explore and unspoiled glades for picnics.

───────────────── ZEPHYR COVE ─────────────────

Pine Wild
600 Highway 50, P.O. Box 11347
Zephyr Cove, NV 89448
702-588-2790 800-822-2790

3 Bedrooms $$$, Min. Stay: 2 Nights,
Visa/MC, Dep. Req'd, •
135 condos, Lo-rise, NoS-yes, Key at sales
office/on site.

Location: Airport: 10 miles; Downtown: 5 min, Need car.

General Facilities: Conf. Rm. Cap.: 30, Hot tub, Tennis, Edgewood Tahoe-2 miles, Boat dock, Baby sitter.

Attractions: South Shore casinos, skiing, snowmobiling, boating, horses, star entertainment.

Shops & Restaurants: Round Hill Mall, Safeway, specialty shops, Zackery's.

New Hampshire

- Franconia
- Lincoln • • Bartlett
- Bretton Woods • Jackson
- Woodstock
- • Gilford
- • Plymouth
- Waterville Valley •
- Weirs Beach •
- Laconia •
- • Weare

BARTLETT

Attitash Mountain Village
Route 302
Bartlett, NH 03812
603-374-6501 800-862-1600

Studio $$, 1 Bedroom $$, 2 Bedrooms $$$,
3 Bedrooms $$$$
Min. Stay 2 Nights, AmEx/Visa/MC, Dep.
Req'd. •
170 condos, Lo-rise, Key at Front desk
H-yes

Location: Airport: 65 miles; Downtown: 6 miles; Need car; Ski lift: Attitash

General Facilities: Full serv., Bus. fac., Conf. rm. cap. 100, Daily maid, Kitchen, Linens, Restaurant on prem., Bar on prem., Game room, Lounge, Baby-sitter, Child planned rec.: Playground

Room Facilities: Pool, Sauna, Hot tub, Tennis, Basketball, TV, Cable, Phone in rm., Crib-Hi-chair, Ind. AC Ctl., Ind. Heat Ctl.

Attractions: Skiing, hiking, sightseeing, amusement areas, snowmobiling, x-country skiing, entertainment

Shops & Restaurants: Major factory outlet area; Doolittle/on-site, Bernerhof

Surrounded by 750,000 acres of White Mountain National Forest, with snow covered mountains for winter skiing, pond ice skating and sleigh rides. The rest of the year, relax in the sparkling sunlight, swim in the pool or river, bike, hike and canoe. Children's playground, tennis and 18-hole courses nearby. The spacious condominiums offer country sophistication with modern conveniences, many with fireplaces, whirlpools, wood stoves and loft bedrooms.

———————————— BRETTON WOODS ————————————

The Townhomes at Bretton Woods
Route 302
Bretton Woods, NH 03575
603-278-1000 800-258-0330

Location: ; Downtown: White Mountains; Ski lift at Nearby

General Facilities: Lounge; Restaurant on premises; Bar on premises

Sports Facilities: Pool; Tennis; Racquetball, ride, hike; 27 holes of golf; Children's programs

Room Facilities: Kitchen

Attractions: Beside Bretton Woods Ski Area, near Cog Railway, Crawford & Franconia Notches; Entertainment

Shops & Restaurants: Outlet shopping nearby, Gift shop; 5 restaurants & 7 lounges on premises

Nestled at the base of the Presidential Mountain Range, The Townhomes at Bretton Woods are the perfect spot for enjoying the great outdoors. The Townhomes are part of the Mount Washington Resort, and guests are welcome to enjoy all Resort amenities—golf, tennis (12 courts), horseback riding, skiing (downhill & cross country), diverse dining, live evening entertainment and special events.

———————————————— JACKSON ————————————————

Nordic Village Resort
Route 16
Jackson, NH 03846
603-383-9101 800-472-5207
FAX: 603-383-9823

Studio $$, 1 Bedroom $$$,
   2 Bedrooms $$$$, 3 Bedrooms $$$$
Min. Stay Ask, Visa/MC, 50% Dep. Req'd.,
Lo-rise, Key at Front desk, P-No

Location: Airport: Boston, 3 hours

General Facilities: Daily maid; Linens

Sports Facilities: Pool; Sauna; Jacuzzi; Tennis; Golf Course nearby

Room Facilities: Kitchen

Attractions: Entertainment

100-acre mountainside resort nestled in the heart of the White Mountains. 1-, 2- and 3-bedroom luxury mountain condominiums. 3 swimming pools, 12-person jacuzzi, rowboats, bonfires, skating, skiing and more. Within minutes of family attractions and major ski areas. Tax-free shopping, PGA golf and fine dining nearby.

—————————————— LACONIA ——————————————

Steele Hill, Phase 1
RFD #1, Box 190
Laconia, NH 03246
603-524-0500

Lo-rise
Pool, Kitchen

Attractions: Racquetball, tennis, golf

500 acres of unspoiled farmland and hardwood forests overlooking Lake Winnipesaukee. Pressure-free, comfortable vacation. Glass solarium surrounding the exterior of the wood-paneled dining room. Amenities building with bar, lounge, weight room and game room.

—————————————— LINCOLN ——————————————

Riverfront Condominiums
Kancanmagus Highway, Box 477
Lincoln, NH 03251
603-745-3441

Rivergreen
P.O. Box 696
Lincoln, NH 03251
603-745-6261 800-654-6183

Pool, Kitchen, Phone in rm.

Attractions: Exercise room, golf

Superior accommodations set alongside the Pemigewasset River. Suites include individual jacuzzis. Free shuttle service to Loon. Pools, sauna, library and enclosed barbecue area.

Village of Loon Mountain
P.O. Box 508
Lincoln, NH 03251
603-745-3401 800-258-8932

Studio $$, 1 Bedroom $$$, 2 Bedrooms $$$,
3 Bedrooms $$$
Min. Stay 2 Nights, AmEx/Visa/MC,
Dep. Req'd. •
220 condos, Key at Registr. office

Location: Airport: 75 mi. Manchester; Need car; Ski lift: Loon Mtn.

General Facilities: Bus. fac., Conf. rm. cap. 100, Restaurant on prem., Bar on prem., Game room, Lounge, Baby-sitter, Child planned rec.: Activities program

Room Facilities: Pool, Sauna, Hot tub, Tennis, Phone in rm., Ind. Heat Ctl.

Attractions: All major area attractions are within 5 miles. Across from a major ski area—41 trails, entertainment

Shops & Restaurants: Mill Front Mall, many small shops; Dickens/gourmet, Common Man

Loon Village is secluded on 240 wooded acres, surrounded by the White Mountain National Forest. A four-season resort with tennis courts, paddle tennis courts, two indoor and two outdoor pools, whirlpools, saunas, ice skating rink, downhill skiing and teen center. Scandinavian furnishings in this centrally located resort, with lounge and bingo. D.G. Wagoner's is the village nightspot with weekend entertainment. Grocery store on the premises.

―――――――――――――――― PLYMOUTH ――――――――――――――――

Cold Spring Resort
RR 3, Box 40
Plymouth, NH 03264
603-536-4600

1 Bedroom $$, 2 Bedrooms $$, 3 Bedrooms $$
1 Bedrm/week $$$$, 2 Bed/week 4$, 3 Bed/
   week 5$
Dep. Req'd.

Location: Ski lift: Loon Mt.

General Facilities: Restaurant on prem., Lounge, Baby-sitter

Room Facilities: Pool, Sauna, Tennis, Kiddie Pool, Golf: 18-hole; TV, Cable, Phone in rm.

Shops & Restaurants: Terrace on the Green

Designed to blend into the lush foliage and Revolutionary heritage of Cold Spring with exquisite interior design and scenic views from every window. All winter and summer sports, exploding autumn colors, trout and salmon fishing. Covered bridges, old stone mills and gem mines and Revolutionary farmhouses for the history buff. The restored Club House, where you can play cards, sit by the fire, or enjoy a cocktail on the terrace, was originally built during colonial days. Terrace on the Green for dining.

―――――――――――――― WATERVILLE VALLEY ――――――――――――――

Black Bear Lodge
Box 357
Waterville Valley, NH 03223
603-236-8371 800-258-8988

1 Bedroom $$
1 Bedrm/week $$$$

Location: Ski lift: 10 min.

General Facilities: Kitchen, Game room

Room Facilities: Pool, Sauna, Tennis, Ice skating, TV, Cable, Phone in rm.

A good place for two couples wishing to share a vacation. Access to Sports Center, game room, indoor pool, sauna and jacuzzi. Fieldstone fireplace in the lobby for socializing. Children under 5 ski free. Get in shape at the fitness center, indoor tennis, racquetball and squash courts. Video arcade and soda fountain.

**Golden Eagle Lodge
Condominiums**
Waterville Valley
Waterville Valley, NH 03223
603-236-4205 800-552-4767

Hi-rise
Kitchen, Linens

Attractions: White Mountain attractions, covered bridges, N.H. Science Center, scenic drives, waterfall

Built to contemporary hotel standards with wood finish exteriors and decorator-furnished interiors offering views of Corcoran's Pond and White Mountain peaks. Within easy walking distance to beach and boating on the pond, indoor sports center, with pools.

─────────────────── WATERVILLE VALLEY ───────────────────

Inns of Waterville Valley
Snowbrook Road, P.O. Box 411
Waterville Valley, NH 03215
603-236-8366

1 Bedroom $$, 2 Bedrooms $$
1 Bedrm/week $$$$, 2 Bed/week 4$
Min. Stay 2 Nights, Visa/MC, Dep. Req'd.
19 condos, Lo-rise, Key at Next door

Location: Airport: 65 miles; Downtown: 22 miles; Need car; Ski lift: Nearby

General Facilities: Daily maid, Kitchen, Linens, Baby-sitter, Child planned rec.: Town
program

Room Facilities: Pool, Sauna, Hot tub, Weight room, Golf: 9-hole adjacent; TV, Cable,
Phone in rm., Crib-Hi-chair, Ind. Heat Ctl.

Shops & Restaurants: Limited; Carnevale's/Northern Italian

*Well-appointed, comfortable condominiums decorated in earth tones. All units have
kitchens with microwaves and in-room jacuzzis and some have hot tubs. In the heart of
the White Mountains; numerous summer activities; winter skiing at Waterville Valley.*

───

The Village Inn
P.O. Box 1
Waterville Valley, NH 03215

───

Windsor Hill Condominiums
Route 49
Waterville Valley, NH 03215
603-236-8321 800-343-1286

Studio $$$, 1 Bedroom $$$, 2 Bedrooms $$$$,
3 Bedrooms $$$$
1 Bedrm/week $$$$, 2 Bed/week 5$, 3 Bed/
week 5$
Min. Stay 2 Nights, AmEx/MC, Dep. Req'd. •
132 condos, Lo-rise, Key at On-site office

Location: Airport: 2 hours; Need car; Ski lift: Nearby

General Facilities: Daily maid, Kitchen, Linens, Baby-sitter, Child planned rec.: Town
recreation ctr.

Room Facilities: Pool, Golf: Waterville Valley; TV, Cable, Crib-Hi-chair, Ind. Heat Ctl.

Attractions: White Mountain attractions, craft fairs, ski swaps, music festivals, ski com-
petitions

Shops & Restaurants: Jugtown Country Store, Post Office, shops; Several fine
restaurants

*Each home has its own private entrance from the outside. Outdoor heated swimming pool
with sun deck, several picnic areas with tables and grills throughout the 10-acre site. Alpine
and cross-country skiing from Thanksgiving into April. 9-hole golf course, 18 clay tennis
courts, 4.5 acre lake with sandy beach, climbing and hiking trails and trout fishing. Town
sponsored recreation program for the whole family.*

─────────────────────────── WEARE ───────────────────────────

Lake Shore Village Resort
744 Reservoir Dr.
Weare, NH 03281
603-529-1800

Lo-rise
Pool, Kitchen

Attractions: Dixfield Notch, Six Gun City, Old Man of the Mountain, The Flume, Lost
River, Polar Caves, Volley Basketball, tennis, golf

*Your warmly furnished cottage overlooks Lake Horace and has a private dock, boat &
motor, fieldstone fireplace and sliding glass windows. Spring fishing, hiking, golf; summer
lake swimming, waterskiing, tennis; fall hiking, hunting, and canoeing.*

Kaanapili Shores

——————————— WEIRS BEACH ———————————

Cedar Lodge at Brickyard Mt.   Studio $$, 1 Bedroom $$$, 2 Bedrooms $$$$
Route 3, P.O. Box 5293   1 Bedrm/week 6$, 2 Bed/week 7$
Weirs Beach, NH 03246   AmEx/Visa/MC, Dep. Req'd.
603-366-4316   23 condos, Hi-rise, Key at Front desk

Location: Airport: Gilford 20 minutes; Downtown: 10 min.; Need car; Ski lift: Loon Mt.
General Facilities: Full serv., Daily maid, Kitchen, Linens, Child planned rec.: Playground
Room Facilities: Pool, Tennis, TV, Cable, Ind. AC Ctl., Ind. Heat Ctl.
Attractions: Boat cruise on Winnipesaukee, train rides, sea plane rides, horses, boating
Shops & Restaurants: K-Mart, Zayre, Star market, Hallmark gift shop; The Manor/American-French

Enjoy serenity, privacy and panoramic views of Lake Winnipesaukee and mountains. Double beds in bedroom, sliding glass doors to balcony and full-size bathtubs. Lodge is set atop Brickyard Mountain to protect you from road noises. Inviting, homey, individually decorated units with pool, tennis, playground and lawn games. Many family activities in nearby Weirs Beach.

──────────── WEIRS BEACH ────────────

Village at Winnipesaukee   2 Bedrooms $$$
Route 3, P.O. Box 5276   Pool, Kitchen, Linens
Weirs Beach, NH 03246
603-366-4878

Attractions: Excursion boat trips, seaplane rides, parachute jumping, kite skiing, the-
atre, museums, volleyball, basketball

*Two-and three-bedroom condominiums with patios or balconies. On-site tennis, picnic
grounds and swimming. Short walk to private beach and dock. Winter skiing, summer
water sports, fall harvest fairs and frosty days, spring flowering fruit trees and lake trout.*

──────────── WOODSTOCK ────────────

Jack O'Lantern Resort   Pool, Kitchen
1-93 Route 3
Woodstock, NH 03251
603-745-8181

Attractions: Tennis, golf

*Beautifully landscaped 250-acre resort along the Pemigewassset River. 6100 yard, par 70,
18-hole golf course and pro shop. Game room, snack bar, and lounge with entertainment.*

Our listings—supplied by the managements—are as complete as possible.
Many of the condos have more features than we list. Be sure to inquire when
you book.

New Jersey

Atlantic City

ATLANTIC CITY

Park Lane
177 S. Illinois Ave.
Atlantic City, NJ 08401
609-344-8277

1 Bedroom $$
1 Bedrm/week 7$
Dep. Req'd.
44 condos, Hi-rise, Key at Office

Location: Airport: 3 miles; Downtown: walk

General Facilities: Full serv., Conf. rm. cap. 50, Daily maid, Kitchen, Linens, Lounge, Baby-sitter

Room Facilities: TV, Phone in rm., Crib-Hi-chair, Ind. AC Ctl.

Attractions: Casinos, shows, Boardwalk, boxing matches, horse racing, Ice Capades, Miss America Pageant

Shops & Restaurants: Downtown shops; Casino restaurants

Comfortable apartments in wicker and cane one block from the beach. Fish, swim, sunbathe, walk on the beach and Boardwalk, and try your hand at games of chance in the 12 casinos. Dine at the casinos and enjoy their nightly entertainment. Guest Services Department for free and discount show and restaurant tickets.

New Mexico

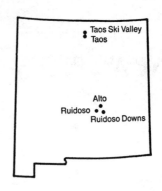

Taos Ski Valley
Taos

Alto
Ruidoso
Ruidoso Downs

─────────── ALTO ───────────

High Country Lodge
P.O. Box 137, Highway 37
Alto, NM 88312
505-336-4321

Lo-rise
Pool, Kitchen

Attractions: Recreation area, tennis

The closest lodging to New Mexico ski areas. Cozy units with fireplaces, covered porches and outdoor barbecue grills. For non-skiers, enclosed pool, spa, saunas, table tennis, video games and pinball machines. Tennis, playground, horseback riding and trout fishing.

─────────── RUIDOSO DOWNS ───────────

Champions Run
P.O. Box 601
Ruidoso Downs, NM 88346
505-378-8080

2 Bedrooms $$$, Lo-rise
Pool, Kitchen, Linens

Attractions: Golf, hiking, fishing, hunting, horseback riding, Ruidoso Downs Race Track, skiing

Walk to the Ruidoso Downs Race Track from these townhome-style condominiums with terraced, spacious floor plans. Two-and three-bedroom homes have wood burning fireplaces, jacuzzis in master bath and microwaves. Ski from Thanksgiving through Easter.

―――――――――――――― RUIDOSO ――――――――――――――

Dan Dee Cabins Resort
310 Main Rd., P.O. Box 844
Ruidoso, NM 88345
505-257-2165 800-345-4848

Studio $$, 1 Bedroom $$, 2 Bedrooms $$$
Min. Stay 3 Days, Disc/Visa/MC •
12 condos, Villas, Key at Office, P-No/H-No

Location: Airport: 20 minutes; Downtown: 1.5 miles; Need car; Ski lift at 15 miles
General Facilities: Full hotel service; Linens; Crib-Hi-Chair
Sports Facilities: Boat, hike, Jeep tours; Links & Cree Meadows GC
Room Facilities: Kitchen; Cable; Fans; Ind.Heat Ctl.
Attractions: Downhill skiing, Ruidoso Down Racetrack, Gambling at Casino, Beautiful natural forest
Shops & Restaurants: Downtown shopping with full range of merchandise; Victoria's Romantic Hideaway-Italian

Experience Ruidoso at its very best—acres and acres of private forest, cottages with fireplaces, cool mountain streams, snowcapped peaks and bear hug hospitality. Located in Ruidoso's beautiful Upper Canyon only steps from stream fishing and access to all recreation sites. Enjoy winter ski packages and summertime seats at Ruidoso Downs in our private box.

High Sierra Condominiums
P.O. Box 4179 H.S.
Ruidoso, NM 88345
505-257-6913

1 Bedroom $$, 2 Bedrooms $$$
Lo-rise

General Facilities: Daily maid; Linens
Sports Facilities: Pool; tennis; basketball
Room Facilities: Kitchen; Phone
Attractions: Space Museum, White Sands Nat. Monument, Valley of the Fires, summer racing, art galleries

High on Camelot Mountain, overlooking lake of the Inn of the Mountain Gods and surrounding hills. Condominiums with laundry rooms, wet bars and fireplaces in the middle of the woods. A hike in the woods may bring you glimpses of deer or wild turkeys.

The Springs Condominiums
1230 Mechem
Ruidoso, NM 88345
505-258-5056

2 Bedrooms $$, 3 Bedrooms $$$
2 Bedrms/week 5$, 3 Bedrms/week 7$
Visa/MC, Dep. Required •
22 condos, Lo-rise, Key at Main office, P-yes/H-yes

Location: Airport: Ruidoso 30 minutes; Downtown: 3 miles; Need car; Ski lift at Apache
General Facilities: Daily maid; Linens; Baby-sitter; Crib-Hi-chair
Sports Facilities: Pool; Hot tub; Horseshoes
Room Facilities: Kitchen; Cable; Ind.Heat Ctl.
Attractions: Flying J Ranch chuckwagon show, Ruidoso Race Track, Ski Apache, Smokey Bear Nat'l Forest
Shops & Restaurants: Art galleries, gift, ski shops, clothing boutiques

Tucked away like a village unto itself, the Springs offers a lifestyle of tall pines, cool, quiet nights and the warm glow of a roaring fire. Year-round attractions in the cool mountains of the Southwest desert and plains, where winter becomes a real wonderland.

---------------------- RUIDOSO ----------------------

West Winds Lodge & Condos
208 Eagle Drive, P.O. Box 1458
Ruidoso, NM 88345
505-257-4031 800-421-0691

1 Bedroom $$, 2 Bedrooms $$, Jr. $$,
3 Bedrooms $$$$, Visa/MC, Dep. 1
Night, •
14 condos, Lo-rise, H-yes, Key at office.

Location: Airport: 20 miles; Downtown: 2 blocks.

General Facilities: Conf. Rm. Cap.: 20, Pool, Hot tub, Creek Meadows, Horse racing.

Room Facilities: Daily maid, Kitchen, TV, Cable, Crib-Hi-chair, Ind. Heat Ctl.

Attractions: Billy the Kid historic tours, Apache Indian Reservation, quarterhorse races, scenic tours.

Shops & Restaurants: Art galleries, gift shops, jewelry and leather, La Lorraine-Fr./Cattle Baron.

Two story condominiums with upstairs loft, modern earth toned furnishings, in a quiet, restful setting. Indoor heated pool and hot tub, Cree Meadows Golf Course and Ski Apache. Horseracing from May to Labor Day, summer festival concert series in June, motorcycle festival, mule racing, street fair and chili cook-off. Space Hall of Fame, ghost towns, Petroglyphs, and Valley of the Fires lava flows.

---------------------- TAOS ----------------------

Hacienda De Valdez
Box 5651
Taos, NM 87571
505-776-2218

2 Bedrooms $$$$, AmEx/Visa/MC, •
13 condos, Lo-rise, Key at office.

Location: Airport: Taos Municipal 10 miles, Need car.

General Facilities: Hot tub, Hiking, fishing, skiing.

Room Facilities: Daily maid, Kitchen, TV, Phone, Ind. Heat Ctl.

Attractions: Rio Grande River & Gorge, Carson National Forest, Taos Plaza Area, Wilderness areas.

Shops & Restaurants: Galleries and shops at Taos Plaza, Indian crafts, Many nearby restaurants.

Nestled in the foothills above the Valdez Valley, these condominiums have unique southwestern design with Spanish tile, fireplaces in every room with firewood provided and fully equipped kitchens. The balconies have spectacular views, outdoor hot tubs, all in a peaceful mountain setting. Located halfway between the town of Taos and Taos Ski Valley for your sight-seeing or skiing enjoyment.

---------------------- TAOS SKI VALLEY ----------------------

The Kandahar
P.O. Box 72
Taos Ski Valley, NM 87525
505-776-2226

1 Bedroom $$, 2 Bedrooms $$$, Kitchen,
Phone.

Attractions: All levels of skiing, Health spa.

Mountain style living in ski-in/ski-out condominiums. Health spa with weight trining center, steam bath and jacuzzi. entertainment and restaurants a few steps away. Sit in front of a crackling fire while you watch your favorite TV shows after a day of skiing.

———————————————————— TAOS ————————————————————

Quail Ridge Inn
P.O. Box 707
Taos, NM 87571
505-776-2211 800-624-4448

Studio $$, 1 Bedroom $$$, 2 Bedrooms
$$$, 3 Bedrooms $$$$
AmEx/Visa/MC, Dep. Required •
110 condos, Lo-rise, Key at Front desk

Location: Airport: Taos–5 miles; Downtown: 4 miles; Need car; Ski lift at Taos

General Facilities: Full serv.; Daily maid; Linens; Baby-sitter; Lounge; Crib-Hi-chair; Restaurant; Bar

Business Facilities: Conf. Room Cap. 125

Sports Facilities: Pool; Sauna; Hot tub; Tennis; Racquetball; Shortie swatters

Room Facilities: Kitchen; Cable; Phone; Ind.Heat Ctl.

Attractions: Taos Ski Vlly., Taos Indian Pueblo, Millicent Rogers Museum, Rio Grande Gorge, art gallery; entertainment

Shops & Restaurants: Arts and crafts, Indian artifacts, clothing; Carl's French Quarter/Cajun

Personal attention from the staff of this modern pueblo-style resort set in the unspoiled country of the Sangre de Cristo Mountains. Southwest adobe condominiums with fireplaces for the cool nights. Tennis and racquetball clinics, instruction and tournaments. Taos area not only has year-round activities from water sports to skiing, but also offers art and music festivals, theatres, lectures and art exhibitions for a true Southwestern vacation experience.

———————————————— TAOS SKI VALLEY ————————————————

Sierra Del Sol
P.O. Box 84
Taos Ski Valley, NM 87525
505-776-2981 800-523-3954
FAX: 505-776-2347

Studio $$$$, 1 Bedroom $$$$,
2 Bedrooms $$$$
Min. Stay 3 Nights, AmEx/Visa/MC, Dep.
Required •
32 condos, Lo-rise, Key at Office on site
No S-yes

Location: Airport: 19 miles; Downtown: 19 miles; Need car; Ski lift at Taos

General Facilities: Daily maid; Linens; Baby sitter; Crib-Hi-chair

Business Facilities: Conf. Room Cap. 30

Sports Facilities: Skiing

Room Facilities: Kitchen; Ind.Heat Ctl.

Attractions: Historic Taos, Taos Plaza, Wheeler Peak Wilderness Area, Carson Nat'l Forest, Taos Pueblo

Shops & Restaurants: Taos art galleries, Indian crafts, jewelry stores

Spacious condominiums with fireplaces only 70 yards away from Taos Ski Valley's main chair lifts, ski shops and ski rentals. In summer, there is trout fishing, nature walks in the forest, art festivals, and Pueblo Indian ceremonies. Raft the Rio Grande, listen to chamber music, or enjoy the hot tubs and saunas. Walking distance to all shops, restaurants and nightlife with on-site parking.

New York

--------------------------------- LAKE GEORGE ---------------------------------

Depe Dene
Lake Shore Dr, Rt. 9N, Box 2422
Lake George, NY 12845
518-668-2788

Lo-rise
Pool, Kitchen, Linens

Attractions: Saratoga Racetrack, Great Escape, Waterslide, Fort William Henry, amusement parks, canoes, shuffleboard, golf

Two-story townhouses located directly on the shoreline of Lake George. All the conveniences of home in a mountain setting. Sit on the beach and watch the activity or use one of the resort's rowboats, kayaks or canoes. Rivers and streams for spring fishing.

Top of the World Townhouses
RR #1, Box 1390
Lake George, NY 12845
518-668-5716

--------------------------------- LAKE PLACID ---------------------------------

Wildwood on the Lake
88 Saranac Avenue
Lake Placid, NY 12946
518-523-2624

------------------------------ LENOX HILL STATION ------------------------------

Club Getaway
Box 606
Lenox Hill Station, NY 10021
212-935-0222

Pool, Daily maid, Kitchen, Linens

Attractions: Covered bridges, Tanglewood, vineyards, antiques, crafts, Torys Cave, archery, fitness center, tennis

Prepaid getaway vacations which include meals, wine, sports, instructions, entertainment and lodging. Set in the lawns and woodland meadows of the Berkshires, surrounded by mountains and overlooking a private lake.

──────────────── MONTAUK, LONG ISLAND ────────────────

Gurney's Inn Resort & Spa
Old Montauk Highway
Montauk, Long Island, NY 11954
516-668-2345 800-832-1131

2 Bedrooms $$$, Lo-rise
Pool, Daily maid, Kitchen, Linens, Phone in rm.

Attractions: Montauk Point lighthouse, golf, tennis, fishing, boating, Marino therapeutic spa

Beach cottages featuring large decks and glass-enclosed sunporches. Custom designed in soft, relaxing sea and sky colors, Italian floor tiles. Convertible sofa bed and fireplace in living room. Adult Health & Beauty Spa with separate male and female pavilions.

──────────────────── SARANAC LAKE ────────────────────

Ampersand Bay Resort
Saranac Lake
Saranac Lake, NY 12983
518-891-3001

1 Bedroom $$, 2 Bedrooms $$$, Lo-rise
Kitchen, Linens

Attractions: Olympic arena, summer ski jumping, chamber music, theatre, climbing, Whiteface Mtn., lake activities

Rustic Adirondack log cabins for four to six people. Carefree vacationing on wilderness rivers and lakes. Motor boats and canoes to rent or bring your own boat for a trip to one of the many islands for a secluded picnic. Fantastic fishing.

Mahana

---------------------- SARANAC LAKE ----------------------

Castle Point Resort
Condominiums
1 Will Rogers Drive
Saranac Lake, NY 12983
518-891-2220

---------------------- SHELTER ISLAND ----------------------

Pridwin Resort (The)　　　　Pool, Kitchen
Crescent Beach
Shelter Island, NY 11946
516-749-0476

Attractions: Golf, charter boats, open boat fishing, charter sailing, billiards, ping-pong, tennis

Comfortable housekeeping cottages in a rural atmosphere between the eastern tips of Long Island. Woodlands, meadows, flowers, wildlife and sandy beaches for sunning and water sports. Electronic indoor games. Summer buffets, cookouts, dancing and entertainment.

---------------------- STAMFORD ----------------------

Deer Run Resort　　　　Studio $$$, 1 Bedroom $$$, 2 Bedrooms $$$$
Route 10, P.O. Box 251　　　AmEx/Visa/MC, Dep. Req'd.
Stamford, NY 12167　　　　45 condos, Villas, Key at Front desk-deposit
607-652-2001 800-252-7317　　H-yes

Location: Airport: Albany—1-¼ hours; Downtown: 3 miles; Need car; Ski lift: Deer Run

General Facilities: Conf. rm., Daily maid, Kitchen, Linens, Restaurant on prem., Bar on prem., Game room, Lounge, Baby-sitter, Child planned rec.: Button Buck Ski Sch.

Room Facilities: Pool, Sauna, Hot tub, Tennis, Skiing, boating, Golf: Stamford Country Cl. near; TV, Phone in rm., Crib-Hi-chair, Ind. AC Ctl., Ind. Heat Ctl.

Attractions: Baseball and Soccer Halls of Fame, James Fenimore Cooper House, Howe Caverns, game farm, entertainment

Shops & Restaurants: Oneonta Mall, Penney's, Jamesway, Nichols, Ames DS; Hidden Inn/seafood steaks

Beautiful lakefront villas in the scenic Catskill Mountains, modern furniture in earth tones, mirrored walls and natural wood paneling around fireplace. On-site Antler Lodge offers fine dining. Day trips to the many area attractions, sports programs, indoor/outdoor heated pools, fishing in two lakes, hiking, camping, canoeing, sailing and bowling.

---------------------- WARRENSBURG ----------------------

Green Mansion Country Club　　1 Bedroom $$, 2 Bedrooms $$$$, Lo-rise
Estate　　　　　　　　Kitchen
Box 370, Green Mansions Road
Warrensburg, NY 12885
516-494-3721

Attractions: Adirondacks, Pack Forest, sporting events

Summer and winter resort in the Adirondacks, adjacent to Pack Forest with tall pines and a spring-fed lake. Fully equipped condominiums with fireplaces, continuous-clean ovens and dishwashers. Many units have stereos and washer/dryers.

North Carolina

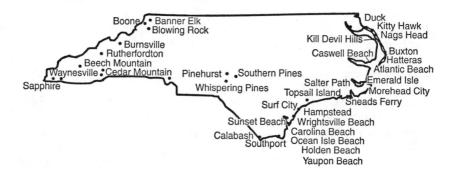

ATLANTIC BEACH

A Place At The Beach
P.O. Box 1140
Atlantic Beach, NC 28512
919-247-2636 800-334-2667

2 Bedrooms $$
Villas

Sports Facilities: Pool; Tennis

Room Facilities: Kitchen

Near Fort Macon State Park on beautifully landscaped grounds with a full range of recreational facilities. The pool has a waterslide and hot tub. Playground area, tennis and sport courts.

Island Beach & Racquet Club
2507 West Fort Macon Rd.
Atlantic Beach, NC 28512
919-247-3600 800-682-3702
FAX: 919-808-2208

Min. Stay Ask, AmEx/Visa/MC
141 condos, Villas, Key at Office on site,
P-No/No S-Yes/H-Yes

Location: Airport: 35 miles; Beachfront

General Facilities: Daily maid; Linens; Baby sitter

Sports Facilities: Pool; Composition tennis courts; Golf within half mile

Room Facilities: Kitchen; Cable; VCR; Phone; Ind.AC.Ctl; Ind.Heat Ctl.

Attractions: Southern tip of Eastern North Carolina's barrier island chain.

Shops & Restaurants: 408 retail stores on the island; 155 restaurants on the island

The Crystal Coast is a 65-mile stretch of natural beaches and dunes, sounds and maritime forests, and rivers and communities offering unlimited recreation for visitors and residents. Aquarium, museums, state parks and national seashore. Fort Macon State Park. We are rich in golf courses, tennis facilities and endless stretches of beach awaiting your footprint.

---------------------------- ATLANTIC BEACH ----------------------------

Whaler Inn Beach Club
3600 Slater Path Rd, P.O. Box 220
Atlantic Beach, NC 28512
919-247-4169

1 Bedroom $$, 2 Bedrooms $$$
1 Bedrm/week 5$, 2 Bed/week 6$
Visa/MC,Dep. 1 Night
46 condos, Hi-rise, Key at Front desk
H-yes

Location: Airport: 30 miles; Downtown: 5 miles; Need car; Beach front

General Facilities: Full serv., Conf. rm. cap. 50, Daily maid, Kitchen, Linens, Game room, Child planned rec.: Supervised games

Room Facilities: Pool, Sauna, Hot tub, Basketball, Volleyball, Golf: Bogue Country Club; TV, Cable, Crib-Hi-chair, Ind. AC Ctl., Ind. Heat Ctl.

Attractions: Dinner and harbor cruises, outer banks still untouched by man, ocean, dining, sightseeing.

Shops & Restaurants: Food Lion, Eckerds, Rose's Department Store; Beaufort House, Blackbeards

Luxurious condominiums at affordable prices on the ocean. Tuesday night dinners for guests, lock-in on Thursday nights for teenagers, sand castle sculpture contests on Fridays. Basketball and volleyball on the property with fine dining and shopping nearby. Supervised games for the children—a real family vacation.

---------------------------- BANNER ELK ----------------------------

Adams Apple
Route 1, Box 298
Banner Elk, NC 28604
704-963-4950 704-963-6325

1 Bedroom $$, 2 Bedrooms $$
Kitchen, Linens

Attractions: Basketball, tennis

An abundance of peace and quiet in these condominiums on the western slope of Grandfather Mountain. Stone fireplaces and private decks. Hiking and fishing, mountain living.

The Highlands at Sugar
P.O. Box 892, Highland Drive
Banner Elk, NC 28604
704-898-9601

1 Bedroom $$, 2 Bedrooms $$, Hi-rise
Pool, Kitchen

Attractions: Grandfather Mountain, hiking, mile-high swinging bridge, Linville Falls, Linville Caverns, weight room, spa, golf

Maagnificent scenery high in the Blue Ridge Mountains. Units with jacuzzis, fireplaces, picture windows, and wet bars. Free shuttle to Sugar Mountain ski slopes. Tennis and horseback riding available on Sugar Mountain.

Mossy Creek at Sugar Mountain
Sugar Mountain Resort, Hwy. 184
Banner Elk, NC 28604
704-898-6311

—————————————— BANNER ELK ——————————————

Sugartop Resort & Country
Club
Rt. 1, Box 397, Hwy. 184
Banner Elk, NC 28604
704-898-6211 800-438-4555

2 Bedrooms $$$
Hi-rise

General Facilities: Linens

Sports Facilities: Pool; exercise room

Room Facilities: Kitchen

Attractions: Golf, tennis, hiking, skiing, Spring Fling, New Year's Eve Torchlight
Parade

*Mountain condominiums with fireplaces, wet bars and covered balconies. Sugar
Mountain skiing with several slopes suited for racing. Ski school for children 5 to 10.
Well-planned recreational programs in summer, as well as golf, tennis, and hiking.*

————————————— BEECH MOUNTAIN —————————————

Four Seasons At Beech
608 Beech Mt. Parkway
Beech Mountain, NC 28604
704-387-4211

Studio $$, 1 Bedroom $$
1 Bedrm/week $$$$
AmEx/Visa/MC, Dep. Required •
35 condos, Lo-rise, Key at Front desk
H-yes

Location: Airport: 56 miles; Need car; Ski lift at Nearby

General Facilities: Daily maid; Linens; Baby sitter; Crib-Hi-chair; Restaurant;
Bar

Business Facilities: Conf. Room Cap. 125

Sports Facilities: Skiing; Beech Mountain–nearby; Skiwee, summer camp

Room Facilities: Cable; Ind.Heat Ctl.

Attractions: 5 ski areas, 6 golf courses, Gorge and Grandfather Mt. scenic areas,
Tweetsie RR Park

Shops & Restaurants: Crafts, Boone Mall, furniture outlet stores; Teaberry's
(American)

*One- and two-room condominiums in a Tudor-style lodge atop Beech Mountain,
directly across from ski area, in America's highest town. Summers are cool with light
breezes to help make the most of the many recreational activities and sightseeing
opportunities.*

The Pinnacle Inn
Beech Mtn. Pkwy.
Beech Mountain, NC 28604
704-387-4276 800-438-2097

──────────── BEECH MOUNTAIN ────────────

The Pinnacle Inn
Beech Mtn. Pkwy.
Beech Mountain, NC 28604
704-387-4276 800-438-2097

──────────── BLOWING ROCK ────────────

Chetola Resort
North Main Street, P.O. Box 205
Blowing Rock, NC 28605
704-295-9301 800-243-8652

1 Bedroom $$, 2 Bedrooms $$
1 Bedrm/week 4$, 2 Bed/week 5$
Min. Stay 2 Nights, AmEx/Visa/MC,
Dep. Req'd. •
60 condos, Villas, Key at Chetola Lodge

Location: Airport: 90 miles; Downtown: 3 blocks; Need car; Ski lift: Nearby

General Facilities: Full serv., Bus. fac., Conf. rm. cap. 75, Kitchen, Linens, Restaurant on prem., Bar on prem., Child planned rec.: Summer day camp

Room Facilities: Pool, Sauna, Hot tub, Tennis, Racquet, fitness center, TV, Cable, Phone in rm., Crib-Hi-chair, Ind. AC Ctl., Ind. Heat Ctl.

Attractions: Waterfalls, hiking, crafts, plays, cultural events, family attractions, entertainment

Shops & Restaurants: Local craft guilds; Claire's-S.C. low country

Set in the mountains adjacent to Blue Ridge Parkway and surrounded by a National Park. Recreation Center with daily planned activities and children's summer day camp. Tennis, racquetball, indoor pool, fitness center, and a lake for trout fishing and canoeing.

Hound Ears Club   P-yes
Box 188
Blowing Rock, NC 28605
704-963-4321

Location: Ski lift: Nearby

General Facilities: Conf. rm. cap. 60, Kitchen, Restaurant on prem., Bar on prem., Baby-sitter

Room Facilities: Pool, Tennis, Golf: Hound Ears Club

Attractions: Tweetsie Railroad, Glendale Springs, Roan Mountain, entertainment

Shops & Restaurants: Antiques, arts and crafts; Hound Ears Club Dining Room

A rather small, four-season resort, remote and secluded, yet offering an atmosphere where service and comfort are at a premium. Intimate dining room done in sea-greens and warm garden colors where Gene Fleri plays the organ. Brown Bagg Lounge with dance floor. The hard-to-find swimming pool is adjoined by a rock grotto and pavilion creating a setting of unsurpassed natural beauty. Stables and bridle trails a few miles away. Scenic golf course.

──────────── BLOWING ROCK ────────────

Swiss Mountain Village
Flat Top Road, Rt. 2, Box 86
Blowing Rock, NC 28605
704-295-3373

Studio $, 1 Bedroom $$, 2 Bedrooms $$
1 Bedrm/week $$$$, 2 Bed/week $$$$,
3 Bed/week $$$$
Min. Stay 2 Nights, Dep. 1 Night •
40 condos, Villas, Key at Office on site
H-yes

Location: Airport: 35 miles; Downtown: 1.5 mile; Need car; Ski lift: Nearby
General Facilities: Daily maid, Kitchen, Linens, Bar on prem., Baby-sitter
Room Facilities: TV, Cable, Crib-Hi-chair, Ind. Heat Ctl.
Attractions: Golf, tennis, horseback, white water rafting, Appalachian Ski Mountain
Shops & Restaurants: Crafts & outlet, chain store, groceries; Many types

Log cabins built of natural materials with rough hewn log walls and native stone fireplaces. Chalets with stairway to the loft over the stone fireplace. Hiking in the forest filled with rhododendron and laurel, and trout fishing with no license required. Attractions in the vicinity include hang gliding, canoe trips, sleigh riding, picnic grounds, outdoor amphitheater, Scottish games, art show, crafts fair, Linville Caverns and Tweetsie Railroad.

──────────────────────────────

Village at Green Park
Goforth Road
Blowing Rock, NC 28605
704-295-9861 800-255-9861

2 Bedrooms $$
2 Bedrms/week 7$
Min. Stay 2 Nights, Dep. Req'd.
12 condos, Villas
No S-yes/P-yes

Location: Airport: 1-2 hours; Downtown: 1.5 mile; Need car; Ski lift: 4 miles
General Facilities: Kitchen, Linens, Restaurant on prem., Bar on prem., Lounge, Baby-sitter
Room Facilities: Pool, Golf: Blowing Rock Golf; TV, Cable, Phone in rm., Crib-Hi-chair, Ind. AC Ctl., Ind. Heat Ctl.
Attractions: Appalachian Summer hosted by Appalachian State U, summer host for NC symphony
Shops & Restaurants: Antique, jewelry, unique shops; The Best Cellar/international

Beautiful villas, tastefully appointed and furnished, overlooking Blowing Rock Golf and Country Club. Adjacent to historic Green Park Inn. Attend the local cultural activities and escape the summer heat.

──────────────── BOONE ────────────────

Smoketree Lodge
P.O. Box 3407
Boone, NC 28607
704-963-6505

1 Bedroom $$, 2 Bedrooms $$

Located 12 miles south of Boone, central to all major ski slopes. Fully furnished condos with HBO and Cinemax. Lobby with stone fireplace and wide-screen TV. Amenities include indoor pool, jacuzzi, saunas and workout area.

─────────────── BOONE ───────────────

Willow Valley Resort
P.O. Box 1782
Boone, NC 28607
704-963-6551

1 Bedroom $$, 2 Bedrooms $$
Pool, Kitchen

Attractions: Skiing, fishing, mile-high hiking, theater, tennis, golf

Modern living in a rustic setting at this all-season resort set in the Appalachian highlands. Away from the hustle and bustle of the city, close to nature with diverse leisure activities. All units are fully equipped and some have washer/dryers and dishwashers.

─────────────── BURNSVILLE ───────────────

Alpine Village
200 Overlook Dr.
Burnsville, NC 28714
704-675-4103

1 Bedroom $$, 2 Bedrooms $$
1 Bedrm/week $$$$, 2 Bed/week 5$
Min. Stay 2 Nights, Visa/MC, Dep. Req'd.
21 condos, Lo-rise, Villas, Key at Office in Clubhouse
H-yes

Location: Airport: 1½ hours; Downtown: 16 miles; Need car

General Facilities: Daily maid, Kitchen, Linens, Game room, Lounge, Baby-sitter

Room Facilities: Pool, Hot tub, Tennis, Hiking, trout fishing, Golf: Mount Mitchell; TV, Phone in rm., Crib-Hi-chair, Ind. Heat Ctl.

Attractions: Blue Ridge Parkway (2 mi.), Biltmore estate, T. Wolfe home, local crafts, Grandfather Mt, entertainment

Shops & Restaurants: Small shops featuring local craftsmen; Albert's-Ger. Beam's-Chinese

Luxurious townhouses with fabulous views from each deck; tennis and heated pool on property. Hiking trails, trout fishing and discounted golf on great Mount Mitchell course; small, quiet and secluded. Surrounded by a national forest, the ideal place for relaxing in the cool mountain air.

Mount Mitchell Lands & Golf Club Lo-rise
7590 Hwy. 80 S.
Burnsville, NC 28714
704-675-4923

Surrounded by the Pisgah National Forest, an hour drive from Asheville, these fully equipped townhouses overlook the golf course. Cool summer days and nights in elevations over 3,000 feet. South Toe River winds through the golf course. Clubhouse and dining room.

─────────────── BUXTON ───────────────

Cape Hatteras Beach Club
Rt. 12 & Old Lighthouse, POB 550
Buxton, NC 27920
919-995-4115

─────────────── CALABASH ───────────────

Carolina Shores Resort
Rt. 179, P.O. Box 2220
Calabash, NC 28459
919-579-7001 800-533-3396

———————————————— CAROLINA BEACH ————————————————

Atlantic Towers   Visa/MC, Dep. Required •
1615 South Lake Park Blvd.   137 condos, Hi-rise, Key at Front desk
Carolina Beach, NC 28428   No S-yes/H-yes
910-458-8313 FAX: 910-458-6074
800-BEACH-40

Location: Airport: 20 minutes; Downtown: 20 min.; Need car; Beach front

General Facilities: Full serv.; Daily maid; Linens; Crib

Business Facilities: Bus. fac.; Conf. Room Cap. 25

Sports Facilities: Game room; Pool; At times

Room Facilities: Kitchen; Cable; VCR; Phone; Ind.AC.Ctl; Ind.Heat Ctl.

Attractions: Historic Wilmington, Battleship N.C., Fort Fisher Historical Site, aquarium, ocean

Shops & Restaurants: Major chain stores, outlets & specialty shops; All types

With the Atlantic Ocean as the front yard, these delightful condominiums are a full-service, guest oriented property. Relax with your family on the sandy beach or by the pool, or visit the many sights in historic Wilmington.

Paradise Tower Resort   1 Night Dep. Req'd. •
901 S. Lake Park Blvd.   37 condos, Hi-rise
Carolina Beach, NC 28428   Key at Tower lobby area, No S-yes/H-yes
919-458-7946

Location: Airport: 20 miles; Downtown: 20 Min.; Need car; Beach front

General Facilities: Full serv.; Daily maid; Linens; Baby-sitter; Crib-Hi-chair

Sports Facilities: Pool; Nearby

Room Facilities: Kitchen; Cable; VCR; Phone; Ind.AC.Ctl; Ind.Heat Ctl.

Attractions: Historic Wilmington, Battleship N.C., Fort Fisher, Aquarium, University of North Carolina

Shops & Restaurants: Major chain stores, specialty shops, outlet stores; All types

Two bedroom, two bath, completely furnished oceanfront condominiums with daily maid service. Rest and relax by the pool or sun and swim in the Atlantic Ocean. For the more ambitious, golf and tennis are nearby. Children are welcome in this family resort.

──────────────── CAROLINA BEACH ────────────────

Spinnaker Point
400 Virginia Ave, P.O. Box 1888
Carolina Beach, NC 28428
919-458-4554 800-334-0454

2 Bedrooms $$, 3 Bedrooms $$
2 Bedrms/week 5$, 3 Bed/week 6$
Min. Stay 2 Nights, Visa/MC, Dep. Req'd. •
42 condos, Lo-rise, Key at Office

Location: Airport: 18 miles; Downtown: 15 miles; Need car; Beach front

General Facilities: Kitchen, Linens, Baby-sitter

Room Facilities: Pool, Hot tub, Tennis, Marina, Golf: Cape Golf—5 miles; TV, Cable, Crib-Hi-chair, Ind. AC Ctl., Ind. Heat Ctl.

Attractions: Charter and cruise boats, live theatre, buggy rides, amusement parks, movies

Shops & Restaurants: Independence Mall, specialty shops, souvenirs; The Steeple-seafood, steaks

The colorful Cape Fear area is fun for the whole family. Villas in mauve and grey or seafoam and cream. Chrome furniture with glass coffee tables, private balconies and bay windows in a colorful setting of natural cypress. 85-acre resort on a peninsula. Plentiful boating, fishing and golf. Huge expanse of preserved marshland, crossed by a boardwalk to the oceanfront. Private marina on the Intracoastal Waterway for convenient boat access.

──────────────── CASWELL BEACH ────────────────

Caswell Dunes
44 Pinehurst Drive
Caswell Beach, NC

3 Bedrooms $$
3 Bedrms/week 4$
Min. Stay 2 Nights, Dep. Req'd.
32 condos, Lo-rise

Location: Airport: 35 miles; Downtown: 30 miles; Need car

General Facilities: Daily maid, Kitchen, Linens

Room Facilities: Pool, Hot tub, Golf: Oak Island Country Club; TV, Cable, VCR, Crib-Hi-chair, Ind. AC Ctl., Ind. Heat Ctl.

Shops & Restaurants: Local beach shops, nautical and clothing

You'll like the bright cool colors of the contemporary beach furnishings in these exquisitely decorated units complete with covered decks and garage. Take the walkways to the beach or pool.

Southern Shore Villas
S.E. 58th Street
Caswell Beach, NC

Min. Stay Ask, Dep. Req'd.
27 condos, Lo-rise

Location: Airport: 35 miles-Wilmington; Downtown: 30 miles; Need car

General Facilities: Daily maid, Kitchen, Linens

Room Facilities: Pool, Hot tub, TV, Cable, Crib-Hi-chair, Ind. AC Ctl., Ind. Heat Ctl.

Shops & Restaurants: Local shops

Condominiums delightfully decorated in mint green and mauve wicker style beach furnishings. Quiet, secluded villas, yet close to shopping, restauants and island activities.

―――――――――――― CEDAR MOUNTAIN ――――――――――――

Sherwood Forest
P.O. Box 156, Hwy. 276
Cedar Mountain, NC 28718
704-885-2091

Villas
Pool, Kitchen

Attractions: Great Smoky Mountains Nat. Park, Pisgah Nat. Forest, Biltmore House and Gardens, boating, fishing, tennis, golf

New villas in the woods, on a trout stream, overlooking the golf course. Woodburning fireplaces, screened porches, open decks, grills, washers and dryers.

―――――――――――――――― DUCK ――――――――――――――――

Barrier Island Station
State Route 1200
Duck, NC 27949
919-261-3525 800-261-3825

2 Bedrooms $$, 3 Bedrooms $$$
2 Bedrms/week 9$, 3 Bed/week 9$
Min. Stay 3 Nights, AmEx/Visa/MC,
    Dep. Req'd.
134 condos, Villas, Key at Guard Gate H-yes

Location: Airport: 60 miles; Downtown: ½ mile; Need car; Beach front

General Facilities: Daily maid, Kitchen, Linens, Restaurant on prem., Bar on prem., Game room, Lounge, Baby-sitter

Room Facilities: Pool, Sauna, Hot tub, Tennis, TV, Cable, Phone in rm., Crib-Hi-chair, Ind. AC Ctl., Ind. Heat Ctl.

Attractions: Wright Bros. Memorial Museum, Lost Colony outdoor drama, fishing, wind surfing, sailing, entertainment

Shops & Restaurants: Small shops; Barrier Island Inn/Steak-fish

While the architecture is Victorian, the furnishings are ultra-modern. Ocean and Sound views, wet bars and jacuzzis, located in a quiet setting. Full-time activities director. A short distance to the ocean for sunning and swimming. Enjoy tennis, windsurfing and sailing.

Maui Kaanapali Villas

—————————————— HAMPSTEAD ——————————————

Belvedere Plantation Golf Club 1 Bedroom $$, 2 Bedrooms $$,
P.O. Box 400   3 Bedrooms $$
Hampstead, NC 28443   1 Bedrm/week $$$$, 2 Bedrms/week 4$,
919-270-2761 800-334-8126   3 Bedrms/week 5$
                                     Visa/MC, Dep. Required •
                                     84 condos, Villas, Key at Belvedere
                                     Plantation, H-yes

Location: Airport: 22 miles; Downtown: 25 miles; Need car

General Facilities: Linens; Lounge; Restaurant

Sports Facilities: Pool; Sauna; Tennis; Belvedere on property

Room Facilities: Kitchen; Cable; Phone; Ind.AC.Ctl; Ind.Heat Ctl.

Attractions: Beaches, marina, saltwater fishing, hunting, Marine Resources
Center, Fort Fisher Park

Shops & Restaurants: Grocery, drug, beauty salon, outlet mall, Penney's;
Bridge Tender/st.-Fraziers

*Villas in a plantation setting with spacious grounds, shaded leisure areas and
boardwalk promenade on a championship golf course. Privacy gate and a 200 slip
marina, plus 3 nine hole golf courses, putting green, driving range, tennis courts and
swimming pool. 15 minute drive to the ocean, or 5 minute boat ride. Surf casting, pier
and deep sea fishing and indoor trolling. Clubhouse includes dining room, lounge,
lockers and showers.*

—————————————— HATTERAS ISLAND ——————————————

Hatteras Cabanas/Dolphin   Studio $$, 1 Bedroom $$, 2 Bedrooms $$,
Realty   3 Bedrooms $$$
P.O. Box 387   1 Bedrm/week $$$$
Hatteras Island, NC 27943   Min. Stay 2 Nights, AmEx/Visa/MC,
919-986-2241 800-338-4775   Dep. Required, 40 condos, Lo-rise,
FAX: 919-986-2908   Key at Office, P-Yes

Location: Airport: 2 miles; Downtown: 1 mile; Need car; Beachfront

General Facilities: Baby-sitter

Sports Facilities: Grills, Picnic areas

Room Facilities: Kitchen; Cable; Ind.AC.Ctl; Ind.Heat Ctl.

Attractions: Deep sea fishing, surf fishing, sail boarding, surfing, lighthouses,
Lost Colony

Shops & Restaurants: Gift, specialty, tackle, boating shops, groceries; Channel
Bass, Breakwater Sonny's

*Offering a variety of the best condos on Hatteras Island. Studio to 4 bedroom. Great
beaches, surfing, fishing, windsurfing. Walk to beach, shops and restaurants. Watch
sunrise over the ocean, sunset over the Pamlico Sound. Hatteras National Seashore*

---------------------- HOLDEN BEACH ----------------------

Ocean Palms
769 Ocean Blvd. West
Holden Beach, NC 28462
919-842-7443

3 Bedrooms $$$
3 Bedrms/week 8$
Min. Stay 3 Nights, Dep. Required, 8
condos, Lo-rise

Location: Airport: 38 miles; Downtown: 35 miles; Need car; Beach front

General Facilities: Daily maid; Baby-sitter; Crib-Hi-chair

Sports Facilities: Pool; Lockwood Folly 4 miles

Room Facilities: Kitchen; Cable; VCR; Phone; Ind.AC.Ctl; Ind.Heat Ctl.

Attractions: N.C. Battleship Memorial, Orton Plantation, Waccamaw pottery, cruises, fishing, golf

Shops & Restaurants: 45 minutes to Wilmington and Myrtle Beach; Calabash/seafood

Three large bedrooms in townhouse condominiums with pastel colors in modern beach decor on the ocean. Family atmosphere for beach and pool fun.

---------------------- KILL DEVIL HILLS ----------------------

Sun Realty Of Nags Head, Inc.
P.O. Box 1630
Kill Devil Hills, NC 27948
919-441-7033 800-334-4745
FAX: 919-441-3245

1 Bedrm/week 5$, 2 Bedrms/week 7$,
3 Bedrms/week 9$
Min. Stay 7 Nights, Visa/MC, 29 condos,
Lo-rise, Key at Sun Realty H-Yes

Location: Need car; Beachfront

General Facilities: Crib-Hi-chair

Sports Facilities: Pool; Sauna

Room Facilities: Kitchen; Cable; VCR; Phone; Ind.AC.Ctl.; Ind.Heat Ctl.

Attractions: Hatteras Island, Wright Brothers Memorial, Elizabethan Gardens, Lost Colony

Shops & Restaurants: Several shopping areas and local shops; Chardo's/Italian, Owens/seafood

A large selection of oceanfront condominiums are available for making a memorable family vacation. Most units offer great ocean views and warm summer breezes. Some units have microwaves, jacuzzis and washer/dryer facilities.

---------------------- KITTY HAWK ----------------------

Heron Cove, Coastal Horizons
4517 Croatan Highway
Kitty Hawk, NC 27949
919-441-8070 800-543-9232

3 Bedrooms $$
3 Bedrms/week 6$
Min. Stay 2 Nights, Dep. Required, 12
condos, Lo-rise H-yes

Location: Airport: 2 hours; Downtown: 2 hours; Need car; Beach front

General Facilities: Daily maid; Linens; Crib-Hi-chair

Sports Facilities: Pool; Nags Head Links

Room Facilities: Kitchen; Cable; Phone; Ind.AC.Ctl; Ind.Heat Ctl.

Attractions: Wright Memorial, Elizabeth II, Lost Colony, Cape Hatteras National Seashore; Entertainment

Shops & Restaurants: Gift shops, shell shops; By Georges/seafood, steaks

Luxury and leisure in these 3-bedroom, 2-bath units with elevator access. Balconies overlook the pool. Join in the weekly barbeques.

─────────────────── KITTY HAWK ───────────────────

Ocean Dunes Condominiums   Studio $
P.O. Box 387   Min. Stay 2 Nights, Visa/MC, Dep. Req'd.
Kitty Hawk, NC   40 condos, Lo-rise, Key at Office on premises
919-986-2241 800-338-4775   P-yes

Location: Airport: 2 miles; Downtown: 1 mile; Beach front

General Facilities: Kitchen

Room Facilities: TV, Cable, Crib-Hi-chair, Ind. AC Ctl., Ind. Heat Ctl.

Attractions: Lighthouse, Wright Brothers, Lost Colony/Roanoke Island, Ocracoke
   Island

Shops & Restaurants: Local shops, groceries, Red & White; Channel Bass/seafood
   Pilot Hse

*Oceanfront condos near fishing pier and gulf stream charter fleet, clean, tranquil beaches,
shopping and restaurants nearby.*

Sea Scape Beach & Golf Villas   2 Bedrooms $$
P.O. Box 276   2 Bedrms/week $$$$
Kitty Hawk, NC 27949   Min. Stay 2 Nights, Visa/MC, Dep. Req'd. •
919-261-3881 800-843-9451   84 condos, Lo-rise, Villas, Key at On-site property
                                      H-yes

Location: Airport: 80 miles; Downtown: 5 miles; Need car

General Facilities: Kitchen, Linens, Restaurant on prem., Bar on prem., Game room,
   Lounge, Baby-sitter

Room Facilities: Pool, Hot tub, Tennis, Mini golf, volleyball, Golf: On 10th fairway; TV,
   Cable, VCR, Phone in rm., Crib-Hi-chair, Ind. AC Ctl., Ind. Heat Ctl.

Attractions: Deep sea, surf and pier fishing, Wright Brothers Memorial, hang gliding,
   wind surfing.

Shops & Restaurants: Sidneys Galleon Esplanade, Outer Banks Mall; Owens Seafood

*Plush contemporary furnishings in these two-bedroom, two-bath condominiums. Balco-
nies with pool, tennis and golf course views. Many local attractions. The area is a fisher-
man's dream. 36 holes of golf per day are included. Perfect for a quiet weekend getaway
or a fun-filled vacation with the kids.*

─────────────────── MOREHEAD CITY ───────────────────

The Breakers   Lo-rise
P.O. Box 736   Pool, Kitchen, Linens, Phone in rm.
Morehead City, NC 28557
919-247-2400 800-334-3157

Attractions: Fort Macon, Cape Lookout, Hampton Mariners Museum, Beaufort, charter
   fishing, marina, tennis, golf

*Oceanfront condominiums with private walkways to the beach, observation decks and
screened balconies. 190 beautiful acres and two miles of sandy beach. High dunes covered
by a dense maritime forest to the ocean's edge. Located in the town of Pine Knoll Shores.*

─────────────── MOREHEAD CITY ───────────────

Notch Estates
P.O. Box 128
Morehead City, NC 28557
417-338-2941

Studio $, 1 Bedroom $$, 2 Bedrooms $$,
   3 Bedrooms $$
1 Bedrm/week 4$, 2 Bed/week 5$, 3 Bed/
   week 6$
Min. Stay 2 Nights, AmEx/Visa/MC,
   Dep. 1 Night
Lo-rise, Key at Notch Inn Office
H-yes

Location: Airport: 50 miles; Downtown: 13 miles; Need car

General Facilities: Conf. rm. cap. 360, Daily maid, Kitchen, Linens, Restaurant on prem., Lounge, Baby-sitter

Room Facilities: Pool, TV, Ind. AC Ctl., Ind. Heat Ctl.

Attractions: Silver Dollar City, Shepherd of the Hills, Table Rock Lake

Shops & Restaurants: Service Merchants Mall, Banister, Carters; Notch/family, Wooden Nickel

150 secluded scenic acres with hiking trails and a private lake. Units decor varies from modern to country. Views of valleys and trees. On-site restaurant and lounge, and minutes away from Music Show and Silver Dollar City.

Sand Castles
Morehead City, NC
919-579-3535

Studio $$, 1 Bedroom $$, 2 Bedrooms $$, 3 Bedrooms $$
1 Bedrm/week $$$$, 2 Bed/week 4$, 3 Bed/
   week 4$
Min. Stay 2 Nights, Dep. Req'd.
156 condos, Lo-rise, Key at Office
H-yes

Location: Airport: Wilmington 45 min.; Downtown: 1 block; Need car; Beach front

General Facilities: Bus. fac., Kitchen, Baby-sitter, Child planned rec.: Play area

Room Facilities: Pool, Sauna, Hot tub, Tennis, Boat docks, fishing, TV, Cable, Phone in rm., Crib-Hi-chair, Ind. AC Ctl., Ind. Heat Ctl.

Attractions: 70 golf courses within 1 hr., fishing, clamming, crabbing, charter fishing, tours

Shops & Restaurants: Gift, liquor, grocery, Myrtle Beach shopping; Twin Lakes/seafood, Calabash

Wide choice of tastefully furnished modern condominiums located on a small family beach. Over a dozen golf courses and restaurants within 10 minutes. A family vacation for those who want an uncrowded and unspoiled beach.

─────────────── NAGS HEAD ───────────────

Ocean Villas
Mile Post 16-¼, P.O. Box 67
Nags Head, NC 27959
919-441-3405

─────────────── OCEAN ISLE BEACH ───────────────

Brick Landing Plantation
Highway 179
Ocean Isle Beach, NC 28459
919-754-4373 800-438-3006
FAX: 919-754-5612

2 Bedroom $$, 3 Bedroom $$$
2 Bedrm/week 5$, 3 Bedrm/week 6$
AmEx/MC/Visa/, Dep. Req'd
27 condos, Lo-rise, Villas, Keys at
Rental office

Location: Airport: 45 minutes; Downtown: 30 miles, Beach front
General Facilities:, Daily maid, Kitchen, Linens, Restaurant on prem., Bar on prem.
Room Facilities: Pool, Hot Tub, Tennis, Swimming, 18-hole championship golf, TV, Cable, Phone in rm., Ind. AC Ctl., Ind. Heat Ctl.
Attractions: Myrtle Beach, Wilmington, nightlife, tourist attractions, beaches, entertainment, pottery.
Shops & Restaurants: Briarcliffe Mall, Barefoot Traders; Calabash/seafood
Master planned community built around a golf course on a 22 foot bluff. Hardwood forests, lakes, ponds and Sauce Pan Marsh. Swimming pool outside your window, beach minutes away. Away from tourist congestion, yet close enough to drive to Myrtle Beach and Wilmington to take advantage of their shopping, restaurants, nightlife, galleries and festivals. 4 Har-Tru tennis courts. Golf packages available. Golf tournaments.

The Winds Beach and Golf Resort
310 E. First Street
Ocean Isle Beach, NC 28459
919-579-6275 800-334-3581

1 Bedroom $$, 2 Bedrooms $$
1 Bedrm/week $$$$, 2 Bed/week $$$$
AmEx/Visa/MC, Dep. Req'd. •
44 condos

Location: Downtown: 2.5 miles
General Facilities: Conf. rm. cap. 45, Kitchen

─────────────── PINEHURST ───────────────

Foxfire Resort & Country Club
P.O. Box 711
Pinehurst, NC 28374
919-295-5555 800-334-9540

1 Bedroom $, 2 Bedrooms $$$
1 Bedrm/week $$$$, 2 Bed/week 5$
AmEx/Visa/MC, Dep. Req'd. •
80 condos, Villas, Key at Front Desk

Location: Airport: 80 miles; Need car
General Facilities: Conf. rm. cap. 200, Daily maid, Kitchen, Linens, Restaurant on prem., Bar on prem., Lounge
Room Facilities: Pool, Tennis, Golf: 2 golf courses; TV, Cable, Phone in rm., Crib-Hi-chair, Ind. AC Ctl., Ind. Heat Ctl.
Attractions: Located in the heart of the North Carolina Sandhills, exciting two-bedroom, bi-level quad

Located in the heart of the North Carolina Sandhills, architecturally designed two-bedroom, bi-level quad villas, with two outdoor decks among the pines near the first tees. Ranch-style Club Villas have fireplaces, garage and screened porches. Pro shop, clubhouse, pool, tennis. Excellent cuisine in the dining room, cocktail lounge, and 36-hole architect-designed championship golf course for the perfect golfing vacation.

PINEHURST

Pinehurst Hotel & Country Club
Carolina Vista, POB 4000
Pinehurst, NC 28374
919-295-6811

Lo-rise
Pool, Kitchen, Linens, Phone in rm.

Attractions: Gun Club, Riding Club, croquet, lawn bowling, biking, walking tours, trap and skeet, tennis, golf

Comfortable furnished condominiums, tastefully decorated. 28 tennis courts amid the pines, 7 golf courses. Horse-drawn carriages, equestrian facility and Gun club with instructor, Annie Oakely. True Southern hospitality in a year-round resort.

PLEASURE ISLAND

The Sands
Wilmington Beach
Pleasure Island, NC 27948
919-441-6993

2 Bedrooms $, Villas
Kitchen

Tastefully decorated villas with private balconies on a wide sandy beach.

RUTHERFORDTON

Cleghorn Plantation Golf Club
Rt. 4, Box 69, Cox Rd.
Rutherfordton, NC 28139
704-287-2091 800-334-1068

SALTER PATH

Summer Winds
Hwy. 58, P.O. Box 100
Salter Path, NC 28575
919-247-2104 800-334-6866

2 Bedrooms $$$, Hi-rise
Pool, Kitchen, Linens

Attractions: Exercise room, tennis

Open airy beach condominiums, views, ceramic tile bath floors, quarry tile in foyer and kitchen, carpeting, pass-through bar to dining area, sound and weather insulated. Sports complex, four pools, two lighted tennis courts.

Please mention *Condo Vacations the Complete Guide* when you reserve your condominium.

──────────────── SAPPHIRE ────────────────

Fairfield Sapphire Valley
4000 Hwy. 64 W.
Sapphire, NC 28774
704-743-3341 800-438-3421

Studio $$, 1 Bedroom $$$, 2 Bedrooms $$$$,
3 Bedrooms $$$$
1 Bedrm/week 6$, 2 Bed/week 8$, 3 Bed/
week 8$
Min. Stay 2 Nights, AmEx/Visa/MC,
Dep. Req'd. •
200 condos, Lo-rise, Key at Guest Registr.
H-yes

Location: Airport: 55 miles; Need car; Ski lift: Nearby

General Facilities: Full serv., Bus. fac., Conf. rm. cap. 80, Daily maid, Kitchen, Linens, Restaurant on prem., Game room, Baby-sitter, Child planned rec.: Sunburst Program

Room Facilities: Pool, Sauna, Hot tub, Tennis, Golf: Holly Forest Golf Course; TV, Cable, VCR, Phone in rm., Crib-Hi-chair, Ind. AC Ctl., Ind. Heat Ctl.

Attractions: Biltmore House & Gardens, rafting, Indian reservation, gem mining, Carl Sandburg Home, entertainment

Shops & Restaurants: Antique, craft, specialty and dress shops; Holly Forest Country Club

A four-season resort in the Blue Ridge Mountains. Country setting, contemporary furnishings in browns, blues, mauves and greens. Recreation Department, Wednesday night B-B-Q, 3 lakes on the property. 8 lighted tennis courts, recreation complex for children, indoor and outdoor swimming pools. Four ski slopes for winter fun and well-equipped ski shop. Scenic mountain trails for horseback riding, hiking or jogging.

──────────────── SNEADS FERRY ────────────────

Chicora Beach Holiday, Inc.
North Topsail Shores, POB 778
Sneads Ferry, NC 28460
800-682-3460 800-222-1536

North Topsail Shores
P.O. Box 778
Sneads Ferry, NC 28460
919-328-0335 800-222-1536

──────────────── SOUTHERN PINES ────────────────

Hyland Hills
4100 U.S. #1 North
Southern Pines, NC 28387
919-692-4434

Two-bedroom, two-bath condominiums ideal for golfers with discounts at 8 sandhills courses. On-site restaurant.

Napili Point

SOUTHPORT

Bald Head Island Mgmt.
P.O. Drawer 10999, 704 E. Moore St.
Southport, NC 28461
919-457-5000 800-443-6305

Studio $$$, 1 Bedroom $$$, 2 Bedrooms $$$,
3 Bedrooms $$$
1 Bedrm/week 6$, 2 Bed/week 6$, 3 Bed/
week 8$
Min. Stay 3 Nights, AmEx/Visa/MC,
Dep. Req'd. •
90 condos, Lo-rise, Key at Front desk

Location: Airport: 40 minutes; Downtown: 20 min.; Beach front

General Facilities: Conf. rm. cap. 50, Daily maid, Kitchen, Linens, Restaurant on prem., Bar on prem., Lounge, Baby-sitter, Child planned rec.: Summer day camp

Room Facilities: Pool, Tennis, Croquet, canoeing, Golf: Bald Head Island Course; TV, Phone in rm., Crib-Hi-chair, Ind. AC Ctl., Ind. Heat Ctl.

Attractions: Orton Plantation, Wilmington, Wacamaw Pottery outlet, Myrtle Beach, entertainment

Shops & Restaurants: Island Chandler-gourmet items, videos, beach toys; The Inn, Peli Deli

Condominiums on a 2,000-acre private island community accessible only by private passenger ferry. No cars allowed on the island, but electric vehicles are available to rent. Various condominiums to rent in this traditional, family beach community. Tennis, golf, pool, 14 miles of beach, croquet, clamming, crabbing, fishing, biking and canoeing.

SUNSET BEACH

Oyster Bay Plantation
900 Shoreline
Sunset Beach, NC 28459
919-579-7181 800-222-1524

Studio $$, 1 Bedroom $$, 2 Bedrooms $$,
  3 Bedrooms $$$
1 Bedrm/week 4$, 2 Bed/week 5$, 3 Bed/
  week 7$
Visa/MC,Dep. Req'd. •
130 condos, Lo-rise, Villas, Key at Office
H-yes

Location: Airport: 35 miles; Downtown: 20 min.; Need car

General Facilities: Bus. fac., Conf. rm. cap. 125, Daily maid, Kitchen, Linens, Baby-sitter

Room Facilities: Pool, Hot tub, Golf: O. Bay & Bricklanding; TV, Cable, VCR, Phone in rm., Crib-Hi-chair, Ind. AC Ctl., Ind. Heat Ctl.

Attractions: Golfing, boating, deep-sea fishing, dining (seafood capital of the world), shopping

Shops & Restaurants: Waccamaw Pottery, Myrtle Square & Briarcliff Malls; Parson's Table/seafood-beef

Truly close to it all, but a true feeling of island living and tranquility amidst a canvas of awesome natural beauty. The Colony at Oyster Bay has 1200 sq. ft. condominiums, 2-bedroom, 2 ceramic tile baths and quarry tile floor kitchens. The Fairway Villas are large with informal and functional floor plans. Lush landscaping and access to the Intracoastal Waterway for boat owners. One mile from the beach.

SURF CITY

Surf
Highway 210
Surf City, NC 28445
919-328-2511 800-255-2233

1 Bedroom $, 2 Bedrooms $$
1 Bedrm/week $$$$, 2 Bed/week $$$$
Min. Stay 2 Nights, Dep. Req'd.
180 condos, Lo-rise, Key at Century 21-Hwy. 50

Location: Airport: 45 minutes; Downtown: 30 min.; Need car; Beach front

General Facilities: Daily maid, Kitchen

Room Facilities: Pool, Golf: 20 minutes; TV, Cable, Crib-Hi-chair, Ind. AC Ctl., Ind. Heat Ctl.

Attractions: Fishing piers, Cotton Exchange, Airlee Gardens, Orton Plantation, USS-N.C.

Shops & Restaurants: Local gift and craft shops, malls; Fish

An exciting resort community on one of the last undeveloped beaches in North Carolina. The beaches can only be reached by bridges across the Intercoastal Waterway. Color-coordinated beach style furnishings. Natural landscaped setting with free form-pool, shaded sitting areas and clubhouse.

―――――――――――――― TOPSAIL ISLAND ――――――――――――――

Topsail Dunes　　　　　　　　　1 Bedroom $$, 2 Bedrooms $$$, 3 Bedrooms
North Topsail　　　　　　　　　　　$$$
Topsail Island, NC　　　　　　　　1 Bedrm/week 4$, 2 Bed/week 5$, 3 Bed/
919-328-0639　　　　　　　　　　　week 7$
　　　　　　　　　　　　　　　　　　Dep. Req'd.
　　　　　　　　　　　　　　　　　　224 condos, Lo-rise, Key at Albert Realty
　　　　　　　　　　　　　　　　　　H-yes

Location: Airport: 35 minutes; Downtown: 30 miles; Need car; Beach front

General Facilities: Kitchen

Room Facilities: Pool, Sauna, Hot tub, Tennis, Golf: North Shore Country Club; TV, Cable

Attractions: Deep-sea fishing, pier fishing, surf fishing, air tour of the island, beaches

Shops & Restaurants: Food Lion, regular shopping mall in Wilmington; Saratoga/ steak and seafood

Topsail Island is for those individuals who want to enjoy the sun, surf, pool and tennis for a quiet laid-back vacation.

―――――――――――――― WAYNESVILLE ――――――――――――――

Ithilien Lodge Condominium　　1 Bedroom $, Lo-rise
Upper Walker Road, Box 987　　　Pool, Kitchen
Waynesville, NC 28786
704-452-2466

Attractions: White-water rafting, mountain trails, lakes, Ghost Town, Cherokee Indian Reservation, exercise room, golf

Large, beautifully furnished units with mountain and valley view from the windows and decks. A real vacation retreat, high in the Great Smoky Mountains.

―――――――――――――― WHISPERING PINES ――――――――――――――

Whispering Pines Resort　　　　1 Bedroom $$, 2 Bedrooms $$
263-B Pine Ridge Drive　　　　　　Pool, Kitchen
Whispering Pines, NC 28327
919-949-3777　800-334-9536

Attractions: N.C. Motor Speedway, horse, harness racing, North Carolina State Zoo, tennis, golf

Located in North Carolina's majestic sandhills, this country club is conceived, designed and built for golfers, but offers other activities as well—all-weather tennis, pool, lake boating and sailing, and fine fishing. The perfect setting for a refreshing vacation.

──────────────── WRIGHTSVILLE BEACH ────────────────

Cordgrass Bay   Lo-rise
527 Causeway Dr, P.O. Box 1040   Pool, Kitchen
Wrightsville Beach, NC 28480
919-256-4516 800-992-6503

Attractions: Tennis

On Shell Island Sound where $_2$ of the land is committed to the conservation of natural landscape and open space. Atlantic on the east, intercoastal waterway on the west and Wrightsville Beach to the south.

One South Lumina   1 Bedroom $$, Hi-rise
P.O. Box 1040   Pool, Daily maid, Kitchen
Wrightsville Beach, NC 28480
919-256-9100

Imaginatively designed exteriors, designer decorated interiors on professionally landscaped grounds. When you're not at the beach, you'll be in the freshwater pool. Ocean views, furnished balconies, covered parking and elevator service.

──────────────── YAUPON BEACH ────────────────

Oak Island Beach Villas   1 Bedroom $$, 2 Bedrooms $$, 3 Bedrooms $$
1000 Caswell Beach Road   1 Bedrm/week 4$, 2 Bed/week 4$, 3 Bed/
Yaupon Beach, NC   week 5$
                               Min. Stay 2 Nights, Dep. Req'd.
                               Lo-rise

Location: Airport: 35 miles; Downtown: 30 miles; Need car; Beach front

General Facilities: Daily maid, Kitchen, Linens

Room Facilities: Pool, Hot tub, Golf: Oak Island adjacent; TV, Cable, Crib-Hi-chair, Ind. AC Ctl., Ind. Heat Ctl.

Attractions: Historical attractions, fishing, beach activities

Shops & Restaurants: Local shops

Each unit is beautifully decorated with wicker furniture in bright fabrics. Units conveniently located to the pool and jacuzzi.

Oklahoma

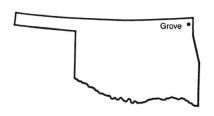
Grove

GROVE

Meghan Coves
P.O. Box 1868
Grove, OK 74344
918-786-4444

2 Bedrooms $$
Pool, Daily maid, Kitchen, Linens

Attractions: Bowling, movie theater, Cherokee Queen party barge, racquetball, tennis

Cape Cod village townhouses on the wooded shoreline of a 60,000-acre lake with private boat slips. Tennis courts, pools, clubhouse with racquetball courts, fitness center, jogging and walking trails. Fish off the air conditioned, heated fishing dock.

We want to hear from you—any comments regarding the condos or our publication may be noted on the form at the end of the book.

Oregon

Gleneden Beach • Lincoln City
⸱ Welches
Bend
• Sunriver

BEND

Mount Bachelor Village
19717 Mount Bachelor Dr.
Bend, OR 97702
503-389-5900 800-547-5204

1 Bedroom $$, 2 Bedrooms $$$,
3 Bedrooms $$$$, Min. stay 2 nights
Amex, Visa, MC, Key at Front office
134 condos, Lo-rise •

Location: Airport: 18 miles; Downtown: 2 minutes; Need car; Ski lift: 18 miles

General facilities: Full serv., Conf. Rm. (cap. 50), Daily maid, Kitchen, Linens, Game room

Room facilities: TV, Cable, Phone, Crib, A/C, Heat, Fireplaces

Sports facilities: Pool, Tennis, Whitewater rafting, Health spa, fishing

Attractions: Mt. Bachelor & Cascade Lks area, High Desert Museum, Smith Rock State Park, Paulina Peak

Shops & Restaurants: 2 malls, Fred Meyer, Shopko, sporting goods, gift shops, Pine Tavern/steaks & seafood

Mt. Bachelor Village offers luxury condominium lodging in a quiet woodland setting. All condominiums have fully equipped kitchens, fireplaces, cable TV & daily housekeeping services. Our units sleep 4-6 people on a nightly basis. Pool, hot tub, tennis courts, 2.2 mile scenic nature trail along Deschutes River. New River Ridge Condominiums offer breathtaking views, 2 or 3 bedrooms, and many amenities. Mt. Bachelor Village located ½ miles from downtown Bend and 18 miles from Mt. Bachelor Ski Area.

The Inn of the Seventh Mountain
P.O. Box 11207
Bend, OR 97709
503-382-8711

1 Bedroom $$$$, 2 Bedrooms $$$$
Lo-rise

General facilities: Daily maid, Kitchen, Linens

Room facilities: Phone

Sports facilities: Pool, Ice skating

Attractions: Skiing, white water rafting, patio boat tours, canoe float trips, fishing, mt. bike tours

Comfortably decorated units with fireplaces in a beautiful alpine setting. 14 miles from Mt. Bachelor with its Outback Super Express chair. Shuttle service to mountain. Warm, friendly staff to make your vacation experience complete. Full range of summer activities.

————————————— GLENEDEN —————————————

Cavalier by the Sea
P.O. Box 58
Gleneden, OR 97388
503-764-2352

——————————————— LINCOLN CITY ———————————————

Ocean Terrace Condominium   1 Bedroom $$
4229 S.W. Beach Ave.   AmEx/Visa/MC, Dep. Required •
Lincoln City, OR 97367   41 condos, Lo-rise, Key at Office No S-yes
503-996-3623 800-648-2119

Location: Airport: 90 miles; Need car; Beach front

General Facilities: Daily maid; Linens; Crib-Hi-chair

Sports Facilities: Pool; Golf and tennis near

Room Facilities: Kitchen; Cable; Ind.Heat Ctl.

Attractions: Ocean activities, whale watching, surf fishing, horseback riding, beachcombing

Shops & Restaurants: Gift shops

Individually owned and decorated condominium units, some with oceanfront view, with an indoor swimming pool. Located near four golf courses, top-rated restaurants, art galleries and wine tasting facilities. Try surf or deep-sea fishing, beachcombing, kite flying or go on a picnic.

————————————————— SUNRIVER —————————————————

Sunriver Resort   Studio $$, 1 Bedroom $$$,
P.O. Box 3609   2 Bedrooms $$$, 3 Bedrooms $$$
Sunriver, OR 97707
503-593-1221 800-547-3922
FAX: 503-593-4683

General Facilities: Linens

Sports Facilities: Pool; Tennis; Nature Center, Canoeing

Room Facilities: Kitchen; Phone

Attractions: 54 holes of Championship Golf. Whitewater rafting, horseback riding, skiing @ Mt. Bachelor

15 miles south of Bend, 300 days of sunshine, snowcapped Mt. Bachelor, lush forests, golf, tennis, skiing, kids klub, nature center, fishing guide, shopping mall, 2 pools, restaurants, all at the Sunriver Resort. Daily ski shuttle, ski and rental shop.

──────────── WELCHES ────────────

Rippling River
68010 E. Fairway Ave.
Welches, OR 97067
503-622-3101 800-547-8054

1 Bedroom $$, 2 Bedrooms $$$
Pool, Kitchen

Attractions: Skiing, golf, tennis, fishing, bicycling, hiking

Come and enjoy the clean mountain air, fantastic scenery and year-round activities. All the comforts of home with all the vacation amenities you'd ever want. Lounges for beverages and entertainment, casual to elegant dining rooms. Easy access to three skiing areas.

Please mention *Condo Vacations the Complete Guide* when you reserve your condominium.

Pennsylvania

Scotrun
Greentown Tamiment
Lake Harmony Lackwaxen
Reeders Hawley Tannersville
Buck Hill Falls
Analomink Shawnee on the Delaware

Champion
Somerset Bedford Springs

---------------------- ANALOMINK ----------------------

Alpine Village
Analomink, PA 18320
800-233-8240

2 Bedrooms $$$, Villas
Kitchen

Attractions: Mineral & Gem Museum, Mine Replica, 1867 Chapel, Petrified Gardens

Ski to the slopes from your charming Swiss chalet. Slopeside chalets with indoor pools, steam and whirlpool baths. "Just for Kids" programs at Alpine Mountain. Separate trails for advanced and beginner skiers. Year-round ice skating at Penn Hills.

Penn Estates
In the Poconos
Analomink, PA 18320
717-424-8795 800-233-4122

2 Bedrooms $$$$, Villas
Pool, Kitchen, Linens

Attractions: Roller skating, horse racing, bowling, horseback riding, golf, gym, spa, hiking, tennis, golf

Villas offering indoor pool with whirlpool in a tropical setting. Microwaves, trash compactors, Thermasol steam and whirlpool baths. Restaurant with take-out service. Live entertainment in Reflections Nite Club. So much to do you'll never want to leave.

———————————— CHAMPION ————————————

Seven Springs Mountain Resort Studio $$$, 1 Bedroom 3$, 2 Bedrooms 4$,
R.D. #1   3 Bedrooms 5$, 1 Bed/week 4$,
Champion, PA 15622   2 Bed/week 5$, 3 Bed/week 7$
814-352-7777 800-458-2313   Min. stay 2 nights, Dep. req'd
                                   Key at Lodge front desk
                                   500 condos, Villas, H-yes

Location: Airport: 75 miles; Downtown: 17 miles; Need car; Ski lift: 1 mile

General facilities: Bus. fac., Conf. Rm. (cap. 1500), Daily maid, Kitchen, Linens, Animal walk/minigolf, Baby-sitter, Restaurant, Bar, Game room, Lounge, Sauna, Hot tub

Room facilities: TV, Cable, Phone, Crib-Hi-chair, Ind. AC. Ctl, Ind. Heat Ctl.

Sports facilities: Pool, Tennis, Mini-golf, Bowling

Attractions: Fallingwater, white water raft., Fort Ligonier, state parks, "whoola" hoop contest, darts, entertainment

Shops & Restaurants: 12 shops-boutiques onsite, drug, grocery, K-Mart, Helen's/French, Amr. Italian

Modern contemporary villas and townhouses situated among the scenic Laurel Highland Mountains. Activities Staff offers varying activities each day, dining, dancing and entertainment. Indoor pool, mini golf, bowling alleys, racquetball & health spa, petting zoo, game rooms, sports massage, water sports, beauty parlor and roller skating. Summer or winter there's always something to do, or you can do nothing but enjoy the relaxed family atmosphere.

———————————— FARMINGTON ————————————

Nemacolin Woodlands Resort 1 Bedroom $$$, 2 Bedrooms $$$$,
Rte. 40, P.O. Box 188   3 Bedrooms $$$$, Amex, Visa, MC
Farmington, PA 15437   Key at Front desk
412-329-8555 800-422-2736   70 condos, H-yes •

Location: Airport: Airstrip on-site; Downtown: 70 miles

General facilities: Full serv., Conf. Rm. (cap. 300), Daily maid, Kitchen, Linens, Baby sitter, Restaurant, Bar, Game room, Lounge, Sauna, Skiing

Room facilities: TV, Cable, Phone, Crib-Hi-Chair, Ind. AC. Ctl., Ind. Heat Ctl.

Sports facilities: Pool, Tennis, Woodlands Golf Links, Health spa, Croquet

Attractions: Fallingwater, Ft. Necessity, Laurel Caverns, Ohiopyle State Park, entertainment

Shops & Restaurants: 5 restaurants on property, Golden Trout/nouvelle cuisine

Luxury mountain resort nestled on 550 wooded acres deep in the breath-taking Laurel Mountains of Pennsylvania. Its many facets include three lakes; Executive Conference Center with 200 seat amphitheater; individualized pampering at the World Class Spa; 18-hole PGA Golf Course; the Golf Academy is one of the top learning centers in the country; and five unique dining experiences.

Please mention *Condo Vacations—the Complete Guide* when you reserve your condominium.

——————————————— HAWLEY ———————————————

Tanglewood Lakes
P.O. Box 257
Hawley, PA 18428
717-226-3000

1 Bedroom $$, 2 Bedrooms $$$

General facilities: Kitchen, Linens

Sports facilities: Pool, tennis, Skiing, rec. room

High quality accommodations with a friendly staff to assist you. Skiing in season at property slopes. Daily planned activities, docks for your boat, recreation room, snack bar and ski lodge.

——————————— MARSHALLS CREEK/BUSHKILL ———————————

The Fairway Villas
P.O. Box 1379
Marshalls Creek
Bushkill, PA 18335
717-588-6669 800-343-8676

2 Bedrooms $$$
2 Bed/week 5-8
Min. stay 2 nights, Visa, MC
120 condos, Lo-rise,
Key at Log Cabin (on-site)

Location: Airport: Newark—2 hours, Downtown: Allentown—1 hour, Ski lift: On-site

General facilities: Conf. Rm. (cap. 1200), Daily maid, Kitchen, Child planned rec., Baby sitter, Restaurant, Bar, Game room, Lounge

Room facilities: TV, Cable, VCR, Phone, Crib-Hi-chair, Fireplace, Jaccuzzi

Sports facilities: IN/OUT Pool, IN/OUT Tennis, 18 hole Champ Golf Course, Rafting, Hiking

Attractions: Bushkill Falls "The Niagara of Pennsylvania", Delaware Water Gap, Amusement Parks.

Shops & Restaurants: Pocono outlet complex (40 stores), American Candle Factory., The Weathervane International Menu

Located at Fernwood Resort and Country Club and neighbors 70,000 acres of Delaware Water Gap National Recreational Area. Enjoy the comfort of your luxury vacation villa and the excitement of the full recreational facilities. See the beauty of our resort in any season in the Pocono Mountains of Pennsylvania. There is something for everyone at The Fairway Villas.

The Fairway Villas, Marshalls Creek, PA

-------------------- PITTSBURGH --------------------

Bahamas Home Rentals
230 Lawrence Ave.
Pittsburgh, PA 15238
412-828-1048
FAX: 412-781-0607

1 Bedroom $$, 2 Bedrooms $$$,
3 Bedrooms $$$$.

General Facilities: Fishing guides, Water skiing, Baby sitter.

Attractions: Fishing, golf, tennis, boating, trips to caves, deserted cays.

Shops & Restaurants: Food shopping always nearby, shopping areas, Bahamian, German, Chinese.

Over 100 cottages, condos, villas and even private islands. Locations vary from extremely private areas (where skinny dipping is OK) to areas near resorts and/or casinos. Most are on the many pristine beaches of the Bahamas, and accommodations vary from economical to luxurious. Amenities vary with the property, but every effort will be made to see that your home or condo has everything you need for your particular interests and requirements.

-------------------- SOMERSET --------------------

Hidden Valley Resort
RD 4, Box 243, 1 Craighead Dr.
Somerset, PA 15501
800-443-6454 800-458-0175
FAX: 814-443-1907

1 Bedroom $$$$, 2 Bedrooms $$$$, Jr. $$$,
3 Bedrooms $$$$, AmEx/Visa/MC, Dep.
1 Night.
All Villas, NoS-yes, H-yes, Key at front desk.

Location: Airport: 75 miles; Downtown: 12 miles.

General Facilities: Bus. fac., Conf. Rm. Cap.: 350, Lounge, Pool, Hot tub, Sauna, Child planned rec., 16 slopes, Tennis, 18-hole golf, fitness trail/health club, Baby sitter, Restaurant, Bar.

Room Facilities: Daily maid, Kitchen, TV, Cable, Phone, Ind. AC. Ctl., Ind. Heat Ctl.

Attractions: Frank Lloyd Wright's Fallingwater, Laurel Caverns, Ft. Ligonier, Storybook Forest.

Shops & Restaurants: Outlet stores, antiques, ceramics, crafts, entertainment, Brass Duck/continental.

Villas and townhouses with beautifully appointed rooms designed for maximum convenience on a 2,000 acre resort community in the Laurel Highlands of southwestern Pennsylvania, one hour from Pittsburgh. Fresh mountain air in this all-season resort with 12 tennis courts, 16 ski slopes, 18-hole golf course. Complete conference center. Fine dining at the Hearthside Restaurant.

We want to hear from you—any comments regarding the condos or our publication may be noted on the form at the end of the book.

Rhode Island

Newport

🐚 Block Island

―――――――――――――――――― BLOCK ISLAND ――――――――――――――――――

Island Manor Resort
Chapel St, Box 400
Block Island, RI 02807
401-466-5567

1 Bedroom $$, Lo-rise
Daily maid, Kitchen, Linens

Attractions: Settler's Rock and North Light, The Maze, Clay Head Cliffs, Lapham wildlife estate, Bicycles

A nature lover's island paradise. Trails through pines, flowers and ponds, rolling hills, stone fences, wildlife, view cliffs and crescent beach. Efficiency units with kitchettes, and one bedroom suites. Run by the McCabe family who will be happy to help you.

―――――――――――――――――――――― NEWPORT ――――――――――――――――――――――

The Newport Bay Club
America's Cup Avenue, Box 1440
Newport, RI 02840
401-849-8600

1 Bedroom $$$, 2 Bedrooms $$$$, Hi-rise
Kitchen, Phone in rm.

Attractions: Nearby health club, racquetball, swimming, Nautilus, waterfront, docks, antiques, museums

You are in the heart of Newport Bay, on the waterfront, and within walking distance to shops, antiques, museums, restaurants and nightclubs when you stay here. Suites with deluxe marble baths and jacuzzis, or two-level townhouses with balconies on both levels.

―――

Newport Onshore
379 Thames
Newport, RI 02840
401-849-8553 800-842-2480

1 Bedroom $$, 2 Bedrooms $$, Hi-rise
Pool, Kitchen

Attractions: Newport Harbor, marina

On Thames Street, directly on Newport Harbor with its seventy-five slip marina. Classic, contemporary outside architecture, landscaped quadrangle and pool with harborfront lawn. All units have two private sun decks, fireplaces, and double whirlpool tubs.

Paki Maui

NEWPORT

The Wellington Yacht Club
543 Thames at Wellington
Newport, RI 02840
401-849-1770

Studio $$, 1 Bedroom $$$, 2 Bedrooms $$$$
1 Bedrm/week 10$, 2 Bed/week 10$
Min. Stay 2 Nights, AmEx/Visa/MC,
Dep. Req'd.
50 condos, Lo-rise, Key at Office
H-yes

Location: Airport: 45 minutes; Downtown: 2 blocks

General Facilities: Kitchen, Linens, Baby-sitter, Child planned rec.: Pool parties

Room Facilities: Pool, Sauna, Tennis, Health club, Golf: Several courses nearby; TV, Cable, VCR, Phone in rm., Crib-Hi-chair, Ind. AC Ctl., Ind. Heat Ctl.

Attractions: Mansion tours, antique shopping, beaches, boating, music festival, shows, trolley tours, entertainment

Shops & Restaurants: Benettons, Brick Market shops, Bannisters Wharf; Clare Cooke House-Black Pearl

Harborfront condominiums with water view. Enjoy the excitement of Newport's nightlife or the leisurely atmosphere of Newport's historical sites, sailing, shopping, and antiquing. Children's splash parties, barbecues, sailing charters, cocktail parties, and complimentary continental breakfast.

South Carolina

Surfside Beach — N. Myrtle Beach, Myrtle Beach

Pawleys Island
Georgetown
Charleston — Edisto Island
Hilton Head Island

─────────────── CHARLESTON ───────────────

Seabrook Conference Resort
P.O. Box 32099
Charleston, SC 29417
800-922-2401 800-845-2475

Studio $$, 1 Bedroom $$$,
2 Bedrooms $$$$-, 3 Bedrooms 5$
1 Bed/week $$$$, 2 Bed/week 4$,
3 Bed/week 6$
Min. stay 2 nights, Amex, Visa, MC,
Dep. req'd
60 condos, Villas,
Key at Seabrook Reception
No S-yes, H-yes

Location: Airport: Charleston International 60 miles, 45 miles south of historic Charleston, Need car, 0.5 mile to beach, 90 miles north of Savannah, GA

General facilities: Full serv., Bus. fac., Conf. Rm. (cap. 250), Daily maid, Kitchen, Linens, Planned programs, Baby-sitter, Restaurant, Bar, Game room, Lounge, Marina view

Room facilities: TV, Cable, Phone, Crib-Hi-chair, Ind.AC.Ctl, Ind.Heat Ctl., linens, crib and highchairs available for rent, full-size kitchens; some with fireplaces, some jacuzzi tubs

Sports facilities: Pool, Tennis, 2 golf courses, Horses, fishing

Attractions: Equestrian center, bicycles, sailboats, deep-sea charters, fishing & crabbing equipment, entertainment

Shops & Restaurants: Seabrook Shoppe, Village Market, Village Spirits, Island House-Seaview-Capt Sams, restaurant on-site

Located on historic Edisto Island, just a short walk to one of South Carolina's premier beaches for shelling and fossil hunting. Unspoiled, in hurried, quiet, family beach. Edisto Beach State Park is just minutes away. Access to seven miles of beach. Recreation staff plans children's activities, nature exploration, movies and dancing.

--------------------------- CHARLESTON ---------------------------

Wild Dunes—Charleston's   1 Bedroom $$, 2 Bedrooms $$$,
Island   3 Bedrooms $$$$
P.O. Box 1410   1 Bed/week 5$, 2 Bed/week 6$,
Charleston, SC 29402   3 Bed/week 8$
803-886-6000   800-845-8880   Amex, Visa, MC, Dep. 1 night
                                     Lo-rise, Villas

Location: Airport: Charleston 35 min., Downtown: 15 miles, Beach front

General facilities: Daily maid, Kitchen, Linens, Activity programs, Restaurant

Room facilities: TV, Phone, Ind.AC Ctl., Ind.Heat Ctl.

Sports facilities: Pool, Tennis, 2 courses, Yacht Harbor

Attractions: Deep sea fishing, harbor cruises, creek fishing, tennis, golf

Shops & Restaurants: General store, Mt. Pleasant and Charleston shops, Island
   House/seafood, The Club

*Luxuriously furnished, extremely spacious villas by the ocean, golf course, tennis
courts, or lagoon. Convenient to all sports activities. Canoe trips, swimming lessons,
story telling for children. Beachside cabana with snacks and beverages. Floats,
chairs, umbrellas, sailboats and windsurfer rentals. Stocked fresh water lagoons for
fishing, or yacht harbor private charters. Restaurants with specialty menus, and
family cookouts at the beach.*

--------------------------- GARDEN CITY ---------------------------

Water's Edge Resort   1 Bedroom $$$, 2 Bedrooms $$$
1012 N. Waccamaw Dr.   1 Bed/week 7$, 2 Bed/week 10$,
Garden City, SC 29576   3 Bed/week 10$
P.O. Box 8159   Min. stay 3 nights, Amex, Visa, MC,
Myrtle Beach, 29578   Dep. req'd
803-651-0002   800-255-5554   145 condos, Hi-rise,
                                     Key at Front desk
                                     H-yes

Location: Airport: 7 miles, 9 miles south of Myrtle Beach, Ocean front

General facilities: Full serv., Conf. Rm. (cap. 25), Daily maid, Kitchen, Linens,
   Baby sitter, Game room, Lounge, Hot tub

Room facilities: TV, Cable, Phone, A/C, Heat, Ind.Heat Ctl.

Sports facilities: Pool, Nearby child planned rec.

Attractions: Golf, fishing, tennis, boating, Brookgreen Gardens, Carolina Opry,
   Dixie Stampede, family water parks, zoo, miniature golf

Shops & Restaurants: Waccamaw Pottery Outlet Park, shopping malls,
Barefoot Landing, Murrells Inlet (seafood capital of SC)

*Each spacious Water's Edge suite is complete with all of life's necessities and includes
private oceanfront balconies. Enjoy the pools and whirlpools, or sun worship on the
beach. Summer children's activity programs and live entertainment. Minutes from
outstanding sightseeing, shopping and premier golf courses. Golf and honeymoon
packages. Easy to get to, but hard to leave. Sorry, no pets.*

——————————— HILTON HEAD ISLAND ———————————

Continental Club
12 South Forest Beach Dr.
Hilton Head Island, SC 29928
803-842-3224 800-367-8211

1 Bedroom $. 2 Bedroom $$, Lo-rise
Pool, Daily maid, Kitchen, Linens, Phone.

Attractions: 13 award-winning golf courses, Sunday polo, marinas, equestrian centers.

Located on the southern end of an 18 mile-long island, these 16 townhouses are designer decorated with private landscaped courtyards. Swimming pool is just outside your door, and you are right across from the beach. Play tennis at Van de Meer Tennis Center.

Cottages at Shipyard Plantation
P.O. Box 7528
Hilton Head Island, SC 29938
803-686-4424 800-255-2471

1 Bedroom $, 2 Bedroom $$, Lo-rise.
Pool, Daily maid, Linens.

Attractions: Golf courses, tennis, shops, restaurants, fitness center.

New townhomes designed in the Low Country manner, clustered in a private park with shady porches overlooking the lagoons and fairways. Reception center with indoor/outdoor pool, fitness center and racquetball. Immediate access to Shipyard golf, tennis and the beach.

Hilton Head Island Beach Club
40 Folly Field Rd.
Hilton Head Island, SC 29928
803-842-4402 800-845-9508

1 Bedroom $$, 2 Bedrooms $$, Villas.
Pool, Kitchen, Linens.

Attractions: Swimming, tennis, golf, beach.

Marriott Villa Vacations
P.O. Box 6959
Hilton Head, SC 29938
803-785-2040 800-527-3490
FAX: 803-686-3677

2 Bedrooms $$$$, 2 Bedrm/week 13$,
3 Bedrm/week 9$, Min. Stay: 3 Nights,
AmEx/Visa/MC, •
400 condos, Hi-rise, Villas, H-yes, Key at
Marriott Welcome Center.

Location: Airport: 8 miles; Downtown: 35 miles, Need car.

General Facilities: Pool, Sauna, Child planned rec., Tennis, Nearby, boating, sailing, rides, Baby sitter.

Room Facilities: Daily maid, Kitchen, TV, Cable, Phone, Crib-Hi-chair, Ind. AC. Ctl., Ind. Heat Ctl.

Attractions: Golf, tennis, deep sea fishing, bikes, jogging, Savannah, GA, Charleston, SC (100 miles), entertainment.

Shops & Restaurants: All types from specialty shops to factory outlets, Area restaurants.

Marriott Vacation Villas are located throughout Hilton Head Island. Your choice of ocean front, harborside, fairway, lagoons or intracoastal waterway. Private luxury villas with a superb beach, great championship golf, tennis, boating and fishing. Sophisticated shops and restaurants. Great for family vacations or get-away mini-vacations. Packages available.

———————————— HILTON HEAD ISLAND ————————————

Palmetto Dunes
P.O. Box 5606
Hilton Head Island, SC 29938
803-785-1161 800-845-6130

1 Bedroom $$$, 2 Bedrooms $$$$
Lo-rise, Villas

One to four bedroom fully equipped villas in various locations. Large living and dining areas, patios and decks. Private access to three miles of beach, tennis, golf, bicycle and boat rentals. 25 pools in the resort, and kiddie pools for the children.

Sea Pines Resort
Box 7000
Hilton Head Island, SC 29938
803-785-3333 FAX: 803-842-1475
800-SEAPINES

1 Bedroom $$, 2 Bedrooms $$$,
3 Bedrooms $$$
1 Bedrm/week 5$, 2 Bedrms/week 5$,
3 Bedrms/week 5$
Dep. Required, 415 condos, Villas,
Key at Welcoming Center

Location: Airport: Savannah, GA 45 min.; Downtown: close; Oceanfront

General Facilities: Daily maid; Linens; Lounge; Restaurant; Bar

Sports Facilities: Fitness center; Pool; Tennis; Marina, charters; 3 championship courses; Summer Fun for Kids

Room Facilities: Kitchen; Cable

Attractions: 605 acre Forest Preserve, entertainment, summer concerts, art galleries, dinner cruises; entertainment

Shops & Restaurants: Harbour Town, Sea Pines Center, South Beach Marina; Casual & fine dining, outdoor cookouts

Our red and white striped lighthouse in Harbour Town has been welcoming guests at Sea Pines for years. 415 one- to six-bedroom villas and private homes with elegant furnishings, many with golf course, harbour, ocean or marsh views and centrally located to resort amenities. Mild year-round temperatures for all season enjoyment.

––––––––––––––––––– HILTON HEAD ISLAND –––––––––––––––––––

Sea Pines Villas
P.O. Box 6959
Hilton Head Island, SC 29938
803-785-2040 800-527-3490

Villas
Pool, Kitchen, Linens

Attractions: Tennis, golf, deep-sea fishing, sailing, horseback riding, jogging, bird-watching

Privacy and relaxed comfort at various locations within Sea Pines Plantation.

Spinnaker & Southwind at Shipyard
25 Bow Circle, P.O. Box 6899
Hilton Head Island, SC 29938
803-785-4881 800-336-3224

2 Bedrms/week 6$, 3 Bed/week 8$
Min. Stay 7 Nights, Dep. Req'd. •
70 condos, Lo-rise, Key at Poolhouse

Location: Airport: 10 Min./Hilton Head; Need car

General Facilities: Kitchen, Linens, Game room, Lounge

Room Facilities: Pool, Sauna, Hot tub, Tennis, Bikes, playground, TV, Cable, VCR, Phone in rm., Crib-Hi-chair, Ind. AC Ctl., Ind. Heat Ctl.

Attractions: 12 miles of sugar sand beach, 25 golf courses, 300 tennis courts, fishing, boating, horses, entertainment

Shops & Restaurants: 30 shopping plazas, two outlet malls-A. Klein; Harbour-master/cont. & seafood

Delicate summer colors of light pinks, greens & blues accent the designer decorated beauty of each unit. All villas have either golf or lagoon views and are located inside private gates. Free golf and tennis, two blocks to the beach, weekly family cookouts at the pool, children's playground, steam room and nautilus. Many elegant shops and restaurants as well as numerous recreational activities.

––––––––––––––––––––––– HILTON HEAD –––––––––––––––––––––––

Heritage Club at Harbour Town
P.O. Box 6959
Hilton Head, SC 29938
803-785-2040 800-527-3490

Villas
Pool, Kitchen, Linens

Attractions: Golf, tennis, deepsea fishing, sailing, horses, bikes, jogging, beach, exercise equipment

Sophisticated accommodations in luxury villas with two master suites, each with whirl-pool baths. Gas log fireplace, formal dining area and three color TV's. Clubhouse with health and exercise equipment. Harbour Town yatch basin and lighthouse to visit.

––––––––––––––––––––––– MYRTLE BEACH –––––––––––––––––––––––

Jade Tree Cove
200 75th Avenue
Mrytle Beach, SC 29577
803-449-9455

Phone in rm.

Attractions: Tennis

──────────────── MYRTLE BEACH ────────────────

Beach Colony Resort
5308 North Ocean Boulevard
Myrtle Beach, SC 29577
803-449-4010 800-222-2141

Studio $, 1 Bedroom $, 2 Bedrooms $$,
3 Bedrooms $$
1 Bedrm/week $$$$, 2 Bed/week 4$,
3 Bed/week 5$
AmEx/Visa/MC, Dep. 1 Night •
154 condos, Hi-rise, Key at Front desk
H-yes

Location: Airport: 6½ miles; Downtown: 3 miles; Need car; Beach front

General Facilities: Full serv., Conf. rm. cap. 60, Daily maid, Kitchen, Linens, Restaurant on prem., Bar on prem., Lounge, Baby-sitter, Child planned rec.: Summer months only

Room Facilities: Pool, Sauna, Hot tub, Racquet, exercise room, Golf: Pine Lakes; TV, Cable, Phone in rm., Crib-Hi-chair, Ind. AC Ctl., Ind. Heat Ctl.

Attractions: Brookgreen Gardens, deep-sea fishing, dinner cruises, Carolina Opry, Georgetown tours, entertainment

Shops & Restaurants: Waccamaw Pottery outlet, Briarcliffe Mall; Fusco's, Mayor's House/cont.

Oceanfront accommodations conveniently located. Three outdoor and one indoor pool, playing privileges at Pine Lakes Country Club and free tennis at Myrtle Beach Tennis & Swim Club. Summer games and prizes for the children. Ocean setback, complemented by native flora, hibiscus, sea oats and palm fronds, and a boardwalk across the dunes. Outdoor pool bar and grill.

───────────────────────────────

Beach House Golf & Racquet Club
6800 North Ocean Boulevard
Myrtle Beach, SC 29577
803-449-7484

1 Bedroom $, 2 Bedrooms $, Hi-rise
Pool

Attractions: Golf

Condominiums with balcony views of Myrtle Beach and pool. Free tennis at Myrtle Beach Racquet Club, and 25 area golf courses. Restaurant row to the north. Five minutes to the downtown hub.

───────────────────────────────

Bluewater Resort
P.O. Box 3000
Myrtle Beach, SC 29578
803-626-8345 800-845-6994

1 Bedroom $, 2 Bedrooms $$, Hi-rise
Pool, Kitchen

Attractions: Myrtle Beach Pavillion, water parks & slides, Brookwood Gardens, Wildlife Park, mini golf, racquet-exercise room, golf

Vast array of apartments, suites, condominiums and villas on Myrtle Beach. Five indoor and outdoor whirlpools, 5 outdoor pools, extra large indoor pool with glass covered removed in summer and a special private pool for children.

Sands of Kahana

———————————— MYRTLE BEACH ————————————

Caribbean Chelsea House Villas   2 Bedrooms $$, Lo-rise
30th Avenue North   Pool, Kitchen
Myrtle Beach, SC 29577
803-448-7181 800-845-0883

Attractions: Amusement Parks, tennis, fishing, golf, theaters, charter fishing, shuffleboard

You and the children come home relaxed and contented after your vacation at the Caribbean. Swim in the pool and sun on the large wooden deck where you can get lunch and drinks from the poolside bar. Build sandcastles and hunt for shells on the beach.

Carolina Winds   1 Bedroom $, Hi-rise
200 76th Ave. N, Drawer 7518   Pool, Kitchen
Myrtle Beach, SC 29578
803-449-2477 800-523-4027

Attractions: Pavilion, water slides, water sports park, miniature golf, golf, tennis, exercise room

On the beach with an oceanfront pool, one bedroom suites and three bedroom condominiums. Indoor and outdoor whirlpools and indoor pool. Exercise room and large kiddie pool. Free tennis at Myrtle Beach Racquet Club and world famous golf courses. On-site restaurant.

─────────────── MYRTLE BEACH ───────────────

Four Seasons Beach Resort   1 Bedroom $, 2 Bedrooms $
5801 N. Ocean Blvd.
Myrtle Beach, SC 29577
803-449-6441

Sports Facilities: Golf

Room Facilities: Kitchen

Attractions: Grand Strand, Myrtle Beach, water sports

Attractive, comfortable units on the quiet cabana section of the Grand Strand. Lifeguard on duty at the beach, or swim and play water games in the pool. Shops and restaurants nearby in the Myrtle Beach area.

───────────────────────────────────

Sands Beach Club   1 Bedroom $$, 2 Bedrooms $$
9400 Shore Dr.   AmEx/Visa/MC, 1 Night Dep. Req'd. •
Myrtle Beach, SC 29572   225 condos, Hi-rise,
803-449-1531 800-845-6701   Key at Registration desk
FAX: 803-449-1879   H-Yes

Location: Airport: 12 miles; Downtown: 7 miles; Need car; Beachfront

General Facilities: Full hotel service; Linens; Baby sitter; Crib-Hi-chair; Restaurant on premises; Bar on premises

Sports Facilities: Pool; Hot tub; Tennis; Racquet, basketball; Golf Course nearby; Child planned recreation

Room Facilities: Kitchen; Cable; Phone; Ind.AC.Ctl.; Ind.Heat Ctl.

Attractions: 85 championship golf courses in the area, shopping, beach, sightseeing; Entertainment

Shops & Restaurants: Barefoot Landing, Myrtle Square Mall, Waccawaw pottery; Broadway at the Beach- seafood, steaks

Ocean front and ocean view condominiums located on exclusive Shore Drive. Family oriented, free summer children's activity program, indoor/outdoor pool and whirlpool in this all-suite resort hotel. Two tennis courts, racquetball and basketball.

─────────────── N. MYRTLE BEACH ───────────────

Condotels Of America   Min. Stay Ask, AmEx/Visa/MC •
2703 Highway 17 South   150 condos, Hi-rise, Lo-rise, Key at Office,
N. Myrtle Beach, SC 29582   P-No/H-Yes
803-272-8400 800-845-0631
FAX: 803-272-6556

Location: Airport: 20 minutes; Downtown: 20 minutes; Beachfront

General Facilities: Daily maid; Linens; Crib-Hi-Chair

Sports Facilities: Pool; Tennis; Fishing; Possum Trot/Cypress Bay

Room Facilities: Kitchen; Cable; VCR; Phone; Ind.AC.Ctl.; Ind.Heat Ctl.

Attractions: Miles of sandy beach, Barefoot Landing, Alabama Theatre, Restaurant Row, Briarcliffe Mall

Shops & Restaurants: Belk, Penneys, hundreds of unique shops at malls; Italian, Mexican, Seafood, Japanese near

Spacious beyond compare, Condotels has more living area than any hotel room. Our second home condos are sweeter than "suites," making them the choice accommodation for today's vacationers. Condotels' 2-, 3- and 4-bedroom homes provide over 1000 sq.ft. of living space. Beautiful furnishings and accessories decorate every living room, the center of family activities. Relax and spread out on a comfortable sofa or sink into an easy chair. Plenty of room for everyone to gather and share a great time!

──────────────── MYRTLE BEACH ────────────────

Ocean Forest Villa Resort   2 Bedrooms $$, 2 Bed/week 7$
5601 North Ocean Blvd.   Amex, Visa, MC, Dep. 1 night
Myrtle Beach, SC 29578   Key at Registration desk
803-449-9661 800-845-6701   243 condos, Villas •

Location: Airport: 8 miles; Downtown: 4 miles; Need car; Beach front

General facilities: Full serv., Daily maid, Kitchen, Linens, Child planned rec.,
Baby-sitter, Hot tub

Room facilities: TV, Cable, Phone, Crib-Hi-chair, Ind. AC. Ctl., Ind. Heat Ctl.

Sports facilities: Pool, Golf nearby

Attractions: 65 championship golf courses nearby, sightseeing tours, 60 miles
of beach

Shops & Restaurants: Waacawaw pottery, Briar Cliff & Myrtle Square Mall,
Barefoot

*Family vacation resort with pool or beach views. Situated in Pine Lakes residential
area. 10 acres, 1,100 feet of sandy beach across Ocean Boulevard. All condominiums
are two bedroom, one queen bed, two twins and a sleeper sofa. Two outdoor pools
and two outdoor whirlpools. Golf packages available.*

───

Ocean Park Condominiums   1 Bedroom $, 2 Bedrooms $$
1905 S. Ocean Blvd.   Hi-rise
Myrtle Beach, SC 29578
803-448-1915 800-624-8539

General facilities: Kitchen, Linens

Sports facilities: Pool, Golf course, Exercise room

Attractions: Myrtle Waves Water Park, Amusement Park, golf, sailing, surfing,
fishing, tennis

*Large variety of floor plans in new luxury units. Kitchens with microwaves and
self-defrosting refrigerators. Glass enclosed indoor pool overlooking the Atlantic and
outside free-form pool. Exercise room with tanning lounge.*

───

Ramada Ocean Forest Resort   Amex, Visa, MC, Dep. 1 night
5523 North Ocean Blvd.   Key at Front desk
Myrtle Beach, SC 29578   193 condos
803-497-0044 800-522-0818   Hi-rise, No S-yes, P-yes, H-yes •

Location: Airport: 8 miles; Downtown: 3 miles; Need car; Beach front

General facilities: Full serv., Conf. Rm. (cap. 100), Daily maid, Kitchen, Linens,
Restaurant, Bar, Lounge, Sauna, Hot tub

Room facilities: TV, Cable, Phone, Crib-Hi-chair, Ind. AC. Ctl, Ind. Heat Ctl.

Sports facilities: Pool, 50 Golf courses in area, Health club

Attractions: Carolina Opry, Brookgreen Gardens, Sculpture Garden, Myrtle
Beach Pavilion, water park

Shops & Restaurants: Waccamaw pottery, Briarcliffe & Myrtle Square Mall,
Gullyfield/seafood

*Luxury oceanfront accommodations in full service hotel. Condominiums have pastel
decor, 2 double beds and private balcony with ocean view. Complimentary airport
van service. Golf and honeymoon packages.*

———————————— MYRTLE BEACH ————————————

Sands Ocean Club
500 Shore Dr.
Myrtle Beach, SC 29577
803-449-6461

Studio $, 1 Bedroom $$, 2 Bedrooms $$,
3 Bedrooms $$$
Amex, Visa, MC, Dep. req'd
Hi-rise

Location: Airport: 8 miles, Downtown: 3 miles, Beach front

General facilities: Kitchen, Seasonal program, Restaurant, Bar, Game room, Lounge, Sauna, Hot tub

Room facilities: TV, Cable, Ind.AC Ctl.

Sports facilities: Pool, Tennis, Pawleys Plantation, Fitness Center

Attractions: Carolina Opry, Brookgreen Gardens, Mt. Olympus Waterslide, Myrtle Beach Pavilion, entertainment

Shops & Restaurants: Myrtle Square Mall, Waccamaw pottery, gift shop, Windows-on-site/seafood-steaks

Suites overlooking The Atlantic Ocean and Grand Strand beaches where you'll soon be swimming or sunbathing. Fully-equipped fitness center for working out or resting in heated whirlpools. Glass enclosed indoor pool. After a hard day playing tennis or golf, sit back and relax at Sandals Lounge with its happy hour, complimentary hors d'oeuvres and nightly entertainment. Also popular is Ocean Annie's beach bar with its's pool parties, bikini contests and live entertainment. Special honeymoon packages.

Be sure to call the condo to verify details and prices and to make your reservation.

——————————— N. MYRTLE BEACH ———————————

Maritime Beach Club
400 N. Ocean Blvd.
N. Myrtle Beach, SC 29582
803-249-3414

1 Bedroom $$, 2 Bedrooms $$, Hi-rise
Pool, Kitchen, Phone in rm.

Attractions: Swim, shell, sail, fish, jog, golf, tennis

Condominiums with full ocean views, ceramic tile entries and baths with raised tubs, private dressing rooms and designer kitchens, in a professionally landscaped setting. A great vacation for children—private exits to beach.

Tilghman Beach & Racquet Club
P.O. Box 315
North Myrtle Beach, SC 29597
803-249-3457 800-334-5061

Lo-rise
Pool, Kitchen

Attractions: Beach, surfing, golf, amusements, fishing pier, tennis

On-site pier and shell-covered beach for fishing, beachcombing or long walks. Oceanfront condominiums with screened porch and balcony off the master bedroom. Children's pool and family picnic area. Lie quietly on the beach and be soothed by the sun and sound of waves.

——————————— PAWLEYS ISLANDS ———————————

Litchfield By The Sea
U.S. Hwy. 17, P.O. Drawer 320
Pawleys Islands, SC 29585
803-237-4225 800-845-1897

2 Bedrooms $$, Hi-rise, Lo-rise, Villas
Pool, Kitchen, Linens

Attractions: Swim, bicycle, sail, fish, Brookgreen Gardens, colonial plantation tours, health club, racquetball, tennis, golf

Wide range of villas and townhomes with varying views and amenities. Each condominium group has its own pool and beach access. Guests may use the Waccamaw House facilities—indoor and outdoor pools, health club, racquetball courts, jacuzzi, lounge and movie theaters.

Please mention *Condo Vacations the Complete Guide* when you reserve your condominium.

────────────── SURFSIDE BEACH ──────────────

Myrtle Beach Resort
P.O. Box 14428, 5905 Frontage Rd.
Surfside Beach, SC 29587
803-828-8000 800-845-0359

Studio $$, 1 Bedroom $$, 2 Bedrooms $$$
1 Bedrm/week $$$$, 2 Bed/week 4$,
  3 Bed/week 6$
AmEx/Visa/MC, Dep. Req'd. •
300 condos, Hi-rise, Lo-rise, Key at Rental office

Location: Airport: 3 miles; Downtown: 6 miles; Need car; Beach front

General Facilities: Full serv., Bus. fac., Conf. rm. cap. 50, Daily maid, Kitchen, Linens, Restaurant on prem., Bar on prem., Game room, Child planned rec.: Peak season activity

Room Facilities: Pool, Sauna, Tennis, 2 exercise rooms, Golf: Deertrack; TV, Phone in rm., Crib-Hi-chair, Ind. AC Ctl., Ind. Heat Ctl.

Attractions: Tennis, golf, beach, Myrtle Beach amusements, Carolina Opry, Brookgreen Gardens, entertainment

Shops & Restaurants: General store, Waccamaw Pottery, Outlet Park; Local seafood restaurants

A 44-acre family resort among woods and lagoons with windswept dunes and sandy beach. Attractive wood bridges and walkways, 6 day and night tennis courts, 5 outdoor pools, oceanfront cabana bar and indoor atrium pool. For real relaxing, spend your time basking in the sun at the beach, watching the children play in the surf. Seasonal nightly entertainment and dancing under the stars. 24-hour security.

Plantation Resort
1250 U.S. Highway 17 North
Surfside Beach, SC 29577
803-238-3556 800-845-5039

Studio $, 1 Bedroom $$, 2 Bedrooms $$, 3 Bed-
  rooms $$
1 Bedrm/week 4$, 2 Bed/week 5$, 3 Bed/
  week 6$
AmEx/Visa/MC
Lo-rise

Location: Airport: M. Beach Jetport; Downtown: minutes

General Facilities: Full serv., Bus. fac., Conf. rm. cap. 120, Daily maid, Kitchen, Linens

Room Facilities: Pool, Sauna, Hot tub, Tennis, Fitness Center, Golf: Deer Track Golf 36-holes; TV, Cable, Phone in rm.

Attractions: The Grand Strand, 40 championship golf courses, beach, tennis

Shops & Restaurants: Myrtle Beach malls, unique low country stores; 1000 area restaurants

Villas with hotel-style amenities and 36 championship holes of golf at your doorstep. Hop on the free beach shuttle bus for your day at the beach. Year-round recreation at the Health and Swim Club with a 70-foot heated, enclosed pool with retractable roof, tennis courts and exercise area where you can take classes in aerobics, water aerobics and weight training. Free jetport pickup and drop-off service.

Tennessee

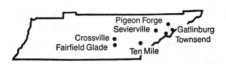

Pigeon Forge
Sevierville • ➤Gatlinburg
Crossville •   Townsend
Fairfield Glade •   Ten Mile

―――――――――――― CROSSVILLE ――――――――――――

Thunder Hollow
P.O. Box 1289
Crossville, TN 38557
615-484-9566

―――――――――――― FAIRFIELD GLADE ――――――――――――

Fairfield Glade—Kensington W.   1 Bedroom $$$, 2 Bedrooms $$$$, Villas
P.O. Box 1500   Pool, Kitchen, Linens
Fairfield Glade, TN 38555
619-484-7521

Attractions: Opryland, Dollywood, Catoosa Wildlife Management Area, Lake St. George
marina, tennis, golf

*A self-contained year-round resort. Two championship golf courses, three pools, Lake St.
George marina and swimming, tennis complex, Dorchester Riding Stables, and hiking on
12,000 acres. Comfortable accommodations for an unhurried life-style.*

―――――――――――― GATLINBURG ――――――――――――

Club Chalet Inn of Gatlinburg
4105 Ski Mountain Road
Gatlinburg, TN 37738
615-436-5536

GATLINBURG

Cobbly Nob	1 Bedroom $$, 2 Bedrooms $$, 3 Bedrooms $$
Route 3, Box 619	1 Bedrm/week 5$, 2 Bed/week 6$
Gatlinburg, TN 37738	Min. Stay 2 Nights, Dep. Req'd. •
615-436-5298	50 condos, Lo-rise, Key at Rental office
	H-yes

Location: Airport: 1 hour; Downtown: 10 min.; Need car; Ski lift: Ober

General Facilities: Full serv., Kitchen, Linens, Restaurant on prem., Bar on prem., Lounge

Room Facilities: Pool, Sauna, Hot tub, Tennis, Golf: Cobbly Nob; TV, Cable, VCR, Phone in rm., Ind. AC Ctl., Ind. Heat Ctl.

Attractions: Surrounded by Great Smoky Mtn. National Park, trout fishing, horses, Dollywood, hiking

Shops & Restaurants: Arts & crafts community, mall, Pigeon Forge; Burning Bush/gourmet

Country furnishings in log cabins with jacuzzi, skylights and stone fireplaces, or golf course condominiums with patios and charcoal grills, or King of the Mountain chalets that accommodate 22 persons, with enclosed spa room with 6-person hot tub. This is a 1,000-acre resort surrounded by the Great Smoky Mountains National Park, minutes from downtown Gatlinburg and ski slopes. 4 pools, tennis, golf course and fishing.

Condo Villas of Gatlinburg	Studio $$, 1 Bedroom $$, 2 Bedrooms $$
201 Parkway	1 Bedrm/week 5$, 2 Bed/week 5$, 3 Bed/
Gatlinburg, TN 37738	week 6$
615-436-4121 800-223-6264	Min. Stay 2 Nights, AmEx/Visa/MC,
	Dep. Req'd. •
	60 condos, Villas, Key at 201 Parkway
	No S-yes

Location: Airport: 35 miles; Downtown: 3 miles; Need car; Ski lift: Nearby

General Facilities: Kitchen, Linens

Room Facilities: Pool, TV, Cable, Phone in rm., Crib-Hi-chair, Ind. AC Ctl., Ind. Heat Ctl.

Attractions: Ski slopes, Dollywood, Great Smoky Mtn. National Park

Shops & Restaurants: Factory Merchants Mall; 50 to 100 restaurants

Log homes in early American surrounded with trees and views of the Great Smokies, or chalet villas in contemporary styling. Large heated pool with waterfall, picnic areas and hiking trails. Villas have cathedral ceilings with wood beams and whirlpool tubs in the bathroom. Security guards on duty day and night. Winter ski packages available.

──────────────── GATLINBURG ────────────────

Deer Ridge Mountain Resort
Route 3, Box 849
Gatlinburg, TN 37738
615-436-2325 800-631-3379

1 Bedroom $$, 2 Bedrooms $$, 3 Bedrooms $$$
1 Bedrm/week 4$, 2 Bed/week 5$, 3 Bed/
    week 7$
Min. Stay 2 Nights, AmEx/Visa/MC,
    Dep. Req'd. •
84 condos, Lo-rise, Key at Reception Center
H-yes

Location: Airport: 60 miles; Downtown: 11 miles; Need car; Ski lift: 13 miles

General Facilities: Full serv., Bus. fac., Conf. rm. cap. 50, Daily maid, Kitchen, Linens, Child planned rec.: Playground Equipment

Room Facilities: Pool, Sauna, Hot tub, Tennis, hiking, skiing, Golf: Bent Creek; TV, Cable, Phone in rm., Crib-Hi-chair, Ind. AC Ctl., Ind. Heat Ctl.

Attractions: Great Smoky Mt. Nat. Park, Dollywood, Dixie Dinner Theater, Passion Play

Shops & Restaurants: Factory Merchants Mall, Smoky Mountain Crafts

Beautiful, fully equipped large suites with private balconies for a spectacular 180-degree view of the Great Smoky Mountains. Relax in the swimming pool, jacuzzi, sauna or steam room, or exercise on the tennis court or the nearby 18-hole golf course.

───

Gatlinburg Summit
Top of Ski View Drive
Gatlinburg, TN 37738
615-436-2600 800-848-4148

───

Gatlinburg Town Square
P.O. Box 887
Gatlinburg, TN 37738

───

Greenbrier Valley Resorts
US 321, Rt. 3, Box 920
Gatlinburg, TN 37738
615-436-2015 800-641-7457

Min. Stay 1 Night, AmEx/Visa/MC,
    Dep. 1 Night •
20 condos, Key at Office
No S-yes/H-yes

Location: Airport: 1 hour 15 minutes; Downtown: 10 miles; Need car; Ski lift: Nearby

General Facilities: Full serv., Bus. fac., Conf. rm., Kitchen, Linens

Room Facilities: Pool, Sauna, Hot tub, Tennis, Golf: Bent Creek; TV, Cable, VCR, Phone in rm., Crib-Hi-chair, Ind. AC Ctl., Ind. Heat Ctl.

Attractions: Great Smoky Mt. National Park, Gatlinburg, Ober Gatlinburg, Dollywood, Pigeon Forge

Shops & Restaurants: Gatlinburg, Outlet malls in Pigeon Forge; Burning Bush/ Teagues/Peddler

Chalets, condos and log cabins surrounded by the unparalleled beauty of the Great Smoky Mountains. A year-round resort offering swimming, tenis, golf, downhill skiing and the entire playground of Great Smoky Mountains National Park. For the adventure-minded there is white-water rafting or tubing or skip stones among the many bubbling brooks.

GATLINBURG

High Alpine Resort
Upper Alpine Way, Rt. 2 Box 786
Gatlinburg, TN 37738
615-436-6643 800-666-6643

Studio $$, 1 Bedroom $$$, 2 Bedrooms $$$$
Min. Stay 2 Nights, AmEx/Visa/MC,
Dep. 1 Night •
36 condos, Lo-rise, Villas, Key at Office
on property
No S-yes/H-yes

Location: Airport: 1 hour; Downtown: 3 miles; Need car; Ski lift: Nearby
General Facilities: Conf. rm., Kitchen, Linens
Room Facilities: Pool, Cable, Phone in rm., Crib-Hi-chair, Ind. AC Ctl., Ind. Heat Ctl.
Attractions: Bus tours of Great Smoky Mountains, Dollywood, Cherokee Reservation
Shops & Restaurants: Several of the largest and best-known outlet malls; Old Heidelberg Castle/German

Located high upon Mount Harrison, half-mile from Ober Gatlinburg, a year-round attraction and ski resort. Condominiums are furnished in earth tones, some with whirlpool tubs and hot tubs. Large decks have views of Mount LeConte and ski slopes. Away from the noise and congestion of downtown, yet convenient to dining pleasures and area attractions.

Highland Condominiums
Campbell-Lead Rd, Rt. 4 Box 369
Gatlinburg, TN 37738
615-436-3547 800-233-3947

1 Bedroom $$, 2 Bedrooms $$$, Lo-rise
Pool, Kitchen, Linens

Attractions: Great Smoky Mountains National Park, Gatlinburg entertainment, tennis

Space, comfort and privacy with the Great Smoky Mountains at your doorstep. One-, two- and three-bedroom condominiums with a bath for every bedroom, wood-stocked fireplace, private entrance and balcony and a whirlpool bath.

Mountain Place Resort
Route 3, Box 756
Gatlinburg, TN 37738

Oak Square at Gatlinburg
990 River Road
Gatlinburg, TN 37738
615-436-7582 800-423-5182

1 Bedroom $$, 2 Bedrooms $$$
Pool, Daily maid, Kitchen, Linens

Attractions: Winter skiing, sledding, Dollywood, ice skating, Great Smoky Mountains National Park

One-and two-bedroom condominiums with wood burning fireplaces and kitchenettes with elevator service. Close proximity to the slopes, walk to restaurants and Aerial Tramway. Gatlinburg Trolley stops at the door to take you on a shopping trip or to Dollywood.

───────────── GATLINBURG ─────────────

Oak Square
990 River Road
Gatlinburg, TN 37738
615-436-7582 800-423-5182

1 Bedroom $$, 2 Bedrooms $$$
1 Bedrm/week 4$, 2 Bed/week 6$
Dep. 1 Night •
60 condos, Hi-rise, Key at Office

Location: Airport: 45 miles; Downtown: 1 block; Ski lift: Ober

General Facilities: Full serv., Conf. rm. cap. 85, Daily maid, Linens

Room Facilities: Pool, Hot tub, TV, Cable, Phone in rm., Crib-Hi-chair, Ind. AC Ctl., Ind. Heat Ctl.

Attractions: Ski lodge, Dollywood, Smoky Mountains National Park

Oak Park is ideally located in downtown Gatlinburg and offers a wide variety of accommodations. Gatlinburg Trolley transports you around the village and to Dollywood. Indoor pool for winter swimming, easy access to the slopes and Aerial Tramway. Suites have wood-burning fireplaces and kitchenettes.

The Summit
Top of Ski View Drive, Box 649
Gatlinburg, TN 37738
615-436-4222 800-231-2701

1 Bedroom $$, 2 Bedrooms $$, Hi-rise
Pool, Kitchen

Attractions: Fishing, swimming, golf, tennis, golf

Winter snow and skiing, summer swimming and fishing, spring hiking and horseback riding along the dogwood, tiger lilies and wildflowers, fall foliage colors, backpacking and fishing, something to do year-round. Condominiums with fireplaces and ski slope views.

Hatteras Inn Cabanas

---------------------- GATLINBURG ----------------------

Town Square Resort Club
Gatlinburg, TN 37738

Tree Tops Resort of Gatlinburg   1 Bedroom $$, 2 Bedrooms $$, Hi-rise
Roaring Fork Rd, P.O. Box 1009   Pool, Kitchen, Linens
Gatlinburg, TN 37738
615-436-6559

Attractions: Great Smoky Mountain National Park, fishing, Dollywood, fitness center, golf

Condominiums with jacuzzis and fireplaces totally tree surrounded and naturally blended into the mountains. 3 blocks from the national park. Nature trails, unspoiled picnic areas, and trout stocked mountain streams where you can forget the pace of everyday life.

---------------------- PIGEON FORGE ----------------------

Mountain Meadows Resort   2 Bedrooms $$, Lo-rise
850 Rolling Hills Dr, P.O. Box 929   Pool, Kitchen
Pigeon Forge, TN 37863
615-428-2897

Attractions: Dollywood, golf, Great Smoky Mountains National Park

Convenience and beauty in a quiet mountain setting surrounded by the Great Smoky Mountains and grassy meadows. Two-bedroom view townhouses with kitchens. Close to Dollywood, six miles of family entertainment, music and crafts.

Oakmont Resort of Pigeon Forge 1 Bedroom $$, 2 Bedrooms $$, Lo-rise
555 Middle Creek Road   Pool, Kitchen, Linens
Pigeon Forge, TN 37863
615-453-3240

Attractions: Dollywood, Gatlinburg Country Club, Old Mill, fishing, Water Circus, exercise room, golf

New, luxury condominiums with private aqua-jet therapeutic whirlpools in the master bath. Hilltop location, half-mile from Dollywood. Join new friends in the recreation room with its kitchenette and stone fireplace, or swim in the indoor/outdoor pool.

Pinecrest Townhomes   Lo-rise
P.O. Box 130, 300 Plaza Way   Kitchen
Pigeon Forge, TN 37863
615-453-6500

Attractions: Dollywood, Great Smoky Mountaind National Park, Old Mill, golf

Two-bedroom townhomes with 2.5 baths, king and queen size beds, balconies and mountain stone fireplaces for romantic evenings. Located among tall pines and minutes from Great Smoky Mountains National Park in a peaceful, scenic setting.

---------------------- SEVIERVILLE ----------------------

Riveredge Village Condominiums
953 Dolly Parton Parkway
Sevierville, TN 37862
615-453-3333

―――――――――――――― TEN MILE ――――――――――――――

The Landing   1 Bedroom $$, 2 Bedrooms $$, Villas
Rt. 2 Box 120   Pool, Kitchen, Linens
Ten Mile, TN 37880
615-334-9600 800-225-5896

Attractions: Tennessee River, Watts Bar Lake, boating, water sports, pontoon boats

Two-bedroom log chalets and one-bedroom modern stone villas on the waterfront. All have porch with spa, wood burning fireplace and outdoor grills. 95-mile lake with pontoon boats. Relaxed gourmet dining in the Yacht Club or floating Sunset Deck.

―――――――――――――― TOWNSEND ――――――――――――――

Riveredge Village Condominiums 2 Bedrooms $$
Townsend, TN 37882   2 Bedrms/week 4$
615-448-6036   Min. Stay 2 Nights, Dep. Req'd.
                                   8 condos, Lo-rise, Key at Office
                                   H-yes

Location: Airport: 30 minutes; Downtown: 2 blocks; Need car; Beach front; Ski lift: 18 miles

General Facilities: Kitchen, Linens

Room Facilities: Pool, Sauna, Hot tub, Biking, Jogging, TV, Cable, Crib-Hi-chair, Ind. AC Ctl., Ind. Heat Ctl.

Attractions: Great Smoky Mt. Nat. Park, Cades Cove

Shops & Restaurants: Pigeon Forge Factory Outlet, Townsend Crafts Mall; Family style

Elegantly decorated two-bedroom suites on the peaceful side of the Smokies. Balconies overlook the Little River and view the mountains. Fish, hike, view wildlife, or relax in the whirlpool or swimming pool.

Our goal is to provide as *complete* a listing of condo vacation properties as possible. If you know of a condo we don't list, please send us their name and address on the form at the back of this Guide.

Texas

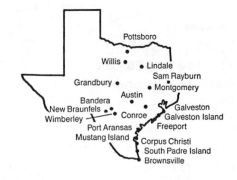

Pottsboro
Willis
Lindale
Sam Rayburn
Grandbury
Montgomery
Bandera
Austin
New Braunfels
Galveston
Wimberley
Conroe
Galveston Island
Port Aransas
Freeport
Mustang Island
Corpus Christi
South Padre Island
Brownsville

AUSTIN

Lakeway on Lake Travis
18 B Schooner Cove
Austin, TX 78734
800-252-3473 800-826-1841

Lo-rise
Pool, Kitchen, Linens

Attractions: Golf, tennis, water sports, fishing, boating

Texas Hill Country location on Lake Travis. Choice of condominiums set in the rolling hills, by the lake or pool. Family recreation among the oaks. Perfect for lazy days on the lake, yet minutes from Austin excitement.

Texas Timeshare in Lakeway
18-B Schooner Cove
Austin, TX 78734
512-261-6663 800-826-1841

2 Bedrooms $$$
2 Bedrms/week 4$
Min. Stay 2 Nights, AmEx/Visa/MC,
  Dep. 1 Night •
18 condos, Villas, Key at Office

Location: Airport: 30 miles; Downtown: 20 mi.; Need car

General Facilities: Daily maid, Kitchen, Linens, Bar on prem., Lounge, Child planned rec.: Summer day camp

Room Facilities: Pool, Hot tub, Tennis, Marina, boat rental, Golf: Live Oak & Yaupon; TV, Cable, Phone in rm., Crib-Hi-chair, Ind. AC Ctl., Ind. Heat Ctl.

Attractions: Hill Country, highland lakes, Sea World of Texas, Capitol Bldg., LBJ Ranch

Shops & Restaurants: Specialty shops, Frost Brothers; Barbara Ellens/homestyle

Contemporary furnished villas for resort living overlooking Lake Travis and Lakeway Marina. Hill Country or pool side settings. Abundant recreational opportunities for the whole family. Great restaurants nearby.

---------------------------- BANDERA ----------------------------

The Bandera Homestead
R.R. #2, P.O. Box 150
Bandera, TX 78003
512-796-3051

1 Bedroom $$, 2 Bedrooms $$
Lo-rise

General facilities: Kitchen

Sports facilities: Pool, Golf course, Volleyball, Horseshoes

Attractions: Historic Bandera, Cowboy Capital of the World, horse racing, Sea World, Camp Verde

Rustic log cabin condos are the 1,800 acre River Ranch. Pools under shade trees, lounge chairs and observation deck. Pavilion for outdoor barbecues overlooking the pools and river. Bandera County is a paradise for nature lovers.

---------------- BROWNSVILLE–RIO GRANDE VALLEY ----------------

Rancho Viejo Resort Country Club
P.O. Box 3918, Hwy. 77 North 83
Brownsville–Rio Grande Valley, TX 78520
512-350-4000   800-292-7263

Studio $$, 1 Bedroom $$,
2 Bedrooms $$$$, 3 Bedrooms $$$$
Amex, Visa, MC, Dep. 1 night
Villas, Key at Hotel front desk •

Location: Airport: Harvinger - 30 min., Downtown: Brownsville 15 min

General facilities: Full serv., Bus. fac., Conf. Rm. (cap. 900), Daily maid, Linens, Restaurant, Bar, Lounge, Hot tub

Room facilities: TV, Cable, Crib-Hi-chair, Ind.AC.Ctl, Ind.Heat Ctl.

Sports facilities: Pool, Tennis, 2 champ. Golf courses, Swimming

Attractions: South Padre Island-30 minutes, shopping in Mexico-20 minutes, zoo, Air Force Museum, entertainment

Shops & Restaurants: Sunrise & Amigo-Land Mall, Valley Vista, Casa Grande Supper Club

Rancho Viejo Resort and Country Club has two championship golf courses, tennis, swimming and fine dining at the Casa Grande Supper Club which has entertainment Thursday through Saturday in season. South Padre Island is 30 minutes away, or be in Mexico in twenty minutes. Swimming pool with waterfall and swim-up bar amidst semi-tropical landscaping. Golf packages available.

---------------------------- CORPUS CHRISTI ----------------------------

Condo on Padre Island Texas
1102 Hazel Dr.
Corpus Christi, TX 78412
512-992-0145 512-882-4731

Studio $$
1 Bed/week $$$$
Min. stay 2 nights
1 condos, Key at Call for info

Location: Airport: 25 minutes, Downtown: 15 minutes, Need car, Canal front

General facilities: Kitchen, Linens, Game room, Lounge, Jacuzzi

Room facilities: TV, Cable, Phone, Children 12+, Ind.AC.Ctl., Ind.Heat Ctl.

Sports facilities: Pool, Tennis, Padre Isles Country Club, Riding, Sailing, Surfing

Attractions: Deep sea fishing, dolphin trips, Port Aransas

Shops & Restaurants: Many fine Mexican & seafood restaurants

This small condo is very peaceful and private, it is truly a get-away and very homey. There is a marina for those who want to bring a boat and a large indoor pool. Just minutes from Port Aransas for deep-sea fishing and good seafood. Texas Jazz Festival held the first week of July at Water-Garden.

──────────── CORPUS CHRISTI ────────────

Fairway Villas   1 Bedroom $$, 2 Bedrooms $$, Villas
14401 Commodore   Pool, Kitchen
Corpus Christi, TX 78418

Attractions: Bayfront Arts & Science Park, Art Museum, Artesian Park, Heritage Park
(historic homes), fishing, tennis, golf

*Luxuriously furnished condominiums adjacent to Padre Island Country Club. A short walk
and you're at the beach.*

Puente Vista   2 Bedrooms $$, Lo-rise
14300 Aloha   Pool, Kitchen, Phone in rm.
Corpus Christi, TX 78418
512-933-7081

Attractions: Tennis, golf, sightseeing boats, surfing, fishing, boat facilities

*All units have waterside decks, and deck or patio overlooking the courtyards and land-
scaped grounds. Area has observation towers for an extended bird's-eye view. 30 feet from
your door are canals for boat docking.*

The Gulfstream   2 Bedrooms $$$
14810 Windward Drive   2 Bedrms/week 4$
Corpus Christi, TX 78418   Min. Stay 2 Nights, AmEx/Visa/MC,
512-949-8061 800-542-7368   Dep. 2 Nights •
          131 condos, Hi-rise, Key at Front desk
          H-yes

Location: Airport: 20 Miles; Downtown: 15 miles; Need car; Beach front

General Facilities: Full serv., Conf. rm. cap. 40, Daily maid, Kitchen, Linens, Game
room, Child planned rec.: Game room

Room Facilities: Pool, Hot tub, Shuffleboard, Golf: Country Club 2 miles; TV, Phone
in rm., Crib-Hi-chair, Ind. AC Ctl., Ind. Heat Ctl.

Attractions: Fishing, national seashores

Shops & Restaurants: Dillards, Jeskes, Penney's, Sears, Mervyns; Wayward Lady-
Country Line BBQ

*Each unit is spacious, tastefully decorated and a short walk across and down the stepped
seawall to the Gulf of Mexico. A large swimming pool, game room for the children, jacuzzi
and shuffleboard. Guest privileges are available on request for the nearby Padre Isles Country Club for golf, tennis, swimming, dining, drinking and dancing.*

Villa Del Sol   1 Bedroom $$, Villas
3938 Surfside Blvd.   Pool, Daily maid, Kitchen
Corpus Christi, TX 78402
512-883-9748 800-242-3291

Attractions: Aransas Wildlife Refuge, ballet, symphony, Art Museum, Museum of
Oriental Cultures, golf

*Beautifully landscaped grounds with palms, flowering shrubs, tropical plants and bedding
plants. Your one-bedroom condominium sleeps 4 adults and 2 children. Satellite TV, spec-
travision, pay premium movies and stereo tape deck. Balconies look out over the Bay.*

--------------------------------- FREEPORT ---------------------------------

Inverness At San Luis Pass 1 Bedroom $$, 2 Bedrooms, Jr. $$,
Route #2, Box 1270 2 Bedrm/week 5$, Min. Stay: 2 Nights,
Freeport, TX 77541 AmEx/Visa/MC, Dep. Req'd.
409-239-1433 40 condos, Lo-rise, Key at front office.

Location: Airport: 68 miles; Downtown: 20 miles, Need car; Beach front.

Room Facilities: Kitchen, Linens, TV, Crib-Hi-chair, Ind. AC. Ctl, Ind. Heat Ctl.

Attractions: TEXSUN sightseeing cruise tours.

Shops & Restaurants: Brazos Mall, Penney's, Dillards, Sears, Windswept/steaks and seafood.

Located on Follet's Island, Inverness has beautiful beaches in a quiet and isolated area. Within an hour and a half drive are Houston, Galveston and Lake Jackson, all of which offer a variety of dining and entertainment. For the fisherman, there are good locations for Gulf or bay fishing.

--------------------------------- GALVESTON ---------------------------------

The Galvestonian 1 Bedroom $$$$, 2 Bedrooms $$$$,
Condominiums 3 Bedrooms $$$$, 1 Bedrm/week 7$,
1401 East Beach Blvd. 2 Bedrm/week 10$, 3 Bedrm/week 10$,
Galveston, TX 77550 AmEx/Visa/MC, •
409-765-6161 713-280-3929 180 condos, Hi-rise, NoS-yes, Key at
FAX: 409-765-8032 lobby/reception.

Location: Airport: 40 miles; Downtown: 1 mile, Need car; Beach front.

General Facilities: Pool, Hot tub, Tennis, Baby sitter.

Room Facilities: Daily maid, Kitchen, TV, Cable, VCR, Phone, Crib-Hi-chair, Ind. AC. Ctl., Ind. Heat Ctl.

Attractions: Near Houston/NASA, historic city, fabled Strand District.

Shops & Restaurants: Galves Mall-3 miles—adequate for most shopping, Gaido's/ seafood.

50 minutes from downtown Houston lies the quaint and fabled city of Galveston with its beaches, historical landmarks and fine dining. The Galvestonian is located beach-side on the Gulf of Mexico, with beach-oriented furnishings and thick pile carpets. Play, fish, tour, dance, walk on the miles of sandy beach, or just relax in the sun.

------------------------------ GALVESTON ISLAND ------------------------------

Seaside Point
7820 Seawall Blvd
Galveston Island, TX 77551
409-744-6200 800-992-1187

Subscribe to our newsletter *Mondo Condo* and hear about the latest special condo vacation values.

Inverness by the Sea
7600 Seawall Blvd.
Galveston, TX 77551
409-740-4066

2 Bedrooms $$, Hi-rise
Pool, Kitchen, Linens

Attractions: Point Bolivar Lighthouse, Galveston Island State Park, Dollhouse Museum, Colonel Paddleboa, exercise room, tennis

Completely furnished two-bedroom suites down to ice makers and stereos. Beachfront property with tennis, exercise room, saunas, pool, rec. room and ll miles of continuous sidewalk. 30 miles of beach for a real family vacation.

The Victorian Condotel
6300 Seawall Blvd.
Galveston, TX 77551
409-740-3555 800-392-1215

1 Bedroom $, 2 Bedrooms $$
1 Bedrm/week $$$$, 2 Bed/week 4$
Min. Stay 2 Nights, AmEx/Visa/MC,
Dep. Req'd. •
330 condos, Lo-rise, Key at Front desk

Location: Airport: Hobby 45 miles; Need car; Beach front

General Facilities: Full serv., Bus. fac., Conf. rm. cap. 200, Daily maid, Kitchen, Linens, Game room, Child planned rec.: Playground

Room Facilities: Pool, Hot tub, Tennis, Playground, TV, Cable, VCR, Crib-Hi-chair, Ind. AC Ctl., Ind. Heat Ctl.

Attractions: Railroad Museum, Marineworld, 1894 Opera House, NASA, Moody Gardens, Sea-arama

Shops & Restaurants: The Strand, Houston/Galleria; Gaidos-seafood

Texas history is at your doorstep in these fully accessorized Victorian suites complete with private balconies overlooking the Gulf. Convenient beaches, fishing pier, shopping and gourmet dining pleasures are nearby.

GRANDBURY

The Ridge Chalets
Route 9, Box 47
Grandbury, TX 76048
817-573-7148

1 Bedroom $, 2 Bedrooms $$, Lo-rise
Kitchen

Attractions: Water sports, tennis

Condominiums on Lake Granbury for full enjoyment of water sports and fishing.

———————————————— HORSESHOE BAY ————————————————

**Horseshoe Bay Country Club
Resort**
Box 7766
Horseshoe Bay, TX 78654
512-598-8561 800-252-9363

Location: Beach front

General Facilities: Restaurant; Bar

Business Facilities: Conf. Room Cap. 250

Sports Facilities: Game room; Pool; Tennis; Sailing, water ski; 3 golf courses

Room Facilities: Kitchen

Attractions: LBJ home, Longhorn Caverns, Falls Creek Winery

Shops & Restaurants: The Captain's Table, Keel Way

Two- and three-bedroom condominiums in this private country club resort with its spring-fed streams, ancient rocks, exotic gardens and miles of shoreline and coves. Fully equipped marina for the boater, and two-tiered pool fed by a waterfall for swimmers. Tennis complex with fitness program consisting of body shape-up classes and aqua aerobics, Equestrian Center and three Robert Trent Jones' designed golf courses.

———————————————— LAGO VISTA ————————————————

Lago Vista Rentals   Min. Stay Ask, Visa/MC
P.O. Box 4986   1 Night Dep. Req'd., Lo-rise
Lago Vista, TX 78645   Key at Rental office, P-No
512-267-0700 FAX: 512-267-9665

Location: Airport: 30 miles; Downtown: 30 miles to Austin; Need car; Lake front

General Facilities: Linens; Baby sitter; Restaurant on premises

Sports Facilities: Pool; Tennis; Water skiing; Point Venture GC nearby

Room Facilities: Kitchen; TV; Phone; Ind.AC.Ctl.; Ind.Heat Ctl.

Attractions: Vanishing River Cruise, San Antonio, The Alamo

Shops & Restaurants: Benton Creek Mall, Lakeline Mall; Out Back Steak House,
    County Line-BBQ

Town homes on Lake Travis. Walk to lake, boat launch marina. Golf courses in Lago Vista and Point Ventura. Near Lakeline Mall. Boat rentals available in area.

─────────────── MONTGOMERY ───────────────

Walden on Lake Conroe
14001 Walden Rd.
Montgomery, TX 77356
409-582-6441

Location: Airport: Houston-1 hour

General facilities: Conf. Rm. (cap. 350), Kitchen, Restaurant

Sports facilities: Pool, Tennis, 72 par Golf course, Yacht harbor

Attractions: Lake Conroe water sports, Reflections III-70' yacht for charters, Sam Houston Nat. Park

Shops & Restaurants: Ship's store, Commodore Room-Cafe on the Green

Resort with seven contemporary complexes of one, two and three bedroom spacious, fully equipped condominiums overlooking the yacht harbor, lagoons or wooded East Texas terrain. Each cluster has it's own pool. 16 tennis courts. Full service marina with rental sail and power boats. Try the driving range across from the golf clubhouse before tackling the par 72 course with a slope rating of 126 from the middle tees.

─────────────── MUSTANG ISLAND, PORT ARANSAS ───────────────

Sandpiper Condos-Mustang   1 Bedroom $$, 2 Bedrooms $$
Island   Hi-rise
Park Rd 53, P.O. Box 1268
Mustang Island, Port Aransas,
TX 78373
512-749-6251

General facilities: Kitchen, Linens

Room facilities: Phone

Sports facilities: Pool

Attractions: Fishing, beach, tennis

A covered porte cochere entry welcomes you upon arrival at this high-rise condominium complex. Suites are individually decorated for a pleasant, relaxing vacation. Elevated boardwalk to the Gulf beach, pool, whirlpool, lanai area, sundecks and tenniscourts.

─────────────── NEW BRAUNFELS ───────────────

Comal River Condominiums   2 Bedrooms $$
Comal St.
New Braunfels, TX 78130

Quiet, relaxing atmosphere under the shade of native trees yet close to all New Braunfels' activities. Woodburning fireplaces and T.V.

---------------------------- NEW BRAUNFELS ----------------------------

Woodlands Condominiums
New Braunfels, TX 78138

Walk out your back door to the 18-hold golf course or the nearby boat ramp to beautiful Canyon Lake.

---------------------------- PORT ARANSAS ----------------------------

Aransas Princess   2 Bedrooms $$$$, 3 Bedrooms $$$$
720 Beach Access Rd. 1-A, Box
309
Port Aransas, TX 78373
512-749-5118 800-531-9225
FAX: 512-749-5120

Sports Facilities: Tennis; Greyhound Race Track; Golf Course nearby

Attractions: Gulf of Mexico, Corpus Christi Bay, intercoastal canal, beach, boating

On the beach, two pools, sauna, jacuzzi, lighted tennis courts, shuffleboard, boardwalk to the beach, fish cleaning room, meeting room and covered parking. Rental units are completely furnished; 2 bedrooms, 2 bedroom plus den, and penthouse. Near Texas State Aquarium and USS Lexington. The finest condominium on Mustang Island. Please call for brochure

---

Beachgate   Lo-rise
Box 116
Port Aransas, TX 78373
512-749-5900

Room Facilities: Kitchen

Four one bedroom apartments on Mustang Island Beach in a natural setting of sand dunes, sea oats and beach morning glories. Resident manager to see to your needs and tell you about island activities.

Beachhead Resort   2 Bedrooms $$
1319 S. 11th St.   2 Bedrms/week $$$$
Port Aransas, TX 78373   Visa/MC, 1 Night Dep. Req'd. •
512-749-6261   34 condos, Lo-rise, Key at Front desk

Location: Airport: 50 miles; Need car; Beach front

General Facilities: Full serv.; Daily maid; Linens; Lounge; Crib-Hi-chair

Business Facilities: Conf. Room Cap. 70

Sports Facilities: Game room; Pool; Tennis

Room Facilities: Kitchen; Cable; Phone; Ind.AC.Ctl; Ind.Heat Ctl.

Attractions: Fishing, boating, beach

Shops & Restaurants: Local shops; Pelican Landing-Seafood

Comfortable, clean, lovely grounds on the beach. Peaceful, serene, close to shopping, fine dining, boating and fishing. A special place for special people who are given special attention.

Victorian Condotel

PORT ARANSAS

Buccaneer Courts
713 Mustang Isl. Rd., Box 507
Port Aransas, TX 78373
512-749-5566

Casa Del Mar   2 Bedrooms $, Lo-rise
104 Dunes Drive, P.O. Box 488   Kitchen, Linens
Port Aransas, TX 78373
512-749-6996

Attractions: Seashore, Horace Caldwell Pier, Port Aransas docks, deep-sea fishing, "Old Mexico"'

Small project with two-bedroom units within the Mustang Island dunes seashore, in a natural setting. No phones, no pool, no pets, just the relaxation of the dunes and beach. Near pier and docks for deep-sea fishing and sailing.

Casadel Beach Hotel & Racquet   1 Bedroom $$, 2 Bedrooms $$$, Hi-rise
P.O. Box 1149   Pool, Kitchen
Port Aransas, TX 78373
512-749-6942

Attractions: Port Aransas fishing village, golf, tennis, water sports, deep-sea, bay and surf fishing, exercise room

On the beach at Mustang Island, beautifully furnished suites with Gulf or pool views from balconies with outdoor furniture. Concrete boardwalk to the beach. 5 miles to Port Aransas for the sport fisherman; trout, flounder and redfish for the bay and surf fisherman.

──────────────── PORT ARANSAS ────────────────

Coral Cay Condominium
1423 11th. Street
Port Aransas, TX 78373
512-749-5111 800-221-4981

Studio $$, 1 Bedroom $$,
  2 Bedrooms $$, 3 Bedrooms $$
1 Bedrm/wk 4$, 2 Bedrms/wk 4$, 3
  Bedrms/wk 5$
AmEx/Visa/MC, Dep. 1 Night
Key at Front office, Lo-rise.

Location: Airport: Corpus Christi; Downtown: minutes away

General Facilities: Full serv., Conf. Rm., Pool, Crib-H-chair

Room Facilities: TV, Daily Maid, Linens, Kitchen, Cable, Phone in rm., Ind. AC Ctl.

Attractions: Port Aransas fishing village, deepsea fishing, jazz, country music, beach.

Shops & Restaurants: Antique shops, art galleries, grocery, spirits, Wharf cafes-seafood restaurant.

Choose your condominium size and location, beachfront, Gulf view or poolside. Native grassees and wild flowers among the landscaped grounds. Just a few blocks away from Port Aransas fishing village with its shops, restaurants and entertainment. Individually decorated condominiums with floor-to-ceiling windows and balconies. Play or rest on the beach and in the Gulf waters.

──

Cline's Landing Condominium
1000 N. Station St, Box 1628
Port Aransas, TX 78373
512-749-5275

2 Bedrooms $$$, 3 Bedrooms $$$$
2 Bedrms/week 7$, 3 Bed/week 10$
Dep. Req'd.
108 condos, Hi-rise, Key at Mgt. office

Location: Airport: Port Aransas; Downtown: minutes

General Facilities: Full serv., Conf. rm. cap. 200, Kitchen, Game room, Lounge, Child planned rec.: Playground

Room Facilities: Pool, Hot tub, Marina

Attractions: Boating, fishing excursions, duck hunting, boat and beach tours, tennis

Shops & Restaurants: Quaint Port Aransas shops; Port Aransas restaurants

Enter the lobby and be impressed with the seven-story atrium graced with trailing philodendron. 1,450 sq. ft. two-bedroom units. Three-bedroom units are 2,075 sq. ft. with walk-in closets, master bathrooms with skylights and jacuzzis. Let the children enjoy the playground while you barbecue your catch of the day at the picnic area. Bristol class marina for Gulf access with slip rentals. Walk for miles on the beach before you settle down to relax on the sand. 24 hr. security and area camera scanning.

─────────────── PORT ARANSAS ───────────────

Dunes Condominium
1000 Lantana Box 1238
Port Aransas, TX 78373
512-749-5155 800-288-3863

1 Bedroom $$, 2 Bedrooms $$
Min. Stay 2 Nights, AmEx/Visa/MC,
Dep. 1 Night •
86 condos, Hi-rise, Key at Front desk, H-yes

Location: Airport: 20 miles; Downtown: 1 mile; Need car; Beach front

General Facilities: Full serv., Bus. fac., Conf. rm. cap. 100, Daily maid, Kitchen, Linens, Lounge

Room Facilities: Pool, Hot tub, Tennis, Shuffleboard, fishing, TV, Cable, Phone in rm., Crib-Hi-chair, Ind. AC Ctl., Ind. Heat Ctl.

Attractions: Charter fishing of all kinds, surf, pier, jetty fishing, entertainment

Shops & Restaurants: Local stores; Pelican's Landing/seafood

Individually decorated condominiums with 200 sq. ft. of Gulf viewing space balconies. The pool is screened from the wind and surrounded with tropical vegetation. Covered lanai area. Steps to the beach and tennis. Port Aransas marina for charter fishing boats.

El Cortes Villas
Mustang Island, Box 1266
Port Aransas, TX 78373
512-749-6206

1 Bedroom $, 2 Bedrooms $$, Villas
Pool, Daily maid, Kitchen

Attractions: Deepsea fishing, surf fishing, beach, tennis, golf

Modern villas behind the sand dunes with private walking acess to the beach. Just a few miles to the fishing port of Aransas.

Executive Keys
Box 1087
Port Aransas, TX 78373
512-749-6272

2 Bedrooms $$, Lo-rise
Pool, Daily maid, Kitchen, Linens, Phone in rm.

Attractions: Fishing, swimming, beach sports, crabbing, volleyball

Comfortable, individually decorated suites for the vacationing family. Three picnic areas with grills. Large pots for boiling crabs/shrimp are available. Two-story townhouse units can also be rented with special weekly rates. A place to get away and enjoy the beach.

Gulf Beach Courts
506 E. Ave. G, Box 778
Port Aransas, TX 78373
512-749-5416

Gulf Shores Condominium
Park Rd. 53, Box 1298
Port Aransas, TX 78373
512-749-6257

Haney's Cottages
225 E. Oakes, Box 171
Port Aransas, TX 78373
512-749-5792

─────────────── PORT ARANSAS ───────────────

Island Retreat Condominium
700 Island Retreat Court, Box 637
Port Aransas, TX 78373
512-749-6222

1 Bedroom $, 2 Bedrooms $, 3 Bedrooms $$
2 Bedrms/week $$$$, 3 Bed/week $$$$
Min. Stay 3 Nights, Visa/MC, Dep. 1 Night •
148 condos, Lo-rise, Key at Office
P-yes

Location: Airport: Corpus Christi; Downtown: 1.5 mile; Need car; Beach front

General Facilities: Full serv., Conf. rm. cap. 100, Daily maid, Kitchen, Linens

Room Facilities: Pool, Tennis, TV, Cable, Phone in rm., Ind. AC Ctl., Ind. Heat Ctl.

Attractions: Texas Gulf Beach and Corpus Christi for big city life

Shops & Restaurants: Surf shops, shell shops and tourist shops; Water Front/seafood

Family-size condominiums decorated in earth tones with wood paneling, accented with Mediterranean styles. Two walkways to the sandy beach on the Gulf of Mexico or the sands of Mustang Island. Swimming pool, spacious parking, and the privacy of your own patio-balcony.

Marine Courts
411 N. Alister, Box 76
Port Aransas, TX 78373
512-749-5509

Mayan Princess Condominium
Park Rd. 53, Box 156
Port Aransas, TX 78373
512-749-5183 800-542-7368

1 Bedroom $$$, 2 Bedrooms $$$
1 Bedrm/week 7$, 2 Bed/week 10$
Min. Stay 2 Nights, Visa/MC, Dep. 2 Nights •
60 condos, Hi-rise, Key at Front desk
H-yes

Location: Airport: 30 miles; Downtown: 25 miles; Need car; Beach front

General Facilities: Full serv., Conf. rm. cap. 50, Daily maid, Kitchen, Linens

Room Facilities: Pool, Hot tub, Tennis, Golf: 8 miles; TV, Phone in rm., Crib-Hi-chair, Ind. AC Ctl., Ind. Heat Ctl.

Attractions: Surf, pier and deep-sea fishing, shelling, beachcombing, boating and sailing, charter boat

Shops & Restaurants: Corpus Christi shops and Port Aransas shops; Numerous seafood restaurants

Nestled in the dunes along Mustang Island, The Mayan Princess is just ten miles from Port Aransas and Corpus Christi. There are three swimming pools and a hot tub outdoors. The beach is only a few yards away. Play golf or tennis or get up early for bird watching.

---------------------- PORT ARANSAS ----------------------

Mustang Island Beach Club	2 Bedrooms $$, 2 Bedrm/week 4$, Min.
Park Rd. 53	Stay: 2 Nights, Visa/MC, Dep. 1 Night, •
Port Aransas, TX 78373	16 condos, Villas, Key at reception center.
512-749-5446	

Location: Airport: 30 miles, Need car.

General Facilities: Pool, Hot tub.

Room Facilities: Daily maid, Kitchen, TV, Cable, Phone, Crib-Hi-chair, Ind. AC. Ctl, Ind. Heat Ctl.

Attractions: Charter fishing, beaches, water sports, shelling, crabbing, bikes, dune buggies, Seafood Cajun style.

Mustang Island Beach Club condominiums are furnished in rattan, glass, and earth-tones of mauve and blues. Vacation activity centers around the beaches and water sports, especially year-round fishing. Many historical sights to visit, or rent three-wheel bikes and dune buggies to explore the undeveloped coastline.

Mustang Isle Apartments	1 Bedroom $, 2 Bedrooms $$.
2100 S. 11th St. Box 37	Lo-rise condos, Kitchen, Linens.
Port Aransas, TX 78373	
512-749-6011	

A small condominium complex on Mustang Isle. All electric kitchens, air conditioning and cable TV. A short walk through the dunes takes you to the beach.

Mustang Towers	2 Bedrooms $$$, 3 Bedrooms $$$$,
Park Rd. 53 Box 1870	2 Bedrm/week 4$, 3 Bedrm/week 5$,
Port Aransas, TX 78373	Visa/MC, Dep. 1 Night, •
512-749-6212 800-343-2772	56 condos, Hi-rise, H-yes, Key at office.
FAX: 512-749-5730	

Location: Airport: 35 miles; Downtown: 6 miles, Need car; Beach front.

General Facilities: Bus. fac., Game room, Pool, Hot tub, Tennis, Volleyball, horseshoe.

Room Facilities: Kitchen, TV, Phone, Cribs, Ind. AC. Ctl., Ind. Heat Ctl.

Attractions: Deep sea fishing, scenic boat cruises, Aransas Wildlife Refuge, 3 hrs. to Mexico, entertainment.

Shops & Restaurants: 2 shopping malls, Penney, Sears, Foleys, K-Mart, Seafood & Spaghetti Works.

A special place where you mark your time by the spectacular sunsets over the Gulf, and sunsets over the Bay. Contemporary furnishings with sea motif, 2 sliding glass doors lead to Gulf view balcony. Miles of sandy beach unspoiled by man. An island retreat. Bi-level pool with waterfall, sundecks, cabanas, and activity room.

PORT ARANSAS

Port Royal Ocean Resort   1 Bedroom $$, 2 Bedrooms $$, 3 Bedrooms $$$
Park Rd. 53, Box 336   Dep. 1 Night
Port Aransas, TX 78373   Hi-rise
512-749-5011 800-847-5659

Location: Downtown: 30 min.; Beach front

General Facilities: Conf. rm. cap. 700, Daily maid, Kitchen, Linens, Restaurant on prem., Bar on prem., Game room

Room Facilities: Pool, Tennis, Shuffleboard volleyball, Golf: Padre Isle Golf Course

Attractions: Port Aransas for deep-sea fishing and charters, Fisherman's Wharf, Marine Science Lab

Shops & Restaurants: Lobby level boutique, gift shop, convenience store; Royal Beachcomber

Professionally decorated with spacious living rooms, sun deck terraces, built-in stereo, whirlpool and steam baths in master suites. 500-foot Royal Blue Lagoon Pool with waterfalls, hidden grottoes, swim-up cabana bars, four whirlpool spas and huge dune water slide. Beach for surfing, swimming and shelling. Royal Beachcomber restaurant and lounge for an evening out.

Sand & Surf Condominium   1 Bedroom $
1423 11th Street, Box 1439   Kitchen, Linens
Port Aransas, TX 78373
512-749-6001

One-bedroom units with two double beds, fully equipped kitchens, dishwasher, disposal, separate bath dressing areas, large linen closet and walk-in closet. Upstairs units have private view balconies. Small room set aside for recreation.

Sandcastle Condominium   1 Bedroom $$, 2 Bedrooms $$$, Hi-rise
Sandcastle Rd. On Beach, Box 1688   Pool, Kitchen, Linens
Port Aransas, TX 78373
521-749-6201 800-727-6201

Attractions: Tennis

View units with sliding glass doors to the balcony. Attractively decorated in rattan and glass with ceiling fans. Wooden walkway to the beach. Pool with lounges and umbrella tables surrounded by lawn, palms and colorful flowers.

Be sure to call the condo to verify details and prices and to make your reservation.

PORT ARANSAS

Sea Gull Condominium
Park Rd. 53, Box 1207
Port Aransas, TX 78373
512-749-4191

1 Bedroom $$, 2 Bedrooms $$, 3 Bedrooms $$$
Min. Stay 2 Nights, AmEx/Visa/MC,
Dep. 1 Night
105 condos, Hi-rise, Key at Front desk
H-yes

Location: Airport: 45 minutes; Downtown: 8 miles; Need car; Beach front
General Facilities: Full serv., Conf. rm. cap. 100, Daily maid, Kitchen, Linens, Child planned rec.: Playground
Room Facilities: Pool, Tennis, Basketball, horseshoes, TV, Cable, Phone in rm., Crib-Hi-chair, Ind. AC Ctl., Ind. Heat Ctl.
Attractions: Beach, trips to Mexico, deep sea and bay fishing
Shops & Restaurants: Groceries, clothes, souvenirs; Spaghetti Works/pasta-seafood

The Sea Gull is an 11-story high-rise located directly on the beach. All units overlook the Gulf of Mexico and are furnished in a luxurious manner. Beach boys set up chaises and umbrellas at no charge—tipping is forbidden. Basketball, volleyball, horseshoes and children's playground are all available at Sea Gull.

Sea Isle Village
1129 S. 11th St., Box 1686
Port Aransas, TX 78373
512-749-6281

1 Bedroom $, 2 Bedrooms $$, Lo-rise
Pool, Daily maid, Kitchen, Linens

Attractions: Beach, fishing

Complex with efficiency to three bedroom apartments. Satellite TV. Pool, boardwalk to beach.

Sea Sands Condominium
1377 S. 11th St., Box 537T
Port Aransas, TX 78373
512-749-6246

1 Bedroom $, 2 Bedrooms $, Lo-rise
Pool, Kitchen, Linens

Attractions: Fishing, beachcombing, swimming

Attractively furnished apartments with living room white brick walls. Lounge around the pool. One block to the Gulf of Mexico for beachcombing, swimming and relaxing.

Spanish Village
200 N. Alister, Box 578
Port Aransas, TX 78373
512-749-5253

Sunday Villas
1900 S. 11th St., Box 1213
Port Aransas, TX 78373
512-749-6480

2 Bedrooms $$, Villas
Pool, Daily maid, Kitchen, Linens

A colony of uniquely designed unattached condominiums in Port Aransas. The beach is a short walk away over the dunes. Pool.

PORT ARANSAS

Teal Harbor Condominium
200 W. Cotter St., P.O. Box F
Port Aransas, TX 78373
512-749-4131

2 Bedrooms $$$, Hi-rise
Pool, Kitchen, Linens

Attractions: Crabbing, surf-fishing, charter boat fishing-touring, boating, beaches, marina

Beautifully designed condominiums along the Texas coast. Unit access is by key-operated elevators serving two units, monitored by closed circuit TV. Marina with boatslips 23' x 70', and resident Harbor Master.

The Pelican
1107 S. 11th St., Box 1690
Port Aransas, TX 78373
512-749-6226

2 Bedrooms $, 3 Bedrooms $$
2 Bedrms/week $$$$, 3 Bed/week $$$$
Visa/MC,Dep. 2 Nights •
65 condos, Lo-rise, Key at Office, H-yes

Location: Airport: 1 mile; Downtown: ⅓ mile; Need car; Beach front
General Facilities: Daily maid, Kitchen, Linens, Baby-sitter
Room Facilities: Pool, Sauna, Golf: 18 miles; TV, Cable, Phone in rm., Ind. AC Ctl., Ind. Heat Ctl.
Attractions: Horseback riding, fishing tournaments, sunset cruises, wildlife refuge, Lighthouse, entertainment
Shops & Restaurants: Islander-gifts, souvenirs, Pat Magees, sun wear; Spaghetti Works, Tortuga Flats

A family-style condominium complex in a sleepy little fishing village accessed from Aransas Pass by free auto ferries. Playground, badminton court and swimming pool are enclosed in a large, privately fenced yard. Everything for the fisherman, or just spend your time on the beach, collecting shells, sunning, and swimming. Water aerobics from June to August, playground and badminton court. Spacious surroundings for kite flying or frisbee throwing, or just enjoying the view.

POTTSBORO

Tanglewood on Texoma Resort Hotel
Highway 120
Pottsboro, TX 75076
800-833-6569

Visa/MC, •
120 condos

Location: Airport: DFW Airport; Downtown: 5 miles
General Facilities: Conf. rm. cap. 135, Kitchen, Restaurant on prem., Bar on prem.
Room Facilities: Pool, Tennis, Riding, boating, Golf: 18-hole course; TV, Phone in rm., Ind. AC Ctl., Ind. Heat Ctl.
Attractions: President Eisenhower's birthplace, Lake Texoma, entertainment
Shops & Restaurants: Midway Mall, Kelly Square, The Depot; The Point/cont.-Pompanos

On tree-covered hills, situated on the shore of beautiful Lake Texoma, Tanglewood on Texoma offers the perfect setting for that perfect vacation. Lake recreational activities, fine cuisine in the Commodores Room, cocktails in the Yacht Club or high atop the nine-story tower overlooking the lake in the Moonraker. Dance floor and planned holiday activities.

──────────── SAM RAYBURN ────────────

Rayburn Country Resort　　1 Bedroom $$, 2 Bedrooms $$, Villas
P.O. Box 36　　　　　　　　　　Pool, Kitchen
Sam Rayburn, TX 75951
409-698-2444

Attractions: Jones Country Music Shop, water sports, fishing, sailing, badminton, horse-shoes, tennis, golf

Recreational development among pines, dogwoods, magnolias and azaleas with water sports and fishing on clear Sam Rayburn Lake. Robert Trent Jones designed golf course, and four all-weather, lighted tennis courts.

──────────── SOUTH PADRE ISLAND ────────────

Bahi'a Mar Resort　　　　　Hi-rise
Park Road 100, P.O. Box 2280　Pool, Kitchen
South Padre Island, TX 78578
512-943-1343

Attractions: 30-minute drive to Matamoros, Mexico, tennis

Bahi'a Mar Resort on the "top of Texas" offers two-and three-bedroom condominiums for weekly or monthly rental. On a subtropical island near the beach, with a lagoon, pool, tennis and Gulf fishing.

Island Estates Condominium
112 Oleander St.
South Padre Island, TX 78597

Padre South Resort　　　　2 Bedrooms $$, Hi-rise
1500 Gulf Blvd, P.O. Box 2338　Pool, Kitchen, Linens
South Padre Island, TX 78597
512-761-4951

Attractions: 30 minutes to Old Mexico, Confederate AFB with WWII planes, golf

Full-service vacation resort with efficiencies or two-bedroom suites. Balconies with Gulf and Laguna Madre Bay views. Mild surf for getting your feet wet, white sand beach for sunning. Barbecue area, patio/deck area with gazebos, indoor/outdoor bars.

South Padre Hilton Resort　2 Bedrooms $$$$
500 Padre Blvd, P.O. Box 2081
South Padre Island, TX 78597
512-761-6511　800-292-7704

Location: Beach front
General Facilities: Kitchen
Room Facilities: Tennis

Two-bedroom condominiums on a quarter mile of sparkling beachfront. Year-round package values.

———————————————— WILLIS ————————————————

Landing At Seven Coves
700 Kingston Cove
Willis, TX 77378
713-222-6865

——————————————— WIMBERLEY ———————————————

Woodcreek Resort   Lo-rise
No. 1 Woodcreek Drive   Pool, Kitchen
Wimberley, TX 78676
512-847-2221 800-252-9303

Attractions: Boating, canoeing, fishing, hiking, biking, hayrides, bonfires, barbecues, health spa, tennis, golf

Texas hill country townhomes for nature lovers. Swim, play tennis, golf, or use the health spa. Marina for paddle boating and canoeing. Explore the area by foot, bicycle or horseback. For a special dinner, dine in the Sam Houston Dining Room in a teepee or jail.

Enter your favorite condo in our "Condo of the Year" contest (entry form is in the back of the book).

Utah

Salt Lake City • Park City
Alta
Snowbird

---------------------------------- ALTA ----------------------------------

Black Jack Condominium Lodge
Alta
Alta, UT 84092
801-742-3200

1 Bedroom $$$$, 2 Bedrooms $$$$
Kitchen, Linens

Attractions: Skiing

Midway between Alta and Snowbird. Mountain view living rooms, fireplaces with wood provided and kitchens with trash compactors. Lodge with fireplace and sunken hearth, ski locker room. Four-wheel drive to take you to ski areas in the morning.

---------------------------------- PARK CITY ----------------------------------

Acclaimed Lodging
P.O. Box 3629
Park City, UT 84060
801-649-3736 800-552-9696

2 Bedrooms $$$, 3 Bedrooms $$$
Min. Stay 4 Nights, AmEx/Visa/MC,
Dep. 1 Night •
18 condos, Lo-rise, Key at Park City Central
P-yes

Location: Airport: 30 miles; Downtown: 25 miles; Need car

General Facilities: Full serv., Kitchen, Linens, Restaurant on prem., Bar on prem., Baby-sitter

Room Facilities: Pool, Sauna, Hot tub, Tennis, Ski, hike, fish, Golf: Park Meadows Golf; TV, Cable, Phone in rm., Ind. Heat Ctl.

Attractions: 3 ski areas within a 3-mile radius, snowmobiles, backpacking, fishing, entertainment

Shops & Restaurants: Historic Main Street in Park City; Deer Valley Cafe, Mariposa

Fully equipped two-level townhouses within the Park City Racquet Club complex. Dinner/sleigh rides available on the premises, cross-country skiing tours, just one mile from Park City ski lifts on the City bus route.

—————————————— PARK CITY ——————————————

Blooming Enterprises Property Studio $$$, 1 Bedroom $$$$,
P.O.Box 2340, 1647 Shortline Rd.   2 Bedrooms $$$$, 3 Bedrooms 5$
Park City, UT 84060   1 Bedrm/week 10$, 2 Bedrms/week 10$,
801-649-6583 800-635-4719   3 Bedrms/week 10$
FAX: 801-649-6598   Min. Stay Ask, AmEx/Visa/MC •
                                   50 condos, Villas, Key at Central office,
                                   P-No/No S-Yes/H-Yes

Location: Airport: SLC, 45 minutes; Downtown: SLC, 45 minutes; Need car; Ski lift
   at 3 miles
General Facilities: Daily maid; Linens; Baby sitter; Crib-Hi-Chair
Room Facilities: Kitchen; Cable; Phone; Ind.AC.Ctl; Ind.Heat Ctl.
Attractions: Park City and Deer Valley Ski Resorts within 3 miles of all condos.
Shops & Restaurants: Elegant Park City's Historic Main St., Factory Stores Mall;
   River Horse Cafe-gourmet

Exclusive lodging at Park City and Deer Valley Ski Resorts. Blooming Enterprises
offers a wide variety of condominiums ranging from economy studio apartments to
ultra-deluxe 6-bedroom ski lodges. Rates start at just $125/night and range to
$3,000/night. All properties have full kitchens, TVs, private phones and excellent
locations. Most have fireplaces, hot tubs, VCRs, stereos and designer furnishings. Fine
quality lodgings in a beautiful mountain setting.

Blue Church Lodge &   Studio $$, 1 Bedroom $$$,
Townhouses   2 Bedrooms $$$, 3 Bedrooms $$$$
P.O.Box 1720   1 Bedrm/week $$$, 2 Bedrms/week $$$,
Park City, UT 84060   3 Bedrms/week $$$$
801-649-8009   Min. Stay 3 Nights, Visa/MC, Dep.
                                    Required •
                                    12 condos, Hi-rise
                                    Key at Prior instructions

Location: Airport: 40 minutes; Downtown: 30 min.; Ski lift at Park City
General Facilities: Daily maid; Linens; Lounge; Crib-Hi-chair
Sports Facilities: Game room; Hot tub
Room Facilities: Kitchen; Cable; Phone; Ind.Heat Ctl.
Attractions: Downhill and cross-country skiing, snowmobiling, ice skating, bal-
   looning
Shops & Restaurants: Main Street shopping located 1 street from lodge; Mr.
   Hunan/Chinese

The Blue Church Lodge offers quaint country charm with some antique repli-
cas,located in the heart of Park City's historic district within walking distance of Main
Street with its shops, restaurants and nightlife. Indoor spa and table tennis in the
game room. Golfing and other outdoor sports in summer. Winter brings skiing,
snowmobiling, ice skating, sleigh rides, helicopter skiing and cross-country skiing on
groomed tracks.

———————————— PARK CITY ————————————

Coalition Lodge
P.O. Box 75, 1300 Park Avenue
Park City, UT 84060
801-649-8591

2 Bedrooms $$$
2 Bedrms/week 7$
AmEx/Visa/MC, Dep. Req'd.
5 condos, Lo-rise, Key at Office #6

Location: Airport: 35 minutes; Downtown: 1 mile; Ski lift: Park City
General Facilities: Daily maid, Kitchen, Linens
Room Facilities: Sauna, TV, Crib-Hi-chair, Ind. Heat Ctl.
Attractions: Hot air ballooning, snowmobiling, skiing, hiking, fishing, hunting, golf, tennis
Shops & Restaurants: Old town major shopping zone; 39 excellent restaurants
Large size, designer furnished condominiums in an old west mining town. Warm., friendly atmosphere. 3 minutes from Park City ski area. Free bus service in front of the lodge to all ski areas, outside ski lockers. Fine restaurants and shops on a free bus route.

Courchevel
P.O. Box 680128
Park City, UT 84068
801-649-9598 800-453-5789

1 Bedroom $$
3 Bedrms/week $$$$
Min. Stay 2 Nights, AmEx/Visa/MC, Dep. 1 Night •
26 condos, Lo-rise, Key at Park City Central

Location: Airport: SLC 35 miles; Downtown: 1 mile; Ski lift: Nearby
General Facilities: Daily maid, Kitchen, Linens, Child planned rec.: Local child care
Room Facilities: Alpine skiing, TV, Cable, Phone in rm., Crib-Hi-chair, Ind. Heat Ctl.
Attractions: Park City, historic silver mining town, gambler's trips to Nevada, steam train.
Shops & Restaurants: Unique shops and boutiques in Park City; Huggery-seafood buffet
Units are decorated with a French accent to create a warm cozy atmosphere. Free city-wide bus route to Park City, walk to ski lifts. U.S. Film Festival at Park City in January followed by celebrity ski races and snow sculpture contest. Fall Oktoberfest and hot air balloon festival in the Fall. Park City nightlife with dance bands and folk singers.

Edelweiss Haus
P.O. Box 495, 1482 Empire Ave.
Park City, UT 84060
801-649-9342 800-438-3855

1 Bedroom $$, 2 Bedrooms $$
1 Bedrm/week 4$, 2 Bed/week 5$
AmEx/Visa/MC, Dep. Req'd. •
45 condos, Hi-rise, Key at Front office

Location: Airport: 35 miles; Downtown: 1 mile; Ski lift: Park City
General Facilities: Conf. rm. cap. 30, Kitchen, Linens
Room Facilities: Pool, Sauna, Hot tub, Winter-summer sports, TV, Cable, Phone in rm., Crib-Hi-chair, Ind. Heat Ctl.
Shops & Restaurants: Local resort shops; All types
Located 250 yards from Park City ski area, these condominiums are decorated in earth tones, brown and white. Outdoor heated swimming pool and jacuzzi. Close to market, ski shops and restaurants.

———————————— PARK CITY ————————————

Intermountain Lodging
P.O. Box 3803
Park City, UT 84060
801-649-2687 800-221-0933

Studio $, 1 Bedroom $, 2 Bedrooms $$, 3 Bedrooms $$$
Min. Stay 3 Nights, AmEx/Visa/MC,
Dep. Req'd. •
150 condos, Lo-rise, Key at At complexes
No S-yes/H-yes

Location: Airport: 26 miles; Downtown: 1 mile; Ski lift: Park City

General Facilities: Full serv., Bus. fac., Conf. rm. cap. 25, Daily maid, Kitchen, Linens, Baby-sitter, Child planned rec.: Ski school-day care

Room Facilities: Pool, Skiing, mtn. sports, TV, Cable, VCR, Phone in rm., Crib-Hi-chair, Ind. Heat Ctl.

Attractions: Nordic and alpine skiing, boating, golf, tennis, ballooning, sleigh and hay rides, entertainment

Shops & Restaurants: Alex's/French

Comfortable, deluxe condominium units centrally located to all activities. Balconies overlooking mountains and ski resort. Fine accommodations at reasonable rates located in America's best mountain resort area.

Tamarron

---------------------- PARK CITY ----------------------

Park Meadows Racquet Club   2 Bedrooms $$, 3 Bedrooms $$$
P.O. Box 680128   2 Bedrms/week 4$, 3 Bed/week 5$
Park City, UT 84068   Min. Stay 2 Nights, AmEx/Visa/MC,
801-649-9598 800-453-5789   Dep. 1 Night •
                                   180 condos, Lo-rise, Key at 1700 Park Avenue
                                   P-yes

Location: Airport: SLC 35 miles; Downtown: 2 miles; Ski lift: Nearby

General Facilities: Daily maid, Kitchen, Linens, Restaurant on prem., Bar on prem., Lounge

Room Facilities: Pool, Sauna, Hot tub, Tennis, Aerobics classes, Golf: Park Meadows Golf-near; TV, Cable, Phone in rm., Crib-Hi-chair, Ind. Heat Ctl.

Attractions: 3 golf courses within 6 miles, Park City, Mormon Tabernacle, Nevada gambling trips

Shops & Restaurants: Unique shops and boutiques in Park City; Alex's/French-continental

Traditional style, 3 levels, sliding doors to deck and lots of grassy area for play. Sauna, swimming pool and hot tub available for a fee. On-site Park City Racquet Club public facilities. Approximately 1.5 miles from Jack Nicklaus-designed Park Meadow Golf Course. Horseback riding, windsurfing, riding the rapids and helicopter skiing.

Park Plaza/Park Regency
P.O. Box 3988
Park City, UT 84060
800-553-1818 801-649-0870

Park Station Condominium Hotel Studio $$, 1 Bedroom $$, 2 Bedrooms $$$,
P.O. Box 1360   3 Bedrooms $$$$
Park City, UT 84060   AmEx/Visa/MC, Dep. Req'd. •
801-649-7717 800-367-1056   80 condos, Hi-rise, Key at Front desk
                                     H-yes

Location: Airport: 40 minutes; Downtown: 2 blocks; Ski lift: Nearby

General Facilities: Full serv., Conf. rm. cap. 50, Daily maid, Kitchen, Linens, Babysitter

Room Facilities: Pool, Sauna, Hot tub, Tennis, TV, Cable, VCR, Phone in rm., Crib-Hi-chair, Ind. AC Ctl., Ind. Heat Ctl.

Attractions: Alpine & cross-country skiing, water skiing, swimming, sailing, hiking, golf, tennis

Shops & Restaurants: Clothing, gifts, art, liquor, food, ski equipment; Philippes-French

Located next to Park City ski area's town lift. Within easy walking distance of the restaurants, shops and nightlife of the historic Main Street district. Finest hotel services in a luxurious condominium environment.

─────────────── PARK CITY ───────────────

Powderwood Resort
6975 N. 2200 W.
Park City, UT 84060
801-649-2032 800-223-7829
FAX: 801-649-8619

1 Bedroom $$, 2 Bedroom $$$
Min. Stay 3 Nights, AmEx/MC/Visa/
Other CC, Dep. 1 Night
192 condos, Lo-rise, Keys at Rental
office, No S-yes,

Location: Airport: 30 miles; Downtown: 25 miles

General Facilities: Full serv., Kitchen, Linens, Baby sitter, Gameroom, Lounge.

Room Facilities: Pool, Sauna, Hot Tub, Tennis, Gym, jogging trail, 5 minute drive, Cable, Phone in rm., Ind. Heat Ctl.

Attractions: Arnold Palmer Golf Course, horses, helicopter tours, ballooning, fishing, hiking, entertainment.

Shops & Restaurants: Shopping centers, supermarkets, Cisero's-Italian

All units have gas log fireplaces, sliding glass doors to private balconies, and queen-sized beds in the master bedroom. Continental breakfast and wine and cheese parties. This 3 year-old project has a clubhouse with a 40" color TV, electronic organ, pool table, card-backgammon table and two fireplaces. Whirlpool in a covered gazebo, steam room fitness room and volley ball and badminton court. Shuttle buses to ski resorts. Both summer and winter activites at this total resort.

───

Prospector Square Hotel
2200 Sidewinder Dr, Box 1698
Park City, UT 84060
801-649-7100 800-453-3812

1 Bedroom $$$, 2 Bedrooms $$$$, 3 Bedrooms
$$$$
Hi-rise, Key at Office

Location: Airport: SLC 30 minutes; Downtown: minutes; Ski lift: Park City

General Facilities: Full serv., Bus. fac., Conf. rm. cap. 330, Daily maid, Kitchen, Linens, Restaurant on prem., Child planned rec.: Ski area ski school

Room Facilities: Pool, Sauna, Hot tub, Tennis, Athletic Club, Golf: Two courses Park City; TV, Cable, Phone in rm.

Attractions: Park City, Deer Valley and Park West Ski areas, music, climbing, golf, tennis alpine slide, entertainment

Shops & Restaurants: Park City's 80 unique shops and galleries; Grub Steak-on-site/seafood/stk

1890's mining town atmosphere in the Wasatch Mountains, Prospector Square Hotel features three-bedroom condominiums which sleep eight. Outstanding ski vacation for all abilities. Athletic club, in-room movies, Grub Steak restaurant with Sunday Buffet Brunch Extravaganza, live entertainment and bar, and complimentary bus service to Park City resorts. Tennis, racquetball and volleyball courts.

─────────────────── PARK CITY ───────────────────

Resort Center Lodging
P.O. Box 3449
Park City, UT 84060
801-649-0800 800-824-5331

Studio $, 1 Bedroom $$, 2 Bedrooms $$, 3 Bedrooms $$$$
AmEx/Visa/MC, Dep. 1 Night •
91 condos, Lo-rise, Key at Resort Center Lodge
H-yes

Location: Airport: 35 miles; Downtown: ¾ mile; Ski lift: Nearby

General Facilities: Full serv., Conf. rm. cap. 385, Daily maid, Kitchen, Linens, Restaurant on prem., Bar on prem., Lounge, Baby-sitter, Child planned rec.: Ski instruction 3 yr

Room Facilities: Pool, Sauna, Hot tub, Tennis, Volleyball, skiing, TV, Phone in rm., Crib-Hi-chair, Ind. Heat Ctl.

Attractions: Ballooning, 3 golf courses within 10 miles, steam train, biking, fishing, brewery tours

Shops & Restaurants: Historic Main St. with boutiques, antiques, gifts; Columbine-fish, seafood

Resort Center offers accommodations with ski-in/ski-out access. Light woods, brass, glass decor with cathedral ceilings and gas fireplaces. Indoor/outdoor pool, sauna, hot tub, steam room fitness center and underground parking. Skater's Center, cross-country and downhill skiing. Summer recreation includes water sports, golf, tennis, hiking and fishing. Unique shops, nightclubs and great dining.

───

Resort Village Plaza
P.O. Box 680128
Park City, UT 84068
801-649-9598 800-453-5789

1 Bedrm/week $$$$, 2 Bed/week 4$
Min. Stay 2 Nights, AmEx/Visa/MC,
Dep. 1 Night •
160 condos, Lo-rise, Key at 1700 Park Avenue

Location: Airport: SLC 35 miles; Downtown: 1 mile; Ski lift: Nearby

General Facilities: Daily maid, Kitchen, Linens, Restaurant on prem., Bar on prem., Child planned rec.: Child care facility

Room Facilities: Hot tub, On-site skiing, Golf: Nearby; TV, Cable, Phone in rm., Crib-Hi-chair, Ind. Heat Ctl.

Attractions: 50 miles to horse racetrack in Evanston, WY, Park City, Mormon Tabernacle

Shops & Restaurants: Unique shops and boutiques in Park City; Columbine/prime rib-stir fry

At the base of the Park City ski area lifts for ski-in, ski-out accessibility. Year-round outdoor heated pool and within walking distance of shops, movie theatres, restaurants, supermarket and ice skating rink. Arrangements can be made for car rentals, lift tickets, ski equipment rentals, baby sitting and "First-Nighter" food packages. Something for everyone from winter skiing to summer activities.

———————————— PARK CITY ————————————

Ridgepoint
P.O. Box 680128
Park City, UT 84068
801-649-9598 800-453-5789

2 Bedrooms $$$, 3 Bedrooms $$$
3 Bedrms/week 6$
Min. Stay 2 Nights, AmEx/Visa/MC,
    Dep. 1 Night •
42 condos, Lo-rise, Key at 1700 Park Avenue

Location: Airport: 35 miles Salt Lake; Downtown: 2 miles; Need car; Ski lift: Nearby

General Facilities: Daily maid, Kitchen, Linens, Child planned rec.: Local care facility

Room Facilities: Pool, Hot tub, Tennis, Alpine skiing, Golf: 3 within 10 miles; TV, Cable, Phone in rm., Crib-Hi-chair, Ind. Heat Ctl.

Attractions: Museums, shops, 3 ski areas within 5 miles, Mormon Tabernacle, genealogy resources

Shops & Restaurants: Park City boutiques, Salt Lake City mall stores; Glitretind-international

Sumptuous condominiums exuding warmth and an alpine ambience. Ski bridge to Deer Valley Resort. Mountain and valley views. 2 miles away, Park City offers many unique shops and restaurants. Summer days are clear and cool and the area is framed by pines, aspen and wildflowers. Outdoor concerts and the Utah Symphony Series and August arts festival at Park City.

Shadow Ridge Resort Hotel
50 Shadow Ridge Street, Box 1820
Park City, UT 84060
801-649-4300 800-451-3031

Studio $$, 1 Bedroom $$, 2 Bedrooms $$
Min. Stay 7 Nights, AmEx/Visa/MC,
    Dep. 2 Nights •
48 condos, Hi-rise, Key at Front desk

Location: Airport: SLC Airport-34 miles; Downtown: 8 blocks

General Facilities: Full serv., Bus. fac., Conf. rm. cap. 250, Daily maid, Kitchen, Linens, Restaurant on prem., Bar on prem., Lounge, Baby-sitter

Room Facilities: Pool, Sauna, Hot tub, Skiing, golf, Golf: Park City Municipal Golf; TV, Cable, VCR, Phone in rm., Crib-Hi-chair, Ind. AC Ctl., Ind. Heat Ctl.

Attractions: Tours-Mrs. Fields Cookie Factory & Schirf Brewery, Timpanogos Cave, Temple Square, skiing, entertainment

Shops & Restaurants: Resort center, Main St. Mall, specialty stores

Four-story brick condominium development with rust, tan and forest green color schemes. Balconies off each sleeping room and private jacuzzi. Weekend entertainment in the lounge. Ski lockers, tuning and hot wax available, and walk to ski runs and Alpine Slide. Water sports in the summer with 3 reservoirs within a half-hour's drive, hayrides and flyfishing in secluded mountain streams, plus four championship golf courses within 15 minutes.

Silver Cliff Village
1485 Empire Avenue, P.O. Box 2818
Park City, UT 84060
801-649-5500 800-331-8652

2 Bedrooms $$, Lo-rise
Kitchen

Attractions: Alpine, x-country skiing-ballooning-golf-tennis-bike tours-sailing-fishing-hiking

Spacious, comfortable condominiums adjacent to Park City ski area. Woodburning fireplace, spa tub in master bedroom, washer/dryer and kitchen microwave. Staff will happily arrange your vacation activities.

——————————— PARK CITY ———————————

Silver King Hotel
P.O. Box 2818
Park City, UT 84060
801-649-5500 800-331-8652

Studio $$, 1 Bedroom $$, 2 Bedrooms $$
Min. Stay 3 Nights, AmEx/Visa/MC,
Dep. Req'd. •
85 condos, Hi-rise, Key at Front desk
H-yes

Location: Airport: 1 mile; Downtown: 35 min.; Need car; Ski lift: Nearby
General Facilities: Full serv., Conf. rm. cap. 150, Daily maid, Kitchen, Linens, Lounge
Room Facilities: Pool, Sauna, Hot tub, Golf: Park City Municipal; TV, Phone in rm.,
Crib-Hi-chair, Ind. AC Ctl., Ind. Heat Ctl.
Attractions: Skiing, snowmobiling, hot air ballooning, golf, tennis, swimming
Shops & Restaurants: Historic Main Street area, Resort Center Mall; Cafe Mariposa-
Cont., Adolphs
*Silver King Hotel is located at the base of the Park City ski area. Fully equipped studios,
one-and two-bedroom suites, and two-bedroom penthouse suites with all the amenities
and services.*

———

Silvertown Condominiums
1505 Park Avenue, P.O. Box 1090
Park City, UT 84060
801-649-9022

1 Bedroom $$, 2 Bedrooms $$$, 3 Bedrooms
$$$
AmEx/Visa/MC, Dep. 1 Night •
13 condos, Key at Office

Location: Airport: 45 minutes; Downtown: 10 blocks; Ski lift: Park City
General Facilities: Kitchen, Linens
Room Facilities: Sauna, Hot tub, Golf: Park City—2 blocks; TV, Phone in rm., Crib-Hi-
chair, Ind. Heat Ctl.
Attractions: Skiing, golf, alpine-slide, recreation water within 1 hour drive
Shops & Restaurants: Grocery store, Main Street shops-10 blocks; Adolfs/Swiss,
Glitretend/fish
Tastefully decorated units in Park City, Utah. Walk to ski lifts.

———

Snowflower Condominiums
P.O. Box 957, 400 Silver King Dr
Park City, UT 84060
801-649-6400 800-852-3101

Studio $$$, 1 Bedroom $$$$, 2 Bedrooms $$$$,
3 Bedrooms $$$$
Min. Stay 7 Nights, AmEx/Visa/MC,
Dep. Req'd. •
142 condos, Lo-rise, Key at Front desk
H-yes

Location: Airport: 45 minutes; Ski lift: Park City
General Facilities: Bus. fac., Conf. rm. cap. 70, Daily maid, Kitchen, Baby-sitter
Room Facilities: Hot tub, Tennis, TV, Cable, Phone in rm., Crib-Hi-chair
Attractions: Skiing, snowmobiling, hot air ballooning, sleigh rides, ice skating, x-
country skiing
Shops & Restaurants: Local shops; Over 42 restaurants
*Summer or winter, something for everyone. Skiers' access to 82 designated trails. On-site
tennis, close to golf, racquetball, swimming, hiking and horses, Park City special events,
shops and restaurants. Units have jetted hot tubs and fireplaces.*

PARK CITY

Stag Lodge
P.O. Box 3000, 8200 Royal St. East
Park City, UT 84060
801-649-7444 800-453-3833

3 Bedrooms 7$
Min. Stay 7 Nights, AmEx/Visa/MC,
Dep. Req'd. •
34 condos, Lo-rise, Key at Front desk
No S-yes/H-yes

Location: Airport: 35 miles; Downtown: 3 miles; Need car; Ski lift: Nearby

General Facilities: Full serv., Conf. rm. cap. 40, Daily maid, Kitchen, Linens, Restaurant on prem., Lounge, Baby-sitter

Room Facilities: Pool, TV, Cable, Phone in rm., Crib-Hi-chair, Ind. Heat Ctl.

Attractions: Ballooning, x-c, Mormon Tabernacle, steam railroad, theatre, sleigh rides

Shops & Restaurants: Main Street shopping; Philippe's/contintental

Luxury units done in a southwestern motif with private hot tubs. On the slopes of Deer Valley Resort for ski-in/ski-out access. Lodge features a highly regarded full-service restaurant.

The Innsbruck
1201 Norfolk, P.O. Box 222
Park City, UT 84060
801-649-9829

1 Bedroom $$, 2 Bedrooms $$$
1 Bedrm/week 5$, 2 Bed/week 7$
Min. Stay 2 Nights, Dep. Req'd. •
8 condos, Lo-rise, Key at On premises

Location: Airport: 35 miles; Downtown: bus 1 mile; Ski lift: Park City

General Facilities: Kitchen, Linens

Room Facilities: Pool, Sauna, Hot tub, Golf: Park City, Park Meadows; TV, Crib-Hi-chair, Ind. Heat Ctl.

Attractions: Skiing, ice skating, golf, tennis, hiking, Alpine Slide

Shops & Restaurants: Park City Main Street unique shops; Baja Cantina/Mexican

A-frame one-bedroom chalets with rough wood walls, conversation pit and gas-burning Franklin stove fireplace. Modern apartments with spiral wrought iron staircases and large sleeping lofts. Mt. Metro shuttle bus takes you to Main Street, Deer Valley ski area and Park City Racquet Club.

The Stein Eriksen Lodge
7400 Lake Flat Road, Box 3779
Park City, UT 84060
801-649-3700 800-453-1302

1 Bedroom $$$$, 2 Bedrooms $$$$, 3 Bedrooms
4$
1 Bedrm/week 5$
AmEx/Visa/MC, Dep. Req'd. •
120 condos, Lo-rise, Key at Front desk, H-yes

Location: Airport: Salt Lake City; Downtown: 30 miles; Ski lift: Deer Vlly

General Facilities: Full serv., Conf. rm. cap. 180, Daily maid, Kitchen, Linens, Restaurant on prem., Bar on prem., Lounge, Baby-sitter

Room Facilities: Pool, Sauna, Tennis, Health club, Golf: Two courses in town; TV, Cable, Phone in rm., Ind. Heat Ctl.

Attractions: Historic Main Street, Alpine slide, Ontario Mine, hiking, tennis, sail boarding, fishing, entertainment

Shops & Restaurants: 86 shops & boutiques on Main Street; Glitretind/European

Overstuffed down comforters and Norwegian pine furniture, gold plated fixtures and terry cloth robes, oversize whirlpool bathtub, fireplace and custom European kitchen. Friendly and informal service, mountain scenery and rustic Norwegian elegance.

——————————— SALT LAKE CITY ———————————

Chamonix Group
3865 S. 3500 E., Suite 206
Salt Lake City, UT 84109
801-262-1299

2 Bedrooms $$$, Lo-rise
Kitchen

Attractions: Gondola, outdoor/indoor tennis, hayrides, mine train ride, Alping Slide, fishing, swimming, skiing, golf

Charming two-story alpine chalets have wood walls and cathedral ceilings for a real mountain feeling. View the mountains from your private sun deck. Private ski room, parking for four vehicles and upstairs loft.

——————————— SNOWBIRD ———————————

The Lodge At Snowbird
Snowbird Resort, Entry 3
Snowbird, UT 84092
801-521-6040

Studio $$$, 1 Bedroom $$$$, 2 Bedrooms 4$
AmEx/Visa/MC, Dep. Req'd. •
120 condos, Hi-rise, Key at Front desk

Location: Airport: 45 minutes; Downtown: 35 min.; Ski lift: Alta

General Facilities: Full serv., Conf. rm., Daily maid, Kitchen, Linens, Restaurant on prem., Bar on prem., Lounge, Baby-sitter, Child planned rec.: Ski season programs

Room Facilities: Pool, Sauna, Hot tub, Tennis, Ski resort, TV, Cable, Phone in rm., Crib-Hi-chair, Ind. Heat Ctl.

Shops & Restaurants: Trolley Square, Shopping malls

Full-size kitchen, fireplace and specially designed sofa beds. Non-ski season rates are less than half the ski season rates.

Please mention *Condo Vacations the Complete Guide* when you reserve your condominium.

Vermont

Stowe
Smugglers Notch •• East Burke
• Bolton Valley •
Bolton
Warren • Fairlee
Waitsfield

Killington
•

• Plymouth
• Rutland

Manchester
Center
•• Stratton Mt.
Rawsonville ••
Wilmington •• West Dover

BOLTON VALLEY

Bolton Valley Resort
Bolton Valley, VT 05477
802-434-2131 800-451-3220

1 Bedroom $$$, 2 Bedrooms $$$$, 3 Bedrooms $$$$
1 Bedrm/week 6$, 2 Bed/week 7$, 3 Bed/week 10$, Min. Stay 2 Nights, 108 condos

Location: Airport: Burlington-19 miles; Downtown: 19 miles; Ski lift: B.Valley

General Facilities: Bus. fac., Conf. rm. cap. 50, Daily maid, Kitchen, Linens, Restaurant on prem., Bar on prem., Lounge, Baby-sitter, Child planned rec.: Nursery, Pied Piper

Room Facilities: Pool, Sauna, Tennis, Sports club-aerobics, Golf: Nearby; TV, Phone in rm., Crib-Hi-chair

Attractions: Shelburne Museum, Champlain Shakespeare festival, Barre granite quarries, tours, cruises, entertainment

Shops & Restaurants: On-site country store, gift shop, Burlington shops; Lindsays/nouveau cuisine

Casually decorated in early American style with fireplaces and decks, located in a self-contained village steps from ski slopes. Restaurants, indoor sports club, tanning bed, masseuse, gift shops. Winter programs for children under 6, including 3 evenings of games, movies and crafts. The only major resort in Vermont offering night skiing. Summer fishing and hiking. The on-site naturalist can take you on a guided nature tour, or get in shape with aerobic and stretch classes.

─────────────── BOLTON ───────────────

Trailside Condominiums
Bolton Valley
Bolton, VT 05477
802-434-2769 800-451-5025

1 Bedroom $$$, 2 Bedrooms $$$$, 3 Bedrooms $$$$
1 Bedrm/week 6$, 2 Bed/week 7$, 3 Bed/week 10$
Min. Stay 2 Nights, Visa/MC, Dep. Req'd.
Lo-rise

Location: Airport: Burlington; Downtown: walk; Ski lift: Bolton V.

General Facilities: Kitchen, Linens, Restaurant on prem., Bar on prem., Lounge, Child planned rec.: Ski lessons/programs

Room Facilities: Pool, Sauna, Hot tub, Tennis, B. Valley sports club, TV, Phone in rm.

Attractions: Novice to expert skiing, cross-country skiing, telemark skiing, Honey Bear day/night care, entertainment

Shops & Restaurants: Bolton Village unique shops, grocery market; Lindsay's/nouvelle cuisine

Condominiums within the Village area, on or near ski trails, with fireplaces and decks/patios. Bolton Valley Sports Club for pre-ski, after-ski and non-skiers. 7 restaurants and cafes with varied menus. James Moore Tavern for an after-ski hot cider and nightly entertainment. Especially for children, Bear's Den ski center, terrain garden for outdoor play, Pied Piper, dinner, movies, games, crafts, and nursery. MAP packages.

─────────────── EAST BURKE ───────────────

Burke Mountain Condominiums
Box 247
East Burke, VT 05832
802-626-3305 800-541-5480

1 Bedroom $$$, 2 Bedrooms $$$$, Lo-rise
Kitchen

Attractions: Skiing, windsurfing, swimming, lake fishing

Choice of 5 slopeside and trailside condominiums with kitchens and TV. Fun ski instruction and races for children and teens. Short drive to area lakes for rest-of-the-year swimming, windsurfing and fishing.

─────────────── FAIRLEE ───────────────

Eagle's Nest Inn & Resort
Lake Shore Road, P.O. Box 308
Fairlee, VT 05045
802-333-4302

AmEx/Visa/MC, Dep. Req'd. •
36 condos, Lo-rise, Key at Lobby front desk
No S-yes/P-yes/H-yes

Location: Airport: 20 miles; Downtown: 2 miles; Beach front; Ski lift: 20 min.

General Facilities: Conf. rm. cap. 100, Daily maid, Kitchen, Linens, Restaurant on prem., Bar on prem., Game room, Lounge, Baby-sitter

Room Facilities: Pool, Sauna, Hot tub, Tennis, Boating, fishing, Golf: 18-hole championship; Phone in rm., Crib-Hi-chair, Ind. AC Ctl., Ind. Heat Ctl.

Attractions: Maple sugar making, antiquing, foliage, Queechee balloonfest, Dartmouth Col, Octoberfest, entertainment

Shops & Restaurants: West Lebanon Shopping Center, J.C. Penny's; Water's Edge/continental

Cozy townhouses with picturesque Vermont scenery, located on Lake Morey. Townhouses are two-story, contemporary to traditional Vermont furnishings, with kitchenettes. Centrally located Lodge for dining, library reading and card or board games. Crystal clear lake makes fishing and water activities a must. Fall foliage, winter skiing, bicycling, horseback riding and ping-pong. Local auctions, antique shops and flea markets.

---------------------------- KILLINGTON ----------------------------

Killington Townhouses　　1 Bedroom $$, 2 Bedrooms $$
R.R. 1, Box 10-A　　　　　　1 Bedrm/week 4$, 2 Bedrms/week 6$
Killington, VT 05751　　　　AmEx/Visa/MC, Dep. Required
802-773-4488　800-822-5011　16 condos, Lo-rise
　　　　　　　　　　　　　　Key at Greenbrier Inn-Rt. 4

Location: Airport: Rutland 15 miles; Need car; Ski lift at Nearby

General Facilities: Linens; Crib-Hi-chair

Sports Facilities: Sauna; Hot tub; Tennis; Badminton, volleyball; Nearby

Room Facilities: Kitchen; Phone; Ind.Heat Ctl.

Attractions: Pico Alpine Slide, Wilson Castle, museums, galleries, Killington gondola, summer theatre,

Shops & Restaurants: Bridgewater Mall, outlets, Rutland stores; Hemingways/nouvelle-Jasons/It.

Luxurious vacation living in decorator-furnished, fully appointed townhouse units. 4 bedroom chalet with wood paneling and ski house decor. Rental includes free use of Cortina Inn Health Spa: indoor pool, sauna, whirlpool, exercise room and 8 tennis courts. Killington Gondola has a view that extends into 5 states and Canada. 6 mountains for skiing, golf, fishing, horses and entertainment within minutes.

---------------------------- MANCHESTER CENTER ----------------------------

Bromley Village　　　　　1 Bedrm/week 4$, 2 Bedrms/week 5$,
Condominiums　　　　　　　3 Bedrms/week 9$
Box 1130　　　　　　　　　　Min. Stay Ask, AmEx/Visa/MC •
Manchester Center, VT 05255　70 condos, Key at Lodging Office,
802-824-5458　800-865-4786　P-No/H-No
FAX: 802-824-5179

Location: Airport: Albany, 1.5 hours; Downtown: Manchester 6 miles; Need car

General Facilities: Linens; Crib

Sports Facilities: Pool; Tennis; Snowmobile, ice skate; Near 4 Golf Courses; Ski school, day care

Room Facilities: Kitchen; Cable; Phone; Ind.Heat Ctl.

Attractions: Summer: Bromley Alpine Slide, Devalkarts Theater, Appalachian Trail. Winter: Skiing

Shops & Restaurants: Outlets: Ralph Lauren, Calvin Klein, Liz Claiborne, 9-West

On-mountain convenience in condominiums with fully-equipped kitchens, linens, cable TV and telephone. Available by the weekend, week, month, or the entire season. You can walk to the heated swimming pool and tennis courts in the summer. In the winter walk to the ski slopes or ride our free shuttle bus. Winter ski packages available.

———————————— PLYMOUTH ————————————

Hawk Inn & Mountain Resort 2 Bedrooms $$$$, 3 Bedrooms $$$$
Route 100, Box 64, NCR 70 Min. Stay 2 Nights, AmEx/Visa/MC, Dep.
Plymouth, VT 05056 Required, Lo-rise
802-672-3811 FAX: 802-672-5067
800-685-HAWK

Location: Airport: Burlington; Downtown: nearby; Ski lift at Nearby

General Facilities: Full hotel service; Linens; Restaurant on premises

Sports Facilities: Pool; Sauna; Hot tub; Tennis; Spa, boats, horses; Woodstock
   Golf Course; Day program

Room Facilities: Kitchen

Attractions: Sailing, canoeing, stables, squash, racquetball, jogging, fishing

Shops & Restaurants: Quaint villages, antiques, crafts, maple syrup; Hawk's
   River Tavern Restaurant

Spectacular award-winning resort with townhouses tucked away in private, wooded sites where you can enjoy the changing Vermont seasons. Ski Killington's six mountains, explore the forest on x-country skis or snowshoes. Skate at the lighted rink, and then to the glass-enclosed spa. Lake Amherst for boating and 300-acre Nature Preserve for riding, hiking and picnicing. Maple syrup in spring, apple cider in fall. New England cuisine at Hawk's River Tavern. Forget your problems, refresh your spirit.

———————————— QUECHEE ————————————

Quechee Lakes Rentals 1 Bedrm/week 5$, 2 Bedrms/week 8$,
P.O. Box 385 3 Bedrms/week 10$
Quechee, VT 05059 Min. Stay 2 Nights, Visa/MC •
802-295-1970 800-745-0042 100 condos, Villas, Key at Rental office,
FAX: 802-296-6852 P-No/No S-Yes

Location: Airport: Lebanon, 20 minutes; Need car; Ski lift at On-site

General Facilities: Linens; Baby sitter; Lounge; Crib-Hi-Chair; Restaurant on
   premises; Bar on premises

Business Facilities: Bus. fac.; Conf. Room Cap. 200

Sports Facilities: Game room; Pool; Sauna; Spa; Tennis; Skate, bike, fishing;
   Highland & Lakeland GC; Childrens rec. programs

Room Facilities: Kitchen; Cable; VCR; Ind.Heat Ctl.

Attractions: Quechee Gorge, Killinton Congola, Dartmouth College, Woodstock
   Vermont; Annual events

Shops & Restaurants: Plaza shopping, J.C. Penneys, Sears; Simon Pearce-ele-
   gant fine dining

Vermont's finest 4-season community—Quechee Lakes, a 5500 acre private resort community located in the beautiful Ottaquechee River Valley is a spectacular combination of elegant homes and luxurious condominiums. The Quechee club offers the best in recreational activities for all age groups. Quechee Lakes also makes a perfect base for day trips thru rural and historic Vermont and New Hampshire. 1- to 4-bedroom fully furnished condominiums are available throughout the Quechee Lakes area.

Jackson Hole Ski Area

SMUGGLERS NOTCH

The Village At Smugglers Notch
Route 108
Smugglers Notch, VT 05464
802-644-8851 800-451-8752

AmEx/Visa/MC, Dep. Req'd. •
279 condos, Lo-rise, Villas, Key at Front desk
H-yes

Location: Airport: 28 miles; Ski lift: Nearby

General Facilities: Full serv., Conf. rm. cap. 300, Kitchen, Linens, Restaurant on prem., Bar on prem., Game room, Lounge, Baby-sitter, Child planned rec.: Camps for kids

Room Facilities: Pool, Sauna, Hot tub, Tennis, Skiing, Golf: Stowe Country Club; TV, Phone in rm., Crib-Hi-chair, Ind. Heat Ctl.

Attractions: Stowe Alpine slide, Ben & Jerry's ice cream factory, Shelburne Museum, Montreal day trips, entertainment

Shops & Restaurants: Antiques & specialty craft stores, Factory outlets; Ilse De France/Crown & Anchor

Self-contained resort village with fully equipped condominium homes in a peaceful mountain setting. Ski resort in winter, summer tennis, family and children's programs. Live entertainment, dancing and movies in the lounge. All day ski camps, summer discovery and adventure camps for children, as well as Alice's Wonderland child care.

―――――――――――――― STOWE ――――――――――――――

Golden Eagle Resort
P.O. Box 1090, Mountain Road
Stowe, VT 05672
802-253-4811 800-626-1010

2 Bedrooms $$
2 Bedrms/week 6$
AmEx/Visa/MC, Dep. 1 Night •
8 condos, Lo-rise, Key at Front office
H-yes

Location: Airport: 40 Miles; Downtown: ½ mile; Ski lift: Stowe

General Facilities: Conf. rm. cap. 60, Daily maid, Kitchen, Linens, Restaurant on prem., Bar on prem., Game room, Lounge, Baby-sitter

Room Facilities: Pool, Sauna, Hot tub, Tennis, Skiing, fishing, hike, Golf: Stone Country Club-near; TV, Cable, Phone in rm., Crib-Hi-chair, Ind. AC Ctl., Ind. Heat Ctl.

Attractions: Concerts-theatre-tennis-golf-horse & dog shows-antique car rally-craft fairs-auctions, entertainment

Shops & Restaurants: Small shops with unique products; Alpine/Bavarian-Partridge/fish

Quiet, scenic Vermont resort, beautifully landscaped gardens and grounds, trout ponds, walking trails, tennis, heated pools, health spa with indoor pool, whirlpool and sauna. Stowe is the ski capital of the East, but also has many summer activities. Visit Morgan Horse Farm., Trapp Family Gardens, the world's largest granite quarry or Shelburne Museum. Movies, Monday night winter wine and cheese parties, summer poolside barbecues, picnic tables and lawn games. Package plans are also offered.

―――――――――――――――――――――――――――――――――――――

Mount Mansfield Townhouses
Mountain Road
Stowe, VT 05672
802-253-7311 800-253-4754

AmEx/Visa/MC, Dep. 1 Night •
100 condos, Lo-rise, Key at Front desk
H-yes

Location: Airport: 40 minutes; Downtown: 6 miles; Ski lift: Stowe

General Facilities: Full serv., Bus. fac., Conf. rm. cap. 200, Daily maid, Kitchen, Linens, Restaurant on prem., Bar on prem., Game room, Lounge, Baby-sitter, Child planned rec.: All season programs

Room Facilities: Pool, Sauna, Tennis, Fitness Center, Golf: Stowe Country Club 4 mi; TV, Cable, Phone in rm., Crib-Hi-chair, Ind. Heat Ctl.

Attractions: Morgan Horse Farm., granite quarry, Lake Champlain, Shelburne Museum, antique car rally, entertainment

Shops & Restaurants: Unique, family or individually owned shops; Toll House-Cliff House-C. Club

Contemporary, slopeside townhouses in a wooded setting in a quaint New England village. Summer water activities on nearby lakes, concerts, theaters, trails, trout streams and ballooning to name a few activities. Fantastic world-class skiing for all levels. Three onsite restaurants and over 30 in Stowe Village to satisfy every taste. Apres-ski entertainment, Fireside Tavern and special events. Special children's programs with nature walks, crafts and ski school. Golf, tennis and resort packages.

—————————————— STOWE ——————————————

Mountainside Resort At Stowe
930 Cottage Club Rd.
Stowe, VT 05672
802-253-8610 800-458-4893
FAX: 800-458-4893

Studio $$, 1 Bedroom $$$,
2 Bedrooms $$$$, 3 Bedrooms $$$$
1 Bedrm/week 4$, 2 Bedrms/week 6$, 3
Bedrms/week 7$
Visa/MC, Lo-rise, Key at Cottage Club Rd.

Location: Ski lift at Stowe
General Facilities: Linens
Sports Facilities: Sauna; Hot tub
Room Facilities: Kitchen; Satel; Phone
Attractions: Skiing, snowboards, Winter carnival, Cross country challenge, ice skating
Shops & Restaurants: Walk to ski shop, convenience store, restaurants; Area restaurants

Individually decorated, fully equipped, firewood provided. Indoor pool, sauna, whirlpool, lounge, wet bar, lighted tennis courts. 3 miles to shopping, entertainment, ice rink, horses. Recreation field has swings, horseshoes, barbeques, picnic tables. Quiet, hillside setting.

—————————————————————————————————————

Stoweflake Resort Townhouses
Box 369
Stowe, VT 05672
802-253-7355 800-253-2232
FAX: 802-253-6858

Studio $$$, 2 Bedrooms $$$$,
3 Bedrooms $$$$
Lo-rise, Key at Reception desk

Location: Airport: Burlington 45 min.; Ski lift at Stowe
General Facilities: Lounge; Restaurant on premises; Bar on premises
Business Facilities: Conf. Room Cap. 250
Sports Facilities: Pool; Sauna; Tennis; Badminton, Fitness center; Stowe Golf Course
Room Facilities: Kitchen
Attractions: Horseback riding, skiing, Lake Elmore, jogging, ice skating, movies, antiques and crafts; Entertainment
Shops & Restaurants: Stowe Villages shops, antiques, crafts; Winfield's-Continental/American, on-site

Year-round resort hosted by the Baraw family. Secluded, luxury units with fireplaces and ski rooms. Step out of you door to cross-country trails. Two mountains for the downhill skier with ski schools and nursery. 2-story suites and cottage apartments also available. Spring flowers and lush summer valleys for picnicking beside mountain streams. Vivid fall colors. Hot air ballooning. Snacks at Charlie B's Vermont decorated bar and lounge with frequent entertainment, romantic candelit dinner at Winfield's.

──────────────── STOWE ────────────────

Topnotch At Stowe　　　　1 Bedroom $$, 2 Bedrooms $$$, 3 Bedrooms
P.O. Box 1260　　　　　　　$$$$
Stowe, VT 05672
802-253-8585　800-451-8686

Location:　Airport: Burlington 45 min.; Downtown: walk; Need car; Ski lift: Stowe

General Facilities:　Full serv., Conf. rm. cap. 200, Kitchen, Linens, Restaurant on prem.,
　　Game room, Lounge

Room Facilities:　Pool, Sauna, Hot tub, Tennis, Exercise room, horses, Golf: Stowe Country Club

Attractions:　Ice skating, tobogganing, country bazaars, auctions, flea markets, craft
　　shows, entertainment

Shops & Restaurants:　Stowe Village boutiques; Topnotch restaurant

*Concierge greets you in the library when you arrive. Retire to your condominium where
you'll find a private library, imported soaps, bath gels and fluffy towels. Be ready for a great
ski vacation. Ice-skate, toboggan or snowshoe for a change of pace. The rest of the year
is equally exciting with tennis, equestrian center, exercise room, swimming, games, putting green and lawn croquet. After a long hike in the woods, dine on the terrace and dance
at the Buttertub Bar.*

Trapp Family Lodge　　　　Pool, Kitchen, Phone in rm.
Stowe, VT 05672
802-253-8511　800-826-7000

Attractions:　Golf, tennis, swimming, concerts, trout fishing, mountain gondola rides,
　　Sports Center

*Units on the hillside, steps away from the Lodge with view decks. Over 40 miles of groomed
cross-country trails and a complete Touring Center, plus Mt. Mansfield for downhill skiing in the winter.*

──────────── STRATTON MOUNTAIN ────────────

Stratton Mountain Resort　　AmEx/Visa/MC
Stratton Mountain, VT 05155　　110 condos, Villas
802-197-2200　800-843-6862

Location:　Airport: Albany, NY 81 miles; Downtown: 18 miles; Ski lift: Nearby

General Facilities:　Conf. rm. cap. 225, Kitchen, Restaurant on prem., Bar on prem.

Room Facilities:　Pool, Sauna, Hot tub, Tennis, Sports center, Golf: Stratton Mt. Country Club; TV, Cable, Phone in rm., Ind. Heat Ctl.

Attractions:　Charming Vermont towns, biking, fishing, skiing, entertainment

Shops & Restaurants:　Stratton Mt. Village, Manchester retail outlets; Mulligans-Sage
　　Hill-Tenderloin

*An award-winning, four-season mountain vacation center in Southern Vermont. All year
long it serves as the favorite location for skiers, golfers, tennis players and sports
enthusiasts. 27-hole of golf surrounded by dramatic mountain scenery, and Lake, Mountain and Forest nines. Fully-equipped pro shop and practice range. Seven restaurants on
the mountain offer a variety of fare and some have dancing and entertainment.*

——————————————— WAITSFIELD ———————————————

Eagles at Sugarbush
Route 100, P.O. Box 180
Waitsfield, VT 05673
802-496-5700

2 Bedrooms $$
2 Bedrms/week 7$
Visa/MC,Dep. Req'd.
16 condos, Villas, Key at Clubhouse Office
H-yes

Location: Airport: Burlington-50 min.; Downtown: ½ mile; Need car; Ski lift: Nearby

General Facilities: Full serv., Kitchen, Linens, Game room, Lounge, Baby-sitter

Room Facilities: Pool, Sauna, Tennis, Racquet/game room, Golf: Sugarbush-near; TV, Cable, Phone in rm., Crib-Hi-chair, Ind. AC Ctl., Ind. Heat Ctl.

Attractions: Skiing, tennis, golf, swimming, fishing, Grand Prix Horse Show, 4th of July fun, entertainment

Shops & Restaurants: Antique and specialty shops, grocery stores; The Common Man-European

Custom-built, individual, contemporary two-thousand-square-foot residences with individual saunas. Backwoods trails and streams for fishing, riding, canoeing or bird-watching, country walks through covered bridges and pastures. Clubhouse with pool, tennis and racquetball, plus multi-million dollar sports center. Some of the finest and most challenging ski runs in the U.S. from novice to professional. Privacy and relaxation in unspoiled Vermont.

———————————————— WARREN ————————————————

The Battleground
Route 17, Sugarbush
Warren, VT 05674
802-496-2288

Pool, Kitchen, Linens, Phone in rm.

Attractions: Skiing at Sugarbush, tennis, Sugarbush Sports Center, swimming, paddle tennis

Arrive at this luxury four-season resort through a rustic covered bridge. Townhouses on 60 wooded acres. Step out on your deck and watch picturesque brooks meander along the valley. Ledgestone fireplace, washer/dryer and color cable TV in your two-bath unit.

Sugarbush Inn
Sugarbush Access Road
Warren, VT 05674
802-583-2301 800-451-4320

Location: Ski lift: x-country

General Facilities: Conf. rm. cap. 225, Kitchen, Restaurant on prem., Bar on prem.

Room Facilities: Pool, Sauna, Hot tub, Tennis, Hiking, fishing, Golf: Sugarbush Golf Course

Attractions: Skiing, hiking, fishing, soaring, polo

Shops & Restaurants: Montpelier shopping; Onion Patch, Main dining room

One-, two-and three-bedroom condominiums in a luxurious, isolated retreat in the Green Mountains. Trout-filled streams, wooden bridges, tennis, indoor and outdoor pools, and outstanding golf course. Nightly seafood bar on the front lawn of the Inn. Winter cross-country skiing.

———————————————— WEST DOVER ————————————————

Timber Creek Townhomes
P.O. Box 191
West Dover, VT 05356
802-464-2323 800-882-5467
FAX: 802-464-8834

1 Bedroom $$$$, 2 Bedrooms $$$$,
  3 Bedrooms $$$$, 1 Bedrm/week 5$,
  2 Bedrm/week 5$, 3 Bedrm/week 7$,
  Min. Stay: 2 Nights, AmEx/Visa/MC,
  Dep. 50%, •
100 condos, H-yes, Key at on-site office.

Location: Airport: 2.5 hours; Downtown: 9 miles, Need car.

General Facilities: Lounge, Pool, Golf: 1 mile, Tennis, Boating, hiking, Babysitter.

Room Facilities: Daily maid, Kitchen, TV, Cable, VCR, Phone, Crib-Hi-chair, Ind. Heat Ctl.

Attractions: X-country skiing, shuttle to Mt. Snow, mountain biking, antiquing, museums, play houses, entertainment.

Shops & Restaurants: Gift shops, factory outlet stores, La Petite Chef/French /American.

Spacious, luxury townhomes with contemporary furnishings, spectacular views of Mt. Snow, fully equipped with optional hot tub or sauna. Two minutes to the lifts via private shuttle bus. Fireplaces, firewood, on-site X-country skiing, full health club facilities with racquetball courts, indoor pool, whirlpool, tanning booth, lounge and more. Scheduled summer activities. Near golf, hiking, boating and fishing.

Subscribe to our newsletter *Mondo Condo* and hear about the latest special condo vacation values.

Virginia

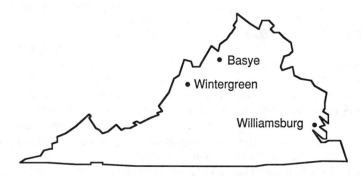

--------- BASYE ---------

The Pine Villas
P.O. Box 76
Basye, VA 22810
703-856-2111

1 Bedroom $$$, 2 Bedrooms $$$.
Kitchen, Linens.

Attractions: Fishing, golf, tennis, horses, skiing, Endless caverna, Orkney Springs.

Chalets, condos and townhouses that sleep 4 to 10 persons. Short walk to amenities, or just off the ski slopes. Recreation room with sauna and jacuzzi. Try grass skiing or windsurf on Lake Laura. Lakes, rivers and national forest to explore.

--------- VIRGINIA BEACH ---------

The Colony Condominium
1301 Atlantic Ave.
Virginia Beach, VA 23451
804-425-8689

2 Bedrooms $$$, 2 Bedrm/week 9$, Min. Stay: 3 Nights.
38 condos, Hi-rise, H-yes, Key at office on property.

Location: Airport: 20 minutes, Need car, Ocean front.

General Facilities: Pool.

Room Facilities: Kitchen, TV, Cable, Crib-Hi-chair, Ind. AC. Ctl., Ind. Heat Ctl.

Attractions: Williamsburg, Bush Gardens, York Town, James Town, historical areas.

Shops & Restaurants: Lynhaven Mall, Sears, Hechts, Wards, Leggetts, Penny's, Lighthouse, Blue Pete's/seafood, Tandoms.

Fully furnished units accommodating six people. Contemporary furnishings. Pool overlooks the ocean. Drive to historic Williamsburg, York Town and James Town. Enjoy deep sea fishing and the many sights and museums in the area.

WILLIAMSBURG

Kingsmill Resort & Conference Ctr
1010 Kingsmill Rd.
Williamsburg, VA 23185
804-253-1703 800-832-5665

Studio $$$, 1 Bedroom $$$$, 2 Bedrooms $$$$, 3 Bedrooms $$$$, 1 Bed/week 7$, 2 Bed/week 10$, 3 Bed/week 10$
Amex, Visa, MC, Dep. 1 night
Key at Front desk
160 condos, Lo-rise, Villas, H-yes •

Location: Airport: Norfolk 40 minutes; Downtown: 5 minutes

General facilities: Full serv., Bus. fac., Conf. Rm. (cap. 360), Daily maid, Kitchen, Linens, Movies, Baby sitter, Restaurant, Bar, Game room, Lounge, Hot tub

Room facilities: TV, Cable, Phone, Crib-Hi-chair, Ind. AC. Ctl., Ind. Heat Ctl.

Sports facilities: Pool, Tennis, 2 Golf courses, Aerobics, Weight training

Attractions: Free shuttle service to Busch Gardens and Williamsburg, Old Country Entertainment Center, lounge music

Shops & Restaurants: Colonial Williamsburg shops, top brand outlets, pottery, Riverview/gourmet LeYaca/French

Luxurious villas set on 2,900 acres on the banks of the James River. Nautilus exercise room, 15 tennis courts, complete Sports Club with indoor and outdoor pools, racquetball courts and 3 golf courses, including the River Course, home of the $1 million Anheuser-Busch Golf Classic. Explore colonial Williamsburg, Jamestown and Yorktown. Choice of casual or elegant dining at this ideal family vacation resort.

———————————— WINTERGREEN ————————————

Wintergreen Resort
P.O. Box 706
Wintergreen, VA 22958
804-325-2200 800-325-2200
FAX: 804-325-6760

1 Bedroom $$$$, 2 Bedrooms $$$$, Jr. $$$,
1 Bedrm/week 7$, 2 Bedrm/week 10$,
3 Bedrm/week 10$, AmEx/Visa/MC,
Dep. 1 Night, •
327 condos, Hi-rise, Lo-rise, Villas, H-yes,
Key at front desk.

Location: Airport: Charlottesville—43miles, Need car.

General Facilities: Bus. fac., Conf. Rm. Cap.: 600, Lounge, Game room, Pool, Hot tub, Sauna, Program & activities, Tennis, 2 18 hole championship golf courses, Spa, equestrian center, Baby sitter, Restaurant, Bar.

Room Facilities: Daily maid, Kitchen, TV, Phone, Crib-Hi-chair, Ind. AC Ctl., Ind. Heat Ctl.

Attractions: Michie Tavern Museum, Stonewall Jackson House, Monticello, Wray Caverns, University of Virginia.

Shops & Restaurants: Gallery of Shops, The Copper Mine, Garden Terrace/Gristmill/The Veranda.

A unique resort experience awaits you at Wintergreen's 11000 acre resort extending from the Blue Ridge Mountains to the valley below. Wintergreen offers recreational facilities for all seasons. The resort features luxurious accommodations and fine dining ranging from continental cuisine to family-style. The resort—43 miles southwest of Charlottesville and 3 hour drive from the nation's capitol—is accessible via interstates 64 or 81.

Wintergreen Resort, Wintergreen, VA

Washington

PORT LUDLOW

The Resort at Port Ludlow
60M #3 Paradise Bay Road
Port Ludlow, WA 98365
206-437-2222   800-732-1239

General Facilities: Conf. rm. cap. 125, Kitchen, Restaurant on prem., Bar on prem., Game room, Child planned rec.: Supervised game room

Room Facilities: Pool, Sauna, Hot tub, Tennis, Bikes, Croquet, Golf: Port Ludlow Golf Course

Attractions: Victorian homes tours, Port Townsend, Hurricane Ridge, sailing on Puget Sound, entertainment

Shops & Restaurants: Harbormaster/seafood

Comfortable condominiums ranging from one bedroom and bath combinations to four-bedroom, four-bath suites, most with a bird's-eye view of the water and hills. Designed for family enjoyment, recreational activities include pools, squash court, tennis courts, saunas, pitch and putt area, and bicycles. Rent a sailboat on Puget Sound or join a sight-seeing tour at the 30-slip marina. Relax in the solitude of the 3500 acres, or participate in nature hikes, raft trips and charter fishing.

ROCHE HARBOR

Roche Harbor Resort   1 Bedroom $$, 2 Bedrooms $$$
P.O. Box 4001   Pool, Kitchen
Roche Harbor, WA 98250
206-378-2155

Attractions: Whale Museum, cruises, English & American Camps, UofW Marine Laboratories, Limekiln Park, volleyball, horseshoes, tennis

Arrive at the island via a two-hour ferry ride for rural charm and romantic escape any time of the year. Mild spring and fall temperatures. Whales return in spring, summer boating, fall salmon fishing and winter scuba diving and beachcombing.

West Virginia

Morgantown

Canaan Valley, Davis

White Sulphur Springs

CANAAN VALLEY, DAVIS

Land of Canaan Vacation Resort
Route 1, Box 291
Canaan Valley, Davis, WV 26260
304-866-4425

2 Bedrooms $$
Min. Stay 2 Nights, MC, Dep. Req'd.
Villas, Key on-site

Location: Airport: 30 miles; Need car

General Facilities: Bus. fac., Daily maid, Kitchen, Linens, Game room, Baby-sitter, Child planned rec.: Activities Director

Room Facilities: Pool, Hot tub, Tennis, Golf: Canaan Valley Resort Park; TV, Cable, VCR, Phone in rm., Crib-Hi-chair, Ind. Heat Ctl.

Attractions: National forest, two state parks, primitive wilderness, Blackwater falls, white water, hunting, entertainment

Shops & Restaurants: None; Oriskany Inn/continental

Modern Broyhill furnishings with oak trim, two-bedrooms with jacuzzi, and tennis, pool and hot tub on the property. Recreation and activities director to help plan your vacation fun. A national forest, two state parks and a primitive wilderness area are minutes away. Canaan Valley State Park boasts ice skating, skiing, golfing, hiking, & bird watching. Enjoy the wildflowers of spring, warm mountain beauty of summer, and fall hunting season. Vacation time is always here.

---------------------- MORGANTOWN ----------------------

Lakeview Resort Club
Route 6, Box 88-A
Morgantown, WV 26505
304-594-1111 800-624-8300

2 Bedrooms $$$$
2 Bedrms/week 7$
AmEx/Visa/MC, Dep. 1 Night •
72 condos, Villas, Key at Sheraton Lakeview

Location: Airport: 8 miles; Downtown: 10 miles; Need car; Ski lift: WHISP Ski

General Facilities: Full serv., Bus. fac., Conf. rm. cap. 300, Daily maid, Kitchen, Linens, Restaurant on prem., Bar on prem., Game room, Lounge, Baby-sitter, Child planned rec.: Games/arts/stories

Room Facilities: Pool, Sauna, Hot tub, Tennis, Fitness Center, Golf: 2 courses on property; TV, Cable, Phone in rm., Crib-Hi-chair, Ind. AC Ctl., Ind. Heat Ctl.

Attractions: White water, summer theatre, state parks, forests, glassmaking, sports & cultural events, entertainment

Shops & Restaurants: Shopping mall and outlet glass factory mall; Reflections on the Lake/Amer.

Contemporary or traditional townhouses done in soft shades of blue, beige, or salmon with cedar and stone exteriors. Complete activities program with activities staff, and games, arts & crafts, stories, movies and entertainment for the children. Two 18-hole golf courses, indoor/outdoor swimming pools, tennis, hot tubs and gourmet dining. A four-season resort for privacy, excitement, and relaxation set in West Virginia's wooded hills.

---------------------- WHITE SULPHUR SPRINGS ----------------------

The Greenbrier
White Sulphur Springs, WV

General Facilities: Kitchen, Restaurant on prem.

Room Facilities: Pool, Sauna, Hot tub, Tennis, Shuffleboard, Golf: 3 golf courses

Attractions: Horse-drawn carriage rides, Droop Mountain, Organ Caves, Pearl Buck's birthplace

Shops & Restaurants: Ryder Cup Grille/Golf Club

Condominiums surrounded by 6500 acres of broad lawns, a profusion of gardens, and acres of eastern deciduous forests. Plethora of activities available, such as horseback riding, jogging, fishing, golf, tennis, shuffleboard, table tennis, lawn bowling, bicycling, swimming and hiking.

Be sure to call the condo to verify details and prices and to make your reservation.

Wisconsin

St. Germain
Minocqua
Eagle River
Egg Harbor
Nekoosa
Sturgeon Bay
Mishicot
Wisconsin Dells
Oconomowoc
Lake Geneva

―――――――――――― EAGLE RIVER ――――――――――――

Chanticleer Inn
1458 East Dollar Lake Rd.
Eagle River, WI 54521
715-479-4486 800-752-9193
FAX: 800-752-9193

Studio $$, 1 Bedroom $$$,
2 Bedrooms $$$$, 3 Bedrooms $$$$
AmEx/Visa/MC •
20 condos, Lo-rise, Key at Front desk,
H-Yes

Location: Airport: 30 miles; Downtown: 3 miles; Need car; Beachfront; Ski lift at cross-country

General Facilities: Full hotel service; Linens; Lounge; Crib-Hi-chair; Restaurant on premises; Bar on premises

Business Facilities: Conf. Room Cap. 80

Sports Facilities: Tennis; Snowmobiling, boating; 5 miles to Golf Course

Room Facilities: Kitchen; Phone; Ind.AC.Ctl.; Ind.Heat Ctl.

Attractions: Nicolet National Forest, on chain of 28 lakes, snowmobile trail, cross-country skiing

Shops & Restaurants: Eagle River shopping; On-site/prime rib/salad bar/full menu

Nestled in the beautiful Northwoods with two sandy beaches close by. A short walk to tennis, volleyball, basketball and badminton. Lovely restaurant and lounge overlooking the water; golf course only 5 miles away. 16 courses within a one-hour drive. A Winter sports paradise, but there's lots to do in the summer too. "Our vacation season never ends!"

Eagle Waters Resort
Box 1509
Eagle River, WI 54521
715-479-4411

1 Bedroom $$
Lo-rise

General Facilities: Daily maid; Linens

Sports Facilities: Pool; Tennis; Eagle Lake, marina; Golf

Room Facilities: Kitchen

Attractions: Eagle chain of lakes water skiing, fishing, sailing, golf, tennis

One bedroom suites with kitchenettes, and lakefront view patios. Peace and quiet in the northwoods air. Lay back and relax by the pool, take to the lake for water fun and fishing, hike or bike in the woods with the wildlife along the nature trail.

---------------------- EAGLE RIVER ----------------------

Safer's Gypsy Villa Resort
950 Circle Dr.
Eagle River, WI 54521
715-479-8644

1 Bedrm/week $$$$, 2 Bedrm/week $$$$,
3 Bedrm/week 7$, Min. Stay: 2 Nights,
Visa/MC, Dep. Req'd, •
21 condos, Lo-rise, P-yes, Key at office.

Location: Airport: 5 miles; Downtown: 4 miles, Need car; Beach front.

General Facilities: Conf. Room, Game room, Hot tub, Sauna, Child planned rec., Lake Forest-near, Baby sitter.

Room Facilities: Kitchen, TV, Crib-Hi-chair, Ind. Heat Ctl.

Attractions: Longest freshwater chain of lakes in the world, gateway to the Nicolet National Forest, entertainment.

Shops & Restaurants: Eagle River-Three River shopping, Persian Paradise, Everetts/French.

Ultra-modern villas with living room cathedral ceilings on beach front. Buildings far apart for privacy, with private docks and free scheduled pontoon boat service to and from the island. Campfire cookouts, music, dancing, treasure hunts, private lakefront and beach with slides, swings, swimming float with spring board. Marina with boat rentals. Year-round activities of all types.

---------------------- EGG HARBOR ----------------------

Landmark Resort & Conf. Center
7643 Hillside Road, P.O. Box 260
Egg Harbor, WI 54209
414-868-3205
FAX: 414-868-2569

1 Bedroom $$$, 2 Bedrooms $$$,
3 Bedrooms $$$$, 1 Bedrm/week 7$,
2 Bedrm/week 8$, 3 Bedrm/week 10$,
AmEx/Visa/MC, •
293 condos, H-yes, Key at front desk.

Location: Airport: Sturgeon Bay–30 min., Need car.

General Facilities: Bus. fac., Conf. Rm. Cap.: 250, Lounge, Pool, Hot tub, Sauna, X country, Tennis, Alpine golf course, Volleyball, Babysitter, Restaurant, Bar.

Room Facilities: Daily maid, Kitchen, TV, Phone, Crib-Hi-chair, Ind. AC. ./Heat Ctl.

Attractions: Historic villages, 5 state parks, beaches, boating, golfing, fishing.

Shops & Restaurants: Delightful shops in nearby villages, varied fish boils.

A 40 acre resort set amidst a natural bluff-top environment, located on the beautiful peninsula of Door County with a 250 mile coastline. Units have contemporary furnishings in blues and bieges with water or woodland views, microwaves and individual hot water heaters. On-site restaurant, unique shopping and all water sports nearby, as well as cross country skiing.

---------------------- LAKE GENEVA ----------------------

Americana Lake Geneva Resort
Hwy. 50
Lake Geneva, WI 53147
414-248-8811

1 Bedroom $$$, 2 Bedrooms $$$$.
Kitchen.

Attractions: Skeet and trap shooting, boating, miniature golf, tennis, skiing, horseback riding, pool.

Resort among 1400 acres of rolling hills and countryside in Wisconsin's Kettle Morraine area. Many year-round recreational and amusement facilities, including skeet and trap shooting, indoor/outdoor tennis, winter skiing, guided trail horseback riding, and canoes.

Lookout Village

———————————————— MINOCQUA ————————————————

The Pointe Resort and Club 1 Bedroom $$, 2 Bedrooms $$, Lo-rise
P.O. Box 1066   Pool, Kitchen
Minocqua, WI 54548
715-356-4431

Attractions: Golf, fishing, lake recreation, x-country skiing, snowmobiling, ice fishing, exercise room

Lakeside condominiums with fireplaces and jacuzzis. Recreation Center has lap pool, exercise room, steam room and whirlpool. Try x-country skiing or ice fishing right outside your door. 1 hour to downhill skiing. Moonlight ski tours, sleigh rides, and festivals.

———————————————— MISHICOT ————————————————

Fox Hills Resort   1 Bedroom $$$, 2 Bedrooms $$$$, Villas
P.O. Box 129   Pool, Daily maid, Kitchen, Linens
Mishicot, WI 54228
414-755-2376

Attractions: Downhill and x-country skiing, charter fishing, horseback riding, tennis, exercise trail, Health Club, golf

Something for everyone all year round. Condominiums feature cathedral ceilings, jacuzzi baths tubs, fireplaces and view patios or balconies. All summer and winter sports. Five minutes to Lake Michigan for sport fishing.

---------------------------- NEKOOSA ----------------------------

Fairway Townhomes   2 Bedrooms 6$
463 Tomahawk Trail   Pool, Kitchen
Nekoosa, WI 54457
715-325-3141

Attractions: Tennis, golf

Located on the tenth fairway, a few hundred feet from the Lake Arrowhead Clubhouse Bar and Restaurant, heated pool and lighted tennis courts. Townhouses with jacuzzi, washer/dryer and fireplace.

---------------------------- OCONOMOWOC ----------------------------

Olympia Village Resort & Spa   Villas
135 Royale Mile Road   Pool, Kitchen, Linens
Oconomowoc, WI 53066
414-567-0311 800-558-9573

Attractions: Summer pool matches, Olympia Stables, water sports, twin movie theaters, fishing, Professional Spa, tennis, golf

Villas with golf, pool, lake or ski views in a forest and lake setting. All the year-round activities you could ever want. Restaurants, cocktail lounges, nightclub entertainment and dancing. Private, sandy beach on Silver Lake.

---------------------------- ST. GERMAIN ----------------------------

Ed Gabes Lost Lake   Lo-rise
Condominiums   Pool, Kitchen, Linens
P.O. Box 24
St. Germain, WI 54558
715-542-3079

Attractions: Fishing, boating, tennis, waterskiing, seaplane rides, x-country skiing, dog sled Races, badminton, shuffleboard

Comfortable units with fully equipped kitchens, barbecues and aluminium boats. Ramp and pier space if you prefer to bring your own boat for water skiing and fishing. Swings and slides for the children.

---------------------------- STURGEON BAY ----------------------------

The Rushes   Lo-rise
Longerquist Rd, 1309 N. 14th Ave   Pool, Kitchen, Linens
Sturgeon Bay, WI 54235
414-839-2730

Attractions: Peninsula Players, sightseeing, golf, Washington Island, fishing, sailing, Exercise room, badminton, tennis

Decorator furnished with private sun deck and natural Door County fieldstone fireplace and patio. Each unit has two TV's and a VCR. 2,800 feet of shore frontage and 8,000-square-foot recreation center. Walk and jog on the woodland trails, practice on the putting green.

———————————— WISCONSIN DELLS ————————————

Villas At Christmas Mountain
S-944 Christmas Mountain Drive
Wisconsin Dells, WI 53965
608-253-1000

2 Bedrooms $$
2 Bedrms/week 6$
Min. Stay 2 Nights, AmEx/Visa/MC, Dep.
   Req'd. •
150 condos, Villas, Key at Hotel lobby
H-yes

Location: Airport: 50 miles; Downtown: 4½ miles

General Facilities: Full serv., Bus. fac., Conf. rm. cap. 250, Daily maid, Kitchen, Linens, Restaurant on prem., Bar on prem., Game room, Lounge, Baby-sitter, Child planned rec.: Activities Directors

Room Facilities: Pool, Sauna, Hot tub, Tennis, Skiing, horses, TV, Cable, Phone in rm., Crib-Hi-chair, Ind. AC Ctl., Ind. Heat Ctl.

Attractions: Many attractions in the area. Crane Foundation, House on the Rock, ski show, boat trips, entertainment

Shops & Restaurants: Craft and goods stores; Many fine restaurants

Modern luxury villas, two fireplaces, whirlpool in master bedroom, Jenair grills on all porches. Resort atmosphere with many local attractions, such as golf, skiing, horseback riding, restaurants, pools and Recreation Center available on-site. Wisconsin's finest four-season resort.

Please mention *Condo Vacations–The Complete Guide* when you reserve your condominium.

Wyoming

- Jackson Hole
- Alta

ALTA

Sioux Lodge at Grand Targhee Resort
P.O. Box SKI
Alta, WY 83422
307-353-2304 800-443-8146
FAX: 307-353-8148

1 Bedroom $$$$, 2 Bedrooms $$$$, Jr. $$$,
3 Bedrooms, 1 Bedrm/week 6$,
2 Bedrm/week 5$, 3 Bedrm/week, Min.
Stay: 3 Nights, AmEx/Visa/MC, •
32 condos, Lo-rise, NoS-yes, H-yes, Key at
lodging office.

Location: Airport: 42 miles; Downtown: 12 miles, Need car.

General Facilities: Conf. Rm. Cap.: 150, Lounge, Pool, Hot tub, Baby and kids' clubs, Tennis, Golf 45 minutes, Riding, massage, Baby sitter, Restaurant, Bar.

Room Facilities: Daily maid, Kitchen, TV, Phone, Crib-Hi-chair, Ind. Heat Ctl.

Attractions: Yellowstone, Grand Teton National Park, Jackson, sleigh rides, horses, hiking, fishing, entertainment.

Shops & Restaurants: Boutiques and galleries in Jackson (45 minute scenic drive), Gourmet, bistro, Mexican.

Grand Targhee has the feel and look of an intimate, Western village, nestled on the sunny, west slopes of the Tetons, 42 miles from Jackson, Wyoming. This year-round resort is known in winter for uncrowded slopes, champagne powder and friendly folk. A NEW adventure is Snowcat skiing daily on 1500 acres of virgin powder! All lodges, restaurants, shops and guest amenities are 50 yards from lifts. Families Welcome!

Sioux Lodge at Grand Targhee Resort, Alta, WY

──────────── JACKSON ────────────

Jackson Hole Racquet Club
Resort
Star Rt. Box 3647
Jackson, WY 83001
307-733-3990 800-443-8616

Studio $$$, 1 Bedroom $$$, 2 Bedrooms
$$$$, 3 Bedrooms $$$$, 1 Bed/week 7$,
2 Bed/week 9$, 3 Bed/week 10$, Min. stay
2 nights, Amex, Visa, MC, Dep. 1 night,
Key at front desk
120 condos, Lo-rise, No S-yes, H-yes •

Location: Airport: 22 miles; Downtown: 8 miles; Need car; Ski lift: Nearby

General facilities: Bus. fac., Conf. Rm. (cap. 120), Daily maid, Kitchen, Linens,
Kinderschule, Baby sitter, Restaurant, Bar, Lounge, Sauna, Hot tub

Room facilities: TV, Cable, Phone, Crib-Hi-chair, Ind. Heat Ctl.

Sports facilities: Pool, Tennis, Teton Pines, Health Club

Attractions: Tours to Yellowstone/Grand Teton Parks. Horses, white water
rafting.

Shops & Restaurants: Numerous art galleries, Ralph Lauren, outlets, Stigler's-
Austrian/US cuisine

*Nestled at the foot of the Teton Mountains; full service, year-round resort; fully
equipped kitchens, washer and dryers; fireplace and sundeck. 4 miles from Jackson
Hole Ski area; 50 miles south of Yellowstone National Park, adjacent to the new
Arnold Palmer 18-hole championship golf course at Teton Pines. Free delivery from
the on-property grocery and liquor store. Wood and stone units with western decor.*

──────────────────────────────

Spring Creek Ranch
Box 3154
Jackson, WY 83001
307-733-8833 800-443-6139

Studio $$$$, 1 Bedroom $$$$
2 Bedrooms $$$$, 3 Bedrooms 4$

General facilities: Daily maid, Kitchen, Linens

Sports facilities: Pool, Tennis, Golf course, Fishing

Attractions: Wildlife sanctuary, Grand Teton Nat. Park, horses, mountain climbing, white-water

*Spring Creek Ranch is just north of Jackson, cattle ranches to the west and National
Elk Refuge on the east. Condominiums in this unhurried resort feature fireplaces
in both living and master bedroom. Detailed, comfortable furnishings with view
balconies.*

Be sure to call the condo the verify details and prices and to make
your reservation.

Canada

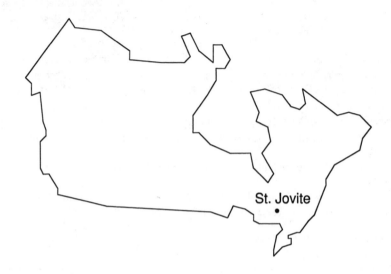

St. Jovite

---------------------- ST. JOVITE, QUEBEC ----------------------

Village Des Soleils at Gray Rocks
P.O. Box 1000
St. Jovite, Quebec, PQ J0T 2H0
819-425-2771 800-567-6767
FAX: 819-425-3006

1 Bedroom $$$$, 2 Bedrooms $$$$, 3 Bedrooms $$$$, 1 Bedrm/week 8$, 2 Bedrm/week 10$, 3 Bedrm/week 10$, AmEx/Visa/MC, • 56 condos, Lo-rise, Key at Gray Rock Le Chateau.

Location: Airport: 1.5 hours; Downtown: 3 miles.

General Facilities: Bus. fac., Conf. Rm. Cap.: 300, Lounge, Pool, Hot tub, Sauna, Child planned rec., Tennis, 18-hole course—1 mile, Health spa, riding, sailing, Baby sitter, Restaurant, Bar.

Room Facilities: Daily maid, Kitchen, TV, Cable, Phone, Crib-Hi-chair, Ind. Heat Ctl.

Attractions: Tremblant Provincial Park, entertainment.

Shops & Restaurants: Clothes, antiques, boutiques, La Couceur/continental.

Village Des Soleils condominiums are one of the accommodation options available to guests of Gray Rocks. This year-round resort is located in the Laurentian Mountains in Eastern Canada. Complete social program with live orchestra, piano bar and comedy club. 22 tennis courts, Alpine and cross-country skiing, complete children's program and a full health spa. Celebrating 85 years of hospitality, price value, variety of activities, convenience and above all service.

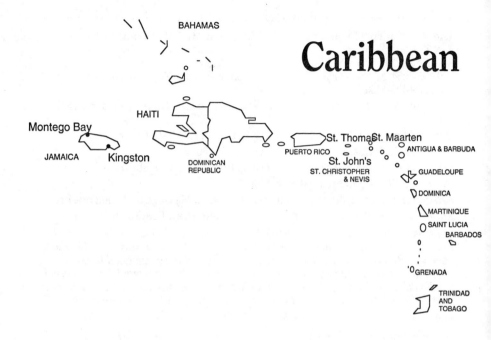

Caribbean

BAHAMAS

HAITI

Montego Bay

JAMAICA Kingston

DOMINICAN REPUBLIC

PUERTO RICO

St. Thomas St. Maarten

ANTIGUA & BARBUDA

St. John's

ST. CHRISTOPHER & NEVIS

GUADELOUPE

DOMINICA

MARTINIQUE

SAINT LUCIA

BARBADOS

GRENADA

TRINIDAD AND TOBAGO

————————— NEGRIL, JAMAICA, W.I. —————————

Crystal Waters Villas
P.O. Box 18, Normal Manley Blvd.
Negril, Jamaica, W.I.,
809-957-4284 800-423-4095
FAX: 809-957-4889

1 Bedroom $$$, 2 Bedrooms $$$$,
3 Bedrooms $$$$
Min. Stay 6 Nights, Visa/MC •
10 condos, Villas, Key at Front desk,
P-No/H-No

Location: Airport: 90 minutes; Downtown: Negril, 5 minutes

Room Facilities: Ind.AC.Ctl.

Attractions: Waterfalls, Boating on the Black River viewing mangroves & crocodiles, Negril lighthouse

Shops & Restaurants: Benneton, Duty free shopping, local art and craft; Le Vendome-French/Jamaican

Comfortable 1-, 2- and 3-bedroom villas in beautiful lush surroundings on mid-section of Negril's 7-mile beach. Each villa with full kitchen, living/dining area, patio and daily housekeeper/cook. Private beach, whirlpool, pool and kids pool. Near restaurants, entertainment, watersports, shopping. Ideal for families, couples and groups of friends. Personalized service and high percentage repeat clientele.

We want to hear from you—any comments regarding the condos or
our publication may be noted on the form at the end of the book.

─────────────── ROADTOWN, TORTOLA ───────────────

The Villas at Fort Recovery　　1 Bedroom $$$, 2 Bedrooms $$$$,
Box 239　　　　　　　　　　　　3 Bedrooms $$$$
Roadtown, Tortola, BVI　　　　　AmEx/Visa/MC •
809-495-4354 800-367-8455　　　10 condos, Villas, Key at In room,
FAX: 809-495-4036　　　　　　　P-No/H-Yes

Location: Airport: 35 minutes; Downtown: Roadtown, 12 min.; Need car; Beachfront

General Facilities: Daily maid; Linens; Baby sitter; Crib-Hi-Chair

Business Facilities: Bus. fac.; Conf. Room Cap. 30

Sports Facilities: Pool; Yoga, snorkerling, boat; Children's library

Room Facilities: Kitchen; Cable; Ind.AC.Ctl.

Attractions: 17th-century Dutch fort on premises. Massage and yoga on-site.

Shops & Restaurants: Supershole Marina, Nanny Cay, Roadtown; Italian

Caribbean seaside resort in Tortola's beautiful west end. Spectacular views of 6 islands. Private beach, swimming pool, historic landmark. Luxury 3–4 bedroom beach house and 1–2 bedroom seaside villas. All include continental breakfast (7 night stay, welcome dinner per person and boat trip), kitchen, maid. Enjoy snorkeling, boating, windsurfing. Expert yoga classes and massages available. Honeymoon package available. Great place for family reunions. ". . . A Bit of Britain in the Sun."

──────────────────── ST. JOHN ────────────────────

Gallows Point Suite Resort　　Studio $$$$, 1 Bedroom $$$$,
P.O. Box 58　　　　　　　　　　2 Bedrooms $$$$
St. John, VI 00831　　　　　　　1 Bedrm/week 10$, 2 Bedrms/week 10$
809-776-6434 800-323-7229　　　Min. Stay 3 Nights, AmEx/Visa/MC •
FAX: 809-776-6520　　　　　　　60 condos, Lo-rise, Villas,
　　　　　　　　　　　　　　　Key at Front desk, P-No/H-No

Location: Beachfront

General Facilities: Full hotel service; Maid; Linens; Restaurant on premises; Bar on premises

Sports Facilities: Pool; Sail, fish, dive, kayak

Room Facilities: Kitchen; Cable; Phone

Shops & Restaurants: Gourmet food shop on-site, jewelry/souvenirs 300 yds away; Paradisio, Ellington, Cafe Roma, Asolare

High quality constructed all-suite apartments. All units are waterfront with spectacular views from each unit. Units sleep up to four persons. Private snorkeling beach, fresh water pool, sun decks. Gourmet concierge shop on premises and Ellingtons Restaurant and Bar. 5 minutes walk to village, shops and restaurants. Totally relaxing and low key vacation.

Please mention *Condo Vacations—the Complete Guide* when you reserve your condominium.

————— KRALENDIJK, BONAIRE, NETHERLANDS ANTILLES —————

Sand Dollar Condominium
Resort
P.O. Box 262
Kralendijk, Bonaire, Netherlands
Antilles, 5997-8738 5997-8760
800-288-4773

Studio $$$$, 1 Bedroom $$$$,
2 Bedrooms $$$$, 3 Bedrooms $$$$
AmEx/Visa/MC •
85 condos, Lo-rise, Key at Front desk, P-No

Location: Airport: 15 minutes; Downtown: 10 minutes; Oceanfront

General Facilities: Full hotel service; Linens; Baby sitter; Crib; Restaurant on premises; Bar on premises

Sports Facilities: Pool; Tennis; Snorkeling, bike, dive; Sand Penny Club

Room Facilities: Kitchen; Cable; Ind.AC.Ctl.

Shops & Restaurants: Seafood, International

Beautiful studio, 1-, 2- and 3-bedroom ocean front condominiums with all the services of a hotel and more. Perfect for families, couples or groups. An exciting world of adventure awaits those who seek the magic of the crystal clear blue tropical sea surrounding Bonaire. Great accommodations, good food, and great diving.

————————————————— ST. CROIX —————————————————

Sugar Beach Condominium
3221 Estate Golden Rock
St. Croix, VI 00820
809-773-5345 800-524-2049
FAX: 809-773-5345

Studio $$, 1 Bedroom $$$,
2 Bedrooms $$$, 3 Bedrooms $$$$
1 Bedrm/week 12$, 2 Bedrms/week 17$,
3 Bedrms/week 17$
Min. Stay 3 Nights, AmEx/Visa/MC, Dep.
Required •
46 condos, Lo-rise, Key at Front desk

Location: Airport: 25 minutes; Downtown: 5 minutes; Need car; Beach front

General Facilities: Linens; Baby sitter; Crib-Hi-chair; Bar

Business Facilities: Conf. Room Cap. 40

Sports Facilities: Pool; Tennis; All water sports; Rental VCR

Room Facilities: Kitchen; Cable; VCR; Phone; Ind.AC.Ctl

Attractions: Watersports, snorkeling, Buck National Island Underwater Park, Seaplane island hopping

Shops & Restaurants: Duty free shops, Cormorant; Coromont Beach Club/continental

Encompassing all the beauty, friendliness, security and tranquility of St. Croix, Sugar Beach is a luxurious beachfront resort uniquely designed and built along a wide stretch of sandy beach. Each condominium has a large terrace with spectacular sea views and fully equipped kitchens. Come join us in your own private Caribbean Villa.

CHRISTIANSTED, ST. CROIX

Colony Cove
221A Golden Rock
Christiansted, St. Croix, VI 00820
809-773-1965 800-828-0746

2 Bedrooms $$$$
Min. stay 3 nights, Amex, Visa, MC
Key at Front desk
60 condos, Lo-rise, H-yes •

Location: Airport: 15 minutes; Downtown: 10 minutes; Need car; Beach front

General facilities: Full serv., Maid 2x/wk, Kitchen, Linens, Baby sitter, Restaurant, Bar, Riding

Room facilities: TV, Cable, Phone, Crib, Ind. AC Ctl,, Decks

Sports facilities: Pool, Tennis, Golf-Carambola-Buccaneer, Parasailing, Snorkeling

Attractions: Whim museum, Buck Island, Danish culture, Scuba diving

Shops & Restaurants: Little Switzerland-duty free shopping, Columbian Emeralas, Top Hat/Danish, Good local restaurants

Deluxe 2-bedroom condos in a quiet beachfront setting by the Caribbean Sea. Enjoy the swimming pool, balconies, air conditioning, cable TV, fully equipped kitchens. Dutyfree shopping in Historic Christiansted. Take a trip to Buck Island on a large catamaran and swim from one of the 10 most beautiful beaches in the world. Go Scuba diving or snorkel the underwater historic landmark.

——————————————— ST. THOMAS ———————————————

McLaughlin-Anderson Villas
100 Blackbeard's Hill, Suite 3
St. Thomas, VI 00802
809-776-0635 800-537-6246
FAX: 809-777-4737

Studio $$$, 1 Bedroom $$$$,
2 Bedrooms $$$$, 3 Bedrooms $$$$
Min. Stay 5 Nights, •
46 condos, Lo-rise, Villas, Key at Meet at
airport No S-Yes/H-Yes

Location: Need car

General Facilities: Maid; Linens; Baby sitter; Crib-Hi-chair

Sports Facilities: Pool; Hot tub; Tennis; Water sports, sailing; Golf Course nearby

Room Facilities: Kitchen; Cable; VCR; Phone; Ind.AC.Ctl.

Attractions: Coral World, Atlantis submarine, sail boats, water sports, explore the Virgin Islands.

Shops & Restaurants: Duty-free shopping in Charlotte Amalie; Alexander's/Austrian with Caribbean

Private vacation villas on St. Thomas, with a wide range of weekly rentals from modest apartments to breathtaking luxurious homes by the sea or high in the hills for island adventurers and beach buffs. All are fully furnished with kitchenware and linens. Guests are met at the airport and escorted to their villa. McLaughlin-Anderson also offers accommodations at St. John, St. Crois, Tortola, Virgin Gorda and Grenada.

———————————————————————————————————————

Ocean Property Management
Box 8529
St. Thomas, VI 00801
809-775-2600 800-874-7897
FAX: 809-775-5901

Studio $$$, 1 Bedroom $$$$,
2 Bedrooms $$$$
Min. Stay 3 Nights, AmEx/Visa/MC •
50 condos, Villas, Key: Arrange with
office, No S-Yes/H-Yes

Location: Airport: 30 minutes; Downtown: 20 minutes

General Facilities: Linens; Crib-Hi-chair

Sports Facilities: Pool; Tennis; Water sports, Fitness ctr; Golf Course nearby

Room Facilities: Kitchen; Cable; Phone; Ind.AC.Ctl.

Attractions: Atlantis submarine underwater tour, Coral World Seaquarium, St. John Island National Park

Shops & Restaurants: Duty-free shops, Tillett Art Gallery; Cafe Normandie/French

A wide variety of studio, 1- and 2-bedrooms suites, completely furnished with fully equipped kitchens. All are located in beachfront resort settings with ocean views, access to resort amenities and short walk to beach. Varied activities at each location include water sports, golf, music, dancing, dining, shuttle service to town and restaurants. 5 minutes from ferries to Tortola and Virgin Gorda. Be as active or as lazy as you wish!

---------------- CHARLOTTE AMALIE, ST. THOMAS ----------------

Secret Harbour Beachfront | Studio $$$$, 1 Bedroom $$$$,
Resort | 2 Bedrooms 4$
6280 Estate Nazareth | Min. Stay Ask, AmEx/Visa/MC •
Charlotte Amalie, St. Thomas, VI | 60 condos, Lo-rise, Key at Lobby
00802 | reception desk, P-No/No S-Yes/H-No
809-775-6550 800-524-2250
FAX: 809-775-1501

Location: Airport: 10 miles; Downtown: 8 miles; Beachfront

General Facilities: Full hotel service; Daily maid; Linens; Baby sitter; Restaurant on premises; Bar on premises

Business Facilities: Conf. Room Cap. 40

Sports Facilities: Pool; Spa; Tennis; Dive shop on-site; Near Mahogany Run Golf

Room Facilities: Kitchen; Cable; Phone; Ind.AC.Ctl.

Attractions: Close to Red Hook shopping and ferry service to St. John. Island tours from resort.

Shops & Restaurants: Quality duty free shops at American Yacht Harbor; 10 major restaurants within 5 miles

Secret Harbour Beachfront Resort is nestled among native palms on a crescent shaped sandy Caribbean beach. It has become famous for its island hospitality and barefoot elegant. Romance for many is the order of the day. Guests enjoy unobtrusive service and superb accommodation in individually designed suites. Situated close to every amenity, its privacy is why guests return year after year.

---------------- CHRISTIANSTED, ST. CROIX ----------------

Gentle Winds | 2 Bedrooms $$$$, 3 Bedrooms $$$$
Pivar at Gentle Winds, 1112 King | Min. Stay 1 Week, •
Christiansted, St. Croix, VI 00820 | 66 condos, Lo-rise, Key at Room or office,
809-778-3400 800-537-6242 | P-No/No S-Yes/H-No
FAX: 809-778-8086

Location: Airport: 15 minutes; Downtown: 15 minutes; Need car

General Facilities: Daily maid; Linens; Baby sitter; Lounge; Restaurant on premises; Bar on premises

Business Facilities: Conf. Room Cap. 40

Sports Facilities: Game room; Pool; Tennis; Volleyball, basketball; Carambola Golf Course

Room Facilities: Kitchen; Cable; VCR; Phone; Ind.AC.Ctl.

Attractions: Salt River Marina (Columbus landing), Buck Island Nat'l Park, Carambola & Buccaneer golf

Shops & Restaurants: Duty free shops downtown is lovely; Carambola-Internat'l, Dino's-Italian

Gentle Winds is a beautiful resort tucked away in a captivating cove on the north shore of St. Croix. Spacious grounds, great snorkeling (look for our 15-year resident "Smiley" the barracuda). We're next door to Salt River—Columbus Landing—great diving—Columbus' anchor is said to be resting here. The perfect island vacation spot. Come visit us!

More Condos

ALABAMA

Alpine Bay Resort Route #2, Box 110-A, Alpine, AL 35014   205-268-9411
DeSoto State Park Route 1, P.O. Box 210, Fort Payne, AL 35967   205-845-5380
Driftwood Towers P.O. Drawer 357, Gulf Shores, AL 36542
Island Winds East Highway 182, West Gulf Shores, AL 36542   205-968-7363
Phoenix, The P.O. Box 1727, Gulf Shores, AL 36542   205-968-7363
Sailboat Bay P.O. Box 2433, Gulf Shores, AL 36542   205-968-6030
Shoreline Towers W. Beach Blvd., P.O. Box 2387, Gulf Shores, AL 36542
205-948-5373
Shores, The 24060 Perdido Beach Blvd., Orange Beach, AL 36561
Southern Shores 18 W. Beach Blvd., Gulf Shores, AL 36542   205-968-6097
The Gulf Shores P.O. Box 1299, Gulf Shores, AL 36542   205-540-2291

ARKANSAS

Club Belvedere P.O. Box 1225, Hot Springs, AR 71902
Copper Mine Lodge Route 6, Box 575, Rogers, AR 72756   501-925-2010
Crown Point 1530 S. Ivory Ln., Horseshoe Bend, AR 72512   501-670-5091
Dawn Hill Resort Dawn Hill Rd., Route 1, Siloam Springs, AR 72716
501-524-9321
Devils Fork Highway 16, Route 1, Greers Ferry, AR 72067
Fairwinds Route 2, Box 425, Eureka Springs, AR 72632   501-253-9465
Greens, The 101 Town Center, Bella Vista, AR 72714   501-855-3741
Hamilton Harbor 203 Sterns Point Rd., Hot Springs, AR 71913   501-767-8300
Heritage Bay Route 6, Highway 12, AR 72756   501-925-2861
Iron Mountain #1 Marina Drive, Arkadelphia, AR 71923   501-246-4310
La Salle Resort Route 4, P.O. Box 485, Mountain Home, AR 72653
Lake Lucerne P.O. Box 441, Eureka Springs, AR 72632   501-253-8085
Lakeshore Resort Highway 270 West, P.O. Box 2540, Hot Springs, AR 71914
Lakeshore Resort P.O. Box 2540, Hot Springs, AR 71914   501-767-8408
Lodge on Whitney Mt. Route 1, 1657 Lodge Drive, Garfield, AR 72732
Mountain Ridge Wonders Dr., Fairfield, AR 72088
North Shore 200 Pretti Point Rd., Hot Springs, AR 71901   501-525-4691
Oak Tree Inn Vinegar Hill, Hwy. 110 West, Heber Springs, AR 72543
501-362-7731
Peal's Resort Route 3, P.O. Box 252, Mountain Home, AR 72653   501-499-5212
Red Bud Valley Route I, P.O. Box 500, Eureka Springs, AR 72632   501-253-9028
Riverview Resort Route 2, Box 475, Eureka Springs, AR 72632   501-253-8367
South Shore Lake 201 Hamilton Oaks Drive, Box 6072, Hot Springs, AR 71902
501-525-8200
South Shore 124 Pine Hill Rd., Hot Springs, AR 71913   501-525-4471
Table Rock 95 Woodsdale Drive, Holiday Island, AR 72632   501-253-7733
Valais-Hi 33 Van Buren, Eureka Springs, AR 72632   501-253-5140
Willow Beach 401 Lake Hamilton Drive, Hot Springs, AR 71902   501-525-4398

ARIZONA

Anasazi Resort 12220 Pardise Parkway S., Phoenix, AZ 85016   602-953-1759
Arizona Biltmore 2525 East Arizona, Biltmore Circle, Phoenix, AZ 85016
602-955-3525

Arroyo Roble   400 N. Highway 89A, P.O. Box NN, Sedona, AZ 86336
602-282-4001
Cedar Court   5215 West Peoria Avenue, Glendale, AZ 85302   602-249-4484
Desert Shadows   14230 N. 19th Avenue, Phoenix, AZ 85020   602-866-9196
Desert Steppes   8485 East 22nd Street, Tucson, AZ 95710   602-298-8485
Fairfield   2580 No. Oakmont Drive, Flagstaff, AZ 86001
Golden Hills   6901 East Broadway, Mesa, AZ 85208   602-832-3202
Greenery, The   1330 W. BroadwayRoad, Tempe, AZ   602-966-7288
Inn at McCormick   7401 N. Scottsdale Road, Scottsdale, AZ 85253
602-948-5050
McKellips Gardens   2601 E. McKellips, Mesa, AZ 85208   602-844-8064
Palmwood Terrace   4915 E. Thomas Road, Phoenix, AZ 85016   602-952-0243
Pinewood Fairway   Walapi Road, Munds Park, AZ 86017
Quail Creek   1651 S. Dobson Road, Mesa, AZ 85208   602-831-6200
Quality Hill, Pinetop, AZ 85935   602-369-0178
Ramada Pima   7330 North Pima Road, Scottsdale, AZ 85258   602-948-3800
Rancho Santa Fe   10201 N. 44th Drive, Phoenix, AZ 85020
602-931-3878
Riviera Park   125 S. Dobson Road, Chandler, AZ   602-963-3092
Sandridge   2835 W. Northern, Phoenix, AZ 85016   602-995-2819
Sands Resort, The   2040 Mesquite Ave., Lake Havasu, AZ 86403   602-855-1388
Shores, The   7401 N. Scottsdale Road, Scottsdale, AZ 85253
Spring Meadows   10030 N. 43rd Ave., Phoenix, AZ 85020   602-264-2626
Sunscape   3500 N. Hayden, Scottsdale, AZ 85251   602-941-1880
Val Vista Gardens   3443 E. University, Mesa, AZ 85208   602-830-4626
Valencia Park   190 W. Valencia, Tucson, AZ 85710   602-294-5090
Windrush Village   1944 West Thunderbird, Phoenix, AZ 85016   602-993-5362

———————————————— CALIFORNIA ————————————————

All Resort   2242 Rosecrans Avenue, Fullerton, CA 92633   714-447-8873
Americana Village   3845 Pioneer Trail, Box 6428, South Lake Tahoe, CA 95729
Aspens & Tetons   1176 Happy Valley Ave., San Jose, CA 95129   408-984-0660
Balboa Park Inn   3402 Park Boulevard, San Diego, CA 92103   619-298-0823
Beach Club Del Mar, Solano Beach, CA 92075
Beach Comber   999 Lakeview, South Lake Tahoe, CA 95702
Beachcomber Resort   999 Lakeview Avenue, South Lake Tahoe, CA 95702
916-544-2426
Biltmore Condos   200 S. Cahuilla Road, Palm Springs, CA 92262   619-325-5281
Blue Whale, The   964 North Strand, Oceanside, CA 92054
Canon Del Sol   400 Abalone Drive, La Selva Beach, CA 95076
Capistrano Surfside   34680 Coast Highway, Capistrano Beach, CA 92624
714-240-7681
Capri By The Sea   P.O. Box 99964, San Diego, CA 92109   619-483-6110
Carlsbad Inn   3075 Carlsbad Blvd., Carlsbad, CA 92008   619-434-7020
Carmel Highland   14455 Penasquitos Drive, San Diego, CA 92129
Casitas Del Monte   2700 South Palm Canyon Drive, Palm Springs, CA 92262
619-320-6589
Channel Island Shores   1311 Mandalay Beach Road, Oxnard, CA 93035
Chinquapin   3600 North Lake Blvd., Box RR, Tahoe City, CA 95730
916-583-6991
Creekside Condominiums   P.O. Box 5097, Bear Valley, CA 95223   209-753-2311
Crown Point View   4088 Crown Point Dr., Box 90008, San Diego, CA 92109
619-272-0676

Desert Breezes 77955 Calle Las Brisas South, Palm Desert, CA 92260
Desert Isle 2555 E. Palm Canyon Drive, Palm Springs, CA 92264 619-327-8469
Desert Vacation 250 W. Vista Chino, Palm Springs, CA 92262 619-323-9898
Donner Pines P.O. Box 2433, Truckee, CA 95734 916-587-4127
Doubletree Hotels P.O. Box 1644, Palm Springs, CA 92263 619-322-7000
Edgewater Shores 180-184 S. Highway 173, Box 537, Lake Arrowhead, CA 92352 714-337-2661
Emerald Pointe 333 North Emerald Drive, Vista, CA 92083 619-726-7331
Executive Suites 725 Pine Street, San Francisco, CA 94108 415-567-5151
Executive Suites 450 N. Mathilda Avenue, Sunnyvale, CA 94086 408-749-8911
Executive Suites 131 Chilpancingo Parkway, Pleasant Hill, CA 94523 415-674-9155
Executive Suites 1033 Hilgard Avenue, #315, Los Angeles, CA 90024 213-208-0141
Fairfield Harbor 1015 Schooner Drive, Ventura, CA 93001
Fountains, The 49599 Monroe Avenue, Indio, CA 92201
Four Seasons 2600 Ave Del Presidente, San Clemente, CA 92672
Golf and Tennis 5300 Waverly Drive, Palm Springs, CA 92264 619-324-5800
Grand Champions 44-600 Indian Wells Lane, Indian Wells, CA 92210 619-341-1000
Harbortown Marina 1050 Schooner Drive, Ventura, CA 93001 805-658-1212
Hawaiian Gardens 1031 Imperial Beach Blvd., Imperial Beach, CA 92032 619-429-5303
Heidelberg Inn P.O. Box 1, June Lake, CA 93529
Helios Townhouses P.O. Box 7054, Mammoth Lakes, CA 93546 619-934-8568
Highlands Inn P.O. box 1700, Carmel, CA 93921 408-624-3801
Indian Palms 49500 Monroe Avenue, Indio, CA 92201
Lagonita Lodge 183 Lagunita Lane, Big Bear Lake, CA 92315 714-866-6531
Lake Arrowhead 188 Rock Lodge Lane, Lake Arrowhead, CA 92352
Lakeland Village P.O. Box 705002, South Lake Tahoe, CA 95705
Laqunita Lodge 183 Lagunita Lane, Big Bear Lake, CA 92315
Lawrence Welk 8858 Lawrence Welk Drive, Escondido, CA 92026
Lodge at Lake Tahoe 3840 Pioneer Trail, Box 5467, South Lake Tahoe, CA 95729
Northstar P.O. Box 2499, Truckee, CA 95734 916-562-1113
Oak Tree Hotels 100 Clocktower Place, #200, Carmel, CA 93923 408-625-4060
Olympic Village P.O. Box 2648, Olympic Valley, CA 95730 916-581-6000
Pacific Grove Plaza 620 Lighthouse Avenue, Pacific Grove, CA 93950 408-373-0562
Pacific Sands 4449 Ocean Boulevard, Pacific Beach, CA 92109 619-483-7555
Pajaro Dunes 2661 Beach Road, Watsonville, CA 95076 408-722-9201
Pala Mesa Resort 2001 Old Hwy., 395, Fallbrook, CA 92028 619-728-5881
Pine Acres Lodge 1150 Jewell Avenue, Pacific Grove, CA 93950
Plaza Resort 2601 Golf Club Drive, Palm Springs, CA 92264
Powell Place 730 Powell Street, San Francisco, CA 94108 415-362-7022
Quail Lodge 8205 Valley Greens Drive, Carmel, CA 93923 408-624-1581
Royce Resort Hotel 34567 Cathedral Canyon Drive, Palm Springs, CA 92264
San Clemente Cove 104 South Ala. Lane, San Clemente, CA 92672
Sands of Indian Wells 75-188 Highway 111, Indian Wells, CA 92110 619-346-8113
Snow Country P.O. Box 7054, Mammoth Lakes, CA 93546 619-934-8568
Snow Lake Lodge 41569 Big Bear Blvd., Big Bear Lake, CA 92315 714-866-8881
Snowbird P.O. Box 7013, Mammoth Lakes, CA 933546 619-934-8270

Solana Beach 614 South Sierra Avenue, Solana Beach, CA 92075 619-755-6651
Southern Cal. 121 South Pacific Street, Oceanside, CA 92054
Spanish Inn, The 640 North Indian Avenue, Palm Springs, CA 92262 619-325-2285
Squaw Tahoe P.O. Box 2612, Olympic Valley, CA 95730
Sun 'n Sno P.O. Box 1919, Kings Beach, CA 95719 916-546-2501
Sun Dunes Villas Washington St. at Interstate 10, Palm Desert, CA 92260
Sweetwater 46765 Bay Club Drive, Indian Wells, CA 92210
Tahoe Donner P.O. Box 2642, Truckee, CA 95734 916-587-6586
Tahoe Tavern 300 West Lake Blvd., Box 82, Tahoe City, CA 95730 916-583-3704
Tahoe Waterfront 953 Ski Run Boulevard, South Lake Tahoe, CA 95702 916-544-3457
Tamarack Beach 3200 Carlsbad Blvd., Carlsbad, CA 92008 619-729-3500
Tennis Club 701 W. Bariso Road, Palm Springs, CA 92262
Village of Squaw Valley 1900 Squaw Valley Road, Olympic Valley, CA 95730
Villas of Palm Springs 1650 Calle Palo Fiero, Palm Springs, CA 92262
Warner Springs Ranch P.O. Box 1D, Warner Springs, CA 29086
Wave Crest 1400 Ocean Avenue, Del Mar, CA 92014 619-755-0100
Winners Circle 550 Via de la Valle, Box 1169, Del Mar, CA 92014 619-755-6666
Winners Circle Resort 550 Via De La Valle, Solano Beach, CA 92014

———————————————— COLORADO ————————————————

AAA Victorian P.O. Box 1797, Breckenridge, CO 80424 303-453-2262
Abrigo 12170 East 30th Avenue, Aurora, CO 303-361-6644
Alpenrose 400 South French, Breckenridge, CO 80424 303-453-2288
Alpine Ridge 3055 Meadow Lane, Steamboat Springs, CO 80477
Aspen Mountain 747 South Galena, Aspen, CO 81611 303-920-3724
Aspen Square 617 East Cooper Avenue, Aspen, CO 81611 800-862-7736
Base 9 Condominiums 800 Broken Lance Drive, Breckenridge, CO 80424 303-453-2262
Best Western 154 Wheeler Pl. Box 3296, Copper Mountain, CO 80443 303-968-2600
Best Western 49617 Highway 550, Durango, CO 81301 303-247-9669
Black Canyon Inn 800 MacGregor Ave, Box 2927, Estes Park, CO 80517 303-586-8113
Breckenridge P.O. Box 2009, Breckenridge, CO 80424 303-453-2222
Brynwood on the River 710 Maraine Avenue, Box 1929, Estes Park, CO 80517
Castle Mountain Lodge 1520 Fall River Road, Box 1948, Estes Park, CO 80517
Chaperral 580 So. French St., P.O. Box 1797, Breckenridge, CO 80424 303-453-2662
Charolay Apartments 15899 E. 13th Place, Aurora, CO 80011 303-364-3005
Chateaux d'Mont 1203 Keystone Rd., P.O. Box 998, Keystone, CO 80435 303-468-0800
Christiania 356 East Hanson Ranch Road, Vail, CO 81657 303-476-5641
Cimarron Lodge Box 756, Telluride, CO 81435
Clack Canyon 800 MacGregor Avenue, Box 2927, Estes Park, CO 80517
Colony at Winter Park 3N County Road 804, P.O. Box 229, Winter Park, CO 80482 303-726-8051
Colorado Elk Run 3555 W. Hwy. 160, Pagosa Springs, CO 81157
Columbine Landing 1175 Overlook Dr., POB 770986, Steamboat Springs, CO 80477 303-879-0465
Copper Valley P.O. Box 3356, Copper Mountain, CO 80443 303-968-2626
Creekside P.O. Box 404, Winter Park, CO 80482

Crested Mt. P.O. Box A, Mt. Crested Butte, CO 81225 303-349-7555
Crestview Place Winter Park Vacations, Box 3095, Winter Park; CO 80482
Denver Suites 8000 E. Girard Avenue, Denver, CO 80231 303-696-9394
Douglas 2264 S. Frontage Rd. W., Vail, CO 81657 303-476-6000
Eagle Point P.O. Box 3040, Vail, CO 81658 303-949-4416
Eagle's Loft 3555 W. Hwy 160, Pagosa Springs, CO 81157
Eagles Nest 101 Golden Edge Rd., Silverthorne, CO 80498 303-468-2837
East Rim 44 Sheol Street, Durango, CO 81301 303-247-5528
Elk Ridge III P.O. Box 247, Crested Butte, CO 81224 303-349-2800
Enzian 610 West Lionshead Circle, Vail, CO 81657
Etta Place Box 1278, Telluride, CO 81435 303-728-4466
Falcon Point P.O. Box 3040, Vail, CO 81658 303-949-4416
Fawn Valley 2760 Fall River Road, Box 3787, Estes Park, CO 80517
303-586-2388
Four Seasons 390 Straight Creek, Dillon, CO 80435
French Ridge 432 S. Ridge St., Breckenridge, CO 80424 303-453-2288
Gasthof Gramshammer 231 East Gore Creek Drive, Vail, CO 81657
303-476-5626
Glen Eden Ranch 54737 Rte. County Rd 129, Box 867, Clark, CO 80428
Golden Peak House 278 East Hanson Ranch Road, Vail, CO 81657
303-476-5667
Greens at Copper Mountain P.O. Box 3001, Copper Mountain, CO 80443
Harbor P.O. Box 774109, Steamboat Springs, CO 80477 303-879-1522
Hideway Village Winter Park Vacations, Box 3095, Winter Park, CO 80482
Holiday Inn P.O. Box 10, Frisco, CO 80443 303-668-5000
Indian Peaks P.O. Box 131, Winter Park, CO 80482 303-726-8047
Inn at Hans's Peak P.O. Box 867, Clark, CO 80428 303-879-3906
Inn-Tervals, Silver Creek, CO 80446
Interlude Village Property Mgmt, Box 5550, Snowmass Village, CO 81615
Lake Dillon 401 W. Lodgepole, P.O. Box 308, Dillon, CO 80435 303-468-2409
Lakeview 62927 Hwy. 40, P.O. Box 4026, Silvercreek, CO 80446 303-887-2131
Landmark, The 610 West Lionshead Circle, Vail, CO 81657 303-476-1350
Lichenhearth Village Property Mgmt, Box 5550, Snowmass Village, CO 81615
Lifthouse 555 East Lionshead Circle, Vail, CO 81657 303-476-2340
Lions Gate Pines 55 Grand County Road, Winter Park, CO 80482 303-726-5771
LionsHead Arcade Vail Resort Rents.605 N. Frontage, Vail, CO 81657
Lodge at Purgatory 49617 Highway 550, Durango, CO 81301 303-247-9669
Lodge at Vail 174 East Gore Creek Drive, Vail, CO 81657 303-476-5011
Lulu City Box 1278, Telluride, CO 81435 303-728-4405
Machins Cottages P.O. Box 2687, Estes Park, CO 80517 303-586-4276
Manitou 2045 South Fir, P.O. Box 276, Telluride, CO 81435 303-728-4311
Mark IX P.O. Box 8409, Breckenridge, CO 80424
McGregor Mountain Box 1969AC, Estes Park, CO 80517 303-586-3457
Meadow Ridge 1 Meadow Mile, P.O. Box 203, Winter Park, CO 80482
303-726-9401
Miles Motel 1250 St. St. Vrain Ave., Estes Park, CO 80517 303-586-3185
Millrace 1000 South Frontage Road W. #200, Vail, CO 81657
Mountain Side 550 Bills Ranch Rd., Frisco, CO 80443 303-668-3174
Needles Purgatory Central Reserv. Box 666, Durango, CO 81302
Nicky's Resort 1350 Fall River Road, Estes Park, CO 80517 303-568-2123
North Star P.O. Box 8800168, Steamboat Springs, CO 80477
Park Meadows 1472 Matterhorn Circle, Vail, CO 81657 303-476-5598
Park Place P.O. Box 1797, Breckenridge, CO 80424 303-453-2262

Pines at Meadow Ridge Winter Park Ranch at E. Meadow Ml, Winter Park, CO 80482 303-726-9401
Plaza at Wood Creek 11 Snowmass Road, P.O. Box 5159, Mt. Crested Butte, CO 81225
Powderhorn Resort 744 Horizon Court, Grand Junction, CO 81506 303-241-1503
Rams Horn Lodge 416 Vail Valley Drive, Vail, CO 81657 303-476-5646
Raspberry House 443 Beaver Dam Road, Vail, CO 81657 303-949-8233
Redwoods P.O. Box 5184, Steamboat Springs, CO 80477
Riva Ridge South P.O. Box 759, Vail, CO 81658 303-476-2233
River Mountain Lodge 100 South Park St., Box 7188, Breckenridge, CO 80424 303-453-4711
Sandstone Creek Club 1020 Vail View Dr., Vail, CO 81657 303-467-4405
Scandinavian Lodge P.O. Box 774484, Steamboat Springs, CO 80477 303-879-0517
Seasons Four P.O. Box 5550, Snowmass Village, CO 81615 303-923-4350
Shadow Mountain 232 W. Hyman Ave., Aspen, CO 81611 303-925-8207
Silverado I Cornerstone Resorts, P.O. Box 9, Winter Park, CO 80482
Silverpick Purgatory Central Reserv. Box 666, Durango, CO 81302
Skier's Edge 5½ Miles S. Hwy. 9, Breckenridge, CO 80424 303-453-0700
Snowblaze Wirsing & Company, P.O. Box 404, Winter Park, CO 80482
Snowmass Inn Box 5640, Snowmass Village, CO 81615 303-923-4202
Snowmass Mountain Village Property Mgmt, Box 5550, Snowmass Village, CO 81615
Solar Vail Vail Resort Rents/605 N. Frontage, Vail, CO 81657
Spruce Lodge P.O. Box 3003, Copper Mountain, CO 80443 303-825-7106
Stanley Hotel P.O. Box 1767, Estes Park, CO 80517 303-586-3371
Sun Song P.O. Box 3123, Winter Park, CO 80482
Sun Vail Vail Resort Rents/605 N. Frontage, Vail, CO 81657
Sunbird Lodge 675 Lionheads Place, Vail, CO 81657 303-476-5264
Tannenbaum 805 S. Columbine Rd., Box 1356, Breckenridge, CO 80424
Thunder Mountain 2030 Walton Creek Rd., Box 771356, Steamboat Springs, CO 80477
Timber Creek P.O. Box 3356, Copper Mountain, CO 80443 303-968-2626
Timberilne P.O. Box 1-2, Snowmass Village, CO 81615 303-923-4000
Timberline P.O. Box 247, Crested Butte, CO 81224 800-821-7613
Treehouse 8500 Ryan Gulch Rd., Silverthorne, CO 80498 303-468-6291
Twilight View Purgatory Central Reserv. Box 666, Durango, CO 81302
Twin Rivers P.O. Box 3123, Winter Park, CO 80482
Vail 21 610 Lionshead Circle, Vail, CO 81657
Valhalla Resort P.O. Box 1439, Estes Park, CO 80517 303-586-3284
Vantage Point 610 Lionshead Circle, Vail, CO 81657
Village Square P.O. Box 3005, Copper Mountain, CO 80443
Wedgewood Lodge 535 Four O'Clock Road, Breckenridge, CO 80424 800-521-2458
Wildrose Lodge 120 Sawmill Road, Breckenridge, CO 80424
Winter Park Lodge 311 County Road 804, P.O. Box 229, Winter Park, CO 80482 303-726-8051
Winter Park P.O. Box 377, Winter Park, CO 80482 303-726-9703
Winterpoint P.O. Box 1797, Breckenridge, CO 80424 303-453-2262
Woodbridge Village Property Mgmt, Box 5550, Snowmass Village, CO 81615
Woodrun V P.O. Box 5550, Snowmass Village, CO 81615 303-923-4350

Woods Manor 0290 Broken Lance Drive, Box 3239, Breckenridge, CO 80424
303-453-6906

―――――――――――――――― DELAWARE ――――――――――――――――

Henlopen Broadwalk and Surf Avenue, Rehoboth Beach, DE 19930
302-227-6409
One Virginia Ave. One Virginia Avenue, Rehoboth Beach, DE 19930
302-227-9533
Rehoboth Gardens Phillips Street, Rehoboth Beach, DE 19971 302-227-3988
Summer Place Rt. 1 & Pennsylvania Ave., Bethany Beach, DE 19930
302-539-1112
Villas of Bethany Tree Top Lane, Bethany Beach, DE 19930

―――――――――――――――― FLORIDA ――――――――――――――――

Alamanda Villa 102 39th Street, Holmes Beach, FL 34217 813-778-4170
Alhoa 605 Riverside Drive, Pompano Beach, FL 33062 305-943-7000
Atlantic Terrace 3529 S. Atlantic Avenue, Daytona Beach, FL 32018
904-767-6447
Bay Club of San Destin P.O. Box 6098, Destin, FL 32541 904-837-8866
Bay Harbor Lodge Route 1, Box 35, Key Largo, FL 33037 305-852-5695
Bay Winds Marina 7345 Bay Street, St. Petersburg, FL 33706
813-367-2721
Baynes Townhouses 8327 Surf Drive, Panama City Beach, FL 32407
Baywatch 1150 Fort Pickens Rd., Pensacola Beach, FL 32561 904-492-0211
Beach Condominium Santa Rosa Island, 8459 Gulf Blvd, Navarre Beach, FL
32561 904-939-2324
Beach Cottage 18400 Gulf Blvd., Indian Shores, FL 33535 813-596-6101
Beach Island 1125 S. Atlantic Ave., Cocoa Beach, FL 32931 305-784-5720
Beach Terrace 5400 Ocean Blvd., Sarasota, FL 33581
Beechwood Terrace 17655 W. Hwy. 98A, P.O. Box 982, Panama City Beach, FL
32401 904-682-4220
Bel-Air Beach Club 780 Estero Blvd., Fort Myers Beach, FL 33931
813-463-7773
Berkshire Beach Club 500 N. A-1-A, Deerfield Beach, FL 33441 305-428-1000
Berkshire By The Sea 126 N. Ocean Blvd., Delray Beach, FL 33444
305-276-8400
Blue Lagoon Resort 99096 Overseas Hwy., Key Largo, FL 33037 305-451-2908
Boca Grande Gulf Boulevard, Boca Grande, FL 33921
Boca Teeca 5800 N.W. 2nd Avenue, Boca Raton, FL 33487 407-994-0400
Bonaventure 200 Bonaventure Blvd, Fort Lauderdale, FL 33304 305-389-8000
Breakers 381 Santa Rosa Blvd., Fort Walton Beach, FL 32548 904-244-9127
Breezy Palms P.O. Box 767, Islamorada, FL 33036 305-664-2361
Bryan's Spanish Cove 13875 S.R. 535, Orlando, FL 32819
Camaron Cove 2402 N. Gulf Blvd., Indian Rocks Beach, FL 34653 813-596-8610
Captiva Hideway 11400 Old Lodge Lane, Box 274, Captiva, FL 33924
813-472-4398
Caribbean Ocean 1885 S. Ocean Boulevard, Delray Beach, FL 33444
305-276-5972
Carlos Pointe 8350 Estero Blvd., Ft. Myers Beach, FL 33931
Carriage House 3200 N. Gulf Blvd., Belleair Beach, FL 34635 813-595-4787
Casa Sierra P.O. Box 10584, Tampa, FL 33679 813-877-4101
Catalina Beach Club 1303 S. Atlantic Avenue, Daytona Beach, FL 32018
904-253-6741

Catalina Beach Resort 1325 Gulf Drive North, Bradenton Beach, FL 33510
813-778-6611
Cedar By The Sea 3311 S. Atlantic Ave., Daytona Beach Shores, FL 32018
904-767-6445
Charlotte Bay 23128 Bayshore Road, Charlotte Harbor, FL 33980 813-627-2300
Checca Lodge Box 527, Islamorada, FL 33036 305-664-4651
Chrystal Beach 8115 Thomas Dr., Panama City Beach, FL 32407 904-235-2142
Clearwater Beach Resort 678 S. Gulfview Blvd., Clearwater Beach, FL 33515
813-441-3767
Coconuts Apartments 100 73rd Street, Holmes Beach, FL 34217 813-778-2277
Commander Beach Club 3100 Ocean Dr., Riviera Beach, FL 33404
305-848-3441
Commodore Beach Club 13536 Gulf Boulevard, Madeira Beach, FL 33708
813-392-2213
Commodore, The 4715 Thomas Drive, Panama City Beach, FL 32407
Coquina 6100 Estero Blvd., Ft. Myers Beach, FL 33931
Coral Harbour Club P.O. Box 2338, Key Largo, FL 33037 305-852-3246
Coral Shores Resort 17030 Gulf Blvd., N. Redington Beach, FL 33708
813-397-6608
Coral Tides 580 Briny Ave., Pompano Beach, FL 33062 305-785-4481
Costa Del Sol 4220 El Mar Drive, Lauderdale-by-the-Sea, FL 33308
305-776-6900
Creciente 7150 Estero Blvd., Ft. Myers Beach, FL 33931
Creston House 5930 A1A South, St. Augustine, FL 32084 904-471-0825
Daytona Resort 1200 Ruger Place, Daytona Beach, FL 32018
DeVille 794 Sundial Court, Ft. Walton Beach, FL 32548
Disney World 1 Magnolia Palm Drive, Lake Buena Vista, FL 32830
305-824-2270
Doral Ocean Beach 4833 Collins Avenue, Miami, FL 33140 305-532-3600
Eden House 7700 Estero Blvd., Ft. Myers Beach, FL 33931
Emerald Isle Club 770 Sundial Court, Fort Walton Beach, FL 32548
904-244-2534
Englewood Beach 2000 Bayview Blvd., Englewood, FL 34223 813-474-7171
Englewood Beach Place 1480 Gulf Boulevard, Englewood, FL 34223
813-474-8392
Executive Bay Club 801 North Swinton, Delray Beach, FL 33444 305-272-8927
Fairview Isles 6655 Estero Blvd., Fort Myers, FL 33931
813-463-9358
Fantasy Island 3205 S. Atlantic Ave., Daytona Beach Shores, FL 32018
904-761-9302
Faro Blanco Marina 1996 Overseas Hwy., Marathon, FL 33050 305-743-9018
Flamingo Lodge Marina P.O. Box 428, Flamingo, FL 33030 305-253-2241
Florida Bay Club Mile Marker 103.5, Key Largo, FL 33037 305-451-0101
Florida Fantasy 1249 South Highway 427, Longwood, FL 32750 407-332-3372
Florida Vacation 2770 Poinciana Blvd., Kissimmee, FL 33040 305-396-6010
Four Seasons 13070 Gulf Blvd., Madeira Beach, FL 33708 813-399-2255
Foxwood 556 Foxwood Boulevard, Englewood, FL 34223 813-474-9338
Freelancer 103100 Overseas Hwy., Key Largo, FL 33037 305-451-0349
Galt Ocean Club 3800 Galt Ocean Drive, Fort Lauderdale, FL 33308
800-547-5516
Gemini Beach 14691 W. Highway 98, Panama City Beach, FL 32407
Georgian Inn 759 South Atlantic Avenue, Ormond Beach, FL 32074
904-677-6043

Gilbert's Resort 107900 Overseas Hwy., Key Largo, FL 33037 305-451-1133
Golden Arms 601 N. Atlantic Avenue, New Smyrna Beach, FL 32069
904-428-2641
Grand Cypress 60 Grand Cypress Blvd., Orlando, FL 32819 407-239-4600
Grand Shores West 17350 Gulf Blvd., N. Redington Beach, FL 33708
813-397-5594
Grove Condominiums 30 Andrews Avenue, Delray Beach, FL 33483
407-276-7729
Gulf Gate Resort 111 50th Ave. West, St. Petersburg Beach, FL 33706
813-367-5696
Gulf Winds 1199 Fort Pickens Road, Pensacola Beach, FL 32561 904-923-5337
Harbor Arms 19823 W. Hwy. 98, Panama City Beach, FL 32407 904-234-5895
Harbor Club at Palm Coast 201 Clubhouse Dr., Palm Coast, FL 32037
904-445-1809
Harbor Pointe Bay Beach Lane, Ft. Myers Beach, FL 33931
Harbortown 7092 Placida Road, Cape Haze, FL 33946 813-697-4800
Hibiscus 4780 Highway A1A South, St. Augustine Beach, FL 32084
904-471-6848
Hidden Harbor 2396 Overseas Hwy, Marathon, FL 33050 305-743-5376
Holiday Beach Resort 4765 Gulf of Mexico Drive, Longboat Key, FL 34228
813-383-3704
Holiday Shores 2617 S. Atlantic Ave., Daytona Beach Shores, FL 32018
904-761-6553
Holley-King Resort Route #5, P.O. Box 79-K, De Funiak Springs, FL 32433
904-892-5914
Hollinsed House 609-611 Southard Street, Key West, FL 33040 305-296-8031
Hollywood Sands 2404 N. Surf Rd., Hollywood, FL 33019 305-925-2285
Hoover Vacation 2426 Skan Court, Orlando, FL 32809 305-843-0703
Hurricane Resort 4650 Overseas Hwy., Marathon, FL 33050 305-743-2393
Indian Key U.S. Hwy 1, P.O. Box 1860, Islamorada, FL 33036 305-664-8801
Islamorada Inn 87760 Overseas Hwy, Islamorada, FL 33036 305-852-9376
Island Gulf 13912 Gulf Blvd., Madeira Beach, FL 33708 813-398-6786
Island House Hwy A1A So. at Mary Street, St. Augustine, FL 32084
904-471-0153
Island House A1A South at Mary Street, St. Augustine, FL 32084 904-471-0153
Island's End 8400 Estero Blvd., Ft. Myers Beach, FL 33931
Islander Resort Box 766, Islamorada, FL 33036 305-664-2031
Islander 17006 Gulf Blvd., North Redington Beach, FL 33708 813-391-0171
Key Colony P.O. Box 24, Key Colony Beach, FL 33051 305-289-0821
Key Colony Point 1133 W. Ocean Dr., Box 99, Key Colony Beach, FL 33051
305-743-7701
Key West Beach Club 1500 Atlantic, Key West, FL 33040
Kon Tiki Resort Rt. 1, Box 58, Islamorada, FL 33036 305-664-4702
La Jolla Resort Rt. 1, Box 51, Islamorada, FL 33036 305-664-9213
La Plaza 106 San Souci/999 Ft. Pickens Rd., Pensacola Beach, FL 32561
904-932-5410
La Siesta Resort P.O. Box 573, Islamorada, FL 33036
Lake Ida 2524 N. US Highway 17, Winter Haven, FL 33881 813-293-0942
Lani Kai Bay 1401 Estero Blvd., Fort Myers Beach, FL 33931
813-463-3111
Leeward Townhouses 7829 Surf Drive, Panama City Beach, FL 32407
Lemon Bay Breezes 1401 S. McCall Road, Englewood, FL 33533 813-475-6509
Lermitage 200 Bradley Place, Palm Beach, FL 33480 305-659-3177

Lido Beach   1234 Ben Franklin Drive, Sarasota, FL 34236   813-388-3733
Lighthouse   748 S. Fletcher Road, Amelia Island, FL 32034   904-261-4148
Lighthouse Cove   1406 N. Ocean Blvd., Pompano Beach, FL 33062
305-941-3410
Lighthouse Resort   219 Lighthouse Road, Sanibel Island, FL 33957
813-472-4162
Lime Tree Bay   Box 839, Islamorada, FL 33036   305-664-4740
Marina Del Mar   P.O. Box 1050, Key Largo, FL 33037   800-253-3483
Marine Terrace   1018 N. Atlantic Avenue, Daytona Beach, FL 32018
904-253-2000
Marriott's Royal Palms   World Center Drive, Orlando, FL 32821
Marriott's Sabal Palms   8805 World Center Drive, Orlando, FL 32821
Matecumbe Resort   US Highway 1, Marker 76.5, Islamorada, FL 33036
Maverick, The   458 South Atlantic Avenue, Ormond, FL 32074   904-672-3550
Melbourne House   227 Australian Avenue, Palm Beach, FL 33480   305-655-7015
Merriweath ˜ Resort   115 N. Atlantic Blvd, Fort Lauderdale, FL 33304
305-462-5356
Midnight Cove   6302 Midnight Cove Rd. Siesta Key, Sarasota, FL 34242
813-349-3004
Miracle Mile Resort   9450 S. Thomas Drive, Panama City Beach, FL 32407
904-234-3484
Misty Harbour   7904 Surf Dr., Panama City Beach, FL 32407   904-234-5947
Moorings, The   Route 1, P.O. Box 116-A, Islamorada, FL 33036   305-664-4708
Native Son, The   1950 S. Ocean Blvd., Pompano Beach, FL 33062   305-942-2800
Native Sun   1950 S. Ocean Ave., Pompano Beach, FL 33062
Nautical Watch   3420 Gulf Boulevard, Belleair Beach, FL 34635   813-595-4747
Navarre Towers   8271 Gulf Blvd., Navarre Beach, FL 32561 · 904-939-2011
Oakwater Cove   6005 N. Beach Road, Englewood, FL 33533   813-474-2319
Ocean Club   21 Dondanville Road, St. Augustine, FL 32084   904-471-6852
Ocean Club Resort   3100 No. Ocean Drive, Singer Island, FL 33404
407-848-3441
Ocean Holiday   1350 N. Ocean Blvd., Pompano Beach, FL 33062   305-941-0300
Ocean House   7870 A1A South, Crescent Beach, St. Augustine, FL 32084
904-471-0454
Ocean Key House   Zero Duval St., Key West, FL 33040   800-231-9864
Ocean Palms   2601 S. Atlantic Ave., New Smyrna Beach, FL 32069   904-427-6892
Ocean Village   2400 South Ocean Drive, Ft. Pierce, FL 34949
Ocean Villas   1041 A1A South, St. Augustine, FL 32084   904-471-6800
Oceana Garden   1230 Hwy A1A Hillsboro Beach, Pompano Beach, FL 33062
305-427-7100
Oceanside 99   99 S. Atlantic Ave., Ormond Beach, FL 32074   904-673-0234
Oceanview Towers   5205 S. Atlantic Avenue, New Smyrna Beach, FL 32069
904-427-8555
Our House   1001 Beach Road, Sarasota, FL 33581
Outrigger Beach Club   215 S. Atlantic Ave., Ormond Beach, FL 32074
904-672-2770
Outrigger Resort   1402 NE Indian River Drive, Jensen Beach, FL 33457
Oyster Bay Resort   P.O. Box 780899, Sebastian, FL 32978   305-589-6513
Palm Bay Resort   2525 S. Atlantic Ave., Daytona Beach Shores, FL 32018
904-756-1685
Palm Beach Biltmore   150 Bradley Place, Palm Beach, FL 33488   305-832-0600
Palm Beach Hampton   3100 South Ocean Blvd., Palm Beach, FL 33480
305-585-3555

Palms Resort on the Ocean   9449 Collins Ave., Surfside, FL 33154   305-865-3551
Parc Corniche   6300 Parc Corniche Drive, Orlando, FL 32821   407-239-7100
Parc Regent   184 Bradley Place, Palm Beach, FL 33488   305-833-6007
Pavilion, The   1170 Edington Place, Marco Island, FL 33969   813-394-3345
Pelican Inlet   Route 9, Box 79C, Crescent Beach, FL 32084   904-471-0434
Pelican Landing   2700 N.Beach Road, Englewood, FL 34223   813-474-7161
Pelicans Roost   605 Donax Street, Sanibel Island, FL 33957   813-472-2996
Penthouse   10182 Gulf Blvd., Treasure Island, FL 33706   813-360-0827
Pier Point   2170 Highway A1A South, St. Augustine, FL 32084   904-471-3622
Pines and Palms   80401 Old Highway, Islamorada, FL 33036   305-664-4343
Pink Shell   250 Estero Boulevard, Fort Myers Beach, FL 33931   813-463-6181
Pirates Cove, Marathon, FL 33050
Placida Harbour   11000 Placida Road, Placida, FL 33946   813-697-2600
Plantation   P.O. Box 217, Captiva Island, FL 33924   813-472-5111
Plantation   500 Rockley Blvd., Venice, FL 34293   813-493-2146
Pool Villa   Amelia Island Plantation, Amelia Island, FL 32034   904-261-4148
Port Largo   417 Bahia Avenue, Key Largo, FL 33037   305-852-8597
Portside Villas   1299 Fort Pickens Road, Pensacola Beach, FL 32561   904-932-5337
Quality Inn   3850 N. Roosevelt Blvd., Key West, FL 33040   305-294-6681
Quarterdeck   1275 Tarpon Center Drive, Venice, FL 34285   813-488-0449
Ramada Key's End   3420 N. Roosevelt Blvd., Key West, FL 33040   305-294-5541
Regency House   2000 S. Ocean Dr., Hallandale, FL 33009   305-454-2220
Regency Towers   5801 Thomas Drive, Panama City Beach, FL 32408   904-234-2281
Resort Sixty-Six   6600 Gulf Dr., Holmes Beach, FL 34217   813-778-2238
Riviera Club   7500 Estero Blvd., Ft. Myers Beach, FL 33931
Rock Reef   P.O. Box 10, Key Largo, FL 33037   305-852-5334
Rodney Motel   9365 Collins Avenue, Miami Beach, FL 33154   305-864-2232
Royal Atlantic   3743 S. Atlantic Avenue, Daytona Beach Shores, FL 32016   904-254-7500
Royal Oak   2150 Country Club Drive, Titusville, FL 32780   407-269-4500
Sand & Surf   2525 S. Atlantic Ave., Daytona Beach Shores, FL 32018   904-761-4771
Sand Caper   6900 Estero Blvd., Ft. Myers Beach, FL 33931
Sand Castles   911 Gulf Breeze Parkway, Pensacola Beach, FL 32561   904-932-9723
Sand Castles   17214 W. Hwy. 98A, Panama City Beach, FL 32407   904-234-7157
Sandarac   6660-62 Estero Blvd., Ft. Myers Beach, FL 33931
Sandcastle   905 Estero Blvd., Ft. Myers, FL 33931
Sandpiper   6414 Midnight Pass Rd.,Siesta Key, Sarasota, FL 33581   813-346-0922
Sandy Shores   3159 S. Atlantic Ave., Daytona Beach Shores, FL 32018   904-767-7631
Sanibel Arms West   827 East Gulf Drive, Sanibel, FL 33957   813-472-1138
Sanibel Beach Club   626 Nerita Street, Sanibel Island, FL 33957
Sanibel Beach Club   220 Lighthouse Rd., Sanibel Island, FL 33957   813-472-5772
Sanibel Surfside   455 Periwinkle Way, Sanibel Island, FL 33957   813-472-4195
Sans Souci   999 Fort Pickens Road, Pensacola Beach, FL 32561   904-932-5337
Sea Club IV   3229 S. Atlantic Ave., Daytona Beach Shores, FL 32018   904-767-2700
Sea Crest   1129 Seaside Drive, Sarasota, FL 34242   813-349-4200
Sea Dome Resort   Hwy. 98 E. at Airport Rd., Destin, FL 32541   904-837-6137

Sea Oats 1720 Gulf Blvd., Englewood, FL 34223 813-474-3611
Sea Palm Resort 7092 Placida Road, Cap Haze, FL 33946 813-481-3636
Sea Shell 6500 Midnight Pass Road, Sarasota, FL 34242 813-349-1191
Sea Side Villas 4701 Thomas Dr., Panama City Beach, FL 32408 904-234-6587
Sea Winds 901 South Collier Blvd., Marco Island, FL 33937
Seafire 2121 Hill Street, New Smyrna Beach, FL 32169 904-427-4427
Seagull Villas 17735 W. Highway 98-A, Panama City Beach, FL 32407
Seaside 501 Briny Avenue, Pompano Beach, FL 33062 305-941-7650
Seaside Villas 4701 Thomas Drive, Panama City Beach, FL 32407 904-234-6587
Seasons, The 5777767 Major Blvd., Orlando, FL 32819 305-351-6123
Seawatch 6550 Estero Blvd., Fort Myers Beach, FL 33931 813-481-3636
Shell Island 300 Lighthouse Road, Sanibel Island, FL 33957 813-472-4497
Shoreline Villas 23009 W. Highway 98-A, Panama City Beach, FL 32407
Shores, The 22500 West Alt. 98, Panama City Beach, FL 32413
904-234-6591
Siesta Sands 1001 Point of Rocks Rd., Sarasota, FL 34242 813-349-8061
Silver Beach 1025 S. Atlantic Ave., Daytona Beach, FL 32018 904-252-9681
Silver Sands 4865 S. Atlantic Avenue, New Smyrna Beach, FL 32069
Smuggler's Cove 1505 Gulf Dr. N, Bradenton Beach, FL 33510 813-778-6667
Soundside Holiday 19 Via de Luna Dr., Pensacola Beach, FL 32561
904-932-4298
South Seas Club P.O. Box 194, Captiva Island, FL 33924 813-472-5111
South Shore Club 1625 S. Ocean Blvd., Delray Beach, FL 33444 305-276-9514
St. Aug. Ocean 3300 Highway A1A South, St. Augustine, FL 32084
904-471-0932
St. Augustine 1981 A1A South, St. Augustine, FL 32084
Starboard Village 1111 Fort Pickens Road, Pensacola Beach, FL 32561
904-932-5337
Stone Lodge Resort Rt. 1, Box 50, Key Largo, FL 33037 305-852-8114
Suites at Key Largo 201 Ocean Drive, Key Largo, FL 33037 305-451-5081
Sun Caper 7930 Estero Blvd., Ft. Myers Beach, FL 33931
Sunrise Beach Club 1212 North Atlantic Avenue, Daytona Beach, FL 32019
904-252-4633
Sunrise 4141 S. Atlantic Avenue, New Smyrna Beach, FL 32069 904-423-3946
Sunrise Cove 8877 Midnight Pass Road, Sarasota, FL 34242 813-349-4955
Sunset Inn Box 269, Islamorada, FL 33036 305-664-4427
Sunswept 6829 Thomas Drive, Panama City Beach, FL 32407
Surfrider 555 East Gulf Drive, Sanibel Island, FL 33957 813-472-2161
Tarpon Woods 800 Tarpon Woods Blvd., Palm Harbor, FL 33563 813-785-7414
Terra Mar 7100 Estero Blvd., Ft. Myers Beach, FL 33931
Three Lov #9 Beachwood, Amelia Is. Plant., Amelia Island, FL 32034
904-261-4148
Tierra Verde Island 200 Madonna Blvd., Tierra Verde, FL 33715 813-867-8611
Tiki Condominiums 5055 N. Beach Road, Englewood, FL 34223 813-474-7225
Topsider P.O. Box 26, Islamorada, FL 33036 305-664-8031
Tropic Air Resort 75780 Overseas Hwy., Islamorada, FL 33036 305-664-4989
Tropical Isles 5550 S. U.S. 1 FP, Port St. Lucie, FL 34982 305-465-2555
Tropical Reef P.O. Box 409, Islamorada, FL 33036 305-664-4707
Turquoise Reef 1920 Coral Way, Miami, FL 33145 305-854-2415
Turtle Inn 3233 S. Atlantic, Daytona Beach Shores, FL 32018 904-761-0426
Vanderbilt Lagoon 9207 Vanderbilt Drive, Naples, FL 33963 813-597-3079
Vanderbilt Vacation 9467 Gulf Shore Dr., Naples, FL 33963 813-597-1141
Ventura 2301 S. Ocean Blvd., Boca Raton, FL 33432 305-395-5991

Venture Out Route 2, Box 38, Summerland Key, FL 33042 305-745-3233
Via Roma 2408 Gulf Dr., N. Bradenton Beach, FL 34217 813-778-6691
Waters Edge 1860 San Casa Drive, Englewood, FL 34223 813-475-2511
Whispering Sands 8459 Gulf Blvd., Navarre Beach, FL 32561
Windjammer 4244 El Mar Drive, Lauderdale-by-the-Sea, FL 37308
305-776-4232

———————————————— GEORGIA ————————————————

AHC at Beaver Forest Beaver Lake Drive, Ellijay, GA 30540
AHC at Eagles Mountain Route 382, Ellijay, GA 30540
Alpine Crest, Helen, GA 30545
Appalachian Heritage 100 Beaver Lake Drive, Ellijay, GA 30540 404-276-1000
Beaver Forest Chalet 100 Beaver Lake Dr., Beaver Lake Estates, GA 30540
404-276-1000
Igls Innisbruck, Helen, GA 30545
King & Prince Villas P.O. Box 798, St. Simon's Island, GA 31522 912-638-3631
Lake Sinclair P.O. Box 928, Milledgeville, GA 31061 404-444-7137
Pine Mountain Club Chalets Highway 18 West, Pine Mountain, GA 31822
Sea Gate Inn 1014 Ocean Blvd., St. Simon's Island, GA 31522 912-638-8661
Sky Valley Resort Route #3, P.O. Box #1, Gillard, GA 30537 404-746-5301
Villas by the Sea 1175 North Beachview Drive, Jekyll Island, GA 31520
916-635-2521
Yacht Club, The Gainesville Marina, Highway 53, Gainesville, GA 30501
404-399-6400

———————————————— HAWAII ————————————————

Abigale Apartments 2233 Ala Wai Blvd, Honolulu, HI 96815
Alii Kai II Hanalei P.O. Box 3292, Lihue, Kauai, HI 96766 808-826-9988
Aloha Towers 430 Lewers St., Honolulu, HI 96815 714-497-4253
Aloha Towers 2215 Alohea Dr. #16K, Honolulu, HI 96815 808-923-7061
Aoao Maui Kai 106 Kaanapali Shores, Maui, HI 96753 808-661-0394
Banyan Tree, The 76-6268 Alii Drive, Kailua, Kona, HI 96740 808-329-3006
Ching Connection 145 North Kihei Road, Kihei, HI 96753 808-879-7866
Cliffs Club, The 1236 Kapiolani Blvd., Honolulu, HI 96814
Cliffs Club, The P.O. Box 960, Hanalei, HI 96714 800-877-9770
Country Club, Kailua-Kona, HI 96740
Discovery Bay 1778 Ala Moana, Honolulu, HI 96815 808-944-8555
Foster Tower 2500 Kalakaua Ave., Honolulu, HI 96815 714-497-4253
Hale Royale 3788 Honoapilani Highway, Maui, HI 96753 808-669-5230
Ilikai 1777 Ala Moana, Honolulu, HI 96815 714-497-4253
Ka Eo Kai P.O. Box 1109, Hanalei, Kauai, HI 96714 808-826-9833
Ka Eo Kai P.O. Box 3099, Princeville Sta., Princeville, Kauai, HI 96722
808-826-7204
Kahana Outrigger 4521 Lower Honoapiilani Road, Lahaina, Maui, HI 96761
808-669-5544
Kamahana Country Club Drive, Princeville, Kauai, HI 96714 808-826-6747
Kapaa Shore 4-0900 Kuhio Highway, Kappa, Kauai, HI 96746 808-822-3055
Kauna Kai P.O. Box 1109, Hanalei, Kauai, HI 96714 808-826-9833
Keauhou Akahi 78-7030 Alii Drive, Kailue, Kona, HI 96740 808-329-6402
Keauhou Palena, Kailua, Kona, HI 96740
Keauhou Punahele Alii Drive, Kailue, Kona, HI 96740 808-329-6402
Keauhou, Kailua-Kona, HI 96740
Kihei Akahi 2531 S. Kihei Road, Kihei, Maui, HI 96753

Kihei Maui   P.O. Box 1055, Kihei, Maui, HI 96753   808-879-7581
Kona Onenalo, Kailua-Kona, HI 96745
Kona Village   P.O. Box 1299, Kaupulehu-Kona, HI 96745   808-325-5555
Lani Kai   390 Papaloa Road, Kappa, Kauai, HI 96746   808-822-7456
Laule'a Maui, Maui, HI 96753
Lawai Beach   5017 Lawai Road, Kauai, Maui, HI 96746   808-742-9581
Makai Club   P.O. Box 3040, Hanalei, HI 96722
808-524-5972
Malia Kai   75-5855 Walua Road, Kailua, Kona, HI 96740   808-329-6402
Manualoha at Poipu   4480 Ahukini Rd., #2, Lihue, Kauai, HI 96766
808-245-6600
Mauna Lani Point   50 Nohea Kai Drive, Lahaina, Maui, HI 96761   808-667-1400
Mauna Lani Terrace   P.O. Box 4959, Kohala Coast, Hawaii, HI 96743
808-885-6688
Pacific Grand   747 Amana St., Honolulu, HI 96815   808-523-7785
Paniolo   P.O. Box 1109, Hanalei, Kauai, HI 96714   808-826-9833
Puunoa Beach Estates   45 Kai Pali Place, Lahaina, Maui, HI 96761   808-667-1400
Ridge At Kapalua Bay   1 Bay Drive, Kapalua, Maui, HI 96761   808-667-2851
Royal Kahili   76-6283 Alii Drive, Kailua, Kona, HI 96740   808-329-6402
Sea Lodge   P.O. Box 1109, Hanalei, Kauai, HI 96714   808-826-9833
Seaside Surf   440 Seaside Avenue, Honolulu, HI 96815
Shores at Waikoloa, Kaikoloa, HI 96743
Silver's Pacific Monarch   142 Uluniu Ave., Honolulu, HI 96815   808-922-4359
Waikiki Park Heights   2440 Kuhio Avenue, Honolulu, Oahu, HI 96815
808-923-2228
Wailea Vacation   P.O. Box 352, Kihei, HI 96753   808-879-0038
Wailua Bayview   P.O. Box 3292, 320 Papaloa, Kapaa, Kauai, HI 96746
808-822-3651

———————————————— IDAHO ————————————————

Condo del Sol   301 Iberian Way, P.O. Box 744, Sandpoint, ID 83864
208-263-7595
Cottonwood   P.O. Box 659, Sun Valley, ID 83353   800-635-8261
Habitat 2000   P.O. Box 700, Ketchum, ID 83340   208-726-8584
Hill's Resort   Route 5, P.O. Box 162A, Pirest Lake, ID 83856   208-443-2551
Hot Springs   P.O. Box 156, Lava Hot Springs, ID 83246   208-776-5445
Kimberland Meadows   Post Office Drawer C, New Meadows, ID 83654
208-347-2163
Lift Haven Inn   P.O. Box 21, Ketchum, ID 83340   208-726-5601
Lodge Apartments   Sun Valley Co, Sun Valley, ID 83353
800-635-8261
Mill Park Condos   P.O. Box 1062, McCall, ID 83638   208-624-4151
Pine Ridge   P.O. Box 20, Victor, ID 83455
Pioneer Inn   2045 Bogus Basin Road, Boise, ID 83702
Rivers Bend   P.O. Box 1678, McCall, ID 83638
Riverside Condos   P.O. Box 877, McCall, ID 83638   208-634-5610
Schweitzer   P.O. Box 815, Sandpoint, ID 83864   208-265-4576
Snow Creek   Sun Valley Co, Sun Valley, ID 83353   800-635-8261
Timberlake   P.O. Box 1678, McCall, ID 83638
Twin Lakes Village   Route 4, Box V-551, Rathdrum, ID 83858   208-687-1311
Tyrolean   Box 202, Sun Valley, ID 83353   208-726-5336
Villager II   Sun Valley, Sun Valley, ID 83353
Waters Edge   P.O. Box 1678, McCall, ID 83638

White Cloud   Box 535, Sun Valley, ID 83353   208-726-3600

───────────────────── KENTUCKY ─────────────────────

Hideaway Hills   1 Doyle Road, Park City, KY 42160   502-749-9466

───────────────────── LOUISIANA ─────────────────────

Bon Temps Village   659 Bon Temps Roule, Mandeville, LA 70448   504-845-8363
Bonaparte's Quarters   717 Ursulines, New Orleans, LA 70116
Chateau Esplanade   1261 Esplanade Ave., New Orleans, LA 70116
504-944-6300
Chateau Orleans   240 Burgundy Street, New Orleans, LA 70116
Club La Pension   Canal Street, New Orleans, LA 70115   504-528-9254
Courtyards, The   1426-28 Royal St., New Orleans, LA 70116   504-944-8196
Hillcrest Lake   Highway 435, Abita Springs, LA   504-893-4930
Jean Lafitte House   613-617 Esplanade Avenue, New Orleans, LA 70116
504-943-2543
La Maison Charles   3801 St. Charles Ave., New Orleans, LA 70116   504-899-8307
La Maison de la Rive   108 University Place, New Orleans, LA 70115
504-527-5810
Leisure Club   717 Ursulines, New Orleans, LA 70116
Maison Orleans   315 Tchoupitoulas St., New Orleans, LA 70130   504-523-4984
Mardi Gras Manor 1   619 Govenor Nichols St., New Orleans, LA 70116
504-524-0370
North Harbor III   123 N. Shore Circle, Slidell, LA 70458   504-641-5870
Rue Esplanade   633 Esplanade Avenue, New Orleans, LA 70115   504-949-7408

───────────────────── MASSACHUSETTS ─────────────────────

Brant Point Courtyard   Swain Street, Nantucket, MA 02564   617-228-0241
Briarwood   77 Pine Valley Rd., Falmouth, MA 02540   617-540-4366
Cap'n Gladcliff   Route 28, P.O. Box 116, Soukth Yarmouth, MA 02664
617-394-9828
Cape Cod Holiday   Four Seasons Dr., Mashpee, MA 02642   617-477-3377
Edgartown Commons   Pease Point Way, Edgartown, MA 02539
Harbor Landing   Beach Road, P.O. Box 1935, Martha's Vineyard, MA 02568
508-693-2600
Kelley Bay Estates   P.O. Box 1008, West Dennis, MA 02660   617-778-1818
Maeline Townhouse   P.O. Box 337, Bass River, MA 02664   617-394-4939
Ocean Mist   97 South Shore Drive, South Yarmouth, MA 02664   508-398-2633
Outin' Spruce Resort   Meadow St., P.O. Box 177, South Lee, MA 01260
413-243-2353
Oyster Pond   1233 Main Street, Chatham, MA 02633   617-945-1095
Oyster Pond   Route 28, Chatham, MA 02633   508-945-1095
Ponds at Foxhollow   Route 7, Lenox, MA 01240   413-637-1469
Samoset Resort, Rockport, MA
Sea Mist Resort   Great Neck Rd., Mashpee, MA 02649   617-477-0549
Seaside   135 S. Shore Drive, South Yarmouth, MA 02664   617-775-6880
The Harwich Port   558 Main St., Harwich Port, MA 02646   617-432-2424
Wellfleet Salt Box   P.O. Box 162, South Wellfleet, MA 02663

───────────────────── MARYLAND ─────────────────────

Lakewood Resort   P.O. Box 660, McHenry, MD 21541   301-387-4900
Spinnaker   18th & Oceanside, Box 519, Ocean City, MD 21842   301-289-5444
Thunder Island   40th Street and Bayside, Ocean City, MD 21842   301-676-4955
Tranquillity   7 Danforth Court, Towson, MD 21204

---------------------- MAINE ----------------------

Bethel Inn   Village Common, Bethel, ME 04217   207-824-2175
Idlease Guest   Route 9. P.O. Box 3086, Kennebunk, ME 04046   207-985-4460
Lakeview   P.O. Box 173, Rangely, ME 04970
Ocean View   72 Beach Avenue, Kennebunk Beach, ME 04043
Vacationland   Island Falls, Island Falls, ME 04645   207-463-2884

---------------------- MICHIGAN ----------------------

Alpine Resort   1116 W. Gruler Road, Petoskey, MI 40770   616-347-8501
Harborage, The   500 Front Street, Boyne City, MI 49712
Pine Mountain   N3332 Pine Mountain Road, Iron Mountain, MI 49801
Ridgeway   Resort Condominiums Marketing Inc, Hilton Shanty Ck., MI 49615
616-533-6135
Schuss Mountain   Mountain House Condominiums, Mancelona, MI 49659
616-587-9162
Springbrook Hills   P.O. Box 219, Walloon Lake, MI 49796   616-535-2227
Water Street Inn   500 Front Street, Boyne City, MI 49712   616-582-3000

---------------------- MINNESOTA ----------------------

Bluefin Bay   Lake Superior, Tofte, MN 55615   218-663-7296
Chateau LaVeaux   Box 115, Tofte, MN 55615   218-663-7223
Eaglewood   P.O. Box 805, Grand Rapids, MN 55744   218-326-9461
Kavanaugh's Resort   2300 Kavanaugh Drive, S.W., Brainerd, MN 56401
218-829-5226
Myr Mar Lodge   Route 2, Aitkin, MN 56431   218-678-2113

---------------------- MISSISSIPPI ----------------------

Captain Ed's   702 Beach Drive, Gulfport, MS 39507   601-896-3469
Chateau Le Grand   1304 W. Beach Blvd., Biloxi, MS 39530   601-374-8047
Golfing Green   1 Golfing Green Dr., Ocean Springs, MS 39564   601-872-1000
Gulf Towers   940 Central Beach Blvd., Biloxi, MS 39530   601-436-3971
Gulf Towers   824 Central Beach Blvd., Biloxi, MS 39530   601-436-3707
Royal Holiday Beach   3420 W. Beach Blvd. US 90, Biloxi, MS 39531
601-388-7034
Sandcastles   404 West Beach Blvd., Highway 90, Long Beach, MS 39560
Village at Henderson   101 4th Avenue, Pass Christian, MS 39571   601-452-7276
Villas of Hickory Hills   900 Hickory Hill Dr., Gautier, MS 39553   601-497-5150

---------------------- MISSOURI ----------------------

Bass Haven Resort   HCR 1 Box 4480, Shell Knob, MO 65747   417-858-6401
Bay Point Village   Route 72, Box 76, Lake Ozark, MO 65049
Bennett Spring   RT 16, Box 745, Lebanon, MO 65536   800-334-6946
Best Western   State Road KK, Osage Beach, MO 65065   314-348-1735
Breckenridge   Lake Road 54-30A, Osage Beach, MO 65065   314-348-2293
Bridgepoint   Route 72, Box 76, Lake Ozark, MO 65049
Bridgeport   4199 N. Lindbergh Blvd., St. Louis, MO 63044   800-727-0231
Brill's Rainbow Trout   414 N. Sycamore, Branson, MO 65616   417-334-3955
Cooper Creek Resort   HCR 5, Box 2204B, Branson, MO 65616   417-334-4871
E Z Center Motel   1901 W. 76 Highway, Branson, MO 65616   417-334-9732
Elms Resort Hotel   Regent and Elms Blvd., Excelsior Springs, MO 64024
816-637-2141
Five Bees Resort   RR 3, Box 492, Kimberling City, MO 65868
417-739-2012

Greenwood Resorts P.O. Box 944, Kimberling City, MO 65868
Harbor Point Route 72, Box 76, Lake Ozark, MO 65049
Harbortown Resort Route 2, Box 26, Monroe City, MO 63456 314-735-4988
Harbour, The P.O. Box 126, Lake RD. P, Gravois Mills, MO 65037 314-372-3000
Hawk's Nest Lodge Rt. 2, Box 3980, Osage Beach, MO 65065 314-348-1741
Heron Bay Route 72, Box 76, Lake Ozark, MO 65049
Holiday Hills Resort Route 3, Box 282, Branson, MO 65616
Idle Days & Gala P.O. Box 689, Lake Road 54-37, Osage Beach, MO 65065
314-348-2134
Indian Trails HCR 1, Box 996, Branson, MO 65616
Inn at Grand Glaize Hwy 54 at Lake Rd. 40. Box 969, Osage Beach, MO 65065
800-348-4731
Jonathan's Landing 500 Walnut Road, Lake Ozark, MO 65049 314-365-6772
Lakeview Resort HCR 69, Box 505W, Sunrise Beach, MO 65079 314-374-5555
Landing Recreation P.O. Box 38, Monroe City, MO 63456 314-735-4242
Maywood Condominiums P.O. Box 623, Lake Ozark, MO 65049
Notch Estates P.O. Box 128, Branson, MO 65616 417-338-2941
Ozark Mountain Route 3, Box 910, Kimberling City, MO 65686
Pointe Royale P.O. Box 1988-GN, Branson, MO 65616 800-962-4710
Roark Vacation 401 N. Business 65, Branson, MO 65616
Robinwood Route 72, Box 76, Lake Ozark, MO 65049
Rock Harbor Lake Road 5-35, Rt. 3, Box 350, Sunrise Beach, MO 65079
314-374-5586
Southwood Shores 790 Highway HH, Lake Ozark, MO 65049 314-365-4644
Stillwaters Beach HCR 1 Box 958, Branson, MO 65616 417-338-2323
Sullivan Motel 770 West S. Service Rd. Hwy 1-44, Sullivan, MO 63080
314-468-4116
Summerset Inn Lake Road 54-37, Rt. 2, Box 2220, Osage Beach, MO 65065
314-348-5073
Sun Dance Resort P.O. Box 871, Lake Ozark, MO 65049 314-365-2946
Sunset Beach Lake Road 54-22, Box 262F, Osage Beach, MO 65065
314-348-2650
Swiss Villa Resort P.O. Box 27, Lampe, MO 65681 417-779-4111
Three Buoys Route 71, P.O. Box 1870, Camdenton, MO 65720
Treetops Village Business R.R. 54 Highway HH, Lake of the Ozarks, MO
65049 324-365-3333
Tribesman Resort Rt. 1 Box 1032W, Branson, MO 65616 417-338-2616
Waters Edge 576 State Highway HH, Lake Ozark, MO 65049 314-365-5311
Weston Point Route 1, P.O. Box 313, Osage Beach, MO 65065
Wheelhouse Villas Horseshoe Bend/Cherokee Road, Lake Ozark, MO 65049
314-365-5306
Winged Eagle HCR 1 Box 928, Branson, MO 65616 417-338-2314
Wishwood Lake Route 3, Box 145, Galena, MO 65656 417-538-2333
Wrenwood Route 72, Box 76, Lake Ozark, MO 65049

———————————— MONTANA ————————————

Arrowhead P.O. Box 8, Big Sky, MT 59716
Beaverhead Box 1, Big Sky, MT 59716
Fairmont Hot Springs 1500 Fairmont Road, Anaconda, MT 59711
406-797-3241
Golden Eagle Westfork Meadows, Big Sky, MT 59716 406-995-4800
Peaceful Bay Resort, Lakeside, MT 59068
Ptarmigan Village P.O. Box 458, Whitefish, MT 59937 406-862-3594

Rock Creek Mine Grizzly   U.S. 212, Red Lodge, MT 59068   406-446-1111
Rock Creek Mine   Route 2, Box 3500, Red Lodge, MT 59068   406-446-1111
Swan Lake Resort   Route 1, P.O. Box 289, Bigfork, MT 59911
Wildwood   128 Central, Whitefish, MT 59937   406-862-2282
Yellowstone   Box 867, West Yellowstone, MT 59758
406-646-9331

──────────────── NEW HAMPSHIRE ────────────────

Anchorage   RFD #1, P.O. Box 90A, Laconia, NH 03246   603-524-3248
Black Horse   RFD #1, Ashland, NH 03217   603-968-7116
Cranmore Place   P.O. Box 1349, North Conway, NH 03860   603-356-6978
Deer Park Resort   P.O. Box 175, Lincoln, NH 03251   603-745-9040
Eastern Slope Inn   P.O. Box 359, North Conway, NH 03860   603-356-6321
Franconia Notch   Route 18, P.O. Box 480, Franconia, NH 03580   603-823-5536
Holiday Bungalows   RFD 3, Box 123 Weirs Blvd., Laconia, NH 03246
Lincoln Station   Kancanmagus Highway, Box 477, Lincoln, NH 03251
603-745-3441
Summit at Four Seasons   The Summit, Laconia, NH 03246   603-366-4896
Wentworth Resort, Jackson Village, NH 03846   603-383-9700
Wentworth Resort   Route 16-A, Jackson Village, NH 03846   603-383-9700
Windrifter, The   South Main St., P.O. Box 608, Wolfeboro, NH 03894
603-564-1323

──────────────── NEW JERSEY ────────────────

Americana Great Gorge   Box 637, McAfee, NJ 07428   201-827-6000
Brigantine Inn   1400 Ocean Ave., P.O. Box 613, Brigantine, NJ 08203
609-266-2266
Flagship Resort   Grammercy Place & Maine Box 539, Atlantic City, NJ 08404
La Renaissance   Kentucky and Boardwalk, Atlantic City, NJ 08401
609-348-1343

──────────────── NEW MEXICO ────────────────

Angelfire Cabin   P.O. Drawer B, Angel Fire, NM 87710   505-377-2301
Aspen Lodge   101 Upper Terrace Dr., Box 2625, Ruidoso, NM 88345
505-257-2978
Barcelona Court   900 Louisiana Avenue, Albuquerque, NM
505-255-5566
Campanilla Compound   334 Otero, Santa Fe, NM 87501   505-988-7585
Condotel   727 Mech, Ruidoso, NM 88346
Four Seasons   Route 70, P.O. Box 3056 H.S., Ruidoso, NM 88345
Foxfire Lodge   P.O. Box 530, Red River, NM 87558   505-754-2540
Hacienda De San Roberto   P.O. Box 5651, Taos, NM 87571   505-758-8811
Las Brisas De Santa Fe   624 Galisteo Street, Box 1770, Santa Fe, NM 87504
505-982-5795
Lookout Estates   Box 2297, Ruidoso, NM 88345   505-257-5064
Mountain Resorts   106 Bishop, Ruidoso, NM 88345   505-257-2119
Mountain Resorts, Timberon, NM
Mountain Spirit, Angel Fire, NM 87710
Mystic Pines   P.O. Box 2374, Ruidoso, NM 88345   505-258-5426
Otra Vez   202 Galisteo and Water Street, Santa Fe, NM 87501
Pinecliff Villas   P.O. Box 716, Ruidoso, NM 88345
Pinon Park   Box 606 Off Hwy 37, Ruidoso, NM 88345   505-258-4129
Ruidoso   366 Sudderth Drive, Ruidoso, NM 88345   505-257-9600
St. Bernard   Taos Ski Valley, Taos, NM 87525   505-776-8506

Starfire Lodge P.O. Box 135, Angel Fire, NM 87710
Sun Lodge Highway 38, Angel Fire, NM 87710
Tiara Del Sol P.O. Box 3148, Ruidoso, NM 88345 505-257-9232
Willow Tree Lodge P.O. Box 1300, Ruidoso, NM 88345 505-257-2731

──────────────── NEVADA ────────────────

Cambridge Towers 3890 Swenson, Las Vegas, NV 89119
Glenrock P.O. Box 5659, Incline Village, NV 89450 702-831-0266
Grand Flamingo 100 Winnick Avenue, Las Vegas, NV 89109
Holiday Royale 4505 Paradise Road, Las Vegas, NV 89109 702-733-7676
Incline Village P.O. Box 3549, Incline Village, NV 89450 702-831-1515
Jockey Club 3700 Las Vegas Blvd. South, Las Vegas, NV 89109
Kingsbury Crossing P.O. Box 6600, Stateline, NV 89449 702-588-6247
Plaza Resort Club 121 West Street, Reno, NV 89505
Reno Spa Resort 140 Court Street, Reno, NV 89501
Renospa 4310 Paradise Road, Las Vegas, NV 702-737-3700
Royal Aloha 317 Quaking Aspen Lane, Stateline, NV 89449 702-588-5102
Sahara Safari Club 2535 Las Vegas Blvd., Las Vegas, NV 89109
Tahoe Chapparal 400 Fairview Blvd., Incline Village, NV 89450
Tahoe Summit P.O. Box 4917, Stateline, NV 89449
Third Creek 797 Southwood Boulevard, Incline Village, NV 89450
Thunderbird 200 Nicholos Blvd., Sparks, NV 89431
Boulders Resort Lake Shore Dr., RD2, Box 125, Lake George, NY 12845
518-668-5444

──────────────── NEW YORK ────────────────

Briston Harbour Seneca Point Road, Canandaigua, NY 14424 716-396-2400
Edgewater 811 Edgewater Drive, Westfield, NY 14787 716-326-2146
Harbor, Lake Placid, NY 12946 518-523-9704
Hunter Mountain Route 23A, P.O. Box 335, Hunter, NY 12442 518-263-4208
L.P. Club Resort, Lake Placid, NY 12946 518-523-3361
Lake Placid Club Mirror Lake Dr., Lake Placid, NY 12946 518-523-3361
Mount Nevis Hotel 58 Hemlock St., North Tarrytown, NY 10591 914-631-4139
Mountainview 1 Philip Street, Lake George, NY 12845
Queensbury Arms Manor Drive, Glen Falls, NY 12801 518-792-6077
Stevensville, Swan Lake, NY 914-292-8000
Villa Roma, Callicoon, NY 12723 914-887-4880
Whiteface Inn Whiteface Inn Road, P.O. Box 231, Lake Placid, NY 12946
518-523-2551
Windham Ridge P.O. Box 67, Windham, NY 12496 518-734-5800

──────────────── NORTH CAROLINA ────────────────

Accommodations Center 500 Beech Mountain Parkway, Beech Mountain, NC
28604 704-387-4246
Banks, The, Kill Devil Hills, NC 27948
Bears Sugar Area Lodging P.O. Box 875, Highway 184, Banner Elk, NC 28604
704-898-4546
Blue Ridge Village Highway 184, Banner Elk, NC 28604 704-898-5610
Bodie Island Beach Club Mile Post 17, P.O. Box 1115, Nags Head, NC 27959
Captain Quarters 1400 Canal Drive, Carolina Beach, NC 28428
Carolina Temple P.O. Box 525, Wrightsville Beach, NC 28480
Cedar Village P.O. Box 261 Beech Mountain, Banner Elk, NC 28604
704-387-4246
Cherokee Beech Mountain, Banner Elk, NC 28604 704-387-2001

Cherokee Beech Mountain Drive, Banner Elk, NC 28604
Cherokee Hills P.O. Box 647, Murphy, NC 28906 704-837-5853
Christie Village Beech Mountain Parkway, Beech Mountain, NC 28604 704-387-2100
Club Yonalossee P.O. Box 1397, Boone, NC 28604
Eighteen South 4713 North Croatan Highway, Kitty Hawk, NC 27949
Fairfield Atlantic P.O. Box 1140 Ft. Macon Road East, Atlantic Beach, NC 28512
Fairfield Harbour 750 Broad Creek Rd., New Bern, NC 28560 919-638-8011
Fairfield Mountains Route #1, Lake Lure, NC 28746 704-625-9111
Frontier Village Hwy 105 S at Bairds Crk, POB 1782, Boone, NC 28607 704-963-6551
Golden Strand P.O. Box 2011, Kill Devil Hills, NC 27948
Hatteras High Hwy. 12, P.O. Box 163, Rodanthe, NC 27968 919-987-2702
High Dunes Resort P.O. Box 1067, Kitty Hawk, NC 27949
Highlands P.O. Box 892, Banner Elk, NC 28604
Holly Forest 4000 SR 64 W, Sapphire, NC 28744 704-743-3441
Island Resort 500 Ocean Dr., Yaupon Beach, NC 28461 919-278-5644
Island Villas Island Chandler Building, Bald Head Island, NC 28461 919-457-5000
Maggie Valley Country Club Cove, P.O. Box 482, Maggie Valley, NC 28751 704-926-0951
Noel Chalets P.O. Box 630, Blowing Rock, NC 28605
North Pier Ocean 1600 Canal Dr., P.O. Box 1628, Carolina Beach, NC 28428 919-458-4062
Ocean Isle Ocean Isle Beach, Ocean Isle Beach, NC 28459 919-579-7116
Outer Banks Nine Mile Post Beach Rd., Kill Devil Hills, NC 27948 919-441-7036
Pelican Watch United Beach Vacations Box 1926, Carolina Beach, NC 28428
Peppertree Blue Ridge Route 1, Highway 184, Box 126, Banner Elk, NC 28604
Peppertree Resort P.O. Box 760, Maggie Valley, NC 28751 704-926-3811
Peppertree Vacation 1 Hilton Dr., Asheville, NC 28806 704-254-3211
Peppertree's 9 Mile Post Beach Road, Kill Devil Hills, NC 27948
Pine Knoll Shores P.O. Box 736, Salter Path Road, Pine Knoll Shores, NC 28557 919-247-2400
Point Emerald P.O. Box 4220, Emerald Isle, NC 28594
Port Trinitie P.O. Box 1674, Kill Devil Hills, NC 27948
Powder Horn Mountain, Triplett, NC 28686
Royal James Landing Island Chandler Building, Bald Head Island, NC 28461 919-457-5000
Salty Hammocks Highway 421 South, Carolina Beach, NC 28428
Sandpebbles Highway 421 South, Carolina Beach, NC 28428
Sea Colony Complex United Beach Vacations Box 1926, Carolina Beach, NC 28428
Seascape 1608 Carolina Beach Ave., North, Carolina Beach, NC 28428
Shell Island Resort 2700 N. Lumina Avenue, Wrightsville Beach, NC 28480 919-256-5050
Smoketree Lodge P.O. Box 3407, Boone, NC 28607 704-963-6506
St. Regis Resort Box 4000, Sneads Ferry, NC 28460
Station One, Wrightsville Beach, NC 28480
Swan's Quarter Island Chandler Building, Bald Head Island, NC 28461 919-457-5000
The Sails Old Oregon Inlet Road, Nags Head, NC 27959
The Whaler Pine Knoll Shores, P.O. Box 220, Atlantic Beach, NC 28512

Timbercreek Island Chandler Building, Bald Head Island, NC 28461
919-457-5000
Villa Capriani One North Topsail Shores, Sneads Ferry, NC 28460
919-328-1900
Villas Island Chandler Building, Bald Head Island, NC 28461 919-457-5000
Westridge at Sugar, Banner Elk, NC 28604
Windjammer 158 Business Mile Post 15, Nags Head, NC 27959 919-441-4811
Wolf Laurel Resort Route 3, Mars Hill, NC 28754 704-689-4111
Yonahlossee Resort Highway 105, P.O. Box 1397, Boone, NC 28607
704-262-1222

——————————————— OHIO ———————————————

Admiralty Lake & Bay Realty, P.O. Box 291, Port Clinton, OH 43452

——————————————— OKLAHOMA ———————————————

Shangri-La Route 3, Afton, OK 74331
Tiffany House 5505 North Brookline, Oklahoma City, OK 73112 405-943-5769

——————————————— OREGON ———————————————

Baywest 1116 S.W. 51st Street, Lincoln City, OR 97367 503-996-3549
Driftwood Shores 88416 First Avenue, Florence, OR 97439 503-997-8263
Little Whale Cove P.O. Box 49, Depoe Bay, OR 97341 503-765-2120
Mount Bachelor 19717 Mount Bachelor Drive, Bend, OR 97702 800-452-9846
Sands Condominium 1525 N. Harbor Drive, Lincoln City, OR 97367
Starfish Point 140 N.W. 48th Street, Newport, OR 97365
503-265-3751
Tolovana Inn P.O. Box 165, Tolovana Park, OR 97145 503-436-2211

——————————————— PENNSYLVANIA ———————————————

Carriage House Pocono Manor, Box 125, Pocono Manor, PA 18349
717-839-6761
Greenhouse at Fernwood, Bushkill, PA 18324
Nemacolin Woodlands, Village of Farmington, PA 15437 800-422-2736
Penn Vacation Club Penn Estates Dr., Analomink, PA 18320 717-421-1060
Swiss Mountain RD 1, Champion, PA 15622 814-352-7502
The Fairways Villas P.O. Box 1379, Marshalls Creek, PA
The Rittenhouse 210 W. Rittenhouse Square, Philadelphia, PA 19103
215-546-9000
Toftrees Resort One Country Club Lane, Toftrees, State College, PA 16803
813-234-8000
Tree Tops at Fernwood, Bushkill, PA 18324
Wild Acres Lakes, Dingmans Ferry, PA 18323
Wolf Run Manor Box 687 Treasure Lake Hwy. 225 N., DuBois, PA 15801
814-371-9150

——————————————— RHODE ISLAND ———————————————

Inn On Long Wharf 142 Long Wharf, P.O. Box 2000, Newport, RI 02840
401-846-0740
Inn on the Harbor 359 Thamas St, P.O. Box 2000, Newport, RI 02840
401-849-3171
Neptune Vacation Connecticut Avenue, Block Island, RI 02807 401-466-2110
Newport Overlook Bay View Dr., Jamestown, RI 02835 401-423-1886
Oceancliff Ocean Dr., Newport, RI 02840 401-849-9000

——————————— SOUTH CAROLINA ———————————

A Place at the Beach Ocean Boulevard, Windy Hill Sec., North Myrtle Beach, SC 29582 803-272-7376

Atlaya Towers 92 Waccamaw Drive, Garden City, SC 29576

Beach Club 1305 South Ocean Boulevard, Myrtle Beach, SC 29577 803-626-3608

Bohicket Marina 1880 Andell Bluff Blvd., John's Island, SC 29455 803-768-1280

Club Regency 2511 S. Ocean Blvd., Myrtle Beach, SC 29577 803-448-8376

Country Club Villas 1 Fawn Vista Dr., Deerfield Plant, Myrtle Beach, SC 29577 803-651-6300

Deer Track Golf Club P.O. Box 14430, Surfside, SC 29587 803-650-2146

Deercreek P.O. Box 14460, Surfside Beach, SC 29587 803-651-2196

Deercreek 1540 Deercreek Road, Surfside Beach, SC 29575

Fairfield Ocean Ridge P.O. Box 27, King Cotton Road, Edisto Island, SC 29438 803-869-2561

Fiddler's Cove Box 1-M, 45 Folly Field Road, Hilton Head Island, SC 29928

Foxwood Hills Rt. 1, Dr. John's Road, Westminster, SC 29693 803-647-9533

Gauley Falls Dliding Rock Rd., Rt #3, Box 129F, Pickens, SC 29671 803-878-7929

Golden Isle Villas SR5, Box 1B, Beaufort, SC 29902

Golf Colony Platt Dr., Deerfield Plantation, Myrtle Beach, SC 29577

Isle of Palms 1300 Ocean Blvd., Isle of Palms, SC 29451 803-886-8600

Kiawah Island P.O. Box 2941201, Charleston, SC 29412 803-768-2121

Kingfisher Inn Ocean Boulevard, Garden City Beach, SC 29576 803-651-2135

Marriott's Sea Pines Plantation, Hilton Head Island, SC 29928 803-785-2040

Montego Inn 1301 South Ocean Blvd., Myrtle Beach, SC 29578 803-626-3608

Ocean Cove Club Palmetto Dunes Plantation PO 5628, Hilton Head Island, SC 29928

Ocean Creek P.O. Box 1557, North Myrtle Beach, SC 29598 800-922-0755

Ocean Creek 10600 North Kings Highway, Myrtle Beach, SC 29577 803-272-3511

Ocean Dunes P.O. Box 2035, 74th Avenue N., Myrtle Beach, SC 29577 803-449-7441

Ocean Forest Colony 5900 Ocean Blvd., Myrtle Beach, SC 29577 803-449-9604

Ocean Point 250 Ocean Point Drive, Fripp Island, SC 29920 803-838-2309

Palmetto Beach 2511 S. Ocean Blvd., Myrtle Beach, SC 29577

Peppertree 305 S. Ocean Blvd., N. Myrtle Beach, SC 29582 803-249-3591

Peppertree Fawn Vista Drive, Deerfield Pl., Myrtle Beach, SC 29577

Polynesian 10th Ave. South & S.Ocean Blvd., Myrtle Beach, SC 29577 803-448-1781

Port O'Call Shipyard Plantation, Hilton Head Island, SC 29928

Port Royal Plantation Box 7000, Hilton Head Island, SC 29928 704-681-3671

Possum Trot P.O. Box 297 US 17 N., Myrtle Beach, SC 29477 803-448-2308

Regency Towers 2511 S. Ocean Blvd., Myrtle Beach, SC 29577 803-448-8516

Riptide Beach Club P.O. Box 3478, Myrtle Beach, SC 29577 803-448-1486

Schooner II 2108 N. Ocean Blvd., Myrtle Beach, SC 29577 803-448-6229

Southwind Shipyard Plantation, Hilton Head Island, SC 29928

Spicebush N. Sea Pines Dr., Hilton Head Island, SC 29948 803-785-2040

Village P.O. Box 1024, Hilton Head Island, SC 29925

Waipani II Resort 6th-7th S. Ocean Dr. Blvd., N. Myrtle Beach, SC 29582
803-272-4956
Waopani Resort 600 S. Ocean Blvd., North Myrtle Beach, SC 29582
Wayward Winds 2609 South Ocean Blvd., Myrtle Beach, SC 29577
803-448-5121
Wedgefield Plantation 100 Manor Drive SR 701N, Georgetown, SC 29440
803-546-8585
Yachtsman, The 1400 N. Ocean Blvd., Myrtle Beach, SC 29577 803-448-4448

———————————————— SOUTH DAKOTA ————————————————

Barefoot Terry Peak, HC 37, Box 924, Lead, SD 57754 605-584-1577
Terry Peak Lodge HC 37, Box 917, Lead, SD 57754

———————————————— TENNESSEE ————————————————

Banner Real Estate 204 Gay Street, Erwin, TN 37650 615-743-2433
Boardwalk on the Lake P.O. Box 1289, Crossville, TN 38555
Cumberland Gardens P.O. Box 95, Crab Orchard, TN 37723 615-484-5285
Fox Run Resort Silver Dollar City Rd, POB 1070, Pigeon Forge, TN 37863
615-453-9800
Gatlinburg Rt. 3 Weber Rd., Gatlinburg, TN 37738 800-222-1738
Hiawatha Manor West P.O. Boz 743, Crossville, TN 38555
Homestead House P.o. Box 367, Gatlinburg, TN 37738 615-436-6166
Laurel Point Rt. 2, Box 649A, Gatlinburg, TN 37738 615-436-3765
Laurel Springs Resort Hwy. 321, P.O. Box 180, Cosby, TN 37722 615-487-2263
Oakmont Resort P.O. Box 1009, Gatlinburg, TN 37738 615-453-3240
Peppertree Laurel Rt. 2, Box 649 Holley Branch Road, Gatlinburg, TN 37738
615-436-4492
Pinecrest 300 Plaza Way, Piegon Forge, TN 37862
Ridgecrest Highway 321, Rt. 2, Box 985, Gatlinburg, TN 37738 615-436-4101
Ski Mountain Chalet P.O. Box 770, Gatlinburg, TN 37738 615-436-7846
Ski View Mountain Resort Route 2, Box 784, Gatlinburg, TN 37738
615-436-5100
Smoky Mountain 356 Circle Dr., Gatlinburg, TN 37738 615-436-9700
Tansi Village Drawer 743, Crossville, TN 38555 615-788-6724
Thunder Hollow P.O. Box 1289, Crossville, TN 38557 615-484-9566
Village Stream P.O. Box 92, Gatlinburg, TN 37738 615-436-6614
Westover Park 401 Club Dr., Sevierville, TN 37862 615-453-1677

———————————————— TEXAS ————————————————

Anchor Resort 14300 South Padre Isl. Box 8314, Corpus Christi, TX 78412
512-949-8141
Aquarius P.O. Box 2640, South Padre Island, TX 78597
Audubon Place 10631 Nacogdoches, San Antonio, TX 512-657-2128
Beachcomber On the Beach, Box 1388, Port Aransas, TX 78373 512-749-6191
Bilmore Courts 100 N. Alister, Box 367, Port Aransas, TX 78373 512-749-5552
Boulevard, The 2441 N.E. Loop 410, San Antonio, TX 512-657-9484
Caribbean Lago Vista Rentals P.O. Box 4986, Lago Vista, TX 78641
Colony Place Resort, West Montgomery, TX
Condominiums a 2901 Central Blvd., P.O. Box 5356, Brownsville, TX 78520
512-544-5302
Country Gold Hwy.274 at FM 148, P.O. Box 529, Kemp, TX 75143 214-498-8533
Galleon of Galveston 9520 Seawall Blvd., Galveston, TX 77551
Galvestonian, The 1401 East Beach Blvd., Galveston, TX 77550 409-765-6161
Gibbs Cottages 400 N. Alister, Box 337, Port Aransas, TX 78373 512-749-5452

Holly Lake Box 358, Dallas, TX 75221
Holly Lake Ranch Farm to Market Rd. 2869, Hawkins, TX 75765 214-769-2138
Inverness at Del Lago 100 La Costa Drive, Montgomery, TX 77356
Inverness at South Padre 5600 Gulf Blvd., P.O. Box 2307, South Padre Island,
TX 78597 512-761-7919
Inverness at Walden 13151 Walden Road, Montgomery, TX 77356
Island House 15340 Leeward Drive, Corpus Christi, TX 78418 512-949-8166
King Fish Courts 1648 S. 11th St. Box 495, Port Aransas, TX 78373
512-749-5527
La Casa Del Sol 15113 Seeward Dr., North Padre Island, TX 78741
Lake LBJ Villages Corner of Out Yonder & Poker Chip, Marble Falls, TX
78654 512-267-1161
Landing at Willis Coves 700 Kingston Cove, Willis, TX 77378
Las Brisas 2530 E. 11th St. Box 1558, Port Aransas, TX 78373 512-749-4752
Le Club Galveston 9520 Seawall Blvd., Galveston, TX 77551 409-744-0086
Leisure Club 14300 Aloha Unit 126, Padre Island, TX 78418
Leisure Club 3001 Ave. KE., Grand Prairie, TX 75050 214-988-8293
Leisure Club Cove St./Horseshoe Bay Box 8467, Marble Falls, TX 78654
Lost Colony Villas Park Rd. 53, Box 196, Port Aransas, TX 78373 512-749-6314
Marisol Apartments 1700 Gulf Blvd., South Padre Island, TX 78597
512-761-1193
Mission Station 4400 Bluemel, San Antonio, TX 512-696-9794
Parkhill 9939 Fredericksburg Road, San Antonio, TX 512-696-2096
Parkland I 108 Coronado P.O. Box 2460, South Padre Island, TX 78597
Pine Forest Inn Hwy. 71 at Loop 150, P.O.B. 576, Bastrop, TX 78602
512-321-3954
Pine Hill Inn Hwy. 155 S., P.O. Box 157, Frankston, TX 75763 214-876-2650
Point Venture Lago Vista Rentals P.O. Box 4986, Lago Vista, TX 78641
Rio Del Valle 1921 S. 8th St., McAllen, TX 78503 512-682-5167
Rock Cottages P.O. Box 517, Part Aransas, TX 78373 512-749-6360
Royale Beach P.O. Box 2809, South Padre Island, TX 78597 512-761-1166
Saida Royale 400 S. Padre Blvd., South Padre Island, TX 78597
San Luis, The 5222 Seawall Blvd., Galveston, TX 77550 409-765-8888
Sea Hawk Inn 103 N. Alister St. Box 604, Port Aransas, TX 78373 512-749-5572
Sea Horse Lodge 501 E. Ave. G Box 216, Port Aransas, TX 78373 512-749-5513
Sea Vista P.O. Box 2460, South Padre Island, TX 78597 512-761-5526
Seascape 116 Polaris Dr., P.O. Box 3702, S. Padre Island, TX 78597
512-761-2288
Shores 1917 American Dr., Lago Vista, TX 78645 512-267-7181
Snapper Courts 120 W. Oaks Box 357, Port Aransas, TX 78373 512-749-5337
Sundial Park Road 53, Port Aransas, TX 78373
Sweetwater Sunchase Condominiums, South Padre Island, TX 78597
Texas Fairway 14117 Commodores Dr., Corpus Christi, TX 78418
Texsun Cottages 307 Ave. G, Box 26, Port Aransas, TX 78373 512-749-5304
Villages Box 7286, Tyler, TX 75711
Vista Grande 1918 American Drive, Lago Vista, TX 78645 512-267-1161
Waterwood Box One, Huntsville, TX 77340 409-891-5211
Westfield Lake 2800 Hirschfield, Spring, TX 713-350-0254

———————————————— UTAH ————————————————

Circle J Club 4065 Jeremy Wood Road, Park City, UT 84060 801-649-0370
Copper Chase P.O. Box 206, Brian Head, UT 84719 801-677-2890
Guinness Chalet P.O. Box 669, Park City, UT 84060 213-598-1371

Iron Blosam Lodge Snowbird, Snowbird, UT 84092 801-742-2222
Kimball, The 150 North Main, Salt Lake City, UT 84102 801-363-4000
Le Concierge P.O. Box 536, Park City, UT 84060 800-824-1672
Mother Lode P.O. Box 536, Park City, UT 84060 801-649-3800
Park Avenue 1650 Park Avenue, P.O. Box 2400, Park City, UT 84060
Park Hotel 605 Main Street, Park City, UT 84060
Park Plaza Resort P.O. Box 3988, Park City, UT 84060 801-649-0910
Park Station 950 Park Avenue, P.O. Box 905, Park City, UT 84060
Parkwest Village P.O. Box 1655, Park City, UT 84060 800-421-5056
Pine Inn P.O. Box 3000, Park City, UT 84060 801-649-4040
Silver Queen P.O. Box 2391, Park City, UT 84060 801-649-5986
Skiers Lodge 1235 Norfolk Avenue, Park City, UT 84060
Sugarplum P.O. Box 2074, Alta, UT 84092
Sugarplum Canyon Services, Box 25, Snowbird, UT 84092
Sweetwater 1255 Empire Avenue, Park City, UT 84060
Three Kings P.O. Box 779, Park City, UT 84060
Turra Murra Snowbird Resort, Snowbird, UT 84092 801-742-2222

────────────────────── VIRGINIA ──────────────────────

Ambassador Place 2315 Atlantic Avenue, Virginia Beach, VA 23451
800-533-1665
Belview Bay Route 1, Box 78, Huddleston, VA 24104 703-297-7532
Bluefields Bay 726 N. Washington St., Arlington, VA 22314
Kingsmill On The James 100 Gulf Club Road, Williamsburg, VA 23185
804-253-3907
Mai Kai Condo 208-C 57th Street, Virginia Beach, VA 23451 804-428-1096
O'Feefe Beach 2068 E. Ocean View Avenue, Norfolk, VA 23503
Powhatan Plantation 3601 Ironbound Rd. . Box 79, Williamsburg, VA 23187
804-220-1200
Retreat by the Sea 901 Pacific Avenue, Virginia Beach, VA 23451 804-425-5273

────────────────────── VERMONT ──────────────────────

Basin Harbor On Lake Champlain, Vergennes, VT 05491 802-475-2311
Bridges Resort Sugarbush Access Road, Warren, VT 05674
Chateau Condominiums Bolton Valley Resort, Bolton, VT 05477 802-434-2131
Contemporary Chalets Route 4, Killington, VT 05751
Emerald Lake Route 1, P.O. Box 475, East Dorset, VT 05253
Hemlock Ridge Killington Road, Killington, VT 05751 802-422-3244
Mill Condominium 145 Main Street, Ludlow, VT 05149 802-228-5566
Notch Brook Resort Notch Brook Road, RRL, Box 1910, Stowe, VT 05672
802-253-4882
Okemo Mountain RFD 1, Ludlow, VT 05149 802-228-8811
Paradise Sugarbush Access Road, Warren, VT 05674
Slopeside Jay Peak Ski Resort, Rte. 242, Jay, VT 05859
Snow Creek Inferno Road, Warren, VT 05674
South Village The Villas, RR1, Box 300, Warren, VT 05674 802-583-2000
Southface Sugarbush Access Rd., Warren, VT 05674
Village Watch Stratton Mt. Road, Stratton, VT 05155
Villages at Killington 418 Killington Road, Killington, VT 05751 802-422-3101
Winterplace Okemo Ski Resort, RFD #1, Ludlow, VT 05149

────────────────────── WASHINGTON ──────────────────────

Grey Gull P.O. Box 1417, Ocean Shores, WA 98569 206-289-3381
Lake Chelan Shores 235 Manson Highway, P.O. Box 602, Chelan, WA 98816

Royal Pacific P.O. Box 756, Ocean Shores, WA 98569 202-289-3306
Sea Fox Racquet 2616 South 224th Street, Des Moines, WA 98198
U.S. Suites 2001 6th Avenue, #1601, Seattle, WA 98121

---------------------------- WISCONSIN ----------------------------

Afterglow Lake P.O. Box 5, Phelps, WI 54554 715-545-2560
Christmas Mountain S-944 Christmas Mountain Road, Wisconsin Dells, WI 53965 608-253-1000
Edgewater 2680 South Shore Road, Land O'Lakes, WI 54540 715-547-3969
Grand View Route 1, P.O. Box 160, Sarona, WI 54870
Haven North, Hurley, WI 54534
Lake Arrowhead 463 Tomahawk Trail, Nekoosa, WI 54457 715-325-3141
Marawaraden Resort Route #1, Sarona, WI 54870 715-354-3855
Treehouse Village, Eagle River, WI 54521

---------------------------- WYOMING ----------------------------

Rendezvous on Wind River P.O. Box 597, Dubois, WY 82513 307-455-2844

---------------------------- CANADA ----------------------------

Cranberry Vacation Box 236, Collingwood, Ontario, L9Y 3Z4
Cuttle's Tremblant Mont Tremblant, Quebec JOT 120, QP JOT 120
Delta Mountain Inn 4050 Whistler Way, Whistler, British Columbia, VON 1BO
Domaine Saint Laurent Cochran Road, CP 180, Compton, Quebec, JOB 1LO
Elkhorn Resort Box 40, Clear Lake, Manitoba, ROJ 2HO 204-848-2802
Grandview-on-the-Lake Huntsville, Ontario
Harbour Inn 1 Poplar Crescent, Lagoon City, Brechin, Ontario LOK 1BO
Horseshoe Valley Horseshoe Valley, RR 1 Box 10, Barrie, Ontario L4M 4YB
Lagoon City Resort Site 2, RR 1, Box 35, Brechin, Ontario, Ontario LOK 1BO 416-361-0000
Le Tremblant Club Cuttle Avenue, Mont-Tremblant, Quebec, JOT 1AO 819-425-2731
Panorama Resort P.O. Box 7000, Invermere, British Columbia, VOA 1KO 604-342-6921
Pinoteau Village Mont-Tremblant, Quebec, JOT 1Z0 800-567-8341
Radium Hot Springs Box 310, Radium Hot Springs, British Columbia, VOA 1MO 604-347-9311
St. Ives on Shuswap Site 30-11, R.R. #1, Chase, British Columbia, VOE 1MO
Whiski Jack Box 344, Whistler, British Columbia, VON 180
Whistler Chalets 204-1650 Duranleau, Granville Island, BC, V6H 3S4
Whistler Resort P.O. Box 1400, Whistler, British Columbia, VON 1BO 604-932-4222

---------------------------- CARIBBEAN ----------------------------

#7 Schooner Bay, Suite 11 Caravelle Arcade, Christiansted, St. Croix, VI
#8 Colony Cove 221a Estate Golden Rock, Christiansted, St. Croix, VI
Abaco Towns by the Sea Box 480 Marsh Harbour, Abaco, Bahamas
Almond Hill Cayman Kai Resort Community, Grand Cayman
Anse Chastanet P.O. Box 215, Soufriere, St. Lucia
Aruba Beach Club Smith Blvd. 53, P.O. Box 368, Orangestad, Aruba, Nassau
Atlantic Beach Hotel P.O. Box F-531, Freeport, Grand Bahama Island
Auberge de la Vielle 97190 Gosier, Guadeloupe, FI
Bahama Breeze Spanish Wells, St. George's Cay, Bahamas
Barbados Beach St. James, Barbados, West Indies 809-425-1440
Bay Garden House, Christiansted, St. Croix, Virgin Islands, 00822 809-773-2211

Bay View Villas P.O. Box SS 6308, Paradise Island, Bahamas 809-326-2555
Beachside Villas, Simson Bay, St. Maarten
Birdcage Walk, Ocho Rios, Jamaica
Bitter End Yacht Club Virgin Gorda, British Virgin Islands 800-872-2392
Bluebeard's Castle P.O. Box 7480, St. Thomas, Virgin Islands
Bonaire Sunset P.O. Box 115, Bonaire, Netherland Antilles 599-7-8291
Butler Bay Plantation Frederiksted, St. Croix, Virgin Islands 00820
Camelot Ocean Blvd., Treasure Cay, Abaco, Bahamas
Candelero Hotel Palmas del Mar, Humacao, Puerto Rico
Candle Reef Christiansted, St. Croix, Virgin Islands 00820
Casa del Mar L.G. Smith Blvd., Oranjestad, Aruba, Nassau
Casablanca Villas Box 2325, St. Thomas, Virgin Islands 00801 809-774-1207
Casuarinas P.O. Box N-4016, Nassau, Bahamas 809-327-7921
Ching Ching Cayman Kai Resort Community, Grand Cayman
Christophers, Ocho Rios, Jamaica
Clear View Sandy Lane, Hamilton Parish, West Indies
Clearview, St. Peter, British West Indies
Club Caribbean P.O. Box 65, Runaway Bay, Jamaica
Club Land'Or P.O. Box SS-6429, Paradise Island, Bahamas 809-326-2400
Coakley Bay Christiansted, St. Croix, Virgin Islands 00820
Colony Cove 221A Golden Rock, St. Croix, Virgin Islands 00820
Coral Shores Villas, Pelican Key, St. Maarten
Coral World Bahamas P.O. Box N-7797, Nassau, Bahamas 809-328-1036
Coral Princess Christiansted, St. Croix, Virgin Islands 00820
Culu-Culu, Ocho Rios, Jamaica
Dian Bay Resort P.O. Box 231, Dian Point, Antigua 809-463-2003
Discovery Bay Hotel Holetown, St. James, British West Indies 809-432-1301
Dorado Naco P.O. Box 162, Playa Dorada, Puerto Plata, Dominican Republic
Dundee Bay Dundee Bay Drive, P.O. Box F-2690, Freeport, Bahamas
Dutch Village L.G. Smith Blvd., Oranjestad, Aruba, Nassau
Edgewater, Ocho Rios, Jamaica
El Refugio, Gibbs Beach, British West Indies
Elfresco Kai Cayman Kai Resort Community, Grand Cayman
Estate Questa Verde Box 278 C'd, St. Croix, VI 00820 809-773-0944
Galleon Beach Club English Harbour, Box 1003, St. John's, Antigua
Garden Villas Treasure Cay, Abaco, Bahamas
Gentle Winds Frederiksted, St. Croix, Virgin Islands 00820
Glitter Bay Hotel Porters, St. James, British West indies
Golden Tulip P.O. Box 290, Great Bay, Philipsburg, St. Maarten
Grand Case Grand Case 97150, Saint Martin, FI
Grand Pavilion P.O. Box 69, Grand Cayman, Cayman Islands, BI
Great House, The P.O. Box 244, St. John's, Antigua
Great House Villas P.O. Box 80, Montego Bay, Jamaica
Guanahani Village P.O. Box 3223, New Providence, Bahamas
Halcyon Cove Hotel P.O. Box 251, St. John's, Antigua
Hamiltonian Hotel Langton Hill, Pembroke, Bermuda
Harbour Heights, Seven Mile Beach, Grand Cayman
Heart's Ease Governor's Harbour, Eleuthera, Bahamas
Heywoods, St. Peter, British West Indies
High Hope Estate, St. Ann's Bay, Jamaica
Holiday Inn Freeport P.O. Box 760, Royal Palm Freeport, Grand Bahama Island

Inn at Mandahl   34 Estate Mandahl, St. Thomas, Virgin Islands
Island Resort   Rum Cay Road, Freeport, Bahamas
Island Place   Cayman Kai Resort Community, Grand Cayman
Jaragua Resort   George Washington Ave., Santo Domingo, Dominican Republic
Jasmine Hill   Cayman Kai Resort Community, Grand Cayman
L'Habitation   P.O. Box 230, St. Martin, FI 97150
Las Palmas, Runaway Bay, Jamaica
Le Meridien   P.O. Box N 10422, Bahamas   809-327-6400
Le Madrepore   Bas du Fort, Face au Frantel, Gosier, Guadeloupe
Leamington Pavilion, St. Peter, British West Indies
Legalion Resort   P.O. Box 4, Marigot, FI
Little Deadman's Cay   Deadman's Cay, Bahamas
Mammee Bay Resort   Arawak Post Office, Ocho Rios, Jamaica
Mariner's Cove   Treasure Cay, Abaco, Bahamas
Mariner   Christiansted, St. Croix, Virgin Islands 00820
Mariners, The   Sandy Ground, Anguilla, BI
Mill Harbour   Golden Rock, Christiansted, St. Croix, Virgin Islands, 00822 809-773-3800
Mullet Bay Resort   P.O. Box 309, Simson Bay, St. Maarten
Munro Beach   P.O. Box SN 99, Southampton, Bermuda, SN BX   809-234-1175
Nassau Beach   P.O. Box N-7756, Nassau, Bahamas
Negril Beach Club   P.O. Box 7, Negril, Jamaica
Ocean Reef Resort   P.O. Box F898, Louise Lane, Freeport, Grand Bahama Island
Ocean Terrace Inn   P.O. Box 65, Portland, St. Kitts
Orange Hill Beach   P.O. Box N-8583, Nassau, Bahamas   809-327-7157
Outrigger   Christiansted, St. Croix, Virgin Islands 00820
Palmas Del Mar   P.O. Box 8755, Humacao, Puerto Rico
Paradise Island   Paradise Island, P.O. Box N10600, New Providence Island, Bahamas
Plantana, Ocho Rios, Jamaica
PLM Azur Hotel Carayou   Pointe du Bout, 07229, Trois-Ilets, FI
PLM Azur Marissol   Bas du Fort 97190 Gosier, Guadeloupe, FI
Point Pirouette   P.O. Box 484, Simson Bay, St. Maarten
Point Pleasant   Estate Smith Bay #4, St. Thomas, VI 00802   809-775-7200
Point on Burgeaux Bay   38 Beacon Hill, St. Maarten
Polamar Gardens   St. Peter, British West Indies
Princess Vacation   West Sunrose Hwy. P.O. Box F207, Freeport, Bahamas
Prospect Reef   P.O. Box 104, Road Town, Tortola, British Virgin Islands
Prospect   48 St. Johns, St. Croix, Virgin Islands 00820
Puerto Plata   Av. Gregorio Loperon, Puerto Plata, Dominican Republic
Queen's Quarters   P.O. Box 770, St. Croix, Virgin Islands 00820
Rainbow Reef   Dover St. Lawrence Gap, Christ Church, BWI   809-428-5110
Ramada Renaissance   P.O. Box 441, St. George's, Grenada
Rockley Resort   P.O. Box Box 35W, Worthing, Christ Church, British West Indies
Romora Bay Club   P.O. Box 146, Harbour Island, Bahamas
Royal Bahamian   P.O. Box 104222, Nassau, Bahamas
Royal Palm   Treasure Cay, Abaco, Bahamas
Runaway Vacation   Rimaway Bay, St. John's, Antigua
Royal Antiguan   Deep Bay, Antigua
Run Cove   Cayman Kai Resort Community, Grand Cayman

San Souci Hotel P.O. Box 103, Ocho Rios, Jamaica
Sand Dollar Treasure Cay, Abaco, Bahamas
Sand Acres Beach Maxwell Coast Road, Christ Church, BWI 809-428-7141
Sandpiper Edwards Avenue, Runaway Bay, Jamaica
Sandy Beach Worthing, Christ Church, British West Indies
Sandy Point Crown Point, Port of Spain, Trinidad & Tobago
Secret Harbour P.O. Box 34, Center Harbor, St. Thomas, VI, 03226
809-775-6550
Sint Maarten Sea Palace Front Street, Philipsburg, St. Maarten, Nassau
Southwinds Hotel St. Lawrence Gap, Christ Church, British West Indies
St. George's Club P.O. Box GE 92, St. George's, Bermuda, GE BX 809-297-1200
Sunny Caribbee Hotel Box 16, Admiralty Bay, St. Vincent, Nassau
Sunrise Beach Club P.O. Box SS-6519, Paradise Island, Bahamas 809-326-2234
Sunrise Beach P.O. Box 6519-S.S., Nassau, Bahamas 809-326-2234
Taino Beach 28 Jolly Roger Dr., Box F3819, Freeport, Grand Bahama Island
Talanquera Vacation Pedro Henriques Urena 67-A, Santo Domingo, DC
Tallyman, The P.O. Box 876, Montego Bay, Jamaica
Terra Nova Mammee Bay Beach Community, Ocho Rios, Jamaica
Tiki Kai Villa Cayman Kai Resort Community, Grand Cayman
Toad Hall Ocean Blvd. Treasure Cay, Abaco, Bahamas
Treasure Beach Paynes Bay, St. James, British West Indies
Tyne Beach Terrace P.O. Box F216, Glover Lane, Freeport, Bahamas
V.I.P House Beacon Hill, St. Maarten
Victoria House Box 636, Seven Mile Beach, Grand Cayman
Villa Kima, Ocho Rios, Jamaica
Villa De Elana, Ocho Rios, Jamaica
Villas in Paradise P.O. Box SS-6379, Paradise Island, Nassau, Bahamas
809-326-2998
Westwind Club P.O. Box N-10481, Cable Beach, Nassau, Bahamas
809-327-7680
Woodbourne Resort 10-11 Discovery Bay, Freeport, Bahamas
Woodbourne Resort 9 Nina Avenue, Freeport, Bahamas
Woodbourne Estates P.O. Box F1098, Freeport, Bahamas
Wykee's World Resort P.O. Box 176, Governor's Harbour, Bahamas
809-332-2701
Xanadu Mammee Bay Beach Community, Ocho Rios, Jamaica
———————————————— MEXICO ————————————————

Acapulco Plaza Costera Miguel Aleman No. 123, Acapulco
Auto Hotel Ritz Calz. Fern. De Magallanes, Acapulco, Guerrero, MX
Bahia Escondida Presa Rodrigo Gomez, Santiago, NL
Balboa Towers Calzada Camaron Sabalo, Esq.Calle, Guerrero, Mazatlan, SI
Brisamar Apartado Postal 473, Playa Azula, Las Brisas, Manzanillo, CL
Caravelle Beach Club Calzado Camaron Sabalo y Cal.Atun, Mazatlan, SI
Castel Palmar Playa El Palmar-Ixtapa, Ixtapa-Zihuatanejo, MX
Club Vacacional Tortuga Costera Miguel Aleman 132, Acapulco, GU
Club Maeva KM 12 Carretera, Apartado, P. 442, Manzanillo-Aeropuerto, CL
Club Lagoon Marina Paseo Kukulcan KM.5.8., Zona Hotelera-Cancun, QR
CP77500
Club Casa Maya Avenue Kukulkan KM 5.5, Cancun, QR
Club Las Hadas P.O. Box 51, Manzanillo, CL
Club Las Perlas Avenida Kukulkan D-01 Blvd. KM2.5, Z.Hotelera-Cancun, QR
Club Caribe-Cancun Ave. Kukulkan s/n Zona Hotelera, Cancun, QR

Club Marina Vallarta Carretera Vallarta-Tepic s/n, Puerto Vallarta, Jalisco, MX
Club Verano Beat Boulevard Cancun 166, Cancun, QR
Club El Pueblito Peninsula de Santiago, Manzanillo, CL
Condesa World Resort Av. Costera Vieja #4, Acapulco, Guerrero, MX
Condomar Vallarta KM 5.5 Carretera al Aeropuerto, Puerto Vallarta, JA
Condomar Acapulco Cattolicos Ave. Costera M. Aleman, Acapulco, GU
Condotel El Dorado Ave. del Mar 117, Sinaloa, MX
Costa Brava Ave. Sabalo Cerritos s/n, Mazatlan, SI
Costa de Oro Beach Calz. Camaron Sabalo s/n P. 130, 82110 Mazatlan, SI
Cuernavaca Hotel Francisco Vila 100, Guernavaca, MR
El Cid Resort Av. Camaron-Sabalo, Box 813, Mazatlan, SI 82110   678 3.3333
Fairwy Cuatro Ave. Fernando de Magallanes 255, Acapulco, Guerrero, MX
Green Ixtapa Paseo de las Golandrinas 88, Ixtapa-Zihuatanejo, GU
Hotel Cancun Viva Paseo Kukulkan, Lote 2 Z Hotelera, Cancun, QR
Hotel Posada Cuernavaca P.d.Conquistador 57 y Alicia 51, Cuernavaca
Hotel Sierra Continental Boulevard Kukulcan, Cancun, QR
Hotel Club Ammaczatlan Calzada Camaron, Sabalo Cerritos, Mazatlan, SI
Hotel Club do Brasil Av. Costera Vieja, Acapulco, Guerrero, MX
Hotel Boca Chica Playa Calletilla s/n, Acapulco, Guerrero, MX
Hotel Granada El Cid Ave. Camaron Sabalo s/n Box 813, Mazatlan, SI
Hotel Rivera Del Sol Lote 1A de la zona Turistica, Ixtapa-Zihuatanejo, GU
Imperial Internatl Vacation Costera Miguel Aleman y Massieu, Acapulco, GU
Hotel Fiesta San Carlos KM 8 Carretera Guaymas San Carlos, Box 828, Nuevo Guaymas, SO
Hotel El Tapatio Blvd. Aeropuerto 4275, Guadalajara 44100, JA
Hyatt Cancun Caribe P.O. Box 353, Zona Hotelara, Cancun, QR
Laguna Cancun Calle Quetzal 11 P 1310 Club Golf, Cancun, QR
Inn at Mazatlan, The Ave. Camaron Sabalo, Box 630, Mazatlan, SI
Islas Del Sol Calzada Camaron Sabalo 969, P 857, Mazatlan, SI
John Newcombe Hotel Plaza Vallarta, Puerto Vallarta, JA
La Mansion Galindo San Jaun Del Rio, Queretaro
Las Brisas Carretera Escenica 5255, Box 281, Acapulco, GU 39868
Los Tules-Viva Vallarta Carretera al Aeropuerto Km 2.5, Puerto Vallarta, JA
Marina de Oro Avenida de las Garzas #1, Puerto Vallarta, JA
Pacific Club Lote F.E. Paseo Colina Pl Hermosa, Ixtapa-Zihuatanejo, GU
Paraiso Del Mar Ave. Sabalo Cerritos s/n, Mazatlan, Sinaloa
Paraiso Mazatlan Avenida Del Atun, Sinaloa
Playasol Girasol Blvd. Kukulkan Km 9 Zona Hotelera, Cancun, QR
Plaza Holiday Club Costera M Aleman Reyes Cattolicos, Acapulco, GU
Posada La Ermita Pedro Vargas 64 San Miguel Allend, Guanajuato
Rosarito Beach Km 27-1/2 Carretera, Tijuana-Ens., Baja California Norte
Suites Costa Dorada Km 142 Carr. Tepic a PTO, Vallarta Bucerias, NT
Tiempo Compartido Vega del Valle Lote 7 Sec L Vegas, Avandaro Valle de Bravo
Torres Mazatlan Vacation Internationale, Puerto Vallarta, Jalisco
Villa Vera Hotel Lomas Del Mar 35, Box 550 & 488, Acapulco, Gro., 39690
Villa Los Arcos Av. Monterrey 195 P. D-115, C. Azul 39690 Acapulco, GU
Villas El Molino Salida R. a Queretaro 1 CP 3700, San Miguel Allende Guanajuato
Villas La Alhambra El Cid A. Camaron Sabalo s/n Fr. El Cid, Mazatlan 82110, SI
Villas del Palmar Avenue Del Tesoro s/n, Manzanillo, Colima

Villas Plaza Cancun Boulevard Cancun Km 11, Cancun, QR
Vista Oceano Private Club Km 1020 Carretera Barra de Nav., Puerto Vallarta, Jalisco, MX

——————————————— THAILAND ———————————————

Baan Somprasong Pattaya 5/1 Soi Charoenkrung 35, New Road, Taladnoi, Bangkok, 10100 2360141
Laem Sai Village 119/5-21 Karon, Phuket 212901-4 113
Phuket Palace 99/64 Moo 4, Patong Beach, Phuket 01-321-0465

Of
Special Interest

―――――――――――― MARINAS ――――――――――――

Still Waters
Dadeville, AL

**Iron Mountain Lodge
& Marina**
Arkadelphia, AR

Table Rock Landing
Holiday Island, AR

**Mountain Harbor
Resort**
Mount Ida, AR

South Seas Plantation
Captiva Island, FL

East Pass Towers
Destin, FL

**Hawk's Cay Resort
and Marina**
Duck Key, FL

**Pirates Bay
Condominium Marina**
Fort Walton Beach, FL

Grenelefe Resort
Grenelefe, FL

Galleon, The
Key West, FL

Longboat Bay Club
Longboat Key, FL

Longboat Key Club
Longboat Key, FL

**Sombrero Resort &
Lighthouse**
Marathon, FL

Marco Bay Resort
Marco Island, FL

Bluewater Bay
Niceville, FL

Perdido Towers
Pensacola, FL

**Indian River
Plantation Resort**
Stuart, FL

River Watch Inn
St. Simons Island, GA

Causeway On Gull
Brainerd, MN

**Breezy Point
International**
Breezy Point, MN

Steele Hill, Phase 1
Laconia, NH

**Belvedere Plantatin
Golf Club**
Hampstead, NC

Beacon's Reach
Morehead City, NC

**Bald Head Island
Resort**
Southport, NC

**White Beauty
Lakeview Resort**
Greentown, PA

Newport Onshore
Newport, RI

**Wellington Yacht &
Racquet, The**
Newport, RI

**Seabrook Conference
Resort**
Charleston, SC

**Wild Dunes -
Charleston's Island**
Charleston, SC

Island Club
Hilton Head Island, SC

Sea Pines Plantation
Hilton Head Island, SC

**Fairfield Glade -
Kensington W.**
Fairfield Glade, TN

**Lakeway on Lake
Travis**
Austin, TX

**Walden on Lake
Conroe**
Montgomery, TX

**Cline's Landing
Condominium**
Port Aransas, TX

**Teal Harbor
Condominium**
Port Aransas, TX

Kingsmill Resort
Williamsburg, VA

**Lake Forest
Recreation Area**
Eagle River, WI

**Safer's Gypsy Villa
Resort**
Eagle River, WI

―――――――――――― FISHING ――――――――――――

Compass Point
Gulf Shores, AL

Inn at Tamarisk
Lake Havasu, AZ

**Nautical Inn Resort &
Conf.Center**
Lake Havasu City, AZ

Roundhouse Resort
Pinetop, AZ

Buena Vista Resort
Hot Springs, AR

**Willow Beach
Lakefront Condos**
Hot Springs, AR

Peal's Resort
Mountain Home, AR

**Brockway Springs
Resort**
Kings Beach, CA

Snowcreek
Mammoth Lakes, CA

**Donner Lake Village
Resort**
Truckee, CA

———————————— FISHING (Cont'd.) ————————————

Inn at Beaver Creek, The
Beaver Creek, CO

Park Plaza Lodge
Beaver Creek, CO

Copper Mountain Resort
Copper Mountain, CO

Spinnaker at Lake Dillon
Dillon, CO

Yacht Club Condominiums, Inc.
Dillon, CO

Tamarron
Durango, CO

Cedar Lodge
Frisco, CO

Tenmile Creek Condominium Resort
Frisco, CO

Soda Springs Ranch Resort
Grand Lake, CO

Bear Claw Condominiums
Steamboat Springs, CO

LaCasa at Steamboat
Steamboat Springs, CO

Lodge At Steamboat, The
Steamboat Springs, CO

Apollo Park at Vail
Vail, CO

Fallridge at Vail
Vail, CO

Manor Vail Lodge
Vail, CO

Beaver Village Condominiums
Winter Park, CO

Amelia Island Plantation
Amelia Island, FL

Palm Island Resort
Cape Haze, FL

Emerald Towers
Destin, FL

Surfside Resort
Destin, FL

Hawk's Cay Resort and Marina
Duck Key, FL

El Galeon Condominium Resort
Englewood, FL

Breakers of Fort Lauderdale, The
Fort Lauderdale, FL

Royal Beach Club
Fort Myers Beach, FL

Grenelefe Resort
Grenelefe, FL

Sand Dollar Resort
Indian Shores, FL

Anchorage Resort & Yacht Club
Key Largo, FL

Moon Bay Condominium
Key Largo, FL

Beach Club Of Marco
Marco Island, FL

Sunrise Bay Resort & Club
Marco Island, FL

Seascape & Sunrise Condominiums
Ormond Beach, FL

Panama City Resort & Club
Panama City, FL

Perdido Towers
Pensacola, FL

Vista Del Mar Condominiums
Perdido Key, Pensacola, FL

Sundial Beach & Tennis Resort
Sanibel Island, FL

Cassine Garden
Seagrove Beach, FL

Sky Valley Resort
Gillard, GA

Pat's at Punaluu Condo
Hauula, HI

Kona Coast Resort
Kailua-Kona, HI

Sea Village
Kailua-Kona, HI

Kihei Surfside Resort
Kihei, Maui, HI

Mana Kai-Maui
Kihei, Maui, HI

Kuhio Shores Condominiums
Koloa, HI

Aston Maui Kaanapali Villas
Lahaina, Maui, HI

Honokeana Cove
Lahaina, Maui, HI

Kaanapali Vacation Rentals
Lahaina, Maui, HI

Maui Kai Condominium
Lahaina, Maui, HI

Paniolo Hale
Maunaloa, Molokai, HI

Colony One at Sea Mountain
Pahala, HI

Stone Hill Condominiums
Ketchum, ID

Elkhorn Resort
Sun Valley, ID

Knob Hill Ridge
Sun Valley, ID

Warm Springs Resort
Sun Valley, ID

Eagle Ridge Inn & Resort
Galena, IL

Southcape Resort and Club
Mashpee, MA

Monomoy Village
Nantucket, MA

Island Country Club Inn
Oak Bluffs, MA

Causeway Harborview
Vineyard Haven, MA

Grand Traverse Resort Village
Acme, MI

—————————————————— FISHING (Cont'd.) ——————————————————

Shanty Creek-Schuss Mtn. Resort
Bellaire, MI

Crystal Mountain Resort
Thompsonville, MI

Pinestead Reef-Vip
Traverse City, MI

Causeway On Gull
Brainerd, MN

Ruttgers Bay Lodge & Conf. Center
Deerwood, MN

Breezy Shores Resort
Detroit Lakes, MN

Sugar Hills Resort
Grand Rapids, MN

Shoreline Oaks
Gulfport, MS

Bentree Lodge
Branson, MO

Idyllwilde Reosrt
Kimberling City, MO

Kimberling Inn Resort & Vacation
Kimberling City, MO

Lake Chalet Resort
Osage Beach, MO

Bay Point Estates
Whitefish, MT

Club Tahoe
Incline Village, NV

Coeur du Lac Condominiums
Incline Village, NV

Forest Pines Rental Agency
Incline Village, NV

Stillwater Cove
Lake Tahoe, NV

Ridge Tahoe
Stateline, NV

Cold Spring Resort
Plymouth, NH

Inns of Waterville Valley
Waterville Valley, NH

Windsor Hill Condominiums
Waterville Valley, NH

High Country Lodge
Alto, NM

Springs Condominiums, The
Ruidoso, NM

West Winds Lodge & Condos
Ruidoso, NM

Champions Run
Ruidoso Downs, NM

Sierra Del Sol
Taos Ski Valley, NM

Gurney's Inn Resort & Spa
Montauk, Long Island, NY

Deer Run Resort
Stamford, NY

Sand Castles
NC

Whaler Inn Beach Club
Atlantic Beach, NC

Four Seasons at Beech
Beech Mountain, NC

Chetola Resort
Blowing Rock, NC

Alpine Village
Burnsville, NC

Barrier Island Station
Duck, NC

Spectrum Investment Group, Inc.
Emerald Isle, NC

Belvedere Plantatin Golf Club
Hampstead, NC

Hattaras Inn Cabanas
Hatteras, NC

Heron Cove
Kitty Hawk, NC

Beacon's Reach
Morehead City, NC

Pinehurst Hotel & Country Club
Pinehurst, NC

Fairfield Sapphire Valley
Sapphire, NC

Bald Head Island Resort
Southport, NC

Oyster Bay Plantation
Sunset Beach, NC

Oak Island Beach Villas
Yaupon Beach, NC

Meghan Coves
Grove, OK

Beachcombers Haven Vacation Rnts
Gleneden Beach, OR

Ocean Terrace Condominium Motel
Lincoln City, OR

Rippling River
Welches, OR

Hidden Valley Resort
Somerset, PA

Wild Dunes - Charleston's Island
Charleston, SC

Beach Colony Resort
Myrtle Beach, SC

Caribbean Chelsea House Villas
Myrtle Beach, SC

Ramada Ocean Forest Resort
Myrtle Beach, SC

Maritime Beach Club
N. Myrtle Beach, SC

Greenbrier Valley Resorts
Gatlinburg, TN

High Alpine Resort
Gatlinburg, TN

Summit, The
Gatlinburg, TN

Gulfstream, The
Corpus Christi, TX

Inverness At San Luis Pass
Freeport, TX

Victorian Condotel, The
Galveston, TX

—————————————— FISHING (Cont'd.) ——————————————

Channelview Condominium
Port Aransas, TX

Cline's Landing Condominium
Port Aransas, TX

Dunes Condominium
Port Aransas, TX

Mayan Princess Condominium
Port Aransas, TX

Mustang Island Beach Club
Port Aransas, TX

Mustang Towers
Port Aransas, TX

Pelican, The
Port Aransas, TX

Port Royal Ocean Resort
Port Aransas, TX

Sea Gull Condominium
Port Aransas, TX

Teal Harbor Condominium
Port Aransas, TX

Rayburn Country Resort
Sam Rayburn, TX

Woodcreek Resort
Wimberley, TX

Acclaimed Lodging
Park City, UT

Coalition Lodge
Park City, UT

Powderwood Resort
Park City, UT

Shadow Ridge Resort Hotel
Park City, UT

Silver King Hotel
Park City, UT

Trailside Condominiums
Bolton, VT

Bolton Valley Resort
Bolton Valley, VT

Eagle's Nest Inn & Resort
Fairlee, VT

Village At Smugglers Notch
Smugglers Notch, VT

Mountainside Resort at Stowe
Stowe, VT

Eagles at Sugarbush
Waitsfield, VT

Anchorage Beach Villas
St. Thomas, VI

Cowpet Bay Village
St. Thomas, VI

Crystal Cove
St. Thomas, VI

Fairway Village at Mahogany
St. Thomas, VI

Harbour House Villas
St. Thomas, VI

Pine Villas
Basye, VA

Land of Canaan Vacation Resort
Canaan Valey, Davis, WV

Safer's Gypsy Villa Resort
Eagle River, WI

Pointe Resort and Club
Minocqua, WI

Fox Hills Resort
Mishicot, WI

—————————————————— SPAS ——————————————————

La Costa Hotel & Spa
Carlsbad, CA

Palm Valley Country Club
Palm Desert, CA

Charter at Beaver Creek, The
Beaver Creek, CO

Tamarron
Durango, CO

Fairfield Pagosa
Pagosa Springs, CO

Inn at Silvercreek
SilverCreek, CO

Trappeurs Crossing
Steamboat Springs, CO

Mountain Haus At Vail
Vail, CO

Vail Hotel and Athletic Club
Vail, CO

Sonesta Sanibel Harbor Resort
Fort Myers, FL

Hollywood Beach
Hollywood, FL

Vistana Resort
Lake Buena Vista, FL

Colony Beach & Tennis Resort
Longboat Key, FL

Naples Bath & Tennis
Naples, FL

Golden Strand Ocean Villa Resort
Sunny Isles, FL

Grand Traverse Resort Village
Acme, MI

Breezy Point International
Breezy Point, MN

Lodge of Four Seasons, The
Lake Ozark, MO

Golden Eagle Lodge Condominiums
Waterville Valley, NH

---------- SPAS (Cont'd.) ----------

Gurney's Inn Resort & Spa
Montauk, Long Island, NY

Seven Springs Mountain Resort
Champion, PA

Hidden Valley Resort
Somerset, PA

Wellington Yacht & Racquet, The
Newport, RI

Plantation Resort
Surfside Beach, SC

Prospector Square Hotel
Park City, UT

Trailside Condominiums
Bolton, VT

Bolton Valley Resort
Bolton Valley, VT

Killington Townhouses
Killington, VT

Woods of Killington, The
Killington, VT

Hawk Inn & Mountain Resort
Plymouth, VT

Golden Eagle Resort
Stowe, VT

Mount Mansfield Townhouses
Stowe, VT

Topnotch At Stowe
Stowe, VT

Stratton Mountain Resort
Stratton Mountain, VT

Kingsmill Resort
Williamsburg, VA

Wintergreen
Wintergreen, VA

Lakeview Resort Club
Morgantown, WV

Jackson Hole Racquet Club Resort
Jackson, WY

---------- GOURMET DINING ----------

Wigwam, The
Phoenix, AZ

Stouffers Cottonwoods Resort
Scottsdale, AZ

La Mancha
Palm Springs, CA

Inn at Aspen
Aspen, CO

Charter at Beaver Creek, The
Beaver Creek, CO

Fairfield Pagosa
Pagosa Springs, CO

Snowmass Club
Snowmass Village, CO

Hollywood Beach
Hollywood, FL

Colony Beach & Tennis Resort
Longboat Key, FL

Villas of Grand Cypress, The
Orlando, FL

Innisbrook
Tarpon Springs, FL

Sea Oaks
Vero Beach, FL

Callaway Gardens
Pine Mountain, GA

Kapalua Bay Hotel & Villas
Kapalua, Maui, HI

Kiahuna Plantation
Koloa, Kauai, HI

Napili Shores Resort
Lahaina, Maui, HI

Kauai Hilton Beach Villas
Lihue, Kauai, HI

Hyannis Harborview Resort
Hyannis, MA

Grand Traverse Resort Village
Acme, MI

Ruttgers Bay Lodge & Conf. Center
Deerwood, MN

Lodge of Four Seasons, The
Lake Ozark, MO

Brookhill Residences
Lake Placid, NY

Britt Real Estate
Duck, NC

Rancho Viejo Resort & Country Cl.
Brownsville, TX

Port Royal Ocean Resort
Port Aransas, TX

Tanglewood on Texoma Resort Hotel
Pottsboro, TX

Woods of Killington, The
Killington, VT

Mount Mansfield Townhouses
Stowe, VT

Kingsmill Resort
Williamsburg, VA

Lakeview Resort Club
Morgantown, WV

Fox Hills Resort
Mishicot, WI

Spring Creek Ranch
Jackson, WY

---------- HORSEBACK RIDING ----------

Still Waters
Dadeville, AL

Fairfield Flagstaff
Flagstaff, AZ

Roundhouse Resort
Pinetop, AZ

Copper Mountain Resort
Copper Mountain, CO

Tamarron
Durango, CO

Cedar Lodge
Frisco, CO

Soda Springs Ranch Resort
Grand Lake, CO

Golden Triangle Condo Resort
Steamboat Springs, CO

Kutak
Steamboat Springs, CO

Trappeurs Crossing
Steamboat Springs, CO

Manor Vail Lodge
Vail, CO

Vail Run Resort
Vail, CO

Villas of Grand Cypress, The
Orlando, FL

Oceana Garden Villas
Pompano Beach, FL

Sky Valley Resort
Gillard, GA

Loreley Resort
Helen, GA

Hana Kai Maui Resort
Hana, Maui, HI

Cliffs at Princeville
Hanalei, Kauai, HI

Molokai Shores
Kaunakakai, Molokai, HI

Aston Kaha Lani
Lihue, Kauai, HI

Stone Hill Condominiums
Ketchum, ID

Elkhorn Resort
Sun Valley, ID

Warm Springs Resort
Sun Valley, ID

Eagle Ridge Inn & Resort
Galena, IL

Island Country Club Inn
Oak Bluffs, MA

Causeway Harborview
Vineyard Haven, MA

Lake Chalet Resort
Osage Beach, MO

McCloud At Incline Village
Incline Village, NV

Cedar Lodge at Brickyard Mt.
Weirs Beach, NH

High Country Lodge
Alto, NM

West Winds Lodge & Condos
Ruidoso, NM

Deer Run Resort
Stamford, NY

Grand View Lodge
Nissova, MN

Swiss Mountain Village
Blowing Rock, NC

Alpine Village
Burnsville, NC

Spectrum Investment Group, Inc.
Emerald Isle, NC

Pinehurst Hotel & Country Club
Pinehurst, NC

Fairfield Sapphire Valley
Sapphire, NC

Ocean Terrace Condominium Motel
Lincoln City, OR

Seabrook Conference Resort
Charleston, SC

Greenbrier Valley Resorts
Gatlinburg, TN

High Alpine Resort
Gatlinburg, TN

Pelican, The
Port Aransas, TX

Tanglewood on Texoma Resort Hotel
Pottsboro, TX

Shadow Ridge Resort Hotel
Park City, UT

Silver King Hotel
Park City, UT

Hawk Inn & Mountain Resort
Plymouth, VT

Village At Smugglers Notch
Smugglers Notch, VT

Topnotch At Stowe
Stowe, VT

Stratton Mountain Resort
Stratton Mountain, VT

Eagles at Sugarbush
Waitsfield, VT

Pine Villas
Basye, VA

Wintergreen
Wintergreen, VA

Safer's Gypsy Villa Resort
Eagle River, WI

Fox Hills Resort
Mishicot, WI

Villas At Christmas Mountain
Wisconsin Dells, WI

Jackson Hole Racquet Club Resort
Jackson, WY

Spring Creek Ranch
Jackson, WY

ROMANCE

Stouffers Cottonwoods Resort
Scottsdale, AZ

La Mancha
Palm Springs, CA

Sundance Villas
Palm Springs, CA

Inn by the Lake
South Lake Tahoe, CA

Crestwood, The
Snowmass Village, CO

Sunset Inn Resort
Islamorada, FL

Vistana Resort
Lake Buena Vista, FL

Loreley Resort
Helen, GA

Hana Kai Maui Resort
Hana, Maui, HI

Kona White Sands
Kailua-Kona, HI

Sea Village
Kailua-Kona, HI

Kapalua Bay Hotel & Villas
Kapalua, Maui, HI

Poipu Kapili
Koloa, Kauai, HI

Napili Shores Resort
Lahaina, Maui, HI

Sands of Kahana
Lahaina, Maui, HI

Kauai Hilton Beach Villas
Lihue, Kauai, HI

Lodge of Four Seasons, The
Lake Ozark, MO

Point Pleasant Resort
PR

Newport Onshore
Newport, RI

Wellington Yacht & Racquet, The
Newport, RI

Sands Ocean Club
Myrtle Beach, SC

Condo Villas of Gatlinburg
Gatlinburg, TN

El Constante
Corpus Christi, TX

Silver King Hotel
Park City, UT

Stein Eriksen Lodge, The
Park City, UT

Killington Townhouses
Killington, VT

Hawk Inn & Mountain Resort
Plymouth, VT

Golden Eagle Resort
Stowe, VT

Point Pleasant
St. Thomas, VI

Sapphire Village
St. Thomas, VI

Roche Harbor Resort
Roche Harbor, WA

Spring Creek Ranch
Jackson, WY

TENNIS

Stella Maris Inn
Long Island,

Bay View Village
Paradise Island,

Still Waters
Dadeville, AL

Boulders Resort
Carefree, AZ

Fairfield Flagstaff
Flagstaff, AZ

Inn at Tamarisk
Lake Havasu, AZ

Nautical Inn Resort & Conf.Center
Lake Havasu City, AZ

Arizona Golf Resort
Mesa, AZ

Arizona Golf Resort & Conf.Center
Mesa, AZ

Hermosa Inn Resort
Paradise Valley, AZ

Pointe at South Mountain, The
Phoenix, AZ

Pointe at Squaw Peak, The
Phoenix, AZ

Pointe at Tapatio Cliffs, The
Phoenix, AZ

Wigwam, The
Phoenix, AZ

Hyatt Regency Scottsdale
Scottsdale, AZ

Scottsdale/Camelback Resort & Spa
Scottsdale, AZ

Stouffer Cottonwoods Resort
Scottsdale, AZ

Villa Serenas
Tuscon, AZ

Bella Vista Village
Bella Vista, AR

Greens, The
Bella Vista, AR

Los Indios
Cherokee Village, AR

Tyrolese Condominiums
Drasco, AR

Fairfield Bay
Fairfield Bay, AR

Heritage Bay Condominiums
Heritage Bay, AR

Table Rock Landing On Holiday
Holiday Island, AR

Table Rock Resort
Holiday Island, AR

Belvedere Resort
Hot Springs, AR

Buena Vista Resort
Hot Springs, AR

———————————— TENNIS (Cont'd.) ————————————

Emerald Isle Condominiums
Hot Springs, AR

Los Lagos
Hot Springs, AR

Sheraton Hot Springs Lakeshore
Hot Springs, AR

SunBay Resort and Condominiums
Hot Springs, AR

The Wharf
Hot Springs, AR

Mountain Harbor Resort and Condo
Mount Ida, AR

Smith's Landing Golf & Racquet
Siloam Springs, AR

La Costa Hotel & Spa
Carlsbad, CA

Carnelian Woods
Carnelian Bay, CA

Winners Circle
Del Mar, CA

Grand Champions
Indian Wells, CA

Indian Wells Racquet Club Resort
Indian Wells, CA

Brockway Springs Resort
Kings Beach, CA

Kings Wood
Kings Beach, CA

1849 Condominiums
Mammoth Lakes, CA

Meadow Ridge
Mammoth Lakes, CA

Snowcreek
Mammoth Lakes, CA

Squaw Valley Lodge
Olympic Valley, CA

Squaw Valley Townhouses
Olympic Valley, CA

Tavern Inn Condominiums
Olympic Valley, CA

Ironwood Country Club
Palm Desert, CA

Lakes Country Club, The
Palm Desert, CA

Monterey Country Club
Palm Desert, CA

PGA West
Palm Desert, CA

Palm Valley Country Club
Palm Desert, CA

Shadow Mountain Resort
Palm Desert, CA

Woodhaven Country Club
Palm Desert, CA

Azure Sky Resort
Palm Springs, CA

Cathedral Canyon Resort
Palm Springs, CA

Doubletree Resort/Desert Princess
Palm Springs, CA

La Mancha
Palm Springs, CA

Palm Springs Marquis
Palm Springs, CA

Racquet Club Of Palm Springs
Palm Springs, CA

Sundance Villas
Palm Springs, CA

San Vicente Resort
Ramona, CA

Rancho La Palmas Country Club
Rancho Mirage, CA

Lakeland Village Beach Resort
South Lake Tahoe, CA

Tahoe Valley Motel & Condominiums
South Lake Tahoe, CA

Christy Hill Resort Rentals
Squaw Valley, CA

O'Neal Associates, Inc.
Tahoe City, CA

Tahoe Marina Lodge
Tahoe City, CA

Tahoe Tavern Condominiums
Tahoe City, CA

Northstar at Tahoe
Truckee, CA

Pajaro Dunes
Watsonville, CA

Alpine Peaks
Aspen, CO

Aspen Alps Condominium Assoc.
Aspen, CO

Aspen Club Lodge
Aspen, CO

Gant, The
Aspen, CO

Prospector at Aspen, The
Aspen, CO

Beaver Creek West
Avon, CO

Charter at Beaver Creek, The
Beaver Creek, CO

Inn at Beaver Creek, The
Beaver Creek, CO

Park Plaza Lodge
Beaver Creek, CO

Poste Mountane at Beaver Creek
Beaver Creek, CO

Beaver Run
Breckenridge, CO

Carbonate Property Management
Copper Mountain, CO

Copper Mountain Inn
Copper Mountain, CO

Copper Mountain Resort
Copper Mountain, CO

—————————————— TENNIS (Cont'd.) ——————————————

The Plaza at Woodcreek
Crested Butte, CO

Buffalo Village
Dillon, CO

Lake Dillon Condotel
Dillon, CO

Swan Mountain Resort
Dillon, CO

Yacht Club Condominiums, Inc.
Dillon, CO

Best Western Lodge and Villas
Durango, CO

Cascade Village Resort
Durango, CO

Purgatory-Village
Durango, CO

Ranch Townhomes, The
Durango, CO

Tamarron
Durango, CO

Nicky's Resort & Lounge
Estes Park, CO

Antlers Realty & Lodging Company
Frisco, CO

Soda Springs Ranch Resort
Grand Lake, CO

Keystone Resort
Keystone, CO

Out Run Condominiums
Mount Crested Butte, CO

Fairfield Pagosa
Pagosa Springs, CO

Desert Princess, The
Palm Springs, CO

Mountainside at Silvercreek
Silver Creek, CO

Inn at Silvercreek
SilverCreek, CO

Wildernest Lodging
Silverthorne, CO

Snowmass Club
Snowmass Village, CO

Snowmass Club Villas, The
Snowmass Village, CO

Lodge At Steamboat, The
Steamboat Springs, CO

Ranch at Steamboat, The
Steamboat Springs, CO

Snow Flower Condominiums
Steamboat Springs, CO

Timber Run
Steamboat Springs, CO

Torian Plum
Steamboat Springs, CO

Trappeurs Crossing
Steamboat Springs, CO

Antlers At Vail
Vail, CO

Coldstream Condominiums
Vail, CO

Lodge at Vail, The
Vail, CO

Manor Vail Lodge
Vail, CO

Simba Resort
Vail, CO

Sonnenalp Hotel
Vail, CO

Vail Racquet Club
Vail, CO

Vail Run Resort
Vail, CO

Hi Country Haus Resort
Winter Park, CO

Lookout Village Condominiums
Winter Park, CO

Meadow Ridge Resort
Winter Park, CO

Meadow Ridge Resort Condominiums
Winter Park, CO

Marco House
Marco Island, FL

Amelia Island Lodging Systems
Amelia Island, FL

Amelia Island Plantation
Amelia Island, FL

Amelia Surf & Racquet Club
Amelia Island, FL

Sea Palm Resort
Cap Haze, FL

Palm Island Resort
Cape Haze, FL

Palm Island Resort
Cape Haze, FL

South Seas Plantation
Captiva Island, FL

Executive/Clearwater House
Clearwater, FL

Ocean Landings Resort
Cocoa Beach, FL

Sutherland Crossing
Crystal Beach, FL

Inn At Deer Creek Racquet Club
Deerfield Beach, FL

Spanish River Resort
Del Rey Beach, FL

International Tennis Resort
Delray Beach, FL

Spanish River Resort & Beach Club
Delray Beach, FL

Beach House Condominiums
Destin, FL

Destin Towers Condominiums
Destin, FL

Edgewter Beach Condominium
Destin, FL

Emerald Towers
Destin, FL

Holiday Beach Resort - Destin
Destin, FL

——————————— TENNIS (Cont'd.) ———————————

Holiday Surf & Racquet Club
Destin, FL

Inlet Reef Club
Destin, FL

Islander Condominium, The
Destin, FL

Jetty East Condominium Assoc.
Destin, FL

Mainsail
Destin, FL

Sandestin Beach Resort
Destin, FL

Sandpiper Cove Resort
Destin, FL

Seascape Resort & Conference Ctr.
Destin, FL

Shoreline Towers and Townhomes
Destin, FL

Surfside Resort
Destin, FL

Waterview Towers
Destin, FL

Hawk's Cay Resort and Marina
Duck Key, FL

Pelican Landing Condominium Asso.
Englewood, FL

Breakers of Fort Lauderdale, The
Fort Lauderdale, FL

Seawatch On The Beach
Fort Myers, FL

Sonesta Sanibel Harbor Resort
Fort Myers, FL

Boardwalk Caper, The
Fort Myers Beach, FL

Pointe Estero
Fort Myers Beach, FL

Seawatch-on-the-Beach
Fort Myers Beach, FL

Windward Passage Resort
Fort Myers Beach, FL

Breakers
Fort Walton Beach, FL

El Matador Condominiums
Fort Walton Beach, FL

Sea Oats Resort Condominium
Fort Walton Beach, FL

Surf Dweller Condominiums
Fort Walton Beach, FL

Grenelefe Resort
Grenelefe, FL

Mission Inn Golf & Tennis Resort
Howey-In-The-Hills, FL

Bay Shores Yacht & Tennis Club
Indian Rocks Beach, FL

Caloosa Cove Resort
Islamorada, FL

Ocean 80 Resort
Islamorada, FL

Turtle Reef II
Jensen Beach, FL

Jupiter Bay Resort & Tennis Club
Jupiter, FL

Marina Del Mar
Key Cargo, FL

Anchorage Resort & Yacht Club
Key Largo, FL

Moon Bay Condominium
Key Largo, FL

La Brisa Condominium
Key West, FL

Fortune Place
Kissimee, FL

Club Sevilla
Kissimmee, FL

High Point World Resort
Kissimmee, FL

Magic Tree Resort
Kissimmee, FL

Orange Lake Country Club Villa
Kissimmee, FL

Orbit One Vacation Villas
Kissimmee, FL

Polynesian Isles Resort
Kissimmee, FL

Resort World Of Orlando
Kissimmee, FL

Westgate Vacation Villas
Kissimmee, FL

Fantasy World Club Villas
Lake Buena Vista, FL

Fantasyworld Club Villas
Lake Buena Vista, FL

Isle of Bali
Lake Buena Vista, FL

Vistana Resort
Lake Buena Vista, FL

Morningstar Condominium
Lauderdale-By-The-Sea, FL

Villas By The Sea
Lauderdale-By-The-Sea, FL

Inverrary House
Lauderhill, FL

Lehigh Resort Club
Lehigh, FL

Sarasota Sands
Lido Beach, Sarasota, FL

Colony Beach & Tennis Resort
Longboat Key, FL

Four Winds Beach Resort
Longboat Key, FL

Gulf Tides of Longboat Key
Longboat Key, FL

Longboat Bay Club
Longboat Key, FL

Longboat Key Club
Longboat Key, FL

——————————————— TENNIS (Cont'd.) ———————————————

White Sands of Longboat
Longboat Key, FL

Veranda Beach Club
Longboat Key, Sarasota, FL

Buccaneer Resort & Yacht Club
Marathon, FL

Cocoplum Beach & Tennis Club
Marathon, FL

Gulfpointe I
Marathon, FL

Hawks Nest, The
Marathon, FL

Marathon Key Beach Club
Marathon, FL

Reef at Marathon, The
Marathon, FL

Sombrero Resort & Lighthouse
Marathon, FL

Key Lime Resort & Marina Club
Marathon Shores, Florida Keys, FL

Charter Club of Marco Beach
Marco Island, FL

Club Regency of Marco Island
Marco Island, FL

Eagle's Nest
Marco Island, FL

Marco Bay Resort
Marco Island, FL

Sea Winds Beach Resort
Marco Island, FL

Surf Club of Marco
Marco Island, FL

Seacoast Towers Apartment Hotel
Miami Beach, FL

Inn at Ravines
Middleburg, FL

Naples Bath & Tennis
Naples, FL

Park Shore Resort
Naples, FL

World Tennis Center
Naples, FL

Beach Resort
Navarre Beach, FL

Sea Woods
New Smyrna Beach, FL

Bluewater Bay
Niceville, FL

Enclave, The
Orlando, FL

Enclave, The
Orlando, FL

Florida Condominiums
Orlando, FL

Orlando International Resort
Orlando, FL

Sonesta Village Hotel on Sand Lak
Orlando, FL

Ventura
Orlando, FL

Villas of Grand Cypress, The
Orlando, FL

PGA National Club Cottages
Palm Beach Gardens, FL

Horizon South II Condominiums
Panama Beach, FL

Panama City Resort & Club
Panama City, FL

Bay Point Yacht and Country Club
Panama City Beach, FL

Dunes of Panama
Panama City Beach, FL

Gulf Highlands Beach Resort
Panama City Beach, FL

Horizon South I Condominiums
Panama City Beach, FL

Horizon South II
Panama City Beach, FL

Landmark Holiday Beach Resort
Panama City Beach, FL

Mariner East & West Condominiums
Panama City Beach, FL

Moondrifter
Panama City Beach, FL

Moonspinner Condominiums
Panama City Beach, FL

Pelican Walk
Panama City Beach, FL

Pinnacle Port Condominiums
Panama City Beach, FL

Portside Resort
Panama City Beach, FL

Sugar Beach
Panama City Beach, FL

Summit, The
Panama City Beach, FL

Sunbird
Panama City Beach, FL

Perdido Towers
Pensacola, FL

Baywatch Condominiums
Pensacola Beach, FL

Holiday Beach Resort
Pensacola Beach, FL

Sabine Yacht & Racquet Club
Pensacola Beach, FL

Tristan Towers
Pensacola Beach, FL

Sandy Key Condominiums
Perdido Key, FL

Sea Spray Luxury Condominiums
Perdido Key, FL

Shipwatch Condominium
Perdido Key, FL

Sundown Condominium
Perdido Key, FL

———————————————— TENNIS (Cont'd.) ————————————————

**Vista Del Mar
Condominiums**
Perdido Key, Pensacola,
FL

Palm Ocean Villas
Pompano Beach, FL

Sea Garden
Pompano Beach, FL

**Surf Rider Resort
Condominium**
Pompano Beach, FL

**Burnt Store Marina
Resort**
Punta Gorda, FL

**Fishermen's Village
Resort Club**
Punta Gorda, FL

San Remo
Redington Shores, FL

Casa Ybel Resort
Sanibel Island, FL

**Executive Services,
Inc.**
Sanibel Island, FL

Hurricane House
Sanibel Island, FL

Sanibel Cottages
Sanibel Island, FL

**Sanibel Siesta
Condominiums**
Sanibel Island, FL

**Sundial Beach &
Tennis Resort**
Sanibel Island, FL

One Seagrove Place
Santa Rosa Beach, FL

Limetree Beach Resort
Sarasota, FL

**Meadows Golf &
Tennis Resort, The**
Sarasota, FL

Meadows, The
Sarasota, FL

Tivoli By The Sea
Sarasota, FL

Beachwood Villas
Seagrove Beach, FL

Cassine Garden
Seagrove Beach, FL

**Oyster Bay Resort &
Club**
Sebastian, FL

Resorts of Sun 'n Lake
Sebring, FL

**Sun'n Lake Estates -
Linkside**
Sebring, FL

House Of The Sun
Siesta Key, Sarasota, FL

**Beach Club At St.
Augustine Beach**
St. Augustine, FL

Captain's Quarters
St. Augustine, FL

Colony Reef Club
St. Augustine, FL

Coquina, The
St. Augustine, FL

Ocean Village Club
St. Augustine, FL

**Ponce de Leon Resort
& Con. Cente**
St. Augustine, FL

**Sand Dollar
Condominiums**
St. Augustine, FL

**Sea Place
Condominiums**
St. Augustine, FL

Spanish Trace
St. Augustine, FL

**St. Aug. Beach and
Tennis Club**
St. Augustine, FL

Summerhouse
St. Augustine, FL

**Tradewinds
Condominiums**
St. Augustine, FL

**Anastasia
Condominiums**
St. Augustine Beach, FL

**Breckenridge Resort
Beach Club**
St. Petersburg Beach, FL

Bay Harbor Club
Stuart, FL

**Harbor Ridge Golf
Club**
Stuart, FL

**Indian River
Plantation Resort**
Stuart, FL

Innisbrook
Tarpon Springs, FL

Land's End Resort
Treasure Island, FL

Sand Pebble Resort
Treasure Island, FL

Voyager Beach Club
Treasure Island, FL

Coralstone Club
Vero Beach, FL

**Reef Ocean Resort,
The**
Vero Beach, FL

Sea Oaks
Vero Beach, FL

**Palm Beach Polo &
Country Club**
West Palm Beach, FL

Sky Valley Resort
Dillard, GA

Loreley Resort
Helen, GA

Callaway Gardens
Pine Mountain, GA

Cloister, The
Sea Island, GA

**Sea Palm Resort Golf
Club**
St. Simons Island, GA

Trbrisa Beach Resort
Tybee Island, GA

Cliffs at Princeville
Hanalei, Kauai, HI

Hanalei Bay Resort
Hanalei, Kauai, HI

Pu'U Po'A
Hanalei, Kauai, HI

Waiakea Villas
Hilo, HI

Aston Waikiki Sunset
Honolulu, HI

Waikiki Banyan
Honolulu, HI

--------------------------- TENNIS (Cont'd.) ---------------------------

Kaanapali Alii
Kaanapali, Maui, HI

Kuilima Estates
Kahuku, HI

Kona Makai
Kailua, Kona, HI

Aston Royal Sea Cliff Resort
Kailua-Kona, HI

Sea Village
Kailua-Kona, HI

White Sands Village
Kailua-Kona, HI

Kapalua Bay Hotel & Villas
Kapalua, Maui, HI

Pono Kai
Kappa, Kauai, HI

Kauhale Makai
Kihei, HI

Aston Kamaole Sands
Kihei, Maui, HI

Aston Maui Hill
Kihei, Maui, HI

Aston Maui Vista
Kihei, Maui, HI

Kihei Alii Kai
Kihei, Maui, HI

Laule'a Maui Beach Club
Kihei, Maui, HI

Leinaala Condominiums
Kihei, Maui, HI

Maalaea Surf Resort
Kihei, Maui, HI

Shores of Maui
Kihei, Maui, HI

Sugar Beach Resort
Kihei, Maui, HI

Aston Shores at Waikoloa
Kohala, HI

Mauna Lani Point
Kohala, HI

Kahala at Poipu Kai
Koloa, HI

Makanui at Poipu Kai
Koloa, HI

Poipu Sands at Poipu Kai
Koloa, HI

Aston Poipu at Makahuena
Koloa, Kauai, HI

Kiahuna Condominium Apts.
Koloa, Kauai, HI

Kiahuna Plantation
Koloa, Kauai, HI

Makahuena at Poipu
Koloa, Kauai, HI

Manualoha At Poipu Kai
Koloa, Kauai, HI

Nihi Kai Villas
Koloa, Kauai, HI

Poipu Crater Resort
Koloa, Kauai, HI

Poipu Kai
Koloa, Kauai, HI

Poipu Kapili
Koloa, Kauai, HI

Aston Kaanapali Shores
Lahaina, Maui, HI

Aston Mahana at Kaanapali
Lahaina, Maui, HI

Aston Paki Maui Resort
Lahaina, Maui, HI

Hoyochi Nikko
Lahaina, Maui, HI

Kaanapali Royal
Lahaina, Maui, HI

Kaanapali Vacation Rentals
Lahaina, Maui, HI

Kahana Villas
Lahaina, Maui, HI

Kapalua Villas
Lahaina, Maui, HI

Kuleana Maui
Lahaina, Maui, HI

Papakea Beach Resort
Lahaina, Maui, HI

Puamana
Lahaina, Maui, HI

Royal Kahana Resort
Lahaina, Maui, HI

Sands of Kahana
Lahaina, Maui, HI

Aston Kaha Lani
Lihue, Kauai, HI

Banyan Harbor Condominium Resort
Lihue, Kauai, HI

Kauai Hilton Beach Villas
Lihue, Kauai, HI

Manualoha at Poipu
Lihue, Kauai, HI

Ke Nani Kai
Maunaloa, Molokai, HI

Paniolo Hale
Maunaloa, Molokai, HI

Kalulakoi Golf Resort
Molokai, HI

Napili Kai Beach Club
Napili Bay, Lahaina, Maui, HI

Colony One at Sea Mountain
Pahala, HI

Wailea Ekahi
Wailea, Kihei, Maui, HI

Wailea Villas
Wailea, Maui, HI

Bitterroot Prorerty Management
Sun Valley, ID

Bluff Condominium
Sun Valley, ID

Elkhorn Resort
Sun Valley, ID

Knob Hill Ridge
Sun Valley, ID

Sun Valley Lodge
Sun Valley, ID

Warm Springs Resort
Sun Valley, ID

French Lick Springs Golf & Tennis
French Lick, IN

TENNIS (Cont'd.)

Vacation Club International
Cadiz, KY

Bethel Inn & Country Club, The
Bethel, ME

Sugarloaf Mountain Resort
Carrabassett Valley, ME

Samoset Village
Rockport, ME

Quay, The
Ocean City, MD

Sea Watch
Ocean City, MD

Ocean Edge Resort
Brewster, MA

Country Village At Jimmy Peak
Hancock, MA

Jimmy Peak Mountain Resort
Hancock, MA

Southcape Resort and Club
Mashpee, MA

Tristram's Landing
Nantucket, MA

New Seabury Cape Cod
New Seabury, MA

Island Country Club Inn
Oak Bluffs, MA

Eastwood At Provincetown
Provincetown, MA

Oak n' Spruce Resort
South Lee, MA

Cove at Yarmouth, The
Yarmouth, MA

Grand Traverse Resort Village
Acme, MI

Shanty Creek-Schuss Mtn. Resort
Bellaire, MI

Crystal Mountain Resort
Thompsonville, MI

Causeway On Gull
Brainerd, MN

Breezy Point International
Breezy Point, MN

Breezy Point Resort Golf Club
Breezy Point, MN

Ruttgers Bay Lodge & Conf. Center
Deerwood, MN

Sugar Hills Resort
Grand Rapids, MN

Village Inn and Resort, The
Lutsen, MN

Breezy Point Resort
Minnetonka, MN

Bentree Lodge
Branson, MO

Pointe Royale Village
Branson, MO

Riverpoint Estates Luxury Condos
Branson, MO

Lake Country Resort & Golf Club
Galena, MO

Kimberling Inn Resort & Vacation
Kimberling City, MO

Lodge of Four Seasons, The
Lake Ozark, MO

Marriott's Tan-Tar-A Resort
Osage Beach, MO

Royal Bahamian Hotel & Villas
Nassau, NA

Club Tahoe
Incline Village, NV

Lakeside Tennis & Ski Resort
Incline Village, NV

Third Creek
Incline Village, NV

Stillwater Cove
Lake Tahoe, NV

Carriage House, The
Las Vegas, NV

Ridge Tahoe
Stateline, NV

Pine Wild
Zephyr Cove, NV

Attitash Mountain Village
Bartlett, NH

Bretton Woods Resort
Bretton Woods, NH

Samoset at Winnipesaukee
Gilford, NH

Steele Hill, Phase 1
Laconia, NH

Village of Loon Mountain
Lincoln, NH

Cold Spring Resort
Plymouth, NH

Black Bear Lodge
Waterville Valley, NH

Lake Shore Village Resort
Weare, NH

Cedar Lodge at Brickyard Mt.
Weirs Beach, NH

Jack O'Lantern Resort
Woodstock, NH

High Country Lodge
Alto, NM

Crown Point Condominiums
Ruidoso, NM

High Sierra Condominiums
Ruidoso, NM

Quail Ridge Inn
Taos, NM

Juniper Hill Villas
Bolton Landing, NY

Brookhill Residences
Lake Placid, NY

Club Getaway
Lenox Hill Station, NY

Long Point Townhouses
New York, NY

—————————————— TENNIS (Cont'd.) ——————————————

Pridwin Resort, The
Shelter Island, NY

Deer Run Resort
Stamford, NY

Grand View Lodge
Nissova, MN

Sand Castles
NC

A Place At The Beach
Atlantic Beach, NC

Sands Villa Resort
Atlantic Beach, NC

Adams Apple
Banner Elk, NC

Pinnacle Inn
Banner Elk, NC

Chetola Resort
Blowing Rock, NC

Hound Ears Club
Blowing Rock, NC

Willow Valley Resort
Boone, NC

Alpine Village
Burnsville, NC

Spinnaker Point
Carolina Beach, NC

Sherwood Forest
Cedar Mountain, NC

Barrier Island Station
Duck, NC

**Belvedere Plantatin
Golf Club**
Hampstead, NC

**Sea Scape Beach &
Golf Villas**
Kitty Hawk, NC

Beacon's Reach
Morehead City, NC

**Brick Landing
Plantation**
Ocean Isle Beach, NC

**Winds Beach and Golf
Resort**
Ocean Isle Beach, NC

**Foxfire Resort &
Country Club**
Pinehurst, NC

**Pinehurst Hotel &
Country Club**
Pinehurst, NC

Summer Winds
Salter Path, NC

**Fairfield Sapphire
Valley**
Sapphire, NC

**Bald Head Island
Resort**
Southport, NC

Oyster Bay Plantation
Sunset Beach, NC

Topsail Dunes
Topsail Island, NC

**Whispering Pines
Resort**
Whispering Pines, NC

Cordgrass Bay
Wrightsville Beach, NC

Meghan Coves
Grove, OK

**Sunriver Lodge and
Resort**
Sunriver, OR

Rippling River
Welches, OR

Penn Hills
Analomink, PA

**Seven Springs
Mountain Resort**
Champion, PA

**White Beauty
Lakeview Resort**
Greentown, PA

**Tanglewood Lakes,
Inc.**
Hawley, PA

**Country Squire
Lakeshore Club**
Lackwaxen, PA

Shawnee Inn
Shawnee-on-Delaware,
PA

Hidden Valley Resort
Somerset, PA

**Wayne Newton's
Tamiment**
Tamiment, PA

Point Pleasant Resort
PR

**Wellington Yacht &
Racquet, The**
Newport, RI

**Seabrook Conference
Resort**
Charleston, SC

**Wild Dunes -
Charleston's Island**
Charleston, SC

Fairfield Ocean Ridge
Edisto Island, SC

Brigantine Quarters
Hilton Head Island, SC

Continental Club
Hilton Head Island, SC

**Hilton Head Island
Beach Club**
Hilton Head Island, SC

Island Club
Hilton Head Island, SC

**Player's Club of
Hilton Head Isl.**
Hilton Head Island, SC

Sea Pines Plantation
Hilton Head Island, SC

Sea Pines Villas
Hilton Head Island, SC

**Spinnaker &
Southwind at Shipyard**
Hilton Head Island, SC

Jade Tree Cove
Mrytle Beach, SC

**Kingston Plantation
Resort**
Myrtle Beach, SC

Sands Beach Club
Myrtle Beach, SC

Sands Ocean Club
Myrtle Beach, SC

**Tilghman Beach and
Racquet Club**
North Myrtle Beach, SC

Litchfield By The Sea
Pawleys Islands, SC

Myrtle Beach Resort
Surfside Beach, SC

Plantation Resort
Surfside Beach, SC

TENNIS (Cont'd.)

Fairfield Glade - Kensington W.
Fairfield Glade, TN

Cobbly Nob
Gatlinburg, TN

Deer Ridge Mountain Resort
Gatlinburg, TN

Greenbrier Valley Resorts
Gatlinburg, TN

Highland Condominiums
Gatlinburg, TN

Riveredge Village Condominiums
Townsend, TN

Lakeway on Lake Travis
Austin, TX

Lakeway on Lake Travis
Austin, TX

Rancho Viejo Resort & Country Cl.
Brownsville, TX

April Sound Country Club
Conroe, TX

Fairway Villas
Corpus Christi, TX

Four Seasons On The Gulf
Galveston, TX

Inverness by the Sea
Galveston, TX

Victorian Condotel, The
Galveston, TX

Ridge Chalets, The
Grandbury, TX

Horseshoe Bay Country Club Resort
Horseshoe Bay, TX

Walden on Lake Conroe
Montgomery, TX

Sandpiper Condos on Mustang Isl.
Mustang Island, Port Aransas, TX

Aransas Princess
Port Aransas, TX

Beachhead Resort
Port Aransas, TX

Casadel Beach Hotel & Racquet
Port Aransas, TX

Dunes Condominium
Port Aransas, TX

El Cortes Villas
Port Aransas, TX

Island Retreat Condominium
Port Aransas, TX

Mayan Princess Condominium
Port Aransas, TX

Mustang Towers
Port Aransas, TX

Port Royal Ocean Resort
Port Aransas, TX

Sandcastle Condominium
Port Aransas, TX

Sea Gull Condominium
Port Aransas, TX

Tanglewood on Texoma Resort Hotel
Pottsboro, TX

Rayburn Country Resort and CClub
Sam Rayburn, TX

Bahi'a Mar Resort
South Padre Island, TX

Woodcreek Resort
Wimberley, TX

Acclaimed Lodging
Park City, UT

Park Meadows Racquet Club
Park City, UT

Park Station Condominium Hotel
Park City, UT

Powderwood Resort
Park City, UT

Prospector Square Hotel
Park City, UT

Resort Center Lodging
Park City, UT

Ridgepoint
Park City, UT

Snowflower Condominiums
Park City, UT

Stein Eriksen Lodge, The
Park City, UT

Lodge At Snowbird, The
Snowbird, UT

Trailside Condominiums
Bolton, VT

Bolton Valley Resort
Bolton Valley, VT

Eagle's Nest Inn & Resort
Fairlee, VT

Woods of Killington, The
Killington, VT

Bromley Village Condominiums
Manchester Center, VT

Hawk Inn & Mountain Resort
Plymouth, VT

Village At Smugglers Notch
Smugglers Notch, VT

Golden Eagle Resort
Stowe, VT

Mount Mansfield Townhouses
Stowe, VT

Stonybrook Resort
Stowe, VT

Stoweflake Resort Townhouses
Stowe, VT

Topnotch At Stowe
Stowe, VT

---------------------- TENNIS (Cont'd.) ----------------------

Stratton Mountain Resort
Stratton Mountain, VT

Eagles at Sugarbush
Waitsfield, VT

Battleground, The
Warren, VT

Sugarbush Inn
Warren, VT

Sugar Beach
St. Croix, VI

Anchorage Beach Villas
St. Thomas, VI

Cowpet Bay Village
St. Thomas, VI

Crystal Cove
St. Thomas, VI

Harbour House Villas
St. Thomas, VI

Mahogany Run Villas
St. Thomas, VI

Pineapple Villas
St. Thomas, VI

Point Pleasant Resort
St. Thomas, VI

Watergate Villas
St. Thomas, VI

Pine Villas
Basye, VA

Kingsmill Resort
Williamsburg, VA

Wintergreen
Wintergreen, VA

Resort at Port Ludlow
Port Ludlow, WA

Roche Harbor Resort
Roche Harbor, WA

Alderbrook Inn Resort
Union, WA

Land of Canaan Vacation Resort
Canaan Valley, Davis, WV

Lakeview Resort Club
Morgantown, WV

Greenbrier, The
White Sulphur Springs, WV

Eagle Waters Resort
Eagle River, WI

Lake Forest Recreation Area
Eagle River, WI

Americana Lake Geneva Resort
Lake Geneva, WI

Fox Hills Resort
Mishicot, WI

Fairway Townhomes
Nekoosa, WI

Olympia Village Resort & Spa
Oconomowoc, WI

Ed Gabes Lost Lake Condominiums
St. Germain, WI

Rushes, The
Sturgeon Bay, WI

Villas At Christmas Mountain
Wisconsin Dells, WI

Jackson Hole Racquet Club Resort
Jackson, WY

Spring Creek Ranch
Jackson, WY

Teton Shadows
Jackson Hole, WY

Teton Shadows
Jackson Hole, WY

---------------------- GOLF ----------------------

Bay View Village
Paradise Island,

Still Waters
Dadeville, AL

Boulders Resort
Carefree, AZ

Fairfield Flagstaff
Flagstaff, AZ

Inn at Tamarisk
Lake Havasu, AZ

Nautical Inn Resort & Conf.Center
Lake Havasu City, AZ

Arizona Golf Resort
Mesa, AZ

Arizona Golf Resort & Conf.Center
Mesa, AZ

Hermosa Inn Resort
Paradise Valley, AZ

Pointe at South Mountain, The
Phoenix, AZ

Pointe at Squaw Peak, The
Phoenix, AZ

Pointe at Tapatio Cliffs, The
Phoenix, AZ

Wigwam, The
Phoenix, AZ

Roundhouse Resort
Pinetop, AZ

Hyatt Regency Scottsdale
Scottsdale, AZ

Scottsdale/Camelback Resort & Spa
Scottsdale, AZ

Stouffer Cottonwoods Resort
Scottsdale, AZ

Villa Serenas
Tuscon, AZ

Iron Mountain Lodge & Marina
Arkadelphia, AR

Bella Vista Village
Bella Vista, AR

Fairfield Bay
Fairfield Bay, AR

Heritage Bay Condominiums
Heritage Bay, AR

Table Rock Landing On Holiday
Holiday Island, AR

Table Rock Resort
Holiday Island, AR

———————————— GOLF (Cont'd.) ————————————

Belvedere Resort
Hot Springs, AR

Emerald Isle Condominiums
Hot Springs, AR

Los Lagos
Hot Springs, AR

Copper Mine Lodge on Beaver Lake
Rogers, AR

Smith's Landing Golf & Racquet
Siloam Springs, AR

La Costa Hotel & Spa
Carlsbad, CA

Grand Champions
Indian Wells, CA

Indian Wells Racquet Club Resort
Indian Wells, CA

Sands of Indian Wells
Indian Wells, CA

Silverado Country Club & Resort
Napa Valley, CA

Ironwood Country Club
Palm Desert, CA

Lakes Country Club, The
Palm Desert, CA

Monterey Country Club
Palm Desert, CA

PGA West
Palm Desert, CA

Palm Valley Country Club
Palm Desert, CA

Woodhaven Country Club
Palm Desert, CA

Cathedral Canyon Resort
Palm Springs, CA

Doubletree Resort/Desert Princess
Palm Springs, CA

La Mancha
Palm Springs, CA

Palm Springs Marquis
Palm Springs, CA

Racquet Club Of Palm Springs
Palm Springs, CA

Sundance Villas
Palm Springs, CA

San Vicente Resort
Ramona, CA

Rancho La Palmas Country Club
Rancho Mirage, CA

O'Neal Associates, Inc.
Tahoe City, CA

Northstar at Tahoe
Truckee, CA

Gant, The
Aspen, CO

Avon Center at Beaver Creek
Avon, CO

Beaver Creek West
Avon, CO

Charter at Beaver Creek, The
Beaver Creek, CO

Inn at Beaver Creek, The
Beaver Creek, CO

Park Plaza Lodge
Beaver Creek, CO

Poste Mountane at Beaver Creek
Beaver Creek, CO

Four Seasons Lodging, Inc.
Breckenridge, CO

Gold Point Condominiums
Breckenridge, CO

Ski Hill Condominiums
Breckenridge, CO

Carbonate Property Management
Copper Mountain, CO

Copper Mountain Inn
Copper Mountain, CO

Copper Mountain Resort
Copper Mountain, CO

Foxpine Inn
Copper Mountain, CO

The Columbine Condominiums
Crested Butte, CO

The Plaza at Woodcreek
Crested Butte, CO

Orofino
Dillon, CO

Snowdance Condominiums
Dillon, CO

Swan Mountain Resort
Dillon, CO

Cascade Village Resort
Durango, CO

Ferringway
Durango, CO

Purgatory-Village
Durango, CO

Ranch Townhomes, The
Durango, CO

Tamarron
Durango, CO

Miles Motel and Cottages
Estes Park, CO

Nicky's Resort & Lounge
Estes Park, CO

Cedar Lodge
Frisco, CO

Keystone Resort
Keystone, CO

Fairfield Pagosa
Pagosa Springs, CO

Desert Princess, The
Palm Springs, CO

Inn at Silvercreek
SilverCreek, CO

Paradise Condominiums
Silverthorne, CO

Wildernest Lodging
Silverthorne, CO

Chamonix at Woodrun
Snowmass Village, CO

—————————————————— GOLF (Cont'd.) ——————————————————

Crestwood, The
Snowmass Village, CO

Enclave, The
Snowmass Village, CO

Snowmass Club
Snowmass Village, CO

Snowmass Club Villas, The
Snowmass Village, CO

Top of the Village
Snowmass Village, CO

Woodrun Place Condominiums
Snowmass Village, CO

Dulany Condominiums
Steamboat Springs, CO

Golden Triangle Condo Resort
Steamboat Springs, CO

Kutak
Steamboat Springs, CO

LaCasa at Steamboat
Steamboat Springs, CO

Lodge At Steamboat, The
Steamboat Springs, CO

Pine Grove Village
Steamboat Springs, CO

Ptarmigan House Condominiums
Steamboat Springs, CO

Ranch at Steamboat, The
Steamboat Springs, CO

Rockies, The
Steamboat Springs, CO

Snow Flower Condominiums
Steamboat Springs, CO

Timber Run
Steamboat Springs, CO

Waterford Townhomes
Steamboat Springs, CO

Winterwood Townhomes
Steamboat Springs, CO

Apollo Park Lodge
Vail, CO

Bighorn Condominium
Vail, CO

Fallridge at Vail
Vail, CO

Holiday Inn At Vail/Holiday House
Vail, CO

Lodge At Lionshead, The
Vail, CO

Lodge at Vail, The
Vail, CO

Manor Vail Lodge
Vail, CO

Montaneros Condominiums in Vail
Vail, CO

Mountain Haus at Vail
Vail, CO

Raintree Inn
Vail, CO

Simba Resort
Vail, CO

Sonnenalp Hotel
Vail, CO

Vail Hotel and Athletic Club
Vail, CO

Vail International
Vail, CO

Vail Racquet Club
Vail, CO

Village Inn Plaza Condominiums
Vail, CO

Willows Condominiums, The
Vail, CO

Hi Country Haus Resort
Winter Park, CO

Iron Horse Resort Retreat
Winter Park, CO

Lookout Village Condominiums
Winter Park, CO

Meadow Ridge Resort
Winter Park, CO

Summit, The
Winter Park, CO

Marco House
Marco Island, FL

Amelia Island Lodging Systems
Amelia Island, FL

Amelia Island Plantation
Amelia Island, FL

Amelia Surf & Racquet Club
Amelia Island, FL

Errol Estate Golf & Country Club
Apopka, FL

La Boca Casa by the Ocean
Boca Raton, FL

Harbortown
Cape Haze, FL

Palm Island Resort
Cape Haze, FL

Palm Island Resort
Cape Haze, FL

South Seas Plantation
Captiva Island, FL

Executive/Clearwater House
Clearwater, FL

Avalon
Deerfield Beach, FL

Inn At Deer Creek Racquet Club
Deerfield Beach, FL

International Tennis Resort
Delray Beach, FL

Beach House Condominiums
Destin, FL

Destin Towers Condominiums
Destin, FL

Edgewter Beach Condominium
Destin, FL

Inlet Reef Club
Destin, FL

Jetty East Condominium Assoc.
Destin, FL

————————————— GOLF (Cont'd.) —————————————

Sandestin Beach Resort
Destin, FL

Sandpiper Cove Resort
Destin, FL

Seascape Resort & Conference Ctr.
Destin, FL

Shoreline Towers and Townhomes
Destin, FL

Surfside Resort
Destin, FL

Waterview Towers
Destin, FL

El Galeon Condominium Resort
Englewood, FL

Fantasy Island Condominiums
Englewood, FL

Tamarind Gulf and Bay Condominium
Englewood, FL

Radisson Ocean Resort
Fort Lauderdale, FL

Seawatch On The Beach
Fort Myers, FL

Sonesta Sanibel Harbor Resort
Fort Myers, FL

Lahaina Inn Resort
Fort Myers Beach, FL

Mariner's Boathouse & Beach Rst.
Fort Myers Beach, FL

Pointe Estero
Fort Myers Beach, FL

Seawatch-on-the-Beach
Fort Myers Beach, FL

Windward Passage Resort
Fort Myers Beach, FL

Breakers
Fort Walton Beach, FL

Sea Oats Resort Condominium
Fort Walton Beach, FL

Grenelefe Resort
Grenelefe, FL

Gulfstream Manor
Gulfstream, FL

Neptune Hollywood Beach Club
Hollywood, FL

Mission Inn Golf & Tennis Resort
Howey-In-The-Hills, FL

Plantation Beach Club-Indian Rive
Hutchinson Island, Stuart, FL

Bay Shores Yacht & Tennis Club
Indian Rocks Beach, FL

Holiday Villas II
Indian Shores, FL

Holiday Villas III
Indian Shores, FL

Sand Dollar Resort
Indian Shores, FL

Turtle Reef II
Jensen Beach, FL

1800 Atlantic
Key West, FL

Fortune Place
Kissimee, FL

Lago Vista Vacation Resort
Kissimmee, FL

Lifetime of Vacations Resort
Kissimmee, FL

Orange Lake Country Club Villa
Kissimmee, FL

Vistana Resort
Lake Buena Vista, FL

Inverrary House
Lauderhill, FL

Lehigh Resort Club
Lehigh, FL

Four Winds Beach Resort
Longboat Key, FL

Gulf Tides of Longboat Key
Longboat Key, FL

Little Gull
Longboat Key, FL

Longboat Key Club
Longboat Key, FL

Veranda Beach Club
Longboat Key, Sarasota, FL

Buccaneer Resort & Yacht Club
Marathon, FL

Casa Cayo Condominiums
Marathon, FL

Gulfpointe I
Marathon, FL

Sombrero Resort & Lighthouse
Marathon, FL

Eagle's Nest
Marco Island, FL

Surf Club of Marco
Marco Island, FL

Seacoast Towers Apartment Hotel
Miami Beach, FL

Inn at Ravines
Middleburg, FL

Naples Bath & Tennis
Naples, FL

Park Shore Resort
Naples, FL

Vanderbilt Vacation Villas
Naples, FL

White Sands Resort Club
Naples, FL

Bluewater Bay
Niceville, FL

Ram Sea I and Ram Sea II
North Redington Beach, FL

Enclave, The
Orlando, FL

Ventura
Orlando, FL

Villas of Grand Cypress, The
Orlando, FL

———————————————— GOLF (Cont'd.) ————————————————

Palm Beach Resort-Beach Club
Palm Beach, FL

PGA National Club Cottages
Palm Beach Gardens, FL

Landmark Holiday Beach Resort
Panama City, FL

Panama City Resort & Club
Panama City, FL

Bay Point Yacht and Country Club
Panama City Beach, FL

Continental Condominiums
Panama City Beach, FL

Landmark Holiday Beach Resort
Panama City Beach, FL

Moondrifter
Panama City Beach, FL

Ocean Towers Beach Club
Panama City Beach, FL

Oceanna Condominiums
Panama City Beach, FL

Pelican Walk
Panama City Beach, FL

Pinnacle Port Condominiums
Panama City Beach, FL

Ramsgate Harbour
Panama City Beach, FL

Top of the Gulf
Panama City Beach, FL

Baywatch Condominiums
Pensacola Beach, FL

Sandy Key Condominiums
Perdido Key, FL

Sundown Condominium
Perdido Key, FL

Sea Garden
Pompano Beach, FL

Sea Side Beach Club
Pompano Beach, FL

Burnt Store Marina Resort
Punta Gorda, FL

San Remo
Redington Shores, FL

Casa Ybel Resort
Sanibel Island, FL

Sanibel Siesta Condominiums
Sanibel Island, FL

Song of the Sea
Sanibel Island, FL

Sundial Beach & Tennis Resort
Sanibel Island, FL

Tortuga Beach Club
Sanibel Island, FL

One Seagrove Place
Santa Rosa Beach, FL

Meadows Golf & Tennis Resort, The
Sarasota, FL

Meadows, The
Sarasota, FL

Tivoli By The Sea
Sarasota, FL

Beachwood Villas
Seagrove Beach, FL

Hidden Beach Villas
Seagrove Beach, FL

Resorts of Sun 'n Lake
Sebring, FL

Sun'n Lake Estates - Linkside
Sebring, FL

Captain's Quarters
St. Augustine, FL

Coquina, The
St. Augustine, FL

Ponce de Leon Resort & Con. Cente
St. Augustine, FL

Summerhouse
St. Augustine, FL

Breckenridge Resort Beach Club
St. Petersburg Beach, FL

Camelot
St. Petersburg Beach, FL

Hideaway Sands Resort
St. Petersburg Beach, FL

Bay Harbor Club
Stuart, FL

Harbor Ridge Golf Club
Stuart, FL

Indian River Plantation Resort
Stuart, FL

Innisbrook
Tarpon Springs, FL

Sand Pebble Resort
Treasure Island, FL

Treasure Shores
Treasure Island, FL

Vanderbilt Beach and Harbour Club
Vanderbilt Beach, Naples, FL

Coralstone Club
Vero Beach, FL

Reef Ocean Resort, The
Vero Beach, FL

Palm Beach Polo & Country Club
West Palm Beach, FL

Sky Valley Resort
Dillard, GA

Loreley Resort
Helen, GA

Callaway Gardens
Pine Mountain, GA

Cloister, The
Sea Island, GA

River Watch Inn
St. Simons Island, GA

Sea Palm Resort Golf Club
St. Simons Island, GA

Cliffs at Princeville
Hanalei, Kauai, HI

Hale Moi Resort
Hanalei, Kauai, HI

Hanalei Bay Resort
Hanalei, Kauai, HI

—————————————— GOLF (Cont'd.) ——————————————

Hanalei Colony Resort
Hanalei, Kauai, HI

Pali Ke Kua at Princeville
Hanalei, Kauai, HI

Paliuli Cottages
Hanalei, Kauai, HI

Pu'U Po'A
Hanalei, Kauai, HI

Aston Island Colony
Honolulu, HI

Aston Waikiki Sunset
Honolulu, HI

Fairway Villa
Honolulu, HI

Waikiki Banyan
Honolulu, HI

Aston Waikiki Beach Tower
Honolulu, Oahu, HI

International Colony Club
Kaanapali, Lahaina, Maui, HI

Maui Eldorado Resort
Kaanapali, Lahaina, Maui, HI

Kaanapali Alii
Kaanapali, Maui, HI

Kuilima Estates
Kahuku, HI

Kona Billfisher
Kailua Kona, HI

Kona Alii
Kailua, Kona, HI

Aston Kona By The Sea
Kailua-Kona, HI

Keauhou Resort Condominiums
Kailua-Kona, HI

Kona Coast Resort
Kailua-Kona, HI

White Sands Village
Kailua-Kona, HI

Waikoloa Villas
Kamuela, HI

Kapaa Sands
Kapaa, Kauai, HI

Plantatin Hale
Kapaa, Kauai, HI

Kapalua Bay Hotel & Villas
Kapalua, Maui, HI

Pono Kai
Kappa, Kauai, HI

Kauhale Makai
Kihei, HI

Kihei Kai Nani
Kihei, HI

Aston Kamaole Sands
Kihei, Maui, HI

Aston Maui Vista
Kihei, Maui, HI

Hale Pau Hana Resort
Kihei, Maui, HI

Kealia Condominium
Kihei, Maui, HI

Kihei Alii Kai
Kihei, Maui, HI

Kihei Surfside Resort
Kihei, Maui, HI

Laule'a Maui Beach Club
Kihei, Maui, HI

Mana Kai-Maui
Kihei, Maui, HI

Royal Mauian
Kihei, Maui, HI

Shores of Maui
Kihei, Maui, HI

Sugar Beach Resort
Kihei, Maui, HI

Aston Shores at Waikoloa
Kohala, HI

Mauna Lani Point
Kohala, HI

Kahala at Poipu Kai
Koloa, HI

Makanui at Poipu Kai
Koloa, HI

Poipu Makai Condominiums
Koloa, HI

Poipu Palms Condominiums
Koloa, HI

Poipu Sands at Poipu Kai
Koloa, HI

Whalers Cove
Koloa, HI

Aston Poipu at Makahuena
Koloa, Kauai, HI

Kiahuna Condominium Apts.
Koloa, Kauai, HI

Kiahuna Plantation
Koloa, Kauai, HI

Makahuena at Poipu
Koloa, Kauai, HI

Manualoha At Poipu Kai
Koloa, Kauai, HI

Nihi Kai Villas
Koloa, Kauai, HI

Poipu Crater Resort
Koloa, Kauai, HI

Poipu Kai
Koloa, Kauai, HI

Poipu Kapili
Koloa, Kauai, HI

Poipu Shores Resort
Koloa, Kauai, HI

Prince Kuhio Resort
Koloa, Kauai, HI

Sunset Kahili Condo Apt.
Koloa, Kauai, HI

Aston Mahana at Kaanapali
Lahaina, Maui, HI

Aston Maui Kaanapali Villas
Lahaina, Maui, HI

Aston Napili Point
Lahaina, Maui, HI

Aston Paki Maui Resort
Lahaina, Maui, HI

Hololani Condo Resort
Lahaina, Maui, HI

Hono Koa Resort
Lahaina, Maui, HI

Honokeana Cove
Lahaina, Maui, HI

————————————— GOLF (Cont'd.) —————————————

Hoyochi Nikko
Lahaina, Maui, HI

Kaanapali Royal
Lahaina, Maui, HI

Kapalua Villas
Lahaina, Maui, HI

Kulakane
Lahaina, Maui, HI

Lahaina Shores Hotel
Lahaina, Maui, HI

Lokelani
Lahaina, Maui, HI

Makani Sands
Lahaina, Maui, HI

Napili Village Hotel
Lahaina, Maui, HI

Noelani
Lahaina, Maui, HI

Nohonani
Lahaina, Maui, HI

Polynesian Shores
Lahaina, Maui, HI

Royal Kahana Resort
Lahaina, Maui, HI

Sands of Kahana
Lahaina, Maui, HI

Valley Isle
Lahaina, Maui, HI

Aston Kaha Lani
Lihue, Kauai, HI

Kauai Hilton Beach Villas
Lihue, Kauai, HI

Manualoha at Poipu
Lihue, Kauai, HI

Makani A Kai
Maalaea Village, Maui, HI

Polo Beach Club
Makena, Maui, HI

Ke Nani Kai
Maunaloa, Molokai, HI

Paniolo Hale
Maunaloa, Molokai, HI

Kalulakoi Golf Resort
Molokai, HI

Napili Kai Beach Club
Napili Bay, Lahaina, Maui, HI

Napili Surf Beach Resort
Napili Bay, Maui, HI

Coconut Inn
Napili, Maui, HI

Colony One at Sea Mountain
Pahala, HI

Mauna Kai
Princeville, Kauai, HI

Sandpiper Village
Princeville, Kauai, HI

Wailea Ekahi
Wailea, Kihei, Maui, HI

Wailea Elua Village
Wailea, Maui, HI

Wailea Villas
Wailea, Maui, HI

Island Sands Resort
Wailuku, HI

Bluff Condominium
Sun Valley, ID

Elkhorn Resort
Sun Valley, ID

Knob Hill Ridge
Sun Valley, ID

Sun Valley Lodge
Sun Valley, ID

Warm Springs Resort
Sun Valley, ID

Eagle Ridge Inn & Resort
Galena, IL

French Lick Spring Villas
French Lick, IN

French Lick Springs Golf & Tennis
French Lick, IN

Bethel Inn & Country Club, The
Bethel, ME

Sugarloaf Mountain Resort
Carrabassett Valley, ME

Samoset Village
Rockport, ME

Will O Wisp
Oakland, MD

Ocean Edge Resort
Brewster, MA

Country Village At Jimmy Peak
Hancock, MA

Jimmy Peak Mountain Resort
Hancock, MA

Breakwaters, The
Hyannis, MA

Southcape Resort and Club
Mashpee, MA

New Seabury Cape Cod
New Seabury, MA

Island Country Club Inn
Oak Bluffs, MA

Oak n' Spruce Resort
South Lee, MA

Oceanside Resort Condominiums
Dennisport, MA

Grand Traverse Resort Village
Acme, MI

Shanty Creek-Schuss Mtn. Resort
Bellaire, MI

Crystal Mountain Resort
Thompsonville, MI

Pinestead Reef-Vip
Traverse City, MI

Causeway On Gull
Brainerd, MN

Breezy Point International
Breezy Point, MN

Breezy Point Resort Golf Club
Breezy Point, MN

Ruttgers Bay Lodge & Conf. Center
Deerwood, MN

Breezy Shores Resort
Detroit Lakes, MN

Edgewater Beach Club
Detroit Lakes, MN

GOLF (Cont'd.)

Sugar Hills Resort
Grand Rapids, MN

Village Inn and Resort, The
Lutsen, MN

Breezy Point Resort
Minnetonka, MN

Pointe Royale Village
Branson, MO

Lake Country Resort & Golf Club
Galena, MO

Idyllwilde Reosrt
Kimberling City, MO

Kimberling Inn Resort & Vacation
Kimberling City, MO

Holiday Shores
Lake Ozark, MO

Lodge of Four Seasons, The
Lake Ozark, MO

Marriott's Tan-Tar-A Resort
Osage Beach, MO

Bay Point Estates
Whitefish, MT

Sunrise Beach Village
New Providence Island, NA

Club Tahoe
Incline Village, NV

Coeur du Lac Condominiums
Incline Village, NV

Forest Pines Rental Agency
Incline Village, NV

L'Ermitage
Incline Village, NV

Lakeside Tennis & Ski Resort
Incline Village, NV

McCloud At Incline Village
Incline Village, NV

Third Creek
Incline Village, NV

Third Creek
Incline Village, NV

Stillwater Cove
Lake Tahoe, NV

Sheffield Inn
Las Vegas, NV

Selective Accommodations
Stateline, NV

Pine Wild
Zephyr Cove, NV

Bretton Woods Resort
Bretton Woods, NH

Steele Hill, Phase 1
Laconia, NH

Rivergreen
Lincoln, NH

Cold Spring Resort
Plymouth, NH

Inns of Waterville Valley
Waterville Valley, NH

Windsor Hill Condominiums
Waterville Valley, NH

Lake Shore Village Resort
Weare, NH

Jack O'Lantern Resort
Woodstock, NH

Aspen Lodge
Ruidoso, NM

Carrizo Lodge
Ruidoso, NM

West Winds Lodge & Condos
Ruidoso, NM

Champions Run
Ruidoso Downs, NM

Juniper Hill Villas
Bolton Landing, NY

Depe Dene
Lake George, NY

Brookhill Residences
Lake Placid, NY

Long Point Townhouses
New York, NY

Pridwin Resort, The
Shelter Island, NY

Deer Run Resort
Stamford, NY

Whaler Inn Beach Club
Atlantic Beach, NC

Highlands at Sugar, The
Banner Elk, NC

Four Seasons at Beech
Beech Mountain, NC

Hound Ears Club
Blowing Rock, NC

Village at Green Park
Blowing Rock, NC

Willow Valley Resort
Boone, NC

Alpine Village
Burnsville, NC

Atlantic Towers
Carolina Beach, NC

Paradise Tower Resort
Carolina Beach, NC

Spinnaker Point
Carolina Beach, NC

Caswell Dunes
Caswell Beach, NC

Sherwood Forest
Cedar Mountain, NC

Belvedere Plantatin Golf Club
Hampstead, NC

Ocean Palms
Holden Beach, NC

Heron Cove
Kitty Hawk, NC

Sea Scape Beach & Golf Villas
Kitty Hawk, NC

Beacon's Reach
Morehead City, NC

Joe Lamb, Jr. & Associates
Nags Head, NC

Brick Landing Plantation
Ocean Isle Beach, NC

Winds Beach and Golf Resort
Ocean Isle Beach, NC

Foxfire Resort & Country Club
Pinehurst, NC

—————————————— GOLF (Cont'd.) ——————————————

**Pinehurst Hotel &
Country Club**
Pinehurst, NC

**Fairfield Sapphire
Valley**
Sapphire, NC

**Bald Head Island
Resort**
Southport, NC

Oyster Bay Plantation
Sunset Beach, NC

Surf
Surf City, NC

Topsail Dunes
Topsail Island, NC

**Ithilien Lodge
Condominium**
Waynesville, NC

**Whispering Pines
Resort**
Whispering Pines, NC

**Oak Island Beach
Villas**
Yaupon Beach, NC

Cavalier By The Sea
Gleneden Beach, OR

**Sunriver Lodge and
Resort**
Sunriver, OR

Rippling River
Welches, OR

Alpine Village
Analomink, PA

Penn Hills
Analomink, PA

**Seven Springs
Mountain Resort**
Champion, PA

**White Beauty
Lakeview Resort**
Greentown, PA

Shawnee Inn
Shawnee-on-Delaware,
PA

Hidden Valley Resort
Somerset, PA

**Wayne Newton's
Tamiment**
Tamiment, PA

**Wellington Yacht &
Racquet, The**
Newport, RI

**Seabrook Conference
Resort**
Charleston, SC

**Wild Dunes -
Charleston's Island**
Charleston, SC

Fairfield Ocean Ridge
Edisto Island, SC

DeBordieu
Georgetown, SC

**Heritage Club at
Harbour Town**
Hilton Head, SC

Continental Club
Hilton Head Island, SC

**Cottages at Shipyard
Plantation**
Hilton Head Island, SC

**Hilton Head Island
Beach Club**
Hilton Head Island, SC

Island Club
Hilton Head Island, SC

Monarch At Sea Pines
Hilton Head Island, SC

**Player's Club of
Hilton Head Isl.**
Hilton Head Island, SC

Sea Pines Plantation
Hilton Head Island, SC

Sea Pines Villas
Hilton Head Island, SC

**Spinnaker &
Southwind at Shipyard**
Hilton Head Island, SC

Beach Colony Resort
Myrtle Beach, SC

**Beach House Golf and
Racquet Club**
Myrtle Beach, SC

Bluewater Resort
Myrtle Beach, SC

**Caribbean Chelsea
House Villas**
Myrtle Beach, SC

Carolina Winds
Myrtle Beach, SC

**Four Seasons Beach
Resort**
Myrtle Beach, SC

**Kingston Plantation
Resort**
Myrtle Beach, SC

**Ocean Park
Condominiums**
Myrtle Beach, SC

**Ramada Ocean Forest
Resort**
Myrtle Beach, SC

Sands Ocean Club
Myrtle Beach, SC

**Schooner Beach and
Racquet Club**
Myrtle Beach, SC

Water's Edge Resort
Myrtle Beach, SC

Maritime Beach Club
N. Myrtle Beach, SC

**Tilghman Beach and
Racquet Club**
North Myrtle Beach, SC

Litchfield By The Sea
Pawleys Islands, SC

Myrtle Beach Resort
Surfside Beach, SC

Plantation Resort
Surfside Beach, SC

**Fairfield Glade -
Kensington W.**
Fairfield Glade, TN

Cobbly Nob
Gatlinburg, TN

**Deer Ridge Mountain
Resort**
Gatlinburg, TN

**Greenbrier Valley
Resorts**
Gatlinburg, TN

Summit, The
Gatlinburg, TN

**Tree Tops Resort of
Gatlinburg**
Gatlinburg, TN

**Oakmont Resort of
Pigeon Forge**
Pigeon Forge, TN

—————————————————— GOLF (Cont'd.) ——————————————————

Pinecrest Townhomes
Pigeon Forge, TN

Lakeway on Lake Travis
Austin, TX

Lakeway on Lake Travis
Austin, TX

The Bandera Homestead
Bandera, TX

Rancho Viejo Resort & Country Cl.
Brownsville, TX

April Sound Country Club
Conroe, TX

Fairway Villas
Corpus Christi, TX

Gulfstream, The
Corpus Christi, TX

Puente Vista
Corpus Christi, TX

Villa Del Sol
Corpus Christi, TX

Four Seasons On The Gulf
Galveston, TX

Horseshoe Bay Country Club Resort
Horseshoe Bay, TX

Inverness Condominium
Montgomery, TX

Walden on Lake Conroe
Montgomery, TX

Aransas Princess
Port Aransas, TX

Casadel Beach Hotel & Racquet
Port Aransas, TX

El Cortes Villas
Port Aransas, TX

Mayan Princess Condominium
Port Aransas, TX

Pelican, The
Port Aransas, TX

Port Royal Ocean Resort
Port Aransas, TX

Tanglewood on Texoma Resort Hotel
Pottsboro, TX

Rayburn Country Resort and CClub
Sam Rayburn, TX

Padre South Resort
South Padre Island, TX

Woodcreek Resort
Wimberley, TX

Acclaimed Lodging
Park City, UT

Innsbruck, The
Park City, UT

Park Meadows Racquet Club
Park City, UT

Powderwood Resort
Park City, UT

Prospector Square Hotel
Park City, UT

Ridgepoint
Park City, UT

Shadow Ridge Resort Hotel
Park City, UT

Silver King Hotel
Park City, UT

Silvertown Condominiums
Park City, UT

Stein Eriksen Lodge, The
Park City, UT

Chamonix Group
Salt Lake City, UT

Bolton Valley Resort
Bolton Valley, VT

Eagle's Nest Inn & Resort
Fairlee, VT

Bromley Village Condominiums
Manchester Center, VT

Hawk Inn & Mountain Resort
Plymouth, VT

Bear Creek Condominiums
Rawsonville, VT

Pico Resort Hotel
Rutland, VT

Village At Smugglers Notch
Smugglers Notch, VT

Golden Eagle Resort
Stowe, VT

Mount Mansfield Townhouses
Stowe, VT

Mountainside Resort at Stowe
Stowe, VT

Stonybrook Resort
Stowe, VT

Stoweflake Resort Townhouses
Stowe, VT

Topnotch At Stowe
Stowe, VT

Trapp Family Lodge
Stowe, VT

Stratton Mountain Resort
Stratton Mountain, VT

Eagles at Sugarbush
Waitsfield, VT

Sugarbush Inn
Warren, VT

Dover Watch at Mount Snow
West Dover, VT

Caribbean View
Christiansted, St. Croix, VI

Crystal Cove
St. Thomas, VI

Fairway Village at Mahogany
St. Thomas, VI

Mahogany Run Villas
St. Thomas, VI

Point Pleasant Resort
St. Thomas, VI

—————————————— GOLF (Cont'd.) ——————————————

Sapphire Village
St. Thomas, VI

Watergate Villas
St. Thomas, VI

Pine Villas
Basye, VA

Kingsmill Resort
Williamsburg, VA

Wintergreen
Wintergreen, VA

Resort at Port Ludlow
Port Ludlow, WA

Alderbrook Inn Resort
Union, WA

Land of Canaan Vacation Resort
Canaan Valley, Davis, WV

Lakeview Resort Club
Morgantown, WV

Greenbrier, The
White Sulphur Springs, WV

Braywood Resort, The
Eagle River, WI

Eagle Waters Resort
Eagle River, WI

Lake Forest Recreation Area
Eagle River, WI

Safer's Gypsy Villa Resort
Eagle River, WI

Americana Lake Geneva Resort
Lake Geneva, WI

Pointe Resort and Club
Minocqua, WI

Fox Hills Resort
Mishicot, WI

Fairway Townhomes
Nekoosa, WI

Olympia Village Resort & Spa
Oconomowoc, WI

Villas At Christmas Mountain
Wisconsin Dells, WI

Jackson Hole Racquet Club Resort
Jackson, WY

Spring Creek Ranch
Jackson, WY

Teton Shadows
Jackson Hole, WY

Teton Shadows
Jackson Hole, WY

Tourism Information

Every state has a great deal of free information available for tourism. Write and ask for their general packet and be sure to mention specific areas you are interested in.

ALABAMA
Alabama Bureau of Tourist & Travel
532 S. Perry St.
Montgomery, AL 36104
800-252-2262

ALASKA
Alaska State Division of Tourism
Department of Economic Development
P.O. Box E
Juneau, AK 99811
907-465-2010

ARIZONA
Arizona Office of Tourism
1100 W. Washington
Phoenix, AZ 85007
602-255-3618

ARKANSAS
Arkansas Department of Parks & Tourism
1 Capitol Mall
Little Rock, AR 72201
800-643-8383

CALIFORNIA
California Office of Tourism
Department of Commerce
1121 L. Street, Suite 103
Sacramento, CA 95814
916-322-1396 or 800-862-2543

COLORADO
Colorado Tourism Board
1625 Broadway, Suite 1700
Denver, CO 80202
303-592-5410

CONNECTICUT
Connecticut Department of Economic Development
210 Washington Street
Hartford, CT 06106
203-566-3385

DELAWARE
Delaware Tourism Office
99 Kings Highway
P.O. Box 1401
Dover, DE 19903
302-736-4271

DISTRICT OF COLUMBIA
Washington D.C. Convention & Visitors Association
1575 Eye Street N.W., Suite 250
Washington, DC 20005
202-789-7000

FLORIDA
Florida Division of Tourism, Visitor Inquiry Section
101 E. Gaines Street, Fletcher Building, Room 422
Tallahassee, FL 32399-2000
904-487-1462

GEORGIA
Georgia Department of Industry & Trade
Box 1776
Atlanta, GA 30301
404-656-3590

HAWAII
Hawaii Visitors Bureau
Waikiki Business Plaza
2270 Kalakaua Avenue
Honolulu, HI 96815
808-023-1811
also 50 California Street, Suite 450
San Francisco, CA 94111
415-392-8173

IDAHO
Idaho Travel Counsel
Hall of Mirrors, Second Floor
700 W. State Street
Boise, ID 83720
800-635-7820

ILLINOIS
Illinois Department of Commerce & Community Affairs
Illinois Travel Information Center
310 South Michigan Avenue, Suite 108
Chicago, IL 60604
312-793-2094

INDIANA
Indiana Department of Commerce, Tourism Development Division
1 N. Capitol, Suite 700
Indianapolis, IN 46204
800-292-6337

IOWA
Iowa Development Commission, Tourism & Travel Division
200 East Grand Avenue
Des Moines, IA 50309
515-281-31000

KANSAS
Kansas Department of Commerce, Travel & Tourism
400 W. Eighth Street, Fifth Floor
Topeka, KS 66603-3957
913-296-2009

KENTUCKY
Kentucky Department of Travel Development
Capital Plaza Tower, 22nd Floor
Frankfort, Ky 40601
502-564-4930

LOUISIANA
Louisiana Office of Tourism
Box 94291 Capitol Station
Baton Rouge, LA 70804-9291
800-334-8626

MAINE
Maine State Division of Tourism
189 State Street
Augusta, ME 04333
207-389-5710

MARYLAND
Maryland Office of Tourist Development
Redwood Tower
217 E. Redwood Street
Baltimore, MD 21202-3316
301-333-6611

MASSACHUSETTS
Massachusetts Department of Commerce & Development
Division of Tourism
100 Cambridge Street
Boston, MA 02202
617-727-3201

MICHIGAN
Michigan Department of Commerce, Travel Bureau
P.O. Box 30226
Lansing, MI 48909
800-543-2937

MINNESOTA
Minnesota Travel Information Center
375 Jackson Street
St. Paul, MN 55101
800-328-1461

MISSISSIPPI
Mississippi Department of Economic Development
Division of Tourism
Box 849
Jackson, MS 39205
800-847-2290

MISSOURI
Missouri Division of Tourism
Truman Office Building
Box 1055
Jefferson City, MO 65102
314-751-4133

MONTANA
Montana Chamber of
   Commerce
1424 Ninth Avenue
Helena, MT 59620
800-548-3390

NEBRASKA
Nebraska Department of
   Economic Development
Division of Travel & Tourism
301 Centennial Mall S., Box 94666
Lincoln, NE 68509
800-228-4307

NEVADA
Nevada Commission on
   Tourism
800 East Williams, Suite 207
Carson City, NV 89710
800-237-0774

NEW HAMPSHIRE
New Hampshire Office of
   Vacation Travel
Box 856
Concord, NH 03301
603-271-2343

NEW JERSEY
New Jersey Division of Travel &
   Tourism
CN 826
Trenton, NJ 08625
609-292-2470

NEW MEXICO
New Mexico Tourism & Travel
   Department
Economic Development &
   Tourism Department
Bataan Memorial Building
Santa Fe, NM 87503
800-545-2040

NEW YORK
New York State Department of
   Commerce
Division of Tourism
   Development
1 Commerce Plaza
Albany, NY 12245
800-225-5697
New York Convention &
   Visitors Bureau Inc.
2 Columbus Circle
New York, NY 10019-1823
212-397-8222

NORTH CAROLINA
North Carolina Travel &
   Tourism Division
Department of Commerce
430 North Salisbury Street
Raleigh, NC 27611
800-847-4862

NORTH DAKOTA
North Dakota Tourism
   Promotion
Liberty Memorial Building
Capitol Grounds
Bismark, ND 58505
800-437-2077

OHIO
Ohio Office of Travel & Tourism
P.O. Box 1001
Columbus, OH 43216
800-282-5393

OKLAHOMA
Oklahoma Tourism &
   Recreation Department
500 Will Rogers Building
Oklahoma City, OK 73105
405-521-2409

OREGON
Oregon State Tourism Division
595 Cottage Street, N.E.
Salem, OR 97310
800-547-7842

PENNSYLVANIA
Pennsylvania State Bureau of
   Travel Marketing
Department of Commerce
Room 453 Forum Building
Harrisburg, PA 17120
800-847-4872

PUERTO RICO
Puerto Rico Tourism Company
301 San Justo St.
Old San Juan, PR 00905
809-721-2400

RHODE ISLAND
Rhode Island Tourism Division
Department of Economic
   Development
7 Jackson Walkway
Providence, RI 02903
401-277-2601

SOUTH CAROLINA
South Carolina Department of
   Parks, Recreation & Tourism
1205 Pendleton St.
Columbia, SC 29202
803-253-6318

SOUTH DAKOTA
South Dakota State Department
   of Tourism
Capitol Lake Plaza
Pierre, SD 57501
800-843-1930

TENNESSEE
Tennessee Department of
   Tourism Development
320 Sixth Avenue N
Nashville, TN 37202
615-741-2169

TEXAS
Texas Tourist Agency
First City Center
P.O. Box 12008
Austin, TX 78711
512-462-9191

UTAH
Utah State Travel Council
Council Hall Capitol Hill
Salt Lake City, UT 84114
801-553-5681

VERMONT
Vermont Travel Division
134 State Street
Montpelier, VT 05602
802-838-3236

VIRGINIA
Virginia Division of Tourism
202 N. Nith Street, Suite 500
Richmond, VA 23219
804-786-4484 or 800-847-4882

WASHINGTON
Washington State Travel
   Development Division
101 General Administration
   Building
Olympia, WA 98504
800-544-1800

WEST VIRGINIA
West Virginia State Travel
   Development Division
Office of Economic &
   Community Development
2101 Washington Stret E., Third
   Floor
Charleston, WV 25305
800-225-5982

WISCONSIN
Wisconsin State Division of
   Tourism
P.O. Box 7606
Madison, WI 53707
608-266-2161 or 800-432-8747

WYOMING
Wyoming State Travel
   Commission
Frank Norris Jr. Travel Center
Cheyenne, WI 83002
800-225-5996

Index

Lanier Travel Guides
In Book Stores Everywhere!

Lanier Travel Guides have set the standard for the industry:

"All the necessary information about facilities, prices, pets, children, amenities, credit cards and the like. Like France's Michelin..." —New York Times.

"Provides a wealth of information needed to make a wise choice." —American Council of Consumer Interest.

Golf Courses — The Complete Guide

It's about time for a definitive directory and travel guide for the nation's 20 million avid golf players, 7 million of whom make golf vacations an annual event. This comprehensive guide includes over 7,000 golf courses in the United States that are open to the public. Complete details, greens fees, and information on the clubhouse facilities is augmented by a description of the golf courses' best features. A beautiful gift and companion to *Golf Resorts — The Complete Guide.* Introduction by Arthur Jack Snyder.

Bed & Breakfasts, Inns & Guesthouses
in the United States and Canada

A best selling classic now in its ninth fully-revised edition. Over 6,000 inns listed and access to over 15,000 guesthouses. Includes specialty lists for interests ranging from birdwatching to antiquing. "All the necessary information about facilities, prices, pets, children, amenities, credit cards and the like. Like France's Michelin ..." — New York Times

All-Suite Hotel Guide
The Definitive Directory

The only guide to the all-suite hotel industry features over 1200 hotels nationwide and abroad. There is a special bonus list of temporary office facilities. A perfect choice for business travellers and much appreciated by families who enjoy the additional privacy provided by two rooms.

Golf Resorts
— The Complete Guide

This first ever comprehensive guide to over 1,000 golf resorts coast to coast. Includes complete details of each resort facility and golf course particulars. Introductions by A.J. Snyder and Fuzzy Zoeller.

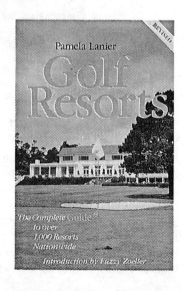

Elegant Small Hotels
— A Connoisseur's Guide

This selective guide for discriminating travelers describes over 200 of America's finest characterized by exquisite rooms, fine dining, and perfect service par excellence. Introduction by Peter Duchin. "Elegant Small Hotels makes a seductive volume for window shopping."
— Chicago Sun Times

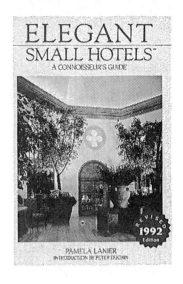

Golf Resorts International

A wish book and travel guide for the wandering golfer. This guide reviews the creme de la creme of golf resorts all over the world. Beautifully illustrated, it includes all pertinent details regarding hotel facilities and amenities. Wonderfuly narrative on each hotel's special charm, superb cuisine and most importantly, those fabulous golf courses. Written from a golfer's viewpoint, it looks at the challenges and pitfalls of each course.

AVAILABLE IN BOOK STORES EVERYWHERE

VOTE

FOR YOUR CHOICE OF
CONDO OF THE YEAR

To the editors of **Condo Vacations, The Complete Guide**:
I cast my vote for "Condo of the Year" for:

Name of Condo _____

Address _____

_____

Phone _____

Reasons _____

_____

_____

I would also like to (please check one):

___ Recommend a new Condo   ___ Comment
___ Critique   ___ Suggest

Name of Condo _____

Address_____

_____

Phone _____

Comment _____

Please send your entries to:
Condo Vacations, The Complete Guide
P.O. Box D
Petaluma, CA 94953

Free Subscription to Mondo Condo Newsletter™

From time to time we will send you a free copy of our Mondo Condo Newsletter that will keep you posted about special Condo travel offers, air and Condo packages, and golf Condo resort packages and family travel specials. This free subscription is available for a limited time only. Subscribe now!

Name _____

Address _____

City _____ State _____ Zip _____

Are you planning a Condo Vacation within the next year? If so, how many adults _____ children _____ ?

Are you interested in receiving information regarding Condos for sale? If so, where? Northeast _____ Southeast _____ Midwest _____ Hawaii _____ Which special areas ?___
_____

Are you golfers? _____ Do you ski? _____

When taking a vacation, do you generally travel by car _____ rail _____ or air _____ ?

Travel Books from
LANIER GUIDES
ORDER FORM

QTY	TITLE	EACH	TOTAL
	Golf Courses—The Complete Guide	$19.95	
	Golf Resorts—The Complete Guide	$14.95	
	Golf Resorts International	$19.95	
	Condo Vacations—The Complete Guide	$14.95	
	Elegant Small Hotels	$19.95	
	Elegant Hotels of the Pacific Rim	$14.95	
	All-Suite Hotel Guide	$14.95	
	The Complete Guide to Bed & Breakfasts	$16.95	
	Family Travel—The Complete Guide	$19.95	
	Sub-Total		$
	Shipping		$3.00 each
	TOTAL ENCLOSED		$

Send your order to:
LANIER PUBLISHING
P.O. Box D
Petaluma, California 94953

Allow 3 to 4 weeks for delivery
Please send my order to:

NAME _____

ADDRESS _____

CITY _____ STATE _____ ZIP _____